DEATH AND CHANGING RITUALS
Function and Meaning in Ancient Funerary Practices

Edited by

J. Rasmus Brandt, Marina Prusac and Håkon Roland

OXBOW | books
Oxford & Philadelphia

First published in 2015. Reprinted in paperback in 2020 in the United Kingdom by
OXBOW BOOKS
The Old Music Hall, 106–108 Cowley Road, Oxford, OX4 1JE

and in the United States by
OXBOW BOOKS
1950 Lawrence Road, Havertown, PA 19083

Paperback Edition: ISBN 978-1-78925-381-8
Digital Edition: ISBN 978-1-78297-640-0

A CIP record for this book is available from the British Library

Library of Congress Cataloging-in-Publication Data

Brandt, J. Rasmus.
   Death and changing rituals : function and meaning in ancient funerary practices / edited by J. Rasmus Brandt, Håkon Roland and Marina Prusac.
      pages cm
   Includes bibliographical references and index.
   ISBN 978-1-78297-639-4
   1. Funeral rites and ceremonies, Ancient. I. Roland, Håkon. II. Prusac, Marina. III. Title.
   GT3170.B73 2014
   393'.93093--dc23
                        2014032027

For a complete list of Oxbow titles, please contact:

UNITED KINGDOM
Oxbow Books
Telephone (01865) 241249
Email: oxbow@oxbowbooks.com
www.oxbowbooks.com

UNITED STATES OF AMERICA
Oxbow Books
Telephone (610) 853 9131, Fax (610) 853-9146
Email: queries@casemateacademic.com
www.casemateacademic.com/oxbow

Oxbow Books is part of the Casemate Group

Front cover: Military grave stele, of Quintus Metius. From Salona. Split, Archaeological museum. Courtesy of the museum. Photo: Tonci Šešer.
The frieze in the upper band: Tarquinia, Tomba del Barone, rear wall. Courtesy of the Ministero per i Beni e le Attività Culturali, Soprintendenza per i beni archeologici dell'Etruria Meridionale, Museo di Villa Giulia. Photo no. MAX 7068 c.

CONTENTS

ACKNOWLEDGEMENTS

The present publication collects 14 out of 18 papers delivered at the international conference, *Ritual Changes, Changing Rituals: Function and Meaning in Ancient Funerary Practices*, held 22–25 May, 2008 at the Museum of Cultural History, University of Oslo, Norway. The editors regret the long production time due to unforeseen health problems among two of its members. The final editing of the manuscript was finished by January 2012.

The conference was born out of an exhibition at the Museum of Cultural History, *Dead Classic*, which had opened just a month earlier. The exhibition was a presentation of artefacts connected with death from the Mediterranean area in the Museum's possession and was the largest exhibition of its kind so far in Norway. The idea was to bring together both prehistorical and historical archaeologists to discuss theoretical and methodological issues for the purpose of testing diverging perspectives on different phenomena of change, both of a short and a long time duration, visible in either archaeological or textual material alone, or in combination. The wide approach to the subject encouraged discussions across some of the traditional chronological and material limits, and called the attention to various observances in past societies, such as beliefs, rituals, performances, commemorations, social norms and transitions, behavioural and mental states, identities, treatment of bodies, pollution and purification, taboos, symbols, traditions, and others. The keywords were ritual, change, and transformation processes. The speakers were personally invited and came from Croatia, France, Germany, Great Britain, Italy, Norway, Romania, and Sweden, though not all working in their country of origin.

The conference was made possible thanks to a generous contribution from the Museum of Cultural History and additional support from The Department of Archaeology, Conservation and History, both at the University of Oslo. The same institutions gave further financial support for the copy-editing of the texts delivered for publication. We are very grateful to both institutions and hope that the present publication can be considered as a small, but visible token of money well spent.

We owe special thanks to the former Director, Prof. em. Egil Mikkelsen, from the Museum of Cultural History, for hosting the Ritual Changes-conference and providing financial guarantees that made the conference possible. Furthermore we wish to thank

Research Advisor, Arve Monsen for enthusiastic support, Johnny Kreutz for the conference website and the administrative staff at the Museum for practical assistance.

Our thanks are also extended to Dr Alex Chepstow-Lusty, who diligently copy-edited all the papers written by the non-native English speakers, and to Dr Adam Lindhagen for help with the index. For any mistakes which remain the editors take the blame.

The publication was already at an advanced stage of preparation when the first publisher realised that the publication was beyond their capacity and we were suggested to use Oxbow Books instead. Sincere thanks go to the staff of Oxbow Books for their professional handling of this publication from the minute they took over production to the final product. These expressions of thanks are also extended to the anonymous peer-reviewers, who made very valuable suggestions to improve the quality of the publication. In particular, we should like to thank Ms Clare Litt and Julie Blackmore, who patiently has supported this publication project in its final, important stages of production.

The Norwegian Research Council generously covered some of the publication costs, a necessity to see the book safely through to print.

Last, but not least, we should like to thank all the participants, who all contributed in making the seminar a successful event, and in particular to those who found the time and energy to rewrite their papers into what makes up this book. We were very touched by their many expressions of thanks afterwards. We will also use this opportunity to forward an excuse to the authors (and to the readers) for the unexpected vicissitudes of production, which has delayed the publication unnecessarily.

J. Rasmus Brandt, Marina Prusac and Håkon Roland
Oslo, January 2013

CONTRIBUTORS

IRINA ACHIM is Researcher at the Department of Greek and Roman Archaeology and Epigraphy at the Archaeological Institute "Vasile Parvan" in Bucharest. She has a Doctoral degree in archaeology from the University of Paris 1, Panthéon-Sorbonne and is presently in charge of a project on the 'Crypt Basilica' of Histria, Constanta County, Bucharest.

SVEN AHRENS is Senior Curator at the Norwegian Maritime Museum, Oslo. He has a Doctoral degree in Classical Archaeology from Humboldt University in Berlin and is presently leading several archaeological projects in Oslo.

ANDREJ BELINSKIJ is working at the Unitary Government Enterprise *Heritage* in Russia. He has among other themes published on Neolithic monuments in the Northern Caucasus.

WILL BOWDEN is Lecturer in Roman Archaeology, University of Nottingham. He has a Doctoral degree from the University of East Anglia and has previously been Lecturer at the University of Reading. A large part of his research is based on the archaeologies of Albania.

J. RASMUS BRANDT is Professor emeritus of Classical Archaeology at the University of Oslo and has been the Director of the Norwegian Institute in Rome. He has conducted several excavations in the Mediterranean on sites such as Ficana and the Palatine in Rome and is presently the leader of a research project at Hierapolis in Turkey.

ANDREA DOLFINI is Lecturer in Later Prehistory and Director of the Centre for Interdisciplinary Artefact Studies (CIAS) at the School of History, Classics and Archaeology, Newcastle University.

CHRIS FOWLER is Senior Lecturer in Later Prehistoric Archaeology at the School of History, Classics and Archaeology, Newcastle University. He has a Doctoral degree from the University of Southampton, and held a postdoctoral research fellowship at the School of Art History and Archaeology at the University of Manchester.

ROBERTA GILCHRIST is Professor of Archaeology at the University of Reading and Head of the School of Archaeology, Geography and Environmental Science. Her publications include *Medieval Life. Archaeology and the Life Course* (2012) and *Requiem: the Medieval*

Monastic Cemetery in Britain (with B. Sloane), which won the British Archaeological Award for best scholarly publication (2005).

HEINRICH HÄRKE is Honorary Professor at the Department of Medieval Archaeology, University of Tübingen. He has formerly been Reader at the Department of Archaeology, University of Reading and Lecturer at the Department of Archaeology, Queens University of Belfast and at the University of Kiel. He has directed excavations in Germany and the Soviet Union and is presently working in Caucasus.

TERJE OESTIGAARD is Associate Professor and the Head of the 'Rural and Agrarian Change, Property and Resources'-cluster at the Nordic Africa Institute, Uppsala, Sweden. His main research focuses on the Nile Basin and the River Nile where he has conducted fieldworks in Egypt, Ethiopia, Tanzania and Uganda.

JOHN PEARCE is Lecturer in Archaeology at the Department of Classics, King's College, London. He was previously a Post-doctoral Researcher at the University of Oxford on the Vindolanda writing tablets, and obtained his Doctoral degree from the University of Durham. His research interests are in Roman archaeology and he has fieldwork experience from Britain, Italy, and Germany.

MARINA PRUSAC is Associate Professor of Classical Archaeology and Keeper of the Collection of Classical Antiquities at the Museum of Cultural History, University of Oslo. She publishes on Roman portraiture and cultural encounters in Illyria/Dalmatia.

ERIC REBILLARD is Professor in Classics and History at Cornell University. He has a Doctoral degree and a Habilitation from the University of Paris 4, Sorbonne, and has previously been researcher at the Centre national de la recherche scientifique, France.

HÅKON ROLAND is Associate Professor and Head of the Section for Numismatics and Classical Archaeology at the Museum of Cultural History, University of Oslo. He wrote his Doctoral thesis on the coinage of Kos and has undertaken excavations at Metropolis in Turkey and Naxos in Greece. He is specialised in international heritage legislation.

LIV NILSSON STUTZ is a Senior Lecturer at The Department of Anthropolgy, Emory University, and has a Doctoral degree from Lund University. She is an editor of the journal *Archaeological Dialogues* and recently edited the *Oxford Handbook of the Archaeology of Death and Burial* in collaboration with Sarah Tarlow. She has taken part of field work and analyses of sites in Scandinavia, Latvia, Jordan, and Portugal.

SARAH TARLOW is Professor of Archaeology at the Centre for Historical Archaeology at the School of Archaeology and Ancient History, University of Leicester. She has a Doctoral degree from Cambridge University and has published extensively on the archaeologies of death and burial. She has recently edited the *Oxford Handbook of the Archaeology of Death and Burial* in collaboration with Liv Nilsson Stutz.

INTRODUCTION
Ritual, Change, and Funerary Practices

J. Rasmus Brandt

For the human being there is only one way into this world, through the woman's womb, but many ways to leave it, from a natural death due to old age, to deadly sicknesses and mortal accidents and disasters, to duels, wars, and meaningless massacres, like the one experienced near Oslo at Utøya on July 22, 2011. Even if there are in general only two ways of getting rid of the corpse: by inhumation (in soil, air, or water) or by cremation, the forms by which the deceased are brought to rest are as many as there are causes of death, from the corpse being left to the decompositional hazards of atmospherical forces, scavenging birds and animals, and insects, to being 'preserved by smoking, embalming, or pickling; they are eaten – raw, cooked, or rotten. . . or they are dismembered and treated in a variety of these ways' (Metcalf & Huntington 1991: 24), to being properly interred.

The funerals, the framework of how to eliminate the corpse, are 'the occasion for avoiding people or holding parties, for fighting or having sexual orgies, for weeping or laughing, in a thousand different combinations' (Metcalf & Huntington 1991: 24). These celebrations, generally termed death rituals, can be performed in many ways from the most simple act of deportment in solitude to the engagement of large masses of people in laborious and creative festivities. By *ritual* in a funerary context we mean a strategy which incorporates all the actions performed and thoughts expressed in connection with a dying and dead person, from the preparatory pre-death stages to the final deposition of the corpse and the post-mortem stages of grief and commemoration. Seeing ritual 'as part of a process of social reproduction' (see the article of Nilsson Stutz) we have chosen to adopt this wide and flexible definition as a reflection of the complex and multiple practices performed in funerary situations, seen both from a chronological and a geographical point of view. In short, the funerary process, or cycle, cover the rites performed from the moment of the biological death of a person to the final interment of the corpse and its thereby social death (Weiss-Krejci 2011: 70–80). It is a large web of ideas turned into actions in a wide variety of expressions.

The central theme of this book, however, is not to look primarily into different funerary practices, their function and meaning, but into the *changes* of such rituals and how they shall be explained. Many practices become more easily visible when looked at through studies of change. In order to approach the problem of funerary changes from a wide variety of situations, scholars from different prehistoric and historical periods (which span from the Mesolithic Period to early modern times, some contributors also drawing parallels to modern society: Nilsson Stutz, Härke/Belinskij, Brandt, Bowden) and working in different geographical areas (which cover the Old World from the Atlantic Ocean to the Caucasus and from the Arctic Sea to the Mediterranean) were asked to give examples from their fields of study and to reflect upon theoretical and methodological issues connected to their case studies. This is a serious challenge to both the editors, the publisher, and the reading public, and has been done on purpose. As editors we find it important to transgress the boundaries of time and place specialisations. Each specialisation develops its own sets of interpretations and 'truths' depending on the availability of physical material and/or textual information. Thus it happens that when a change in one kind of funerary practice in one field of archaeology is interpreted with reference to eschatology and cosmology, a similar change in another field is interpreted as a simple change of trend. Both fields may be right in their interpretations, but some challenges across the specialisation boundaries are necessary to stimulate further research. In fact, three of the contributors, Härke and Belinskij and Gilchrist, address this particular problem of chronological specialisation boundaries and call for more continuity studies as changes are most often not abrupt, but best visible in a *longue durée* perspective.

In difference to other social actions, an organised burial is performed to 'preserve' the deceased for 'eternity'; tombs are therefore the most common discovery in archaeology – and since, in addition, many graves contain furnishings of remarkable workmanship and high spectacular and economic value, burial archaeology has attracted easier funding. The majority of archaeological finds in all museums around the world derive from grave contexts; burial archaeology is therefore perhaps the most thriving discipline of the field. Publications are many (the long bibliographies presented by the present contributors open only a small glimpse into this vast publishing world) and one may ask why a new publication in the field is necessary. By concentrating on change it is our hope that we shall be able to introduce new ways (or old ways in new settings) into the study of the function and meaning of funerary practices and the processes which triggered the changes. Analyses of the cadaver *per se*, like osteology, isotopes, and DNA, will not be considered in this publication, though this does not exclude that observations on the corpse are considered.

In this introductory chapter we should like, not to make a presentation of each singular contribution (for that the reader is advised to read the abstract of each article), rather to pull together some of the theoretical issues and methodological grips used by the contributors, in order to reveal how the articles are bound together despite the wide chronological and geographical framework adopted. This will be done by presenting briefly some concepts related to the central problem of the present publication, as the question about Change and Continuity, and to some of the important elements of the funerary process connected to Belief and Ritual, Body and Deposition, Place and Burial, Performance and Commemoration.

Before doing so, however, it should at once be noted that apart from addressing changes in funerary practices, a change can also be noted in the contributors' approach to the changing rituals problem. In the wake of the intensive debate on processual and post-processual archaeology in the 1970s and 1980s, the archaeologists moved from documenting the funerary material with a view to chronology, geographical origin, and distribution to look at the same material in a social context reflecting status and identity of the dead. In the present publication, independently of each other, the contributors have shifted their focus to the burial itself and the social behaviour, the mental metaphors, and the belief systems hidden in the funerary practices, and whether they can be extracted from the funerary material itself and/or from written evidence – in other words, the focus is shifted more to a study of the content of the practices than of their form.

Change and continuity[1]

The keyword in the present publication is change. But what do we mean by change? Implicitly it means something altered that is seen in relation to what is considered normal/the norm and thus requires an explanation. The purpose of this collection of articles is to document *how* changes manifested themselves in the archaeological/textual material, *why* changes were made and *in what way* they can be explained – whether related to changes in the funerary ceremonies and eschatological ideas *per se* or to other types of changes in the society. While the *how* question will regard the funerary form or the archaeological/textual (= empirical) data, through the questions *why* and *in what way* we may approach the funerery content or the social behaviour and ancient belief systems connected to eschatology and cosmology. However, in such discussions it is important to consider if a change in form necessitates a change in content.

From an archaeological point of view changes can be observed in many ways, most easily visible in a change in the treatment of the dead body from being inhumed to being cremated, or vice versa (Nilsson Stutz, Fowler, Ahrens, Pearce, Rebillard, Achim, Oestigaard); however, the changes may also regard the lay-out and distribution of tombs (Dolfini, Fowler, Achim), the treatment of the deceased in the tomb, whether as a primary or secondary deposition (Nilsson Stutz, Dolfini, Fowler, Oestigaard, Gilchrist), tomb forms and architecture (Fowler, Härke & Belinskij, Ahrens, Pearce, Rebillard, Achim, Bowden, Oestigaard, Gilchrist), themes in funerary pictorial decorations (Brandt), composition of the funerary goods (Fowler, Härke & Belinskij, Pearce, Bowden, Oestigaard), inscription formulas (Ahrens), etc. Though many changes in funerary practices may not be visible in the archaeological material, and only in the textual material (Tarlow, see also Rebillard) – this is a limitation difficult to get round.

What drives a ritual change? As demonstrated by many of the contributors a ritual change is not necessarily related to changes in the belief system (as, for example, witnessed with the conversion to Christianity: Achim, Gilchrist), rather to other social and cultural phenomena (Nilsson Stutz; see also Ahrens), as attitudes to death (Brandt, Rebillard), to the body (Nilsson Stutz, Dolfini, Fowler, Pearce), to tensions between social norms and individual behaviour (Härke & Belinskij, Oestigaard, Tarlow), to mental stress (Bowden), and other factors – in fact the causes of ritual change may often be strongly interlinked, and hence not bound to one single obvious cause (Härke & Belinskij).

How do changes appear? They can be abrupt breaking away from the dominating scheme (Nilsson Stutz), often the result of intentional acts of a social, political, and/ or religious character on a local, regional, or world-wide level (Ahrens, Rebillard, Achim, Bowden, Oestigaard, Gilchrist); and they can be gradual of a *longue durée* (Fowler, Härke & Belinski, Pearce, Tarlow) referring to societal developments and alterations. In some cases a change also appears as a reworking or reinvention of older traditions (Oestigaard, Gilchrist). An observed change in the archaeological material, however, may not necessarily express a change as such, it may also be an expression of continuity. Chris Fowler in an earlier version of his contribution asked in the title: 'The more things change, the more they remain the same?' This is a challenging question, because what often appears to be a change may actually be an expression of the same, only expressed differently. This may be why some of the contributors have used the antonym of change, continuity, as part of their title (Fowler, Brandt, Rebillard; and indirectly Dolfini), whether as an affirmation or as a question.

Belief and ritual

Beliefs are the content of the funerary practices, with rituals the forms in which the content, through the practices, are expressed. The forms can be expressed in many ways through ephemeral actions, such as for example, dance and music, grief and laughter, and through physical material in the form of necropoleis, tombs, furnishings, but also through pictorial presentations of the practices and inscriptions in various media, both within and outside a funerary context.

When studying the physical material preserved we study the material of past actions, or the form of ritual/funerary practices (Nilsson Stutz, Brandt). According to practice theory, well presented by Nilsson Stutz, the understanding of the past actions will ideally reveal how ritual as a process works and the embodied experience of this process, i.e. the active participation in the ritual creates a sense of structure in the participant, through which meaning, inherent in action, is formulated. This means that meaning as such could vary, while the embodied knowledge – the sense of how things are done – was shared, or in other words: the participants would have had a sense of what a 'proper' burial would be like, but they may have projected different meanings to the practices. A similar attitude to the practices, but not expressed in a theoretical framework, can be found also in the contributions by Bowden and Oestigaard, who both, within the established ritual practices, stress the role of the living in conveying messages about the dead person, their relation to the deceased and to other members of the society, to ancestors, to the spiritual world, or in using the deceased as a medium for social outcomes in the reconstitution of society (cf. also Härke & Belinskij).

This interpretative model gives greater flexibility to the interpretations of the funerary data, but does not exclude a bond between the data (i.e. the funerary practices) and the belief systems, whether they are connected to afterlife (Fowler, Härke & Belinskij, Brandt, Gilchrist), to cosmologies concerning the human body (Dolfini), or to other eschatological ideas (Ahrens, Oestigaard, Tarlow). By looking at rituals as a practice, both in social and religious life, they open up a sphere of manifold interpretations, in which negotiations, manipulations, and constructions of political and cosmological orders are active (Oestigaard).

In these examples, belief is presented as a religious, or theological belief, concerning transcendental actions and forces, but belief, or rather 'belief discourses', can also be expressed in different forms, as social, scientific, and folk beliefs; by which they all affect the kinds of rituals that surround the dead body (Tarlow). Tarlow's conclusions are drawn from the study of a wealthy set of written sources, but such a categorisation of beliefs is certainly not only limited to an early modern European society; it may well have been part and package of funerary practices in other societies in other time periods as well – we only have to start looking for them. Taboo may be an important element of such non-religious beliefs (Brandt). Tarlow also makes another observation of interest and contrary to the normal understanding of the relationship of belief and ritual: under certain circumstances ritual action may actually have been more stable than belief.

Body and deposition

The deposition of the dead body is the main objective of all funerary practices; this can be done either by cremation or inhumation. The choice of the one or the other practice has often been related to eschatological ideas and ancient belief systems, but here, as in other aspects of funerary practices, multiple explanations, evaluated case by case, are now more favoured. This comes more to light when a change from one practice to another is considered, but it does not exclude a religious explanation. For example, the Christian insistence on inhumation may well be connected to their belief of resurrection at Judgment Day (Achim, Gilchrist), but the change from cremation to inhumation in the Roman Empire from the 2nd century AD onwards was not the result of Christian thoughts of death and afterlife, but the practice was upheld by them.

The change can rather be ascribed to a change of fashion, as has also been observed in earlier periods when in Rome the mode of deposition changed (Morris 1992: 52–68). Alternatively, the change in the Imperial Period has suggestively also been attributed to a new, pre-Christian concern for the body (Rebillard).

Practical circumstances may often have been the reason for a change of deposition practices, as when in Victorian England, due to over-crowded cemeteries, hygienic considerations, and new furnace technology, cremation (even if contested and causing distress and conflict) gradually became the norm (Nilsson Stutz). In a more distant past, when both practices appear next to each other in the same region or between neighbouring regions, they may not have been considered as something contrary, rather, as in the Greek and Roman Asia Minor, as two options in a multifaceted specter of funerary rites connected to practical considerations, personal preferences, traditions, fashions, and even to migrations (previously the most favoured model among cultural historians to explain the reasons for a change in the deposition mode) (Ahrens; cf. also Achim). Actually, the tendency among a couple of the present authors, in comparison with other contextual evidence, is to downplay the importance of the shifts in such funerary practices (Fowler, Pearce), though it does not eliminate the fact that cremation (more than inhumation) dramatised the transformation of the dead, making it visible to the mourners (Fowler). However, it shall not be excluded that the choice between the one or the other practice can have carried more or less strong ideological implications, especially in times of religious, social, and political upheaval, as in the early Viking Age in Norway, conveying explicit references to funerals, which both break with tradition and at the same time reinvent it (Oestigaard).

Cremation or inhumation was one way of treating the dead body, another was to expose it to disarticulation, i.e. the whole body, or body parts, were disturbed and manipulated, whether at the moment of interment or at a later re-opening of the grave (Nilsson Stutz, Dolfini – in Mesolithic and Neolithic contexts respectively in the Baltic area and Italy), or through reburial in a secondary context (Dolfini; see also Gilchrist). This is a phenomenon which can be followed through all periods, finding its extreme result in charnel houses from the Medieval Period onwards. The explanations for their manipulation may be many. They can, as in the present examples, be connected to questions of the nature of the disarticulated bones, if they were considered of this or the other world, or if they were associated with questions of social control and normalcy (Nilsson Stutz), in which questions of ancestry and group and individual identity may have played an important part (Dolfini). In both case studies can be sensed a view in which bones of dead persons were imbued with some kind of transcendental power, a view still actively maintained, but under a different explanatory umbrella, in early modern Europe through the veneration of saints and martyrs and through folk practices as 'bier-right' and the curative power of the 'dead hand' (Tarlow).

The treatment of the body raises also a question about the soul. Even if not treated in particular in this publication the soul is normally related to ideas of immortality, as among the Etruscans (Brandt) and the Romans, and of resurrection, as among the Christians, in all three examples linked to a preceding death journey. In early Christian thinking only pure souls, not burdened with heavy sins, could find their rest inside a church (Achim), and in later Medieval thoughts the soul could be protected on its purgatory journey by items buried with the dead: in fact, the progress of the soul in judgment appears to have been directly affected by the condition of the corpse in the grave. The experience of the Christian dead in Purgatory was embodied and sensory, and the living could alleviate their suffering by taking the appropriate preparations of the corpse and the grave (Gilchrist) – ideas which were not alien to Etruscan (and Roman) ritual thinking, only enveloped in a different dress. With the Protestants the journey through Purgatory was eliminated – the soul went directly to Judgment, and nothing that the living did could make any difference to the fate of the dead person's soul (Tarlow).

Place and burial

The deposition of the body in most societies was not a chance act; first the place and shape of the tomb had to be decided. In an Etrusco-Roman context a clear distinction was made between the place of the dead and the place of the living. Due to an inherent risk of pollution, all dead (with some exceptions of children in their first months/years of life) were buried outside the space reserved for the dwellings. However, this was a time-defined situation and not observed with the same rigidity within the boundaries of the Roman Empire. The importance of place is underlined in two of the present articles and expresses two modes of change, both connected to the conceptional views of the dead bodies: the first, in a centrifugal movement, from lived towards unlived areas (Dolfini); the other in a contrary, centripetal movement from the unlived back to the lived areas (Achim).

In the Italian peninsula, in the transition between the Neolithic and Copper Age (late 5th/4th millennia BC), burials were gradually moved from the nucleated villages to their peripheral areas before they were gathered in cemeteries located in the landscape. The process may be explained not as a change in the *meaning* of the burial *per se*, but as a change in the *medium* chosen by the society to stress the same group identity which were previously conveyed by co-residence, and which made the body of the dead a major locus for the reproduction of prehistoric society (Dolfini). A similar process of change from isolated burials to the use of collective burial grounds could also be observed in Northumberland, England, in the Early Bronze Age (*c.* 2400–1500 BC), also here underlining the importance of the body, person, and death for the community in the ritualised transformation of the dead (Fowler).

New views on the dead bodies, not as a polluter in the Etrusco-Roman view, but as sacred and holy, permanently purified at the moment of baptism and 'prefiguring the transformed body that would be resurrected into eternal life at the end of time' (Paxton

2011), in early Christian times (and thus linked to a changed belief system) caused an opposite, centripetal movement of the burials from the outside of towns, towards the inside – at first detached from, but later unified with the new cult monuments, the churches. The case study selected concentrates on the *Scythia Minor* and *Moesia Secunda* (present day southeast Romania and northeast Bulgaria) and presents new important data on this process from an area in the periphery of the Roman Empire, an area otherwise not easily accessible and not much known (Achim).

Size and shape of graves, and the composition and wealth of grave goods are generally considered as markers of the deceased's social position and identity. Long descriptions of funerary monuments and physical contents are avoided in this publication. Instead the discussions and interpretations, seen in relation to funerary changes, underline the complex multiple meanings attached to the funerary data. Some interpretations are connected to ritual, worship, and belief systems (Dolfini, Fowler, Brandt, Achim, Gilchrist), others to practical purposes (Ahrens) and the use of traditions (Oestigaard), and others again to social life and behaviour (Pearce, Bowden), interpretations already touched upon in the previous sub-chapter or which will be elaborated a bit further in the next.

Performance and commemoration

The funerary ritual, much like a religious festival, is an orchestrated performance in which the 'programme might evolve in a succession of shifting moods and sentiments, guided by symbolic, that is, imaginative and affective stimulants' (Bouvrie 2012: 62). It covers often a pre-defined period which extends from the physical death of the person solemnised to his/her social death marked by the interment and successive concluding ritual acts. Depending on the associated belief systems the programme guides and modulates the acts and sentiments of family and friends through the ceremony and guarantees the deceased a 'proper' burial. The programme can involve moments of dance and music, weapon fights and erotic plays, weeping and laughter, eating and drinking – Etruscan tomb paintings being a rich treasure for establishing the components of this people's funerary rituals (Brandt).

In societies with a belief system propagating a death journey and a life after death, the duration of the funerary rituals is often considered a liminal period in which the dead subject has not yet become an object of commemoration, but is something in between, and which by Julia Kristeva is referred to as an *abject* (Nilsson Stutz). It is a particularly difficult period for the deceased when he/she is operating in a no-man's land on the way from one kind of life existence to another. The funerary process thus becomes a ritual passage for the deceased, composed of three phases: separation (the pre-liminal phase), transition (the liminal phase), and reintegration (the post-liminal phase). In Etruscan tomb paintings this process can be followed as a parallel journey undertaken by both the deceased and the living mourners in which the actions of the latter shall ease the passage of the former (Brandt). A similar mode of liminal thinking may also be unveiled if mortuary deposits (here in an Early Bronze Age context from England) are studied, not primarily as indicators of social standing and prestige, but reflecting mortuary rites (whether the body was inhumed or cremated) as being the result of a sequence of ritualised actions that transform social relations and identities (Fowler).

Christian beliefs of afterlife and the embodied experience of Purgatory contain elements of a similar thinking: separation (deathbed rites of confession, communion, and the sacrament of extreme unction) and transition (the preparation and dressing of the deceased during which the living were empowered to assist the soul through Purgatory) (Gilchrist), but in difference to the Etruscans (and Romans) the Christian mourners did not participate actively in the liminal ritual performances, and in difference to the Christians the Etruscan reintegration did not contain an element of resurrection of the flesh.

The performed sequence of ritual actions may, as mentioned, be used to orchestrate the sentiments of the mourners, for example, creating ecstatic moods through dance, laughter, and erotic plays (Brandt), but such sentiments are difficult to abstract from the funerary material. However, the material deposited by the participants of the funerary ritual may, apart from a possible social status, also reflect symbolically the identity of the dead embodying and evoking a certain life style (Pearce, in Roman Britain and Belgium/the Netherlands) – or even, through a wide diversity of burial practices, reflect the uncertainties and anxieties that accompanied the adoption of new practices in a rapidly changing world (Bowden, in post-Roman Albania).

Sacrifices and banquets are returning elements of the funerary procedures. Sacrifices of animals, in addition to honouring a particular deity, had a purative effect in societies in which death was considered as pollution, as among the Etruscans and Romans (Brandt). Sacrifices also recall blood, an important element in Etruscan funerary customs, as a blood sacrifice (whether acquired by a slain animal or through fierce human combats) was considered to give immortality to the deceased's soul. In some societies, animals were deposited with the deceased, such as horses in the nomadic Sarmatian phase (2nd century BC–4th/5th century AD) of the Klin-Yar cemetery in the North Caucasus (Härke & Belinskij); a possible human sacrifice from the same period in the same necropolis appears to be an extremely rare occurrence, but together with the animal sacrifice may raise a question of belief in immortality.

In North Africa, in the 3rd century AD, animal sacrifice to the dead gave way to banquets as the focus of ritual attention, but was, as already observed, not the result of a Christianisation of the dead, but an important act of piety (Rebillard). Banquets had also previously been a central element in funerary rituals, in an Etruscan context marking the end of the transitional liminal period of the celebrations (Brandt), perhaps coinciding with an animal sacrifice as seen in Roman usage. In an Early Bronze Age context, animal bones from burials and their environs may comprise direct evidence for foodstuffs consumed by the funerary participants and/or burnt on the cremation pyre (Fowler), the last a habit also observed in a northern European Roman context (Pearce). Animal sacrifice is often considered as an act of purification, a concept which, together with its antonym pollution, is often closely connected with funerary practices (Brandt). In some societies (as in Bronze Age England, and Classical Greece and Rome) cremation may be looked upon as a purifying act and emblematic of physical transformation (Fowler, Ahrens), but in Persian funerary practices an exposure of the body to water and fire was considered as acts of pollution (Ahrens).

Funerary ritual is not only a question of belief (as already discussed), but also of commemoration of the deceased beyond the moment of death and interment. This runs as a leitmotif through most burial practices and is an area of extraordinary complexity as funerary rituals and memorials to the dead send out a multiplicity of messages (Bowden). However, the need for commemoration is perhaps more strongly emphasised in societies in which ancestor cult is important in regularising social and political imperatives. For example, in both Neolithic/Chalcolithic Italy and Early Bronze Age England, ancestor commemoration rituals were crucial to the development of ideas of lineages, identity and personhood (Dolfini, Fowler), basic ideas which are well preserved both in later Etruscan beliefs in afterlife (Brandt), in Roman funerary *Selbstdarstellung* art (Pearce), and Viking Age 'death myths' (Oestigaard).

To conclude, funerary practices (covering the period from the biological to the social death of a person), if looked upon as a web, or rather as a piece of textile built up of vertical threads expressing movement in time and horizontal threads movement in space, they can be said to have a clearly defined frame. The practices, however, consist of threads loosely bound to each other: some threads represent practices which can be followed through both in time and space, some represent practices which can be followed in one time period across large spaces, while others represent threads which are linked to one space over a long period of time; some practices may also appear in one shape, later developing into a different shape, but without changing content. The purpose of this introductory chapter has been to highlight some of these threads and demonstrate how the articles in the present publication are woven together despite the wide chronological and geographical framework chosen. We leave the reader to judge if we have succeeded.

Note

1   I shall in the following presentation often quote or paraphrase sequences from the contributed articles. In order not to split up the text too much with quotation marks I shall only add the name of the author in parenthesis where applicable. Since the aim of this introduction is to show how the articles are bound together in fact and spirit, I hope the readers and the authors will excuse me for using the contributors' own words in this way.

Bibliography

Bouvrie, S. des 2012: 'Greek Festivals and the Ritual Process. An Inquiry into the Olympia-cum-Heraia and the Dionysia', in J. R. Brandt & J. W. Iddeng (eds): *Greek and Roman Festivals. Content, Practice, and Meaning*, Oxford University Press: Oxford, 53–93.

Morris, I. 1992: *Death Ritual and Social Structure in Classical Antiquity*, Cambridge University Press: Cambridge.

Metcalf, P. & Huntington, R. 1991: *Celebrations of Death. The Anthropology of Mortuary Ritual*, 2nd ed., Cambridge University Press: Cambridge.

Paxton, F. S. 2011: see internet: http: //www.deathreference.com/Ce-Da/Christian-Death-Rites-History-of.html (visited 28.10.11).

Weiss-Krejci, E. 2011: 'The Formation of Mortuary Deposits: Implications for Understanding Mortuary Behaviour of Past Populations', in S. C. Agarwal & B. A. Glencross (eds): *Social Bioarchaeology*, Wiley-Blackwell: Chichester & Oxford, 68–106.

1

A PROPER BURIAL
Some Thoughts on Changes in Mortuary Ritual, and how Archaeology can begin to understand them

Liv Nilsson Stutz

What role does ritual play in mortuary practice and the handling of the dead body, and how can we understand ritual change? This article provides an opportunity to explore these fundamental questions through the lens provided by practice theory influenced by ritual theory, and through three case studies: two historical examples of ritual change in the handling of the dead body: the introduction of cremation in Victorian England, and the emergence of the American Way of Death (with embalming and the funeral home), and one prehistoric case: the handling of the death at two Mesolithic cemeteries in southern Scandinavia. It is argued that the focus on practice is especially valuable in archaeology since it is well adapted to the nature of our sources; the material remains of past actions. The author explores the usefulness of the practice focused framework, both to reflect over ritual change and changing rituals in historic periods and prehistoric periods where we are limited to the archaeological sources.

Keywords: American way of death, corpse, Mesolithic Period , mortuary ritual, practice theory, Scandinavia, Victorian England

How can archaeology study and understand ritual change and changing rituals? In order to begin to answer this question we need to understand why people need ritual and what role ritual plays in society. In the past, ritual was often understood as conservative in nature. This view has long been abandoned, but until recently, theory about ritual has (sometimes implicitly) emphasised its role in maintaining existing structures. Today, the focus in ritual studies has shifted toward seeing ritual as part of a process of social reproduction, a process that holds the potential for both continuity and change (Bell 1992). This view on ritual as dynamic and as an integral part of social and cultural reproduction is relevant in archaeology, which since its very beginning has attempted to understand and theorise change within a range of different schools of thought. But while archaeology may be comfortable with the concept of change, it is more challenged when approaching ritual. As opposed to other disciplines tied to the field of ritual theory, archaeology does not have access to the same kind of immediate information about the range of the practices, alongside the thoughts and motivation of the practitioners that are often obtained through written and oral accounts. We are limited to the fragmentary remains of what people in the past were doing. I will argue in this article that while archaeology's fragmentary sources continue to constitute a challenge, the recent developments in ritual theory that emphasise practice point toward an important methodological opportunity.

In archaeology we need a theoretical framework that allows us to reflect on social and ritual dynamics on a general scale and that can be articulated to the nature of our sources. Any kind of model assumes a certain amount of generalisation and is founded on the idea that while every culture, and every individual is unique, the human condition is a shared experience, and the responses we have to different situations to *a certain extent* can be understood through generalising models that allow us to relate to other human beings across cultural and chronological boundaries.

In this article the problem of ritual change takes its departure in the universal experience of death and the encounter with the human cadaver. I argue that while the human responses to death and the cadaver may be extremely variable, all societies deal with death, and the responses tend to be ritual in character. After a general introduction to the theoretical understanding of the role of ritual in society and its particular role in mortuary practices, two historical cases of changing rituals are introduced in order to discuss the dynamic shifts in social practices that constituted the rituals. Finally, the model is tested on a prehistoric case, Mesolithic mortuary practices from Scandinavia.

The liminal cadaver

When a social being dies, the survivors are left not only with the abstract problem of loss and grief, but also with the concrete product of death: a cadaver. Archaeology has tended to overlook this aspect of death and focus only on the reconstruction of the role of the living – often as part of an archaeology more interested in burials for their potential for revealing social roles in life, than in their religious and ritual components. This is unfortunate, because how the body is handled in the mortuary ritual appears to be universally linked to important cultural phenomena that can give us a more complete image of past societies. The handling of the corpse reveals structures tied to attitudes toward the body, the self and other, the dead and the living, culture and nature, order and disorder, and the present, the future and the past, all potentially crucial dimensions of human life. As archaeologists we need to work toward a deeper understanding of these phenomena and how and why the ritual response to death may change over time.

In order to define the cadaver and understand it in a ritual context, I have been inspired by Julia Kristeva's abject theory (1980) and Victor Turner's concept of liminality and anti-structure (1969). Their respective models can be successfully combined in a discussion of the encounter with the cadaver and the process of dealing with it and redefining it through ritual. At death the system of the mindful body and the embodied mind (Csordas 1994; Schepher-Hughes & Lock 1987; Varela et al. 1999; and others) breaks down. The body is no longer a subject engaged in the dialectic of structured and structuring practices which simultaneously, through *hexis*, reproduce social order and embody it to the point of affecting how people feel and think (see Bourdieu 1977: 124; 1980: 117). The dead body that used to incorporate a person, a subject, is now radically changed on several levels. At first, while the cadaver still resembles the person it used to embody in so many ways, it is no longer this person. Moreover, the fact that death constitutes the starting point for an irreversible process of decay and destruction that will disfigure the remains and alter them forever, gives us a clear indication that social control and cultural shaping of the body no longer can be exercised from within, but can only be imposed from the outside. But while the body at death loses its subjective character, it does not immediately acquire an object status. Instead it is located somewhere in between these categories. In fact the cadaver can be perceived as an *abject* in the sense defined by Kristeva (1980). She introduced the term as a psychoanalytical and phenomenological category that builds on the French word *abject*, which designates something repulsive, low and despised (Rehal 1992: 15) and includes associations to the not-desirable, the borderline, and indeed, the viscerally repulsive. The abject is neither subject nor object, but a sort of pseudo-object located in between these defined categories. The human cadaver fits well within this model and Kristeva has actually defined it as 'the ultimate abject' (Kristeva 1980: 11). The lack of obvious separation between the living person and dead body introduces conflicting dimensions of desire and perversion, while the otherness of death causes the cadaver to be designated as taboo and non-object for desire (Rehal 1992: 16). Kristeva makes an important distinction when she points out that it is not the absence of purity or health that defines the abject, but *that which disturbs an identity, a system and an order. That which does not respect the limits, the places, the rules. The in-between, the ambiguous, the mixed* (Kristeva 1980: 12). In other words, the category of the abject is especially useful when reflecting over the power of that which transgresses cultural categories and defies order, rather than as something inherently repulsive (we know for example, that the cadaver is not universally experienced as such). But when contemplating the concept of the embodied mind and the mindful body, invested with an embodied sense of rules and limits, we can begin to sense the danger of the cadaver. Here we have a body that is no longer controlled from within and thus threatens the order of things. Again, it may be important to point out here that this does not automatically mean that the bodily decay necessarily is seen as a horrifying experience. Rather, by acknowledging that death constitutes a crisis, we can also observe that no matter what values or associations are projected on the cadaver in different cultures, all cultures deal with it, albeit in a wide variety of ways.

Being no longer a subject nor an object, the cadaver seems to occupy a position that integrates well into Victor Turner's model of liminality and anti-structure (Turner 1969). The cadaver, being neither fully dead nor alive, neither subject nor object, is clearly a betwixt-and-between category of person/body. It defines a truly liminal category that fits Turner's definition of its two-fold character 'at once no longer and not yet classified' (1969: 96). While Turner's model of *communitas* and anti-structure was developed to understand initiation rites, it can also be transposed to mortuary rituals as rites of passage more generally according to the framework proposed by Arnold van Gennep and which Turner continues to build upon, as rites which transfers an individual from a defined state to different but equally defined state (van Gennep 1981: 4). The need for the ritual stems from the fact that the cadaver has to be separated from the world of the living in order for the survivors to carry on with their lives. The cadaver, described as an abject, liminal phenomenon, threatening the order of society and life, constitutes a problem that has to be solved. Now that culture and society have no place within the body (through *hexis*), culture and society have to be imposed from the outside by others. Through cultural practice, the ritual handling of the dead body effectively transforms it from its identity as a living human being. Through the embodied practices of the survivors, the body of the dead, the cadaver, is ritualised and redefined. The process of ritual redefinition of the deceased – and of the cadaver – tends to generate structural connections with other 'life crises' or rites of passage, where the societal order is recreated and reinforced through embodied ritual practices. As action in response to the crisis of death, the mortuary practices are more or less explicitly linked to basic, embodied attitudes about life and death, and in turn, because these attitudes are connected – through their process of ritualisation – to concepts of self identity, order and disorder, culture and nature, individual and collective, etc., their embeddedness in the structuring structures that give form to society can help us to understand quite much about those structures. These rites of passage allow us to redefine the individual as dead and the abject as object, while at the same time helping us through the crisis that death generates and get on with life. The liminal phase is a time when mourners are allowed to mourn their dead, where life is secondary (Rosenblatt et al. 1976: 89–90). The duration of this period is highly variable within each culture and likely also on an individual level. In fact, on a personal emotional level, the transition often requires more time than is allowed for in the ritual structure (compare de Boeck 1995). But the symbolic transition from one state to the next helps define the borders that are being transgressed and provides a frame of reference for the social structure of the living.

At the same time, death is also the starting point for the processes of decay and decomposition that gradually will consume the body. This process alters the appearance of the cadaver further and thus imposes a time cap on the separation process. Mortuary rituals, in a variety of ways, handle this process as well. In some cultures, like our own, the processes of decay are hidden – our corpses are placed inside coffins or they are rapidly destroyed by fire. In the contemporary US the open casket burial takes the denial of decay to extremes, through embalming and restoring the cadaver so that it closely resembles the living individual in a state of sleep (see below). When we consider cadavers as abjects, we can better understand how they become the focus of the liminal phase of a ritual that aims to pass a person through the life crisis of death. The structural associations of oppositions and contradictions produced in dealing with death and the cadaver seem to stretch out beyond the physical remains of the body. They draw in opposing elements to the cadaver and thus form a symbolic complex that defines good vs. bad death. To control death as well as the dead body defines a ritual instrument for controlling biology and nature in a tight connection to controlling the social death. Thus, the mortuary ritual practices tend to embed the phenomenon of death – along with that of society – into an idea about the eternal order of things. In handling the cadaver in the right way, the survivors affirm the structure at a much more fundamental level than simply restoring a peaceful, effective arrangement of social relationships.

So how is this redefinition of the corpse possible? How does the ritual operate in this context, and how can we understand change in mortuary practices? In order to respond to these questions, we need to turn to ritual theory.

Understanding rituals as practice

Ritual studies have in recent years come to focus increasingly on practice (Bell 1992; de Boeck 1995; Humphrey & Laidlaw 1994; Parkin 1992). The main model draws on the sociology of Pierre Bourdieu (1977; 1980), but has its roots in the early sociological studies of ritual and religious phenomena (e.g., Durkheim 1965 [1915]; van Gennep 1981 [1909]), and the later forms they inspired in social and cultural anthropology (e.g., Rappaport 1999; Turner 1967; 1969). This theoretical framework is very useful for archaeology since it emphasises people's actions rather than prescribed meaning and symbolic content. Like practice theory in general, it does not infer that practices are *meaningless*, but rather than embodied knowledge and bodily practice precedes verbalised meaning. Moreover, while these models build on sociological and anthropological studies and comparisons, they attempt to formulate *how ritual as a process works*. It is assumed that there are certain recurrent elements within ritual that allows us to formulate a series of cross-culturally shared fundamentally human mechanisms integral to the ritual process *per se*, which could be applied within archaeology.

Catherine Bell has proposed a comprehensive, influential and useful theory of ritual practice (1992). She views ritual as a strategic way to act and uses the concept *ritualisation* to distinguish ritual from non-ritual acts. Ritualisation, according to Bell (1992: 7), is a strategic way to act that, which, in the process of being carried out, creates a distinction from other practices, defining this specific practice – in relation to other practices in its social context – as ritual, privileged, significant and powerful. Bell draws on Bourdieu's practice theory framework and sees ritualisation as proceeding in dialectic between practice and structure. The structures that give form to ritual may be said – in the sometimes difficult but carefully formulated language of practice theory – to structure and be structured by actions that tend to generate practices, memories, emotional sensations, symbolic representations, and so on, that display formal relationships organised into binary oppositions, often articulated hierarchically (Nilsson Stutz 2003: 41). Moreover, the structural links between the elements of ritualising practices intertwine into complex chains of associations, and despite the dynamic dialectical variation in ritual practices from one moment to the next, ritualisation generates a feeling of a logical system with a clear, comprehensive, hierarchically organised order. Through this process, a cosmology, i.e. a structured world of significance, is created through this production of separation. Ritual creates a world: a structure that appears to be logical and natural (for similar ideas see for example Turner 1969; Kertzer 1988). Instead of emphasising underlying meaning, this perspective on ritual underlines the process of embodiment. The model emphasises the embodied experience – it is the active participation in the ritual that creates the sense of structure in the participants. This further means that ritual does not express a meaning, nor does it reflect social structure; instead it creates and generates meaning and relationships (Bell 1992: 82; Bourdieu 1977: 120). Since meaning does not exist independent of practice, it is secondary. The ritual does not have to create a coherent and uncontested meaning for the participant; instead it is the embodied action that creates the sense of structure – not the rationalisations that the participants may give for their actions. This does not mean that rituals are meaningless. Perhaps it is better stated that practice theory emphasises a different understanding of meaning, as being inherent in action, which has social-historical consequences – no matter how small or short-term. This broader notion of meaning may be opposed to the classic, linguistically inspired structuralist conception, that meaning in ritual may be directly translated into a verbal reference (Nilsson Stutz 2003: 38). This further means that meaning as such can vary, while the embodied knowledge – the sense of how things are done – is shared. In the case here, it would mean that the participants would have a sense of what a 'proper' burial would be like, but they may still project different meanings to the practices.

What is particularly interesting here is that the model provides a framework to understand ritual *change*. Following practice theory, this model allows considerable potential for flexibility, through reinterpretation and appropriation. Since practice precedes meaning, every ritual event becomes a potential opportunity for reproduction or change. The change can be intentional and clearly break away from the dominating scheme, but it can also be gradual, almost invisible and unintentional, and only in a long term perspective become visible without the participants necessarily being aware of the process as it is taking place.

In the previous section we discussed how the handling of the cadaver constitutes a crucial component of mortuary ritual. When viewing this through the practice theory focused framework proposed by Bell, we can comprehend the treatment of the body as a response to the uncontrollable nature of the cadaver and indeed of death. Through ritualisation the cadaver is redefined into an object that conforms to structured ideas about death and from which the mourners can separate. The ritual practices create an image of death, and a final image of the dead, which conform to and can be articulated with more general ideas about a 'good death' (relating to attitudes to life, death, the dead body etc.) and through these practices the social and cultural structure is reproduced through the structure-practice dialectic. When viewing the mortuary ritual and the ritual redefinition of the cadaver from this perspective, every burial – or every other occasion for a mortuary ritual – becomes an arena for the reproduction of social structure in the widest sense of the term, including not only the classic archaeological categories of social status, gender, etc., but also attitudes to life and death, to the body, to order of society and the wider world, etc. In this way practice theory allows us to link the specific practice of handling the dead to a society's cosmology as a whole. And since every ritual event is a separate occasion in this process, the ritual holds potential for change as well as continuity.

Archaeologically we often see variation in practices and we try to understand this pattern. This kind of variation could be a part of the ritual program which prescribes a proper way to single out different individuals within a group (according to gender, age, social class etc.). Variation may also take other forms: the proper burial may not be possible to carry out (for example if the corpse is missing) or, some individuals may be denied a proper burial as a sanction or punishment. In these cases, differences are viewed as variation within a program. But what about *change*? How can we view the processes of change in the archaeological material within this framework? And how can variation within an existing program relate to long term change? While it would be wrong to assume that all rituals are conservative, it would be equally difficult to assume that change takes place for no particular reason. The production of a new imagery of death must have been articulated with other views within the social structure and operate in a way that would make sense in the past through altered conceptions of death, of the body, of the individual, or as part of shifts in the processes of identification, for example through emulation and aspiration. Change can thus be highly visible in the society where it takes place, or operate in a less visible way and gradually affect the views of what a proper burial and a good death is. In order to illustrate this I will now proceed to discuss two historical cases of change in the handling of the body.

Ritual changes and changing rituals: two historical cases

What does ritual change with regards to mortuary practices look like? Why and how do mortuary rituals change? The framework developed above indicates that mortuary practices are important both for society and for the individuals. If indeed the treatment of the corpse constitutes a an arena for the production of the proper death and for control over death and nature, then changes in that treatment would be a serious matter with repercussions in other dimensions of society as well. To test this assumption I will now briefly discuss two historical cases of mortuary ritual change. Through the examination of the introduction of cremation in nineteenth century England and the development of the American way of death in the twentieth century, I will explore the dynamics involved in changing mortuary ritual.

The shift from inhumation to cremation in 19th century England

In the 19th century, attitudes toward the disposal of the dead changed radically in England. From predominantly disposing of the dead through inhumation, cremation gained not only acceptance but eventually also popularity. Brian Parsons (2005) accounts for the multiple factors that intertwined in this change in the perception of the proper burial. It is often assumed that a religious or eschatological shift underlies ritual change, but the introduction of cremation in nineteenth century England tells a more complex story. Rather than reflecting a religious conversion, the introduction of cremation was situated in a time of social, cultural and technological change which all in different ways contributed to the radical break with the traditional practice of inhumation. Overcrowded urban cemeteries associated with stench and nuisances like drunken grave diggers and the business of body snatchers, were perceived an unattractive place for the liberal and forward thinking reformers that pioneered the movement. They argued for a more hygienic and modern practice of disposing of dead bodies, an attitude which also, and rather typically for this period, occasionally was associated with nostalgia for a very distant past. With the technological development of furnaces that made the cremation process possible to be conducted out of sight and in an efficient manner that reduced the body to cremains within hours also contributed to offering a socially acceptable *kind* of cremation which could be synchronised with the ideals of progress and modernity. While the practice broke off with tradition it also gained support from certain clergy, which allowed for it to be articulated with the Christian faith and as a consequence an alternative for a larger group of society. But even if cremation can be seen as a part of modernity that swept through society more generally, it was still perceived as a radical idea, and the introduction was visible, contested and controversial. In many instances legal indictments were part of the process of the transition (see for example the case of Dr Price, Parsons 2005: 100–7).

When viewed through the lens of practice theory, this ritual change was radical and intentional. Through a clear and visible break with tradition, a new form of 'proper burial' was proposed. It is interesting to note that while certain practices changed radically, other components remained the same. While the reduction of the corpse to cremains in a specially constructed furnace contextualised this death within a world-view that valued progress, modernity, hygiene and technology, the use of coffins and the actual shielding of the observers from the destructive processes anchored these practices within a traditional idea of a proper burial. Moreover, while the destructive power of the flames horrified many (for example, Parsons 2005: 38), cremation was still founded on the idea of a dignified and proper way of handling the body, by keeping it away from the appalling cemeteries, the body snatchers and the unhealthy aspects of decay etc. In this way also, the radical new practice could become articulated with the older tradition. In a way, cremation offered a new way of sustaining a dignified way of dealing with the dead as the surrounding society corrupted the traditional ways of doing so. In this way we can also understand how people eventually came to accept this ritual change: while it broke off with tradition on some levels, it still held on to traditional values. It was probably also important that through the sanction of certain representatives of the clergy, the practice could become embedded within the Christian faith. While we in retrospect might view this new practice as a reflection of change in other areas of society, the practice itself constitutes the act of reproducing that ideal, a reproduction that also would have equal repercussion in other areas of society.

The introduction of cremation in 19th century England illustrates how ritual change can be abrupt and collide with contemporary society in a way that caused distress and conflict. It also provides an example for how mortuary ritual can become a privileged arena for the conflict between different positions in society. Finally, we can also see how a new practice within generations becomes completely embraced by society – something which those of us working with a deep past may need to keep in mind as we observe what form our point of view may appear to be drastic shifts in the archaeological record.

The emergence of embalming and funeral homes in America

The second example of a change in the treatment of the body after death shows a different trajectory. In the early 20th century the attitudes to death and the dead went through a radical transformation in the United States. And just like in the case of cremation in England, the ritual change was not immediately tied to religious changes, but rather a shift in the general attitudes to death and the dead body. Gary Laderman (1996; 2003) who has written extensively on the American death rituals, relates the changes to three main factors: changes in demographic patterns, the rise of hospitals as places of dying, and the growth of modern funeral homes which all contributed to creating a divide between the mourners and the physical remains of the dead (Laderman 2003: 1). As mortality rates dropped and life expectancy improved, death became a rare occurrence, to the point that 'it was easier to imagine the dead than to actually encounter them in everyday life, a common feature of social history up until that time' (Laderman 2003: 1). During the 19th century the development of medicine led not only to lower mortality, but also to changes in *the ways* people died. In the early 20th century the medical profession had assumed power to define death and control the process of death, and where ultimately death was seen as defeat (Laderman 2003, see also Ariès 1981: 583–8).

In this context a new attitude to the dead emerged. Just like medical doctors were the professionals of dying, the funeral directors rose as a new professionalised specialist in the care for the dead. While many complex factors contributed to the separation of the dead and the living, the practice of embalming appears to have become a particularly important one. In the early 19th century, embalming was only carried out in medical faculties, away from the public consciousness as a method to preserve corpses for education and research purposes (Laderman 2003: 6). The technical knowledge of it existed within the medical community, but it was not part of a general approach to death. The technique appears to have become more commonly used at the end of the civil war as the bodies of dead soldiers were embalmed in order to sustain the transportation home for burial. When the body of President Lincoln met the same fate before its transportation from Washington DC to Springfield, Illinois, the practice gradually gained more general acceptance. Eventually it found an important place within the American mortuary ritual of the viewing of the corpse, where it transformed the experience of encountering the dead. Over the course of the 19th century, the viewing of the corpse had become an integral part of the American funeral and instrumental in the struggle to make sense of death (Laderman 2003: 6). Along with social and cultural changes such as concern with sanitation and the fact that people had become highly mobile and needed to travel great distances for a funeral (Laderman 2003: 6), the ritual began to constitute an emerging problem. The art of embalming proposed an immediate and available solution.

As the practice of embalming gained ground a new profession emerged to carry it out. Gradually the treatment of the dead was moved from the private home to the funeral home, a new phenomenon that starts to emerge in the early 20th century. The funeral home provides new place for the ritual – a kind of pseudo-home that provides a professional yet domestic place for the ritual viewing. This 'home away from home' provided the space both for the new treatment of the body and the intimate ritual viewing of the body. At this point, Laderman argues:

> the body had become more than simply a container for the spirit… Under the loving gaze of mourners, the corpse acquired a sacred status that was decidedly material rather than spiritual, and comforting rather than horrifying (Laderman 2003: 22).

The final image of the dead became central to the ritual, and was often documented through photography – and the responsibility to create this image fell upon the funeral director. Embalming also restored bodies after destruction and could present the corpse of the person the way they had lived rather than the way they had died. This art was widely and publicly appreciated. The corpse that 'looked good and was at peace' embodied the good death. This new image of the dead fit the needs of people caught in 'the fast-paced, technologically driven changes in modern society' as they 'longed for a fixed, permanent image of the deceased at peace' (Laderman 2003: 8). It also fit into an increasingly consumerist and capitalist society.

From a practice theory perspective the changes that occurred at the turn of the last century in the United States are extremely interesting. As in the previous example, it is not mainly changes in religious beliefs that drive the ritual change, but rather other social and cultural phenomena, mainly attitudes to death, the body, hygiene and the commodification of specialised services. These values have long-lasting effects on mortuary ritual. Through the generalisation of embalming, the handling of the corpse becomes so complex that it requires special training and equipment and is transferred from the mourners to the funeral director and the funeral home. As a result, not only the dead but also death is removed from proximity with the living. The practice that engages the mourners is now exclusively the viewing of the perfect corpse, staged in order to project an image of peaceful sleep of the unaltered and even perfected body. Again, while we could view these new rituals as mere reflections of changes in society, it is important to see them as an active part of changing these ideas. Every time a dead body was viewed according to the new ritual program, the attitudes were reproduced and reinforced. Death was constantly moved further away from lived experienced and encased in a new artificial mold that through the ritual of viewing came to represent 'real' death.

As opposed to the previous example, this transition is more seamless and gradual, and while critical voices that viewed embalming as unnatural, unnecessary and un-American and that claimed that the profit-making funeral industry was unethical were heard (Laderman 2003: 29), there was not the same intense conflict surrounding the development of embalming and the development of the funeral home in America as at the introduction of cremation in England a few decades earlier.

Both these historical examples illustrate how ritual change takes place in society. The development is complex and draws in multiple aspects of the social and cultural reality. Interestingly, in both cases, religion plays a minor role and tends to just be flexible enough to incorporate the new practices rather than to lead the way to change. In the first case we see how a new ritual is introduced as a controversial idea by a few radical minds and only gradually gains support among the public. In the second case, the change is more gradual and seeps in on all levels of society and gains acceptance without causing general outrage or distress. The cases show the archaeologist that ritual change can take many shapes, but also that it operates on several levels of the social fabric where it needs to make sense in order to gain ground.

Understanding the treatment of the body in the Mesolithic

The previous cases have shown us how complex ritual changes can be, and how many different dimensions become intertwined in the process. There is no reason to think that prehistory was any different. How then can we understand ritual change and changing rituals archaeologically? To approach this question, I will explore the example of Mesolithic cemeteries around the Baltic (this work is based on previous research, for details, please see Nilsson Stutz 2003). Here we do not have the rich record of the historical periods regarding people's emotions, thoughts and attitudes. Instead, we need to try to recreate this social and cultural history, or at least fragments of it, by starting with the practices that we can observe in the archaeological record. The assumption here is that following the ritual theory proposed by Bell, and illustrated in the examples of historical mortuary ritual and ritual change, the mortuary practices would be linked to general attitudes in society toward death, the dead body, ideas about the life, death, the afterlife etc.

During the later phases of the Mesolithic in northern Europe (6th–7th millennium BC), the first formal cemeteries emerge as places for the disposal of the dead (see Fig. 1.1). In places like Vedbæk/Bøgebakken in eastern Denmark (Albrethsen & Brinch-Petersen 1977) and Skateholm in southern Sweden (Larsson 1988), Zvejnieki in northern Latvia (Zagorsikis 1987), and Olenii Ostrov in Karelia (Gurina 1956; O'Shea & Zvelebil 1984), the dead are buried in what appears to be specifically dedicated areas, often close to the occupation sites, in dozens and up to several hundreds. The mortuary rituals at these sites have often been described as complex because of the variation in position and grave-goods placed with the dead. In my work I have looked closer at the practices at Skateholm and Vedbæk/Bøgebakken in detail and also to a certain extent the practices at Zvejnieiki. Instead of focusing on what distinguishes the individuals buried at the sites, I initially wanted to establish a core of practices that the overwhelming majority could be said to share. My focus has been mainly on the ritual treatment of the body which I have reconstructed in detail with the French taphonomical approach to burials called *Archaeothanatology* (Duday 2009).

Overall the burials in Skateholm and Vedbæk/Bøgebakken can be characterised by a practice that appears to emphasise the integrity of the body at the time of disposal. The overwhelming majority of the bodies were buried intact shortly after death. The practice hides or denies the processes of decay and decomposition since the bodies are buried before the postmortem disfiguration has reached an advanced stage. At the time of burial the bodies probably still resembled the living individual. This impression of a remaining subjectivity associated with the body is strengthened by the fact that the bodies often were placed in life-like positions. There are several cases of bodies arranged to look at each other or even hold one another in the grave. In some rare instances the analysis has also shown that the bodies were shielded from the surrounding sediment either by the use of platforms under the body, or wrappings of different kinds. The attention to the integrity of the body could also explain the very few disturbances of the burials, which indicates that the burial place was known and respected. In some rare instances disturbances have occurred, and it is interesting to note that in these cases there is no visible trace of any attempt to correct the disturbance (like we often witness in Medieval cemeteries). Maybe the body of the dead after a long time in the ground had completed its transition from subject and abject to object, and the disturbance was therefore unproblematic. It is of course also possible that since this kind of disturbance was rare, there might not have been a prescribed way to deal with it.

Within this core of practices that respects the body, we can see a significant amount of variation. The bodies are placed in different positions, and they are accompanied by different kinds of deposits – often artifacts, but also ochre, possible food items, etc. This variation can be understood as being linked to each of the buried individuals. Every time a burial is carried out an attempt is made to create a proper burial and a good death. The variation regarding position and burial goods could be seen in this perspective as a variation within the core of practices, sometimes as a reproduction, and sometimes potentially also as a way to distinguish the dead or highlight an aspect of their identity.

But some burials break away from the established norm in other ways that may indicate a tension within the attitudes to death and the dead body. At Skateholm, three individuals appear to have been burned before disposal at the cemetery. In another case, grave 28 in Skateholm, the analysis has shown how the body was buried in a way that facilitated the removal of several bones from the grave after the process of decomposition was terminated (for more details of the study, see Nilsson Stutz 2003). This indicates that while the processes of decomposition and decay were hidden at the time of burial of the dead, they were intimately known and could be controlled and exploited. Here the dry bones of the dead have been removed from the burial probably to become reintroduced into the world of the living. We may ask ourselves if they at this point represented the dead individual whose body was buried in a way that indicates premeditation of this removal, or if they represented the world of the dead. Had the transition from subject to object of death been completed at this point, or would these bones forever be considered abject? The presence of human bones on Mesolithic occupation sites raises questions about how common these practices may have been as a parallel to the burial practices that respect the body's integrity.

Another interesting case to discuss here is burial 13 in Skateholm where the incomplete and partially disarticulated remains of a body were found in a constrained space. The analysis has revealed that the remains were disposed of when the cadaver was still fresh, which indicates that the individual must have been cut up in pieces. There are several possible interpretations to this burial. Maybe the dismemberment was part of the ritual practice and contributed to actively separate this individual from a 'proper' burial, maybe as a case of a scapegoating strategy. This would open up to a discussion of the role of ritual as an instrument of social control. But it is also possible to propose the opposite hypothesis: the body may have been violated at the time of death and the mortuary practices may have hidden this state by burying the remains with a container that shielded the mourners from the real state of the remains. In this case the ritual practice would be an example of trying to recreate certain fundamentally important aspects of the burial ritual, as it would be experienced at the time of disposal, as an attempt to create normalcy.

When looking at the Mesolithic cemeteries we can also track a certain amount of change, both over time and space. When looking at change over time, Skateholm constitutes an interesting example. Here two chronological phases can be distinguished. For the older phase the individuals are distinguished by a variation in grave-goods. The things placed with the dead are both more varied and more numerous. In the second phase, grave-goods appear to become less instrumental in the distinguishing of individuals, and instead the position of the body shows greater variability. Here it is possible to track a change in the way in which the proper burial is staged, and possibly in the way in which the individual is marked at the time of separation from the living. At the same time the integrity of the body continues to be a central feature emphasised in the burial. This indicates that while certain things are negotiable for change, others are not. Again, this indicates that the integrity of the body and the life like arrangement at the time of separation probably was a fundamental component of mortuary ritual and the attitudes to death and the dead body.

When taking a wider perspective on changing rituals it is interesting to compare the pattern in southern Scandinavia to what we can observe in the eastern Baltic. Here the Mesolithic burials show many interesting similarities to the Scandinavian practices. However, when extending the perspective chronologically contrasts emerge. During the Neolithic Funnel Beaker Period in southern Scandinavia (*c.* 4000–2700 BC) collective mortuary practices associated with megaliths were embraced, practices which are also highly associated with the fragmentation of the individual body. The ritual practices at Zvejnieki remain in the same cemeteries and while the position of the body changes and the grave goods changes (for a summary of the changes in the burial practices over time, see Zagorska 2006), the respect for the individual body remains at the center of the archaeological image of the mortuary ritual, perhaps eventually giving way for a focus on location and place as the cemetery filled up. Maybe the change to collective burials and extensive manipulation of the body in southern Scandinavia has deep roots in the local Mesolithic practice of occasionally manipulating human bones as was shown in burial 28 in Skateholm described above. Here, we can begin to discuss how ritual variation at a certain point in time may constitute practices that ritual change can articulate with and thus be viewed as a continuation of traditional ways or at least as a continuation of an accepted variation. For example, maybe the occasional ritual manipulation of body parts in the Mesolithic (for which we do not know the extent) were crucial in rendering the more extensive manipulation of the dead seen in later periods socially possible and acceptable. Here the examples of historical examples of ritual change (for example the cases described above) can help us understand the dynamic processes of changing ritual in prehistoric settings.

Concluding remarks

In this article I have attempted to propose a way in which archaeology can approach the question of ritual change. The practice theory based ritual theory provides a framework for thinking about how ritual operates in society, and it also gives us a framework to reflect over the dynamics of ritual change. I have limited my exploration to mortuary ritual, but I believe that the overall theoretical model is valid also for other ritual practices. The historical examples serve as inspiration to think about mortuary ritual and how change in the treatment of the body may be contested in one context and almost seamlessly accepted in another. Still, the examples of modern cremation practices in England and embalming and open-casket viewing in the United States underscore how – because all societies must deal with ritually redefining their dead – changes in mortuary ritual reflect dynamic changes in the rich fabric of attitudes linking aspects of death (such as decay) to the surrounding culture. Thus, we can make sense of these changes within their cultural contexts. Finally the prehistoric example serves as a test case to see just how we can approach these issues archaeologically – principally by turning the approach around, starting with the practices, rather than with the history of shifts in social attitudes. In this way, the focus on material traces of ritual practices can help us to reconstruct what people in the past were doing in order to handle their dead ritually, allowing us to interpret a sort of social history that reveals long-term attitudes to death and to the dead body.

Bibliography

Albrethsen, S. E. & Brinch-Pedersen, E. 1977: 'Excavations of a Mesolithic Cemetery at Vedbæk, Denmark', *Acta Archaeologica*, 47.1: 9–54.

Ariès, P. 1981: *The Hour of our Death*, Alfred A. Knopf: New York.

Bell, C. 1992: *Ritual Theory. Ritual Practice*, Oxford University Press: Oxford.

Bourdieu, P. 1977: *An Outline of a Theory of Practice*, Cambridge University Press: Cambridge.

Bourdieu, P. 1980: *Le sens pratique*, Les Editions de Minuit: Paris.

Csordas, T. (ed.) 1994: *Embodiment and Experience*. Cambridge University Press: Cambridge.

De Boeck, F. 1995: 'Bodies of Remembrance: Knowledge, Experience and the Growing of Memory in Llunda Ritual Performance', in G. Thinès & L. de Heusch (eds): *Rites et Ritualisation*, Librairie Phlisophique J. Vrin: Paris, 113–38.

Duday, H. 2009: *The Archaeology of the Dead. Lectures in Archaeothanatology.* Oxbow Books: Oxford.

Durkheim, E. 1965 [1915]: *The Elementary Forms of Religious Life*, The Free Press: New York.

Gurina, N. 1956: 'Olenostrovski mogilnik', *Materialy i issledovaanyia po arheologgi SSR* 47.

Humphrey, F. & Laidlaw, J. 1994: *The Archetypal Actions of Ritual. A Theory of Ritual Illustrated by the Jain Rite of Worship.* Oxford: Oxford University Press.

Kertzer, D. L. 1988: *Ritual, Politics and Power*, Yale University Press: New Haven.

Kristeva, J. 1980: *Pouvoirs de l'horreur*, Editions de minuit: Paris.

Laderman, G. 1996: *The Sacred Remains. American Attitudes toward Death 1799–1883*, Yale University Press: New Haven.

Laderman, G. 2003. *Rest in Peace. A Cultural History of Death and the Funeral Home in Twentieth-Century America*, Oxford University Press: Oxford.

Larsson, L. 1988: *The Skateholm Project I, Man and Environment*, Regiae Societatis Humaniorum Litterarum Lundensia LXXIX: Lund.

Nilsson Stutz, L. 2003: *Embodied Rituals and Ritualized Bodies. Tracing Ritual Practices in Late Mesolithic Burials*, Acta Archaeologica Lundensia 46: Lund.

O'Shea, J. & Zvelebil, M. 1984: 'Olenostrovski mogilnik: Reconstructing the Social and Economic Organization of Prehistoric Foragers in Northern Russia', *Journal of Anthropological Archaeology* 3: 1–40.

Parkin, D. 1992: 'Ritual as Spatial Direction and Bodily Division', in D. de Coppet (ed.): *Understanding Rituals*, Routledge: London, 421–28.

Parsons, B. 2005: *Committed to the Cleansing Flame. The Development of Cremation in Nineteenth-Century England*, Spire Books: Reading.

Rappaport, R. 1999: *Ritual and Religion in the Making of Humanity*, Cambridge University Press: Cambridge.

Rehal, A. 1992: "Förord", in J. Kristeva: *Fasans makt. En essä om abjektionen*, Daidalos: Göteborg, 7–24.

Rosenblatt, P. C., Walsh, R. P. & Jackson, D. A. 1976: *Grief and Mourning in a Cross-Cultural Perspective*, Human Relations Area Files.

Schepher-Hughes, N. & Lock, M. 1987: 'The Mindful Body: A Prolegomenon to Future Work in Medical Anthropology', *Medical Anthropology Quarterly* 1: 6–41.

Turner, V. 1967: 'Betwixt and Between: The Liminal Period in Rites de Passage', in V. Turner (ed.): *The Forest of Symbols. Aspects of Ndembu Ritual*, Cornell University Press: Ithaca, 93–111.

Turner, V. 1969: *The Ritual Process. Structure and Anti-Structure*, Aldine de Gruyter: Hawthorne, NY.

van Gennep, A. 1981 [1909]: *Les rites de passage. Étude systématique des rites*, Picard: Paris.

Varela, F. J., Thompson, E. & Rousch, E. 1999: *The Embodied Mind. Cognitive Science and Human Experience*, MIT Press: Cambridge.

Zagorsikis, F. 1987: Zvejnieku akmens laikmeta kapulauks. Zinātue: Riga.

Zagorska, I. 2006: 'Radiocarbon Chronology of the Zvejnieki Burials', in L. Larsson & I. Zagorska (eds): *Back to the Origin. New Research in the Mesolithic-Neolithic Zvejnieki Cemetery and Environment in Northern Latvia*, Acta Archaeologica Lundensia: Lund, 91–113.

2

NEOLITHIC AND COPPER AGE MORTUARY PRACTICES IN THE ITALIAN PENINSULA
Change of Meaning or Change of Medium?

Andrea Dolfini

For Gianni Bailo Modesti – In Memoriam

The goal of this paper is to reassess the changes in mortuary practices documented in the Italian peninsula during the late 5th and 4th millennia BC, at the transition between Neolithic and Copper Age. For much of the Neolithic, burial was carried out within the nucleated village in the form of a relatively simple performance, which started with the interment of an articulated body and ended, in most cases, with the disturbance of the grave and the scattering of the dry bones. In the late and final Neolithic, however, burial was increasingly undertaken at peripheral or otherwise distinct areas within villages, and by the early Copper Age it was moved to purpose-built extramural cemeteries. Moreover, disarticulation practices became increasingly complex in this time period, and caused most of the deceased to lose their individuality. Finally, the Copper Age saw the appearance of the first richly furnished burials, which are often interpreted as markers of growing social inequality. It is argued in this paper that the emergence of the cemetery as a separate locus for the performance of burial does not depend on radical changes in the political structure of society. Rather, it would mark a profound modification in the symbolic toolkit used by prehistoric society to express individual and group identity as well as beliefs concerning the human body. In other words, it is not a change in the meaning of burial per se that we are witnessing in the Copper Age but a change in the medium chosen by society to stress overarching ideas of group identity, which were previously conveyed by co-residence in the nucleated village. However, since social relations derive their meanings from the practices through which they are articulated, modifications

Andrea Dolfini

to the social understanding of burial did emerge from the changing media employed for their expression. The most important of these concerns the body of the deceased, which Copper Age communities turned into a major locus for social reproduction.

Keywords: body, burial, identity, Italy, mortuary practices, Neolithic, Copper Age.

Introduction: burial, politics, and identity

A central avenue of investigation in funerary archaeology claims that changes in burial rituals are to be explained with changes in the political structure of society. Explorations into the political aspects of burial were especially favoured by processual archaeologists in the 1970s and early 1980s. This tradition of studies can be traced back to Binford (1971), who famously maintained that burial directly reflects the structure of society, and that differences in funerary treatment are informative about power inequalities and social hierarchy amongst the living. He also argued that the social persona of the deceased, or the composite of a person's social identities recognised as appropriate for consideration in death, would vary according to their lifetime rank.

Working within a similar research milieu, Tainter (1978) introduced the concept of energy expenditure into mortuary analysis. He claimed that the more energy is expended by mourners during all stages of the funerary performance – be it in the lavishness of the funeral, the monumentality of the grave or the quantity of goods deposited therein – the higher is the standing of the deceased within their community. In a similar vein, Saxe (1970) argued that cemeteries are established by corporate groups to legitimise their rights to access restricted resources, for ancestors provide a powerful medium to support political claims. Finally, O'Shea (1981) assessed the viability of mortuary data as an indicator of 'vertical' (i.e. hierarchy-driven) and 'horizontal' (i.e. descent-driven) social distinctions. By examining changes in burial patterns at a number of native cemeteries in the American Central Plains, he found that ranking would emerge quite clearly from variations in the mortuary record while the 'horizontal' dimensions of society would be more difficult to identify.

In the last three decades, these concepts have been applied to investigating the changes in funerary customs which occurred in the Italian peninsula during the late/final Neolithic and early Copper Age (*c.* late 5th and 4th millennia BC). Burial, in particular, was widely employed as a proxy for two major phenomena that were thought to characterise prehistoric Italian society at this important juncture: the rise of social ranking and the establishment of political claims over land or other restricted resources.

In numerous works dedicated to the Italian Copper Age, Cazzella (1992; 1998; 2003a) argued that the appearance of richly furnished burials would reflect the emergence of structural inequalities within prehistoric society. In particular, he interpreted the practice of burying adult males with rich sets of tools and weapons as a marker of a 'Big Man' society, in which men competed for power through the accumulation of prestige-giving goods. Since power could not be transmitted by descent in societies of this kind – he argued – the funerals of these individuals were marked by acts of conspicuous consumption whereby the symbols of their lifetime authority were removed from circulation. Thus, the burying of 'Big Men' would have sanctioned the opening of a new power contest within their communities. Similar readings were championed by Barker (1981), Guidi (2000), and Peroni (1989; 1996), and greatly contributed to shaping scholarly interpretations of Copper Age society in the central Mediterranean region.

With regard to the politics of resource procurement and land use, Skeates (1995: 229) noted that the earliest Copper Age cemeteries to be found in east-central Italy lay at the heart of the agricultural zone stretching through valley bottoms and coastal lowlands. Following Saxe (1970) and Bradley (1981), he proposed interpreting this evidence as the archaeological correlate of the political claims made by emerging elites over arable land and pastures. However, he tempered his reading by pointing out that graves in this period presented no exterior monumental aspects. Therefore, he argued, such claims might have had a rather limited outreach, and were perhaps intended more for the immediate funeral audience than for society at large. Notably, such interpretations were not solely put forward for the fertile valley bottoms of middle Adriatic Italy, but were also extended to the rugged landscape of southern Tuscany and northern Latium, where arable land is historically scarce. For example, it was suggested that Ponte San Pietro, a Copper Age cemetery in this region, had been purposefully established near now-depleted copper and antimony deposits, perhaps as a way to claim access to critical ore sources (Giardino et al. 2011). The fortune of such readings is most apparent in a recent synthesis of research on the Italian Neolithic, in which the rise of corporate burial in the 5th millennium BC is ascribed to the need to legitimise control over valuable resources by placing the dead in the landscape (Pessina & Tiné 2008: 304).

The limits of these approaches, which tend to equate funerals with a social arena for power contests, have been revealed by an alternative tradition of mortuary analysis stemming from contemporary social theory (Bourdieu 1977; Giddens 1984). For the purpose of this work, two lines of critique can be isolated within this tradition of study. The first challenges the assumption that modifications in burial practices are induced by changes in the political configuration of society. The second argues that politics provide just one of the many answers that could be given to questions of mortuary variability and ritual change.

Processual archaeologists tended to see the fossil record as directly reflecting the dynamic behaviour of people in the past. This prompted a frantic quest for 'middle range theories' which were thought to provide meaningful links between past and present (Binford 1977; Schiffer 1987; Trigger 2006: 414–15). In mortuary archaeology, in particular, a key component of middle range theories consisted of Saxe's (1970) and Binford's (1971) concept of the social persona whereby the deceased were rather mechanistically reduced to the sum of the social roles they had maintained in life. Dissatisfactions with this standpoint have been voiced by many a scholar (Barrett 1990; 1994; Hodder & Hutson 2003; Parker Pearson 1982; 1999; Thomas 1999;

Ucko 1969). A common point of their critiques to the Binford-Saxe agenda is that 'social systems are not constituted of roles but by recurrent social practices' (Parker Pearson 1982: 100). Social theory emphasises that roles are not defined once and for all, but are continuously created and re-enacted through daily practice (Bourdieu 1977; Giddens 1984). As such, they are open to negotiation and reworking in all spheres of social life including, of course, funerals. This implies that no direct relationship can be postulated between burial and the political structure of society. Rather, both burial and politics are to be conceptualised as strategic engagements that contribute, subtly or openly, to the making and breaking of the fabric of society.

The second line of critique stresses that politics represent at best one of the possible angles for approaching the study of mortuary practices (Robb 2007b). Far from being solely concerned with status and power contests over restricted resources, funerals are increasingly understood as powerful media for social communication, which have the capability to convey several messages at once: cosmological and religious beliefs, the well-being or crisis of the social group, ideas concerning the body and personhood, and the place occupied by the dead within an idealised life-cycle (Bloch 1971; Fowler 2010; this volume; Gnoli & Vernant 1982; Goody 1962; Metcalf & Huntington 1991; Robb 2002). In particular, a fruitful strand of this research tradition claims that burial acts as a meaningful arena for defining, challenging and reworking people's identity (Barraud et al. 1994; Brück 1995; 2001; Shanks & Tilley 1982; A. Strathern 1981; M. Strathern 1988).

Identity is an ambiguous concept that refers to the recognition of the self at both individual and group level (Diaz-Andreu & Lucy 2005; Meskell 2001). Individual identity is often conceptualised in terms of gender, age, status, and other aspects of human life which are deemed central to the self-understanding of people. However, identity is far more complex and multi-layered a concept than it might appear in the first instance. For example, it has been pointed out that each person embodies several facets of identity at the same time, each facet interacting and recombining with the others in potentially infinite ways (Meskell 2002; 2007). Moreover, Fowler (2004; 2008) drew our attention to the fact that the ideas of individual personhood and the bounded body underpinning personal identity in Western society are historically contingent. In other cultures, persons may be conceived of as partible and permeable, or as made from a combination of distinct substances, or indeed as resulting from the encounters and relationships in which one would engage in the course of their lives. This suggests caution in extending our own ideas of identity to non-Western societies.

Other aspects of identity are by definition relational. This is the case of class, caste, religion, and ethnicity. Interestingly, group identity is no less open to contrasting definitions than individual identity. In a seminal work, Jones (1997) convincingly argued that the culture-historical agenda that characterised prehistoric archaeology for the best part of the 20th century was shaped by Western ideas of 'people' and 'culture'. She claimed in particular that the normative and bounded idea of the ethnic group elaborated in Europe during the 18th and 19th centuries is specific to our own society, and cannot be extended uncritically to the prehistoric past. On the contrary – she argued – ethnic identity must be understood as a dynamic and contested notion, which is continually recreated and renegotiated through social practice. A similar interpretive framework has also been proposed for religion and the reworking of identity following colonial encounters (Edwards 2005; Edwards & Woolf 2004; Insoll 2007).

A common point of these investigations lies in recognising that identity cannot be understood in isolation, but only as something that is articulated through social relations. Lying at the intersection between personal ideas of the self and cultural representations of society as an orderly cosmos, identity is constantly challenged and redefined through social reproduction. Hence, it is on the dynamic interplay between individual beliefs and societal values that we must focus our attention if we are to explore how identity was conceptualised in the prehistoric past.

In this paper, I shall apply the ideas of identity hitherto discussed to investigate the profound modifications in mortuary practices, which occurred in the Italian peninsula (broadly defined as the landmass lying south of the Apennines) during the late 5th and 4th millennia BC (Fig. 2.1). I will argue, in particular, that the rise of the cemetery in this time period is not to be interpreted as a marker of major social changes, but 'merely' as the emergence of a new medium to express the same principles of group identity and solidarity which were previously conveyed by co-residence in nucleated villages. I will also maintain that the changing role of mortuary practices brought about, and in turn rested upon, a new understanding of the human body, which was conceived of as a more partible and permeable entity than had been previously. In turn, novel ideas of the body allowed prehistoric communities to inscribe social change into the very bones of the deceased, thus naturalising it through reference to a seemingly immutable ancestral cosmos.

The Italian Neolithic: the age of the village

To the archaeological imagination, the Italian Neolithic is the age of the village (Robb 2007a: 76). This is best exemplified by the substantial *villaggi trincerati* (ditched villages) brought to light in the Apulian Tavoliere, the hinterland of Matera, and southeast Sicily since the late 19th century (Pessina & Tiné 2008). Typically measuring between 80 m and 300 m in diameter, with a few much larger, these substantial settlement sites were surrounded by series of round or elliptical ditches, which sharply divided the inner inhabited space from the outer landscape (Fig. 2.2).

At Lagnano da Piede, for example, five concentric ditches, some of which were certainly in use at the same time, encircled a 5 ha village; within it, a series of C-shaped interrupted ditches enclosed smaller areas that are normally interpreted as domestic compounds (Mallory 1984–87). At Passo di Corvo, one of the largest and best investigated *villaggi trincerati* in the Tavoliere, the settled area marked by the C-shaped ditches was surrounded by three large enclosures, the outer extending about 6 km out

Andrea Dolfini

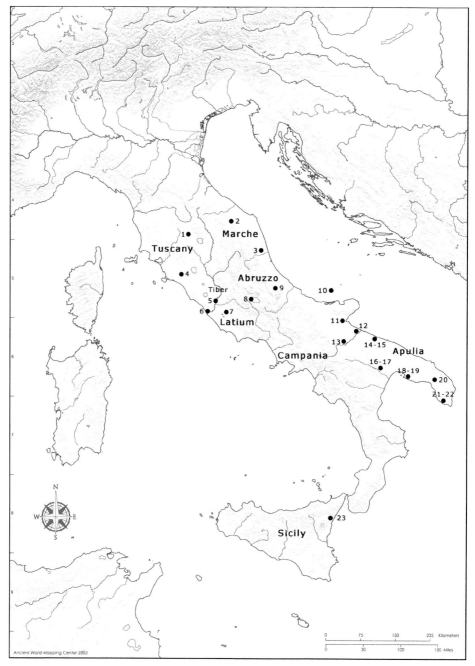

Fig. 2.1. Map of the sites mentioned in this paper. 1: Pienza; 2: Conelle di Arcevia; 3: Ripoli; 4: Ponte San Pietro; 5: Casale del Cavaliere; 6: Maccarese; 7: Quadrato di Torre Spaccata; 8: Ortucchio; 9: Grotta dei Piccioni; 10: Cala Tramontana; 11: Passo di Corvo; 12: Pulo di Molfetta; 13: Lagnano da Piede; 14: Balsignano; 15: Cala Colombo; 16: Murgecchia; 17: Serra d'Alto; 18: Masseria Bellavista; 19: Scoglio del Tonno; 20: Arnesano; 21: Samari; 22: Serra Cicora; 23: Bronte.

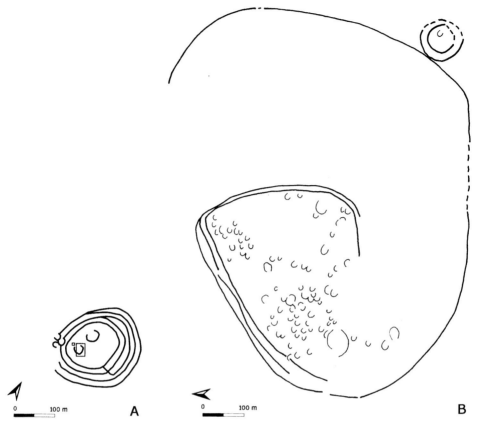

Fig. 2.2. Neolithic ditched enclosures from the Apulian Tavoliere. A: Lagnano da Piede; B: Passo di Corvo (Pessina & Tiné 2008, modified).

of the village to encircle what is thought to be the community's farmland (Tiné 1983). Although ditched villages are typically found in southern Italy and Sicily, structured enclosures separating the inhabited space from the landscape are relatively common in the Italian Neolithic (Pessina & Tiné 2008: 154). For instance, traces of wooden palisades were unearthed at Pienza in the middle Tyrrhenian peninsula, and dry-stone walls encircled the inhabited area at Pulo di Molfetta and other contemporary sites in southeast Italy (Radina 2002). Similar arrangements are also known at northern Italian sites (e.g. Degasperi et al. 1998), but these lie beyond the scope of this paper.

The debate over the meaning of Neolithic enclosures has traditionally focused on the Apulian evidence, which is the most intensively researched (Brown 1991; Skeates 2002). In this region, ditches have been variously interpreted as structures built for defence (Robb 2007a: 94; Trump 1966: 42), herd containment or corralling (Jones 1987; Whitehouse 1968), the drainage and perhaps catchment of water (Bradford 1950; Gravina 1975; Tiné 1983), and the symbolic demarcation of community boundaries

(Cassano & Manfredini 1983; Morter & Robb 1998). Micromorphology has revealed that water did flow in the ditches of Passo di Corvo and other Apulian sites (Pessina & Tiné 2008: 155), but it is doubtful whether water management was the intended goal of ditch building given the porosity of the base sediment, the high number of interrupted enclosures, and the frequency of villages built on relatively high ground (Manfredini 1972; Skeates 2002). It must perhaps be recognised that all interpretations have their own difficulties and limitations, and ditches may have served a plurality of functions (Robb 2007a: 94).

Whatever their practical role, it is fair to say that ditches must have provided Neolithic people with a discernible boundary between the inhabited village and the landscape (Pessina & Tiné 2008: 154; Robb 2007a: 94; Skeates 2002). Interestingly, recent research has shown that ditches were not built once and for all, but were continuously maintained through a series of practices encompassing filling as well as digging; meaningful acts of deposition including burial were also carried out at Neolithic ditches (Conati Barbaro 2007–08). It is not hard to imagine that such practices would have strongly contributed to reinforcing the common identity of the village community, and would have also helped to develop a cultural distinction between 'insiders' and 'outsiders'. Furthermore, similar concepts of boundedness and separation can be discerned in the C-shaped ditches surrounding household compounds. These might have informed ideas of intra-kin bonds vis-à-vis the collective identity of the village population. Significantly, mortuary practices carried out in the ditches would have further contributed to defining these structures as liminal boundaries that separated not only a group from another, but also the living from the dead (Skeates 2002: 178).

The centrality of the village for the Neolithic way of life is further emphasised by the frequent occurrence of burials (or scattered human remains) at open settlements and inhabited caves, the latter being especially common in the central Apennines (Grifoni 2003; Skeates 1997). Neolithic burial practices are extremely varied and do change remarkably in both space and time. Nonetheless, two recurrent features can be recognised in the Italian peninsular record. Firstly, for much of the Neolithic, the basic burial rite consisted of the primary inhumation of crouched individuals in earthen pits, stone-lined trenches or slab-built cists without durable goods (Fig. 2.3). Secondly, primary burial was frequently followed by the intentional or unintentional disturbance of the grave, which caused human remains to be disarticulated, fragmented, and finally dispersed within or outside the village (Pessina & Tiné 2008; Robb 2007a). The secondary treatment of bodies could take several forms ranging from the reburial of selected bones (e.g. at Samari: Cremonesi 1985–86) to their cremation (e.g. at Balsignano: Radina 2002). Acts of ancestor commemoration were also enacted at Neolithic villages. These focused on either the skull, which was sometimes removed from an otherwise complete burial (e.g. at Cala Colombo: De Lucia et al. 1977), or the undisturbed individual grave. The intentionality of the latter practice can be postulated in those cases where the undisturbed body is contained in a durable stone structure, which would have served as a visible marker for the perpetuation of ancestral memory.

Fig. 2.3. Neolithic primary burials in earthen pits and stone-lined trenches. A: Passo di Corvo; B: Balsignano, tomb 2 (Pessina & Tiné 2008, modified).

Gender is normally not stressed in the Italian Neolithic (except for a statistically significant tendency to bury males on their right-hand sides and females on their left-hand: Robb 1994a), but age occasionally is. Adult burials are slightly more numerous than children's and were left undisturbed more frequently. Moreover, children and juveniles were usually excluded from skull curation and other acts of veneration, seemingly because their untimely death had prevented their becoming ancestral beings (Robb 2007a: 63). However, unequal preservation of children and adult bone might have concurred to creating such a scenario, and caution must be taken in interpreting data that might be distorted by a sample bias.

Following Gnoli and Vernant's (1982) concept of the 'good death', Robb (2002) proposed interpreting the multifarious burial patterns of the Italian Neolithic according to their responding to an ideal life narrative, against which the circumstances of death would have been judged and the prescribed funerary rituals would have been performed (Fig. 2.4). Individual burial within villages or inhabited caves would have marked the normal deathway in Neolithic Italy. For most of the deceased, and with near-certainty for children and juveniles, this would have been followed by the disturbance of the grave and the dispersal of the bones, which would have marked the transformation of the dead into a non-individualised 'ancestral presence' for the village community. In a few cases, however, the social being of the deceased would have been preserved for remembrance and veneration by retaining their skulls or other selected remains. Finally, extraordinary circumstances of death would have compelled the performance of exceptional mortuary treatments. For example, epidemics and warfare would have

Andrea Dolfini

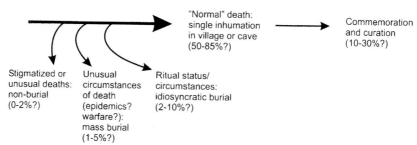

Fig. 2.4. Burial pathways in the early and middle Neolithic of the Italian peninsula (Robb 2002).

dictated mass burial at special locales, and the stigmatised dead would have been left unburied. The latter practices is probably documented at Passo di Corvo, where a young woman was found lying face-down at the bottom of a well (Tiné 1983).

Two notable points emerge from Robb's reconstruction of the Neolithic burial programme. Firstly, burial and ancestor commemoration rituals were overwhelmingly performed at villages or other inhabited sites. Ditches and houses would have provided special foci for primary and secondary burial[1], although human remains are generally found wherever domestic activities were carried out, seemingly as a part of the normal detritus of daily life. Secondly, the disturbance and dispersal of human remains were probably the consequence, either wanted or unwanted, of an array of mundane tasks such as digging new pits and building new houses. However, some ancestors were singled out for individualised remembrance either by removing selected bodily remains from their graves or by consciously avoiding disturbing their tombs, for these would have been permanently inscribed in the village landscape and social fabric. It stems from both considerations that burial, both primary and secondary, was not conceptualised as qualitatively different from the rest of the day-to-day accomplishments carried out in the village, but just as one of these accomplishments – doubtless an important one. This strongly reinforces the impression that Neolithic identity and social life would have revolved around an overarching principle of co-residence within the bounded village (Robb 1994b; 2007a). Importantly, the principle was ample enough to include the newly as well as the more distant dead, whose incorporation into a village-centred cosmos would have secured the well-being and orderly reproduction of the community.

From village to cemetery: the late Neolithic and Copper Age

The picture hitherto sketched gradually changed during the late and final Neolithic (*c.* 4500–3600 cal. BC), when burial was increasingly performed at peripheral or otherwise distinct locales within the village as to signify separation from daily life. Moreover, mortuary rites became more complex and formalised, with special regard to secondary practices of bone manipulation and reburial. The first appearance of this long-term trend can be traced back to the late Serra d'Alto phase in the advanced middle Neolithic (Pessina & Tiné 2008: 287). In this period, small segregated burial areas were first established at sites such as Serra Cicora and Murgecchia, either at the edge of villages or, significantly, at abandoned settlement sites (Conati Barbaro 2007–08; Ingravallo 2004; Lo Porto 1998). The earliest-known cemetery proper was also founded on the outskirts of Pulo di Molfetta, a large open settlement in Apulia. Excavations carried out at this site in the early 20th century brought to light over 50 stone-lined tombs, in which a staggering variety of primary and secondary inhumation rituals had been performed, and durable goods had occasionally been placed with the dead. Interestingly, certain tombs were found devoid of any human remains. These might be interpreted as either cenotaphs or temporary repositories for burials that were later moved elsewhere (Mosso 1910; Radina 2002).

This trend gained momentum from the late 5th millennium BC. In the southern peninsula, cemeteries were established away from domestic sites at Masseria Bellavista, Scoglio del Tonno and Cala Tramontana (the latter on the Tremiti islands), and also at Bronte in Sicily (Palma di Cesnola 1967; Privitera 2012; Quagliati 1906). The high frequency of secondary burials and the growing standardisation of good assemblages witnessed at these sites openly anticipate characters that will become widespread in the Copper Age. The first hypogeal chambers reminiscent of Copper Age rock-cut tombs also appeared in the advanced 5th/early 4th millennia BC at a handful of sites including Arnesano, Serra d'Alto-Fondo Gravela and perhaps Scoglio del Tonno (Manfredini 2001; but see Pessina & Tiné 2008: 289–91 for problems of interpretation).

In the central peninsula, key evidence for this transitional phase has been yielded by the large aggregation site at Ripoli. Here, a distinct cemetery area was constructed in the unusual form of nine linear cavities cutting across the centre of the village. At least 45 individuals were buried in them, their number in each trench varying from one to 14. Skeates (1995) reconstructed a complex ritual process that would have started with the deposition of the bodies, left uncovered to decompose in the graves. Then, certain bodies would have been disarticulated and eventually all trenches would have been filled up with selected artefacts and the remains of funerary feasts. However, this reading is debated due to the scarce information available for the site, which was investigated over 100 years ago (Grifoni 2003). Caves continued to be used for burial in the late 5th and early 4th millennia BC. Even at these sites, however, interment and bone manipulation rites were progressively moved away from the cave mouths where domestic life concentrated to be increasingly performed in the deeper recesses. This pattern is particularly apparent at Grotta dei Piccioni in Abruzzo, where primary and secondary inhumation, skull deposition, and other ritual activities were all carried out at the bottom of the cave (Cremonesi 1976).

From about 3800 cal. BC, in the final Neolithic and early Copper Age, the lengthy process of separation of the dead from the living described above was brought to an end. Burial was finally moved out of domestic sites and cemeteries were created in the landscape as separate and often secluded locales for the performance of funerals and other mortuary rituals. Based on regional difference, burial was practised in rock-cut

Fig. 2.5. Rinaldone-style chamber tomb from Ponte San Pietro, west-central Italy (Miari 1995).

chamber tombs, uninhabited caves (or uninhabited parts of otherwise occupied caves) and, to a lesser extent, trench graves (Cocchi Genick 2009). Particularly informative in this respect is the evidence provided by the so-called Rinaldone and Gaudo funerary traditions, which were first elaborated in this time period (Cazzella & Silvestrini 2005; Passariello et al. 2010). Whereas the former is found all over central Italy with special foci in the central Tyrrhenian region and the Marche lowlands, the latter flourished in southwest Italy up to the lower Tiber valley (Carboni 2002). Both traditions are typified by small rock-cut chamber tombs preceded by entrance shafts or short corridors, and sealed by removable slabs. The new tomb structure allowed mourners to access the grave in order to carry out reburial practices and ancestor veneration rites (Fig. 2.5).

The new mortuary programme emerging at the onset of the Copper Age was characterised by an unprecedented degree of ritual elaboration (Conti et al. 1997; Dolfini 2004). Evidence from Rinaldone-style burial chambers, albeit not uniform, suggests that the ritual process was generally divided into the following steps:

1. Interment of a fleshed and often furnished individual in crouched position, normally placed on the left-hand side regardless of their gender;
2. Manipulation of the dry bones, which were removed (partly or totally) from the grave and probably circulated within the cemetery;
3. And reburial of selected bones (usually skull and long bones), which were stacked along the tomb walls or near the entrance with the remains of other individuals (Table 2.1).

Table 2.1. The Copper Age burial programme as documented by Rinaldone-style chamber tombs, central Italy.

	INTERMENT	MANIPULATION	REBURIAL
	TIME ⟶		
T I M E	Interment of an articulated body, crouched on their left-hand or right-hand side	Manipulation or removal of the skull	Reburial of the skull
	Interment of further articulated bodies	Manipulation or removal of the upper body; the lower limbs are left in situ	Reburial of the upper body, reorganised
		Manipulation or removal of skull and limbs; spine/ribs (and occasionally feet) are left in situ	Reburial of the entire body, reorganised
		Manipulation or removal of the entire body; tiny bone fragments are (unintentionally?) left in situ	Reburial of the entire body, which is reorganised and mixed with other bodies
			Reburial of long bones and skulls of several bodies, stacked together

Interestingly, the new burial process seems to have necessitated the intermediate step to be especially elaborate. This was marked by a mind-boggling variety of bone manipulation practices ranging from the mere removal of the skull from an otherwise articulated skeleton to the complete transgression of the bodily boundaries by means of disarticulation and, more occasionally, bone fragmentation. Goods were also removed from the grave at this stage to be circulated, fragmented, and occasionally re-deposited with secondary burials.

Similar rituals were also performed in the chamber graves and entrance shafts of the Gaudo cemeteries (southwest Italy), although a greater stress was placed here on disarticulation and bone handling/circulation (Bailo Modesti 2003; Bailo Modesti & Salerno 1998). Likewise, cemeteries were divided into clusters of tombs in which descent groups would have interred their deceased and venerated their ancestors (Fig. 2.6). Such overarching similarities between Rinaldone and Gaudo burial programmes suggest that, in most of the Italian peninsula, Copper Age mortuary practices would have followed a common tripartite structure involving the interment of the fleshed body, the manipulation and circulation of the dry bones after the flesh had naturally decayed, and the final reburial of selected bones with other ancestral remains. Crucially, the fact that all stages of this process are seemingly found in the extant burial record suggests that the Copper Age mortuary programme was not intended to be linear or equifinal, for not all individuals ended up being disarticulated, and those who did were rearranged in extremely diverse manners. It would thus appear that unlike burial and manipulation practices were applied to different individuals based on their social identity and personhood as well as, presumably, the circumstances of their death. If we try to discern a meaningful pattern in the multifarious burial record of Copper Age Italy, an opposition is easily noticed between the relatively small number of individuals that were left undisturbed in the grave and the vast majority of the deceased, whose bodies were, to a smaller or greater extent, transgressed and reworked (Dolfini 2006a; 2006b). The number of possible outcomes of bodily disarticulation practices is also noteworthy, and seems to greatly exceed the spectrum of choices available to Neolithic society.

Gender and age were sometimes stressed in burial through the deposition of stereotyped sets of goods. Typically, men were disposed of with flint, groundstone or copper-alloy tools and weapons while women and children were accompanied by small ornaments including necklaces, pins, and conical V-bored buttons. To a lesser extent, gender and age were also expressed through body arrangement. In the Copper Age, however, the focus was not placed on body orientation as in the Neolithic, but on manipulation, since men were left articulated more often than women and children (Bailo Modesti & Salerno 1998: 183; Dolfini 2006a; 2006b). Moreover, whereas gender-specific goods were mostly placed with articulated burials, disarticulated and selected remains were either left unfurnished or were provided with gender-neutral goods such as copper awls and fragmented pots. This seems to suggest that gender and age, as well as presumably other elements of a person's identity, had to be removed during the ritual process in order to integrate the new dead into a non-individualised and perhaps undifferentiated community of the ancestors (Dolfini 2004; Skeates 1995). However, in striking *contrappunto* to this widespread practice, the personal identity of a relatively small number of individuals, mostly adult males, was carefully preserved by leaving their bodies not only undisturbed, but also fully furnished with the complete panoply of goods with which they had been buried in the first place.

In parallel to the rise of the cemetery as a place to be exclusively devoted to the performance of mortuary rites, the long-lived nucleated village seems to disappear from

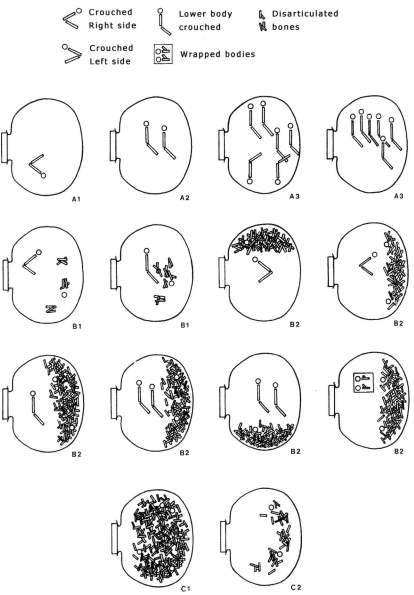

Fig. 2.6. Outline of Copper Age mortuary practices as documented by Gaudo-style chamber tombs, southwest Italy (Bailo Modesti & Salerno 1998, modified).

the Italian landscape, or at any rate to become rarer. Substantial villages are replaced by dispersed and often short-lived settlements, isolated dwellings, and seasonally inhabited caves and open-air stations. This trend is apparent at several late Neolithic sites across the peninsula, where sizeable habitation sites give way to rather insubstantial settlements whose features often amount to a handful of pits, cobblestone floors, and

Table 2.2. Changes in settlement and burial patterns in the Neolithic and Copper Age of the Italian peninsula, c. 6th–3rd millennia BC.

	Early and Middle Neolithic	**Late Neolithic and Copper Age**
Settlement	Long-lived nucleated villages and (permanently?) inhabited caves	Short-lived settlements and seasonally inhabited caves; a number of substantial settlements; aggregation sites?
Burial place	Within villages, especially near houses or in ditches	In cemeteries built at the edge of villages or in extramural cemeteries
Grave structure	Earthen pits, stone-lined trenches and slab-built cists	Rock-cut chamber tombs and burial caves; a number of trench graves
Primary burial	Inhumation of a crouched individual lying sideways	Inhumation of a crouched individual lying sideways
Secondary burial	Removal of skull; intentional and unintentional bone scattering; occasional reburial of selected bones	Great variety of manipulation and reburial practices; frequent reburial of selected bones (see Table 2.1)
Gender and age	Loosely defined by body orientation and burial treatment	Strictly defined by stereotyped grave goods and, more occasionally, burial treatment
Ancestor rituals	Skull curation in villages; veneration of undisturbed bodies?	Wide array of bone and artefact manipulation practices at cemeteries; veneration of undisturbed bodies?

hearths (Anzidei et al. 2002; Grifoni et al. 2001; Manfredini et al. 2005a; Moscoloni 1992). The trend continues well into the Copper Age at sites such as Quadrato di Torre Spaccata, Casale del Cavaliere, and Maccarese (Anzidei & Carboni 1995; Boccuccia et al. 2000; Manfredini 2002). Copper Age sites often lie close to one another on river terraces, and it is uncertain whether this should be interpreted as evidence of the same community moving to neighbouring unexploited soils or smaller groups dwelling nearby (Cazzella 1992; Gianni 1991; Moscoloni & Silvestrini 2005). In either case, however, the outcome is similar: from the late 5th millennium BC, and increasingly so during the 4th and 3rd millennia BC, communities were generally smaller and villages left fainter footprints in the landscape than they did in the early and middle Neolithic.

The demise of the nucleated village during the late Neolithic and Copper Age was long considered to be a consequence of growing seasonal mobility due to intensified pastoralism, which is especially apparent in the Apennine uplands (Barker 1981; Maggi 1998; 2002; Maggi & De Pascale 2011). Recent research has nuanced this picture by showing that lowland alluvial plains and fertile river valleys were intensively cultivated, and villages in these areas were often substantial and long-lived (Anzidei et al. 2011; Fugazzola Delpino et al. 2007; Laforgia & Boenzi 2011; Maniscalco & Robb 2011). A small number of villages were also surrounded by walls, ditches and palisades, which are normally interpreted as defence structures (Cazzella 2003b; Cazzella & Moscoloni 1999; Cerqua 2011; Cipolloni Sampò 1988; Manfredini et al. 2005b). However, notwithstanding the possibility that some communities might have continued to dwell together in large numbers during the Copper Age, some of the large upland sites including Conelle and Ortucchio might be interpreted as seasonally inhabited aggregation sites, where a dispersed population would have gathered to exchange livestock and goods, arrange marriages, and perhaps carry out youth initiation rites in which red deer and wild boar were hunted (Robb 2007a; Whitehouse 1992b). Moreover, some of the alleged defence works appear to have been maintained for very short periods of time (e.g. Cerqua 2011), thus casting doubts over their actual or intended function.

The salient features of the long-term changes outlined in this section are summarised in Table 2.2.

E pluribus, unum

The modifications in settlement and burial patterns hitherto discussed lend themselves to several possible interpretations. As we have seen above, the rise of corporate burial in the late Neolithic and Copper Age might be read as a new political strategy aiming to express ownership or inheritance claims over land and other restricted resources (Pessina & Tiné 2008; Skeates 1995). While this remains a perfectly possible scenario, it is not clear whether land was actually a rare commodity in the sparsely inhabited Neolithic and Copper Age world, perhaps with the exception of a few densely populated areas in the Adriatic lowlands. Moreover, if burial was employed as a strategy for political control, we should ask ourselves why the sourcing locales of obsidian and greenstone – some of the most prized and most widely exchanged materials in the late Neolithic world – were not protected by a 'firewall of ancestors', but lay apparently open for anyone to exploit.

Another long-standing tradition of studies argues that the richly furnished male burials making their appearance in the Copper Age ought to be seen as the first markers of social inequality. By displaying the prestigious tools and weapons acquired through prowess in combat and control of long-distance exchange routes, tribal leaders and 'Big Men' would have expressed their power according to the new ethos of the 'prestige goods economy' (Barker 1981; Cazzella 1992; 1998; 2003a; Guidi 2000). However, if prestige was gained through the procurement of exotic materials such as obsidian and greenstone, why did the far-reaching exchange networks of these goods flourish in egalitarian Neolithic society and crash dramatically in supposedly unequal Copper Age, where emerging tribal leaders would have needed them the most to justify power and social control? The demise of obsidian and greenstone exchange is often interpreted as the consequence of the emerging 'trade' in metal, which would have become the new, pervasive symbol of social prominence. Yet, failing to recognise the *unlike* function and social role of obsidian and copper tools in Italian prehistoric society, this reading leaves much to be desired; it also underestimates the fact that, in Copper Age Italy, metal did not circulate as extensively as obsidian and greenstone (Dolfini 2010).

I would propose here an alternative, heterodox explanation for the momentous shifts in settlement and burial patterns discussed in this paper. It is my contention that this phenomenon does not indicate any radical change in the political structure of prehistoric society. Rather, it marks a profound modification in the symbolic toolkit used by society to express individual and group identity as well as beliefs and cosmologies concerning the human body. In other words, it is not a change in the underlying 'meaning' of burial that we are witnessing here, but a change in the *medium* chosen by society to represent and reproduce itself. However, since social relations derive their meanings from the practices through which they are articulated, it would be wrong to presume that changes in the expression of burial did not cause any change in its social understanding. As we shall see in the remainder of the article, alterations to the Neolithic burial programme rested upon a wholesale re-signification of the human body, which was turned into one of the core symbolic resources deployed by society to reproduce itself.

In the early and middle Neolithic, the village acted as the principal locus for the enactment of social life. Burial was performed within the bounded village as one of the many practices, both ritual and mundane, which helped to define social relations and a sense of being in the world. When afforded archaeologically visible formal inhumation, the dead were laid, crouched and (mostly) unfurnished, in simple pits, stone-lined trenches or slab-built cists. Bodies were arranged according to loosely defined yet fairly recurrent norms dictating orientation and burial treatment, which would have responded to shared ideas concerning cosmology and identity including gender and age. Over time, most of the graves were disturbed and the dry bone dispersed, possibly during the performance of daily tasks. In a few cases, however, selected bodily remains were formally reburied, either during one-off special ceremonies or as a part of calendrical rites.

It would appear that the disturbance of the grave and the scattering of the bones responded to overarching cosmological principles dictating that all traces of the individual identity be erased during the ritual process. In this way, the individualised deceased were turned into a non-individualised ancestral presence that would have guaranteed the well-being and orderly reproduction of the village community. A principle of group solidarity and continuity was expressed through the Neolithic burial programme, in which the community took precedence over the individual (Shanks & Tilley 1982; Skeates 1995). The burying and scattering of human remains near houses, in ditches, and at other inhabited locales would have strongly contributed to the self-representation of the group as a bounded social body, and a common sense of belonging would have emerged from dwelling in a space where, from living memory, the community had interred, manipulated, and reburied its dead. Importantly, these practices were fully integrated into the daily life of the village. Burying and commemorating the dead was just one of the many tasks that were carried out at domestic sites together with the building and burning of houses, the digging and filling of ditches, the erection of palisades and so on. In Neolithic Italy, burial was not conceptualised as qualitatively different from other social practices, but just as one of the possible media – doubtless an important one – that communities had at their disposal for reproducing the core principle underpinning social life: co-residence in the bounded village.

In the late Neolithic, and increasingly so in the Copper Age, the tie between co-residence and the common history of the group split apart (Robb 1994b: 49). In most of peninsular Italy, the long-lived enclosures that had so conspicuously embodied Neolithic life disappeared from the landscape, only to be replaced by smaller and more scattered settlements, isolated houses, and seasonally inhabited caves or open-air stations. Due to their insubstantial structures, their short occupation span and, above all, their failure to accommodate the whole community within the same inhabited space, domestic sites lost their previous centrality as loci for the reproduction of group identity. Even for those communities that continued to dwell in large villages, co-residence seems to have lost its earlier importance, possibly due to an economic regime that required a higher degree of seasonal mobility. Under these circumstances, a new medium had to be found around which social relations could coalesce. Interestingly, late Neolithic society did not actually conjure the new medium out of thin air, but – as human societies habitually do – picked it from the spectrum of cultural resources that were already at hand. It is perhaps unsurprising that the choice fell on burial due to its long-standing role as a prime means for ascribing group identity and structuring social interaction. All that was required in the new circumstances was to realign the old mortuary rituals to the changing needs of increasingly mobile communities, and turn one of the many media of social reproduction into the core medium around which group identity could newly crystallise. This was a process of cultural selection, not of outright invention: *E pluribus, unum.*

The changing role of burial brought about a number of important modifications to the enactment and social understanding of funerary practices. The first was the invention of the cemetery, which emerged in the cultural landscape of late Neolithic Italy as the principal locus for the performance of funerals and ancestor rites. As we have seen above, this was concomitant to the slow but inexorable waning of the nucleated village as a cultural resource. It could perhaps be said that the demise of the village *necessitated* the cemetery to be invented insofar as smaller and more dispersed groups did require meaningful places to gather periodically in order to bury their dead, commemorate their ancestors, and ultimately reinforce the common genealogic ties that the new lifestyle had loosened. Yet such a dramatic change in the topography of burial did not rest upon a wholesale alteration in its meaning, but on an unprecedented surge in its importance as a medium for the reproduction of group identity and social relations. This is neatly indicated by the fact that the basic tenets of the Neolithic burial programme were carried through into the new era, albeit in an 'augmented' form. As previously, the dead were laid sideways in the grave and oriented or manipulated according to their gender, age, and presumably the circumstances of their death. As previously, the loss of individual identity through disarticulation was recognised to be the chief avenue for incorporating the new dead into the collective cosmos of the ancestors. And just as previously, 'special' ancestors were singled out for individual remembrance and veneration by leaving their bodies undisturbed in the grave, although the importance of this practice grew over time (Dolfini 2006a; 2006b).

The second change concerns the structure and nature of mortuary practices. Primary and secondary burial rites grew increasingly complex in the Copper Age, to a degree that has no parallels in the Neolithic world. This phenomenon can perhaps be explained by considering that, since the ancestors had become the core medium of social reproduction, a fairly simple funerary rite no longer responded to the novel needs of Copper Age communities. Genealogy had to be played up in order to tie together the threads of a common history that the new role of the village had thrown into jeopardy, and the ancestors, either real or conveniently 'rediscovered', were the obvious means for doing so (Robb 1994b; 2007a). In the 4th and 3rd millennia BC, people increasingly defined themselves by handling, circulating, breaking, selecting, mixing and reburying the physical bodies of their ancestors in a mind-boggling array of ritual practices. Formally, such practices would have been justified by a richer and subtler categorisation of the identity of the deceased (e.g. in terms of gender: Barfield 1998; Robb 2007a; Whitehouse 1992a; 1992b; 2001). At a deeper level, however, they were motivated by the novel desire and, indeed, social need to stress group identity and genealogic ties. In turn, the new mortuary rites required a grave structure that could periodically be accessed by the mourners: the Copper Age chamber tomb was thus born. Nevertheless, the old order was recognisably preserved within the new; for the segmentary structure of Neolithic society as expressed by the C-ditched village compounds was recreated in the cemetery in the form of separate tomb clusters where kin-groups would have buried their own dead and commemorated their own ancestors (Robb 1994b: 49).

The final and perhaps deepest change lay in the social understanding of the human body. Following Robb (2002), I have argued above that Neolithic burial was enacted according to an ideally linear programme dictating the articulated body to be disarticulated and dispersed amongst the living. However, linearity was lost in the growing complexity of Copper Age mortuary performances, as indeed was the prior (ideal) equi-finality of the burial programme. Not only were now bodies transgressed and fragmented in entirely new ways, but for the first time it was also perfectly possible to 'interrupt' the disarticulation process before its 'natural' end marked by the complete reorganisation of the body and the scattering or reburial of selected remains. Yet none of the seemingly interrupted acts of bodily manipulation found in Copper Age chamber graves is to be understood as an unfinished inhumation process. Rather, it must be recognised that all dead, be they articulated or reorganised, isolated or inextricably mixed together, selected or fragmented, underwent the ritually correct and definitive burial afforded by their personhood and identity (Dolfini 2006a: 61).

It could be suggested that, in the Italian Copper Age, the body was reconceptualised as a more partible and transgressible entity than it had been previously, and that body parts and substances would have been given specific qualities and meanings (Chapman 2000; Chapman & Gaydarska 2007; Fowler 2004; 2008; Jones 2005; Strathern 1988). Body parts could also be extracted from the dead to be employed in a range of interactions and ritual exchanges, and objects could be paired up with them, and presumably circulated with them, in mutually reinforcing signification processes (Dolfini 2004; Lucas 1996). It is not inconceivable to think that such an extensive reconfiguration of the dead might reflect broader changes in the social understanding of the living. At a time of sweeping economic and social change a mighty effort was seemingly made to represent the social body as unchanging by intensifying burial and ancestor rituals, and the tension between old and new order was thus naturalised by reference to the physical body of the dead. In this way the body, and in particular the ancestral body, became the surface on which identity, and the social relations previously expressed by the nucleated village, could newly be inscribed.

Concluding remarks

In this paper I have proposed an alternative reading for the dramatic transformations affecting prehistoric Italian society at the transition between Neolithic and Copper Age, in the late 5th and 4th millennia BC. In particular, I claimed that the momentous changes in settlement and burial patterns occurring in this time period need not indicate any radical modifications in the political structure of society. Rather, they seem to mark a profound discontinuity in the symbolic toolkit deployed by communities and kin-groups to express identity and social relations in a changing world. Since co-residence in the nucleated village could no longer be used to express a common sense of belonging and being in the world, a new medium had to be found to replace it. Perhaps unsurprisingly, the choice fell on burial, which had been employed since the early Neolithic as a prime means for structuring social interaction. Thus, I would argue, the unprecedented surge in mortuary practices witnessed at this time seems to reflect a change in the role of burial as a medium for expressing individual and group identity, not a wholesale modification in its underlying 'meaning'.

However, the new role fulfilled by burial triggered three important changes that progressively eroded, and ultimately altered, the underlying principles of Neolithic social reproduction. The first is the invention of the cemetery, which emerged in the cultural landscape of the late Neolithic as the principal locus for funerals and ancestor rites; the second lies in the structure and nature of mortuary practices, which grew increasingly complex and elaborate in order to reinforce the genealogic ties that the new, more mobile lifestyle would have unwound; and the third is a general modification in the social configuration of the human body, which was reconceptualised as a more partible and permeable entity than it had been previously. Herein lies the most significant alteration in the meaning of mortuary practices, for new ideas of identity and personhood would have been naturalised through reference to the ancestral body. In a mighty effort to represent a fast-changing society as unchanging, prehistoric Italian communities realigned the old mortuary practices to the new social needs, and inscribed on the human body the unresolved tension between the old and the new order.

Acknowledgments

I wish to thank J. Rasmus Brandt, Marina Prusac and Håkon Roland for inviting me to the 'Ritual Changes and Changing Rituals' conference in Oslo, and for providing the opportunity to publish my research within this volume. I am also grateful to Chris Fowler, Alessandra Manfredini, John Robb, and an anonymous reviewer for commenting upon earlier drafts of this article, and wish to thank Giovanni Carboni and Claudio Giardino for sending relevant material. All opinions and errors are mine.

Note

1   The term 'secondary burial' is used in this work to signify the secondary stage of a funerary rite, which in the Italian Neolithic and Copper Age normally entailed the reorganisation, manipulation, selection, and reburial of dry bones. The term is never used here in the sense of 'addition of burials in a context that already contains one set of remains', as often intended in British prehistory.

Bibliography

Anzidei, A. P. & Carboni, G. 1995: 'L'insediamento preistorico di Quadrato di Torre Spaccata (Roma) e osservazioni su alcuni aspetti tardo-neolitici ed eneolitici nell'Italia centrale', *Origini* 19: 55–255.

Anzidei, A. P., Carboni, G. & Celant, A. 2002: 'Il popolamento del territorio di Roma nel Neolitico recente/finale: aspetti culturali ed ambientali', in Ferrari & Visentini (eds), 473–82.

Anzidei, A. P., Carboni, G., Carboni, L., Catalano, P., Celant, A., Cereghino, R., Cerilli, E., Guerrini, S., Lemorini, C., Mieli, G., Musco, S., Rambelli, C. & Pizzuti, F. 2011: 'Il Gaudo a sud del Tevere: abitati e necropolis dell'area romana', in *Atti della XLIII Riunione Scientifica dell'Istituto Italiano di Preistoria e Protostoria*, Istituto Italiano di Preistoria e Protostoria: Florence, 309–21.

Bailo Modesti, G. 2003: 'Rituali funerari eneolitici nell'Italia peninsulare: l'Italia meridionale', in *Atti della XXXV Riunione Scientifica dell'Istituto Italiano di Preistoria e Protostoria*, vol. I, Istituto Italiano di Preistoria e Protostoria: Florence, 283–97.

Bailo Modesti, G. & Salerno, A. 1998: *Pontecagnano. La Necropoli Eneolitica: L'Età del Rame in Campania nei Villaggi dei Morti*, Istituto Universitario Orientale: Naples.

Barfield, L. 1998: 'Gender Issues in North Italian Prehistory', in R. D. Whitehouse (ed.): *Gender in Italian Archaeology: Challenging the Stereotypes*, Accordia Research Institute: London, 143–56.

Barker, G. 1981: *Landscape and Society: Prehistoric Central Italy*, Academic Press: London.

Barraud, C., de Coppet, D., Itenau, A. & Jamous, R. 1994: *Of Relations and the Dead: Four Societies viewed from the Angle of their Exchanges*, Berg: Oxford.

Barrett, J. C. 1990: 'The Monumentality of Death: The Character of Early Bronze Age Mortuary Mounds in Southern Britain', *World Archaeology* 22.2: 179–89.

Barrett, J. C. 1994: *Fragments from Antiquity: An Archaeology of Social Life in Britain, 2900–1200 BC*, Blackwell: Oxford.

Binford, L. R. 1971: 'Mortuary Practices: Their Study and Potential', in J. A. Brown (ed.): *Approaches to the Social Dimensions of Mortuary Practices* (Memoirs of the Society for American Archaeology 25): 6–29.

Binford, L. R. 1977: 'General Introduction', in L.R. Binford (ed.): *For Theory Building in Archaeology*, Academic Press: New York, 1–10.

Bloch, M. 1971: *Placing the Dead: Tombs, Ancestral Villages, and Kinship Organization in Madagascar*, Seminar Press: London.

Boccuccia, P., Carboni, G., Gioia, P. & Remotti, E. 2000: 'Il sito di Casale del Cavaliere (Roma) e l'Eneolitico dell'Italia centrale: problemi di inquadramento cronologico e culturale alla luce della recente datazione radiometrica', in M. Silvestrini (ed.): *Recenti acquisizioni, problemi e prospettive della ricerca sull'Eneolitico dell'Italia centrale*, Regione Marche: Ancona, 231–47.

Bourdieu, P. 1977: *Outline of a Theory of Practice*, Cambridge University Press: Cambridge.

Bradford, J. S. P 1950: 'The Apulia Expedition: An Interim Report', *Antiquity* 94: 84–95.

Bradley, R. 1981: 'Various Styles of Urn: Cemeteries and Settlement in Southern England *c.* 1400–1000 BC', in Chapman et al. (eds): 93–104.

Brown, K. 1991. 'A Passion for Excavation: Labour Requirements and Possible Functions for the Ditches of the "villaggi trincerati" of the Tavoliere, Apulia', *Accordia Research Papers* 2: 5–30.

Brück, J. 1995: 'A Place for the Dead: The Role of Human Remains in the Late Bronze Age', *Proceedings of the Prehistoric Society* 61: 245–77.

Brück, J. 2001: 'Body Metaphors and Technologies of Transformation in the English Middle and Late Bronze Age', in J. Brück (ed.): *Bronze Age Landscapes: Tradition and Transformation*, Oxbow Books: Oxford, 149–60.

Carboni, G. 2002: 'Territorio aperto o di frontiera? Nuove prospettive di ricerca per lo studio della distribuzione spaziale delle facies del Gaudo e di Rinaldone nel Lazio centro-meridionale', *Origini* 24: 235–301.

Cassano, S. M. & Manfredini, A. (eds) 1983: *Studi sul Neolitico del Tavoliere della Puglia: indagine territoriale in un'area-campione*, British Archaeological Reports, International Series 160: Oxford.

Cazzella, A. 1992: 'Sviluppi culturali eneolitici nella penisola italiana', in Cazzella, A. & Moscoloni, M. (eds): *Neolitico ed Eneolitico* (Popoli e Civiltà dell'Italia Antica 11), Biblioteca di storia patria: Rome, 349–643.

Cazzella, A. 1998: 'Modelli e variabilità negli usi funerari di alcuni contesti eneolitici italiani', *Rivista di Scienze Preistoriche* 49: 431–45.

Cazzella, A. 2003a: 'Rituali funerari eneolitici nell'Italia peninsulare: l'Italia centrale', in *Atti della XXXV Riunione Scientifica dell'Istituto Italiano di Preistoria e Protostoria*, vol. I, Istituto Italiano di Preistoria e Protostoria: Florence, 275–82.

Cazzella, A. 2003b: 'Aspetti e problemi dell'Eneolitico in Abruzzo', in *Atti della XXXVI Riunione Scientifica dell'Istituto Italiano di Preistoria e Protostoria*, Istituto Italiano di Preistoria e Protostoria: Florence, 221–38.

Cazzella, A. & Moscoloni, M. 1999: *Conelle di Arcevia: un insediamento eneolitico nelle Marche*, Gangemi: Rome.

Cazzella, A. & Silvestrini, M. 2005: 'L'Eneolitico delle Marche nel contesto degli sviluppi culturali dell'Italia centrale', in *Atti della XXXVIII Riunione Scientifica dell'Istituto Italiano di Preistoria e Protostoria*, vol. I, Istituto Italiano di Preistoria e Protostoria: Florence, 371–86.

Cerqua, M. 2011: 'Selva dei Muli (Frosinone): un insediamento eneolitico della facies del Gaudo', *Origini* 33: 157–248.

Chapman, J. 2000: *Fragmentation in Archaeology: People, Places and Broken Objects in the Prehistory of the South-Eastern Europe*, Routledge: London.

Chapman, J. & Gaydarska, B. 2007: *Parts and Wholes: Fragmentation in Prehistoric Context*, Oxbow Books: Oxford.

Chapman, R., Kinnes, I. & Randsborg, K. (eds) 1981: *The Archaeology of Death*, Cambridge University Press: Cambridge.

Cipolloni Sampò, M. 1988: 'La fortificazione eneolitica di Toppo Daguzzo (Basilicata)', *Rassegna di Archeologia* 7: 557–58.

Cocchi Genick, D. 2009: *Preistoria*, QuiEdit: Verona.

Conati Barbaro, C. 2007–08: 'Custodire la memoria: le sepolture in abitato nel Neolitico italiano', *Scienze dell'Antichità* 14(1): 49–70.

Conti, A. M., Persiani, C. & Petitti, P. 1997: 'I riti della morte nella necropoli eneolitica della Selvicciola (Ischia di Castro – Viterbo)', *Origini* 21: 169–85.

Cremonesi, G. 1976: *La Grotta dei Piccioni di Bolognano nel quadro delle culture dal Neolitico all'Età del Bronzo in Abruzzo*, Giardini: Pisa.

Cremonesi, G. 1985–86: 'Samari (Gallipoli)', *Rivista di Scienze Preistoriche* 40: 424–25.

Degasperi, N., Ferrari, A. & Steffè, G. 1998: 'L'insediamento neolitico di Lugo di Romagna', in Pessina & Muscio (eds): 117–24.

De Lucia, A., Ferri, D., Geniola, A., Giove, C., Maggiore, M., Melone, N., Pesce Delfino, V., Pieri, V. & Scattarella, V. 1977: *La comunità Neolitica di Cala Colombo presso Torre a Mare, Bari*, Società per lo Studio di Storia Patria per la Puglia: Bari.

Diaz-Andreu, M. & Lucy, S. 2005: 'Introduction', in Diaz-Andreu et al. (eds): 1–12.

Diaz-Andreu, M., Lucy, S., Babić, S. & Edwards, D. N. (eds.) 2005: *The Archaeology of Identity*, Routledge: London.

Dolfini, A. 2004: 'La necropoli di Rinaldone (Montefiascone, Viterbo): rituale funerario e dinamiche sociali di una comunità eneolitica in Italia centrale', *Bullettino di Paletnologia Italiana* 95: 127–278.

Dolfini, A. 2006a: 'Embodied Inequalities: Burial and Social Differentiation in Copper Age Central Italy', *Archaeological Review from Cambridge* 21.2: 58–77.

Dolfini, A. 2006b: 'L'inumazione primaria come sistema simbolico e pratica sociale', in N. Negroni Catacchio (ed.), *Preistoria e Protostoria in Etruria: Atti del VII Incontro di Studi*, II, Centro Studi di Preistoria e Archeologia: Milan, 461–72.

Dolfini, A. 2010: 'Metalwork Exchange in Chalcolithic Italy: Fact or Fiction?', Paper presented at the 16th Annual Meeting of the European Association of Archaeologists (Den Haag 2010).

Edwards, D. N. 2005: 'The Archaeology of Religion', in Diaz-Andreu et al. (eds): 110–28.

Edwards, C. & Woolf, G. 2004: 'Cosmopolis: Rome as World City', in C. Edwards & D. Edwards (eds): *Rome the Cosmopolis*, Cambridge University Press: Cambridge, 1–20.

Ferrari, A. & Visentini, P. (eds) 2002: *Il declino del mondo neolitico*, Comune di Pordenone: Pordenone.

Fowler, C. 2004: *The Archaeology of Personhood: An Anthropological Approach*, Routledge: London.

Fowler, C. 2008: 'Fractal Bodies in the Past and Present', in D. Borić & J. Robb (eds): *Past Bodies: Body-Centred Research in Archaeology*, Oxbow Books: Oxford, 47–57.

Fowler, C. 2010: 'Pattern and Diversity in the Early Neolithic Mortuary Practices of Britain and Ireland: Contextualising the Treatment of the Dead', *Documenta Praehistorica* 37: 1–22.

Fugazzola Delpino, M. A., Salerno, A. & Tinè, V. 2007: 'Villaggi e necropoli dell'area "Centro Commerciale" di Gricignano d'Aversa – US Navy (Caserta)', in *Atti della XL Riunione Scientifica dell'Istituto Italiano di Presitoria e Protostoria*, Istituto Italiano di Preistoria e Protostoria: Florence, 521–37.

Gianni, A. 1991: 'Il farro, il cervo ed il villaggio mobile', *Scienze dell'Antichità* 5: 99–161.

Giardino, C., Guida, G. & Occhini, G. 2011: 'La prima metallurgia dell'Italia centrale tirrenica e lo sviluppo tecnologico della facies di Rinaldone: evidenze archeologiche e sperimentazione', in *Atti della XLIII Riunione Scientifica dell'Istituto Italiano di Presitoria e Protostoria*, Istituto Italiano di Preistoria e Protostoria: Florence, 181–86.

Giddens, A. 1984: *The Constitution of Society: Outline of the Theory of Structuration*, University of California Press: Berkeley.

Gnoli, G. & Vernant, J.-P. 1982: *La mort, les morts dans les sociétés anciennes*, Éditions de la Maison des Sciences de l'Homme: Paris.

Goody, J. 1962: *Death, Property and the Ancestors: A Study of the Mortuary Customs of the Lo Dagaa of West Africa*, Tavistock: London.

Gravina, A. 1975: 'Fossati e strutture ipogeiche dei villaggi neolitici in agro di S. Severo', *Attualità Archeologiche* 1: 14–34.

Grifoni, R. 2003: 'Sepolture neolitiche dell'Italia centro-meridionale e loro relazione con gli abitati', in *Atti della XXXV Riunione Scientifica dell'Istituto Italiano di Preistoria e Protostoria*, vol. I, Istituto Italiano di Preistoria e Protostoria: Florence, 259–74.

Grifoni, R., Radi, G. & Sarti, L. 2001: 'Il Neolitico della Toscana', in *Atti della XXXIV Riunione Scientifica dell'Istituto Italiano di Preistoria e Protostoria*, Istituto Italiano di Preistoria e Protostoria: Florence, 57–70.

Guidi, A. 2000: *Preistoria della complessità sociale*, Laterza: Roma.

Hodder, I. & Hutson, S. 2003: *Reading the Past: Current Approaches to Interpretation in Archaeology*, 3rd edition, Cambridge University Press: Cambridge.

Hodder, I. (ed.) 1982: *Symbolic and Structural Archaeology*, Cambridge University Press: Cambridge

Ingravallo, E. 2004: 'Il sito Neolitico di Serra Cicora (Nardò, Lecce): note preliminari', *Origini* 26: 87–119.

Insoll, T. 2007: 'Introduction: Configuring Identities in Archaeology', in Insoll (ed.): 1–22.

Insoll, T. (ed.) 2007: *The Archaeology of Identities: A Reader*, Routledge: London.

Jones, A. 2005: 'Lives in Fragments? Personhood and the European Neolithic', *Journal of Social Archaeology* 5: 193–224.

Jones, G. D. B. 1987: *Apulia I: Neolithic Settlement in the Tavoliere*, Society of Antiquaries: London.

Jones, S. 1997: *The Archaeology of Ethnicity*, Routledge: London.

Laforgia, E. & Boenzi, G. 2011: 'Nuovi dati sull'Eneolitico della piana campana dagli scavi A.V. in provincia di Napoli', in *Atti della XLIII Riunione Scientifica dell'Istituto Italiano di Presitoria e Protostoria*, Istituto Italiano di Preistoria e Protostoria: Florence, 249–55.

Lo Porto, F. G. 1998: *Murgia Timone e Murgecchia* (Monumenti Antichi dei Lincei 30), Accademia dei Lincei: Rome.

Lucas, G. 1996: 'Of Death and Debt: A History of the Body in Neolithic and Early Bronze Age Yorkshire', *Journal of European Archaeology* 4: 99–118.

Maggi, R. 1998: 'Storia della Liguria fra 3600 e 2300 avanti Cristo (età del Rame)', in A. Del Lucchese & R. Maggi (eds): *Dal diaspro al bronzo*, Luna: La Spezia, 7–28.

Maggi, R. 2002: 'Pastori, miniere, metallurgia nella transizione fra Neolitico ed età del Rame: nuovi dati dalla Liguria', in Ferrari & Visentini (eds): 437–40.

Maggi, R. & De Pascale, A. 2011: 'Fire making Water on the Ligurian Apennines', in M. Van Leusen, G. Pizziolo & L. Sarti (eds): *Hidden Landscapes of Mediterranean Europe*, British Archaeological Reports, International Series 2320: Oxford, 105–12.

Mallory, J. P. 1984–87: 'Lagnano da Piede I: An Early Neolithic Village in the Tavoliere, *Origini* 13: 193–290.

Manfredini, A. 1972: 'Il villaggio trincerato di Monte Aquilone nel quadro del neolitico dell'Italia meridionale', *Origini* 6: 29–154.

Manfredini, A. 2001: 'Rituali funerari e organizzazione sociale: una rilettura di alcuni dati della facies Diana in Italia meridionale', in M. C. Martinelli & U. Spigo (eds): *Studi di Preistoria e Protostoria in onore di Luigi Bernabò Brea*, Museo Archeologico Regionale Eoliano: Lipari, 71–87.

Manfredini, A. (ed.) 2002: *Le dune, il lago, il mare: Una comunità di villaggio dell'età del Rame a Maccarese*, Istituto Italiano di Preistoria e Protostoria: Florence.

Manfredini, A., Sarti, L. & Silvestrini, M. 2005a: 'Il Neolitico delle Marche', in *Atti della XXXVIII Riunione Scientifica dell'Istituto Italiano di Preistoria e Protostoria*, vol. I, Istituto Italiano di Preistoria e Protostoria: Florence, 197–208.

Manfredini, A., Carboni, G., Conati Barbaro, C., Silvestrini, M., Fiorentino, G. & Corridi, C. 2005b: 'La frequentazione eneolitica di Maddalena di Muccia (Macerata)', in *Atti della XXXVIII Riunione Scientifica dell'Istituto Italiano di Preistoria e Protostoria*, vol. II, Istituto Italiano di Preistoria e Protostoria: Florence, 433–44.

Maniscalco, L. & Robb, J. 2011: 'L'organizzazione dello spazio durante l'età del rame in Italia meridionale, Sicilia e Malta', in *Atti della XLIII Riunione Scientifica dell'Istituto Italiano di Presitoria e Protostoria*, Istituto Italiano di Preistoria e Protostoria: Florence, 279–85.

Meskell, L. 2001: 'Archaeologies of Identity', in Hodder, I. (ed.): *Archaeological Theory Today*, Polity Press: Cambridge, 187–213.

Meskell, L. 2002: 'The Intersections of Identity and Politics in Archaeology', *Annual Review of Anthropology* 31: 279–301.

Meskell, L. 2007: 'Archaeologies of Identity', in Insoll (ed.): 23–43.

Metcalf, P. & Huntington, R. 1991: *Celebrations of Death*, 2nd edition, Cambridge University Press: Cambridge.

Miari, M. 1995: 'Il rituale funerario della necropoli eneolitica di Ponte S. Pietro (Ischia di Castro, Viterbo)', *Origini* 18: 351–90.

Morter, J. & Robb, J. 1998: 'Space, Gender and Architecture in the Southern Italian Neolithic', in R. D. Whitehouse (ed.): *Gender in Italian Archaeology: Challenging the Stereotypes*, Accordia Research Institute: London, 83–94.

Moscoloni, M. 1992: 'Sviluppi culturali neolitici nella penisola italiana', in A. Cazzella & M. Moscoloni (eds): *Neolitico ed Eneolitico* (Popoli e Civiltà dell'Italia Antica 11), Biblioteca di Storia Patria: Rome, 9–348.

Moscoloni, M. & Silvestrini, M. 2005: 'Gli insediamenti eneolitici delle Marche', in *Atti della XXXVIII Riunione Scientifica dell'Istituto Italiano di Preistoria e Protostoria*, vol. I, Istituto Italiano di Preistoria e Protostoria: Florence, 421–31.

Mosso, A. 1910: 'La necropoli neolitica di Molfetta', *Monumenti Antichi dei Lincei* 20: 237–356.

O'Shea, J. 1981: 'Social Configurations and the Archaeological Study of Mortuary Practices: A Case Study', in Chapman et al. (eds): 39–52.

Palma di Cesnola, A. 1967: 'Il neolitico medio e superiore di San Domino (Arcipelago delle Tremiti)', *Rivista di Scienze Preistoriche* 22: 349–91.

Parker Pearson, M. 1982: 'Mortuary Practices, Society and Ideology: An Ethnoarchaeological Study', in Hodder (ed.): 99–114.

Parker Pearson, M. 1999: *The Archaeology of Death and Burial*, Sutton: Phoenix Mill.

Passariello, I., Talamo, P., D'Onofrio, A., Barta, P., Lubritto, C. & Terrasi, F. 2010: 'Contribution of Radiocarbon Dating to the Chronology of Eneolithic in Campania (Italy)', *Geochronometria* 35: 25–33.

Peroni, R. 1989: *Protostoria dell'Italia continentale: la penisola italiana nelle età del Bronzo e del Ferro* (Popoli e Civiltà dell'Italia Antica 9), Biblioteca di storia patria: Rome.

Peroni, R. 1996: *L'Italia alle soglie della Storia*, Laterza: Rome.

Pessina, A. & Muscio, G. (eds) 1998: *Settemila anni fa… il primo pane: ambienti e culture delle società neolitiche*, Museo Friulano di Storia Naturale: Udine.

Pessina, A. & Tiné, V. 2008: *Archeologia del Neolitico. L'Italia tra VI e IV millennio a.C.*, Carocci: Rome.

Privitera, F. 2012: 'Necropoli tardo-neolitica in contrada Balze Soprana di Bronte', in *Atti della XLI Riunione Scientifica dell'Istituto Italiano di Preistoria e Protostoria*, Istituto Italiano di Preistoria e Protostoria: Florence, 543–56.

Quagliati, Q. 1906: 'Tombe neolitiche in Taranto e nel suo territorio', *Bullettino di Paletnologia Italiana* 30: 17–49.

Radina, F. (ed.) 2002: *La Preistoria della Puglia. Paesaggi, uomini e tradizioni di 8000 anni fa*, Adda: Bari.

Robb, J. E. 1994a: 'The Neolithic of Peninsular Italy: Anthropological Synthesis and Critique', *Bullettino di Paletnologia Italiana* 85: 189–214.

Robb, J. E. 1994b: 'Burial and Social Reproduction in the Peninsular Italian Neolithic', *Journal of Mediterranean Archaeology* 7.1: 27–71.

Robb, J. E. 2002: 'Time and Biography: Osteobiography of the Italian Neolithic Lifespan', in Y. Hamilakis, M. Pluciennik & S. Tarlow (eds): *Thinking Through the Body: Archaeologies of Corporeality*, Kluwer Academic/Plenum: London, 153–71.

Robb, J. E. 2007a: *The Early Mediterranean Village: Agency, Material Culture, and Social Change in Neolithic Italy*, Cambridge University Press: Cambridge.

Robb, J. E. 2007b: 'Burial Treatment as Transformations of Bodily Ideology', in N. Laneri (ed.): *Performing Death*, The Oriental Institute of the University of Chicago: Chicago, 287–97.

Saxe, A. 1970: *Social Dimension of Mortuary Practices*, Unpublished Doctoral Dissertation, University of Michigan: Ann Arbor.

Schiffer, M. B. 1987: *Formation Processes of the Archaeological Record*, University of New Mexico Press: Albuquerque.

Shanks, M. & Tilley, C. 1982: 'Ideology, Symbolic Power and Ritual Communication: A Reinterpretation of Neolithic Mortuary Practices', in Hodder (ed.): 129–54.

Skeates, R. 1995: 'Transformations in Mortuary Practice and Meaning in the Neolithic and Copper Age of Lowland East-Central Italy', in W. H. Waldren, J. A. Ensenyat & R. C. Kennard (eds): *Ritual, Rites and Religion in Prehistory*, British Archaeological Reports, International Series 611: Oxford, 211–37.

Skeates, R. 1997: 'The Human Use of Caves in East-Central Italy during the Mesolithic, Neolithic and Copper Age', in C. Bonsall & C. Tolan–Smith (eds): *The Human Use of Caves*, British Archaeological Reports, International Series 667: Oxford, 79–86.

Skeates, R. 2002. 'The Social Dynamics of Enclosure in the Neolithic of the Tavoliere, Southeast Italy, *Journal of Mediterranean Archaeology* 13.2: 155–88.

Strathern, A. 1981: 'Death as Exchange: Two Melanesian Cases', in S. Humphries & H. King (eds): *Mortality and Immortality: The Archaeology and Anthropology of Death*, Academic Press: London, 205–23.

Strathern, M. 1988: *The Gender of the Gift*, University of California Press: Berkeley.

Tainter, J.A. 1978: 'Mortuary Practices and the Study of Prehistoric Social Systems', in M. Schiffer (ed.): *Advances in Archaeological Method and Theory* 1: 105–41.

Thomas, J. 1999: *Understanding the Neolithic*, Routledge: London.

Tiné, S. 1983: *Passo di Corvo e la Civiltà Neolitica del Tavoliere*, Sagep: Genoa.

Trigger, B. G. 2006: *A History of Archaeological Thought*, 2nd edition, Cambridge University Press: Cambridge.

Trump, D. H. 1966: *Central and Southern Italy before Rome*, Thames and Hudson: London.

Ucko, P. J. 1969: 'Ethnography and Archaeological Interpretation of Funerary Remains', *World Archaeology* 1(2): 262–80.

Whitehouse, R. D. 1968: 'Settlement and Economy in Southern Italy in the Neothermal Period', *Proceedings of the Prehistoric Society* 34: 332–66.

Whitehouse, R. D. 1992a: 'Tools the Manmaker: The Cultural Construction of Gender in Italian Prehistory', *Accordia Research Papers* 3: 41–53.

Whitehouse, R. D. 1992b: *Underground Religion: Cult and Culture in Prehistoric Italy*, Accordia Research Institute: London.

Whitehouse, R. D. 2001: 'Exploring Gender in Prehistoric Italy', *Papers of the British School at Rome* 68: 49–96.

3

CHANGE AND CONTINUITY IN EARLY BRONZE AGE MORTUARY RITES
A Case Study from Northumberland

Chris Fowler

This article offers a new exploration of how archaeologists can deploy an anthropological perspective on the sequential nature of rites of passage (from pre-liminal rites through liminal phases to post-liminal rites) when interpreting mortuary evidence. Combining a detailed examination of a large and previously neglected dataset of Northumbrian Terminal Neolithic/Chalcolithic and Early Bronze Age mortuary deposits, c. 2450–1500 BC, with a novel reading of van Gennep's Rites of Passage, *it argues that while those pre-liminal rites closest to the liminal phase generally have the most impact in shaping the mortuary evidence, such deposits may also project desirable aspects of identity towards the post-liminal rites, and provide the dead with key media to assist in those latter rites. Drawing out an often-overlooked aspect of van Gennep's anthropological model, it argues that the work of the post-liminal incorporation of the dead into a new community may be deferred to non-living agents (the community of the dead, deities, etc), and then explores the implications of differences in such post-liminal practices for the Northumbrian Early Bronze Age evidence. It argues that the often-acknowledged shift from 'inhumation' to cremation during the period was perhaps of lesser importance in terms of understandings of the body, person and death than a contemporary shift from isolated burials to the use of collective burial grounds where a community of the dead could physically incorporate the deceased during the mortuary rites carried out by the living. It also places the change from inhumation to cremation and from isolated to communal burial places within the context of enduring trends in the funerary rites that transformed the dead, in particular highlighting key media deployed repeatedly throughout the period in effecting the ritualised transformation of the dead. In so doing it maps out precisely what changed and what remained the same during hundreds of years of prehistoric mortuary practices.*

Keywords: burial grounds, cremation, Early Bronze Age, inhumation, mortuary rites, Northumberland, rites of passage

Introduction

A wealth of current research is focused on British Terminal Neolithic/Chalcolithic and Early Bronze Age mortuary evidence.[1] Our understanding of the chronology of funerary practices and assemblages of this period is being enhanced through programmes of radiocarbon dating (e.g. as part of the *Beaker People Project* directed by Mike Parker Pearson, and, for Scotland, through the *Dating Cremated Bones* project led by Alison Sheridan (2007a; 2007b)) and has benefitted from a thorough reappraisal of the chronology of Beaker pottery by Stuart Needham (2005). Human remains are being examined in analyses of mobility patterns, diet and health (Montgomery et al. 2007; Jay & Richards 2007; and see Sheridan 2008 for summary). Artefact assemblages are also being re-analysed in detail, investigating contact over distance and considering the implications of the scarcity, manner of deposition, association and distance from point of origin of the objects for Early Bronze Age identities (e.g. Needham & Woodward 2008), as well as considering what the artefact assemblages can tell us about ritual activity (e.g. Woodward et al. 2005). Attempts are also being made to refine the chronology of monuments, which were often the scene of mortuary activity (e.g. Garwood 2007), and to explore the detailed sequences of activity at such monuments (e.g. Owoc 2001; 2005). At the same time, sophisticated theoretical approaches to the role of mortuary practices in negotiating social relations have been developed, and several authors have attempted to examine the relational construction of Early Bronze Age identity through mortuary rites (e.g. Brück 2004; 2006; Fowler 2005; Jones 2002; 2008; Owoc 2001; 2005). These studies emphasise how persons emerge from different strategies in social relations (which deploy material culture in differing ways), consider the metaphors involved in mortuary rites, and stress the nature of the mortuary context as a venue for ritualised transformation. There are also calls to consider the mortuary evidence in greater detail in order to move beyond the idea that distinct periods of the Neolithic and Bronze Age can be characterised by singular forms of mortuary practice (Fowler 2005; Gibson 2004; 2007). Such approaches to bodies, persons, and mortuary practices have not yet been applied together in detailed regional analysis drawing on the emerging chronologies mentioned above.

   In order to build up a contextual appreciation of mortuary rites at a regional level I have been examining the evidence from Northumberland with many of these analytical and interpretative developments in mind. This area of Britain has often been neglected in national syntheses of Neolithic and Early Bronze Age archaeology. Some recent research (e.g. the *Ritual in Early Bronze Age Grave Goods* project, directed by John Hunter; Woodward et al. 2005) considers evidence from some specific Northumbrian sites, but none is directed towards a detailed analysis of this region. While levels of preservation vary significantly within the county, there is a history of research with reliable recording stretching back into the mid nineteenth century. I have produced a database of information from published records of excavations of Early Bronze Age mortuary deposits from the eighteenth, nineteenth and twentieth centuries, including a corpus of work by William Greenwell, and some unpublished material.[2] The results analysed in this chapter draw on information from 127 sites (Fig. 3.1),[3] where a reasonable excavation record exists for 298 separate mortuary deposits. This information has now been incorporated into a broader regional analysis elsewhere by including comparable evidence from Tyne and Wear and County Durham (Fowler 2013a; 2013b), and these results will be considered elsewhere alongside contemporary evidence from southeast Scotland (Fowler & Wilkin in prep.). A programme of osteoarchaeological re-analysis and some radiocarbon dating of later prehistoric human remains currently in Tyne and Wear Museums collections has also just been completed, improving the resolution of the chronological patterns discussed here (Gamble & Fowler 2013a; 2013b). This article was initially drafted before all of this work was completed, but subsequent analyses confirm the picture of both the ritual transformation of the dead and the transformation of mortuary rites themselves during the Early Bronze Age in Northumberland.

In this article I will characterise trends in Northumbrian mortuary rites *c*. 2500–1500 BC. In so doing I will provide a contextual analysis of the decline in 'inhumation'[4] practices and the growing dominance of the deposition of cremated remains since this is often taken as the key change in mortuary practice during the period. Certain artefacts often accompanied specific mortuary practices and this provides some basis for a chronological scheme based on dating programmes and typological analyses of these artefacts and practices elsewhere in Britain. In Northumberland only between two and four burials included Beakers with cremated remains (some scraps of 'calcined bones' in the two cists at Dilston Park with respectively two and three Beakers (Gibson 1906), and clearly cremated remains in two of the cists at Low Hauxley (Waddington 2010)), the earliest Beaker burials (those before *c*. 2250 BC) were mainly those of adults, and the majority of crouched burials with Beaker pottery that date to *c*. 2250–1950 BC were oriented east–west. Earlier Beaker burials, and those buried with copper-alloy flat rivetted daggers, tended to remain as isolated burials while later burials of all kinds tended to occur in burial grounds such as cist cemeteries or sites marked with round mounds. The overall picture is one of specific practices associated with specific object types, and as the range of burial practices became more diverse so did the range of objects from which the grave accompaniments were chosen (though not the number of objects in any one grave), until *c*. 1750–1500 BC when a more restricted range of artefacts were placed in pits with cremated remains. From *c*. 2200/2100 BC Food Vessels sometimes accompanied burials that were not cremated, sometimes accompanied or contained

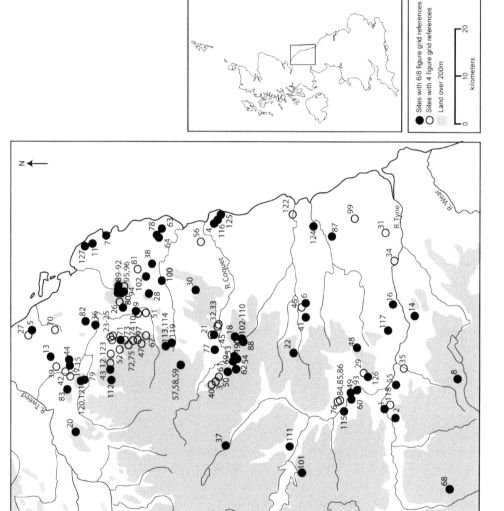

Gw - Greenwell site number; GwUn - Greenwell unnumbered site (numbered according to Kinnes & Longworth, 1985)

1. Allerwash cist, Newbrough NY871673
2. Altonside cist, Haydon Bridge NY856649
3. Alwinton cairn (Gw203) NT9305
4. Amble cist NU273052
5. Ancroft cist (GwUn11) NU041456
6. Angerton cist, Hartburn NZ100848
7. Benthall cairn NZ237289
8. Birkside Fell cairn NY934512
9. Blawearie kerbed cairn (Eglingham, Gw200) NU08172229
10. Blawearie satellite cairn 1 NU0822
11. Bluebell Inn cist, Seahouses NU215315
12. Bowchester cist, Humbleton Farm NT9728
13. Bowsden West Farm cist NT984414
14. Broomhill cist, High Mickley NZ076606
15. Broomhill kerbed cairn (Ford, Gw187) NT965370
16. Broomhouses barrow (Prudhoe, Ovingham Gw214) NZ099655
17. Broomridge 2 (GwUn15) NT9437
18. Burgh Hill 1 (Gw208, Rothbury) NU023005
19. Burgh Hill 2 (Gw209, Rothbury) NU0200
20. Carham cist, Howburn (GwUn30) NT821357
21. Cartington Farm, Rothbury NU0305
22. Catcherside cairn, Kirkwhelpington (Gw211) NY992877
23. Chatton barrow 1 (Gw190) NU0228
24. Chatton barrow 2 (Gw191) NU0228
25. Chatton barrow 3 (Gw192) NU0228
26. Chatton Sandyford kerbed cairn, Sandyford Moor NU1026.
27. Cheswick cist (GwUn16) NU0346
28. Cheviot Walk Wood cemetery NU10161960
29. Chollerton barrow (Gw213) NY9572
30. Corby's Crags rock-shelter NU12800965
31. Crag Hall cists, Jesmond NZ2567
32. Debdon Farm cairn 1, Cartington Fell (Gw206) NU0504
33. Debdon Farm cairn 2, Cartington Fell (Gw207) NU0504
34. Denton cist NZ1965
35. Dilston Park cists NY9663
36. Doddington cist (Gw189) NU005310
37. Dour Hill cist, Byrness NT794021
38. Elsnook cist NU183187
39. Etal Moor barrow (Ford Gw184) NT9640
40. Farnham cist (GwUn10) NT9206
41. Fawns cairn, Kirkwhelpington (Gw210) NZ007853
42. Ford barrow (Gw186) NT9538
43. Gains Law Ring Cairn NT956282
44. Goatscrag rock-shelter NT977371
45. Great Tosson Quarry cists (GwUn22) NU030005
46. Green Leighton barrow, Hartburn (Gw212) NZ0986
47. Greenhill cist, Ilderton (GwUn23) NU022
48. Grundstone Law barrow (GwUn24) NZ004734
49. Gunnerton cist (GwUn25) NY905750
50. Harbottle Peels cairn (GwUn26) NT9404
51. Harehope Hill cairn, Eglingham (Gw201) NU0820
52. Haugh Head cist, Wooler NU0026
53. Hedley Wood cist (GwUn27) NT985006
54. Hepple cairn, Rothbury (GwUn29) NT980000
55. Hexham Golf Course cist NY922649
56. High Buston Cist NU2308
57. High Knowes cairnfield A cairn 2 NT967121
58. High Knowes cairnfield B ring ditch NT967121
59. High Knowes cairnfield A small henge NT967121
60. Holybush Field cist NY894746
61. Holystone Common cairn 1 (Gw204) NT950020
62. Holystone Common cairn 2 (Gw205) NT961004
63. Howick cist cemetery NU25851657
64. Howick Heugh ring cairn NU237171
65. Humbleton Burn House cist Unknown
66. Huntlaw Quarry cist, Belsay Unknown
67. Jubilee Wood cist, Roddam NU0320
68. Kirkhaugh barrow, Alston NY700503
69. Kirkhill NY975007
70. Kyloe Quarry cist NU0440
71. Lilburn Hill Farm cemetery NU020263
72. Lilburn Hill Farm, North Cairnfold Field cists NU0124
73. Lilburn Hill Farm, East Cairnfold Field cists NU0225
74. Lilburn South Steads cist, West Lilburn NU0223
75. Lilburn Tower Farm, West Lilburn NU0124
76. Low Shield Green Crag barrow NY8879
77. Low Trewitt barrow NU001047
78. Lowstead Ground cist, Howick NU245175
79. Milfield North henge NT934348
80. Millstone Hill kerbed cairn NU088261
81. North Charlton cairn NU1722
82. North Hazelrigg cist NU06053345
83. Pace Hill cemetery (Crookham) NT913375
84. Pitland Hills, Birtley, Barrow 1 NY8879

85. Pitland Hills, Birtley, Barrow 2 NY8879
86. Pitland Hills, Birtley, Barrow 3 NY8879
87. Plessy Mill (GwUn36) NZ241793
88. Ravensheugh cairn NZ015989
89. Rayheugh cairn 1, Lucker Moor (Gw193 Bamburgh) NU116268
90. Rayheugh cairn 2, Lucker Moor (Gw194 Bamburgh) NU117267
91. Rayheugh cairn 3, Lucker Moor (Gw195 Bamburgh) NU118267
92. Rayheugh cairn 4, Lucker Moor (Gw196 Bamburgh) NU118264
93. Reaverhill Farm cist NY907737
94. Rosebrough Moor Cairn 1 (Gw197 Rosebrough I) NU118260
95. Rosebrough Moor Cairn 2 (Gw198 Rosebrough II) NU1326
96. Rosebrough Moor Cairn 3 (Gw199 Bamburgh) NU1326
97. Roseden Edge cairn (GwUn39, Rosedean) NU0221
98. Sandyford Park cist Unknown
99. Seghill cist (GwUn40) NZ2874
100. Shipley cist, Alnwick NU145165
101. Smalesmouth cist (GwUn41) NY731858
102. South Charlton Cairn NU157200
103. Spital Hill cairn 1 NZ020992
104. Spital Hill cairn 2 NZ018990
105. Spital Hill cairn 3 NZ026998
106. Spital Hill cairn 4 NZ0299
107. Spital Hill cairn 5 NZ0299
108. Spital Hill cairn 6 NZ0299
109. Spital Hill cairn 7 NZ0299
110. Spital Hill cairn 8 NY792885
111. The Sneep cist, Tarset Burn NY792885
112. Tom Tallon's Grave (Tantallon's Grave) (GwUn43) NT932280
113. Turf Knowe North cairn NU006157
114. Turf Knowe South NU006157
115. Warkshaugh Farm barrow (Warkshaugh (GwUn44)) NY867765
116. Warkworth cairn (Gw296) NU277043
117. Well House Farm cist NZ04046676
118. West Wharmley cist NY8866
119. Wether Hill cists NU013145
120. Whitton Hill henge 1 NT933347
121. Whitton Hill henge 2 NT933347
122. Woodhorn cist (GwUn46) NZ2988
123. Wooler cist (GwUn44) NY9928
124. Bedlington NZ263815
125. Low Hauxley NU284018
126. Middle Gunnar Peak NY915750
127. Seafield Farm NU216320

Fig. 3.1. Locations of the sites analysed within this study.

cremated bone, and were contemporary with some Beaker burials. Some burial practices were locally distinctive, such as north–south burials with jet ornaments, late Beaker pottery or Food Vessels in northern Northumberland after *c.* 2100 BC, often at burial grounds that were monumentalised. From *c.* 2000 BC Enlarged Food Vessel Urns (or Vase Urns) and Collared Urns joined the mix, and these were only found containing cremated remains, sometimes the mixed remains of multiple individuals. I will argue that equally as important, if not more so, than the rising deposition of cremated remains from *c.* 2150 BC is an increasingly tendency to combine the remains of the dead at a single locale or even in the same vessel or cist. While 'inhumation' did largely give way during the period to cremation, which accentuated the visible transformation of the body, this developed on and extended a trend of producing closer physical relations between the bodies of the dead during inhumations after *c.* 2200 BC. This in turn declined at the very end of the sequence. Detailed analysis also suggests continuities in some key features of the mortuary rites throughout much of the period whether these involved remains that had or had not been cremated before deposition.

In this analysis I explore the implications of van Gennep's model of the structure of rites of passage (from pre-liminal rites through liminal phases to post-liminal rites) by considering each Early Bronze Age mortuary deposit as the result of a sequence of ritualised actions. I argue that while those pre-liminal rites closest to the liminal phase generally have the most impact in shaping the mortuary evidence, such deposits also project desirable aspects of identity cited in the pre-liminal rites towards the post-liminal rites, and provide the dead with key media to assist in those latter rites. Drawing out an often-overlooked aspect of van Gennep's anthropological model, I argue that the work of the post-liminal incorporation of the dead into a new community may be deferred to non-living agents (the community of the dead, deities, etc), and then explore the implications of differences in such post-liminal practices for the Northumbrian Early Bronze Age evidence. I will first examine patterns in mortuary rites where the remains of the dead are buried without being cremated, before analysing mortuary rites involving cremation. In each case I will consider the fragmentary evidence for sequences of ritualised events from the preparation of the body to the closing of the mortuary deposit. I will consider elements of continuity in these mortuary practices alongside the changes in the material result, experiences and effects these events produced. I argue that the often-acknowledged shift from 'inhumation' to cremation during the period was perhaps of lesser importance in terms of understandings of the body, person and death than a contemporary shift from isolated burials to the use of collective burial grounds where a community of the dead could physically incorporate the deceased during the mortuary rites carried out by the living. I also place the change from 'inhumation' to cremation and from isolated to communal burial places within the context of enduring trends in the funerary rites that transformed the dead, in particular highlighting key media deployed repeatedly throughout the period in effecting the ritualised transformation of the dead. I will suggest that certain media were repeatedly deployed in transforming the body, resulting in presentations of idealised identities and desired relationships in the mortuary context, certain aspects of which changed relatively little over time. In so doing I map out precisely what changed and what remained the same during hundreds of years of prehistoric mortuary practices.

Early Bronze Age mortuary practices as *rites de passage*

The perspective on mortuary rites adopted in this chapter is strongly anthropological in basis, following van Gennep's (1960) and Turner's (1969) identifications of a tripartite structure to rites of passage. Van Gennep argues that each rite of passage has three phases: pre-liminal, liminal and post-liminal. Turner argues that the pre-liminal phase involves the affirmation of existing identities and relationships (e.g. dressing the dead, visiting the body) leading up to the separation of the person(s) undergoing the rite from others in the community. The identity presented during this affirmation relies on the perceptions of those among the community doing the affirming and, importantly, may stress the most desirable aspects of the identity of the deceased since the dead are prepared for their post-liminal reincorporation into the community of the dead, the afterlife, or whatever is hoped or expected to be the next stage in existence (see also Fowler 2013c). For that reason, in the analysis that follows I have resisted arguing that how the dead were prepared for the grave tells us only about the pre-liminal rites: transformations made at this stage, materials presented to the dead at this stage, prefigure the expected and hoped-for post-liminal rites which might take place in the afterlife or among the dead. Thus, in the Northumbrian Early Bronze Age analysis, I consider that the media of each practice provides a material conduit linking together all three phases of the ritual: the materials offered up for deposition in pre-liminal rites were *presented towards* the next stage of existence and as such are more than just residues of the first stage of the ritual. Incrasingly, such deposition arguably formed part of the post-liminal reincorporation of the dead.

Following the separation of the living and the dead at the end of the pre-liminal phase, the identities of, and relationships between, mourners and the deceased are further transformed during the liminal phase of the ritual. During this phase the deceased body is also usually physically transformed, for instance through mummification, cremation or decay, though this may go unseen by (most of) the living as the deceased has been physically separated from them. Turner stresses that a sense of community or belonging ('communitas') binds those who experience the transformation together – this might cement a community of mourncrs, but could also charactcrisc thc way that the dead are transformed in the same way as those who died before them or share the same burial ground and thus transfer the recently deceased into a community of the dead. The liminal phase may be lengthy, meaning that identities may be in flux for some time, including after the body has been buried. Certain activities may be prohibited during the liminal phase and these prohibitions may surround how mourners act with regards to the living as well as the recently deceased.

The final, post-liminal phase of ritual activity involves the reincorporation of the persons undergoing the rite into a wider community (of the living and/or the dead) and the acknowledgement of their new identities and relationships. Yet the key agents in the post-liminal reincorporation of the dead may be divinities, supernatural beings or a community of the dead (Fowler 2013c). For instance, in some belief systems the dead must be judged by divine agents before entering the afterlife, and this was certainly the case during the Bronze Age in Egypt; indeed, Van Gennep himself draws on the Ancient Egyptians as an example (van Gennep 1960: 157–59). Mummification, and the provision of the dead with a panoply of goods in the tomb, were directed towards this reincorporation by the divinities for the dead, even though these practices took place before the dead were fully separated from the living and the tomb was closed. Rites of incorporation may also take place among the living, freeing widows or widowers from mourning obligations and restrictions for instance and bringing the whole community of survivors together.

The Chalcolithic and Early Bronze Age mortuary practices under discussion in this chapter can be seen as culturally-specific rites of passage, and changed over time. While we could argue that all of these rites sought to affirm, transform, and present a new identity for the dead as their place in the cosmos was renegotiated, changes in practice over time are important. The symbols and spaces deployed in the rites, the techniques by which persons and bodies were transformed, and the duration of the ritual process could all potentially have changed over time, altering the experiences of mourners and the relationship between the deceased and certain places, objects, and communities of the dead. For instance, the length of time that the liminal phase lasts might vary to the extent that the deceased may be incorporated into a new community soon after death or this might be deferred (as arguably occurred in the Medieval Catholic conception of an afterlife following Resurrection and Judgement). The new status the dead attained is often (though not always) a desirable one: the dead are either elevated to new planes of existence or exist alongside the living in a new and special form (Turner 1969: 166–69). Thus, the production of a desired identity is a key aspect of the transformations undertaken in rites of passage (cf. Fowler 2013c). Yet in order to interpret past mortuary rites meaningfully we also need to consider the significance of symbols used and the place of those symbols as they move through or are introduced within a narrative sequence of events which includes acts of affirmation, transformation and reincorporation into a community of living and/or dead persons (Turner 1967; 1969). As explained above, features of the archaeological remains studied here cannot always be neatly attributed to one stage or another in the ritual process, and many materially connected different phases of the process. Rituals are complex, and may employ successive stages in which statements are made and then later reflected on, recontextualised and revised. Thus, interpretations of Early Bronze Age mortuary deposits have to be built contextually: we cannot simply assume that the body as it is presented in the grave affirms identity in life, but need to consider how identities were transformed through the mortuary sequence. Below I focus on the decisions made in treating the dead that have left material traces, and what inferences can be drawn about mortuary rituals from these traces. Changes in how various stages of the rite were conducted, in the symbols used, or in how, say, an act like deposition might articulate pre-liminal separation, liminality and post-liminal reintegration, are significant in considering changes in how persons were transformed following death. I have divided the evidence into the interment of uncremated and then cremated human remains in order to discuss the broad long-term trend in changing mortuary rites and assess the relative significance of this change in funerary practice.

Mortuary rites involving the interment of uncremated human remains

Most of the burials from the region that were not cremated date to *c.* 2450–1950 BC, some to *c.* 1950–1750 BC (Fowler 2013a: chapter 4; Gamble & Fowler 2013a). Thirty-four mortuary deposits included Beaker pottery, which was mainly current in the region *c.* 2300–1900 BC,[5] and 27 of these were associated with bones that had not been burnt. Forty burials of remains which had not been cremated included various types of Food Vessel, which were in use *c.* 2200–1700 BC. Twenty-two of these 73 burials were recorded as 'probable inhumations' where no bone had survived in the cist or grave, and it is possible that cremated bones found in the corners of the cists at Dilston Park (Gibson 1906) and at Haugh Head (Collingwood & Cowen 1948) shared these cists, which were the size of cists usually containing crouched burials, with one or more burials that have not survived.

Preparing the body for the grave[6]

There are numerous finds of personal ornaments in Early Bronze Age burials across northern Europe suggesting that the dead were often buried dressed. In Northumberland there are only a few cases where corpses were buried wearing personal ornamentation that survived to the time of recovery. Those objects which have survived indicate that some features of dress may have varied by age and sex. However, as explained below, it does not appear that hierarchical status categories were frequently marked out for the dead, and I would suggest that we need to consider a range of explanations for the presence of all 'grave goods', including that these were deployed as key symbols at various stages in the funerary narrative. Here I consider each type of artefact individually.

An assemblage including a gold basket-shaped ornament (probably a hair-clasp but sometimes seen as an 'ear-ring') was recovered from centre of Kirkhaugh barrow (Maryon 1936). The area where the artefacts were found was covered with earth, while cairn stones comprised the sides and the very top of the monument suggesting that the body was placed on the land surface, possibly in an organic container (e.g. wooden coffin) which was then covered, largely with stone slabs (Fig. 3.2). This is unusual as almost all the other Northumbrian mortuary deposits in the dataset were found in graves or cists

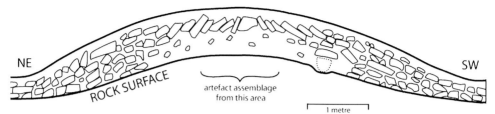

NE

SW

ROCK SURFACE

artefact assemblage
from this area

1 metre

Fig. 3.2. Section through the Kirkhaugh barrow (redrawn from Mryon 1936: 210 by Sheila Severn Newton).

cut into the ground. While poor preservation might account for the absence of bodies in the fabric of other barrows, there are very few artefacts and no personal ornaments from such locations that might alert us to the presence of such bodies. Kirkhaugh is the only confirmed example in the region of a Beaker burial with a complex assemblage of grave goods: a flint barbed and tanged arrowhead, six worked flint flakes, two flint cores and 'a number of' unworked flakes, a fragment of a whetstone, part of a flat sandstone rubber, and a nodule of iron pyrites, as well as an All Over Cord decorated Beaker crushed under a large stone (Maryon 1936: 211; Cowen 1966: 219–22; Tait 1965: 16). The flint 'saw' (Maryon 1936: 215) is a fabricator, probably used along with the lump of iron pyrites as a 'strike-a-light'.[7] The fabricator, the arrowhead, several of the flakes and one of the cores are of same blue–grey mottled flint. Perhaps the flint objects were knapped nearby and the debris buried along with the artefacts during the funeral, or perhaps the deceased carried the flakes as 'blanks'. Specialist analysis concluded that 18 flint objects were struck from a single piece of flint in grave 203 at Barrow Hills, Oxfordshire (Brück 2004: 317–18). That burial was also accompanied by a nodule of iron pyrites. The production and use of such tools might have formed an important part of the funerary sequence, and a vital accompaniment for the deceased. At Kirkhaugh it could be inferred that the deceased was provided with the means to hunt and cook in the next stage of existence. The Kirkhaugh burial connects with a burial tradition that was widespread yet rare across Britain *c.* 2500–2250 BC, and one which was not applied extensively throughout society in Northumberland.

The other notable example of personal ornamentation is a complete necklace of at least 100 jet beads (4 barrel-shaped, 4 flattened barrel-shaped, 92 discoid) found in a cist at Blawearie (Greenwell 1877: 419–20; Kinnes & Longworth 1985: 103). No bone survived, but from the size of the cist it seems likely that a body was deposited in a crouched position wearing this necklace. The Blawearie necklace appears to comprise a full set of matching beads, but incomplete necklaces and small numbers of beads or even single beads have been found in Northumberland. John Barrett (1994: 121–22), Anne Woodward (2002), and Andrew Jones (2002) have all argued that some necklaces from this period were broken up and only sections placed in graves or cists. They suggest that necklaces might be taken apart and restrung, combining parts from different original necklaces in ways that might trace or construct biographical relations between persons. In some cases necklaces were composed from beads of differing materials, as at Shrewton Barrow 5J in Wiltshire (Barrett 1994: 121–22), and Brück (2004: 314–16) describes how bone, jet, and amber beads from different necklaces played different roles in a funeral by cremation at Bedd Branwen burial H on Anglesey. No necklaces or collections of beads composed of differing materials have been found in Northumberland, but there are deposits with one or a small number of beads which require explanation. I return to the use of beads in cremation deposits later, but one jet or shale bead was found at Well House Farm cist (Gates 1981) and eight shale beads were found with the unburnt bones of a 'woman' (a mid-nineteenth century analysis) and what sounds like a flat riveted blade at Angerton (Cowen 1966). At Kyloe cist the middle third of a jet necklace was missing (50 barrel-shaped beads and six spacer plates were recovered) while only about half of the sherds from a Bowl Food Vessel were recovered from this cist (Brewis 1928; Newman 1976). The cist was discovered and opened by workmen quarrying the site and the beads had to be collected from various people who had taken them from the site, so poor recovery seems likely to account for the partial remains (the remains of the Bowl Food Vessel also show both fresh and old breaks).

It is important to consider the preservation and recovery of jet objects because this issue clearly affects our interpretation of the frequency and value of these items, as well as whether necklaces were deliberately fragmented during mortuary practices. Alison Sheridan and Mary Davis (2002: 822–23) have shown that some spacer-plate jet necklaces are composed only partly of true jet, with added beads of cannel coal, and suggest this resulted from a history of necklace curation and repair. They suggest that jet necklaces were prestigious items exported across northern Britain. The beads were fairly fragile, and individual beads might be lost or broken – when this happened they were replaced with beads made of local materials. The description of the (now lost) Angerton beads suggest seven spacer plates and a v-perforated button (Cowen 1966: 227) and these might either represent exotic jet fixtures of a necklace otherwise composed of more local organic elements which did not survive to recovery or poor recovery in which smaller beads were missed. Jet can become friable and fragments could easily be missed during nineteenth and earlier twentieth century excavations where sieving was not practiced. On the other hand, the (probably complete) jet necklace from Blawearie survived even though no human bone did, and finds of one or a very small number of smaller beads in a burial seem genuine reflections of what was deposited: it would seem unlikely that taphonomic processes have claimed an entire necklace bar one to four beads. While it remains possible that some necklaces were pulled apart during funerals and only some of the beads accompanied the corpse to the grave, for deposits of cremated bone some beads may have dropped through the pyre during cremation to be collected up with the remains (Sheridan 2010). Other beads might have been retained by the living, commemorating the deceased and linking them in chains of continuing relationships. Alternatively the living might have donated beads from their necklaces to the dead as a symbol of their loss (Fowler 2004: 72–76), or might have burst necklaces apart at the graveside, from which some beads or sections fell into the grave.

It is impossible to know the sex of the person buried with the Blawearie necklace as no bone survives and the other instances where jet beads accompanied burials suffer similar problems with bone preservation. Yet in Scotland and Yorkshire jet necklaces are clearly associated with female burials (Sheridan & Davis 2002: 816; Pierpoint 1980: 224, 228). Necklaces (of varying materials) were perhaps worn in producing a certain kind of adult female identity, or perhaps thought to have apotropaic effects relevant to women's bodies – indeed jewellery may serve to symbolically protect people (e.g. the Beng use of necklaces, bracelets and other strings of beads on infants – Gottlieb 2004: 113–15, *inter alia*). In studying Medieval burials, Gilchrist (2008) suggests that various objects accompanying the dead acted as amulets designed to cure ills or protect bodies for their resurrection, while burning or consuming crushed jet was believed to cure afflicted female bodies in the Roman Period (Allason-Jones 1996: 15). Dressing the dead in special materials might have been intended to have protective effects rather than or as well as designating some particular status.

In five cases bodies were accompanied by v-perforated jet buttons. An adult woman was buried in a cist at Lilburn South Steads (West Lilburn) with a large Shepherd type 6a button with beading at the edge as well as a bronze knife-dagger and sherds from a Short-Necked Beaker (Collingwood et al. 1946; Shepherd 2009: 359). When discovered the bones and the vessel were already broken. Two jet buttons (Shepherd type 1 and 2) were found with Beaker sherds next to a disturbed grave at Chatton Sandyford (Jobey 1968; Shepherd 2009: 358). No bone survived here. Three Food Vessel burials which had not been cremated included jet buttons: bone survived in two cases and one was identified in the nineteenth century as an adult male, the other as possibly an adult female (Greenwell 1872; 1877; Shepherd 2009: 358–59). V-perforated jet buttons potentially had several uses: Shepherd (2009: 346–48) identifies examples of dress fasteners (especially as a toggle on a loop of material), necklace fasteners (e.g. for necklaces made of organic materials), and pouch fasteners. Any of these options are possible for the Northumbrian examples, and their position with respect to the body was not recorded. Shepherd (2009) reports four cases of sets of buttons ranging from six to 20, though not all of these were produced as sets: one of the six buttons from Rameldry, although all of similar size and shape, was made not of jet like the others but of lizardite (not found in Yorkshire). The six buttons show varied wear patterns. It is therefore possible that the set was assembled over time during life or from different donors at the grave (Baker et al. 2003). While there are pairs in Northumberland, there are no cases where sets of buttons survive, and it does not appear that these were showy ornaments woven into clothes in large number. It seems further possible – though this cannot be substantiated – that buttons were used (or re-used) as toggles to tie a shroud or hide around the body. A bone pin accompanied some uncremated[8] bones in a cist, and may have held a shroud in place or may have been a dress fitting. Worked calfskin scraps were recovered from two burials (Doddington cist, and the coffin burial in a cist at Cartington: Dixon 1913; Greenwell 1877: 411), but it is unclear whether these were from clothing, shrouds, body coverings or other items. Ashbee (1960: 93) identifies shrouds wrapping a small number of burials across Britain, mostly in cases where log coffins have also survived. A recently-excavated cist at Langwell Farm, Strath Oykel, included the remains of a woman wrapped in a cow hide and accompanied by a rod of hazel and some basketry; the remains were radiocarbon dated to *c.* 2200–1880 BC (Lelong 2012). If shrouds or coverings were present then bodies were secluded during pre-liminal rites before or as they were placed in the grave, but even if these bodies were placed clothed in the grave then they were 'wrapped' when deposited.

It seems that the majority of bodies were prepared for the grave wearing garments with organic fixtures or fixed with small, unostentatious pins and buttons. Some wore necklaces, but token beads were perhaps tucked in with other bodies or fell into the deceased's clothing, shrouds or graves as mourners broke necklaces. Beads and buttons were valued objects, but perhaps also had personal, magical/medical and/or historical value. The button at Lilburn South Steads is larger than average, and complete necklaces were probably very eye-catching. Personal ornaments may have been associated with membership of particular gender and age categories, and may potentially have carried implications about social relations with people from distant places. Such categories of things and persons, and the extent of social differentiation probably varied during the period and within the region (Fowler 2013a: chapter 6). There are few signs of other kinds of personal ornaments or dress items found elsewhere in Britain: for instance, no stone bracers, belt-rings or belt-hooks have been found in the region. In common with the rest of Britain, copper alloy axeheads were not placed with the dead. Three mortuary deposits which were excluded from my database due to a poverty of contextual information included personal ornaments: a jet spacer plate from a cist on Simonside, two bronze bracelets from a cairn on Cooper's Hill, two gold basket-shaped ornaments from a barrow near Alnwick. There are also a small number of these sites which contained flint or bronze knives and/or arrowheads since lost, and there are stray finds of personal ornaments from the Bronze Age reported from the county, including two large amber beads or 'terminals' from Simonside (Cowen 1966), and 13 gold beads from Redesdale, but these may not have come from mortuary contexts. It is notable that all but one of the jet ornaments were found in northern Northumberland where jet buttons were found in three north–south oriented cists (along with Food Vessels), and a jet necklace in a fourth, while jet buttons are also associated with one of the north–south late Beaker graves at Chatton Sandyford (see below). Indeed, only two cists contained jet artefacts without being oriented north–south, and one of those was northeast–southwest. Thus, if these objects were associated with distant contacts and/or prestige then such identities were focussed around the Milfield Basin in areas rich in rock carvings and overlooking approaches to a complex of henge monuments (particularly from the south).

Not everyone was buried during the Early Bronze Age in Britain, and it is possible that burial practices in some periods were mainly reserved for adult men, begging the question of what form the funerary rites for women and children, as well as other men, took (Brück 2003: 181). In Northumberland, all the Beaker burials likely to date before *c.* 2000/1950 BC where the age of the individual was recorded were of adults with one exception (Bluebell Inn, Seahouses). While some cists where no bone was recovered were 60 cm long or less, making it difficult to see how they could have contained entire adult's bodies, none of these contained Beakers dating to before *c.* 1950 BC. In the 17 cases where the age of the individual is recorded for burials with Food Vessels five are subadults. No dress ornaments have been recovered with their remains, but the same can be said for the vast majority of all the burials in the region.

In some cases there were different or further steps in the preparation of the body before deposition and not all British Early Bronze Age mortuary practices resulted in the burial of an intact dressed body (Petersen 1972; Fowler 2005; Gibson 2004; 2007). Aside from cremation and possibly the charring of already decayed body parts or bones, British mortuary practices include the burial of bodies probably in states of decay and/ or the burial of body parts rather than complete bodies (e.g. Horsbrugh in Peeblesshire, see Petersen et al. 1974), and, as Gibson (2007: 57) convincingly illustrates, exposure of the corpse to the elements prior to burial which in many cases would be hard to detect. There are relatively few cases in Northumberland where curation, manipulation or deliberate fragmentation of corpse or skeleton can be conclusively demonstrated, but both the preservation conditions and the preconceptions of nineteenth and earlier twentieth century excavators that burials were of whole bodies immediately following death need to be taken into account here. Both of these factors are likely to influence our view of the numerous cases where partial remains or no remains were recovered from graves, and we tend to perceive these by default as single burials. A small quantity of fragmented bones from two cists at Dilston Park were described as 'partially burnt' (Gibson 1906: 142), and may have resulted from cremation of bodies or from the burning of bones. Scorching on bones suggests that other burials were subjected to burning after the flesh had decayed naturally and reports of burnt stones and soils at other sites suggest that burning took place within the cist (Gamble & Fowler 2013a). In some cases this occurred before mounds covered the burials (Fowler 2013a: 152–53) – this will be discussed below as a feature of liminal or post-liminal rites or later activity at mortuary sites. The few clear examples of bodily fragmentation in the Northumbrian corpus could all result from later intercession with the grave rather than initial preparation of the body, but disarticulation or attrition of the body before deposition is equally possible and it is worth considering one example here. Bones from the lower half of a body were found in a cist at Allerwash, Newborough; the pelvis was placed where the skull should be in a crouched burial, with a tibia to the east of it and the other bones to the west (Fig. 3.3). The excavators state '[o]nly the lower half of the skeleton was deposited, and at a time when it was already in a skeletal condition' (Newman & Miket 1973: 92). Osteological re-analysis of these remains tentatively

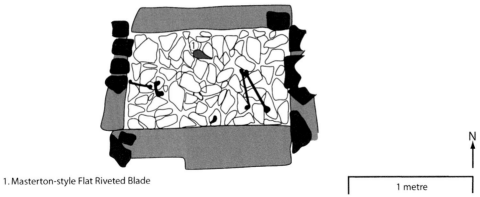

1. Masterton-style Flat Riveted Blade

N

1 metre

Fig. 3.3. Allerwash cist, Newborough (redrawn from Newan & Miket 1973: 89 by Sheila Severn Newton).

concurs that the remains were likely deposited after decaying elsewhere and reveals the individual is more likely male than, as originally thought, female (Gamble & Fowler 2013a: 52). This burial, like several where bodily integrity was compromised, was accompanied by a bronze dagger.

Choosing the location for burial

Early sites seem to have been mainly single, isolated, cists. In some cases cemeteries of cists developed before 2000 BC, and towards *c.* 2000 BC new monuments were not always built following each death. Instead, existing sites were commonly re-used, though there are some examples of isolated cist burials that may date after 2000 BC. After *c.* 2250 BC it was seemingly acceptable to bury successive bodies at the same locale, potentially some time after it was first marked with a burial. Where cists were found without mounds or other cists in the immediate vicinity, 32 contained remains that had not been cremated while only two contained cremations. Cists and graves containing burials where the remains were not cremated had very wide distribution across the landscape, though many were close to rivers or streams (Fowler 2013a: chapter 5). The choice of location for the grave did not simply relate to geographical features, but also to historically meaningful places, particularly after *c.* 2250 BC. Some were placed in cemeteries with previous burials, and others were deposited at pre-existing monuments, especially after *c.* 2100 BC, perhaps suggesting that the act of deposition had come to conjoin the separation of the deceased from the living and their incorporation with the dead more visibly than before. In a couple of cases successive burials occurred in the same cist. For instance, a large cist with an oversized cover slab at Dour Hill was the scene of two successive burials: the body of a child about eleven years old interred with a Vase Food Vessel and a burnt hazelnut shell was severely disturbed and so decayed that only tooth fragments remained from the individual. The second deposit yielded skull and mandible fragments from an infant six to nine months old, and sherds from a Bowl Food Vessel (Jobey & Weyman 1977).

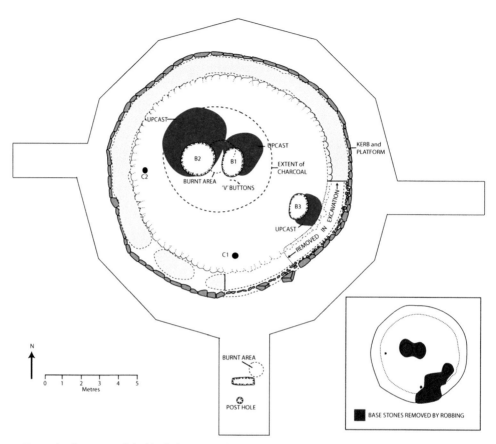

Fig. 3.4. Chatton Sandyford kerbed cairn (redrawn from Jobey 1968: fig. 2 by Sheila Severn Newton).

Two sites in northern Northumberland exemplify the complex history of burial sequences in relation to monuments after *c.* 2250 BC (sequences which also often include cremation deposits): Chatton Sandyford (Jobey 1968) and Blawearie (Hewitt & Beckinsall 1996). At Chatton Sandyford (Fig. 3.4) stakes were driven into the ground and burning resulted in a dense lens of charcoal at the centre of the area. A grave was cut and filled here, and while it was later robbed an S-profile globular Beaker (probably dating to *c.* 2050–1850 BC) and two v-perforated jet buttons were found in disturbance next to the grave. A deeper grave was cut next to this one and partly through its mound, and this grave contained a similar Beaker, but no bones survived. A third grave was dug 2 m to the southeast of these two – this was robbed also, but contained sherds of a Beaker which probably dates to *c.* 2250–1950 BC. All three burials were covered with a round cairn, which rested against a platform ring with kerb of flat slabs. This ring may have predated some or all of the aforementioned activities. Two cremation deposits were later inserted into the cairn. While the sequence of deposition between

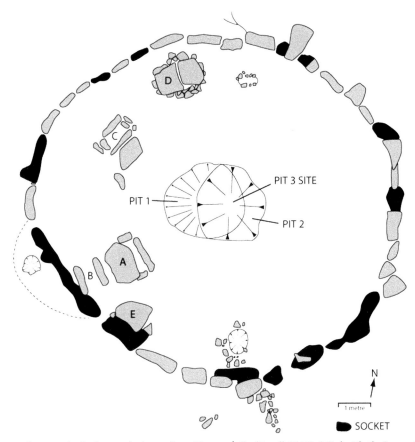

Fig. 3.5. Blawearie kerbed cairn (redrawn from Hewitt & Beckinsall 1996: 261 by Sheila Severn Newton).

burials 1 and 2 and burial 3 is unclear, the location was chosen repeatedly for burial and mound construction, forming a circumscribed community of the dead.

At Blawearie (Fig. 3.5) a pit was dug, perhaps to remove the stump of a tree, and a second pit was of a size and shape to hold a large post. A kerbed round cairn was constructed with this feature at its centre, creating a circular enclosure. Later (according to the excavators, though it seems equally possible that this predated the construction of the cairn) a pit was dug through the central pit and a cist inserted. Three of five later cists, one of which contained the jet necklace discussed earlier and a flint knife, another of which held a Vase Food Vessel, were built using slabs removed from the kerb of the cairn. Kerbstones were removed from the southwest of the kerb. A pit excavated in the gap contained charcoal and burnt bone, and its sides were a strong red colour, suggesting this was the scene of a cremation pyre or that bone was burnt within this pit (cf. Gibson 2007: 58), and was then capped by a low cairn. Thus, while the construction of the kerb and cairn might have followed an initial central burial, the majority of deposition at the site involved later return to and alteration of a historically meaningful place. Furthermore, the place chosen for the earliest burial may already have had specific meaning – the excavators argue that a large tree had stood in the area of the cairn and oak charcoal was strewn across the centre of the site before the first pits were dug (cf. the location of a ring ditch around a tree and the eventual location of Raunds barrow 6 over the area centred on the tree (Harding & Healy 2007: 213–14)). At Blawearie, the aggregation of a community of the dead within a stone kerb partly fragmented that kerb, and deployed those kerb-stones in building containers for the dead. The kerb was initially a boundary, perhaps circumscribing liminal transformations. Fragments of the kerb connected the dead with one another and with the kerb, simultaneously ending the pre-liminal phase of the mortuary rite for those burials and setting up conditions for the reincorporation of the deceased into a community of the dead in a post-liminal phase. Over time the site itself moved from a place of liminal transformation to a locale associated with the transformed, ancestral dead.

Both of these sites have a complex history, and burying the dead was only one element in that history. The pre-liminal rites therefore situated the deceased in time and space before their liminal transformation, and increasingly this time and place was relative to other dead persons and elaborate architecture. Owoc (2001; 2005) has suggested that cairns and barrows can be understood as projects that incorporated human remains alongside other materials within a set of cosmologically sanctioned principles, rather than simply as mortuary monuments (cf. chapters in Last 2007). While I focus here on the funerary process, I agree with Owoc's suggestion that funerals need to be put in a broader context of activity. For instance, at Chatton Sandyford the creation of a cairn or barrow closed off the dead, but each grave had already been capped, suggesting that the cairn construction was part of some other narrative structure encompassing these burials. One aspect of that narrative might have been the post-liminal reincorporation of the dead (collectively) into a community of the ancestral dead. This happened sometime after each of the first two burials was covered with a cairn that separated them from the living, ending a phase in the funerary sequence. It is also possible that the architecture of these sites related to a particular (circular and cyclical) model of the cosmos. Thus, the narrative related individual death and mortuary transformation with a growing sense of communal ancestry. While this may have supported the claims to importance by certain lineages or other groups within the community, the overall narrative is rather different from one concerned with the expression of individual power and status that archaeologists have often perceived when describing Early Bronze Age burials (cf. Brück 2004; Fowler 2005).

Preparing the grave for the body

Throughout Northumberland almost all of the cists were dug into the earth rather than free-standing, and far more cists are known than graves. Cist burials first appeared early on in the sequence, probably before 2300 BC, developing contemporaneously with the same practice across eastern Scotland – such 'short cists' are far rarer in Yorkshire than

Table 3.1. The orientation of cists and grave pits containing Beakers (n = 19) and Food Vessels (n = 20) in Northumberland. Beakers likely to post-date 1950 BC are marked *

Orientation	Head to the…	No. Beaker burials	No. Food Vessel burials
E–W	E	4	1
	W	2	4
	Unknown	4(*1)	6
	Total E–W =	**10**	**11**
ENE–WSW	ENE	0	0
	WSW	0	0
	Unknown	1	1
	Total ENE–WSW	*1*	*1*
N–S	N	0	1
	S	0	0
	Unknown	4 (*1)	3
	Total N–S =	**4(*1)**	**4**
NE–SW	NE	0	1
	SW	1	0
	Unknown	0	3
	Total NE–SW	**1**	**4**
NNE–SSW	NNE	0	0
	SSW	0	0
	Unknown	0	0
	Total NNE–SSW	**0**	**0**
NW–SE	NW	0	0
	SE	0	0
	Unknown	3(*2)	2
	Total NW–SE	**3(*2)**	**2**
WNW–ESE	WNW	0	0
	ESE	0	0
	Unknown	0	0
	Total WNW–ESE	**0**	**0**
NNW–SSE	NNW	0	0
	SSE	0	0
	Unknown	0	1
	Total NNW–SSE	**0**	**1**

in the northeast of England. The cists are indeed short – most are between 0.80 m and 1.20 m in length – requiring those burying the dead to squeeze them into place. The paving of cist floors varied: two were paved with pebbles – in one case these were embedded in clay. A clay floor was found in another cist, while clay was also used to seal the joins between slabs in at least five cists all of which were located fairly near to burns or rivers; three of these cists yielded preserved bronze knives/daggers, and if the clay joint lining had enhanced preservation in these cases this might suggest that more blades were buried than have survived. A bedding (or perhaps wrapping?) of rushes was found in the Allerwash cist, and a layer of bracken was recovered in the Cartington coffin. In most cases, therefore, the grave was clearly designed to encase the dead in stone and earth, and possibly wrap them in other materials, and place them below the level of the land-surface.

Ten out of the 19 Beaker graves and cists where orientation was recorded were oriented east–west (see Table 3.1), all of them dating to *c.* 2300–1950 BC, while three of the four Beaker burials where orientation is recorded that can be identified on a typological basis as later than this exhibit other orientations. For Food Vessel burials eastwest orientations were favoured but north–south and northeast–southwest and northwest–southeast orientations are also evident. In general, we could suggest that cist orientation varied more by period than by style of vessel, though we currently lack a firm enough chronology for Food Vessels to test this. Some variation may also relate to the practices of localised kin groups: all of the 14 cists and graves oriented north–south lie in the north of the county. Pierpoint (1980: 247–48) also noticed regional patterns for the placement of bodies in Food Vessel burials in Yorkshire.

Placing the body in the grave

Conditions of preservation may mean that graves or bodies placed on the ground and then covered with barrows may have been overlooked in previous excavations, and it is also likely (based on the numbers found) that many of the dead were not buried at all. But where we find burials, it appears that the dead were laid into very small graves and short cists, usually crouched in an almost foetal position. Of the 53 cases where uncremated human remains were recovered, 20 were specifically described as crouched burials and the dimensions of the graves and cists suggests this was the case for the vast majority of the remains that were not cremated prior to deposition.

While most Beaker burials were laid on an east–west axis some were placed with heads to the east and some to the west. Burials with Beakers typologically identified as being later than *c.* 2250 BC or with Food Vessels exhibited a preference for heads placed to the west end of the grave (see Table 3.2). Among the crouched burials where the bone was preserved and the placement of the Beaker was recorded, there was a preference for placing Beakers near to the head. The number of recorded instances where the sex of the remains and the placement of Beaker are recorded is only three, but the Beaker was placed behind the head for two females and in front of the face for one male. Within the small number of Food Vessel burials, for which accurate information on bodily position and object location exists, three adult males lay with their heads to the west and a vessel near the head, while the only female for which information exists shares the orientation, but the vessel was placed at her feet. Alexandra Tuckwell's (1970; 1975) analysis of artefact positioning in East Yorkshire graves, which deploys a far larger dataset, suggests that ceramics were mostly placed around the head, but she was unable to connect any patterns with sexual differentiation.

Overall, crouched burials were most often positioned so as to face south in the grave, whether the head lay to the east with the body lying on its left side (which seems to be more common for earlier burials) or to the west with the body lying on its right side (as is more common in later burials). A southeasterly orientation to the face accords with the direction of the sunrise during the part of the year including the winter months and southwest to winter sunsets, while south is the position which gets

Table 3.2. Details of the orientation of the body in the grave, grave goods and side that the body was placed on where recorded, showing details of sex where identified (all are adults)

Head at	Side buried on	Facing	No. males (artefact types where present)	No. females (artefact types where present)	No. unknown sex (artefact types where present)	Total	Comparison with patterns in Yorkshire identified by Tuckwell (1975)
E	Left	S	2 (1 Food Vessel)		3 (2 Beakers (c.2300–2100, 2200–2000 BC), 1 Food Vessel)	5	Matches most Beaker males
W	Right	S	3 ?Males (2 Food Vessel, 1 knife-dagger)	2 (1 Beaker c. 2200–2000 BC prob. Food Vessel)	1 (awl, no vessel)	6	Matches some Food Vessel males & most Beaker females
NE	Left	SE	1 c.23–57, no artefacts, c. 2279–2040 BC (Gamble & Fowler 2013a)			1	
NW	Right	SW		1 (Beaker c. 2300–2100 BC)		1	
SW	Left	SW			1 (c. 2450–2200 BC)	1	
E	Right	N			1 (Beaker c. 2300–2100 BC)	1	
W	Left	N	2 (1 Beaker c. 2300–2100 BC), plus 1 ?male (Food Vessel)	1 (dagger)		3	

most sun for most of any day. The dead were arguably oriented with respect to these events, though in differing ways. While there is insufficient evidence for an analysis of difference in orientation by sex, such patterns as can be detected may be parallel with a distinction between male and female noted in Yorkshire, Aberdeenshire, and east central Scotland (Tuckwell 1975: 101–2; Shepherd 1989; Wilkin 2009: 39–40). This division is, however, set within the larger pattern of shared orientation of the face to the south in each region.

While most of the dead were provided with vessels, some were interred with other objects. Two women were interred with bronze blades (knife-daggers[9]) as were three males (two flat riveted blades, one flat riveted knife-dagger), and three with bodies for which sex was not identifiable. Some of the human remains buried with copper alloy daggers,[10] show signs of attrition or disturbance. I have already discussed the Allerwash partial burial. At Reaverhill cist only some of the bones of an adult male were recovered along with a bronze flat riveted blade – the site had been disturbed, though it is not clear when (Jobey et al. 1965: 66), and some of the bones were scorched (Gamble & Fowler 2013a: 55–6). At Bowchester (Humbleton Farm) the individual buried with a flat riveted dagger exhibited two lesions through the parietal bone, with the jaw and left femur also showing signs of disease (Short 1931). A body interred in North Charlton cist 2 was described as having a dagger lying on its chest (Tate 1891). These blades may or may not have been personal possessions of the deceased, but in some cases could also be artefacts placed in the grave during the separation of the dead from the living at the end of the pre-liminal phase of the ritual. In other words, knives cut away the dead from the living. In other cases they may have been introduced during a later intercession with the body – perhaps if the funeral was not considered sufficiently effective in severing ties with the living and transforming the dead. In such cases they may have been effective in ending the liminal phase of mortuary transformation.

Scrapers were found with five burials and a cluster of four scrapers was found near to a further cist. The only sexed remains to be found with a scraper (two scrapers, in fact, along with a Short-Necked Beaker (probably *c.* 2300–2100 BC) and five flint flakes) was a female buried in The Sneep cist (Hedley 1892). Scrapers may be used in working hides, and if hides were prepared to cover or shroud the dead, then these tools could have been associated with the mortuary rite. Fragmented objects and materials were found in some graves: for instance, flint fragments were found with 13 burials. In four of these cases flint fragments accompanied flint knives or scrapers and could potentially be seen as waste from artefact production on site, though this requires further analysis. In Cartington cist, a body was either dressed in stitched calfskin or kidskin garments or possibly 'wrapped in the skin of a kid or calf' (Grinsell 1953: 250) and placed in a crouched position on a layer of bracken in a log coffin (radiocarbon dated to 2340–2060 BC: Jobey 1984) along with sherds from a Beaker, a scraper and some flint fragments (Dixon 1913: 81–82). The coffin was lowered into a cist which was then covered with 'a course of arches' and a stone cairn (Dixon 1913: 81). This deposit illustrates successive episodes of concealment or containment from wrapping the body in hide clothing or a shroud to placement in a shaped log coffin, lowering it into and sealing a stone chamber, and the erection of a cairn. In the process the body of the deceased was incrementally removed from contact with the living – but as the body became hidden from them the deceased was presenced in the landscape through the capping stone cairn towards the end of the funerary sequence.

There are a couple of cases where multiple bodies might have been buried in the same feature at the same time, where bodies were added to existing graves (as at Dour Hill, discussed above), or where bones from another body seem to have been buried along with a corpse. The two cists at Dilston Park contained two and three Beakers respectively with some partially burnt bone, while at Haugh Head a Vase Food Vessel was tucked away in the northeast corner of the 1 m long east–west oriented cist with two scraps of cremated bone. In these cases the cists were all large enough for crouched burials, and it is possible that the burnt bone accompanied uncremated remains which have since decayed. At Grundstone Law a cist contained incomplete sets of bones from two bodies (Greenwell & Embleton 1862). A third body was laid out on the cover of the cist which was covered by a barrow – it is possible that some of the bones from this individual had intruded into the cist so it is difficult to confirm multiple burial, but the presence of the two bodies confirms at least successive burial and the burial in the cist reads as though it was not an intact body when interred. Thus, some bodies might have been laid out with parts of others and projected together towards their post-liminal incorporation into a community of the dead.

Ending the act of deposition

The bodies of the dead were perhaps on display in their grave or cist for a period of time, but graves were filled in and cists were covered with large stone slabs, secluding the dead. Earlier burials in cists were rarely covered with earth, sand or other similar materials, and the bodies were sealed in place simply with a cover slab. Later burials, after *c.* 2150 BC, were more commonly immersed in the earth as cists were more often backfilled, again concealing the bodies and setting up different conditions for bodily transformation (Fowler 2013a: chapter 6). In at least ten cases an episode of burning occurred before a cist or grave containing a burial which had not been cremated was sealed. For instance, burnt planks covering burials are suggested in two probable grave pits at Milfield North henge (Harding 1981), while at Howick cist 4 a 'burnt residue' was attached to the underside of the cover slab and the fill included reddened clay and charcoal (Waddington et al. 2005: 77), while several other excavators refer to fire-cracked stones, black soil and/or charcoal in cists that either contained burials that had not been cremated or where no bone survived, and some of these were sealed by mounds in the Early Bronze Age (Fowler 2013a: 152–53). Cists were typically capped with a single large flat slab, finally secluding the deceased: between the heavy cover and the tight fit of the body in the cist, the burial architecture gives the impression of holding the dead in place and preventing any possibility of their moving from that position. Indeed, cists (and cairns) might be interpreted as technologies devised to keep the dead in place, while also allowing for the potential to re-examine or remove the remains if necessary. Cist pits were backfilled with stones and earth. At Low Trewitt North Moor and Well House Farm cist these stones and earth seem to have been burnt (Bate 1912; Gates 1981). Many cists were covered with low mounds of stone, perhaps after an intervening period. Between the closing of the cist and the construction of the cairn at Dour Hill the soil around the cist was burnt (Jobey & Weyman 1977: 204). If the earlier stages of the ritual involved some display of the dead, later phases involved seclusion and separation, perhaps successive episodes of containment, and sometimes the severing of the dead from the living through various means including knives and fire. These activities repeatedly and gradually separated the dead from the living at the onset and perhaps sometimes the conclusion of the liminal phase of the mortuary process.

Returning to the grave?

The possibility to monitor the remains of the dead was provided by burying them in cists with cover slabs and while it is difficult to say whether the dead were examined in this way, there are few instances where remains were interfered with. Successive deposition was rare. As noted above, some of the dagger graves show signs of disturbance to the human remains within. Two of the long-bones from the adult female body in the Lilburn South Steads cist were split longitudinally when found and the excavators report that the contents of the cist were jumbled up and the bones out of their correct anatomical positions (Collingwood & Cowen et al. 1946). The fact that no small bones were recovered at Allerwash favours the interpretation that the remains were partial when deposited, rather than that bones were removed from the grave (Gamble & Fowler 2013a) – though it is possible that this was a 'reburial' of bones from another grave site. If bodies were secluded and their transformation was hidden or deferred through the act of burial, then returning to a grave and interceding with the dead might have formed a special final phase in a mortuary process restricted to only a few, or beliefs about certain events might have led people to return to graves in special cases.

Mortuary rites involving the interment of cremated human remains

I now want to consider the mortuary rites surrounding deposits of burnt or cremated bone. It seems that the deposition of cremated remains did not occur frequently between *c.* 2500 and *c.* 2250 BC. This does not mean that no cremations took place, but that cremated bones were not usually deposited in cists or graves nor even inserted into cairns or mounds during this period. Further dating is needed to know exactly when cremation deposition with Food Vessels began in the region but it is possible this was contemporary with crouched burials from either as early as *c.* 2250 BC or as late as *c.* 2100 BC. Cremation deposits associated with various types of Food Vessel in the region have been radiocarbon dated to from *c.* 2000–*c.* 1700 BC, while examples with reliable dates from Scotland and Yorkshire suggest that Food Vessels were current there from *c.* 2200–2150 BC to *c.* 1700–1600 BC (see Sheridan 2004; 2007b).[11] Collared Urn deposits have been dated to *c.* 2000–*c.* 1500 BC. Thirty-five cremation deposits from my study sample were interred with Food Vessels of various kinds, 13 with Collared Urns (two also with Accessory Vessels), three with Accessory Vessels only, and two with Cordoned Urns (both of which contained the remains of children). Ceramic vessels were not present with 57 collections of cremated remains, though organic containers can be deduced from accounts of some of these. Six unurned cremation deposits have been dated and all of these are from between *c.* 2000 and *c.* 1600 BC, but it may be that some of the others not placed in cists date from the Middle Bronze Age (Brück, pers. comm.). Cists seem to have housed cremated remains with or without vessels *c.* 2100–1750 BC (Fowler 2013a: 155–59), after which cists were seldom constructed. It is interesting to compare this continuity in the use of cists for both 'inhumations' and cremations with Middle Bronze Age central Europe, where there are examples of cremated bones and grave goods laid out horizontally within graves in the same way as earlier unburnt burials had been (Sørensen & Rebay 2008). Cremated remains do not seem to have been 'laid out' in this way in Northumberland, but the use of short cists did endure for some time before giving way to the use of round pits, some of which were lined with stone.

There are important differences in the process, experience and result of cremating the dead compared with burying an intact body, but despite these differences, I will illustrate that similarities between cremation and 'inhumation' rites were maintained in several ways. I will also illustrate that the shift to cremation was one part of an ongoing long-term process of transformation in funerary practices that took place throughout the Early Bronze Age in the region and which increasingly combined the remains of the dead in the same locale.

Preparing the body for the pyre

It is possible that bodies were prepared for the pyre in a similar way to those prepared for the grave. Jet burns like coal so necklaces or buttons attached to the body would largely be destroyed by a pyre (Sheridan, pers. comm.), and it is possible that jet ornaments were more numerous than the surviving evidence would suggest. While this does not diminish the fact that the raw material only originates in a small part of Yorkshire, and it seems very likely that jet was highly sought after, it may not be the case that wearing jet necklaces marked a particular *hierarchical* status in Northumberland. If we envisage jet items as prestigious gifts we also need to remember that such prestige goods can be widespread in communities using them, particularly where they are emblematic of achieving an adult gendered identity.

Bone pins were found burnt and broken in seven cases and one bronze pin or awl fragment was found. The pins may have fastened shrouds and/or garments. Other objects passed through the pyre: two flint knives were recorded as burnt, one or more burnt flint fragments were described in nine cases, and a damaged barbed-and-tanged arrowhead was found with the cremated remains of a 2–3 year old child at Cheviot

Walk Wood (Stopford et al. 1985: 123). The child would obviously not have been able to use this item: it may have been a gift and/or an emblem of a desired identity for the dead in a way comparable to the adult-sized rings deposited with a 4–5 year old child at grave 919 in Barrow Hills, Oxfordshire (Brück 2004: 314). It is also possible that it had been shot into the infant.

Cremating the body

There is at present little information on Northumbrian Early Bronze Age cremation technology. Records of the types of wood used are scarce, though they include ash, oak, cherry and hazel. Where such information is recorded some remains are described as thoroughly cremated, while others are described as scorched and blackened or poorly cremated. Cremation would have been a vivid and dramatic event (Downes 1999; Williams 2004), which transformed the body in a very visible and tangible way. As van Gennep points out, cremation rapidly dissolves the body and separates out different aspects of the person in an act that separates the living from the dead but also different elements of the dead person from each other: '[a]s for the destruction of the corpse itself (by cremation, premature putrefaction, etc.), its purpose is to separate the components, the various bodies and souls' (van Gennep 1960: 164). As Jane Downes (1999; 2005) has discussed, bodily materials are dramatically transformed and redistributed in the world through cremation practices. The soft components of the body are burnt away, sending elements of the person up into the sky as smoke. Bones may also be partially reduced to ash, and (where deposition occurred) remaining bones were collected up in baskets, bags, boxes, or pots and deposited in the earth. Thus, cremation divided up the body and directed bodily substances to different places. Cremation also transformed the dead corpse to cleaned bone rapidly, making the transformation of the dead visible much more quickly than with a crouched burial. It is possible, however, that bodies were burnt some time after death (as suggested for one of the cremations at Horsburgh, Peebleshire: Petersen et al. 1974), and it is equally possible for bodies to be curated for some time prior to burial so neither process *necessarily* involves a different duration in the mortuary process. While the experience of cremation is clearly different to that of burial without cremation, the significance of this difference may lie in more in the memories and experiences of the living than in differing beliefs about the fate of the dead. It is also worth considering that, as Gibson (2007: 58) points out, the cremation of entire bodies on pyres is not the only way that 'cremated' bone might enter the archaeological record: for instance, body parts or defleshed bones might be burnt within pits. But in most cases in Northumberland sufficient combinations of bones and/or quantity of bone have been recovered to suggest the cremation of a relatively intact body.

Collecting the remains and combining cremated bones

The act of cremation might radically transform the body, finally separating the fleshed body of the deceased from the living, but further transformations followed in cases where the bones of the deceased were interred in the ground. Charcoal was found along with bone among most cremations, so pyre debris was not carefully sifted out from the bones during the collection of remains. A variety of vessels were used to hold the bones and convey them to the grave. Almost all of the 35 Food Vessels found with cremated bones originally contained rather than just accompanied bones.

Five Food Vessels held what were definitely the mixed remains of two individuals, and four of these were Enlarged Food Vessel Urns, or Vase Urns. Three of the 15 deposits with Collared Urns definitely held the cremated bones of more than one individual. One cist (Spital Hill cairn 7 cist 2) contained cremated remains from more than one individual along with fire-reddened soil and fire-cracked stones, suggesting the burial of the remains of a nearby pyre (Dixon 1892: 27–29). Some pyre sites were probably used for several cremations, and some bones left behind from earlier cremations were scooped up when bones from a later cremation were being collected. This may account for why only one fragment of 1 kg of cremated bone from Blawearie cairn 1 cist E was identified as from a child, while the rest was attributed to an adult (Hewitt & Beckensall 1996: 268), for instance, though other explanations are possible (e.g. that the child's bone was curated by the adult prior to death). Differences in the colour and condition of cremated bones within a single deposit may suggest commingling of bones from successive cremations, though these need not have taken place at the same locale: for instance, the scorched and blackened bones of an adult in cremation deposit 4 at Cheviot Walk Wood can be distinguished from the well-cremated bones of a child in the same deposit (Stopford et al. 1985: 122). By contrast, the cremated bones from three adults and a child found in a Collared Urn at Kirkhill were 'well intermixed when deposited in the urn' (Barlow & Wright in Miket 1974: 186): the four bodies might have been cremated together, or the bones from four separate cremations might have been brought together and commingled. Thirteen of the 21 multiple cremation deposits combined adult and child remains, but as Petersen et al. (1974: 49) warn it would be much easier for excavators to detect this combination than the remains of more than one child, or more than one adult. Thus, this pattern suggests the number of multiple cremation deposits is likely to be higher than has been recorded, rather than that the bones of children and adults were most often combined during or after cremation. Nonetheless, we can consider the kinds of relationships between two or more people whose bones shared a single urn – perhaps the connections between their bodies were more significant than the boundaries between them. The fact that multiple cremation deposits are far more common than multiple 'inhumations' also bolsters the idea that communities of the dead became more nucleated throughout the period. It may even suggest that the reincorporation of the deceased into a community of the dead was something that began *before* burial occurred.

It is hard to say how often some bones were deliberately left out of urns, or sets of bones divided up and deposited in more than one location, or how pyre debris was treated. Brück (2003; 2006) has suggested that cremated bones might have been split up and portions taken by different groups of mourners. This is certainly possible though it would be extremely difficult to detect in the Northumbrian corpus. The use of pyre debris – such as that found at Turf Knowe North (McKinley 1998) – also provides a potential avenue of future research (McKinley 1997; Downes 2005), but was often overlooked in past excavations.

While Collared Urns frequently contained objects along with human remains, most Food Vessel Urns did not (those that did most commonly held flint knives), while Enlarged Food Vessel Urns never contained artefacts. Not all of the items placed in the urns were burnt, and some deposits were accompanied by other unburnt objects. In five cases where a flint knife accompanied cremated remains – and a bone knife at Middle Gunnar Peak – it had clearly not been burnt. A flint knife was found within the top of a layer of bones in an 'urn' at Spital Hill cairn 7 cremation deposit 1 (Dixon 1892: 28). These knives were seemingly added *after* the dead had been transformed, after the remains had been gathered and either before they were deposited or, as seems likely for burials that were not cremated, during the act of deposition or terminating the deposition of remains and marking the point at which those remains were covered up and removed from any further contact. I would suggest that the addition of these knives after the body was processed illustrates a similarity with 'inhumation' deposits, indicating a trend which continued throughout the period: knives or daggers cut away the dead and/or were presented with the deceased towards whatever entities oversaw their incorporation into a community of the dead. While it can only be speculation, it is possible that the burnt knives (and any bronze knives which did not survive the pyre) were also placed with the dead immediately prior to cremation, again as part of a ritual severing of the dead from the living.

Selecting place of cremation and/or deposition

While some cremation deposits were isolated burials covered with their own cairns, as at Birkside Fell (Tolan-Smith 2005), and some became the first deposit at a site that attracted further deposition of cremated remains, the majority of cremation deposits were placed at sites which had seen previous deposition and were often inserted into existing cairns and barrows, at henge monuments, or in pits or cists alongside other pits or cists in cemeteries. Some of these were cut into natural knolls as at Pace Hill (Stopford et al. 1985), while at Goatscrag cremations, two within Enlarged Food Vessel Urns, were buried in a rock shelter (Burgess 1972). Most of the cairns and barrows containing cremation deposits show a complex history of use and re-use. For instance, at Pitland Hills barrow 1 the barrow was a complex, possibly multi-phase construction which covered a rock-cut cist with a crouched burial accompanied by a hammer-stone and Vase Food Vessel and a second grave with no surviving remains or finds. Between these two cists were found a number of cup-marked stones. The excavator wrote '… where most of the cup-incised stones were found, the fires of cremation and of the funeral feast had raged with great fierceness' (Rome Hall 1887: 280), and it was here that two cremation deposits, one child and one adult, were found. The barrow yielded 17 cup-marked stones in total which might have been deposited in commemorative activities, perhaps involving mound construction, and/or as part of one or more funerals.

Depositing the remains

Food Vessels containing cremated bones were largely recovered from cists and occasionally in pits, some inverted, some upright. In one case a cremation deposit in a Food Vessel at Pace Hill was accompanied by a jet necklace (Stopford et al. 1985: 125–26), of which Greenwell (1868: 196 n) writes '... a necklace of jet beads, of varied form, was found strung around the neck of an urn...', while at Ford three jet beads and a jet button (Shepherd type 2) were found near the rim of a Collared Urn containing the cremated bones of an adult (possibly female) and a burnt flint knife. Here necklaces, or parts of them, were placed around the neck of the urn, suggesting a conceptual equivalence between the human body and the vessel, which I return to below. Enlarged Food Vessel Urns are rare (only seven have been found), but exhibit a very specialised pattern of usage: all were placed, upside down, in pits at natural places (rock outcrop, rock shelter) or within cairns and in one case on top of an existing cist, but never in cists. Collared Urns were buried either inverted or upright in cists or pits. The shift from cists to burial only in urns like these may result from a growing sense that the cremation itself, and containment in the vessel, were sufficient to separate the dead from the living during and at the end of the liminal rites, and lend credence to the idea that deposition had by now become a feature of post-liminal incorporation.

Not all cremation deposits were contained in pots. Some heaps or tight dumps of bone were probably placed in baskets, bags or other organic containers. Fifty-six (or 66%) of all mortuary deposits at cairns and barrows were located in the southerly quadrant of the site (i.e. between southeast and southwest), and 42 of these southerly deposits were cremations. Of these, 30 did not include any ceramics. Thus, those remains not contained with a hard skin were especially likely to be placed in a southerly direction, which I would describe as an auspicious direction for the dead throughout the period due the shared choice of the south as the most common direction that bodies were laid to face in crouched burials. The emphasis on the south continued well into the later part of the Early Bronze Age with Collared Urn and Cordoned Urn cremation deposits from cairns lying either at the centre of the site or in the southerly quadrant, and it is possible that at least some of the 30 unurned deposits date to even later in the Bronze Age where the southerly quadrant of barrows were commonly used for mortuary deposition (Ashbee 1960: 84–85; Brück pers. comm.). Locations for deposition were therefore carefully chosen for cremated remains just as bodily position was meaningful for crouched burials, and according to a continuous focus on southerly direction.

Ending the act of deposition

The act of deposition often ended in a similar way as it had for 'inhumations', with the construction of a cairn or replacement of earth or stones over the burial deposit. Symbolic media of separation were sometimes also deployed towards the end of the act of deposition. At Gains Law boulders covered the cist and a flint knife was found within this covering layer. At Birkside Fell a burnt or burning plank of wood was placed over the mouth of the Collared Urn in a pit containing remains from two adults (Tolan-

Smith 2005; Fig. 3.6). A cairn then covered this. Cremated remains often accumulated at a site so that those cairns and barrows over *c.* 3 m in diameter covered and attracted multiple deposits, and the remains of one body seldom remained isolated from those of others. While in some cases pyre debris suggests that deposition immediately followed a local cremation, in other cases acts of deposition might be separated from the funeral by days or years, and monuments may have acted as foci for interactions with the long dead, including via votive offerings of the cremated bone of the recently deceased.

What changed, and what remained the same?

What are the long-term patterns that we can deduce from these mortuary deposits? During the earlier part of the period rules of deposition were rigid, typified by infrequent, single and isolated Beaker burials, mainly of adults. From *c.* 2250 BC to 1900 or perhaps 1800 BC there was greater diversity in mortuary practices that ended in the deposition of remains: cists or graves exhibited a wider variety of orientations with some local variation and some change over time away from the predominance of east–west burial, children appear more frequently in the burial record, and both cremated and unburnt bones were deposited. Smaller cists were more common after *c.* 2150 BC, as were cists backfilled with soil. Cremation, which had perhaps been practiced during the earlier part of the period but not followed by deposition of remains, was increasingly applied to bodies that would then also receive burials in cists; in a rare case at Low Hauxley cremated remains in a cist were accompanied by a Beaker, and radiocarbon dating indicates this took place some time between 2010 and 1875 BC (Waddington 2010). Cremation deposits were also placed in or with Food Vessels, perhaps from *c.* 2150 BC. Eventually during the early second millennium cists were abandoned, and urns containing the dead were enlarged. Within the diversity, then, there were chronologically and regionally distinct patterns – such as the emergence of north–south burials in northern Northumberland after *c.* 2200 BC – and even some rigid orthodoxies such as the specific rules about placement of and the containment of cremated bone and artefacts in Enlarged Urn Food Vessels. It is possible that the change in emphasis from 'inhumation' to cremation took place quickly some time between 2100 and 1900 BC, but there are examples of cremation and 'inhumation' from throughout that period and probably even later. There is a clear trend towards the nucleation of the dead after 2250 BC and especially between 2000 and 1700 BC: first at cemeteries, cairns and barrows, and later by combining the remains of the dead in single features or deposits. Some trends in the presentation and transformation of the dead continued even when others changed. Funerals are organised according to cosmological principles, and we can see some of these principles forming a thread throughout most of the period, despite the changes outlined here. In what follows I shall interpret these and other changes outlined earlier in the chapter in terms of continuing yet mutating cosmological principles applied to understanding bodies, persons, and communities during mortuary transformations. I will argue for sporadic but relatively

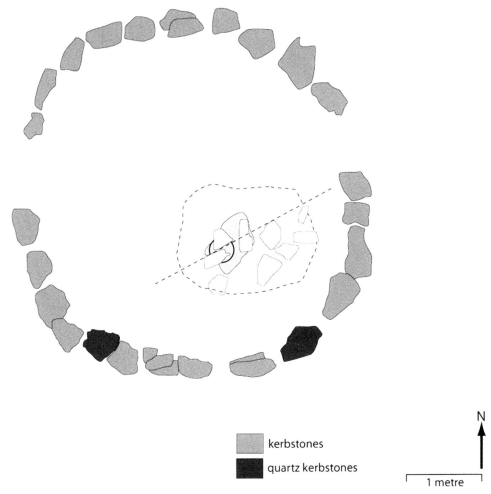

Fig. 3.6 Birkside Fell kerbed cairn: the location of cremation deposit; the Collared Urn cremation deposit in situ (redrawn from Tolan-Smith 2005: 58–60 by Sheila Severn Newton).

gradual change in varying aspects of mortuary rites through much of the period, and consider the implications for the duration and nature of the liminal phase of mortuary rites and the changing effects of post-liminal rites in particular.

Why deposit human remains?

In understanding these changes we need to ask a vital question: why bury the remains of the dead at all? In this chapter I have adopted the conventional stance that most – if not necessarily all – of these deposits were produced as parts of funerals, but that does not explain why some were buried while others were not. As Gibson (2004; 2007) puts it, Beaker burials provide a 'veneer' to the broader mortuary practices of much of the period many of which did *not* involve burying human remains. While I do not doubt that many more burials took place than have survived to be recovered so far, it seems likely that other people must have died and had funerals but their remains were not buried.

Thus, we need to explain the rather unusual activity of depositing these remains, and consider whether differing explanations might best fit the evidence from different parts of the period. Conventionally, accounts of the period argue that those buried were the social elites, though exactly what privileges (beyond sometimes acquiring objects with distant origins), roles, duties, and responsibilities characterised those elites is seldom discussed. Rather than being persons of high status in a hierarchical sense, we can envisage various possibilities for adults buried with Beakers before 2250 BC and perhaps *some* of those who remains were deposited from *c.* 2250 to 1500 BC. They might, for instance, have held a specific social and/or religious role within the community (e.g. a role of guardianship), they might have followed a particular religion or social code (potentially entwined with a distinct sense of their origins or affinities) and/or they might have been perceived as attaining a position of ancestry as they had children who reached adulthood before they died. Indeed, perhaps some cremated remains were only deposited after it was deemed that a state of ancestry had been attained, even if that was some time after the death of the individual. Another possibility is that certain causes of death (by disease or violence or deaths that were sudden and unexplained) rather than certain identities necessitated the burial of bodies or purified bones – the most disturbing deaths requiring the deposition of the remains in elaborate ceremonies, perhaps. Humphrey Case (2004: 204) offers a further interesting suggestion: that burials were part of a 'dialogue between the living and the dead' in which the community were at pains '... to assert their participation in activities desirable for the wellbeing of the group both living and dead...'. Although Case's emphasis on single burials as celebrations of individual identity for those of 'elite' status does not sit well with much of the Northumbrian evidence, his argument that the concerns of the living can be seen in the treatment of the dead is extremely useful and I think that we can trace those concerns through funerary practices in the Northumbrian Early Bronze Age. Before *c.* 2200 BC the dead were separated from the living during the act of burial, and were often left isolated from the remains of other dead persons. Between *c.* 2200 and *c.* 2000 BC it was more likely that the dead were buried in a locale alongside the remains of other people, or that their remains would soon be joined by others. The physical incorporation of the dead into a local community was increasingly apparent. During this period and for centuries to follow the components of the dead body were increasingly separated out, as well as separated from the living, through the act of cremation. Cremation itself was probably a feature of the liminal phase of the rite of passage, transforming the body and the person. Deposition may have become associated with the reincorporation of the dead into a new community, part of a post-liminal phase of activity. This may have been so too for the earlier isolated crouched burials, but these people were not incorporated into a *local* and physical community of the dead. Indeed, it is possible that post-liminal rites for early crouched burials were not carried out by the living in a way that left any trace on the grave site, or even that the living left such reincorporation to non-human forces. Acts of funerary deposition were perhaps, like votive deposits, intercessions between living and dead in which valued material was removed from the sphere of the living and given to the community of the dead. Furthermore, the construction of monuments over mortuary deposits extended mortuary rituals through time and embedded them in space, providing visible opportunities for the production of communities of the dead within the landscape. Not only were the living increasingly involved in the post-liminal rites of the dead, those rites became sedimented in the unfolding histories of each monument. Whether or not those burying a corpse in a cist towards the end of the third millennium expected that person to be incorporated into a new community by human agency or supernatural means, increasingly towards the outset of and during the first quarter of the second millennium living human communities worked to ensure such reincorporation. As a whole we can perceive different ways of relating to the dead in the changing mortuary practices throughout the period; burials were perhaps always a way of dealing with certain deaths, but the length of time a complete funeral took and the ways it was knitted together with other events – such as other funerals, or the transformation of place – changed.

Changing the direction of the dead, maintaining cosmological patterns

Burying the dead fixed them in place. Early isolated single burials (i.e. early burials, especially Beaker burials) were buried alone in places that may have had personal, historical, and/or religious or cosmological significance but were not burial grounds. The use of certain mortuary technologies and material culture might have tied burials like Kirkhaugh in with distant communities, alive and dead, more than with a local community of the dead, as became more common in later periods. All burials ended with the seclusion of the dead from the living, but for isolated burials this left any incorporation of the dead into a new community unobserved. The dead were not united with the bodies of others who had died before them. If, as has often been suggested, these burials directed the dead towards an otherworld or afterlife along with gifts or possessions to sustain them there, or for them to offer to the beings existing there, then this incorporation of the dead into a new community either occurred in a time and place removed from the graveside, or the dead were understood to be distributed throughout the landscape, perhaps reincorporated into the world of the living (locally or more distantly – particularly if early Beaker identities were associated with relatively 'foreign' origins). Later in the period two things changed: the dead were more likely to be placed in the same locale as those who died before them, and their bodies were often visibly transformed before deposition. I will consider the creation of a physical community of the dead in a later section, and here focus on how the bodies of the dead were transformed and directed through mortuary activity.

Cremating the dead sent bodily substances into the sky as smoke and ash, and bones were collected up and deposited. This vertical dimension to the transformation of the dead was an extension from the 'downward' movement of the dead in earlier burials (and it is worth considering that some of these were placed in upland locales or local prominences), suggesting communication with forces in the sky as well as under the earth. Since the body was no longer intact, bodies were not aligned in the grave in the same way as before. Yet, because burials increasingly took place at pre-existing circular sites like ring cairns, henges, or round cairns and barrows, direction could be expressed in terms of where the deposit was placed in respect to the centre of the monument. It is difficult to detect any consistent patterning for crouched burials at round sites, though many were near the centre, and specific senses of relatedness may perhaps have played a part in such location. For crouched burials patterns of bodily orientation within the grave are far clearer than location with respect to the centre of circular sites. Cremation deposits favoured the southern quadrant, just as crouched burials were arranged to face south within their graves. Both sets of practices presented the dead as facing the sun for the longest part of the year: with crouched burials, the whole body was sent underground, but respecting this direction; with cremations flesh was burnt away and bones placed underground, but oriented towards the sun. For both burnt and unburnt remains the centre of a cairn or barrow was also a common position for deposition. The points where sun shines longest and where the sun first appeared and last disappeared in the bleakest months were the most appropriate locations or orientations for the dead. Thus, a religious concern for the path of the sun could be seen as emerging early in the period and continuing into the Middle Bronze Age (cf. Kaul 1998; Kristiansen & Larsson 2005: fig. 167). We could even speculate that cremations and burials took place at specific auspicious times of the day or even in some cases, year. Thus, a continuity in cosmological principles is discernible.

Changing media of funerary transformations, maintaining desirable social relations

Grave goods may be present for a range of reasons, but locating the material culture of these mortuary deposits within the structure and sequence of mortuary rites provides us with an important perspective with which to view some of these objects. Over 93% of all deposits included fewer than three objects. However, we have to accept that many organic materials have not survived and thus some of the complexity and attendant symbolism of the mortuary rites have been lost. Working with what has survived, in some few cases the dead were accompanied with special collections of objects and some of these may have been made for the grave or produced to be used in preparing the body, grave furniture, and grave, as seems likely at Kirkhaugh. The Kirkhaugh burial probably did cite a specific kind of prestigious identity for the dead, and much later in the period some of the burials with jet or bronze daggers in northern Northumberland may have been part of the emergence of a desired set of identities for a specific section of the community, which possibly drew on associations with the historical ritual complexes and rock art panels in this part of the county. These identities were significantly localised even though they drew on some materials, objects and monument types that had distant origins and were shared with distant places. Other grave goods might have been deposited in order to cultivate an identity which was desired for the dead but not achieved in life, as may be the case with the arrowhead placed with the cremated remains of a 2–3 year old child, who would not have been able to use it. Some sexual differentiation is evident in the use of jet necklaces, which generally seem to be associated with women. In some cases objects may have been gifts to the dead, designed to maintain relations beyond death and elicit further gifts from the dead in the future. The bodies of the dead themselves may even be perceived as gifts, owed to divine powers who had given them life and offered over to them following death.

Some of the objects buried with the dead can be seen as emblems of desirable conduct, and as designating and ensuring the social efficacy of the dead person. This might include knives, scrapers, arrowheads, and other tools. Yet the most common of all grave goods were ceramic vessels. This ubiquity suggests a close affinity between the human body and the ceramic vessel. There was a shift over the long term from bodies accompanied by small vessels probably containing food and/or drink, to the containment of cremated human remains in a larger vessel. Ceramics increasingly replaced the skin and flesh of the dead in containing the bones. Pots were important in the acts of consumption through which bodies were fed. Recent lipid analysis of British Beakers suggests that dairy products were consumed (Šoberl et al. 2009: 9), though it is not clear whether these were from porridge-like meals or fermented milks. Šoberl et al. (2009), who also reported that Collared Urns found in funerary contexts exhibited significant accumulations of lipid-rich residues, suggested these vessels were in use for a long time in the domestic sphere before they were used to house the bones of the dead. We might suggest that a vessel which had 'fed' a person with vital substances in life was in turn used to contain vital substance following death. The placement of beads around the neck of vessels containing cremated remains at Pace Hill and Ford illustrate this equation of bodies with vessels. Arguably ceramic vessels acted as new, hard and enduring skins, replacing the corruptible flesh which had been burnt away as the container of enduring human bone. That bone was then 'fed' into a community of the dead through special places, fed to the ancestors just as the benevolence of the ancestors had provided the current world for the living and left them crops and animals (cf. Oestigaard's (2000) interpretation of Iron Age Scandinavian cremations as sacrifices of cooked persons to the gods).

But while it might be tempting to perceive a move from inhumation-as-burial to cremation-as-offering (cf. Lucas 1996), we could equally suggest that the remains of the dead formed special offerings to other beings throughout the period. Ceramics were not the only containers of the dead. Almost all of the earlier burials were in cists, and the few that were not were probably in log coffins or other organic containers. Brück (2004: 318–19) has interpreted this emphasis on 'wrapping and containment' as potentially: protecting the dead and objects associated with them (she provides examples from elsewhere in Britain of objects that were often sheathed, boxed or bagged); keeping secret from some mourners exactly what was being deposited; bringing together bundles of things through which relations could be traced; and/or weaving a sense of community through these nested collections of contained objects in the grave. We could also add that this containment was *successive*, creating stages of gradual separation of the living from the dead through the funerary rites. In some cases, as at Cartington, the dead might have been secluded in many successive stages during the pre-liminal rites. Cists and coffins gave way to ceramic vessels as containers of the dead (or aspects of the dead) over the long term as how and when the dead were secluded and transformed in the funerary rite changed. So, while in the earlier part of the period the offering was a discrete bundle, later on the elements of the body were distributed to different locales, shared between the sky and the earth, and bones were used to build physical communities of the dead. These are important differences. When set against the background of continued containment of the dead the move to cremation may denote some shift in religious beliefs – for instance, the adoption or re-alignment of a tripartite model of the cosmos (heavens, earth, underworld) into which different aspects of the dead person now had to be distributed, or a need to visibly ensure the transformation of the dead which had previously been left to unseen forces – but by itself it need not necessarily constitute a *major* revision to understandings of personhood, the body, death and ancestry. The spread of cremation may relate to a change in beliefs about the fate of the dead or the structure of the cosmos or a change in how the dead were prepared for this fate or in how it was demonstrated to the living that the dead were relocated in this cosmos. The transformation of the dead was increasingly demonstrable prior to burial.

Some of the objects in the mortuary deposits were potentially used in transforming the dead by preparing the body for the grave or pyre: scrapers for preparing hides, toggles and pins for tying shrouds. Flint knives and bronze daggers were sometimes introduced late in the mortuary rite at the end of the point of contact between the living and the dead. It is possible that the presence of knives, like that of burning planks covering the mortuary deposit, was a graphic statement of the separation of the living and the dead, ending one phase of the rite of passage and beginning the next. Symbols used in rites of passage, such as the vessel and the knife, probably had broader meanings derived from their everyday features and uses. Knives may have been emblematic of cutting ties but also of killing animals, preparing food and dividing it for sharing. Cutting is necessary to share food and thus sustain and renew the body. Knives were also used to cut away a part of the communal body, a person whose remains were increasingly likely to be offered to a community of the dead. Pain and grief might also then be associated with knives. The transformation of the deceased, particularly those whose bodily substances had been divided, may have drawn widely on this ambiguous motif. Burning was also often an important part of the mortuary process, either of the body or else lighting a fire above a grave or elsewhere before placing burnt residues in graves. Burning often purifies and is emblematic of physical transformation: like cutting it is destructive but also necessary for the preparation of food, reiterating the connection between mortuary transformations and food preparation.

Mortuary acts such as burning, containment, and severing may suggest an anxiety over contact with the dead and ritualised acts of separation in a complex emotive process which successively articulated remembering and forgetting while idealising and transforming the identities of the dead. I would suggest that the symbols used celebrated those relations people (and things) engaged in throughout their lives. As well as pots and knives we could consider that cattle were referred to through the hide shrouds or garments that encased the corpses, combining human and animal skins. Broken quernstone fragments were also incorporated into five cairns, citing the production of food or drink from cereal crops. Many of the relations referred to throughout do not seem to be relations of dominance, competition, or aggression, which are the types of relations which have often been the focus of studies of Early Bronze Age mortuary deposits elsewhere (e.g. Heyd 2007). Preservation undoubtedly has a factor to play, but the dearth of arrowheads, copper-alloy axe heads (excluded from burials across the country) and battleaxe heads (of which there is only one buried with human remains), and absence of bracers, belt-hooks, and other objects commonly explained as symbols of warriors or others of high status cannot be explained by preservation alone. Either these objects were not part of the common repertoire of those buried in Northumberland in the Early Bronze Age, or such objects were excluded from burial. This is not to deny the importance of hunting or fighting as social activities foundational to identity, but to highlight their limited currency in the mortuary record. Overall I would suggest that the Northumbrian mortuary rituals spoke more often of how the person was embedded in the world and celebrated desirable social relations: cutting, cooking, drinking, giving, sharing, sociality. This did not change significantly throughout the period.

Changing communities of the dead

Perhaps the most major change during the period was from isolated burials at various places in the landscapes to cemeteries and cairns used repeatedly for deposition of human remains. This is evident with some of the later burials of uncremated remains (e.g. Chatton Sandyford) as well as with cremations, and it seems likely that the accumulation of remains that were not cremated in a single place either pre-dated or was contemporary with the widespread use of cremation. This nucleation of burials created visible communities of the dead before and during the same periods as there was an increase in commingling remains in a single deposit, even within a single vessel. How could we characterise those communities and what are the implications for understanding personhood?

The increasing commingling or nucleation of the remains of the dead suggests a way of tracing relations between the living and the dead that produced lineages, or at least groups, of ancestors. The identities of the living were perhaps increasingly constructed in relation to such lineages or groups, and their position with respect to their ancestors was revised by placing their remains within the same burial sites. This deposition drew out their ancestral connections after individual features of their personhood had commemorated and transformed (cf. Bloch 1989; Fowler 2004: 79–100). We could argue that a collective sense of ancestry was produced through each funeral which first acknowledged the relational identity of the deceased, enacted key transformations upon the body and person, and elevated them to the status of belonging to a community of ancestors. These acts also transformed places as they transformed the dead. At Pitland Hills earlier funeral grounds were used in later cremations and turned into cairns. At Blawearie the kerb to the cairn was dismantled and the stones used as cist cover slabs, while at Chatton Sandyford two separate low mounds were eventually united under a single larger cairn, closing off the burial ground within a kerbed cairn. Later on cremation deposits were inserted, renewing connections with the ancestral dead. Not all of these reworkings of burial grounds were necessarily expected by those who first buried the dead at these locales; *they* may have deferred the final transformation of the dead to other powers without imagining the roles their human successors would play in the reincorporation of the dead.[12] Turf Knowe North provides an excellent example: here a burial cairn was seemingly ploughed over, rediscovered, reworked and re-used, and then ploughed over again in a long-term Early Bronze Age sequence (Adams & Carne 1997).

Early Bronze Age communities pursued a series of different strategies in the presentation of the dead, placement in the landscape, congregation of the dead and monumentalisation of mortuary locales. In some regions clearly divergent strategies have been identified. Peters (2000) suggests that the Stonehenge landscape was home to two communities: the locals who maintained discrete mortuary traditions over the long term, and an elite community who buried their dead with exotic goods in prominent monuments elevated above a ceremonial landscape. Although some burial practices did become localised in some centuries no such clear split is evident in Northumberland; rather there were changing local strategies in mortuary rites and in the construction of mortuary monuments (Fowler 2013a: 250–52). Perhaps cairns or barrows were constructed by communities at times when it was thought important to do so in making social, political and/or religious statements, or when senses of family (for instance) came to focus on the congregation of dead family members. Rather than perceiving burials without mounds or in inconspicuous locales or without knives or necklaces as of lower status than those with mounds or prominent locations or such grave goods, we might consider that different strategies were followed as other choices were made. For example, the man subjected to bodily modification and buried with a dagger at Allerwash, did not join a community of the dead, was not joined by later burials, and does not seem to have formed the basis for a significant grave marker: his burial need not be seen as reflecting hierarchical status, but may relate to other distinctions between the dead in which some bodies could be brought together, while certain bodies required a different treatment. Changing cosmological beliefs might also affect choice of landscape location (Field 1999), as might the creation of distinct senses of community (Edwards 2006) in certain sub-regions. Some communities, able to challenge any claims to elevated status, might shun the practice of burying single individuals under prominent large mounds and favour other practices (cf. Skoglund 2008). Perhaps elevated hierarchical statuses were less important at funerals than a broader sense of community, and perhaps such statuses were infrequent and unstable in Early Bronze Age Northumberland. Overall, I would suggest that changes in mortuary practices can be understood as changes in how communities of the living related to communities of the dead and other beings through the funerary transformation of the recently deceased. While this probably had political currency, we cannot assume that this politics was always one of competitive hierarchical status acquisition and need also to consider beliefs about 'good' and 'bad' deaths, religious codes and other cultural concerns.

Conclusion

I would suggest that in Early Bronze Age Northumberland some aspects of the form and role of mortuary rites stayed the same over time, even though there were some significant changes in who was buried, how visibly and rapidly their bodies were transformed, and whether they were buried singly or with the remains of others. Mortuary rites carefully separated the dead from the living while transforming them both. In providing a vehicle for such personal transformations mortuary rites also referenced the desirable relations that connected up the social world and shaped each person. The notion of a community of the dead sharing the same place was stronger after *c.* 2100 BC than earlier, but there were continuities over the long term too: for instance a consistent practice of orienting the dead facing towards the south, though in differing ways. There were also repeated instances of practices which, while they may not be verified as a dominant trend, nonetheless recurred over the long term, such as the introduction of knives late in the mortuary sequence or the fact that while the deposition of remains that had not been cremated gave way to cremation many of the key symbols of the rite were already present in the earlier period, such as setting fire to grave sites or placing burnt materials in cists. Material culture in mortuary deposits may potentially relate to any of the phases of the ritual process, and indeed the introduction of material media early on in the ritual projected those media through to the later stages, so that acts in the pre-liminal rites set up conditions for the post-liminal reincorporation of the dead. Some objects were involved in the ritual transformation of the dead, but the inclusion of these objects (and others, like necklaces) in graves may also suggest aspirations about desirable identities, social relations and practices. Throughout the period, many of the objects chosen seem related to the ability to provide food; to share, process, and serve it. Vessels commonly accompanied the dead: earlier on as containers of food or drink, perhaps providing the dead with the ability to share in the afterlife or in acknowledgement of debt to the deceased and/or hope of a return gift; and later as containers of cremated bone, replacing a corruptible skin with an incorruptible one through the mortuary process. In both practices the bodies of the dead themselves could have been offered up to divine beings with whom the living were locked in relations of debt and gift-giving. Thus, I have suggested that grave goods may have a range of roles and meanings from devices used to cite and produce identities to tools used in acts of ritual transformation. They might be gifts or possessions, they may have been associated with certain social practices and roles, and they might have had valued biographies or magical or apotropaic effects. Indeed, they may be many or all of these things at once, and it would be a mistake to read them only in one way. Nonetheless, while tracing changes in mortuary practices over time, I have illustrated how many of the relationships produced through practices cited in the funerary rites can be seen as convivial and co-operative rather than competitive.

I have also suggested that while the emergence of cremation is often seen as the most major change in the period, the consequences of cremating the dead are not *necessarily* very different from burial without cremation. In both cases, before the rites of separation were concluded the deceased were presented with what they needed to assume a new identity and be incorporated into a new community of the dead. To that extent they were initially transformed by the community of mourners during the pre-liminal rites. Yet successful reincorporation was perhaps hoped for rather than certain, particularly earlier in the period when the dead were buried alone in the landscape. The assumption of a new status might have been completed or celebrated in activities that took place off-site and at other times, or it might have been left in the hands of divine forces. Cremation need not necessarily have accelerated nor slowed the funeral sequence as unburnt bodies could *potentially* be curated for as long as cremated bones, or lie in the ground awaiting others to join them before they could be incorporated into a close community of the dead; but cremation dramatised the transformation of the dead, making it visible to mourners. Cists fell out of use as the flesh of the dead was now burnt away and the bones contained by urns; there was no need to hold bodies 'in place' with constricting chambers and heavy cover slabs, nor the potential to re-examine decaying remains. The deposition of the bones may have marked the assumption of the dead into a new status in a much more direct and assured way than burial without cremation did. However, this is less a feature of cremation-followed-by-depostion *per se*, and more a factor of the phenomena of burying remains in *communal* burial grounds: something that might have preceded the introduction of cremation-before-deposition, or might be contemporary with it. The production of nucleated communities of the dead in cist cemeteries, cairns and barrows transformed the dead into members of a community of ancestors more visibly, physically and completely than before.

These results illustrate the importance of considering mortuary rites as a sequence of actions that transform social relations and identities. They illustrate the usefulness of approaches that perceive funerary rites as transformations to identity (rather than simply reflections of identity) and the value of applying recent typological and dating studies to even the older records of excavations of Bronze Age mortuary deposits at a regional level. Characterising change and continuity through time is only possible by appreciating shifts in the form and content, the timing and effect of each phase in an overall sequence of mortuary rites. This may be difficult to observe through the records of past excavations and may not be evident in some of the archaeological remains that survive to be recovered, but sufficient information does exist to make the detailed reconstruction of changing prehistoric mortuary rites a priority in coming years. Building up such regional pictures will provide the opportunity for more detailed analysis of the interaction between regions, and support a more rich and varied appreciation of changing ritual transformations for the dead along with more subtle inferences about European Early Bronze Age concepts of the body, person and community.

Acknowledgments

I would like to thank Lindsay Allason-Jones and Andrew Parkin for providing information on and access to artefacts held at the Great North Museum, and Peter Carne for information on the Turf Knowe excavations. I thank Joanna Brück, Andrea Dolfini, Jan Harding, Oliver Harris, and Alison Sheridan for providing comments on a draft version - their comments helped improve this chapter enormously, and any errors or unsubstantiated arguments in the published version are entirely my own doing. Thanks also to Sheila Severn Newton for producing the illustrations.

Notes

1   The period covered is *c.* 2450–1500 BC, encompassing the Terminal Neolithic or Chalcolithic (Allen et al. 2012) as well as the Early Bronze Age. I have retained the term Early Bronze Age in the title for this piece for the sake of simplicity. While there is little evidence for copper with these burials there is good reason to see the burials here as part of wider changes in Britain associated with 'Chalcolithic' or early Beaker burials. While this could be discussed under the heading of a Terminal Neolithic, referring to the current text as a discussion of Neolithic and Early Bronze Age mortuary rites would claim too much ground. Regardless of the problems with the term Chalcolithic, it seems necessary to acknowledge a distinctive set of practices emerging *c.* 2450–2250 BC in Britain. All dates in this chapter are calibrated radiocarbon years BC (cal. BC).

2   A database of Chalcolithic and Early Bronze Age mortuary deposits from Northumberland, Tyne and Wear and County Durham has been lodged on-line with the Archaeology Data Service (Fowler 2013b).

3   A small number of recently-excavated sites with good preservation and high-quality records are currently excluded awaiting a complete set of post-excavation reports (e.g. Low Hauxley).

4   The term inhumation implies burial in the earth, and as such it is an imprecise term on at least two counts: first, cremated remains were also placed in the earth, and second, many cist burials were not backfilled with soil, so that the remains were not in contact with earth at all. For that reason I shall refer to burials except where the remains were directly covered with earth.

5   Beaker vessels have been placed within date ranges based on the typology of Needham (2005) and chronology from Needham (2005) and Healy (2012): full details of the identification of vessels to type is provided elsewhere (Fowler 2013a; 2013b). Based on typology only six of the Northumbrian Beakers from excavated deposits, one from Elsnook (Bosanquet

1933), one from Low Hauxley, and two from Chatton Sandyford (see below), and two from Milfield North henge (Harding 1981), match Needham's (2005) late styles of Beaker, which probably date to *c.* 2100–1850 cal BC (Healy 2012).

6   I will use the term grave in this chapter to refer to an excavated grave or a cist used as a grave.

7   Alison Sheridan suggested considering this may be a fabricator, and it compares closely with one from Rudston barrow burial 6 (BM 79 12-9 1060, Kinnes & Longworth 1985: 76).

8   This category here includes burials where the bones show signs of scorching but the body was clearly laid in the grave as a crouched burial.

9   Flat riveted daggers and blades probably date to between 2200 and 1900 BC (see Baker et al. 2003; Sheridan 2007b), knife-daggers probably had currency within the period *c.* 2200 BC to *c.* 1600 BC (see Sheridan 2007b).

10   There are further examples of burials recorded with bronze daggers from sites not included in the database due to poverty of information for comparative contextual analysis (2), and stray finds of daggers from Northumberland (5). There are also 27 bronze daggers or knife-daggers known from SE Scotland (Baker et al. 2003).

11   Cremated bone from one Enlarged Food Vessel Urn from Turf Knowe North has provided a date of *c.* 2490–2200 cal BC, but this is far earlier than other dates associated with Food Vessels, and the site is both complex and still being prepared for publication.

12   As noted in peer review of this chapter, there is potentially more that could be said about how the timing of site elaboration and the materials used related to post-liminal rites. This might be best explored through barrows from other regions (e.g. as explored by Owoc [2001; 2005]), however, as there is relatively little detailed information on the materials used in Northumbrian barrows and cairns. Some sequences of activity at specific sites, including some glimpses of the timing and material composition of mound elaboration in northeast England is explored elsewhere (Fowler 2013a: chapters 5 and 6).

Bibliography

Adams, M. & Carne, P. 1997: *The Ingram and Upper Breamish Valley Landscape Project, Interim Report 1997*, Archaeological Services, University of Durham: Durham.

Allason-Jones, L. 1996: *Roman Jet in the Yorkshire Museum*, Yorkshire Museum: York.

Allen, J., Gardiner, J. & Sheridan, J. A. (eds) 2012: *Is there a British Chalcolithic? People, Place and Polity in the Late Third Millennium*, Oxford: Prehistoric Society Research Paper 4.

Ashbee, P. 1960: *The Bronze Age Round Barrow in Britain*, Phoenix: London.

Baker, L., Sheridan, J. A. & Cowie, T. G. 2003: 'An Early Bronze Age "Dagger Grave" from Rameldry Farm, near Kingskettle, Fife', *Proceedings of the Society of Antiquaries of Scotland* 133: 85–123.

Barrett, J. 1994: *Fragments from Antiquity: An Archaeology of Social Life in Britain, 2900–1200 BC,* Blackwell: Oxford.

Bate, D. M. A. 1912: 'On a North Northumberland Barrow and its Contents', *Proceedings of the Society of Antiquaries of Scotland* (4th Series) 10: 15–26.

Bloch, M. 1989: 'Death and the Concept of the Person', in S. Cederroth, C. Corlin & J. Lindstrom (eds): *On the Meaning of Death,* Cambridge University Press: Cambridge, 11–29.

Bosanquet, R. C. 1935: 'The Ellsnook Tumulus near Rock', *Archaeologia Aeliana* (4th Series) 6: 146–49.

Brewis, P. 1928: 'A Bronze Age Cist at Kyloe, Northumberland', *Archaeologia Aeliana* (4th Series) 5: 26–29.

Brück, J. 2003: 'Early Bronze Age Burial Practices in Scotland and Beyond: Differences and Similarities', in G. Barclay & I. A. G. Shepherd (eds): *Scotland in Ancient Europe: The Neolithic and Early Bronze Age of Scotland in their European Context*, Society of Antiquaries of Scotland: Edinburgh, 179–88.

Brück, J. 2004: 'Material Metaphors: The Relational Construction of Identity in Early Bronze Age Burials in Ireland and Britain', *Journal of Social Archaeology* 4: 307–33.

Brück, J. 2006: 'Death, Exchange and Reproduction in the British Bronze Age', *European Journal of Archaeology* 9.1: 73–101.

Burgess, C. B. 1972: 'Goatscrag: A Bronze Age Rock Shelter Cemetery in North Northumberland. With Notes on other Rock Shelters and Crag Lines in the Region', *Archaeologia Aeliana* (4th Series) 50: 15–70.

Case, H. 2004: 'Bell Beaker and Corded Ware Culture Burial Associations: A Bottom-up rather than Top-down Approach', in A. Gibson & A. Sheridan (eds): *From Sickles to Circles: Britain and Ireland at the Time of Stonehenge*, Tempus: Stroud, 201–14.

Collingwood, E. F. & Cowen, J. D. 1948. 'A Prehistoric Grave at Haugh Head, Wooler', *Archaeologia Aeliana* (4th Series) 26: 47–54.

Collingwood, E. F., Cowen, J. D. & Bernard Shaw A. F. 1946: 'A Prehistoric Grave at West Lilburn', *Archaeologia Aeliana* (4th Series) 24: 217–29.

Cowen, J. D. 1966: 'Prehistoric Notes', *Archaeologia Aeliana* (4th Series) 44: 209–35.

Dixon, D. D. 1892: 'Notes on the Discovery of British Burials on the Simonside Hills, Parish of Rothbury, in Upper Coquetdale, Northumberland', *Archaeologia Aeliana* (2nd Series) 15: 23–36.

Dixon, D. D. 1913: 'Donations to the Museum: Cartington Oak Coffin, etc.', *Archaeologia Aeliana* (3rd Series) 6: 79–84.

Downes, J. 1999: 'Cremation as a Spectacle and a Journey', in J. Downes & T. Pollard (eds): *The Loved Body's Corruption: Archaeological Contributions to the Study of Human Mortality*, Cruithne Press: Glasgow, 19–29.

Downes, J. 2005: *Cremation Practice in Bronze Age Orkney*, unpublished PhD Thesis: Sheffield University.

Edwards, B. 2006: *Liminality, Identity and the Dead: The Burial Monuments of Later Neolithic and Early Bronze Age Coquetdale, Northumberland*, unpublished MA Dissertation: Durham University.

Field, D. 1999: 'Barrows, Cairns and Harmony in the Prehistoric Landscape of Northumberland', in P. Frodsham (ed.): *We were always chasing Time: Papers presented to Keith Blood Northern Archaeology* 17/18: 35–40.

Fowler, C. 2004: *The Archaeology of Personhood: An Anthropological Approach*, Routledge: London.

Fowler, C. 2005: 'Identity Politics: Personhood, Kinship, Gender, and Power in Neolithic and Early Bronze Age Britain', in E. Casella & C. Fowler (eds): *The Archaeology of Plural and Changing Identities: Beyond Identification*, Kluwer Academic/Plenum Press: New York, 109–34.

Fowler, C. 2013a: *The Emergent Past: A Relational Realist Archaeology of Early Bronze Age Mortuary Practices*. Oxford University Press: Oxford.

Fowler, C. 2013b: *Chalcolithic and Early Bronze Age Burials in Northeast England*. Dataset. Archaeology Data Service. Digital Object Identifier 10.5284/1017128.

Fowler, C. 2013c: 'Identities in Transformation: Identities, Funerary Rites and the Mortuary

Process', in L. Nilsson Stutz & S. Tarlow (eds): *The Oxford Handbook of the Archaeology of Death and Burial,* Oxford University Press: Oxford.

Fowler, C & Wilkin, N. in prep.: 'What can the Chalcolithic and Early Bronze Age Mortuary Evidence from Northeast England and Southeast Scotland tell us about Social Networks across and beyond this Area?', in R. Crellin, C. Fowler & R. Tipping (eds): *Prehistory without Borders: The Prehistoric Archaeology of the Tyne-Forth Region.*

Gamble, M. & Fowler, C. 2013a: 'A Re-Assessment of Human Skeletal Remains in Tyne and Wear Museums: Results and Implications for interpreting Early Bronze Age Burials from Northeast England and beyond', *Archaeologia Aeliana* 42: 47–80.

Gamble, M. & Fowler, C. 2013b: *Osteological Analysis of Early Bronze Age human skeletal Remains in Tyne and Wear Museums,* Archaeology Data Service: York. Digital Object Identifier 10.5284/1017462.

Garwood, P. 2007: 'Before the Hills in Order stood: Chronology, Time and History in the Interpretation of Early Bronze Age Round Barrows', in J. Last (ed.): 30–52.

Gates, T. 1981: 'A Food Vessel Burial from Well House Farm, Newton, Northumberland', *Archaeologia Aeliana* (5th Series) 9: 45–50.

Gibson, A. 2004: 'Burials and Beakers: Seeing beneath the Veneer in Late Neolithic Britain', in J. Czebreszuk (ed.): *Similar but Different: Bell Beakers in Europe,* Adam Mickiewicz University: Poznań, 173–91.

Gibson, A. 2007: 'A Beaker Veneer? Some Evidence from the Burial Record', in Larsson & Parker Pearson (eds): 47–64.

Gibson, J. 1906: 'Some Notes on Prehistoric Burials on Tyneside and the Discovery of Two Cists of the Bronze Period in Dilston Park', *Archaeologia Aeliana* (3rd Series) 2: 126–49.

Gilchrist, R. 2008: 'Magic for the Dead? The Archaeology of Magic in Later Medieval Burials', *Medieval Archaeology* 52: 119–59.

Gottlieb, A. 2004: *The Afterlife is where we come from: The Culture of Infancy in West Africa,* Chicago University Press: Chicago.

Greenwell, W. 1868: 'Notes on the Opening of an Ancient British Tumuli in North Northumberland in 1863 and 1865', *History of the Berwickshire Naturalists' Club* 5: 195–96.

Greenwell, W. 1872: 'On Two Ancient Interments at Wooler and Ilderton', *History of the Berwickshire Naturalists' Club* 6: 415–20.

Greenwell, W. 1877: *British Barrows: A Record of the Examination of Sepulchral Mounds in various Parts of England,* Clarendon Press: Oxford.

Greenwell, W. & Embleton, D. 1862: 'Notes on a Tumulus and its Contents at Rundstone Law', *Transactions of the Tyneside Naturalists Field Club* 6: 34–39.

Grinsell, L. V. 1953: *The Ancient Burial Mounds of England,* Institute of Geological Sciences: London.

Harding, A. F. 1981: 'Excavations in the Prehistoric Ritual Complex near Milfield, Northumberland', *Proceedings of the Prehistoric Society* 47: 87–135.

Harding, J. & Healy, F. 2007: *The Raunds Area Project: A Neolithic and Bronze Age Landscape in Northamptonshire,* English Heritage: Swindon.

Healy, F. 2012: 'Chronology, Corpses, Ceramics, Copper and Lithics', in Allen et al. (eds): 144–63.

Hedley, R. C. 1892: 'A Prehistoric Burial at the Sneep, North Tyndale', *Archaeologia Aeliana* (2nd Series) 15: 49–53.

Hewitt, I. & Beckensall, S. 1996: 'The Excavation of Cairns at Blawearie, Old Bewick, Northumberland', *Proceedings of the Prehistoric Society* 62: 255–74.

Heyd, V. 2007: 'Families, Prestige Goods, Warriors and Complex Societies: Beaker Groups of the Third Millennium cal. BC along the Upper and Middle Danube', *Proceedings of the Prehistoric Society* 73: 327–79.

Jay, M. & Richards, M. 2007: 'The Beaker People Project: Progress and Prospects for the Carbon, Nitrogen and Sulphur Isotopic Analysis of Collagen', in Larsson & Parker Pearson (eds): 77–82.

Jobey, G. 1968: 'Excavations of Cairns at Chatton Sandyford, Northumberland', *Archaeologia Aeliana* (4th Series) 46: 5–50.

Jobey, G. 1984: 'The Cartington Coffin: A Radiocarbon Date', *Archaeologia Aeliana* (5th series) 12: 235–37.

Jobey, G., Smith, D. & Tait, J. 1965: 'An Early Bronze Age Burial on Reaverhill Farm, Barrasford, Northumberland', *Archaeologica Aeliana* (4th Series) 43: 65–75.

Jobey, G. & Weyman, J. 1977: 'A Food Vessel Burial on Dour Hill, Byrness, Northumberland', *Archaeologica Aeliana* (5th Series) 5: 204–7.

Jones, A. 2002: 'A Biography of Colour: Colour, Material Histories and Personhood in the Early Bronze Age of Britain and Ireland', in A. Jones & G. MacGregor (eds): *Colouring the Past*, Berg: Oxford, 159–74.

Jones, A. 2008: 'How the Dead live: Mortuary Practices, Memory and the Ancestors in Neolithic and Early Bronze Age Britain', in J. Pollard (ed.): *Prehistoric Britain*, Blackwell: Oxford, 177–201.

Kaul, F. 1998: *Ships on Bronzes: A Study in Bronze Age Religion and Iconography*, National Museum of Denmark: Copenhagen.

Kinnes, I. A. & Longworth, I. H. 1985: *Catalogue of the Excavated Prehistoric and Romano-British Material in the Greenwell Collection*, British Museum: London.

Kristiansen, K. & Larsson, T. 2005: *The Rise of Bronze Age Society: Travels, Transmissions and Transformations*, Cambridge University Press: Cambridge.

Last, J. (ed.) 2007: *Beyond the Grave: New Perspectives on Barrows*, Oxbow: Oxford.

Larsson, M. & Parker Pearson, M. (eds) 2007: *From Stonehenge to the Baltic: Living with Diversity in the Third Millennium BC*, British Archaeological Reports, International Series 1692: Oxford.

Lelong, O. 2012: 'Langwell Farm, Strath Oykel', *Past* 72: 12–14.

Lucas, G. 1996: 'Of Death and Debt: A History of the Body in Neolithic and Early Bronze Age Yorkshire', *Journal of European Archaeology* 4: 99–118.

Maryon, H. 1936: 'Excavation of Two Bronze Age Barrows at Kirkhaugh, Northumberland', *Archaeologia Aeliana* (4th Series) 14: 207–17.

McKinley, J. 1997: 'Bronze Age "Barrows" and Funerary Rites and Rituals of Cremation', *Proceedings of the Prehistoric Society* 63: 129–45.

McKinley, J. 1998: *Breamish Valley, Ingram, Northumbria: Cremated Bone Reports*, Salisbury: Trust for Wessex Archaeology Ltd.: Salisbury.

Miket, R. 1974: 'Excavation at Kirkhill, West Hepple, 1972', *Archaeologia Aeliana* (5th Series) 2: 153–87.

Montgomery, J., Cooper, R. & Evans, J. 2007: 'Foragers, Farmers or Foreigners? An Assessment of Dietary Strontium Isotope Variation in Middle Neolithic and Early Bronze Age East Yorkshire', in Larsson & Parker Pearson (eds): 65–75.

Needham, S. 2005: 'Transforming Beaker Culture in North-West Europe: Processes of Fusion and Fission, *Proceedings of the Prehistoric Society* 71: 171–218.

Needham, S. & Woodward, A. 2008: 'The Clandon Barrow Finery: A Synopsis of Success in an Early Bronze Age World', *Proceedings of the Prehistoric Society* 74: 1–52.

Newman, T. G. 1976: 'The Jet Necklace from Kyloe', *Archaeologia Aeliana* (5th Series) 4: 177–82.

Newman, T. G. & Miket, R. F. 1973: 'A Dagger-Grave at Allerwash, Newbrough, Northumberland', *Archaeologia Aeliana* (5th Series) 1: 87–95.

Oestigaard, T. 2000: 'Sacrifices of Raw, Cooked and Burnt Humans', *Norwegian Archaeological Review* 33.1: 41–58.

Owoc, M-A. 2001: 'The Times they are a-changin': Experiencing Continuity and Development in the Early Bronze Age Funerary Rituals of Southwestern Britain', in J. Brück (ed.), *Bronze Age Landscapes: Tradition and Transformation*, Oxbow: Oxford, 193–207.

Owoc, M-A. 2005: 'From the Ground Up: Agency, Practice, and Community in the southwestern British Bronze Age', *Journal of Archaeological Method and Theory* 12: 257–81.

Pierpoint, S. 1980: *Social Patterns in Yorkshire Prehistory, 3500–750 BC*, British Archaeological Reports, British Series 74: Oxford.

Peters, F. 2000: 'Two Traditions of Bronze Age Burial in the Stonehenge Landscape', *Oxford Journal of Archaeology* 19.4: 343–58.

Petersen, F. 1972: 'Traditions of Multiple Burial in Late Neolithic and Early Bronze Age England', *Archaeological Journal* 129: 22–55.

Petersen, F., Shepherd, I. A. G., & Tuckwell, A. 1974: 'A Short Cist at Horsbrugh Castle Farm, Peebleshire', *Proceedings of the Society of Antiquaries of Scotland* 105: 43–62.

Rome Hall, G. 1887: 'On some Cup-Incised Stones found in an Ancient British Burial Mound at Pitland Hills, near Birtley, North Tynedale', *Archaeologia Aeliana* (2nd Series) 12: 268–83.

Shepherd, A. 1989: 'A Note on the Orientation of Beaker Burials in North-East Scotland', *Proceedings of the Society of Antiquaries of Scotland* 119: 79–81.

Shepherd, I. A. G. 2009: 'The V-bored Buttons of Great Britain and Ireland', *Proceedings of the Prehistoric Society* 75: 335–69.

Sheridan, J. A. 2004: 'Scottish Food Vessel Chronology revisited', in A. Gibson & A. Sheridan (eds): *From Sickles to Circles: Britain and Ireland at the Time of Stonehenge*, Tempus: Stroud, 243–67.

Sheridan, J. A. 2007a: 'Scottish Beaker Dates: The Good, the Bad and the Ugly', in Larsson & Parker Pearson (eds): 91–123.

Sheridan, J. A. 2007b: 'Dating the Scottish Bronze Age: "There is clearly much that the Material can still tell us"', in C. Burgess, P. Topping & F. Lynch (eds): *Beyond Stonehenge: Essays on the Bronze Age in Honour of Colin Burgess,* Oxbow: Oxford, 162–81.

Sheridan, J. A. 2008: 'Towards a fuller, more nuanced Narrative of Chalcolithic and Early Bronze Age Britain 2500–1500 BC', *Bronze Age Review* 1: 57–78.

Sheridan, J. A. 2010. 'Cremating Miss Piggy: An experimental Bronze Age-style Cremation'. *Contribution to 'A lad o'pairts', Day Conference in Memory of Ian Shepherd*. http://www.aberdeenshire.gov.uk/archaeology/projects/IanShepherdConferencePapers-WebVersion.pdf

Sheridan, J. A. & Davis, M. 2002: 'Investigating Jet and Jet-like Artefacts from Prehistoric Scotland: The National Museums of Scotland Project', *Antiquity* 76: 812–25.

Short, D. C. 1931: 'A Bronze Age Cist at Humbleton, Wooler', *History of the Berwickshire Naturalists Club* 27.3: 385–90.

Skoglund, P. 2008: 'Stone Ships: Continuity and Change in Scandinavian Prehistory', *World Archaeology* 40.3: 390–406.

Šoberl, L., Pollard, J. & Evershed, R. 2009: 'Pots for the Afterlife: Organic Residue Analysis of British Bronze Age Pottery from Funerary Contexts', *Past* 63: 6–8.

Sørensen, M. L. S. & Rebay, K. 2008: 'From Substantial Bodies to the Substance of Bodies: Analysis of the Transition from Inhumation to Cremation during the Middle Bronze Age in Europe,' in J. Robb & D. Borić (eds): *Past Bodies: Body-centred Research in Archaeology*, Oxbow: Oxford, 59–68.

Stopford, J., Weyman, J., Ford, B. & Miket, R. 1985: 'Two Cemeteries of the Second Millennium B.C. in Northumbria', *Archaeologia Aeliana* (5th Series) 13: 117–31.

Tait, J. 1965: '*Beakers from Northumberland*', Oriel Press: Newcastle-Upon-Tyne.

Tate, J. 1891: 'Sepulchral Remains on North Charlton', *History of the Berwickshire Naturalists Club* 13: 269–72.

Tolan-Smith, C. 2005: 'A Cairn on Birkside Fell: Excavations in 1996 and 1997', *Archaeologia Aeliana* (5th Series) 34: 55–65.

Tuckwell, A. 1970: *The possible Significances of the Orientation and Positioning of Skeletons in the round Barrows of the Yorkshire Wolds*, unpublished MA Thesis, University of Edinburgh.

Tuckwell, A. 1975: 'Patterns of Burial Orientation in the Round Barrows of Eastern Yorkshire', *Bulletin of the University of London Institute of Archaeology* 12: 95–123.

Turner, V. 1967: *The Forest of Symbols: Aspects of Ndembu Ritual*, New York: Cornell University Press.

Turner, V. 1969: *The Ritual Process: Structure and Anti-Structure*, Aldine: Chicago.

van Gennep, A. 1960: *The Rites of Passage*, Routledge and Kegan Paul: London.

Waddington, C. 2010: *Low Hauxley, Northumberland: A Review of Archaeological Interventions and Site Condition*, Archaeological Research Services Ltd Report 2010/25.

Waddington, C., Bailey, G., Boomer, I. & Milner, N. 2005: 'A Bronze Age Cist Cemetery at Howick, Northumberland', *Archaeological Journal* 162: 65–95.

Wilkin, N. 2009: *Regional Narratives of the Early Bronze Age. A Contextual and Evidence-led Approach to the Funerary Practices of East-Central Scotland*, unpublished M.Phil Thesis, University of Birmingham.

Williams, H. 2004: 'Death warmed up: The Agency of Bodies and Bones in Early Anglo-Saxon Cremation Rites', *Journal of Material Culture* 9.3: 263–91.

Woodward, A. 2002: 'Beads and Beakers: Heirlooms and Relics in the British Early Bronze Age', *Antiquity* 76: 1040–47.

Woodward, A., Hunter, J., Ixer, R., Maltby, M., Potts, P., Webb, J., Watson, J. & Jones, M. 2005: 'Ritual in some Early Bronze Age Grave Goods', *Archaeological Journal* 162: 31–64.

CAUSES AND CONTEXTS OF LONG-TERM RITUAL CHANGE
The Iron Age to Early Medieval Cemetery of Klin-Yar (North Caucasus, Russia)

Heinrich Härke & Andrej Belinskij

The discussion of change tends to prioritise sudden, marked change over the gradual development and transformation of behaviour and institutions, but it is probably fair to say that the latter is far more common in human societies. At the site of Klin-Yar, it is possible to observe the evolution of grave construction and mortuary ritual across three cultural phases, from the Late Bronze Age to the Early Middle Ages.

This evolution comprises continuous elements as well as observable changes and developments. Changing ideas about the afterlife and tensions between social norms and individual behaviour may have affected the changes. But the key factors behind the overall pattern of evolution appear to be a series of interlinked changes: immigration leading to economic change which, in turn, led to social change; the latter was, at the same time, affected by the wider geo-political context of the region.

This case study highlights two points: (1) causes of ritual change may often be strongly interlinked, and it may therefore be misleading to look for a single obvious cause; and (2) marked changes in the wider contexts may not always be reflected in pronounced changes in mortuary ritual.

Keywords: Alans, burial ritual, Koban Culture, ritual change, Sarmatians

The archaeological study of change is one of the most fascinating areas of the discipline because it rests on one of its strengths: the long-term perspective which makes changes stand out more clearly than they would when observed within the context of a shorter period. But there are a number of problems associated with studying change. One is that we tend to think of 'change' in terms of sudden and marked change whereas most

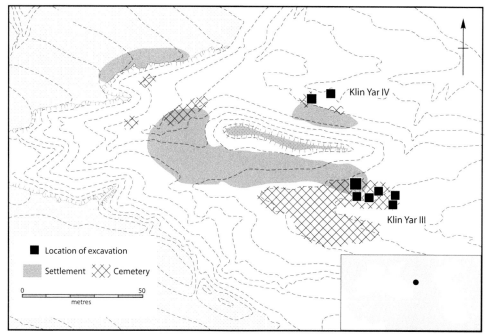

Fig. 4.1. Site map of Klin-Yar, with location of excavations 1994–96 (drawn by M. Mathews, Reading).

change in human societies tends to be slow, gradual and cumulative – something which is often more in the nature of evolution. In fact, changes over a long period appear more marked mainly because the long-term perspective has the effect of collapsing them into seemingly shorter and more pronounced events.

This, in turn, is linked to the second problem. Archaeologists are better at observing difference and studying variation, than at observing change and studying processes of transformation. The reasons for this are twofold, and they are rooted in the structure of the discipline and in the nature of the archaeological evidence. The discipline is split into specialisms which have traditionally been defined by chronology more than by any other factor, and specialists in the one or the other period feel uneasy transgressing into other periods because of their lack of familiarity with evidence and debates there. The consequence is that phases of change and transition between the chronological blocks tend to be studied from one side or the other, or not at all, but rarely as a whole. The fragmentary and incomplete nature of the archaeological evidence tends to exacerbate the problem. This evidence presents us with a series of isolated 'snapshots' of past situations rather than a complete 'film' of unfolding stories in the past. Thus, we infer processes of transformation from differences between the 'snapshots', and causes of change from contextual information. Even where the 'snapshots' are reasonably close to one another, the chronological resolution of our dating evidence will often make it difficult or even impossible to follow a transformation step by step; very often, it will be century by century, or if we are lucky, decade by decade.

The specific subject of ritual change poses a third problem: to what extent can we separate, or even distinguish, ritual change from other types of change? Can we study ritual change on its own? In many societies, there appears to be a link between funerary ritual and the type of economy (pers. comm. Tony Walter, Bath). Processualists have postulated that social organisation determines the complexity of mortuary rites (Binford 1971), which implies that social change may, or should, entail ritual change. Political change has recently been the cause of ritual change in Russia where the collapse of the Soviet Union was followed by a massive return of orthodox ritual in worship and burial (Merridale 2000). And recent cases of migration in, or into, Europe have demonstrated that migrants often (though not always) bring their own styles of ritual with them, linking ritual change to population change (Jonker 1996).

Some of the issues discussed above will be explored in this paper which looks at a case of ritual change within a single cemetery site over the best part of two millennia, with a focus on processes of transformation and their causes. Particular attention will be paid to interrelated aspects of change in order to see how ritual change may be interlinked with other changes in society. This, in turn, may help to identify the causal factors at work in the transformational processes.

Klin-Yar: site and evidence

Klin-Yar is located in the chalk and sandstone hills of the Russian North Caucasus, outside the old spa town of Kislovodsk in the region of Stavropol. A narrow, steep-sided sandstone plateau (called Paravos, or 'The Locomotive') has produced settlement traces of Late Bronze/Early Iron Age (Koban Culture) and Early Medieval (Alanic) date. Further settlement areas of Koban and Alanic date are located on the upper slopes around the plateau. Extensive burial grounds with Koban, Sarmatian and Alanic graves occupy the lower slopes (Fig. 4.1). It is the presence of three cultural and chronological phases in the cemeteries which has made Klin-Yar a key site for regional archaeology, and it makes it an ideal case for the study of change.

Phase at Klin-Yar	*Designation*	*Period/Absolute date*
1 Koban Culture	Late BA/Early IA	10th–4th century BC
2 Sarmatian	Late IA/Roman IA	2nd century BC–4th/5th century AD
3 Alanic	Early Middle Ages	4th/5th 8th century AD

Excavations carried out before 1993 uncovered some 350 graves, most of them dating to the Late Bronze/Early Iron Age, but also about 100 Sarmatian and Alanic graves, providing one of the largest samples of undisturbed Alanic burials in the entire North Caucasus (the terms 'Sarmatian' and 'Alanic' are used here primarily as chronological, not as ethnic labels). Joint Anglo-Russian fieldwork in cemeteries III and IV undertaken by the Regional Heritage Unit 'Nasledie' and the University of Reading added another

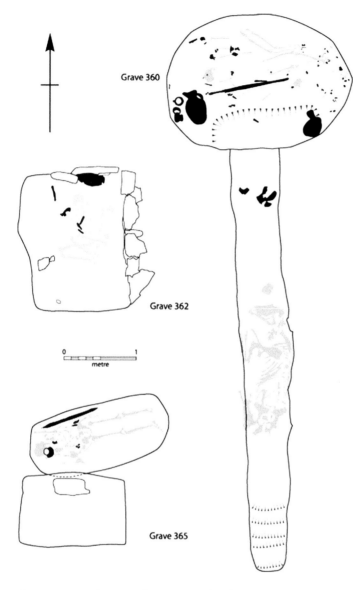

Grave 360

Grave 362

Grave 365

Fig. 4.2. Plans of graves from the three phases represented in the Klin-Yar cemeteries: Koban Period (grave 362), Sarmatian (grave 365) and Alanic (grave 360) (drawn by M. Mathews, Reading).

52 graves, with more than 100 individuals (Härke & Belinsky 2000; 2008; Belinskij & Härke forthcoming). This new fieldwork also identified an elite plot of rich Late Sarmatian and Early Alanic catacombs. The full extent of the Klin-Yar cemeteries can currently only be guessed at, but it is probably somewhere between 1000 and 3000 graves. Cultural contacts shown in grave-goods are wide-ranging, from Central Asia to Mesopotamia and Byzantium. In the Alanic Period, a branch of the Silk Road is thought to have led past Klin-Yar to the mountain passes of the Caucasus.

In the first phase of the site, the Koban-Period inhabitants of Klin-Yar practised inhumation with grave-goods in rectangular grave pits (Fig. 4.2). These pits were regularly cut, quite shallow, and sometimes stone-lined and/or covered with flagstones. Each grave contained a single body, deposited crouched on the side. Gender differences within the burial rite were marked. As a rule, males had been deposited on the right side, females on the left; this is part of a long-standing East European tradition reaching back to the Late Neolithic (Häusler 2003; Sofaer-Derevenskij 1997). There was a limited range of grave-goods which, again, show marked differences between the genders. Males were buried with weapons (usually a spearhead) and tools (knife and whetstone), females with dress and body ornaments (headdress, glass or amber beads, bronze pins). One male adult burial (skeletal sex determination checked and confirmed) with female grave-goods (large bronze pin and nine glass beads) was also unusual in the deposition of the body which had been bunched up in a corner of the grave, and in the placing of a pottery vessel underneath the bent left knee (grave 355) (Fig. 4.3); this may be one of the 'shaman' burials which have occasionally been suggested in cases of Koban-Period cemeteries (pers. comm. S. L. Dudarev, Armavir; Belinskij & Härke, forthcoming). The most frequent grave deposit, common to both genders, was a single pottery vessel; this was found with the majority of Koban burials at Klin-Yar. Wealth was indicated by more elaborate items within this range, such as a decorated axe in a male burial (grave 362) and bronze bracelets and a necklet in a female burial (grave 366). Previous excavations had produced some more exotic items, including Assyrian helmets and Scythian artefacts, highlighting that Klin-Yar belongs to the contact zone between the steppes to the north, and developed civilisations to the south, of the Caucasus mountains.

In the second (Sarmatian) phase, the local burial rite was characterised by inhumation in a small underground chamber (catacomb), usually with the body extended on the back and provided with some grave-goods (Fig. 4.2). The chamber was accessed by a pit or a short corridor (*dromos*) which was in most cases aligned east–west; in a few cases, the ritual deposition of a horse 'skin' (head-and-hooves) was observed on or in the *dromos*. The entrance to the chamber from the *dromos* was always blocked with large stones. Most Sarmatian chambers contained only a single body, and many double burials were constructed by linking single-burial chambers with a short dromos. In some cases of Late Sarmatian catacombs, two bodies had been buried in the same chamber. In contrast to the preceding period, gender was signalled now only through grave-goods: some males had been buried with weapons, many females with dress ornaments (earrings, beads) and a mirror; pottery vessels and horse sacrifice were gender-neutral depositions. Within the narrow range of grave-goods, wealth indicators were few and unspectacular; they included an iron long sword for males (e.g. grave 365), and gold ornaments for females (e.g. grave 379). The most notable feature of the Sarmatian burial rite at this site was variation from grave to grave, and an absence of standardisation.

The Alanic ritual in the third phase was similar to the Sarmatian, but more elaborate. The standard burial rite continued to be dressed inhumation, with an increased range and quantity of grave-goods. The catacombs were larger and deeper now and occasionally had additional features such as pits or niches; dromoi were longer and predominantly orientated around north–south, with the entrance at the northern end blocked with

Fig. 4.3. Photograph of the possible 'shaman' burial in Koban grave 355 (photo H. Härke).

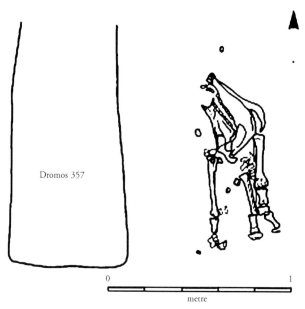

Dromos 357

0   1
metre

Fig. 4.4. Plan of horse 'skin' deposition 1/1995 next to the dromos of Alanic catacomb 357 (drawn by M. Mathews, Reading).

large stones (Fig. 4.2). In the majority of cases, Alanic catacombs contained more than one body, and occasionally as many as four. There is clear evidence of re-opening of chambers and later deposition of bodies and grave-goods, suggesting that the catacombs were used as family or kin group vaults. This is highlighted by cases of large catacombs with single bodies where space had been left for later depositions (e.g. in grave 371). Sacrificial depositions in or on the *dromos* became more frequent and varied in the Alanic phase, frequently including pottery, less often weapons or parts of horse harness.

Gender associations of Alanic grave-goods are less easy to identify because of multiple burials and mixed inventories in the chambers, but items found on the bodies indicate that grave-goods were gendered along Sarmatian lines: males had weapons, and boot and belt fittings, while females had been buried with dress ornaments and textile bags. There was, however, some overlap, with a single earring found in the cases of a couple of men, and a large knife or short sword found next to, at least, one woman. Pottery, wooden household items and horse harness were found in the head and foot ends of chambers, possibly implying that they were gender-neutral objects. The most conspicuous indicator of wealth was the sacrificial deposit of an entire horse in the dromos; these cases were concentrated in the elite plot. Glass vessels, bronze cauldrons and Byzantine coins (of late sixth/early seventh century date) were found only in the richest graves at Klin-Yar (e.g. grave 360).

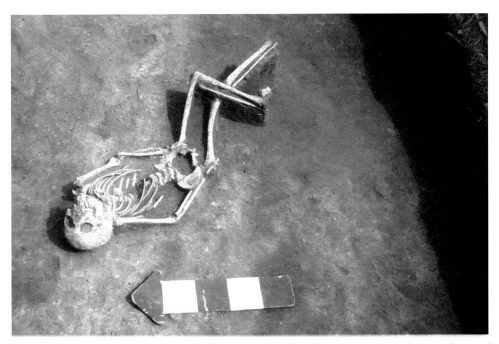

Fig. 4.5. Skeleton of an adolescent (grave 385), a possible human sacrifice in the topsoil above the dromos of Late Sarmatian catacomb 386 (photo H. Härke).

In addition to the graves, there were some ritual features in the cemetery which were not always clearly associated with particular graves; virtually all of them appear to be of Sarmatian or Alanic date. One was a *dromos* without a chamber, but with a horse 'skin' deposition on top; this may have been intended as a cenotaph. Three horse 'skin' depositions between the graves and a separate horse burial without a human body (grave 367) suggest the conduct of post-burial ritual in cemetery III (Fig. 4.4). The most intriguing of these ritual features was the skeleton of an adolescent (grave 385) deposited in contorted position above the backfilled *dromos* of a Late Sarmatian catacomb (grave 386) (Fig. 4.5). This may well have been a human sacrifice although such cases are extremely rare in other Sarmatian and Alanic cemeteries of the region.

Discussion: ritual change at Klin-Yar

There are marked changes as well as clear continuities in the mortuary ritual at Klin-Yar. Features found across all three phases, over some two millennia, are inhumation rite and grave-goods custom. While, from an archaeological perspective, these are profound continuities, the list of observable changes is considerably longer.

First, there was a development from Koban grave pits (phase 1) to Sarmatian/Alanic underground chambers (catacombs; phases 2 and 3). This coincided with a shift from single burial (phase 1) to multiple burial, first in the shape of linked single-burial chambers (phase 2), then with several bodies in one chamber (from late in phase 2, and throughout phase 3). Consecutive double burial, in turn, meant continued use and re-use of burial chambers, possibly as family or kinship vaults (from late in phase 2, and throughout phase 3). Parallel to these three developments and innovations, it is possible to observe, across all phases, an increasing complexity of funerary ritual in graves until it reached a peak in the rich Alanic catacombs (phase 3). With the sacrificial depositions between the graves, we may also see the appearance of commemorative ritual at this site (from phase 2 or 3).

Perhaps the most intriguing change, though, was a 'pendulum' change in the overall ritual package from standardisation (phase 1, Koban Culture) to variety (phase 2, Sarmatian) and back to standardisation (phase 3, Alanic). Like all the other changes, this seems to have been a slow and gradual process, in each case over decades or even centuries, with more marked transitions from phase 1 to 2, and more gradual, incremental developments from phase 2 to 3.

The key question, as with all processes of change and transformation, relates to the reasons and causes of the processes. The following discussion will attempt a deductive approach, looking at the possible causes of change, and then considering which of the observed changes might be explained by them. This will include factors suggested by the editors of the present volume, as well as other factors which may be relevant in late prehistoric and early historic processes of change.

Mortuary ritual is often thought to be determined by ideas about cosmology and the afterlife; changing ideas should, therefore, affect the shape (or perhaps just the meaning?) of ritual. Such change might well explain the abandonment of the crouched body position in Koban graves which is so strikingly reminiscent of the foetal position, but is also a sleeping position. Eschatological change may also be a factor in the appearance of burial chambers which could be thought of as 'underground houses'. The inhabitants of North Ossetia, generally accepted as the direct descendants of the Alans of the North Caucasus and living a couple of hundred kilometres to the east of Klin-Yar, put small brick models of houses into their graves (Kalojev 2004). However, that may be a modern innovation because the religion of Iranian nomads (including Sarmatians and Alans) is generally thought to be linked to fire and the sun (Frye 1962), not to houses and underground spaces. The disposal of the dead in rural Iran today is by exposure at designated places and on purpose-built platforms (seen at Yazd in 2004; pers. comm. Hubertus Härke, Vaasa).

Personal preferences are always likely to have some impact on funerals, and the tension between social norms and individual behaviour is typical of funerary ritual in all societies (pers. comm. Tony Walter, Bath). This tension could explain the changing patterns of standardisation versus variety (the 'pendulum' change) which can be observed at Klin-Yar. Perhaps, Sarmatians were greater individualists than Koban people and Alans, or to put it another way, the standardising populations before and after the Sarmatians had a tighter social control.

At Klin-Yar, population change appears to be closely linked to ritual change. The skeletal evidence suggests that the Sarmatians at this site are likely to be immigrants from the southern Urals (possibly a male-only immigration) who mixed with the native Koban population (Belinskij & Härke forthcoming). The Alans, too, were new arrivals in the region, introducing new male and female phenotypes; there are differences in the stable isotope patterns of the Alanic populations buried in cemeteries III and IV, respectively, suggesting the existence among the local Alans of, at least, two sub-groups of possibly different origins (Belinskij & Härke forthcoming). Interestingly, though, the limited Sarmatian immigration led to a more marked change in burial ritual than the apparently more extensive Alanic influx which was followed by gradual change and a development of existing ritual themes. The presence of Alanic sub-groups might help to explain subtle differences in grave construction, grave-goods, and funerary ritual between cemeteries III and IV as well as their separate locations on either side of the rock formation.

Economic change was associated with the population change, and the former may well have been the primary factor of change. The native Koban people were agriculturalists while the biological evidence of the Sarmatians suggests the lifestyle of horse nomads and the diet of livestock breeders (Belinskij & Härke forthcoming). In the Alanic Period, the economy appears to have been mixed, including agriculture and herding. It is probably significant that settlements of Koban and Alanic date have been found in the vicinity of the Klin Yar cemeteries, but none of Sarmatian date. An *a priori* observation would be that the two sedentary populations (Koban and Alanic) had a more standardised ritual than the nomadic population of the intervening Sarmatian Period.

This may be as significant as the fact that a ritual emphasis on horse sacrifice and horse burial appeared with the transition from Koban agriculturalists to Sarmatian nomads. With the next economic change, from the Sarmatian livestock economy to the mixed economy of the Alans (but starting in the Late Sarmatian Period), we see the emergence of family or kin group vaults and of commemorative ritual in the cemeteries. Again, this link is probably significant because agricultural societies tend to emphasise family links because these define land ownership and give access to land. A final economic factor involved in ritual changes at Klin-Yar may be the Early Medieval branch of the Silk Road which ran along the North Caucasus, and passed through the Kislovodsk Basin in the seventh century AD (Ierusalimskaya 1992). This could have contributed to the exceptional burial wealth found at Klin-Yar in the first half of the seventh century.

Economic factors seem to have engendered social change, with a noticeably greater social differentiation in the Alanic Period (phase 3 at Klin-Yar). This is particularly visible in the elite plot of cemetery III which boasts a concentration of wealth indicators: 14 horse and horse 'skin' depositions, three bronze cauldrons, four glass vessels, as well as the most elaborate underground architecture and the largest burial chambers at the site (Fig. 4.6). Greater social hierarchy was expressed in a more complex, but at the same time more standardised, burial ritual, and possibly in human sacrifice (grave 385, cf. above). Gender was symbolised to some extent in the ritual of all three phases at Klin-Yar (Härke 2000), but least of all (only by the few grave-goods) in the second, Sarmatian phase. This may be linked to social patterns of Iranian-speaking nomads, which are also signalled by the discovery of 'amazon' burials elsewhere in Scythian and Sarmatian contexts (Guliaev 2003).

Political change is often associated with economic and social change, be it as cause or consequence. Some grave-goods in rich Alanic catacombs, such as Byzantine coins (in graves 341 and 363) and an Iranian glass vessel (in grave 360), are a clear reflection of the position of the North Caucasus Alans between the Byzantine and Iranian regional powers, and of the Alanic military service for both of them at various times (Savenko, in Belinskij & Härke forthcoming). Finally, the changing patterns of standardisation and variation in mortuary ritual across the three phases at Klin-Yar may well reflect differences between settled societies in the process of early state formation (perhaps in the Koban Period, and most likely in the Alanic), on the one hand, and nomadic immigrants (Sarmatians), on the other.

Concluding remarks

Many of the possible explanations discussed above make eminent sense in explaining ritual change at Klin-Yar and elsewhere, but the key point surely is that the possible causal factors are all strongly interlinked: immigration brought in new populations with different economies and possibly with a new religion; economic change led to social change; and changes in the wider political context reinforced social and economic change. This interlinkage is probably in the nature of mortuary ritual which itself

Fig. 4.6. Analytical plan of the Sarmatian–Alanic elite plot in cemetery III of Klin-Yar (drawn by M. Mathews, Reading).

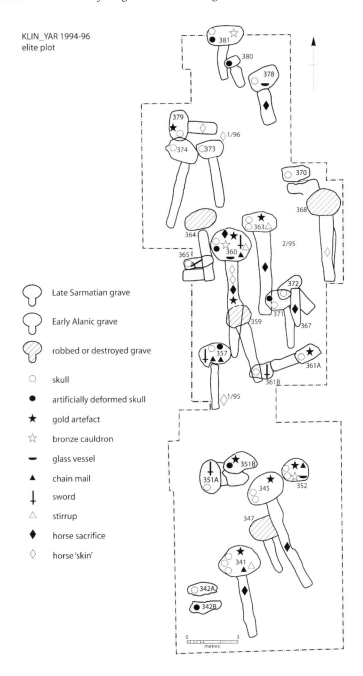

KLIN_YAR 1994-96
elite plot

Late Sarmatian grave

Early Alanic grave

robbed or destroyed grave

○ skull

● artificially deformed skull

★ gold artefact

☆ bronze cauldron

— glass vessel

▲ chain mail

↓ sword

△ stirrup

◆ horse sacrifice

◇ horse 'skin'

is complex and reflects a multitude of very different aspects, including ideas about afterlife and pollution, personal factors such as individual biographies and mourners' emotions, kinship and family links as well as social relations, status, and access to positions and land.

Sometimes even a short-term, dramatic change of behaviour and attitude in the encounter with death may not have an obvious single cause. The public mourning of Princess Diana in Britain, a country not previously known for public hysteria on such occasions, is a case in point: sociologists of death are still debating the reasons for this entirely new phenomenon which surprised everyone at the time, and nobody more so than the academic specialists (Walter 1999). If this focused look at the development of burial ritual at a single site over a long period of time tells us anything, it is probably that we should not be looking for single causes of gradual change, and perhaps not even of marked change, in mortuary behaviour.

Bibliography

Belinskij, A. B. & Härke, H. forthcoming: *The Iron Age to Early Medieval Cemetery of Klin-Yar: Excavations 1994-96* (Forschungen in Eurasien), Deutsches Archäologisches Institut: Berlin.

Binford, L. 1971: 'Mortuary Practices: Their Study and their Potential', *American Antiquity* 36.3.2: 6–29.

Frye, R. N. 1962: *The Heritage of Persia* (Bibliotheca Iranica, Reprint Series, 1), Mazda Publishers: Costa Mesa, California.

Guliaev, V. 2003: 'Amazons in the Scythia: New Finds at the Middle Don, Southern Russia', *World Archaeology* 35.1: 112–25.

Härke, H. 2000 (with A. B. Belinskij & N. Stoodley): 'Die Darstellung von Geschlechtergrenzen im frühmittelalterlichen Grabritual: Normalität oder Problem?', in W. Pohl & H. Reimitz (eds): *Grenze und Differenz im frühen Mittelalter* (Österreichische Akademie der Wissenschaften, Phil.-Hist. Klasse, Denkschrift 287 = Forschungen zur Geschichte des Mittelalters 1), Verlag der Österreichischen Akademie der Wissenschaften: Vienna, 181–96.

Härke, H. & Belinskij, A. 2008: 'Trauer, Ahnenkult, Sozialstatus? Überlegungen zur Interpretation der Befunde im Gräberfeld von Klin-Yar (Nordkaukasus, Russland)', in C. Kümmel, B. Schweizer & U. Veit with M. Augstein (eds): *Körperinszenierung – Objektsammlung – Monumentalisierung: Totenritual und Grabkult in frühen Gesellschaften* (Tübinger Archäologische Taschenbücher 6), Waxmann: Münster, New York, München & Berlin, 417–30.

Häusler, A. 2003: 'Urkultur der Indogermanen und Bestattungsriten', in A. Bammesberger & T. Vennemann with M. Biewswanger & J. Grzega (eds) *Languages in Prehistoric Europe*, Universitätsverlag Winter: Heidelberg, 49–83.

Härke, H. & Belinsky, A. 2000: 'Nouvelles fouilles de 1994–1996 dans la nécropole de Klin-Yar', in M. Kazanski & V. Soupault (eds): *Les sites archéologiques en Crimée et au Caucase durant l'Antiquité tardive et le haut Moyen Age* (Colloquia Pontica 5), Brill: Leiden, 193–210.

Ierusalimskaya, A. A. 1992: *Kavkaz na shelkovom puti* (exhibition catalogue), State Hermitage: St Petersburg.

Jonker, G. 1996: 'The Knife's Edge: Muslim Burial in the Diaspora', *Mortality* 1.1: 27–43.

Kalojev, B. A. 2004: *Osetiny. Istoriko-etnograficheskoe issledovanie*, Nauka: Moscow.

Merridale, C. 2000: *Night of Stone: Death and Memory in Russia*, Penguin: London.

Sofaer-Derevenski, J. 1997: 'Age and Gender at the Site of Tiszapolgár-Basatanya, Hungary', *Antiquity* 71: 875–89.

Walter, T. (ed.) 1999: *The Mourning for Diana*, Berg: Oxford.

5

PASSAGE TO THE UNDERWORLD
Continuity or Change in Etruscan Funerary Ideology and Practices (6th–2nd Century BC)?[1]

J. Rasmus Brandt

For Axel Seeberg (1931–2011) who taught me to ask questions

Arnold van Gennep's pioneering study on rites-de-passage *more than a century ago (1908 [1960]) has only relatively recently been applied to Etruscan cultural studies and, in particular, opened up new aspects and interpretations of Etruscan funerary practices and iconography, as expressed in tomb paintings and sculpture. However, apart from definitions of funerary real and mental spaces, discussions on ancestral ideology, and occasional studies of one or more tombs and selected pictorial themes and details, no investigation has tried to apply van Gennep's model in order to understand in greater detail the preserved Etruscan tomb paintings in coherence. The present study is a meagre attempt to remedy somewhat this defect, and it was carried out with references to Mary Douglas' observations on taboos, pollution, and purification (1966 [2005]) and to two additional important concepts in ritual studies: content and form.*

The investigation begins by returning to a central question in Etruscan tomb painting: the change in tomb iconology from merry revellers in the 6th/5th centuries BC to monstrous nether world scenes in the 4th century BC and later. In the past, this marked change was interpreted from either a political or an eschatological point of view. However, with the discovery of a new tomb at Tarquinia some 25 years ago, Tomba dei Demoni Azzurri, *dated to 450–430 BC (or slightly later), these views have been somewhat modified. The aim of the present paper is thus to review some of the data on Etruscan painted tombs from the Archaic to Hellenistic times and discuss, with a view to van Gennep and Douglas, if the changes in iconology are due to a change in ritual content or only in form.*[2]

Keywords: Content, eschatology, Etruria, form, funerary rituals and practices, iconography, paintings, pollution, purification, rites-de-passage, sculpture, taboo.

> 'Access to ancient Greek society is severely limited by the quantity and nature of our sources. So the study of … Greek attitudes towards death present even greater difficulties than is normally the case in the history of collective representations; and it is necessary to use as many types of evidence and methodological tools as possible.'[3]

So Christiane Sourvinou-Inwood wrote in 1981 about Greek attitudes towards death. The situation of the sources available since then has not improved considerably. If it is difficult to understand attitudes towards death in Greece, a cultural area for which we have both literary and archaeological sources, the situation in Etruria, where written sources are nearly absent or at best secondary, collected and presented by non-Etruscan writers, is even worse. Thus it becomes more necessary 'to use as many types of evidence and methodological (and I should add theoretical) tools as possible.'

The nether world – the Etruscan questions

To understand the function and meaning of Etruscan funerary practices our main sources lie in archaeology and art. For a long time a specific problem has tormented scholars: how to explain a profound iconological change occurring in Etruscan funerary art around the middle of the 4th century BC. At this time the Archaic and Classical presentations of merry scenes with banquets, athletic games, and dancing taking place in this world move to presentations from the nether world,[4] where we meet Aita[5] (Hades), Phersipnai[6] (Persephone), and ugly demons, the most frequent ones named Charu(n) and Vanth.[7]

What was the reason for this iconological shift? Before trying to answer the question, let us take a very quick look at the historical situation in Etruria from the Late Archaic to the Hellenistic Period. At the beginning of this period the Etruscan dominance and/ or influence in Italy was at its maximum extending from its core area between the rivers Arno and Tiber (Fig. 5.1), northwards into the Po valley and southwards into Campania. In 474 BC, off Cumae in the Bay of Naples, the Etruscans lost in a sea battle against Syracuse, and thus also gradually lost control over the shipping routes towards their home country. In 396 BC the first Etruscan city, Veii, fell to Roman expansionist politics; at the same time from the north Celts made incursions deep into Etruscan territory. In 351 BC, after seven years of atrocious conflict with Rome, Tarquinia signed a 40 year truce, but at the time of its expiry in 311 BC the Romans were back. This was the beginning of a conquest policy, which in the course of a few generations would see all Etruscan cities subjected to Roman political hegemony.

The reason for the iconological change in Etruscan funerary art has for a long time been proposed by two main lines of explanation:

1. The political explanation: From an optimistic view of life, the Roman and Celtic incursions into Etruscan territory in the early 4th century BC brought about political instability and a general uncertainty about the future. The introduction of the scenes from the nether world was accordingly the result of a general pessimistic view of life spreading through the Etruscan society during this time and the following generations.[8]

2. The eschatological explanation: This connects the iconological change to the introduction of new ideas about the afterlife into Etruria, especially as formulated by the expanding mystery cults, such as Pythagorism and Orphism.[9] The influence is said to have come to Etruria in particular from southern Italy, where, from the middle of the 4th century BC, appeared a series of funerary vases depicting Underworld scenes with Hades, Persephone, and Orpheus.[10] Alternatively, the change in pictorial motifs is explained as 'un radicale cambiamento nelle strutture mentali.'[11]

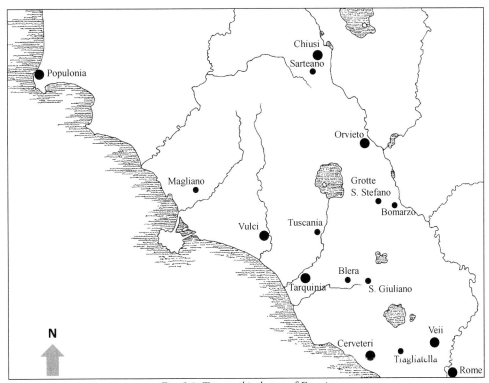

Fig. 5.1. Topographical map of Etruria.

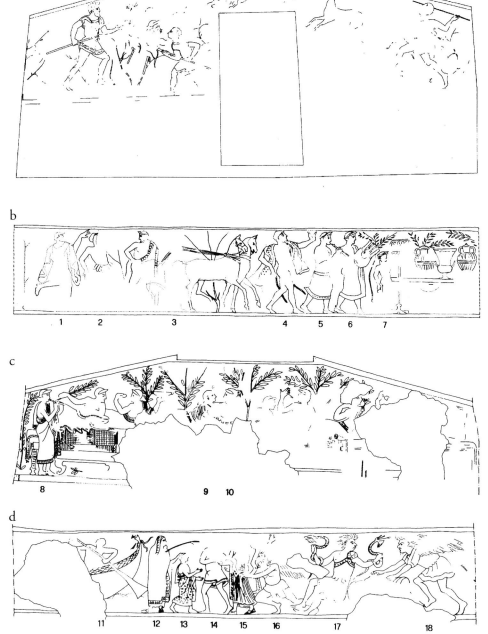

Fig. 5.2. Tarquinia, T. dei Demoni Azzurri: *a) entrance wall; b) left wall; c) right wall; d) rear wall (line drawings from Adinolfi et al. 2005a: 46, fig. 1 (= a); Cataldi 1989:152, figs 108–10 (= b, d, c); with kind permission of Ministero per i Beni e le Attività Culturali, Soprintendenza per i beni archeologici dell'Etruria Meridionale, Museo di Villa Giulia).*

In 1985, a new painted tomb was discovered at Tarquinia, the *T. dei Demoni Azzurri* (phase 4), but unfortunately not well preserved in all its details (Figs 5.2a–d):[12]

Entrance wall (Fig. 5.2a): badly preserved; probably hunting scenes.[13]

Left wall (Fig. 5.2b): From left (i.e from the entrance wall): A procession moving right with two dancers (1–2) following in the footsteps of a man about to enter a two-horse chariot (or biga) (3); up front another dancer(?) with a forked branch in his right hand (4), together with a flute (5) and a kithara player (6); a tree separates the procession from a small, young servant (7) standing by a *kylikeion*, or table with different kinds of wine vessels for mixing and serving.[14]

Rear wall (Fig. 5.2c): The *kylikeion* scene on the left wall mediates the transition to the banquet scene on the rear wall; from left: a flute player (8), followed by four *klinai*, the first and the two last ones with male couples, the second one with a woman and a man (9–10); midway a young servant; trees in the background.[15]

Right wall (Fig. 5.2d): This is the wall which has given the name to the tomb; from right (i.e. from the entrance wall): a winged demon climbs a rock (18), another (not winged) (17) sits with two bearded snakes in his hands looking back at the first demon. A third winged demon (16) pushes a woman (15) guided by the hand of a fourth one (14); they are met by a young boy (13) and a veiled woman (12). Behind the woman is a boat with a rudder and an unnamed person (11) on board. This last scene bears a clear resemblance to the Greek Charon shipping dead souls to Hades across the river Styx, demonstrating well from where this unique pictorial theme in Etruscan art was borrowed. We are in a hereafter setting beyond the tomb.[16]

On stylistic grounds, correlated with the date of the fragmentary remains of objects found in the grave and in the backfill of its entrance (the tomb had already been violated when excavated), the paintings have been dated to 450–430 BC (or slightly later);[17] this is some 2–3 generations earlier than other tomb paintings considered to show scenes from the nether world.[18]

This tomb has quieted, but not fully silenced, the supporters of a political explanation for the iconological change;[19] for the supporters of the eschatological explanation nothing has changed, except for the date of the earliest influences of nether world mysteries from areas outside Etruria.

What are the reasons for this iconological change in Etruscan funerary art? Are they due to a ritual change, to changing rituals, or shall we look at the change, not as a change in the Etruscan perception of life after death, but rather as a continuity?

To answer this I shall apply two concepts to keep apart when studying material culture in social contexts: content and form.[20] *Content* is related to the cosmological ideas, myths, and *aitia* with which members of a society use to explain social customs and phenomena. *Form*, on the other hand, is the way in which the content is presented. Content is less liable to be exposed to change than form (thus being synchronic in character), and a change of form (being diachronic in character) does not necessarily indicate a change in content. Likewise, celebrations containing similar forms do not necessarily have the same content. However, by equating content and form one risks to give synchronic answers to diachronic phenomena.[21] My point of departure is thus not to look primarily on what impact external political situations and/or eschatological ideas may have had on the Etruscans' vision of death and afterlife, but rather to look at the Etruscans' visions of death as a social phenomenon and process to which the surviving relatives gave expression.

The *content* in the present funerary context are the ideas which the Etruscans had about death and afterlife, in other words their eschatology. The *form* is the way in which the Etruscans expressed their ideas of death and afterlife in funerary material and practices, which in the present context means the pictorial themes in painted tombs, as, for example, dances, games, processions, banquets, erotic plays, etc., or, in other words, the funerary iconography. Similar themes can be found in contemporary funerary sculpture in the shape of sarcophagi, ash urns, and grave markers and these will be referred to as the arguments are disclosed. The material to be examined here represents the ideas of the elite, but they are not necessarily much different from the beliefs of the other contemporary social groups of the same society, which through time appropriated many of the elite's forms of expression.[22]

The purpose of this presentation is not to look at tomb paintings (and some sculpture) as isolated monuments, but to investigate if there is a common idea or content, a kind of common denominator, behind the monuments which bind them all together – the guiding concepts in the presentation being ritual practices and iconography.

Tarquinia, with its great corpus of preserved tomb paintings, will be used as a test case, but tomb paintings were only one form through which eschatological ideas were transmitted. The Etruscan cities had each its own way of expressing funerary form, but if these different forms also expressed different eschatological contents shall not be considered. However, the cities were not isolated nuclei without external contacts, I should therefore expect that the differences in form is not the result of major differences in the Etruscans' experiences of death, rather of local traditions and physical milieus. The few tomb paintings found in other cities like Cerveteri, Chiusi, Orvieto, Veii, Vulci, and others (see Appendix A) (Fig. 5.1), follow all thematically the Tarquinian model and may thus be used as an argument to sustain the postulation.

Off to Greece – an iconographical connection

All societies are bounded by a set of common rules, norms, and values; some are juridical written in law codices and checked by established control bodies, others are ethical and maintained by common consent through controlling concepts like honour, taboo, purity, etc. While the first can normally only be changed by the same powers which implemented them, the others can change gradually by manipulating and challenging the controlling concepts of the common consent – a sort of social self-criticism, be that conscious or unconscious.

As for taboos, for example, let us, within the argument of death, see how this has changed over some generations within our own Western society. As a guide, I shall use how death has been presented for over a century in crime stories on film and TV. In early films blood was in short supply at murder scenes. The viewing public and the victim on the screen were respected and spared from undue violence. With Arthur Penn's film *Bonnie and Clyde* in 1967 the old taboo was broken. The final shoot-out of the two folk heroes was shown as realistically as possible, and since then there has been no limit to how much blood has flooded the Big Screen. However, the corpses as such were respected, no matter how much violence they had been exposed to. Today, when the TV set has become an ever-present guest at the dinner table in many homes, in a number of soap operas, you are invited into the forensic departments, where, in the name of realism and science, post-mortem examinations are served as the main side-dish. But this cinematic change in presenting the dead has not changed our visions of death and the possible world beyond.

In many ancient societies a presentation of the world beyond death may have been considered a taboo. In the Greek society, for example, the nether world is described by Homer in the 11th song in the *Odyssey*, but in the poem's near contemporary Geometric Period, figural presentations of ceremonies of death are confined to *prothesis*- and *ekphora*-scenes on grave markers in the shape of amphorae and kraters.[23] An early 6th century BC Corinthian kotyle shows Herakles, accompanied by Hermes, in a confrontation with Persephone and Hades, the last one running off towards the left, while the guardian dog Kerberos heads off to the right.[24] But this presentation of the Underworld is an exception. It is not till the last quarter of the same century that figures of the Underworld, like Hades,[25] Persephone (in her Underworld state),[26] Kerberos,[27] Sisyphos,[28] Thanatos,[29] Hypnos,[30] and Charon[31] begin to appear with some frequency on Athenian black- and red-figure vases, though not all always in their Underworld habitat. In the following century Charon in his boat takes the lead on a group of white ground lekythoi produced in particular for funerary uses at home.[32] Furthermore, in southern Italy, at Lokri, in this early 5th century BC, terracotta plaques had also taken up the Underworld theme with Persephone on a throne alone or together with Hades receiving other gods and young girls.[33] So, when Polygnotos painted his *Nekyia* in the Cnidian lesche at Delphi in the second quarter of the 5th century BC,[34] he built on an already established tradition, but his painting may have given new impetus to the theme even if, despite the fame of the murals, 'there was no systematic dissemination of the *Nekyia* images into the repertory of images used in Attic vase-painting'.[35] The reason may be that the painting was exhibited in a place far away from the important vase production centres and could not easily be copied.

However, it appears that the transition into the world beyond did not find much enthusiasm with the Greeks. Having overcome the taboo of revealing the secrets of the other world the Athenian artists did not carry the theme any further. Charon's presence in funerary art and the dead heroes became a short interlude. By the end of the 5th century BC the white lekythoi had been replaced by sculpted grave stones, which in the figural representations brought the funerary motifs solidly back into the world of the living. It was only from the middle of the 4th century BC, with the Apulians in southern Italy, that the Underworld theme would find further development. In a series of large amphora and volute krater grave markers Hades and Persephone appear under a large white-painted *naiskos* or temple-pavilion in the midst of many Greek heroes, including Orpheus, normally placed close to the reigning couple of the Underworld.[36]

In *T. dei Demoni Azzurri* (phase 4) we recognised Charon and his boat, a motif certainly borrowed from the Greek sphere, whether from the white lekythoi or through some other channels.[37] The rocky landscape is a curiosity, but could have been inspired by Sisyphos' punishment scenes, in which an Underworld rock (defining the borders of the otherworldly space) is present;[38] the demon furthest to the right even borrows the climbing posture from the punished Greek to underline the massive expanse of the borderline area. The central demon, without wings, has been identified with Eutynomos in Polygnotos' *Nekyia*, the corpse eating demon sitting on a vulture's hide at the entrance to the Greek Underworld – here transformed into a human figure with a vulture's talon and beak.[39] In sum, elements are borrowed from Greek models, but they have been transformed into what appears to be a pictorial world of the afterlife which is mainly Etruscan. One might suggest that the Greek pictorial world has functioned only as a catalyst for changing the Etruscan world thereafter from an abstract idea into a more apprehensive image.

So far the *T. dei Demoni Azzurri* is unique within the Etruscan funerary pictorial repertoire. In later presentations Charon – or Charu(n) – has left his boat and exchanged the steering oar for a mallet, as shown in a few 5th century BC Felsinian grave stelae.[40] The mallet was used to unbolt and bolt the door into the Underworld: thus the old ferryman has become its guardian.[41] He works alone or is accompanied by the female Vanth, who also often moves alone. The three nameless demons in the *T. dei Demoni Azzurri* may reappear among named or unnamed demons in other funerary contexts, and underline that the Etruscans imagined the other world peopled by ugly, more or less terrifying demons, whose presence, as we shall see, was mainly to make sure the deceased should reach his/her destination.

Back to Etruria the liminal way – some further iconographical considerations

The Etruscan pictorial world is characterised by a syncoptic or acronymistic narrative style, which means that the number of iconographical elements are heavily reduced in order to impart a message to the viewer. This becomes especially apparent when we now shall pass from Greek iconographical borrowings and Etruscan syncoptic narrative styles to the transformation of the Greek Underworld into the Etruscan apprehension of this otherworldly space. To do this we shall have to ask: *What are the important pictorial themes in Etruscan funerary art from the 6th and the 5th centuries BC, before the emergence of the nether world scenes?* – No two tombs are alike in their combination of pictorial themes, but seen together some singular pictorial motifs (here called parameters) are more common than others, here listed chronologically as they appear in the tomb paintings (for details, see Appendix B):

A. Heraldic birds and animals, both real and mythical; animal battle scenes in a heraldic setting; Gorgoneia; 'lararium' type snakes.
B. Subjects alluding to sea/water: boats/ships, dolphins, hippocamps, sea/water snakes, Tritons, waves.
C. Closed doors: squared or arched.
D. Unconventional scenes: *cornuto* sign, bodily fluid emission scenes, erotic scenes, scenes with reference to laughter, phallus bird, purification sacrifices, pygmies – and (in a Hellenistic grave) skeletons in boxes.
E. Banquets, often accompanied by music (in both this world and the Underworld).
F. Dances, most often accompanied by music.
G. Scenes with blood, visible and potentially visible: Phersu, flogging, boxers, wrestlers, warriors, fights, and killings.
H. Athletic games (excluding boxers and wrestlers: see parameter G), tug of war, and chariot races.
I. Ritual objects: *thymiateria* and oversized kylikes.
J. Horsemen (excluding mythical contexts and hunting scenes).
K. Hunting scenes.
L. Prothesis and related scenes.
M. Weapon (or Pyrrhic) dances.

What do these scenes refer to? – For some scholars the pictorial motifs in Etruscan funerary paintings refer to funerary rituals,[42] in which case they may refer to rituals which took part after the moment of death, but before the interment of the deceased, whether the body was inhumed or cremated. This means at the moment when, following Arnold van Gennep's model on passage rites, both the deceased and the participants in the funerary ceremony found themselves in the liminal phase of transition, between the phase of separation (the moment of death) and the phase of reintegration (after the interment of the deceased).[43] In funerary rites this transitional phase was the most critical, during which all participating members normally found themselves temporarily suspended from normal social life;[44] they were in a border land in which strong powers and dangers were released and in which abnormal activities connected to dirt, obscenities, and lawlessness symbolically were just as relevant for the performance of the rites as were more normal actions.[45]

Societies reacted in different ways to this liminal period. An example close to our own time from Rome illustrates this well, as described by an eyewitness, when Pope Clemens IX died on December 9, 1669. At the announcement of death the big Capitol bell started to peal and continued without interruption for three full days and nights – until the Pope's body had been transferred from the Quirinal, where he died, to St Peter's.[46] In these days the situation in Rome became 'unsafe due to robbery, murder, and similar non deadly assaults, in that no justice was held, nor malefactors arrested.' Every person had to see to their own protection till the bell stopped, when 'the inquisition' duly followed. But whatever protection was arranged, much mischief and many homicides occurred; at this occasion three persons, in fact, were deliberately trampled to death by horses.[47]

According to van Gennep 'those funeral rites which incorporate the deceased into the world of the dead are most extensively elaborated and assigned the greatest importance.'[48] Since the Etruscans appear to have been much concerned about the afterlife, it may not come as a surprise that tomb paintings and sculpture refer to this critical transitional phase. But what did the transitional rituals consist of, what was their significance, and how was this told in figurative terms?

The moment of death triggered a set of social mechanisms and funerary actions in which the deceased should be honoured according to his/her social standing and merits. At the same time the corpse became a source of pollution, which had to be counteracted with rituals of purification,[49] and measures had to be taken in order to help the deceased on his/her journey to the other world. Accordingly, in this liminal phase the funerary actions were of a threefold nature: honouring of the dead, alleviation of the deceased's journey to the Underworld, and purification of the funerary celebrants – at times the three kinds of actions may have overlapped.

The parameters listed above may thus be divided into three funerary physical and mental spheres regarding the deceased. Of these parameters heraldic animals (A) and banquets (E) dominate on the rear wall, while the other parameters are spread out on the other three walls without following a strongly repetitive pattern:

1. The celebration of the deceased: death, honour, and afterlife (parameters B, C, H, J, K, L, M)
2. The liminal journey of the deceased: actions and counteractions (parameters A, D, F, G)
3. The interment of the deceased: purification and reintegration (parameters E, I)

The division is artificial; it was not organised as such in the minds of the Etruscans. The parameters and their meaning are separated into modern, virtual compartments in an attempt to discover some sort of organisational pattern in the use of the pictorial motifs – and through this pattern discover the Etruscan view on death and the meaning of their funerary practices as conveyed through art expressions.

The celebration of the deceased: death, honour, and afterlife

The pictorial themes in this first group of parameters refer to the deceased (parameters K and L), to the celebrations of the deceased (parameters H and M), to the tomb (parameter C), and the journey to the Underworld (parameters B and J).

Fig. 5.3. Tarquinia, T. del Morente, *rear wall (with kind permission of Ministero per i Beni e le Attività Culturali, Soprintendenza per i beni archeologici dell'Etruria Meridionale, Museo di Villa Giulia; photo no. 138666).*

The deceased and death: Hunting and prothesis (parameters K and L)

On Greek Geometric funerary vases, *prothesis-* and *ekphora-*scenes dominated the pictorial repertoire, and *prothesis-*scenes were a recurring theme in Attic vase-painting similarly later.[50] In the Archaic-Classical *cippus* base reliefs from Chiusi *prothesis-*scenes are not uncommon,[51] but in tomb paintings they are rare. Only three examples are known, all from Tarquinia: *T. del Morto* (phase 2:89), *T. del Morente* (phase 2:88) (Fig. 5.3), and *T. del Letto Funebre* (phase 3:82).[52] Emotional expressions like wailing occur,[53] but here it appears not to be a theme of great interest and concern. The tomb paintings (and funerary reliefs) demonstrate that the dead corpse was displayed in honourable circumstances (on a kind of *lit de parade*), but apparently it was not the moment of death (or the presentation of the dead), nor the interment of the dead (never presented pictorially) which concerned the Etruscans most, rather what happened in between these two events – in this funerary liminal phase. Though this does not mean that the deceased did not figure in funerary paintings and sculpture. We shall give more examples of their presence later.

Hunting scenes have no immediate reference to funerary practices, but may refer to the social status of the deceased, that is a person of the élite with whom hunting was

Fig. 5.4. Chiusi, T. della Scimmia, *entrance wall, corner with right right wall (with kind permission of American Academy in Rome, Photographic Archive; photo no. Moscioni 10534).*

not only an exciting game, but also an expression of social adherence. Such pictorial scenes may thus be considered part of the honours paid to the deceased (cf. Fig. 5.2a).

Honour: Athletic games and weapon dances (parameters H and M)

Funerary games in the shape of chariot races and athletic competitions most likely were introduced from Greece and performed in honour of the dead – a practice presumably reserved for the élite. It is assumed that such contests more had the character of celebrating the dead than being part of a funerary liminal ideology.

Likewise weapon dances – or Pyrrhic dances – were imported from Greece, or perhaps, more precisely, from Athens. In connection with the introduction of democracy at Athens in the late 6th century BC, the city's most important religious festival, the yearly Panathenaia, was reformed both in its organisation and programme. One reform was the introduction of Pyrrhic dances, performed as a competition between *phylai* – in this way tying the new political and administrative organisation to ritual performances. Attic black figure vases demonstrate that the Pyrrhic dances were not only performed during the yearly festival, but also at funerals.[54] From here the new fashion may also have reached Etruria, though whether the Etruscans incorporated it only as a new, fashionable athletic game or transformed it into a meaningful element

Fig. 5.5. Tarquinia, T. degli Auguri, *rear wall (with kind permission of Ministero per i Beni e le Attività Culturali, Soprintendenza per i beni archeologici dell'Etruria Meridionale, Museo di Villa Giulia; photo no. MAX7042).*

of their funerary liminal ideology, perhaps with reference to blood (see below), is at present difficult to decide (Fig. 5.4).

Afterlife I: False doors (parameter C)

T. dei Demoni Azzurri (phase 4) was the earliest Etruscan tomb to depict an explicit reference to the world of the dead, but it was not the first tomb to refer to a world beyond that of the living. It is generally agreed that painted false doors of the *dorica* type (i.e. with marked, vertical door jambs and horizontal lintel) on the tomb walls 'symbolise the boundary between the worlds of the living and of the dead'[55] (Fig. 5.5). The false door motif appears already in the earliest paintings from the first half of the 6th century BC at Tarquinia, dies out in the second quarter of the following century, but reappears, now arched, in a new setting, from the second half of the 4th century BC.[56] In its first phase, it is most often combined with scenes of dance and music (parameter F) or boxers/wrestlers and other kinds of fighting scenes (parameter G), often with blood running; in its second phase, the door is associated with the nether world demons Charu(n) and Vanth. However, is it conceptually the same door? An answer shall be given later. For the time being suffice it to look at the false door as an entrance to the world beyond, an entrance which can only be entered after the time of death.

Afterlife II: Water scenes and horsemen (parameters B and J)

A long series of pictorial elements, either narratively or purely decoratively, allude to sea/water: boats/ships, dolphins, hippocamps, sea/water snakes, Tritons, waves (parameter B).[57] These motifs are most often interpreted as symbols referring to the journey made by the deceased on his/her way to the Underworld.[58] The Greeks had to cross the river Styx to arrive at Hades; Acheron, giving name to the *Acherontic Books* (containing the *sacra Acheruntia* or the Etruscan 'Rituals of the Underworld'[59]), was the name of one of the major rivers of the Etruscan Underworld. Apparently in both cultures the crossing of water was considered as part of the approach to the world of the dead, but the way a Greek or an Etruscan crossed these waters may not have been the same. These pictorial elements, referring to the hereafter liminal journey, presented in a very syncoptic way, are the only ones which can be followed through every phase of Etruscan tomb paintings from Archaic to Hellenistic times, though varying in popularity from one period to another.[60] In these scenes we have mentally penetrated the false door (parameter C) and moved into the first stage of an Etruscan vision of life after death.

   For part of the liminal journey the dead were accompanied by one or more horsemen (parameter J), 'the traditional Etruscan allegorical representation of the voyage to the Underworld',[61] at times interpreted as the Dioscuri, the protectors of travellers,[62] or passage/door gods.[63] This is well expressed in *T. del Barone* (phase 2: 44) (Fig. 5.6). On the rear wall (*c*) of the tomb is depicted, flanked by two horsemen, a bearded man carrying a large kylix in his out-stretched left hand, and with the right he accompanies a young flute player. In front of, but separated from them by a single-stemmed tree, stands a woman in a long dress with a veiled *tutulus*;[64] she has raised both hands in some kind of greeting gesture. The music signals a sacred act with the very large kylix (parameter I) possibly referring to a funerary libation. The single stemmed tree(?) divides the space in two, as it can also be observed on a slightly later bronze mirror where a tree distinguishes between outside and inside.[65] The veiled woman appears as the 'object' of the libation, but not as a living person; she has already crossed the border and it is offered to her in an otherworldly space. This central scene is in its turn separated from the horsemen by branched trees, placing them in still a different funerary space. The horsemen reappear on both sidewalls: on the right wall (*a*) the two horsemen stand antithetically, each with his horse; on the left wall (*b*) they flank the dead *tutulus* woman already met on the rear wall (*c*). In their function as attendants of the deceased to the Underworld the walls can be read as three stages in a death journey narrative: the horsemen's preparation for the journey (right wall); the moment of their departure together with the dead woman (left wall); and the dead woman's safe arrival in the Underworld, made possible through the funerary rites and sealed with the duly performed sacrifices and libations.[66] If this interpretation is valid, already by the end of the 6th century BC in Etruria can be observed a vision of the deceased's journey in the liminal space between this world and the Underworld, a world which iconographically had not yet found its pictorial expression. However, the trees separating the horsemen from the central scene on the rear wall signify that the horsemen belong to the liminal space, not to the world of the living, nor to the Underworld.

The horsemen are thus attendants of the deceased. At times there are more than two appearing in a kind of procession, as visible in *T. delle Iscrizioni* (phase 2:74) (Fig. 5.7) and *T. dei Pigmei* (phase 4:97). In none of these 'processions' can the deceased be identified. We should therefore look at the horsemen only as attendants, symbolically representing the deceased on her/his liminal journey, and not search for the deceased among them.

It may seem strange to see persons appearing in the same painting representing both the deceased and the bereaved, but this constellation can be followed all through the Etruscan tomb paintings. In *T. dei Giocolieri* (phase 2:70), for example, the person seated on a *sella curulis*, dressed in the regal *toga purpurea*, to the right on the rear wall, may by his attributes be identified with the deceased person – perhaps a magistrate[67] (Fig. 5.8). In *T. degli Auguri* (phase 2:42) a similarly dressed person on the right wall, accompanied by a young slave carrying his *sella curulis* (cf. Figs 5.5 & 5.13 left) may likewise be the presentation of another deceased magistrate.[68] In a world where either the Underworld was still a taboo, or the society lacked a proper picture of it, the deceased is present overseeing that the funerary rites, made to help him on his otherworldly journey, are held in a proper way. Later the deceased can be found in funerary processions, both as a charioteer and on foot, often carefully guarded by the death demon Charu(n).[69]

The liminal journey of the deceased: actions and counteractions

In the first group of parameters we found references to the deceased's social status (and the honours which followed that) and to the journey of the dead, accompanied by horsemen towards the Underworld, made in a space beyond this world, marked by false doors. What happened in this journey of the dead the 6th and 5th century BC tomb paintings do not reveal – instead the paintings may show some of the actions and counteractions the living funerary celebrants engaged in to help the deceased on his/her journey, as already indicated.

In the following I shall concentrate in particular on four pictorial themes listed for the liminal journey: heraldic birds and animals (parameter A), unconventional scenes (parameter D), dancing (parameter F), and scenes referring to blood (parameter G) – in order to see what function they may have had in the set of actions the Etruscans established to counteract the dangers and fears they believed were set loose at the time of death.

An important key to the reading of the tomb paintings in this light is *T. della Fustigazione* (phase 3:67),[70] in which heraldic animals, dancing, blood, and the unconventional are all present: In the pediment of both the entrance and rear wall are presented heraldic animal fights. The rear and the side walls all have a central false door

Fig. 5.6. Tarquinia, T. del Barone: a) right wall; b) left wall; c) rear wall (with kind permission of Ministero per i Beni e le Attività Culturali, Soprintendenza per i beni archeologici dell'Etruria Meridionale, Museo di Villa Giulia; photo nos. 8909D (a), 8903D (b), MAX 7068 (c)).

Fig. 5.7. Tarquinia, Tomba delle Iscrizioni, *left wall, corner with rear wall (with kind permission of American Academy in Rome, Photographic Archive; photo no. Moscioni 24111).*

Fig. 5.8. Tarquinia, T. dei Giocolieri, *rear wall (with kind permission of Ministero per i Beni e le Attività Culturali, Soprintendenza per i beni archeologici dell'Etruria Meridionale, Museo di Villa Giulia; photo no. 138598).*

Fig. 5.9. Tarquinia, T. della Fustigazione, *right wall (with kind permission of Ministero per i Beni e le Attività Culturali, Soprintendenza per i beni archeologici dell'Etruria Meridionale, Museo di Villa Giulia; photo nos. 117722 (a), 117723 (b)).*

flanked by various figures and figure scenes. On the rear wall the door is flanked on the left by a dancing kithara-player with an amphora standing on the ground in front of him, on the right by a male dancer with a large kylix in his right extended hand. Two boxers, ready to fight each other, flank the real door on the entrance wall, while on the left wall the false door is flanked on the left by a dancer with a kylix held high above his head, and on the right by a flute player. The right wall presents two erotic scenes (Fig. 5.9): on the left a naked woman with *tutulus*(?) 'embraces a young man amorously, while a bearded man tries to penetrate her from behind'[71]; on the right a naked woman, also with a *tutulus*(?) bends forward towards the hip region of a half-naked man with a satisfied smile (is she performing a fellatio?), while at the same time she is beaten with a whip on a stick by a half-naked young man who approaches from behind and has placed his other hand on her buttocks. – The heraldic animals and the dancing are easily recognisable, the blood is represented by the boxers and the flogged woman, and the unconventional scenes by the two erotic groups, of which the last one may even contain an element of laughter.

Actions: Heraldic animals and birds (parameter A)
Heraldic birds and animals (both real and mythological ones), including animal battle scenes in heraldic settings (cf. Figs 5.5, 5.8, 5.17, 5.24), Gorgoneia, and 'lararium' type snakes (Fig. 5.22) are the most numerous pictorial motifs in the tomb paintings.[72] They are nearly always to be found in the rear pediment of the tomb, perhaps the most important pictorial space – 'similar to temple pediments ... apparently considered to be a superhuman, sacred space'.[73] Heraldic animals and birds figure often in Etruscan art from the Orientalising Period (from the 8th century BC onwards) borrowed from Greek and other Eastern sources. The Archaic presentation of them is often maintained in the tombs, as if to underline their age and apotropaic powers.[74] In their apotropaic powers they were presumably considered both as guardians of the tomb and of the deceased, not only in a generic way, but perhaps in particular as protectors against the strong transcendental powers and dangers released at the moment of death. In this way they helped the deceased on her/his journey to the Underworld.

Counteraction I: Dancing (parameter F)
The dancing scenes in Etruscan tombs are characterised by being individual for both men and women, often underlined by separating trees: never do the dancers touch each other, nor do they act in a concerted manner[75] (Figs 5.10, 5.15, 5.23b). Each dancer determines his/her own actions. The dances are 'spirited, strenuous, even unrestrained', with great gesticulations, but they often lack the Dionysiac frenzies.[76] All the same the Dionysiac label is often given to these dances, whether directly or indirectly, by referring to the dancers as *komasts* (among whom women participated only occasionally).[77] However, one must be careful when giving Greek terms to Etruscan scenes. Not all spirited, unrestrained dances are necessarily Dionysiac. In his analysis of the Chiusan

Fig. 5.10. Tarquinia, T. dei Baccanti, *left wall (with kind permission of Ministero per i Beni e le Attività Culturali, Soprintendenza per i beni archeologici dell'Etruria Meridionale, Museo di Villa Giulia; photo no. 8893D).*

cippus base reliefs, Jean-René Jannot distinguished between two categories of funerary dances: those he named 'a programme' and free dances, each having its own function within the funerary rituals.[78] The tomb paintings may also be inserted into such a pattern; however, since my interpretative approach is slightly different from that of Jannot, I should like to make a distinction between three possible contexts of dancing, in most cases accompanied by music: a barbiton, a flute, a kitharos, a lyre, or by a combination of two or more musical instruments:

1. Dionysiac *komasts*: In this group the merry revellers are all men and all, or most of them, carry their own vase used for containing, serving, or drinking wine, as in *T. delle Iscrizioni* (phase 2:74) (see Fig. 5.19), but in no other tomb.

2. Ritual performance: In many tombs one or occasionally two male dancers carry a large kylix, most often close to the body (as on the rear wall of *T. dei Baccanti* (phase 2:43)) or on an out-stretched arm (as on the rear wall in *T. 5591* (phase 3:154)). It is carried out-stretched in the same way by the central male figure in *T. del Barone* (phase 2:44) (Fig. 5.5c), a scene which has no reference to drinking and dancing, but, as we saw above, rather to libation. In such scenes the accent is most likely more on the kylix as a ritual object rather than as a merry-making drinking cup.[79]

3. Spirited, unrestrained dancing: Both male and females perform without drinking vessels, the women at times having brought *krotala*, or castanets along.[80] Here

occurs an overlap with the ritual performers, as occasionally a spirited dancer carries the large kylix, perhaps the result of a narrative syncoptic style, which has combined the spirited dance and the ritual performance in one picture. It is interesting to note that none of the dancers on the Chiusian cippus base reliefs ever carry a wine vessel.

If in this last group of dancing, wine does not play a central role, could it be that the spritited dance was not performed to celebrate Dionysos, but had another particular function within the funerary ritual?

Wine is not essential for spirited and unrestrained dancing; it can also be created through the rhythm of the music, castanets, and a competitive togetherness. In a funerary context dance could be used to express sorrow and wailing by pulling hair, scratching cheeks, tearing clothes, or chest beating, but this is not the case here.[81] Dance could also be performed to 'express a desire to turn ... attention away from the contemplation of death, which holds only fear, sorrow, and uncertainty ...'[82], or in its bodily expression of motion, order and joy, it could be experienced as an antithesis to the 'still, lifeless, polluting corpse.'[83] However, in many societies, spirited dancing has also been used to come in contact with transcendental forces. I therefore suggest, as a theory, that in Etruscan funerary practices the dance may have been considered important because through the dance the performers could be brought into a trance, which in the next instance could bring them in contact with such forces outside their own body and cognitive world; forces which in one way or the other could be warded off, or perhaps even manipulated to help the deceased on his/her journey to the Underworld.[84]

In the year 364 BC a plague broke out in Rome. Scenic entertainments were instituted as a last effort to appease the wrath of the gods. At this occasion, Livy (7.2) tells, also mimes (lat. *ludiones*), accompanied by flutes, were brought in from Etruria to perform dances – 'not ungraceful evolutions in the Tuscan fashion'. Apparently Etruscans were famous for their dancing and the effect it could have on transcendental forces.[85]

Counteraction II: Scenes referring to blood (parameter G)

According to the late Roman author Arnobius, in the *Acherontic Books*, the Etruscans promised 'that by the blood of certain animals, divine souls (*animae*) become endowed with certain numinous spirits and they would be led away from the laws of mortality.'[86] In other words, a blood sacrifice was able to give immortality to dead souls.[87]

No tomb painting displays an animal sacrifice,[88] but on a funerary relief from Chiusi an ox/cow is brought forward to an altar, certainly in order to be sacrificed (Fig. 5.11). The fire on the top of the altar is lit and next to it is placed a *thymiaterion*, or incense burner;[89] incense was used for purification, an important act in connection with sacrifices. – So when *thymiateria* appear in Etruscan tombs (parameter I),[90] most famous being the one in *T. dei Giocolieri* (phase 2:70) (Fig. 5.8),[91] they refer symbolically to funerary acts of purification (in which also a blood sacrifice could have been performed). What is actually portrayed in the painting of the *T. dei Giocolieri* is difficult to say, but

*Fig. 5.11. Paris, Louvre Ma 3610, funerary relief from Chiusi (copied from http://commons.wikimedia.org/
wiki/File:Louvre,_frammento_di_urna_cineraria_da_chiusi,_con_scena_di_sacrificio.JPG#metadata, under
the terms of the* GNU Free Documentation Licence).

Fig. 5.12. Chiusi, Tomba della Scimmia *entrance wall, left side (with kind permission of American Academy
in Rome, Photographic Archive; photo no. Moscioni 10498).*

an interesting guess would be that after purification, a game was instituted by which
competitors tried to extinguish the purification fire by throwing round objects – and
perhaps a certain funerary privilege or attention was awarded the winner.[92]

Fig. 5.13. Tarquinia, T. degli Auguri, *right wall (reconstruction drawing; with kind permission of American Academy in Rome, Photographic Archive; photo no. Moscioni 24133).*

If no animal blood sacrifice has been recorded in the tomb paintings, scenes with the flowing of human blood are not infrequent, as in some scenes with wrestlers and boxers[93] (Figs 5.12, 5.13, 5.23) in an erotic flogging scene (Fig. 5.9),[94] in ferocious games led by a masked person named Phersu (Fig. 5.13),[95] to which should be added also a late decapitation and combat scene.[96] The armed, blood-running combats, visible in Lucanian tomb paintings from the 4th century BC (mainly), most likely belong to the same cognitive world.[97] Could such blood-thirsty scenes have served the same purpose as the animal sacrifices, to give immortality to the deceased's soul?[98] At death the blood stops running; flowing blood in a ritual context would thus be a symbol of life. Tertullian's observation that '… earlier, since it was believed that the spirits of the dead could be appeased with human blood, they used at funerals to sacrifice prisoners of war or slaves of poor quality…', may be a reflection of this kind of thinking.[99]

This may in the next instance explain why gladiatorial combats grew out of funerary games,[100] and why such combats (*munera*) continued to be a returning ingredient in later Roman funerary ceremonies and commemorative feasts for dead persons. Their popularity among the public eventually turned these spectacles into shows arranged to attract political support (in some cases on the pretext of being funerary or commemorative), and over time lost their strong funerary connection.[101] Instead the gladiator became an example of 'male self-control in the face of death',[102] and thus an old funerary ritual of life gradually changed into a display of death, in which was created a tension between the fight as *spectaculum* and the fight as *exemplum*.[103] The old tension between death and the life-giving blood, procured through fighting, was thus buried.

Counteractions III: Unconventional scenes (parameter D)

The unconventional scenes, which appear to have reference to disorder and pollution, purification and apotropaic magic, I have divided into two generic groups with reference to the body:

1. Scenes referring to bodily functions I: erotic and bodily fluid emission scenes

Erotic scenes may seem out of context in a funerary situation, but they do appear even if not frequently. The oldest Etruscan funerary item with reference to sexual play is the Etrusco-Corinthian jug (630–600) found in a chamber tomb at Tragliatella, inland from Cerveteri. In an incised frieze around the vase appear two male-female copulation acts, one placed above the other – the exact meaning much discussed.[104] In tomb paintings sexual acts of various sorts are documented: in *T. dei Tori* (both a threesome with two males and one female and a twosome male-male copulation act)

Fig. 5.14. Tarquinia, T. dei Tori: *a) erotic scene from the rear wall (with kind permission of Ministero per i Beni e le Attività Culturali, Soprintendenza per i beni archeologici dell'Etruria Meridionale, Museo di Villa Giulia; photo no. 138714); b) erotic scene from the rear wall (with kind permission of American Academy in Rome, Photographic Archive; photo no. Moscioni 24120).*

Fig. 5.15. Tarquinia, T. delle Leonesse, *rear wall, detail (with kind permission of Ministero per i Beni e le Attività Culturali, Soprintendenza per i beni archeologici dell'Etruria Meridionale, Museo di Villa Giulia; photo no. IMG_0096).*

(phase 2:120) (Fig. 5.14); *T. della Fustigazione* (two threesome acts with two males and a female, one with a possible anal penetration, the second with a possible fellatio-act) (phase 3:67) (Fig. 5.9); *T. 4260* (badly damaged, but on the side walls traces of two- and threesome erotic groups) (phase 3:156); and *T. delle Bighe* (among others, scenes of foreplay and copulation between young males) (phase 3:47). In *T. delle Leonesse* (phase 2:77) a young, black-haired woman, without *tutulus*, in light, translucent dress dances to the rhythm of her castanets up against a young, blond, naked man carrying a jug matching her movements (Fig. 5.15) – the scene exudes of eroticism, but the erotic play is not so explicit as presented in the other paintings. With her left hand the woman makes a *cornuto*-sign, perhaps warding off evil.[105]

Mary Douglas in her discussion of pollution and taboo considered the body as a model for any confined system, the body openings thus being the border areas considered vulnerable and exposed to danger.[106] Therefore, copulations and the emission of bodily fluids can in metaphorical terms be considered as transgressions of the borders of the social and cultural order, causing pollution and disorder, which need to be repaired by acts of purification. The strange defecation scene in *T. dei Giocolieri* (phase 2:70) (Fig. 5.16) may be seen in the same context: having transgressed the borders of the body, the bodily wastes become a metaphorical picture of the pollution and disorder caused in the liminal area of the funerary process, when the social and cultural order has been abolished.[107] On the right entrance wall to *T. delle Iscrizioni* (phase 2:74), a white-haired man with a round belly, presented in the act of urinating into a low basin (Fig 5.17),[108] might be explained along the same lines – the ritual aspect of this act underlined by the ribbon tied around the head of the man's penis.

The *thymiaterion* used in *T. dei Giocolieri* (Fig. 5.8) could therefore well be an expression of the purification acts implemented to repair the disorder in the liminal space caused by the border transgressions. However, the copulation scenes (Figs 5.9, 5.14) may at the same time refer to a transcendental dimension caused by orgasm. At that particular moment are released forces in the body, which bring the performers into a transcendental space outside him-/herself, where he/she may come in contact with transcendental forces with which the safe journey of the dead soul could be negotiated and defended. Orgasm, as well as dancing, are thus only two different ways of getting into contact with the other world; sometimes, as perhaps implied by the erotic dance in *T. delle Leonesse* (Fig. 5.15) the one may lead to the other, a phenomenon observed in primitive societies,[109] and not unknown (in a secular way) in both a Roman Late Republican[110] and a modern disco culture. In such a setting the males sitting under the stands in *T. delle Bighe*, shall perhaps not be interpreted as servants,[111] but as males performing disorderly ritual acts in a funerary liminal context.

A further tomb, *T. del Topolino* (phase 2:119) may also belong to the same conceptual world, but with a different twist: on the left side wall flies a phallus-bird (Fig. 5.18),[112] a motif borrowed directly from Greek models.[113] The bird having an apotropaic function may have been included to ward off the liminal evils and dangers – the possible ejaculation of semen,[114] a sign of orgasm, being an indirect reference to the transcendental space in which these evils and dangers belonged.[115]

However, it is wise to show some prudence in putting all scenes of apparently similar content under the same interpretative umbrella. Each scene has to be evaluated in its proper pictorial context. Returning to *T. delle Iscrizioni* (phase 2:74) it cannot be excluded that the urinating scene described above may have had a completely different meaning. The white-haired man, facing left, raises his right hand in a gesture of greeting(?), in the left he carries a long stick with a split end (symbol of an official position?). Opposite him a naked boy bends forward holding a short stick in each hand, giving the scene a further narrative content (Fig. 5.17). On the left entrance wall two naked men stand gesticulating on either side of a round table, discuses hanging on the wall. Above the head of the urinating man is written his family name: Matve. The same family name, together with the first name Larth, appears above the head of the front white-haired *komast* on the right wall, the only one carrying wreaths.[116] He is naked(?)[117] and presented slightly isolated from the other *komasts* (also they are named through inscriptions) on the same wall (Fig. 5.19). The two white-haired persons appear to be the same, possibly the deceased. Carlo Ruspi in his drawing of the entrance wall did not notice the white-haired man's fluid emission jet and he interpreted the object held by the naked boy in his left hand, not as a stick, but as a fish.[118] For this reason the two scenes on the entrance wall have been seen as part of a sacrificial act,[119] a situation which

Fig. 5.16. Tarquinia, T. dei Giocolieri, *left wall, detail (with kind permission of Ministero per i Beni e le Attività Culturali, Soprintendenza per i beni archeologici dell'Etruria Meridionale, Museo di Villa Giulia; photo no. 138600).*

cannot be sustained anymore (and which, by the way, was never shown so directly in tomb paintings). However, the scene, in its narrative context, may not be seen as part of a disorderly, liminal act either. Since the urine appears to be collected in a basin, should we perhaps rather see the scene as an expression of a symbolic ceremonial act, in which the stress is not on the urination, rather on the urine, which has a disinfecting property and since it belonged to the deceased, could have been used with extra effect in some purification act in the course of the funerary practices?[120]

2. Scenes referring to bodily functions II: laughter

Did the Etruscans laugh? Most likely so, but what made them laugh? That is a question containing many restrictive impediments of definition: the lack of a comic literature and of a more subtle knowledge of the Etruscan language, the reliance on visual media most of which come from funerary contexts, the lack of a homogeneous people and culture, and finally, who makes the joke, the client or the patron?[121] The observations are right, but is a funerary context really an impediment to display humour?[122] Perhaps it is just the context in which humour shall be sought.

In Rome, actors dressed as satyrs could form part of the aristocratic funeral processions.[123] They preceded the bier, mimicking and hence mocking the serious

Fig. 5.17. Tarquinia, T. delle Iscrizioni, *entrance wall (water colour copy in Ny Carlsberg Glyptotek, Copenhagen; with kind permission of the museum; photographer Ole Haupt).*

Fig. 5.18. Tarquinia, T. del Topolino, *rear wall, detail (with kind permission of Ministero per i Beni e le Attività Culturali, Soprintendenza per i beni archeologici dell'Etruria Meridionale, Museo di Villa Giulia; photo no. 8741D).*

Fig. 5.19. Tarquinia, T. delle Iscrizioni, *parts of the right and the rear wall (to the left) (with kind permission of American Academy in Rome, Photographic Archive; photo no. Moscioni 24113).*

Fig. 5.20. Tarquinia, T. dei Pigmei, *left wall (with kind permission of Ministero per i Beni e le Attività Culturali, Soprintendenza per i beni archeologici dell'Etruria Meridionale, Museo di Villa Giulia; photo no. 9125D).*

Fig. 5.21. Tarquinia, T. degli Auguri, *left wall (reconstruction drawing; with kind permission of American Academy in Rome, Photographic Archive; photo no. Moscioni 24139).*

movements of the others in a dance called the *sicinnis*. What is more, comic merriment formed part of at least one emperor's funeral, as the one arranged for Vespasian. As was the practice, a leading mime, in this case the *archimimus* Favor, donned the death mask of the emperor *and mimicking, as is the practice, the deportment and speech of the dead man,* [he] *asked the imperial procurators who were there, in front of everyone, how much the funeral and procession had cost. When he heard '10 million sesterces,' he retorted, 'Give me* (i.e. Favor himself) *100 and you can throw my* (i.e. Vespasian's) *body into the Tiber'*.[124] Parody and laughter was thus incorporated as an important element in the Roman ritual practices surrounding the deceased in his liminal state of transition. Was it also so in an Etruscan context?

Laughter promotes solidarity and it releases stress and eases social and personal tensions,[125] a situation not uncommon in funerary ceremonies. Through laughter you could conceal your real feelings and to the rest of the community show that you were in control of yourself. Such a control situation was, for example, some years ago observed with great dismay in a Danish court murder case regarding honour. A Pakistani father had organised his whole family, friends, and employees to track down his young daughter and boy-friend who had brought shame on the family. During very sensitive witness hearings the public, including the accused persons and family, were brought to an adjoining chamber to follow the hearings via internal loudspeakers. In the eyes of the public, instead of guilt and penitence, the involved persons reacted incredibly to the hearings with laughter. This was their way to subdue real feelings and a way to save face in the eyes of their own family and countrymen.[126]

Laughter in funerary situations creates contradictory feelings; laughter improves your mood in a moment of distress and could thus well be regarded as an appropriate liminal condition of emotional disorder. However, laughter is also another bodily action in which you can lose control of your senses and come in contact with transcendental forces. Laughter could have had many functions within an Etruscan funerary context; the allusions to it made in their funerary art may confirm this. The examples are few, but perhaps significant – more situations may escape our attention, since the Etruscans' sense of humour and body language is still a field of study to be explored more closely.

The most obvious theme appears in the *T. dei Pigmei* (phase 5:97),[127] in which pygmies fight large cranes (Fig. 5.20), a theme well known from Greek literature and art,[128] here presented as a hilarious fight between undersized, clumsy humans and oversized birds. The motif appears at the end of the left wall in a crammed space above a loculus and thus fitted the wall well; it was inserted between a procession of six horsemen (starting on the entrance wall: parameter J) and the rear wall banquet (parameter E). The pygmies lived at the end of the world[129] and could well have functioned as a *trait d'union* between a liminal funerary escort and the banquet in the world beyond,[130] but this does not eliminate the comic aspect of the fight, as also clearly present in contemporary Greek presentations.[131]

Fights, athletics, and acrobatics are a fertile field for puzzlement and laughter, as, for example, the small acrobat squatting on the head of a big charioteer, who tries to control a biga in *T. del Guerriero* (phase 5:73). The control of the horses is taken over by another small acrobat, who sits on the back of one of the horses. Is this an athletic competition or a burlesque game arranged to create laughter?

Another example is taken from *T. degli Auguri* (phase 2:42). Here on the right wall we have already met Phersu directing a ferocious game between a dog and a man with a covered head. On the left wall Phersu reappears, alone, next to a man running and two boxers facing each other. Running away with a raised, closed fist, but looking back, he imitates in an exaggerated, parodying manner both the runner and the opening gestures of the two boxers (Fig. 5.21).[132] Mockery, of which this is a very good example, is a common and primitive way of creating laughter and well known from later Roman political life.[133] In *T. del Pulcinella* (phase 2:104), Phersu mimics in accentuated movements a runner and at Chiusi in *T. della Scimmia* (phase 3:25), pictured as a dwarf, he mimics a flute player, who stands opposite him and plays for a weapon dancer (Fig. 5.4).[134] In *T. del Gallo* (phase 5:68), a masked man in a fell-jacket dances with a woman; he imitates the unrestrained dance of a satyr, she that of a maenad. The mask is not that of Phersu, rather (if the practice can originally by ascribed to some Etruscan funerary custom[135]) a death mask, donned a person to mimic the participants in the funerary ceremonies in the dance similar to that which the Romans called *sicinnis*, or to impersonate in a burlesque way the dead person, as happened in Vespasian's funerary procession just described above.

A more sophisticated scene of imitation to create laughter may be a detail in the rear wall motif in *T. dei Vasi Dipinti* (phase 2:123) (Fig. 5.22): The picture is dominated by a man-woman symposium scene; to the left, in smaller dimension is depicted a well-dressed young woman sitting on a *diphros*, or stool, dressed in the same way as the symposium lady in a long chiton, with a mantle, a *tutulus* hair-dress, and large disc-shaped ear-rings. In her lap sits a naked young man with a dove in his hand. The dove confirms the erotic character of the scene,[136] but the situation is thrown upside down – normally a naked *hetaira* will court a man, but here a naked 'gigolo' appears to court a soberly dressed woman. If this was the message, the first astonishment of the viewer most likely would have turned into laughter.[137]

Erotics and bodily necessities have always been a fertile field for expressing wittiness and humour, but here, as in the other cases of interpretation presented above, it is difficult to draw a precise line between what is ritual and what is not; sometimes the two fields of interpretation overlap, sometimes it may not be a question of either-or, but rather of both-and. The defecating man in *T. dei Giocolieri* (phase 2:70) (Fig. 5.16) is one such instance of difficult interpretation – the scene draws the smile from a modern viewer, but was this the artist's/patron's intention with regard to their contemporary viewers? And what about the urinating old man to the right of the entrance in *T. delle Iscrizioni* (phase 2:74) (Fig. 5.17)? In the right erotic scene in *T. della Fustigazione* (phase 3:67) (Fig. 5.9b), in which the whipped, naked woman apparently performs a fellatio on the right male, his blissful, 'transcendental' smile evokes a reciprocal smile from the modern viewer (and also from the ancient one?). At the same time the naked woman

Fig. 5.22. Tarquinia, T. dei Vasi Dipinti, *rear wall (water colour copy by L. Schultz; with kind permission of Deutsches Archäologisches Institut, Rome, photo no. 2013.0207; photographer H. Behrens).*

appears as unclean, using her mouth in sexual play,[138] and about to be penetrated from behind(?) by another. – Was humour also the purpose of one of the erotic scenes in *T. dei Tori* (phase 2:120) (Fig. 5.14b)? Above the door into the right back chamber a human-headed bull charges towards a homoerotic couple – the anal penetrator turns round and does not see the approaching danger, while the penetrated, who sees it, tries to hide behind a slender tree, but is unable to move.[139]

Also the phallos-bird in *T. del Topolino* (Fig. 5.18), weighed down by heavy testicles and with a tuft of black hair where the erect penis meets the wings of the bird (an unusual creature in Etruscan art), may have called for a smile or laughter. And we may also ask, if not for a humorous touch, what was the function of the mouse balancing on a branch to the left of the closed door on the end wall. Further, three small, grey mice play(?) with a man lying on his stomach in the pediment of the *T. delle Olimpiadi*, perhaps another humorous touch without further significance.

In this part of the presentation we have discussed a selected number of funerary scenes as an integrated part of the funerary ceremonies connected to liminality, that is actions taken by the funerary participants in order to ease the journey of the deceased towards the Underworld at a time when disorder and pollution threatened both the deceased and the society of the living. This could partly be done through the flowing of blood as a means of offering immortality to the dead soul. Another way was through spirited, unrestrained actions, dancing, laughter, and orgasm to get in contact with the deceased's transcendental, liminal world in order to negotiate with the sinister and dangerous forces which were active there. But this liminal period of agonising social disorder and pollution could not last – it had to come to an end – and make sure that the deceased reached his/her goal. This was accomplished through acts of purification and ritual reintegration.

The interment of the deceased: purification and reintegration

Death in a Roman context was synonymous with pollution, both of the place in which it occurred and of the persons who came in contact with the dead body, both directly and indirectly (as, for example, through eye-contact). Many measures were taken to protect and purify both places and persons from the social exclusion and isolation that followed the contact with death. This must certainly also have been the case with the Etruscans, with their ideas (or the content) of death and pollution being similar, but the form in which they found their expressions perhaps somewhat different. The acts of protection and purification were adopted to neutralise the pollution, which appeared in different forms in the course of the transitional rites that characterised the funerary process, their aim being both to help the soul of the dead person to find its way to the world beyond and to restore the imbalance created in society at the moment of death and to reintegrate the bereaved into society.[140]

Two sorts of pictorial scenes referring to purification and reintegration can be detected in the tomb paintings: the presence or the carrying of ritual objects (parameter I) and the banquet (parameter E). In addition, more pictorial elements (more or less hidden) in the tomb paintings may have carried references to purification even if not treated as separate parameters in the present context. The many pictorial allusions to water (parameter B)[141] referring to the journey to the Underworld, including a passage of water, could well also have contained a reference to purification, as water has a strong purifying power. Another element of purification was laurels, so often pictured in the tomb paintings, separating scenes and figures in their various tasks, in particular in connection with the liminal actions.[142]

Purification: Ritual objects (parameter I)
Ritual objects are few and far between. Only two objects reappear with some frequency: *thymiateria*, or incense burners, and large kylikes.

The *thymiateria*, used for purification in connection with animal sacrifices (cf. parameter G) and to repair the disorder in the liminal space caused by border transgressions (parameter D), have already been discussed above,[143] but they appear also in contexts with athletic/chariot games (*T. delle Bighe* (phase 3:47) and *T. della Scimmia* (phase 3:25), underlining the ritual character of these funerary ceremonials, and with banquets (*T. del Biclinio* (phase 4:46)).[144] In the last tomb, the *thymiaterion* appears on the rear wall, to the left of a false door, together with two trees and a servant, juxtaposing a servant and a *kylikeion* with vases on the other side of the door. The *kylikeion* refers to a banquet, which in this grave is not painted on the rear, but on the side walls. The presence of the *thymiaterion* underlines the ritual aspect of the banquet, in which purification was part of the ritual – or, alternatively, it functioned as a symbol for the banquet being itself a funerary purification ritual. In *T. Golini I* (phase 6:32) at Orvieto, a *thymiaterion* is also placed on the *kylikeion*, again underlining the ritual character of the accompanying banquet scene, though this time the scene

Fig. 5.23. Tarquinia, T. dei Leopardi, *a) left wall; b) right wall (with kind permission of Ministero per i Beni e le Attività Culturali, Soprintendenza per i beni archeologici dell'Etruria Meridionale, Museo di Villa Giulia; photo no. 224066 (a) and 224069 (b)).*

is not placed in this world, but in the Underworld with Aita and Phersipnai present. It appears thus that the *thymiaterion*, as a ritual object could be used both in this and in the Underworld (presumably symbolically referring to the purifications among the mourners in the world of the living), but it is never found in the liminal space of the journey to the Underworld. Apparently during this critical part of the funerary ceremonies no acts of purification were performed.

Kylikes are carried both in banquets and in dancing scenes, though in some cases the kylix is presented oversized. Such large kylikes find their confrontation in some Tarquinian tombs from the late 6th century BC in the shape of a few Attic red-figure examples with a diameter of 0.37–0.52 m,[145] that is about the double size of a normal drinking cup. They may have been included among the grave finds because of their ritual function, perhaps in connection with a wine offering during the deposition of the dead and before the closing of the grave.

The kylix carried in the *T. dei Leopardi* (phase 3:81) is a good example to support this argument (Fig. 5.23a): on the left wall of the tomb, a kithara- and a fluteplayer are followed by four men carrying respectively a staff and an alabastron, an open box (*pyxis*)[146] and a low bowl or mirror, a jug and a bowl, and a ladle, some, if not all objects, serving ritual purposes. On the right wall (Fig. 5.23b), a man carrying a large, black kylix, is followed by a flute player, a lyre-player and two more persons, who are more walking than dancing. If seen together the two side walls refer to a funerary procession, most likely sacrificial, in which the kylix may indicate the imminent wine offering act of purification at the grave before it is closed.

A similar argument was put forward in connection with the *T. del Barone* (phase 2:44) when discussing the accompanying horsemen (parameter J):[147] on the rear wall the central man with a large kylix in his out-stretched hand performed a libation act for the deceased woman confronting him (Fig. 5.6c) – or perhaps more precisely, he made the final offering to his wife, before he ritually sealed the tomb, symbolically affirming that the dead soul had reached its final destination, the Underworld. When the grave was closed – the final act in the ceremonies could be undertaken, the banquet.

In a possible total of ten tombs,[148] though in each case in a different setting, the large kylix is carried close to the body or stretched out, obliquely, or on edge; in the last case this is as if to underline that an action is about to begin by filling the cup from a volute krater in front – or that the action has already been performed. Large kylixes are at times also used by the central figure at the depicted symposia, where they may appear as simple drinking cups, or, in a narrative syncoptic way, refer to a ritual act already performed before the funeral banquet, which in itself is another ritual act.

A third ritual object, the double axe, often used to slaughter sacrificial animals, should also be mentioned, but it appears perhaps only in two very early tombs, *T. della Nave* at Cerveteri (phase 1:7) and *T. Campana* at Veii (phase 1:176), and shall not be considered any further here.[149]

Reintegration: Banquets (parameter E)

The by far dominant pictorial theme in the Etruscan tomb paintings was heraldic animals (parameter A), followed by the banquet, both occupying nearly exclusively the rear wall of the tomb. In *T. delle Leonesse* (phase 2:77) the banquet occupies the sidewalls, the rear wall reserved for an enormous bronze volute krater, a symbol of the dead buried in an urn in the niche cut in the wall below.[150] In *T. del Biclinio* (phase 4:46) the banqueters also occupy the sidewalls of the tomb, but here they are symbolically tied to the rear wall through the presence of a *kylikeion*.

The banquet could consist of one or more *klinai* carrying male-female or male-male couples, at times assisted by young servants, at times by musicians – and thus follows (with the exclusion of the male-female couple) more or less the original Greek pictorial scheme. In the tombs, the banquet scenes started in the pedimental field of the rear wall, as can be seen in the phase 2 tombs *T. Bartoccini* (45), *T. Tarantola* (114), *T. della Caccia e Pesca* (50), *T. del Topolino* (119), *T. 5039* (60), *T. delle Olimpiadi* (92), *T. 5898* (167), *T. del Frontoncino* (66), and *T. 4780* (157). However, in *T. 1999* (141) around 510 BC, banquet scenes moved down to cover the entire wall below and remained there.[151]

The ritual character of the banquet is demonstrated by *T. del Biclinio*, in which the rear wall scene with the *kylikeion* is balanced by a *thymiaterion* on the other side of the central, false door. In *T. dei Leopardi* (phase 3:81) the sacrificial procession on the side walls ends with the banquet scene on the rear wall (Fig. 5.24), demonstrating an interesting sequence of events, in which the funerary sacrifices, generally of a purificatory character at the end of the ceremonies, as revealed above, precede the banquet. The banquet scene thus appears as the final ritual act of the funerary ceremonies, and as the last ceremony it signals the end of the deceased's liminal journey to the Underworld. Through this final ritual act the deceased has been received and reunited with his ancestors in the world where Aita and Phersipnai reign. At the same time, the banquet functions as a reintegration of the bereaved into society, now cleansed from the pollution absorbed in the liminal phase of the ceremonies.

The banquet is thus the most important ritual act of the funerary ceremonies (see also Fig. 5.22). This explains the motif's popularity and for the same reason, as the final funerary act, why it occupies the rear wall – and why it also decorated the lids of an endless number of sarcophagi and ash urns.[152] The other walls in the tomb, when a banquet scene is presented, portray scenes either with reference to the deceased's life and honours offered to him/her, or to liminal actions and counteractions, or both, hence the funerary ceremonies leading up to the integration of the deceased in the Underworld and the reintegration of the living back into society.

The banquet scene in its early period always belongs to this world,[153] but with the *T. dei Demoni Azzurri* (phase 4) a change appears. On the left wall is presented a procession with three dancers, two musicians and, in the central part, a biga with a man about to enter (Fig. 5.2b). The biga, not being part of a competition, most likely belongs to the deceased. Here, as in earlier tombs we participate in an action of this world (the dancers and musicians) in which the deceased participates. On the right

Fig. 5.24. Tarquinia, T. dei Leopardi, *rear wall (with kind permission of Ministero per i Beni e le Attività Culturali, Soprintendenza per i beni archeologici dell'Etruria Meridionale, Museo di Villa Giulia; photo no. 224067).*

wall we are already in the world of the death journey, crowded with death demons and an encounter by the boat, which carries the deceased (here in the shape of a woman) to the Underworld (Fig. 5.2d).[154] The rear wall is occupied by a banquet, four *klinai*, three with man-man couples, the second from left with a man-woman couple, perhaps referring to the two deceased persons: the man in biga on the left wall and the woman by the boat on the right wall (Fig. 5.2c). Both scenes on the side walls belong to the liminal phase of the celebrations: on the left a procession for the deceased man with dancing and music taking part in this world to help; on the right, the deceased woman on her infernal journey. The final result of both actions is the banquet. On the left wall the earthly liminal phase finishes with a final banquet (with the deceased couple present) to seal the tomb and cleanse the participants in the funeral of their final death pollution; on the right the liminal death journey finishes in the Underworld, where the arrival likewise is celebrated by a banquet. The two banquets occur simultaneously, but according to the side wall being read, the banquet depicted belonged either to one or the other world.

This kind of dichotomous reading of the same scene is not unique. In the slightly later *T. dei Pigmei* (phase 5:97) on the entrance and the left wall are presented six

Fig. 5.25. Tarquinia, T. dell'Orco II, *detail (with kind permission of Ministero per i Beni e le Attività Culturali, Soprintendenza per i beni archeologici dell'Etruria Meridionale, Museo di Villa Giulia; photo no. 315).*

riders[155] moving towards the rear wall with six banqueters, only interrupted by a funny Geranomachia scene (battle between pygmies and cranes) (Fig. 5.20). This has been interpreted collectively as the deceased's otherworldly journey; the Underworld could only be reached after having passed the Land of the Pygmies.[156] On the right wall a procession of magisterial character moves towards the same rear wall. Both side wall scenes refer to the liminal phase of the funerary ceremonies: the one on the right wall to the world of the living; the one on the left to the otherworldly journey of the deceased. According to which wall is read their goal is the same: the final purificatory banquet for the living and the welcome banquet for the deceased, respectively.

Less than a couple of generations later, just after the middle of the 4th century BC, the banquet scene has moved definitely to the Underworld with Aita and Phersipnai participating in the celebrations, as visible in *T. Golini I* (phase 6: 32) and *T. dell'Orco II* (phase 6: 94) (Fig. 5.25). By this time a new pictorial world has emerged in the tomb paintings, a world which iconographically has little or nothing to do with the earlier scenes.

A new world – down under

The new pictorial world which emerges in Etruscan tomb paintings from around the middle of the 4th century BC (even if some parameters have already appeared in singular examples previously) can be summarised as follows:

N.   Demons in various guises: as winged *genii*, Charu(n), Lasa?, Tuchulcha, or Vanth, though in most cases unnamed.

O. Processions (see also parameter J: Horsemen): in a ritual setting, the deceased in a chariot, magisterial processions.
P. Encounters (reunions beyond this world).
Q. The Underworld with Hades/Aita and Persephone/Phersipnai present.
R. Underworld mythological figures.

The motifs all carry a reference to the liminal world of the journey (parameters N–P) or to the Underworld itself (parameters Q–R). Most of the old pictorial themes die out in the course of the 4th century BC; only a few, parameters B and C, linger on into the following two centuries (Tables 5.1 and 5.2): the water scenes with a renewed vitality, while the doors appear in a new setting.

The liminal journey I: Demons (parameter N)

The most common and also characteristic motif in this new phase of tomb paintings are demons of various sorts, some named, some not. Their *fluorit* was in the second half of the 4th and in the 3rd century BC and they vanished in the course of the 2nd century BC. However, winged demons have been recorded as early as in the second half of the 6th century BC, as in one of the terracotta plaques of the Campana series from Cerveteri, but it was not till the following century that they appeared in a proper tomb context.[157] In *T. dei Demoni Azzurri* (phase 4) they appear for the first time in full measure: four in all, none of them named (Fig. 5.2d). One of them stands in a boat, like the Greek Charon, ready to ship the deceased across the river Styx, but this is the only time a Greek model is used for such an otherworldly scene.

Fig. 5.26. Tarquinia, T. degli Anina, *entrance wall (with kind permission of Ministero per i Beni e le Attività Culturali, Soprintendenza per i beni archeologici dell'Etruria Meridionale, Museo di Villa Giulia; photo no. 160562).*

Table 5.1. Distribution of Etruscan tomb paintings in numbers within each phase (1–8) according to the pictorial parameters (A–R).

Phase: total graves	A	B	C	D	E	F	G	H	I	J	K	L	M	N	O	P	Q	R	Total scenes
1. 625–550: 13	09	02	03	–	–	–	–	–	?	?	–	–	–	–	–	–	–	–	14
2. 550–500: 47	38	15	09	10	16	15	08	03	09	04	02	02	–	–	–	–	–	–	131
3. 500–450: 27	16	04	06	03	15	19	11	10	07	06	01	01	08	02	01	–	–	–	110
4. 450–400: 14	09	03	01	–	10	09	–	02	01	02	07	–	02	02	03	01	–	–	52
5. 400–350: 14	07	01	–	03	09	07	01	02	01	04	01	01	02	01	–	01	–	–	41
6. 350–300: 15	08	09	01	02	07	01	02	–	01	01	–	–	–	12	04	02	02	02	54
7. 300–200: 15	01	06	02	–	–	–	–	–	–	–	–	–	–	10	04	02	–	01	26
8. 200– : 11	01	02	03	–	–	–	01	–	–	–	–	–	–	07	07	05	–	–	25
Total 156	89	42	25	18	57	51	23	17	19	18	11	04	12	34	19	11	02	03	455

Table 5.2. Distribution of Etruscan tomb paintings in percentages within each phase (1–8) according to the pictorial parameters (A–R).

Phase: total graves	A	B	C	D	E	F	G	H	I	J	K	L	M	N	O	P	Q	R	Total
1. 625–550: 13	64	14	21	–	–	–	–	–	?	?	–	–	–	?	–	–	–	–	99
2. 550–500: 47	29	11	07	08	12	11	06	02	07	03	02	02	–	–	–	–	–	–	100
3. 500–450: 27	15	04	05	03	14	17	10	09	06	05	01	01	07	02	01	–	–	–	100
4. 450–400: 14	17	06	02	–	19	17	–	04	02	04	13	–	04	04	06	02	–	–	100
5. 400–350: 14	17	02	–	07	22	17	02	05	02	10	02	02	05	02	–	02	–	–	97
6. 350–300: 15	15	16	02	04	13	02	04	–	02	02	–	–	–	22	07	04	04	04	101
7. 300–200: 15	04	22	07	–	–	–	–	–	–	04	–	–	–	37	15	07	–	04	100
8. 200– : 11	04	08	12	–	–	–	04	–	–	–	–	–	–	27	27	19	–	–	101
Total 156	20	09	05	04	13	11	05	04	04	04	02	01	03	07	04	02	0+	01	99+

The fierce-looking Etruscan Charu(n) with a hawk-beak shaped nose and dressed in a short chiton, often winged, sometimes carrying snakes, seems to have borrowed his name from the Greek model (Figs 5.26 and 5.28). In an early version, he was donned with a paddle/rudder,[158] the symbol of the Greek ferryman, but in his Etruscan function as gate keeper he soon changed this for a mallet used to bolt and unbolt the gate to the Underworld. His female counterpart, the sweet-looking Vanth, is also dressed in a short chiton, boots, and carries torches to light the way for the deceased to the Underworld (Fig. 5.26). Her name appeared in writing on an aryballos from Vulci from about 600 BC, but it is not till the 5th century BC that we find a first possible pictorial presentation of her presented as a winged demon attending the seated or semi-reclining deceased in a Chiusine funerary statue group.[159]

Both Vanth and Charu(n) are shown, either alone flanking real or false doors in the grave, or they accompany deceased persons whether present in the world of the living or in that of the infernal liminal space. A third demon, Tuchulcha, only named once in the *T. dell'Orco II* (phase 6:94), also fierce-looking like Charu(n), is present in the Underworld of Aita and Phersipnai, but he appears to be the only demon present in the Underworld.[160] Both Vanth and Charu(n), as well as other demons, seem to be able to move both in the world of the living and in the liminal infernal world, but they never appear in scenes of the Underworld itself.[161]

The liminal journey II: Processions (parameter O)

Processions of some sort appear in various ways in the tomb paintings. An early kind can be observed in *T. dei Leopardi* (phase 3:81) (Figs 5.23a–b), in which men and women carrying ritual objects move in a parallel way on both side walls towards the banquet on the rear wall. This procession, singular of its kind, as observed above, appears to be of a sacrificial character.

In *T. dei Demoni Azzurri* (phase 4) on the left wall a man entering a biga is visible (Fig. 5.2b). Its triumphal spirit anticipates a theme popular in later Etruscan funerary art, though it is more or less contemporary with two other tombs showing a similar theme in Tarquinia, *T. Francesca Giustiniani* (phase 4:65; on the rear wall) and *T. Querciola I* (phase 4:106; on the entrance wall, above the door). If the interpretation of these three tombs is right, in all the tombs the deceased is placed in the liminal phase of the funerary celebrations among scenes of dancers and musicians. The theme with a chariot can be followed through the 4th century BC in *T. Golini I* (phase 6:32), *T. Golini II* (phase 6:33), and *T. degli Hescanas* (phase 6:34), but then disappears in favour of processions on foot.[162] In these paintings the biga is placed definitely in an otherworldly sphere; the liminal journey in two cases (*T. Golini II* and *T. degli Hescanas*) underlined by the running wave border (parameter B) on the chariot itself.

An early procession on foot can be witnessed in *T. Golini II*, where on the left wall it is inserted between the biga on the left side of the door and a banquet at the end of the side wall. In the procession are officials (carrying their signs of office) and musicians, a composition followed up in later tombs and often referred to as magisterial processions,[163]

Fig. 5.27. Tarquinia, T. del Tifone, *right wall (reconstruction drawing; with kind permission of American Academy in Rome, Photographic Archive; photo no. Moscioni 24084).*

perhaps including a *eulogy* given in the forum to celebrate specially deserved members of the society. In such processions, but not present in the Golini tomb, the deceased is accompanied by one or more death demons.

When the death demons disappear from the paintings, as in *T. del Convegno* (phase 8:58) and in *T. del Tifone* (Fig. 5.27), the *processus magistratualis* has turned from being a liminal procession, with reference to the infernal, to becoming a commemorative one in this world.[164] The procession has been individualised, with the deceased present as if alive, which he was symbolically in Roman funerary processions where a member of the family carried his death-mask.[165] The final stage of this pictorial process is visible, for example, in the Late Republican marble relief from Amiternum which displays a funeral procession with the deceased carried on a funeral coach.[166] Hence, we are back to where we started to trace the pictorial tradition, the *ekphora* on the Geometric vases in Athens.

The liminal journey III: Encounters (parameter P) – with a return to the False doors (parameter B)

Scenes which I prefer to call encounters are despite their easy identification perhaps one of the more enigmatic in Etruscan funerary art. They show people that meet, normally in the presence of one or more death demons, named or not, most often recognised as Charu(n) with his mallet and Vanth with her torches.[167] In most cases the encounter happens in front of a closed, arched door.[168] The problem, much discussed, regards whether the scenes portray a farewell situation between the deceased and bereaved relatives in this or in the infernal, liminal world, or a reunion situation between the deceased and ancestors in the same infernal world.[169] One answer to the question may lie in the identification of the closed, arched door.

The doors in the tomb paintings rightly 'symbolise the boundary between the worlds of the living and of the dead,'[170] but the paintings show two kinds of doors: the traditional *porta dorica* with vertical door jambs and horizontal lintel, a type which appeared already in the 6th and lasted into the 3rd century BC (Fig. 5.5); and the arched door having the shape of a city gate (Fig. 5.28), which appeared only in scenes of encounters from the 3rd century BC onwards. Do these refer to different doors and, if so, to which of these did Charu(n) have the 'key'?

The Etruscans operated with three spaces in their funerary ideology: the space of the living, the space of the infernal, liminal journey, and the Underworld of Aita and Phersipnai proper. The presence of the arched door may mean that the shape was chosen to distinguish it conceptually from the *porta dorica*, which in earlier tomb contexts had acquired a specific meaning. Since the Etruscans pictorially had no specific vision of the Underworld till after the middle of the 5th century BC, I would postulate that the *porta dorica* led to the space which apparently was the most significant one for the Etruscans – the infernal, liminal space in which the deceased met the most serious challenges on the way to the Underworld,[171] in which the ancestors domiciled. The arched gate, when the visual idea of the Underworld began to develop, thus was chosen to mark the entrance to Aita's reign. Charu(n), who could move in both the space of

Fig. 5.28. Tarquinia, T. Querciola II *(with kind permission of Deutsches Archölogisches Institut, Rome, photo no. D-DAI-ROM-83.1096).*

the living and of the infernal, liminal journey, but not in the Underworld itself, had the 'key' to both doors.

The scenes with arched doors were therefore linked to the second space, that of the infernal, liminal journey. While the deceased could still move and be present in the world of the living, the Etruscan tomb paintings give no explicit example of the living moving about in infernal spaces. Thus, it is likely that the encounters be considered as a reunion between the deceased and his/her ancestors. That would in a liminal way of thinking, as clearly demonstrated by the tomb paintings, be the most reassuring result of the liminal actions and counteractions taken by the bereaved to secure the deceased a safe arrival down under.

As Charu(n) also his companion Vanth could only move in the space of the living and of the infernal, liminal journey. This is well expressed in the Hellenistic sarcophagus of Hasti Afunei: at the left end a female demon, named Culśu, exits the arched door of the Underworld while Vanth waits outside together with the named deceased who, after his death journey, here is reunited with his ancestors.[172]

The Underworld: Aita and Phersipnai and mythological figures (parameters Q and R)

The liminal phase of the funerary ceremonies in this world ended with a banquet (parameter E); for the deceased on his/her infernal journey it ended with a parallel banquet in the Underworld in the presence of Aita, Phersipnai, and the ancestors. While the banquet of the living was a most popular motif (appearing at least 56 times on the tomb walls), in only two tombs is the proper Underworld presented, in *T. Golini I* (phase 6:32) at Orvieto and in *T. dell'Orco II* (phase 6:94) at Tarquinia (Fig. 5.25); furthermore, in only two tombs do we find depicted mythological scenes from the Underworld: again in *T. dell'Orco II* (the dead heroes from Troy) and in *T. François* at Veii ((phase 6:178): the two heroes Amphiaros and Sisyphos). It seems therefore that the result of the funerary ceremonies was not the main concern for the bereaved, rather that the deceased arrived there safely through the liminal journey.

In a few instances (*T. dei Demoni Azzurri* (phase 4) (Fig. 5.2c) and *T. dei Pigmei* (phase 4:97)) the banquet on the rear wall could be read as both the banquet of the living and as that of the ancestors, depending on which side wall was read: the one with motifs referring to this world, or the one with motifs referring to the world beyond. In *T. Golini II* (phase 6:33) only two out of five preserved *klinai* have banqueters (the persons even named) preserved. The close parallel in motifs with the slightly older *T. Golini I* makes it possible that on one of the remaining three *klinai* Aita and Phersipnai could have been present.

Content: Continuity or change? A liminal conclusion

Religious festivals are generally explained as an event of joy offering public excitement.[173] Funerary rituals (like the religious festivals) are an orchestration of sentiments by actions, which bring the mourners from a situation of grief and gloom through emotional experiences of transcendental character to relief and joy in the concluding banquet. The deceased is put to final rest in the tomb and certainty has been achieved that he/she has arrived safely in the Underworld received by his/her ancestors.

The basic model for the orchestration of sentiments, as extracted from the interpretation of the parameters A–R, lies in the Etruscan apprehension of three funerary spaces in which death and afterlife took place:

1. The space of the living, i.e. this world, in which the death occurred and in which the funerary rituals and practices were performed. In addition to the mourners, the deceased could also participate in this space, as well as the death demons Charun and Vanth, but not the ancestors.
2. The liminal space beyond this world, i.e. the space in which the deceased travelled to reach the Underworld. In this space the deceased, Charun and Vanth, as well as ancestors of the deceased could participate, but not the bereaved relatives.
3. The space of the dead, i.e. the Underworld in which Aita and Phersipnai reigned. Here the deceased, ancestors, dead heroes and other dead persons could participate, as well as demons like Tuchulcha and Culśu, but apparently not Charun and Vanth.

From the moment of death to the arrival in the Underworld the movement of the deceased through these three spaces adheres well to van Gennep's three stage *rites-de-passage* model: phase of separation (the moment of death in this world), phase of transition (the liminal journey), and phase of reintegration (the arrival in the Underworld). These three steps coincided also with the funerary practices performed by the bereaved relatives and friends, who at the moment of death (phase of separation) started the prescribed funerary rituals (phase of transition) which ended with the interment and sacrifices (phase of reintegration).

The travel in the liminal space, between the moment of death and the entrance into the Underworld, was for the deceased the most critical phase when he/she was exposed to the dangers of transcendental forces. The mourners, through prescribed rituals containing dance, erotic plays, laughter, and spilling of blood, could challenge and avenge these forces to help the deceased arrive safely in the Underworld. Death caused pollution among the mourners, an unpleasant condition which had to be countered with acts of purification. In their polluted, transitional state the mourners were isolated from the community and could behave out of the norms performing abnormal activities connected to dirt, obscenities, and lawlessness, activities most, if not all, aimed at helping (with all means necessary) the deceased on his/her liminal passage. The reintegration was celebrated, both among the mourners and for the deceased's arrival in the Underworld, with a joyous banquet.

The idea of a liminal space and the space of the dead did not arrive in Etruria through Pythagorism or Orphism spreading from southern Italy in the mid-4th century BC,[174] when the pictorial presentation of these two spaces gained popularity. Nor did these

Fig. 5.29. Veii, T. Campana, *rear wall (copied from L. Canina:* L'antica città di Veii, *Rome 1847, pl. 31).*

ideas arrive through Greek channels a couple of generations earlier with the *T. dei Demoni Azzurri* (Figs 5.2a–d); they were already present in the minds of the Etruscans by the end of the 6th century BC, as well demonstrated by the *T. del Barone* (Figs 5.6a–c). Here we encounter for the first time all three funerary spaces – that of the living in the man (husband) with the large kylix and the young flute-player, that of the liminal space with the horsemen accompanying the deceased woman (wife), and that of the dead, the wife who receives from her husband the concluding (and reintegrating) funerary sacrifice, symbolised by the kylix. In this tomb, as well as in *T. delle Iscrizioni* the followers of the deceased are horsemen (Fig. 5.7), but in contemporary Etruscan vase-paintings they appear also as winged demons.[175]

To this can be added two further pictorial observations, which may sustain the early Etruscan idea of a nether world: 1) an aryballos from Vulci from about 600 BC, which carries the inscription: *I am the beautiful offering to Vanth* – one of the nether world female demons;[176] and 2) the near contemporary *T. Campana* at Veii.

Flanking the door into the inner tomb chamber, the paintings in *T. Campana* are divided into two pairs of superimposed panels (Fig. 5.29). Below on both sides: various real and imaginary animals. Above to the left: a seated panther turned right, looking back; a naked rider moving towards the right. Above to the right: moving towards the left a man in waist cloth carrying a double-axe on his left shoulder; behind him a horse with a small naked rider and a small panther resting on the horse hindquarters; on the further side of the animal another man walking holding high the reins of the horse, also he naked, and a dog. The scenes have been interpreted both as Hephaistos' return, as hunting, and as the journey of the dead to the Underworld.[177] – The real and imaginary animals are typical of the Corinthian vase-painting, they have no reference to hunting nor to Hephaistos, but may have had an apotropaic function (parameter A).[178] The double-axe carried by the front man top right does not belong to hunting, but it is one of Hephaistos' attributes. However, the double-axe is also a ritual object

Fig. 5.30. Florence, Archaeological Museum, funerary stele inv. 75840, from Vulci (with kind permission of La Soprintendenza per i Beni Archeologici della Toscana – Firenze).

used for slaughtering animals at sacrifices (parameter I), an important element of funerary rituals.[179] The two riders, if not hunters, nor followers of Hephaistos, may thus be an early reference to accompanying horsemen (parameter J). In that case the tomb paintings match ideologically well the Vanth-aryballos: here is presented an early scene of the deceased's liminal journey, the deceased being the man, the tallest of them all, walking on the further side of the horse in the top right panel.[180]

This interpretation may be further sustained by a slightly later (early 6th century BC) grave marker from Vulci, now in Florence (Fig. 5.30).[181] The stele is composed of three superimposed panels: in the top panel a man walks towards the left on the inside of a horse, holding the reins high, as in the *T. Campana* painting – there as here perhaps the deceased accompanied by horsemen, here symbolically present through the horse only (parameter J); in the middle panel is a sfinx turned right, most likely in the function as an apotropaic animal (parameter A); in the bottom panel a bird perches on ox-back, the ox (turned left) again perhaps carrying reference to the funerary sacrifice, as already witnessed in a later Chiusan funerary relief.[182]

To these monuments from the same early period may also be added an ivory chest from a tomb at Chiusi[183] and two stone grave markers from Bologna,[184] all showing scenes with a person mounting/ inside a chariot, by some interpreted as the infernal journey. The interpretations may be questionable, but if right, from an ideological point of view, they are not anachronistic.

At what time then did the Etruscans develop these ideas on the afterlife and a liminal space? At present the pictorial world can give no further clues. However, Arnold van Gennep sustained that in societies where travel made up a part of the afterlife ideas, the deceased's:

> survivors are careful to equip him with all the necessary material objects – such as clothing, food, arms, and tools – as well as those of a magico-religious nature – amulets, passwords, signs, etc. – which will assure him a safe journey or crossing and a favourable reception…[185]

At least as early as the Bronze Age, Villanovan (pre-Etruscan) graves contained equipment connected with the serving and drinking of liquids together with other household objects, jewellery, and weapons; some of the objects often in miniature form, some most likely carrying a strong symbolic meaning whether of a religious and/or social kind. This custom continued into the Etruscan Period with an ever increasing sumptuous quantity of the deposited objects. Thus there are, according to van Gennep's postulate above, good reasons to believe that from an early date the Villanovans and the Etruscans already had the idea of an afterlife connected to a nether world journey after death. And we may add that the banquet service becoming more and more prominent in the Iron Age tombs may be a reflection of the same or similar eschatological ideas as the banquet scenes in the Etruscan tomb paintings. Parallel with this development, in the Iron Age, appear the first dwellings of the dead in the form of terracotta/bronze houses (*capanne*) and subsequently the deceased person in various representations (as terracotta and bronze figurines, on reliefs, in *canopic* urns, etc.) with and without mourners.[186]

In addition, when the early, large tumuli graves appeared in Etruria in the early 6th century BC (see especially at Cerveteri), it is noteworthy that many of the first grave chambers were placed in the NW sector of the tumulus, or in the quadrant of the heavenly space – as defined by the Etruscan *templum*, the sacred area of the augurs, formalised in the *disciplina etrusca* – which was reserved for the gods of the nether world.[187]

Together, all these elements strengthen the argument that the Etruscan idea of an afterlife and an Underworld was not a 5th century BC Greek or a 4th century BC southern Italian import, but was an integral part of Etruscan mental and cultural life from an early non-clearly definable date. The appearance in funerary contexts of pictorial motifs with relevance to the world beyond life in the 5th/4th centuries BC was thus not the result of the introduction of new ideas about afterlife into Etruria; the motifs expressed continuity, not change. However, the viewpoint shifted from presenting the funerary rituals performed in the world of the living for helping the deceased on his/her journey to the Underworld to presenting the deceased's journey in the liminal, infernal space itself. The afterlife content was the same, only the form in which it was presented had changed.

But why did the form change? Since the eschatological explanation, as presented in the introduction, has no longer any sense, the change could perhaps be due to the political instability and a general uncertainty about the future in Etruria from the early 4th century BC. However, to stay in the context of funerary rituals and afterlife, another explanation needs to be considered – an explanation which lies on the mental level and regards pictorial visualisations and taboos. I would suggest that the Etruscans, if they had an idea of liminal journeys and afterlife, either did not have a visual idea of what the liminal space and the Underworld looked like (except that the journey required a passage of water – see parameter B), or that, if they did have a vision of the liminal space and the Underworld, a depiction of them was considered a taboo, perhaps connected with ominous outcomes.[188] Under Greek influence in the second part of 5th century BC, this taboo was challenged and gradually disappeared. But contrary to the situation in Greece, where Underworld scenes in a funerary context disappeared towards the end of the same century, in Etruria, they were transformed into their own afterlife visions, gained popularity and by the middle of the 4th century BC had become the most common pictorial motif in funerary art.

The model presented here is an attempt to read Etruscan tomb paintings in their entirety and it may well be expanded, as has also been done along the way, to other forms of Etruscan funerary art.[189] The parameters A–R may likewise be extended to incorporate other pictorial motifs as our knowledge of the ideas lying at the base of Etruscan funerary art is further developed. Some may find that I have interpreted some iconographical elements too narrowly in a funerary context, excluding the many possible Greek connections, especially to Greek deities, assimilated into the Etruscan religious world or not. This has been done on purpose, in order to see if there could be an Etruscan answer to the most often unchallenged Greek connections. The importance is to start the interpretations within an Etruscan funerary context and mentality and from there expand, if necessary, to larger overviews incorporating other parts of the Etruscan society and history, not forgetting the initial context.[190]

In his delightful and in many ways visionary book *Etruscan Places*, D. H. Lawrence, close to the end of the last chapter, wrote that 'the Etruscans are not a theory or a thesis. If they are anything, they are an *experience*. And the experience is always spoilt. Museums, museums, museums, object-lessons rigged out to illustrate the unsound theories of archaeologists, crazy attempts to co-ordinate and get into a fixed order that which has no fixed order and will not be co-ordinated! It is sickening! Why must all experience be systematised? Why must even the vanished Etruscan be reduced to a system? They never will be.'

Lawrence may well be right – as a writer of fiction – but as archaeologists we shall never let experience end only as a personal sensation. Rather we shall through trial and error, continue to systemise and organise the material culture of the past and put forward theories. Only in that way will we be able to expand our knowledge about a time that was. Through theories and resulting dialogues we may open new insights into the world of the Etruscans, which perhaps was not so romantically disorderly as we might at first think.

Appendix A: List of tombs containing motifs referring to parameters A-R

Phases: **1**: 650–550; **2**: 550–500; **3**: 500–450; **4**: 450–400; **5**: 400–350; **6**: 350–300; **7**: 300–200; **8**: after 200[1]

BL = Blera; BO = Bomarzo; CH = Chieti; CV = Cerveteri; GS = Grotte S. Stefano; MA = Magliano in Toscana (loc. Le Ficaie); OR = Orvieto; PO = Populonia; SA = Sarteano; SG = S. Giuliano (loc. Chiusa Cima); TQ = Tarquinia; VE = Veii; VU = Vulci. – c. = con

Tomb and Place		Phase	A	B	C	D	E	F	G	H	I	J	K	L	M	N	O	P	Q	R	Cat.
T.d. Anatre	VE	1	x																		175
Nameless tomb	CV	1	x																		12
T.d. Animali Dipinti 1[2]	CV	1	x											?							3
T.d. Leoni Dipinti[3]	CV	1	x																		6
T.d. Nave	CV	1			x																7
T. Cima	SG	1	x																		37
T.d. Stile Orientalizzante	CH	1	x																		26
T. Dei[4]	MA	1	x	x										?							30
T. Campana[5]	VE	1	x									?									176
T.d. Pantere[6]	TQ	1	x																		96
T. 6120[7]	TQ	1			x																171
T.d. Capanna	TQ	1			x																52
T. Marchese	TQ	1			x																85
T.d. Tori[8]	TQ	2	x	x			x														120
T. 939	TQ	2	x																		133
T. 1646	TQ	2	x																		139
T. Labrouste	TQ	2	x	x	x																75
T.d. Leoni Rossi	TQ	2	x																		80
T.d. Leoni di Giada	TQ	2	x		x																79
T.c. Porte e Felini	TQ	2	x		x																101
T.d. Leonesse[9]	TQ	2	x	x			x	x	x												77
T c. Zampa di Felino	TQ	2	x																		126
T. 356	TQ	2	x																		129
T.d. Leoni	TQ	2	x																		78
T. d. Auguri[10]	TQ	2	x		x	x				x	x										42
T. 3011	TQ	2		x																	145
T. Bartoccini	TQ	2	x	x			x														45
T.d. Fiore di Loto	TQ	2	x																		63
T. Stefani[11]	TQ	2	x	x																	112
T. Tarantola	TQ	2	x				x														114
T.d. Tritoni	TQ	2			x																122
T. 3986	TQ	2	x																		151
T.d. Mare	TQ	2	x	x																	86

Tomb and Place	Phase	A	B	C	D	E	F	G	H	I	J	K	L	M	N	O	P	Q	R	Cat.
T.d. Iscrizioni[12]	TQ	2	x		x	x?		x	x		x?	x									74
T.c. Dioniso e Sileni	TQ	2	x					x													59
T.d. Caccia e Pesca[13]	TQ	2	x	x				x	x					x							50
T.d. Topolino	TQ	2	x	x	x		x	x	x		x										119
T. 5039	TQ	2						x													160
T.d. Giocolieri	TQ	2	x	x		x		x			x										70
T. c. Alberelli e Corone	TQ	2	x																		38
T.d. Olimpiadi	TQ	2			x	x	x		x	x	x										92
T. 5898	TQ	2		x				x													167
T. d. Morto[14]	TQ	2	x					x			x		x								89
T.d. Baccanti[15]	TQ	2	x			x		x			x										43
T.d. Barone[16]	TQ	2	x	x						x	x										44
T. Cardarelli	TQ	2	x		x			x	x		x										53
T.d. Cacciatore	TQ	2	x						x				x								51
T.d. Frontoncino[17]	TQ	2	x					x													66
T. 4780	TQ	2						x													157
T. 1999	TQ	2	x	x			x	x	x												141
T. 3098	TQ	2	x					x													146
T. 1000	TQ	2						x													135
T.d. Pulcinella[18]	TQ	2	x			x		x	x			x									104
T.d. Vasi Dipinti[19]	TQ	2		x		x	x	x			x										123
T.d. Vecchio[20]	TQ	2	x					x													124
T.d. Porta di bronzo	TQ	2			x			x													100
T.d. Maestro d. Olimpiadi	TQ	2	x					x	x	x											83
T.d. Morente[21]	TQ	2	x					x					x		x						88
T.d. Antilopi	TQ	2	x																		41
T.d.'Argilla	CV	2	x					x													4
T. 5591	TQ	3	x					x			x										164
T.d. Pirrichisti	TQ	3				x					x				x						99
T.d. Fustigazione	TQ	3	x		x	x		x	x		x										67
T.d. Citaredo[22]	TQ	3	x		x			x	x		x										57
T.d. Bighe[23]	TQ	3	x				x	x	x	x	x					x					47
T.d. Teschio	TQ	3	x		x			x	x												116
T. 4255	TQ	3	x		x			x			x										155
T. 4260	TQ	3				x	x														156
T.d. Caccia	CH	3												x			x				14
T.d. Pozzo a Poggio Renzo	CH	3	x				x														24
T.d. Montollo	CH	3						x	x	x		x									17
T.d. Scimmia[24]	CH	3	x	x		x			x	x	x	x					x				25
T.d. Orfeo ed Eurydice[25]	CH	3					x	x													18
T.d. Poggio Gaiella	CH	3								x											23
T.d. Leopardi[26]	TQ	3	x				x	x			x							x			81

Tomb and Place	Phase	A	B	C	D	E	F	G	H	I	J	K	L	M	N	O	P	Q	R	Cat.
T.d. Triclinio[27]	TQ 3	x	x			x	x				x									121
T.d. Letto funebre[28]	TQ 3	x	x			x	x	x	x		x		x	x						82
T. dipinta	GS 3		x			x	x		x					x?						29
T. Paolozzi	CH 3							x	x											21
T.d. Poggio al Moro	CH 3	x		x		x	x	x	x					x						22
T.d. Fiorellini	TQ 3	x				x	x													64
T.d. Colle Casuccini[29]	CH 3			x		x	x	x	x					x						15
T. 994	TQ 3					x	x													134
T. 3988[30]	TQ 3					x														152
T. 4813[31]	TQ 3	x				x	x								x					158
T. 4021	TQ 3	x				x														153
T. without name	TQ 3	x					x	x	x	x				x						173
T. without name	TQ 4	x																		172
T.d. Caccia al Cervo	TQ 4	x				x	x				x		x							49
T. Francesca Giustiniani[32]	TQ 4	x					x		x		x	x				x				65
T.d. Scrofa nera[33]	TQ 4					x	x					x								108
T.d. Demoni azzurri[34]	TQ 4		x			x	x					x			x	x	x			-
T.d. Biclinio[35]	TQ 4	x		x			x			x	(x)									46
T. 5513	TQ 4	x				x	x													162
T. Maggi	TQ 4	x				x	x						x							84
T. 2015	TQ 4	x				x														142
T. 5517	TQ 4					x							x							163
T.d. Nave	TQ 4			x		x	x													91
T.d. Pulcella[36]	TQ 4	x				x							x							103
T. Querciola I[37]	TQ 4	x				x	x		x		x	x			x					106
Grotta dipinta	BL 4		x																	1
T. 1200	TQ 5					x		x												137
T. 3713[38]	TQ 5						x		x											149
T. 130	TQ 5					x														-
T. 808	TQ 5					x														130
T.d. Gallo	TQ 5	x			x	x	x													68
T.d. Gorgoneion	TQ 5	x														x				71
T.d. Guerriero	TQ 5	x				x	x	x	x		x		x	x						73
T. 2327[39]	TQ 5					x	x					x								143
T. 3242	TQ 5						x						x							147
T. 3442	TQ 5											x								-
T. 3697	TQ 5	x				x														148
T. 6071	TQ 5	x				x	x					x								169
T. 1560	TQ 5	x					x					x								138
T.d. Pigmei	TQ 5	x	x		x	x						x								97
T. Golini I[40]	OR 6					x			x						x	x		x		32
T.d.'Orco I[41]	TQ 6		x			x								x						93

Tomb and Place	Phase	A	B	C	D	E	F	G	H	I	J	K	L	M	N	O	P	Q	R	Cat.
T.d.'Orco II[42]	TQ	6															x			x	x	94
T. Guasta	TQ	6					x										x					72
T. Golini II[43]	OR	6	x	x			x										x	x				33
T. François[44]	VU	6	x						x								x				x	178
T.d. Hescanas[45]	OR	6	x	x		x	x										x	x	x			34
T.d. Ceisinie[46]	TQ	6	x	x													x					56
T.d. Quadriga Infernale[47]	SA	6	x	x			x										x					-
Grotta dipinta	BO	6		x																		2
T.d. Sarcofagi	CV	6	x	x																		10
T.d. Triclinio	CV	6	x	x		x	x															11
T.d. Mercareccia I[48]	TQ	6	x						x			x?					x		x?			87
T. 4836[49]	TQ	6			x												x					-
T.d. Scudi[50]	TQ	6		x			x										x	x				109
T. Bruschi[51]	TQ	7		x								x?					x	x				48
T.d. Tappezzeria[52]	TQ	7															x?					113
T.d. Onde Marine	CV	7		x																		8
T.d. Rilievi	CV	7															x					9
T.d. Mercareccia II	TQ	7															x	x				87
T.d. Festoni[53]	TQ	7		x													x					62
T. Campanari[54]	VU	7															x	x				177
T. Querciola II[55]	TQ	7			x	x											x		x			107
T.d. Anina[56]	TQ	7															x					40
T.d. Caronti[57]	TQ	7				x											x					55
T.d.'Orco III[58]	TQ	7																			x	95
T.d. Martinella	CH	7?																x				16
T.d. Corridietro	PO	7		x																		35
T.d. Delfini	PO	7		x																		36
T. 4912[59]	TQ	7															x					159
T. c. Donna . . .[60]	TQ	7	x?															x?				60
T.d. Eizenes[61]	TQ	8			x												x					61
T. Tartaglia[62]	TQ	8			x												x		x			115
T.d. Cardinale[63]	TQ	8			x				x								x	x	x			54
T. c. Nave	TQ	8			x																	90
T.c. Processione di Cibele	TQ	8																x				102
T.c. Teste di Charun[64]	TQ	8															x	x?	x?			117
T.d. Tifone[65]	TQ	8	x	x													x	x				118
T.d. Convegno[66]	TQ	8																x				58
T. 5512[67]	TQ	8															x	x	x			161
T. 5636[68]	TQ	8			x												x		x			165
T.d. Alsina	TQ	8																x				39

Appendix A – Notes

[1] Steingräber 1985, dates the latest painted tombs to the 2nd c. BC, but there is a tendency in later literature on Etruscan tomb paintings to push this limit back into the 3rd c. BC (see, for example, Sacchetti 2000; Franzoni 2011). I have for the latest paintings maintained Steingräber's dating, mainly to underline that they belong to the latest phase of the paintings.

[2] The painting, in addition, contains a man and a man running with a bow, both of difficult interpretation and perhaps not relevant to the listed parameters.

[3] In addition: a 'potnios theron' between two lions (cf. also T. Stefani (phase 2: 112) at Tarquinia).

[4] In addition: archer on horseback.

[5] Moltesen & Weber Lehmann 1992: 85–87.

[6] Weber-Lehmann 2004b, *c.* 600 BC. – The head between the panthers has been interpreted both as an animal head and as Medusa. For the last interpretation, see Krauskopf 1988a: 331.4, 340.

[7] Fiorini 2007: 134, Table 1, dates this tomb to 560 BC.

[8] Moltesen & Weber Lehmann 1992: 71–72.

[9] Moltesen & Weber Lehmann 1992: 24–27.

[10] Moltesen & Weber Lehmann 1992: 75–76; Weber-Lehmann 2004c, 530–520.

[11] For the motif, see also Phase 1: *T.d. Leoni Dipinti* (6).

[12] Blanck & Weber-Lehmann 1987: 61–74; Moltesen & Weber Lehmann 1992: 63–65.

[13] Blanck & Weber-Lehmann 1987: 82; Moltesen & Weber Lehmann 1992: 21–24; Weber-Lehmann 2004d: 520–510.

[14] Blanck & Weber-Lehmann 1987: 74–81; Moltesen & Weber Lehmann 1992: 42–43; the large kylix is carried on edge, i.e. at 90 degrees, not able to contain liquid (Steingräber 1985: 336, fig. 232).

[15] Blanck & Weber-Lehmann 1987: 94–97; Moltesen & Weber Lehmann 1992: 40–42.

[16] Blanck & Weber-Lehmann 1987: 82–90; Moltesen & Weber Lehmann 1992: 68–71.

[17] Also known as T. 2002.

[18] Moltesen & Weber-Lehmann 1992: 77–78.

[19] Blanck & Weber-Lehmann 1987: 90–94; Moltesen & Weber Lehmann 1992: 57–59. – Note that one of the amphoras on the kylikeion carries a scene with a person between two horses, giving association to parameter J and to the *T.d. Barone* (phase 2:44).

[20] Moltesen & Weber Lehmann 1992: 60–61.

[21] Moltesen & Weber Lehmann 1992: 61–62.

[22] Blanck & Weber-Lehmann 1987: 118–25; Andreae 2004a: 490–480.

[23] Blanck & Weber-Lehmann 1987: 97–117; Moltesen & Weber Lehmann 1992: 65–68.

[24] Blanck & Weber-Lehmann 1987: 198–203; Moltesen & Weber Lehmann 1992: 80–82.

[25] Blanck & Weber-Lehmann 1987: 204.

[26] Blanck & Weber-Lehmann 1987: 125–28; Moltesen & Weber Lehmann 1992: 31–33.

27 Blanck & Weber-Lehmann 1987: 129–58; Moltesen & Weber Lehmann 1992: 36–40.

28 Moltesen & Weber Lehmann 1992: 33–36; Scala 1997: a *theoxonia* for the Dioscuri; Weber-Lehmann 2004e.

29 Blanck & Weber-Lehmann 1987: 204–7; Moltesen & Weber Lehmann 1992: 78–80.

30 The tomb, according to Steingräber 1985: 374, makes 'einen merkwürdig pasticcio-artigen Eindruck und sind möglicherweise eine moderne Fälschung.'

31 Steingräber 1985: 375, a very early example of winged juveniles in Etruscan wall-painting.

32 Moltesen & Weber Lehmann 1992: 73–75.

33 Weber-Lehmann 2004f, 460–450.

34 See in particular: Cataldi Dini 1989, pls 39–41, figs 107–110; Adinolfi et al. 2005a; 2005b. See also Sacchetti 2000: 128.1, second half of the 5th c.

35 The hunting scene appears on a rolled-out *rotulus* held by one of the banqueting women.

36 Moltesen & Weber Lehmann 1992: 27–29.

37 Blanck & Weber-Lehmann 1987: 159–75; Moltesen & Weber Lehmann 1992: 29–31; Prayon 2004: 48, late 5th c BC; Cerchiai 2010.

38 The kylix is held on edge.

39 Also called *T. Bertazzoni*.

40 Blanck & Weber-Lehmann 1987: 176–82; Moltesen & Weber Lehmann 1992, 83–85; Sacchetti 2000: 130.4, mid 4th c. BC.

41 See also preceding note; Sacchetti 2000: 128–29.2, second quarter 4th c. BC; for the *gens* Murina as possible owners, see Morandi & Colonna 1995.

42 Moltesen & Weber Lehmann 1992: 52–56; Sacchetti 2000: 129–30.3, mid 4th c. BC.

43 Sacchetti 2000: 130–31.5, mid 4th c. BC.

44 Blanck & Weber-Lehmann 1987: 207–15; Moltesen & Weber Lehmann 1992: 87–88; Sacchetti 2000: 131.6, second half 4th c. BC.

45 The central scene on the rear wall (badly preserved) may refer to a 'Purifikationsopfer am Altar?' (Steingräber 1985, 288), which, if the case, will be a unique presentation in Etruscan tomb painting.

46 Sacchetti 2000: 131.7, second half 4th c. BC.

47 Millet 2005; 2007.

48 Thematically there appears to be a distinction between the choice of motifs in the Upper chamber (here called I) and the Lower chamber (here called II).

49 Linington & Serra Ridgway 1997, I: 112–14.70, 152; II, pl. 104.a; Sacchetti 2000: 132.10, late 4th/early 3rd c. BC.

50 Blanck & Weber-Lehmann 1987: 183–88; Moltesen & Weber Lehmann 1992: 46–50; Tassi Scandone 2001: 44, third quarter of 4th c. BC; Prayon 2004: 50, 59, beginning of 3rd c. BC.

51 Blanck & Weber-Lehmann 1987: 189–96, early 3rd c. BC; Vincenti 2007: 102, late 4th/early 3rd c. BC; Sacchetti 2000: 138–39.13 and Tassi Scandone 2001: 45, first half 3rd c. BC; Prayon 2004: 59, 300/250.

52   Haumesser 2007: 58, 66, end 4th c. BC; Sacchetti 2000: 132.9, late 4th/early 3rd c. BC.
53   Sacchetti 2000: 139–40.14, mid 3rd c. BC.
54   Steingräber 1985: 384, does not view the throning man and standing women as Aita and
      Phersipnai (parameter Q), rather as the dead husband and his wife; Sacchetti 2000: 147–
      48.24, 3rd c. BC.
55   Blanck & Weber-Lehmann 1987: 196–98; Sacchetti 2000: 140.15, mid 3rd c. BC.
56   Sacchetti 2000: 132, 134.11, second/third quarter 3rd c. BC.
57   Haumesser 2007: 77, early 3rd c. BC; Sacchetti 2000: 134, 136–38.12, second/third
      quarter 3rd c. BC.
58   Moltesen & Weber-Lehmann 1992: 52–56.
59   Sacchetti 2000: 140, 142.16, mid 3rd c. BC.
60   Full name: *T. con Donna con Diadema, Cimbali, Uomo su Elefante* – only known from
      descriptions: perhaps a procession, though some want to see both Bacchus and Cybele
      among the participants.
61   Sacchetti 2000: 144.21, end 3rd c. BC.
62   Sacchetti 2000: 144.20, third quarter 3rd c. BC. – Cf. also Sacchetti's note 10, p. 157.
63   Morandi 1983; Moltesen & Weber Lehmann 1992: 51–52; Peruzzi 2007. – Sacchetti
      2000: 145, 147.23, 3rd c. BC.
64   Sacchetti 2000: 144–45.22, 3rd c. BC.: 'scena di "viaggio nell'Aldilà" probabilmente
      nella forma di un "corteo magistratuale".'
65   Cristofani 1971a; Moltesen & Weber Lehmann 1992: 43–46; Sacchetti 2000: 142, 144.19
      and Tassi Scandone 2001: 48, third quarter 3rd c. BC; Prayon 2004: 51, 59, after mid 3rd
      c. BC; Massa-Pairault 1996: 216, last quarter 3rd c. BC.
66   Tassi Scandone 2001: 46, first half 3rd c. BC.
67   Sacchetti 2000: 141.17, mid 3rd c. BC.
68   Sacchetti 2000: 142.18, third quarter 3rd c. BC.

Appendix B: Pictorial parameters

List of the pictorial parameters A-R including in the footnotes some details on their distributions (the number between brackets refers to the catalogue number in Steingräber 1985):

A. Heraldic birds and animals, both real and mythical; animal battle scenes in a heraldic setting, Gorgoneia,[191] 'lararium' type snakes.[192]
B. Subjects alluding to sea/water: boats/ships,[193] dolphins,[194] hippocamps,[195] sea/water snakes,[196] Tritons,[197] waves.[198]
C. Closed, false doors: squared or arched.[199]
D. Unconventional scenes: *cornuto* sign,[200] bodily fluid emission scenes,[201] erotic scenes,[202] scenes with reference to laughter,[203] phallus bird,[204] purification sacrifice,[205] pygmies[206] – and skeletons in boxes.[207]
E. Banquets, often accompanied by music (in this world, in both this and the Underworld,[208] in the Underworld[209]).
F. Dance, most often accompanied by musicians.[210]
G. Scenes with blood, visible and potentially visible: Phersu,[211] flogging,[212] boxers,[213] wrestlers,[214] warriors, fights, and killings.[215]
H. Athletic games (excluding boxers and wrestlers: see parameter G),[216] tug of war,[217] chariot races,[218] and horse jumpers.[219]
I. Ritual objects: *thymiateria*[220] and oversized kylikes.[221]
J. Horsemen (excluding mythical contexts and hunting scenes).[222]
K. Hunting scenes.[223]
L. Prothesis and related scenes.
M. Weapon (or Pyrrhic) dances.
N. Demons in various guises: as winged *genii*,[224] Charu(n),[225] Lasa?,[226] Tuchulcha,[227] Vanth,[228] in most cases unnamed.[229]
O. Processions (see also parameter K: Horsemen): in a ritual setting,[230] the deceased in chariot,[231] magisterial processions,[232] or processions in general.[233]
P. Encounters (reunion beyond this world).
Q. The Underworld with Hades/Aita and Persephone/Phersipnai present.
R. Underworld mythological scenes.

Notes

1   The ideas presented in this article were conceived many years ago, but needed a seminar to be born in writing. Not being an Etruscologist by profession I had no up-to-date knowledge about *l'état des affaires* when I started writing it, but soon discovered that Torelli 1997a and 1997b (with an English off-spring in 1999, which I shall use as the main reference) had already started to develop a similar kind of thinking. In 2007, the year before our seminar in Oslo, the journal *Ostraka* presented an issue with a series of articles on late Etruscan painting, including an article by Fiorini 2007, in which he further developed Torelli's

initial ideas. The reader will find much agreement between our respective articles, but there are also some basic divergences, which seen together will hopefully open up further discussions on the interpretation of the Etruscan tomb paintings. However, others have also been thinking along similar lines, as, for example: Spivey & Stoddart 1990: 110–20; Prayon 2004; Leighton 2004: 113–21; Krauskopf 2006; Weber-Lehmann 2012. – I am most grateful to prof. Eric Hostetter and to the anonymous peer-reviewer for having read the ms. in typescript and for having presented some useful suggestions.

2   At the end of the article, in Appendix A, is presented a simple catalogue of all the painted tombs of interest for the present arguments. The catalogue, arranged chronologically according to phases (8 in all), builds on Steingräber 1985 (including his catalogue numbers) with the addition of a few tombs discovered later – The Italian names of the tombs will be used (*T.* = *Tomba*). In the running text all references to the tombs described by Steingräber 1985 will be made by the phase + Steingräber's cat. no., for example: *T. degli Auguri* (phase 2: 42); new tombs, not registered by Steingräber 1985, will only be referred to by (phase), and in a footnote the main publications will be entered.

3   Sourvinou-Inwood 1981: 15.

4   I distinguish between 'nether world'/'the hereafter' and 'Underworld'; the first concepts refer generically to the infernal world, the other specifically to the world in which Hades/Aita and Persephone/Phersipnai reign.

5   Krauskopf 1988b; de Grummond 2006: 229.

6   Mavleev 1994; de Grummond 2006: 229.

7   For a generic description of them, see, for example, Jannot 1991; 1997; 1998: 79–81; de Grummond 2006: 213–25.

8   For an abridged research history on this question, see Krauskopf 1987: 11–12, note 1; 2006: 73. Cf. also Roncalli 2000: 362; Weber-Lehmann 2004a: 125.

9   Bremmer 2002: 11–26. The Orphic-Pythagorean influence in Etruscan tomb-painting was first suggested by Weege 1921: 22–56, and contradicted (receiving little attention) by van Essen 1927: 41, 80–82. For an abridged research history on this question, see Krauskopf 1987: 11, note 1; 2006: 73; Steingräber 2006: 191–94. Cf. also Jannot 1998: 58, 69–70; Leighton 2004: 117, 119, 165; and more generically Bernabé & Jiménez San Cristóbal 2008.

10   See, for example, Pensa 1977.

11   Cristofani 1989: 27.

12   First published by Cataldi Dini 1987, followed up by further publications, as listed below.

13   Cataldi Dini 1989: 151; Adinolfi et al. 2005a: 46, 52–53, fig. 1; however, Torelli 1997a: 143; 1997b: 83; 1999: 157, opts for funerary games.

14   Cataldi Dini 1989: 151, pls 40b–41, fig. 108; Adinolfi et al. 2005a: 46–48. – See also Steingräber 2006: 163 (fig.).

15   Cataldi Dini 1989: 151, fig. 109; Adinolfi et al. 2005a: 46–48.

16   Cataldi Dini 1989: 151, pls 39, 40a, fig. 110; Adinolfi et al. 2005a: 46, 48–52, fig. 2. – See also Roncalli 1997: 37–44; Steingräber 2006: 177, 181 (figs).

17   Adinolfi et al. 2005a: 46; 2005b: 445; recently this date has been lowered to 430–420 BC (Torelli 2007: 149). Prayon 2004: 48, 59, dates the paintings to the first half of the 4th c. BC.

18   Though note the slightly later (420–400 BC) bronze handle of Orvietan origin from Tomb

169 C at Spina; here Aitia may be presented: Hostetter 1986: 20–27, cat. 4, pls 6a–d, 7a–d and colour plate 1.

19 Ronacalli 2000: 362.
20 Instead of the word *form* some will perhaps be more comfortable with the word *behaviour*.
21 Brandt 2006: 44–45; 2012a: 140–42; cf. also Seeberg 1995: 6–7.
22 See also Jannot 1998: 69–70.
23 Coldstream 1968: 29–90 *passim.*
24 Woodford & Spier 1992: 25.1 with fig.
25 Lindner et al. 1988.
26 Güntner 1997.
27 Woodford & Spier 1992.
28 Oakley 1994.
29 Bažant 1994.
30 Bažant 1997.
31 Sourvinou-Inwood 1986; Oakley 2004: 113.
32 According to Oakley 2004: 113–14, starting from the 460's BC in two examples by the Tymbos Painter, but particularly frequent from after the middle of the century.
33 Prückner 1968: 75–84; Lissi Caronna et al. 2007.
34 Described by Pausanias, *Description of Greece* 10.28–31. For modern authors, see, for example, Robertson 1975: 266–70; Stansbury-O'Donnell 1990; Castriota 1992: 89–95, 118–27.
35 Stansbury-O'Donnell 1990: 234. – See, Cerchiai 2010 (with furher literature) for a possible Etruscan loan.
36 See note 10 above.
37 Adinolfi et al. 2005a: 48, though note that according to Rendeli 1996: 16, no Attic vase presenting Charon has been found in Etruria, and certainly not any white ground lekythoi, which were produced nearly exclusively for the Attic market (note, however, Hostetter 1986: 42, who mentions two white lekythoi found at Spina).
38 De Grummond 2006: 212–13, referring to Roncalli 1996; 1997.
39 Cataldi Dini 1989: 151; Roncalli 1996: 48; cf. also Krauskopf 1987: 22, 42 with note 113.
40 Ducati 1910: cols. 417.106, 441–49.169, pl. 5; Haynes 2000: 307–8, fig. 248. – Cf. also note 7 and Sassatelli 1984; Cerchiai 1995; and also Hostetter 1986: 22 of a possible syncretism between Charun and Turms Aitas, the messenger of Aitas.
41 Cf. Jannot 1997: 141–42; Serra Ridgway 2000: 307–8.
42 Cristofani 1989: 27; Torelli 1999; Prayon 2004: 45; Weber-Lehmann 2012.
43 Van Gennep 1908 [1960: 146]; Morris 1992: 8–10. See, also Cristofani 1987: 192; 1989: 27; Spivey & Stoddart 1990: 116–17; Torelli 1999: 152, 156–57; Weber-Lehmann 2004a: 124; Krauskopf 2006: 74–75.
44 Van Gennep 1908 [1960: 148].
45 Douglas 1966 [2002: 119–21].
46 As reported by the Norwegian student Hans Hansen (Johannes) Lilienskiold (ms. 211r) on a visit to Rome that same winter. A Danish student, Holger Jacobæus, some years later, reported the same, specifying that the period without law lasted from the time of the Pope's death to the transfer of his body to St Peter's (Maar 1910: 118).

47 Lilienskold ms. 211r; see also Brandt 2002: 173–74. For a further, modern description of the disorders, see, for example, Boiteux 1997: 46–47, 49. Such customs may go back to Early Medieval times (Paravicini-Bagliani 2000: 99–107, 150–55) becoming a sort of passage rite, as suggested by Ginzburg 1987.

48 Van Gennep 1908 [1960: 147].

49 For issues of purification in general, see Douglas 1966 [2002]; in Greece, see, for example, Cole 2004: 30–37, 105–6; in Rome, see, for example, Brandt 2012b: 153–54; 2014.

50 Shapiro 1991.

51 Jannot 1984a: 368–73.

52 A possibly fourth scene can be observed in *T. delle Iscrizioni* (phase 2: 74) where on the right wall, close to the entrance wall, a man directs a young boy carrying branches; on the ground line, lying higher than all other ground lines in this tomb, thus signalling a scene of some importance, rest two sets of two pillows. The scene could thus refer to the *lit de parade*, where the pillows refer to the (two?) deceased person(s) (as in the *T. del Letto Funebre*) and the young boy carry branches to be used for the purification of the home after the dead(s) has/have been carried away.

53 See at Tarquinia: *T. degli Auguri* (phase 2: 42), *T. del Citaredo* (phase 3: 57), and *T. del Pulcinella* (phase 2: 104); cf. also Hostetter 1986: 42. On early mourning in Etruria, see Taylor 2011.

54 See, for example, Poursat 1968; Delavaud-Roux 1993; Ceccarelli 1998; in Etruria, see Camporeale 1987.

55 Steingräber 2006: 66; Torelli 1999: 153; Prayon 2004: 54–57; though, see also Staccioli 1980, Jannot 1984b, and Serra Ridgway 2000: 310: 'It is ... quite possible to recognize in the Tarquinian false doors a double symbolism ...: they are meant to be seen as the sign of the tomb, which – as the home of the dead – is in itself at the same time an allusion to Hades ...'

56 Naso 1996: 417–20 (see also Steingräber 2006: 66) counted 18 tombs with false doors at Tarquinia (Torelli 1999: 150, arrived only at 17), among which figure two undated tombs not included in my catalogue in Appendix A: T. 12 (Naso 1996: 200.59) and T. 2202 (Naso 1996: 207.99).

57 For a distribution of the singular elements on the painted tombs, see the list of parameters in Appendix B.

58 Boosen 1986: 58–63, 129–33, 177–82, 217–22, 232; Krauskopf 1987: 14 with notes 4–6; Jannot 1998: 76–78; Haynes 2000: 223. Cf. also Hostetter 1986: 22–23, the water element signalled by a water drop.

59 Jannot 1998: 71–88; de Grummond 2006: 209–33, esp. p. 209. – See also Massa-Pairault 1998.

60 See *Tables 5.1–5.2* on p. 144.

61 Torelli 1999: 150.

62 Colonna 1996; Torelli 1997a: 138; 1997b: 79 (note the slight difference in the two texts). Cf. also Cristofani 1989: 29; Krauskopf 2006: 76–77; Steingräber 2006: 98. Cf. also a bronze handle of a volute krater from Tomb 128 at Spina: Hostetter 1986: 18–19, cat. 2, pls 4a–d, 5a–c.

63 De Grummond 2006: 191, while Haynes 2000: 236 refers to them as 'saviors and mediators between this world and the next'.

64 According to Bonfante 2009: 189, *tutulus* is a kind of hair-dress and not the melon-shaped hat which normally has adopted this name. In this study, however, I shall use the traditional denomination to describe the hat.

65 *CSE* 1995: 25.16, fig. p. 101. Cf. also Haynes 2000: 240, fig. 195; Weber-Lehmann 2004e: 147, fig. 5.

66 For other interpretations, see, for example, Åkerström 1981: 24–33; Walberg 1986; Massa-Pairault 1992: 84–85. For a more recent and much different interpretation based, in the present context, on doubtful Greek sources, see Amann 1998.

67 Torelli 1999: 148.

68 Torelli 1999: 147–48.

69 See parameter N, pp. 143, 145; and Appendix B. – Cf. also note 40.

70 See also Moretti 1966: 135–41 (plates inclusive) (*T. 1701*); Steingräber 2006: 114–15 (figs).

71 So described by Haynes 2000: 234. The paintings are partially blackened in the most strategic areas, but the situation is made worse by the lack of a proper publication and an attempt to make a careful description of what actually goes on in this and the following scene.

72 See *Tables 5.1–5.2* on p. 144. – For the Gorgoneis and 'lararium' snakes in the graves, see the distribution signalled in Appendix B. With 'lararium' snakes I mean snakes as often found in the lararia-paintings at Pompeii and other places (see, for example, Brandt 2010), with a crest on the head and/or a 'beard'. In Italian they are often referred to as *serpenti agatodemoni*. – See also Harari 2011.

73 Cf. Torelli 1999: 155.

74 Izzet 2007: 93, 98. For a different twist to the question, see Roncalli 2000: 349, 351.

75 Only in one instance do a man and a woman dance up against each other, the scene being more erotic than spirited, see *T. delle Leonesse* (phase 2: 77). – For a very early example of a ring-dance on a funerary relief from Chiusi, see Jannot 1984a: 8, Cat. A,1, figs 62, 64 (8th c. BC).

76 Johnstone 1956: 46–47.

77 As, for example, Torelli 1999: 150–57; Fiorini 2007: 135–41. See also Dobrowolski 1990, who, in addition, defines Dionysos as a chthonic deity. – On the Greek *komos* and *komasts*, see, for example, Greifenhagen 1929; Seeberg 1971; Carpenter 1986: 85–90; Peschel 1987; Lissargue 1990.

78 Jannot 1984a: 314–40, esp. pp. 314–20.

79 See also parameter I, p. 137, 139, and Appendix B.

80 For details, see Appendix B, parameter F. – A *krotola* dancer appears also on a utensil stand from Tomb 128 at Spina, see Hostetter 1986: 32–33, cat. 8, pls 11b–d, 12a–c, 91a, and colour pl. 2.

81 This does not mean that such lamentations were not performed, as visible on a funerary ash urn from Chiusi (early 5th c. BC): see, for example, Jannot 1998: 62–63, fig. 29.

82 Metcalf & Huntington 1991: 57.

83 Lonsdale 1993: 258.

84 We have no reference to such Etruscan forces, but Vergil, *Aenid* 6.273–94, described, as referred by Krauskopf 2006: 75, 'monsters and spirits who can endanger human beings and drive them into the Realm of the Dead dwell there: War, Disease, Anxiety, Grief,

Fear, Discord, Poverty, Hunger, and other figures. The spirits who have their abode here can exercise their powers all on earth, which is why they live in the intermediate zone. In a more abstract manner they have a function similar to that of the Etruscan demons: 'they conduct men into the Underworld' – or perhaps not conducting, rather making the conduct difficult. Vergil's presentation may be a fossilised picture of an earlier Etruscan view of undesirable real and abstract forces.

85 Note, however, that these *ludiones* appear to be of a different kind than the initiated persons, who participated in the celebrations of Dionysos, as described by Livy (39.8–18) in the famous Roman decree on the Bacchanalia of 186 BC.

86 Arnobius, *Adversus Nationes* 2.62; cf. de Grummond 2006: 209, who also refers to a similar idea expressed in Homer, *Odyssey* 11.34–50, when Odysseus 'slits the throat of sheep so that the blood may flow down into a pit and be drunk by the souls in the Underworld. When they drink the blood, they are then able to talk to Odysseus, that is, they are literally *animated*' (cf. Burkert 1985: 59–60). On blood sacrifice, see also von Vacano 1957: 30.

87 See de Grummond 2006: 209–10. – On pure and impure blood in Greece, see Cole 2004: 137–40 *passim*.

88 Note, however, that Cristofani 1987: 198, tried to restore the presence of a ram or pig in *Tomba dell'Orco II* (phase 6: 94) at Tarquinia, a restoration supported by Roncalli 1997: 44–45.

89 Jannot 1984a: 23–25.5 (B, I, 5, *b*) (Louvre 3611 according to catalogue, wrongly numbered 3610 on illustration), fig. 105. On the accompanying relief (B, I, 5, *a*), fig. 106, another burning altar with a *thymiaterion* separates two banquet scenes, one with reclining silens, the other with reclining young and old men. – As this article went to press I discovered that Jannot (2010: 70–71) now questions the authencity of the relief. However, the connection between *thymiaterion* and altar (where bloody sacrifices were performed) is not exceptional in an Etruscan context (on *thymiateria* and their use, see Ambrosini 2002: 59–68 (text sources), 69–96 (images, also with altars)). – For Etruscan sacrificial procedures in general, see Jannot 1998: 54–56. Cf. also Dionysius of Halicarnassus, *Roman Antiquities* 7.72.13, for *thymiateria* carried in Roman sacrificial processions (Jannot 1998: 58).

90 *Thymiateria* are recorded in a game context in the following tombs: *T. dei Giocolieri*, Tarquinia (phase 2: 70), *T. delle Bighe*, Tarquinia (phase 3: 47; see also Thuillier 1997b: 375, fig. 4 to the right; Ambrosini 2002: 69), *T. della Scimmia*, Chiusi (phase 3: 25), *T. del Biclinio*, Tarquinia (phase 4: 46; see also Dobrowolski 1989; Steingräber 2006: 162–63, recently dated to the second/third quarter of the 5th c. BC and not to the 4th c. BC). For an Underworld presentation, see *T. Golini I*, Orvieto (phase 6: 32), placed on the *kylikeion* at a banquet with Aita and Phersipnai present.

91 See also Haynes 2000: 230–31.

92 More or less as the balancing game *acroamata* as suggested by Torelli 1999: 148 with reference to D'Agostino 1993; see also Haynes 2000: 231, and Ambrosini 2002: 69–73.

93 The streaming blood in boxing scenes are also remarked by Jannot 1998: 66.

94 *T. della Fustigazione* (phase 3: 67): Moretti 1966, fig. on p. 138 (*T. 1701*); Steingräber 2006: 114–15 (figs).

95 On Phersu, see, for example, Bomati 1986; Jannot 1993a; Emmanuel-Rebuffat 1997; Avramidou 2009. – For Phersu-scenes, see, from Chiusi: *T. della Scimmia* (phase 3: 25), and two cippus base reliefs: Jannot 1984a: 58 (C, 1, 27, *b*), fig. 197; Thuillier 1997a:

254–55, figs 1 and 6 (480/470); and from Tarquinia: *T. degli Auguri* (phase 2: 42); *T. delle Olimpiadi* (phase 2: 92); *T. del Pulcinella* (phase 2: 104); and perhaps *T. 1999* (phase 2: 141; Moretti 1966: 87–91 (plates inclusive)); cf. also *T. del Gallo* (phase 5: 68) in which a masked man dances with a spirited woman, though most likely he shall not be identified with Phersu (see below, p. 135).

96 *T. François*, Vulci (phase 6: 178): cf., for example, Buranelli 2004; Andreae 2004b; Weber-Lehmann 2005b).

97 Pontrandolfo & Rouveret 1992, 54–58 and the histograms figs 45–46, p. 68. The Lucanian painted tombs from the Paestum area in S. Italy make up to some 80 out of a total of *c.* 700 tombs excavated (p. 17). They were composed of stone slabs and contained normally more than one motif. Armed combat scenes ('duello') was the most popular figurative motif, present in 33 tombs, with blood-streaming boxing scenes ('pugilato') as a good runner up, present in 22 tombs.

98 As also suggested by Jannot 1998: 67.

99 Tertullian, *De spectaculis* 12.

100 Ville 1981: 1–19, esp. 9–19.

101 On gladiatorial games, see, for example, Edwards 2007: 46–77.

102 Bergmann 1999: 22.

103 Edwards 2007: 53.

104 Helbig 1966: 343–45.1529; Menichetti 1992: 27–29 (*hieròs gámos*); Haynes 2000: 97–99; latest, see the discussion by van der Meer 2011: 71–74.

105 From Chiusi, only one erotic scene – on a sarcophagus – is known: four silens play with three naked women with *tutuli*; a standing copulation scene where she is carried high in the air, a fellatio-act, and a bed-lying copulation scene, all accompanied to the tunes of a double flute (Jannot 1984a: 23.5 (B, I, 5, *c*), fig. 107 (Louvre 3603): 'peu après 520' (p. 302)). This relief, however, belonging to the same sarcophagus as the one referred to in note 89, is now also considered not to be authentic (Jannot 2010: 71).

106 Douglas 1966 [2002]: 142, 150. I am grateful to Lene Os Johannessen (2010), for having drawn my attention to this part of Douglas' thoughts. Cf. also Cole 2004: 94, 101, 111–13: sexual activity as pollution in Greece.

107 Torelli 1997a: 126, 'scena scurrile di *apotropaion*, un gesto cioè destinato a esorcizzare il male e i rischi di sventure' (in 1997b: 67, the important second part of the sentence was omitted). – The two heraldically black birds, in their ominous apparition, placed next to the defecating scene may be read as a warning to the amused and confused onlookers of the seriousness of the liminal situation, but they could also be considered as a sign to ward off the liminal dangers inherent in the defecating act.

108 Moltesen & Weber-Lehmann 1992: 64, fig. 1.58; cf. also Prayon 2004: 62. The man is described as ityphallic, but the downward directed position of his penis and the curved, continuous jet of bodily fluids give more the impression of urinating rather than an act of ejaculation (when the semen will be ejected in thrusts).

109 Metcalf & Huntington 1991: 54–59, 113, 117, 119, 184.

110 Corbeill 1996: 135–39.

111 As, for example, by Steingräber 1985: 297.

112 See also the original, but questionable opinion of Cerchiai 2001, who gives the pediments a Dionysiac interpretation and in the mouse sees an allusion to erotic pairing off.

113 Keuls 1993: 76–77, 80: Attic phallic birds, interpreted merely as 'a phallic joke'.

114 Moltesen & Weber Lehmann 1992: 65, followed by Prayon 2004: 63, note 63, suggest that the bird may be depicted in an act of ejaculation, while also a curved jet of fluids has suggestively here been discerned in the painting.

115 If, however, the postulated beam should be interpreted as an act of urinating (though a difficult action in an aroused state), the emission of bodily fluids could again be interpreted as belonging to a disorderly act.

116 Wreaths occur frequently in tomb contexts, carried or hanging from the horizontal architectural feature lines above (cf. *T. del Barone*, Fig. 5.6), and may have had a significance similar to that of garlands, later more common (on garlands, see Serra Ridgway 2000: 307–9).

117 So according to Carlo Ruspi's drawing of the wall (Blanck & Weber-Lehmann 1987: 63, fig. 4), but in the water colour painting presented in Moltesen & Weber Lehmann 1992: 65, fig. 1.59, he appears to carry a short garment around his hips.

118 For the drawings, see, for example, Blanck & Weber-Lehmann 1987: 67–68, figs 9–10.

119 As suggested by Steingräber 1985: 322 ('Opferszene?'), and carried further by Torelli 1999: 152.

120 Urine used as a disinfectant liquid in connection with wounds, blisters, bee-stings, and insect- and snakebites is generally known; in some cultures urine is also used as a potion for internal use to strengthen health. Urine is a bodily fluid like blood, but in difference to blood which runs in a closed system, urine runs in an open system and is ejected. Both systems stop at death. We know next to nothing about the Etruscans view of the body, but the presence of the deceased as urinating may contain reference to a belief in which the urine as a bodily fluid was essential to living and in that function included as part of the funerary practices.

121 Whitehead 1996: 9–13.

122 Whitehead 1996: 12.

123 Dionysius of Halicarnassus, *Roman Antiquities* 7.72.12.

124 Suetonius, *Divus Vespasianus* 19.2. Translation borrowed from Purcell 1999: 190, note 9.

125 For a short introduction to modern theories on laughter, see Clarke 2007: 2–11; cf. also Seeberg 1995: 3.

126 Wikan 2008: 81–82. On such and other problematic life situations in general, see Wikan 1990.

127 Harari 2004: 173; 2005: 86. For a close description of the tomb, see Weber-Lehmann 2005a; cf. also Steingräber 2006: 160–61 (figs).

128 See, latest Steingräber 1999; Harari 2004.

129 Homer, *Iliad* 3.3–7; cf. Herodotus 3.14.

130 Harari 2004: 178; 2005: 88. See also p. 142 below.

131 Steingräber 1999: 39–40.

132 Jannot 1993a: 288, note 21; Haynes 2000: 233.

133 Corbeill 1996: 9–10, 14–56 (with special reference to physical peculiarities).

134 See parameter M, pp. 116–17, and Appendix B.

135 The Etruscan origin of Roman funerary practices is still a field of study with few secure inputs – for a general discussion, see, for example, Flower 1996: 339–53.

136 D'Agostino 1983: 7; 1987: 216; Small 1994: 88–89.

137 For similar topsy-turvy situations, see the erotic scenes in the Suburban baths at Pompeii, as interpreted by Clarke 2007: 194–204. Massa-Pairault 1992: 88, however, draws to attention representations of Aphrodite and Adone and interprets the scene as a comment on *felicitas*.

138 For a Roman situation, cf. Clarke 2007: 193–94, 196–98.

139 As suggested by Whitehead 1996: 26–27.

140 For some examples from the Roman world, see Bodel 1994 (inscription from Puteoli); 2000: 135–44; Lindsay 2000: 154–60. See also Hope 2000.

141 See above, p. 118

142 On laurels in tombs at Tarquinia, see, for example, Simon 1973; Jannot 2005: 540 and note 53. The connection with Apollo in this instance is not necessary, the purifying power of the laurel in a funerary context being more important. Fontaine 2009: 374–75, suggests that in *T. d. Caccia e Pesca*, in the first room the trees are not laurels but myrtles, associating the trees with Aphrodite and the orgiastic dance, but the myrtle, at least in a Greek setting, has also a funerary and re-creative function (Furley 1981: 169; Brandt 2012a: 150), perhaps a more appropriate association in a funerary context.

143 See pp. 125–26, 132 and 130 in connection with *T. dei Giocolieri* (phase 2: 70); and Appendix B.

144 Add also a relief base from Florence (Museo archeologico nazionale inv. 86508), in which the incense burner is placed next to the *kliné* in a banquet scene: Jannot 1984a: 102, drawing B *ad* fig. 353; Ambrosini 2002: 74, fig. 6.

145 *CVA*, III, I, pls 2–3, 4–5, 6–7

146 For the pyxis, cf. also the box carried on the Florence relief base (see note 144), both of ritual character

147 See pp. 118–19, and Appendix B.

148 See parameter I, Appendix B.

149 For a further note on *T. Campana*, however, see pp. 150–51.

150 Torelli 1999: 152–53.

151 Torelli 1999: 151 Table 1, 154. Note that in an earlier tomb (*c.* 520), *T. delle Leonesse* (phase 2: 77), the banquet is displayed on the side walls, as also in *T. 1000* (phase 2: 135), *c.* 500 BC.

152 Krauskopf 2006: 70.

153 Torelli 1999: 156, interprets the banquet scene in the lower frieze in *T. delle Bighe* (phase 3: 47) as belonging to the Underworld, which it can not do. The dancers, not being *komasts*, are not dancers accompanying the deceased, but dancers of this world performing acts in the liminal phase of the funerary rituals to help the deceased on his/her way to the Underworld. The two friezes of the tomb do not necessarily distinguish between an earthly (the athletic games above) and a sub-earthly space (the banquet and dancing) below, rather between two phases in the liminal funerary practices: the phase of honours (above) and the phase of liminal actions (below).

154 Note that on the left wall the deceased is male, on the right wall female. Could the tomb have been made for a married couple, the man representing the social status of the couple in this world, the woman encountering the ancestors (including an earlier dead son?) in the

liminal world? – Prayon 2004: 48–49, note 19, seems unduly careful in his interpretation of the scene by the boat as either a meeting scene or as one of farewell (cf. parameter P below). – See also the comments of Massa-Pairault 1992: 92.

155 For riders/horsemen, see parameter J, pp. 118–19 above, and Appendix B.

156 Harari 2005: 88.

157 Krauskopf 1987: 19–20, 25–33. Note, however, a late 6th c. Etruscan black-figure hydria showing winged demons accompanying a dead couple (Bentz 2008: 162–64.241).

158 See note 40. – For a catalogue of Charun in Etruscan art, see latest Mavleev & Krauskopf 1986, with an updated version of presentations in tomb paintings by Sacchetti 2000.

159 Cristofani 1975: 42.12, pl. 29.1–2. – For presentations of Vanth, see Paschinger 1992; Boujibar 1997.

160 Jannot 1993b: 79–80; Harari 1997.

161 On the left entrance wall of *T. dell'Orco II* another demon with mallet is present, apparently in a Sisyphos scene. Sisyphos' mountain represents the border of the Underworld (cf. above p. 112) and the demon's presence by the entrance door may thus be seen as a liminal area in which he could move.

162 Prayon 2004: 46–50, 58.

163 Cf. Appendix B, parameter O.

164 Menzel & Naso 2007: 39–40; cf. also Prayon 2004: 50–51; Tassi Scandone 2001: 44–48; Lambrechts 1959: 182–85.

165 Polybius, *Histories* 6.53.

166 See, for example, Toynbee 1971: 146–49, pl. 11.

167 For possible forerunners without demons, see *T. del Barone* (phase 2: 44) and *T. del Gorgoneion* (phase 5: 71).

168 See Appendix B, parameter C. – For arched doors, see also Scheffer 1994; Vaccaro 2011.

169 For recent discussions, see, for example, Davies 1985, esp. 630–32, 639; Serra Ridgway 2000: 311–12; Prayon 2004: 51–59; Krauskopf 2006: 74–75; see also Massa-Pairault 1992: 192–93.

170 See note 55.

171 As also explicitly suggested by Torelli 1999: 152 in his discussion on *T. delle Iscrizioni* (phase 2: 74), but which distinction is less explicit in his further discussion on the false doors. Though one important clarification may be necessary: in *T. delle Iscrizioni* there are three false doors all placed centrally, one on the rear wall, one on each of the side walls. Between the door on the left and the one on the rear wall, four horsemen and one person on foot move forward. This is balanced by a group of *komasts*, accompanying the deceased, moving in the same direction between the door on the right wall and that on the rear one. The horsemen (parameter J) belong to the infernal, liminal world, the *komasts* do not; however, through their dance, together with the deceased, they act in the liminal sphere of the funerary ceremonies and thus counterbalance the horsemen, but in this world.

172 Krauskopf 2006: 67, fig. V.1 (with further references), wrongly defines the scene as a farewell between the deceased and living relatives.

173 See, for example, des Bouvrie 2012: 56–57.

174 Note that only twice do we find Hades and Persephone present in the large repertoire of late Classic and Hellenistic paintings and sculpture, in *T. dell'Orco II* (phase 6: 94) and *T. Golini I* (phase 6: 32). In neither of these nor other scenes from the Etruscan hereafter

do we find the *naiskos* from the Apulian vases present, nor Orpheus. On possible earlier Orphism, see Leighton 2004: 117, 119, while on later Orphic and Pythagorean ideas of purification, see p. 165.

175 See, for example, a hydria in Bonn dated 525–500 BC: twice: three winged demons accompany a couple veiled wrapped in a large mantle (Bentz 2008: 162–64.241).

176 Boujibar 1997: 173 with references to the discussions on the aryballos.

177 For earlier references, see Steingräber 1985: 382–83. Add Torelli 1985: 321 (hunting); Pfiffig 1975: 172–73; Dohrn 1983: 133–36; Colonna 1989: 22–23; Moltesen & Weber-Lehmann 1992: 85–87; Torelli 1997a: 134; Prayon 2004: 62–63 (Underworld journey); Haynes 2000: 89–90 (either or); see also Massa-Pairault 1992: 32–33, who suggests a funerary game.

178 Further underlined by the panther resting on the horse hindquarters.

179 Our interpretation of the object is based entirely on its shape as copied in the water-colour, not on a study of the ruined frescoes themselves. This raises a question, even if anachronistic, as we know the situation to-day, if the object originally was not a double-axe, but a mallet – thus turning the double-axe carrier into a demon (parameter N), who we later know under the name of Charun.

180 Cf. also Dohrn 1983: 133.

181 *Treasures* 2004, 98.155 (Museo archeologico nazionale di Firenze, inv. 75840).

182 Cf. note 89. The bird is a curiosity to which I can give no answer – but the connection between birds and auspices may be considered. The two black birds on the left wall of *T. dei Giocolieri*, may perhaps belong to the same kind of ideological thinking. – Cf. also the Chiusan reliefs in Torelli (ed.) 2000: 564, no. 77, and Jannot 2010: 56–57, no. 5.

183 Cristofani 1971b; Torelli 1997b: 134.

184 Montanari in Montanari (ed.) 1987: 35–36, fig. 19a; M. Marchesi in *Principi etruschi* 2000, 338.444–45 with figs.

185 Van Gennep 1908 [1960: 153–54].

186 Jannot 1998: 72–81; Prayon 2004: 64. – For a synthesised presentation of early tombs and grave goods, see also Krauskopf 2006: 78; van der Meer 2011: 45–56.

187 Prayon 1975: 85–90; 1991: 1287; Torelli 1986: 230–31; cf. also Brandt 1997: 163–64.

188 Sannibale 2012: 101, says that the world beyond (*l'Aldilà*) for the Etruscans down to the Archaic Period appeared as 'una dimensione, piuttosto che un luogo'.

189 Jansen 2010, in a recent MA-thesis presented at the University of Oslo, was able to demonstrate that similar ideas were expressed in many of the figural motifs on Late Etruscan ash urns.

190 Krauskopf 2006: 78 finished her article with a cautionary quotation from van Gennep 1908 [1960: 146]: 'Funerals are further complicated when within a single people there are several contradictory or different conceptions of the afterlife which may become intermingled with one another, so that their confusion is reflected in rites'. Here lies buried a difficult challenge not to be overlooked.

191 Phase 3: T.d. Scimmia (25), T.d. Poggio al Moro (22). – Phase 4: T.d. Pulcella (103). – Phase 5: T.d. Gorgoneion (71).

192 Phase 6: T. Golini II (33), T.d. Hescanas (34), T.d. Cesinie (56), T.d. Quadriga Infernale (-). – On 'lararium' snakes, see note 72.

193 Phase 1: T.d. Nave CV (7). – Phase 2: (T.d. Caccia e Pesca (50)). – Phase 4: T.d. Nave TQ (91). – Phase 8: T. con Nave (90).

194 Phase 1: T. Dei (30). – Phase 2: T.d. Leonesse (77), T. Bartoccini (45), T.d. Caccia e Pesca (50), T. 5898 (167), T.d. Barone (44). – Phase 3: T.d. Letto Funebre (82). – Phase 6: T.d. quadriga Infernale (-), Grotta dipinta (2), T.d. Sarcofagi (10). – Phase 7: T. Bruschi (48), T.d. Delfini (36). – Phase 8: T.d. Tifone (118).

195 Phase 2: T.d. Tori (120), T. Labrouste (75), T.d. Leonesse (77), T.3011 (145), T. Bartoccini (45), T. Stefani (112), T.d. Tritoni (122), T.d. Mare (86), T.d. Topolino (119), T. 5898 (167), T.d. Barone (44), T.d. Vasi Dipinti (123). – Phase 5: T.d. Pigmei (? 97). – Phase 6: Grotta dipinta (2), T.d. Sarcofagi (10), T.d. Triclinio (11). - Phase 7: T.d. Festoni (62).

196 Phase 2: T. 1999 (141), T.d. Vasi Dipinti (123). – Phase 3: T.d. Scimmia (25).

197 Phase 2: T. Stefani (112), T.d. Tritoni (122), T.d. Mare (86). – Phase 8: T. con Nave (90).

198 Phase 2: T.d. Leonesse (77), T.d. Caccia e Pesca (50); T.d. Giocolieri (70). – Phase 3: T.d. Triclinio (121), T.d. Letto Funebre (82), T. dipinta (29). – Phase 4: Grotta dipinta (1). – Phase 6: T.d. 'Orco I (93), T.d. Scudi (109), T. Golini II (33), T.d. Hescanas (34), T.d. Ceisinie (56), T.d. Quadriga Infernale (-), Grotta dipinta (2), T.d. Sarcofagi (10), T.d. Triclinio (11). – Phase 7: T. Bruschi (48), T.d. Onde Marine (8), T. Querciola II (107), T.d. Corridietro (35). – Phase 8: T.d. Tifone (118).

199 For arched doors, see Phase 7: T. Querciola II (107). – Phase 8: T.d. Eizenes (61), T.d. Cardinale (54), T. Tartaglia (115), T. 5636 (165).

200 Phase 2: T.d. Leonesse (77).

201 Phase 2: T.d. Iscrizioni (74), T.d. Giocolieri (70).

202 Phase 2: T.d. Tori (120), T.d. Leonesse (77), T.d. Baccanti (? 43), T.d. Vasi Dipinti (123). – Phase 3: T.d. Fustigazioni (67), T.d. Bighe (47), T. 4260 (156).

203 Phase 2: T.d. Tori (120), T.d. Auguri (42), T.d. Iscrizioni? (74), T.d. Topolino (119), T.d. Giocolieri (70), T.d. Olimpiadi (92), T. d. Pulcinella (104), T.d. Vasi Dipinti (123). – Phase 3: T.d. Fustigazione (67), T.d. Scimmia (25). – Phase 5: T.d. Gallo (68), T.d. Guerriero (73), T.d. Pigmei (97).

204 Phase 2: T.d. Topolino (119).

205 Phase 6: T.d. Hescanas (34).

206 Phase 5: T.d. Pigmei (97).

207 Phase 6: T.d. Triclinio (11).

208 Phase 4: T.d. Demoni Azzurri (-). – Phase 5: T.d. Pigmei (97).

209 Phase 6: T. Golini I (32), T.d.'Orco I (93), T. Golini II (33), T.d. Scudi (109), T.d. Hescanas (? 34).

210 For women dancers with *krotala*: Phase 2: T. delle Leonesse (77), T.d. Vasi Dipinti (123). – Phase 3: T.d. Citaredo (57), T.d. Teschio (116), T. 4255 (155, the krotala used by a male dancer), T.d. Triclinio (121), T.d. Poggio al Moro (22), T.d. Colle Casuccini (15). – Phase 4: T. Francesca Giustiniani (65). – Phase 5: T.d. Gallo (68), T. 2327 (143).

211 Phase 2: T.d. Auguri (42), T.d. Olimpiadi (92), T. 1999? (141), T.d. Pulcinella (104). – Phase 4: T. Maggi (? 84).

212 Phase 3: T.d. Fustigazione (67).

213 Phase 2: T.d. Auguri (42), T.d. Iscrizioni (74), T.d. Olimpiadi (92), T. Cardarelli (53), T. d. Maestro d. Olimpiadi ?(83). – Phase 3: T.d. Fustigazione (67), T.d. Citaredo (57), T.d. Bighe (47), T.d. Teschio (116), T.d. Montollo (17), T.d. Scimmia (25), T.d. Letto Funebre

(82), T.d. Poggio al Moro (22), T.d. Colle Casuccini (15), T. without name (173). – Phase 5: T.d. Guerriero (73).

214 Phase 2: T.d. Auguri (42). – Phase 3: T.d. Bighe (47), T.d. Montollo (17), T.d. Scimmia (25), T.d. Poggio al Moro (22), T.d. Colle Casuccini (15).

215 Phase 2: T.d. Cacciatore (51). – Phase 3: T. Paolozzi (21). – Phase 6: T. François (178). – Phase 8: T.d. Cardinale (54).

216 Phase 2: T.d. Auguri (42), T.d. Olimpiadi (92), T.d. Maestro delle Olimpiadi (83). – Phase 3: T.d. Bighe (47). T.d. Montollo (17), T.d. Poggio Gaiella (23), T.d. Letto Funebre (82), T. Paolozzi (21), T.d. Poggio al Moro (22). – Phase 4: T.d. Francesca Giustiniani (65). – Phase 5: T.d. Guerriero (73).

217 Phase 2: T.d. Auguri (42).

218 Phase 2: T.d. Olimpiadi (92), T.d. Maestro delle Olimpiadi (83). – Phase 3: T.d. Bighe (47), T.d. Montollo (17), T.d. Scimmia (25), T.d. Letto Funebre (82), T. dipinta? (29), T.d. Poggio al Moro (22), T.d. Colle Casuccini (15). – Phase 5: T. 1200 (137), T.d. Guerriero (73).

219 Phase 2: T.d. Maestro delle Olimpiadi (83). – Phase 3: T.d. Scimmia (25), T. without name? (173 – or parameter J).

220 Phase 2: T.d. Giocolieri (70). – Phase 3: T.d. Bighe (47), T.d. Scimmia (25). – Phase 4: T.d. Biclinio (46). – Phase 6: T. Golini I (32: in the Underworld).

221 Phase 2: T.d. Iscrizioni? (74), T.d. Topolino (119), T.d. Olimpiadi (92: on the ground in the pediment), T.d. Morto (89), T.d. Baccanti (43), T.d. Barone (44), T. Cardarelli (53), T.d. Vasi Dipinti (123). – Phase 3: T. 5591 (164), T.d. Fustigazione (67), T.d. Citaredo (57), T.d. Leopardi (81), T. without name (173). – Phase 5: T. 3713 (149).

222 Phase 1: T. Campana (the two men on horseback are under this parameter signalled with a question mark, since their exact meaning is not clear; see also pp. 150–51).

223 Phase 1: T.d. Animali dipinti 1 (man with bow) and T. Dei (man with bow on horseback), are under this parameter both signalled with a question mark, since their exact meaning is not clear.

224 Phase 3: T.d. Caccia (14). – Phase 4: Grotta dipinta (103). – Phase 5: T.d. Guerriero (73).

225 Phase 4: T.d. Demoni Azzurri (-). – Phase 6: T. Golini I (32), T. Golini II (33), T. François (178). – Phase 7: T. Bruschi (48), T.d. Caronti (55), T. Campanari (177), T.d. Anina (40). – Phase 8: T.c. Teste di Charun (117).

226 Phase 8: T.d. Tifone (118).

227 Phase 6: T.d.'Orco II (94).

228 Phase 6: T. François (178). – Phase 7: T.d. Anina (40).

229 Phase 3: T. 4813 (158: winged). – Phase 4: T.d. Demoni Azzurri (-). – Phase 6: T. Golini I (32), T.d.'Orco I (93), T. Guasta (72), T. Golini II (33), T.d. Scudi (109), T.d. Hescanas (34), T.d. Ceisinie (34), T.d. Quadriga Infernale (-), T.d. Marcareccia I (87), T. 4836 (-). – Phase 7: T. Bruschi (48), T.d. Rilievi (9), T.d. Mercareccia II (87), T.d. Festoni (62), T. Querciola II (107), T. 4912 (159). – Phase 8: T.d. Eizenes (61), T. Tartaglia (115), T.d. Cardinale (54), T.d. Tifone (118), T. 5512 (161), T. 5636 (165).

230 Phase 1: T. Campana (this parameter is signaled with a question mark since the exact meaning of the scene is not clear; see also pp. 150–51). – Phase 3: T.d. Leopardi (81). – Phase 8: T.c. Processione di Cibele (102: the scene is only known from descriptions; if rightly interpreted it is unique in Etruscan tomb painting).

231 Phase 4: T. Francesca Giustiniani? (65), T.d. Demoni Azzurri (-), T. Querciola I? (106).
    – Phase 6: T. Golini I (32), T. Golini II 33), T.d. Hescanas (34).
232 Phase 6: T.d. Scudi (109). – Phase 7: T. Bruschi (48). – Phase 8: T.d. Tifone (118), T.d.
    Convegno (58), T.d. Alsina? (39).
233 Phase 7: T.d. Mercareccia II (87), T. Campanari (177), T. con Donna ...? (60). – Phase 8:
    T.d. Teste di Charun? (117), T. 5512 (161).

Bibliography

Adinolfi, G., Carmagnola, R. & Cataldi, M. 2005a: 'La Tomba dei Demoni Azzurri: Le pitture',
    in Gilotta (ed.), 45–56.
Adinolfi, G., Carmagnola R. & Cataldi, M. 2005b: 'La Tomba dei Demoni Azzurri. Lo scavo di
    una tomba violata', in *Dinamiche di sviluppo delle città nell'Etruria meridionale. Veio, Caere,
    Tarquinia, Vulci* (Atti del XXIII Convegno di studi etruschi ed italici), Istituti editoriali e
    poligrafici internazionali: Pisa & Roma, 431–53.
Åkerström, Å. 1981: 'Etruscan Tomb Painting – an Art of Many Faces', *Skrifter utgivna av
    Svenska institutet i Rom 4°* (Opuscula Romana 13) 37: 7–34.
Amann, P. 1998: 'Die Tomba del Barone. Überlegungen zu einem neuen ikonologischen
    Verständnis', *Studi Etruschi* 64: 71–93.
Ambrosini, L. 2002: Thymiateria *etruschi in bronzo di età tardo classica, alto e media ellenistica*
    (Studia Archaeologica 113), "L'Erma" di Bretschneider: Rome.
Andreae, B. 2004a: 'Tomba del Citaredo. Das wiedererstandene Grab des Kitharaspielers aus
    Tarquinia', in Andreae, Hoffmann & Weber-Lehmann (eds), 154–61.
Andreae, B. 2004b: 'Die Tomba François. Anspruch und historische Wirklichkeit eines
    etruskischen Familiengrabes', in Andreae, Hoffmann & Weber-Lehmann (eds), 176–207.
Andreae, B., Hoffmann, A. & Weber-Lehmann, C. (eds) 2004: *Die Etrusker: Luxus für das
    Jenseits – Bilder vom Diesseits – Bilder vom Tod* (exhibition catalogue: Bucerius Kunst Forums
    und des Museums für Kunst und Gewerbe Hamburg, 13. Februar bis 16. Mai 2004),
    Hirmer Verlag: Munich.
Avramidou, A. 2009: 'The Phersu Game revisited', *Etruscan Studies. Journal of the Etruscan
    Foundation* 12: 73–87.
Bažant, J. 1994: 'Thanatos', in *LIMC* VII: 904–08, pls 616–18.
Bažant, J. 1997: 'Hypnos', in *LIMC* VIII: 643–45, pls 398–99.
Bentz, M. (ed.) 2008: *Rasna. Die Etrusker. Eine Ausstellung im Akademischen Kunstmuseum
    Antikensammlung der Universität Bonn*, Michael Imhof Verlag: Petersberg.
Bergmann, B. 1999: 'Introduction: the Art of Ancient Spectacle', in Bergmann & Kondoleon: 9–35.
Bergmann, B. & Kondoleon, C. (eds) 1999: *The Art of Ancient Spectacle* (Studies in the History
    of Art 56, Center for Advanced Study in Visual Arts. Symposium Papers 34), National
    Gallery of Art: Washington.
Bernabé, A. & Jiménez San Cristóbal, A. I. 2008: *Instructions for the Netherworld. The Orphhic
    Gold Tablets* (Religions in the Graeco-Roman World 162), Brill: Leiden & Boston.
Blanck, H. & Weber-Lehmann, C. (eds) 1987: *Malerei der Etrusker in Zeichnungen des 19.
    Jahrhunderts*, Verlag Philipp von Zabern: Mainz am Rhein.
Bodel, J. 1994: *Graveyards and Groves. A Study of the* Lex Lucerina (American Journal of
    Ancient History 11 (1986), published in 1994).
Bodel, J. 2000: 'Dealing with the Dead. Undertakers, Executioners and Potter's Fields in
    Ancient Rome', in Hope & Marshall, 128–51.

Boiteux, M. 1997: 'Parcours rituels romains à l'époque moderne', in M. A. Visceglia & C. Brice (eds): *Cérémonial et rituel à Rome (XVIe–XIXe siècle)* (Collection de l'École française de Rome 231), École française de Rome: Rome, 27–87.

Bomati, Y. 1986: 'Phersu et le monde dionysiaque', *Latomus* 45: 21–32.

Bonfante, L. 2009: 'Ritual Dress', in M. Gleba & H. Becker (eds): *Votives, Places and Rituals in Etruscan Religion. Studies in Honor of Jean MacIntosh Turfa*, Brill: Leiden & Boston, 183–91.

Bonghi Jovino, M. & Chiaramonte Treré, C. (eds) 1987: *Tarquinia: richerche, scavi e prospettive* (Atti del convegno internazionale di studi: La Lombardia per gli Etruschi, Milano 24–25 giugno 1986), Edizioni ET: Milan.

Boosen, M. 1986: *Etruskische Meeresmischwesen. Untersuchungen zu Typologie und Bedeutung* (Archaeologia 59), Giorgio Bretschneider Editore: Rome.

Boujibar, N. el Khatib 1997: 'Vanth', in *LIMC* VIII: 173–83, pls 122–27.

Brandt, J. R. 1997: 'Space and Orientation. Some Observations on Settlement Organization in Iron Age Latium', *Acta ad archaeologiam et artium historiam pertinentia, series altera* 9: 144–69.

Brandt, J. R. 2002: 'Hans Hansen Lilienskiold. A Norwegian Traveller to Italy 1669–1670. A Portrait of a Man and his Time', *Analecta Romana Instituti Danici* 28: 163–79.

Brandt, J. R. 2006: 'Votives and Veneration. Athena, Hellotis, and Europa at Gortyna', in C. C. Mattusch, A. A. Donohue & A. Brauer (eds): *Common Ground: Archaeology, Art, Science and Humanities. Proceedings of the XVIth International Congress of Classical Archaeology, Boston, Aug. 23–26, 2003*, Oxbow: Oxford, 44–48.

Brandt, J. R. 2010: '*Sacra privata* in the Roman *domus* – Private or Public? A Study of Household Shrines in an Architectural Context at Pompeii and Ostia', *Acta ad archaeologiam et artium historiam pertinentia* 23: 57–118.

Brandt, J. R. 2012a: 'Content and Form. Some Considerations on Greek Festivals and Archaeology', in Brandt & Iddeng (eds), 139–98.

Brandt, J. R. 2012b: 'From Sacred Space to Holy Places. The Christianization of the Roman Cityscape: some Reflections', *Orizzonti. Rassegna di archeologia* 13: 151–56.

Brandt, J. R. 2014: 'Blood, Boundaries, and Purification. On the Creation of Identities between Memory and Oblivion in Ancient Rome', in B. Alroth & C. Scheffer (eds): *Attitudes towards the Past in Antiquity: Creating Identities* (Acta Universitatis Stockholmiensis/Stockholm Studies in Classical Archaeology 14), Stockholm, 201–16.

Brandt, J. R. & Iddeng, J. W. (eds) 2012: *Greek and Roman Festivals. Content, Practice, and Meaning*, Oxford University Press: Oxford.

Bremmer, J. N. 2002: *The Rise and Fall of the Afterlife. The 1995 Read-Tuckwell Lectures at the University of Bristol*, Routledge: London & New York.

Buranelli, F. 2004: 'Die Kopien des Gemäldezyklus der Tomba François von Carlo Ruspi im Museo Gregoriano Etrusco des Vatikan', in Andreae, Hoffmann & Weber-Lehmann (eds), 168–75.

Burkert, W. 1985: *Greek Religion*, Harvard University Press: Cambridge, MA.

Camporeale, G. 1987: 'La danza armata in Etruria', *Mélanges de l'École française de Rome, Antiquité* 99: 11–42.

Carpenter, T. H 1986: *Dionysian Imagery in Archaic Art. Its Development in Black-Figure Vase Painting*, Clarendon Press: Oxford; Oxford University Press: New York.

Castriota, D. 1992: *Myth, Ethos, and Actuality: Official Art in Fifth-Century B.C. Athens*, The University of Wisconsin Press: Madison.

Cataldi Dini, M. 1987: 'La Tomba dei Demoni Azzurri', in Bonghi Jovino, M. & Chiaramonte Treré, C. (eds), 37–42.

Cataldi Dini, M. 1989: 'Tarquinia. Tomba dei Demoni Azzurri', in *Pittura etrusca*: 150–53.

Ceccarelli, P. 1998: *La pirrica nell'antichità greco romana: Studi sulla danza armata*, Istituti editoriali e poligrafici internazionali: Pisa & Rome.

Cerchiai, L. 1995: '*Daimones* e Caronte sulle stele felsinee', *La Parola del Passato* 50: 376–94.

Cerchiai, L. 2001: 'La Tomba del Topolino', *AION – Annali di archeologia e storia antica. Istituto universitario orientale. Dipartimento di studi del mondo classico e del Mediterraneo* 8: 99–104.

Cerchiai, L. 2010: 'Riflessi della grande pittura nell'iconografia etrusca del VI e V secolo', in I. Bragantini (ed.): *Atti del X Congresso Internazionale Association Internationale pour la Peinture Murale Antique (AIPMA)*, Università degli Studi di Napoli 'L'Orientale': Naples, 105–11.

Clarke, J.R. 2007: *Looking at Laughter. Humor, Power, and Transgression in Roman Visual Culture, 100 B.C.–A.D. 250*, University of California Press: Berkely, Los Angeles & London.

Coldstream, J. N. 1968: *Greek Geometric Pottery. A Survey of Local Styles and their Chronology*, Methuen & Co.: London.

Cole, S. G. 2004: *Landscapes, Gender, and Ritual Space. The Ancient Greek Experience*, University of California Press: Berkeley, Los Angeles & London.

Colonna, G. 1989: 'Gli Etruschi e l'"invenzione" della pittura', in *Pittura etrusca*: 19–25.

Colonna, G. 1996: 'Il *dokanon*, il culto dei Dioscuri e gli aspetti ellenizzanti della religione dei morti nell'Etruria tardo-arcaica', in L. Bacchielli & M. Bonanno Araventinos (eds): *Scritti di antichità in memoria di Sandro Stucchi*, vol. II (Studi Miscellanei 29), "L'Erma" di Bretschneider: Rome, 165–84.

Corbeill, A. 1996: *Controlling Laughter: Political Humour in the Late Roman Republic*, Princeton University Press: Princeton, NJ.

Cristofani, M. 1971a: *Le pitture della tomba del Tifone* (Monumenti della pittura antica scoperti in Italia, sez. I: La pittura etrusca. Tarquinii fasc. V), Istituto Poligrafico dello Stato Rome, Libreria dello Stato: Rome.

Cristofani, M. 1971b: 'Per una nuova lettura della pisside della Pania', *Studi Etruschi* 39: 63–89.

Cristofani, M. 1975: *Statue-cinerario chiusine di l'età classica* (Archaeologica 1), Giorgio Bretschneider Editore: Rome.

Cristofani, M. 1987: 'Pittura funeraria e celebrazione della morte: il caso della Tomba dell'Orco', in Bonghi Jovino & Chiaramonte Treré (eds), 191–202.

Cristofani, M. 1989: 'Celebrazioni della morte nella pittura funeraria etrusca', in *Pittura etrusca*: 27–31.

CSE 1995: *Corpus speculorum etruscorum*, Bundesrepublik Deutschland 4, Staatliche Museen zu Berlin, Antikensammlung 2 (by G. Zimmer, J. Riederer & H. Rix), Hirmer Verlag: Munich.

CVA s.a.: *Corpus vasorum antiquorum*, Italy 25, Tarquinia 1 (published in 1956 or just before).

D'Agostino, B. 1983: 'L'immagine, la pittura e la tomba nell'Etruria arcaica', *Prospettiva. Rivista di storia dell'arte antica e moderna* 32: 2–12.

D'Agostino. B. 1987: 'L'immagine, la pittura e la tomba nell'Etruria arcaica', in C. Bérard, C. Bron & A. Pomari (eds): *Images et société en Grèce ancienne: l'iconographie comme méthode d'analyse* (Actes du Colloque international, Lausanne 8–11 février 1984: Cahiers d'Archéologie Romande 36), Institut d'archéologie et d'histoire ancienne, Université de Lausanne: Lausanne, 215–19.

D'Agostino, B. 1993: 'La Tomba della Scimmia. Per una lettura iconografica delle immagini etrusche', in *La civiltà di Chiusi e del suo territoro* (Atti del XVII Convegno di Studi Etruschi ed Italici, Chianciano Terme, 28 maggio–1° giugno 1989), Leo S. Olschki Editore: Florence, 193–202.

Davies, G. 1985: 'The Significance of the Handshake Motif in Classical Funerary Art', *American Journal of Archaeology* 89: 627–40.

De Grummond, N. T. 2006: *Etruscan Myth, Sacred History, and Legend*, University of Pennsylvania, Museum of Archaeology and Anthropology: Philadelphia.

Delavaud-Roux, M. H. 1993: *Les danses armées en Grèce antique*, Publications de l'Université de Provence: Aix-en-Provence.

De Puma, R. D. & Small, J. P. (eds) 1994: *Murlo and the Etruscans. Art and Society in Ancient Etruria*, The University of Wisconsin Press: Madison.

Des Bouvrie, S. 2012: 'Greek Festivals and the Ritual Process. An Inquiry into the Olympia-cum-Heraia and the Dionysia', in Brandt & Iddeng (eds), 53–93.

Dobrowolski, W. 1989: 'La Tomba del Biclinio', in *Secondo congresso internazionale etrusco, Firenze 26 Maggio–2 Giugno 1985. Atti*, Giorgio Bretschneider Editore: Rome, vol. I: 205–12.

Dobrowolski, W. 1990: 'La Tomba dei Sacerdoti danzanti a Corneto', in H. Heres & M. Kunze (eds): *Die Welt der Etrusker. Internationales Kolloquium 24.–26. Oktober 1988 in Berlin*, Akademie-Verlag: Berlin, 307–13.

Dohrn, T. 1983: 'Die Blüte der Malerei in Etrurien', in D. Metzler, B. Otto & C. Müller-Wirth (eds): *Antidoron. Festschrift für Jürgen Thimme zum 65. Geburtstag am 26. September 1982*, Verlag C. F. Müller: Karlsruhe.

Douglas, M. 1966 [2002]: *Purity and Danger. An Analysis of Concept of Pollution and Taboo*, Routledge: London & New York 1966 [2005].

Ducati, P. 1910: 'Le pietre funerarie felsinee', *Monumenti Antichi* 20, cols. 361–728.

Edwards, C. 2007: *Death in Ancient Rome*, Yale University Press: New Haven & London.

Emmanuel-Rebuffat, D. 1997: '*Hercle* aux Enfers', in Gaultier & Briquel (eds), 55–67.

Fiorini, L. 2007: 'Immaginario della tomba. Retaggi arcaici e soluzioni ellenistiche nella pittura funeraria di Tarquinia', *Ostraka* 16.1: 131–47.

Flower, H. I. 1996: *Ancestor Masks and Aristocratic Power in Roman Culture*, Clarendon Press: Oxford.

Fontaine, P. 2009: 'Observations à propos de la Tombe de la Chasse et de la Pêche à Tarquinia', in S. Bruni (ed.): *Etruria e Italia Preromana. Studi in onore di Giovannangelo Camporeale*, F. Serra: Pisa & Rome, 371–78.

Franzoni, F. 2011: 'Alcune annotazioni sulla cronologia delle tombe tarquiniesi dipinte di III secolo', in La Torre & Torelli (eds), 361–85.

Furley, W. D. 1981: *Studies in the Use of Fire in Ancient Greek Religion*, Arno Press: New York.

Gaultier, F. & Briquel, D. (eds) 1997: *Les Étrusques. Les plus religieux des hommes. État de la recherche sur la religion étrusque* (Actes du colloque international. Galeries nationales du Grand Palais 17–18–19 novembre 1992), Documentation française: Paris, 373–90.

Gilotta, F. (ed.) 2005: *Pittura parietale, pittura vascolare. Ricerche in corso tra Etruria e Campania* (Atti della Giornata di studio, Santa Maria Capua Vetere, 28 maggio 2003), Arte Tipografica Editrice: Naples.

Ginzburg, C. 1987: 'Saccheggi rituali. Premesse a una ricerca in corso', *Quaderni storici* 22: 615–36.

Greifenhagen, A. 1929: *Eine attische schwarzfigurige Vasengattung und die Darstellung des Komos im VI. Jahrhundert*, Gräfe und Unzer: Königsberg in Preussen.

Güntner, G. 1997: 'Persephone', in *LIMC* VIII: 956–978, pls 640–53.

Harari, M. 1997: 'Tuchulcha', in *LIMC* VIII: 97–98.

Harari, M. 2004: 'A Short History of Pygmies in Greece and Italy', in K. Lomas (ed.): *Greek Identities in the Mediterranean. Papers in Honour of Brian Shefton* (Mnemosyne Suppl. 246), Brill: Leiden & Boston, 163–90.

Harari, M. 2005: 'La Tomba n. 2957 di Tarquinia, detta dei Pigmei: *Addenda et corrigenda*', in Gilotta (ed.), 79–91, colour pls 11–16.

Harari, M. 2011: 'Perché all'inferno cresce la barba ai draghi', in La Torre & Torelli (eds), 387–97.

Haumesser, L. 2007: 'La tombe de la Tapisserie et la tombe des Charons: le décor peint des tombe tarquiniennes à deux niveaux', *Ostraka* 16: 55–78.

Haynes, S. 2000: *Etruscan Civilization. A Cultural History*, British Museum Press: London.

Helbig W. 1966: *Führer durch die öffentlichen Sammlungen klassischer Altertümer in Rom*, vol. II, Verlag Ernst Wasmuth: Tübingen.

Hope, V. M. 2000: 'Contempt and Respect. The Treatment of the Corpse in Ancient Rome', in Hope & Marshall, 104–27.

Hope, V. M. & Marshall, E. (eds) 2000: *Death and Disease in the Ancient City*, Routledge: London & New York.

Hostetter, E. 1986: *Bronzes from Spina I. The Figural Classes: Tripod, Kraters, Basin, Cista, Protome, Utensil Stands, Candelabra and Votive Statuettes*, Verlag Philipp von Zabern: Mainz am Rhein.

Izzet, V. 2007: *The Archaeology of Etruscan Society*, Cambridge University Press: Cambridge.

Jannot, J.-R. 1984a: *Les reliefs archaïques de Chiusi* (Collection de l'École Française de Rome 71), École Française de Rome: Rome.

Jannot, J.-R. 1984b: 'Sur les fausses portes étrusques', *Latomus* 43: 273–83.

Jannot, J.-R. 1991: 'Χαρων et Charun. A propos d'un démon funéraire étrusque', *Comptes rendus des séances: Académie des inscriptions & belles-lettres*, 443–64.

Jannot, J.-R. 1993a: 'Phersu, Phersuna, Persona. À propos du masque étrusque', in *Spectacles sportifs et scéniques dans le monde étrusco-italique* (Actes de la table ronde organisée par l'Équipe de recherches étrusco-italiques de l'UMR 126 (CNRS, Paris) et l'École française de Rome, Rome, 3–4 mai 1991), Collection de l'École française de Rome 172: Rome, 281–320.

Jannot, J.-R. 1993b: 'Charun, Tuchulcha et les autres', *Mitteilungen des Deutschen Archäologischen Instituts, Römische Abteilung* 100: 59–81.

Jannot, J.-R. 1997: 'Charu(n) et Vanth, divinités plurielles?', in Gaultier & Briquel (eds), 139–66.

Jannot, J.-R. 1998: *Devins, dieux et demons. Regards sur la religion de l'Étrusque antique*, Antiqva e Picard: Paris (English translation by Jane Whitehead: *Religion in Ancient Etruria*, The University of Wisconsin press: Madison 2005).

Jannot, J.-R. 2005: 'Banqueteurs aux mains vides. Absences, immatérialités, gestes vides: a propos de quelques images du banquet funéraire étrusque', *Revue des Études Anciennes* 107: 527–41.

Jannot, J.-R. 2010: 'Les reliefs de Chiusi. Mise a jour de nos connaissances', *Mélanges de l'École française de Rome* 122: 51–72.

Jansen, M. 2010: *Blod og grenser: en undersøkelse av utvalgte motiver på sen-etruskiske askeurner fra Volterra og Chiusi* (Blood and Boundaries: An Examination of some Selected Motifs on Late Etruscan Ash Urns from Volterra and Chiusi), MA-thesis, Oslo.

Johannessen, L.O. 2010: 'I grenseland i det arkaiske Hellas' (In Borderland in Ancient Greece), *Primitive tider* 12: 15–26.

Johnstone, M. A. 1956: *The Dance in Etruria. A Comparative Study*, Leo S. Olschki Publisher: Florence.

Keuls, E. C. 1993: *The Reign of the Phallus: Sexual Politics in Ancient Hellas*, University of California Press: Berkeley.

Krauskopf, I. 1987: *Todesdämonen und Todengötter im vorhellenistischen Etrurien. Kontinuität und Wandel* (Istituto di Studi Etruschi ed Italici, Biblioteca di "Studi Etruschi" 16), Leo. S. Olschki Editore: Florence.

Krauskopf, I. 1988a: 'Gorgones in Etruria', in *LIMC* IV: 330–45, pls 188–95.

Krauskopf, I. 1988b: 'Hades/Aita', in *LIMC* IV: 394–99, pls 225–28.

Krauskopf, I. 2006: 'The Grave and Beyond in Etruscan Religion', in N. T. de Grummond & E. Simon (eds): *The Religion of the Etruscans*, University of Texas: Austin, 66–89.

Lambrechts, R. 1959: *Essai sur les magistratures des républiques étrusques* (Études de philologie, d'archéologie et d'histoires anciennes publiées par l'Institute historique Belge de Rome 7), Bruxelles & Rome.

La Torre, G. F. & Torelli, M. (eds) 2011: *Pittura ellenistica in Italia e in Sicilia. Linguaggi e tradizioni* (Atti del convegno di studi, Messina, 24–25 settembre 2009) (Archaeologica 163), Giorgio Bretschneider Editore: Rome.

Leighton, R. 2004: *Tarquinia. An Etruscan City*, Duckworth: London.

Lilienskiold ms.: *Johannes Lilienskiolds reisejournal 1668–1670, ii Deel, Rom*, ms. in the University Library in Bergen: 'nr. 35 fol. 2'.

LIMC: *Lexicon iconographicum mythologiae classicae*, Artemis Verlag: Zürich & Munich, 9 double vols., 1981–1997.

Lindner, R., Dahlinger, S.-G. & Yalouris, N. 1988: 'Hades', in *LIMC* IV: 367–94, pls 210–25.

Lindsay, H. 2000: 'Death Pollution and Funerals in Rome', in Hope & Marshall (eds), 152–73.

Linington, R. E. & Serra Ridgway, F. R. 1997: *Lo scavo del Fondo Scataglini a Tarquinia*, 2. vols., Comune di Milano. Settore cultura e spettacolo, raccolte archeologiche e numismatiche: Milan.

Lissarrague, F. 1990: 'Around the *krater*', in O. Murray (ed.): *Sympotica. A Symposium on the Symposion*, Clarendon Press: Oxford & Oxford University Press: New York, 196–209.

Lissi Caronna, E., Sabbione, C. & Vlad Borrelli, L. (eds) 2007: *I pinakes di Locri Epizifiri. Musei di Reggio Calabria e di Locri* III.1–2 (Atti e memorie della Società Magna Grecia, Quarta serie III, 2004–2007), Società Magna Grecia: Rome.

Lonsdale, S. H. 1993: *Dance and Ritual in Greek Religion*, Johns Hopkins University Press: Baltimore & London.

Maar, V. 1910: *Holger Jacobæus' Rejsebog (1671–1692), med Understøttelse af Den grevelige Hjelmstierne-Rosencroneske Stiftelse, udgivet efter Originalhaandskriftet*, Copenhagen.

Massa-Pairault, F.-H. 1992: *Iconologia e politica nell'Italia antica. Roma, Lazio, Etruria dal VII al I secolo a.C.*, Longanesi: Milan.

Massa-Pairault, F.-H. 1996: *La cité des Étrusques*, CNRS Editions: Paris.

Massa-Pairault, F.-H. 1998: '*Libri acherontici – Sacra Acheruntia*. Culture grecque et etrusca disciplina', *Annali della Fondazione per il Museo "Claudio Faina"* 5: 83–103.

Mavleev, E. 1994: 'Phersipnei', in *LIMC* VII: 329–32.

Mavleev E. & Krauskopf, I. 1986: 'Charu(n)', in *LIMC* III: 225–36, pls 174–85.

Menichetti, M. 1992: 'L'*oinochóe* di Tragliatella: Mito e rito tra Grecia ed Etruria', *Ostraka* 1: 7–30.

Menzel, M. & Naso, A. 2007: 'Raffigurazioni di cortei magistratuali in Etruria. Viaggi nell'Aldilá o processioni reali?' *Ostraka* 16: 23–43.

Metcalf, P. & Huntington, R. 1991: *Celebrations of Death. The Anthropology of Mortuary Ritual*, 2nd ed., Cambridge University Press: Cambridge.

Minetti, A. 2005: 'La Tomba della Quadriga Infernale di Sarteano', *Studi Etruschi* 70: 135–59.

Minetti, A. 2007: 'La tomba dipinta di Sarteano', *Ostraka* 16: 79–91.

Moltesen, M. & Weber-Lehmann, C. 1992: *Etruskische Grabmalerei. Faksimiles und Aquarelle. Dokumentation aus der Ny Carlsberg Glyptotek und dem Schwedischen Institut in Rom*, Verlag Philipp von Zabern: Mainz am Rhein (German version of *Copies of Etruscan Tomb Paintings in the Ny Carlsberg Glyptotek*, Ny Carlsberg Glyptotek: Copenhagen 1991).

Montanari, G. B. (ed.) 1987: *La formazione della città in Emilia-Romagna. Prime esperienze urbane attraverso le nuove scoperte archeologiche* (exhibition catalogue Museo civico archeologico, Bologna, 27 settembre 1987–24 gennaio 1988), Nuova Alfa Editoriale: Bologna.

Morandi, A. 1983: *Le pitture della tomba del Cardinale* (Monumenti della pittura antica scoperta in Italia, sez. I, fasc. VI), Rome.

Morandi, M. & Colonna, G. 1995: 'La *gens* titolare della tomba tarquiniese dell'Orco', *Studi Etruschi* 61: 95–102.

Moretti, M. 1966: *Nuovi monumenti della pittura etrusca*, Lerici Editori: Milan.

Morris, I. 1992: *Death-Ritual and Social Structure in Classical Antiquity*, Cambridge University Press: Cambridge.

Naso, A. 1996: *Architetture dipinte. Decorazioni parietali non figurate nelle tombe a camera nell'Etruria meridionale (VII-V sec. a.C.)*, "L'Erma" di Bretschneider: Rome.

Oakley, J. H. 1994: 'Sisyphos', in *LIMC* VII: 781–87, pls 564–67.

Oakley, J. H. 2004: *Picturing Death in Classical Athens: The Evidence of the White Lekythoi*, Cambridge University Press: Cambridge.

Paravicini-Bagliani, A. 2000: *The Pope's Body*, The University of Chicago Press: Chicago (Engl. translation of Italian original: *Il corpo del Papa*, Giulio Einaudi editore s.p.a.: Turin 1994).

Paschinger, E. 1992: *Die etruskische Todesgöttin Vanth* (Österreichisches archäologisches Institut in Wien, Sonderschriften 20), Verlag: Verband der Wissenschaftlichen Gesellschaften Österreichs: Vienna.

Pensa, M. 1977: *Rappresentazioni dell'oltretomba nella ceramica apula*, "L'Erma" di Bretschneider: Rome.

Peruzzi, B. 2007: 'La Tomba del Cardinale', *Ostraka* 16: 105–14.

Peschel, I. 1987: *Die Hetäre bei Symposion und Komos in der attisch-rotfigurigen Vasenmalerei des 6.–4. Jahrh. v. Chr.*, P. Lang: Frankfurt am Main & New York.

Pfiffig, A. J. 1975: *Religio etrusca*, Akademische Druck- und Verlagsanstalt: Graz.

Pittura etrusca 1989: *Pittura etrusca al Museo di Villa Giulia nelle foto di Takashi Okamura* (Studi di archeologia pubblicati dalla Soprintendenza archeologica per l'Etruria meridionale 6), De Luca: Rome.

Pontrandolfo, A. & Rouveret, A. 1992: *Le tombe dipinte di Paestum*, Panini: Modena.

Poursat, J. C. 1968: 'Les representations de danse armée dans la céramique attique', *Bulletin Correspondance Hellenique* 92: 550–615.

Prayon, F. 1975: *Frühetruskische Grab- und Hausarchitektur* (Mitteilungen des Deutschen Archäologischen Instituts, Römische Abteilung, Suppl. 22), F. H. Kerle: Heidelberg.

Prayon, F. 1991: '*Deorum sedes*. Sull'orientamento dei templi etrusco-italici', *Archeologia Classica* 63: 1285–95.

Prayon, F. 2004: '*Reditus ad maiores*. Ein Aspekt etruskischer Jenseitsvorstellungen', *Mitteilungen des Deutschen Archäologischen Instituts, Römische Abteilung* 111: 45–67.

Principi etruschi 2000: *Principi etruschi tra Mediterraneo ed Europa* (exhibition catalogue Museo civico archeologico, Bologna, 1 ottobre 2000–1 aprile 2001), Marsilia: Venice.

Prückner, H. 1968: *Die lokrischen Tonreliefs. Beitrag zur Kultgeschichte von Lokroi Epizephyrioi*, Verlag Philipp von Zabern: Mainz am Rhein.

Purcell, N. 1999: 'Does Caesar mime?', in Bergmann & Kondoleon (eds), 181–93.

Rendeli, M. 1996: '*Anagoghe*', *Prospettiva. Rivista di storia dell'arte antica e moderna* 83–4: 10–29.

Robertson, C. M. 1975: *A History of Greek Art*, Cambridge University Press: Cambridge.

Roncalli, F. 1996: 'Laris Pulenas and Sisyphus: Mortals, Heroes and Demons in the Etruscan Underworld', *Etruscan Studies. Journal of the Etruscan Foundation* 3: 45–64.

Roncalli, F. 1997: 'Iconographie funéraire et topographie de l'au-delà en Étrurie', in Gaultier & Briquel (eds), 37–54.

Roncalli, F. 2000: 'Painting', in Torelli, M. (ed.), *The Etruscans*, Bompiani: Milan, 345–64.

Sacchetti, F. 2000: '*Charu(n)* nella pittura funeraria etrusca', *Ocnus* 8: 127–64.

Sannibale, M. 2012: 'Riti, simboli e religione. Le aristocrazie etrusche e la communità dei vivi oltre la vita', in A. Mandolesi & M. Sannibale (eds): *Etruschi. L'ideale eroico e il vino lucente*, Electa: Milan, 87–101.

Sassatelli, G. 1984: 'Una nuova stele felsinea', in P. Delbianco (ed.): *Culture figurative e materiali tra Emilia e Marche. Studi in memoria di Mario Zuffa*, Maggioli: Rimini, 107–37.

Scala, N. 1997: 'La Tomba del Letto funebre di Tarquinia. Un tentativo di interpretazione', in *Prospettiva. Rivista di storia dell'arte antica e moderna* 85: 46–52.

Scheffer, C. 1994: 'The Arched Door in Late Etruscan Funerary Art', in De Puma & Small (eds), 196–210.

Seeberg, A. 1971: *Corinthian Komos Vases* (Institute of Classical Studies, Bulletin Suppl. 27), London.

Seeberg, A. 1995: 'From Padded Dancers to Comedy', in A. Griffiths (ed.): *Stage Directions: Essays in Ancient Drama in Honour of E. W. Handley* (Bulletin of the Institute of Classical Studies, supplement 66), London, 1–12.

Serra Ridgway, F. R. 2000: 'The Tomb of the Anina Family. Some Motifs in Late Tarquinian Painting', in D. Ridgway, F. R. Serra Ridgway, M. Pearce, E. Herring, R. D. Whitehouse & J. B. Wilkins (eds), *Ancient Italy in its Mediterranean Setting. Studies in Honour of Ellen Macnamara* (Accordia Specialist Studies on the Mediterranean), 301–16.

Shapiro, H. A. 1991: 'The Iconography of Mourning in Athenian Art', *American Journal of Archaeology* 95: 629–56.

Simon, E. 1973: 'Die Tomba dei Tori und der etruskischen Apollonkult', *Jahrbuch des Deutschen Archäologischen Instituts* 88: 27–42.

Small, J.P. 1994: 'Eat, drink, and be Merry', in De Puma & Small (eds), 85–94.

Sourvinou-Inwood, C. 1981: 'To die and enter the House of Hades: Homer, before and after', in J. Whaley (ed.): *Mirrors of Mortality. Studies in the Social History of Death*, Europa Publications: London, 15–39.

Sourvinou-Inwood, C. 1986: 'Charon', in *LIMC* III: 210–55, pls 168–74.

Spivey, N. & Stoddart, S. 1990: *Etruscan Italy*, Batsford: London.

Staccioli, R. A. 1980: 'Le finte porte dipinte nelle tombe arcaiche etrusche', *Quaderni dell'Istituto di archeologia e storia antica, Università di Chieti*, 1: 1–17.

Stansbury-O'Donnell, M. D. 1990: 'Polygnotos' *Nekyia*. A Reconstruction and Analysis', *American Journal of Archaeology* 94: 213–35.

Steingräber, S. (ed.) 1985: *Etruskische Wandmalerei*, Belser Verlag: Stuttgart & Zürich (Italian translation: *Catalogo ragionato della pittura etrusca*, Jaca Books: Milan 1985).

Steingräber, S. 1999: 'Zum ikonographischen und hermeneutischen Wandel von Pygmäen- und speziell Geranomachiedarstellungen in vorhellenistischer Zeit (6.–4/3. Jh. v. Chr)', *Mediterranean Archaeology* 12: 29–41.

Steingräber, S. 2006: *Abundance of Life. Etruscan Wall Painting*, The J. Paul Getty Museum: Los Angeles.

Tassi Scandone, E. 2001: *Verghe, scuri e fasci littori in Etruria. Contributi allo studio degli Insignia Imperii* (Istituto nazionale di studi etruschi ed italici, Biblioteca di 'Studi Etruschi' 36), Istituti editoriali e poligrafici internazionali: Pisa & Rome.

Taylor, L. 2011: 'Mourning becomes Etruria: Ritual Performance and Iconography in the Seventh and Sixth Centuries', *Etruscan Studies. Journal of the Etruscan Foundation* 14: 39–54.

Thuillier, J.-P. 1997a: 'Un relief archaïque inédit de Chiusi', *Revue Archéologique*, 243–60.

Thuillier, J.-P. 1997b: 'Dieux grecs et jeux étrusques', in Gaultier & Briquel (eds), 373–90.

Torelli, M. 1985: *L'arte degli etruschi*, Editori Laterza: Rome-Bari,

Torelli, M. 1986: 'La religione', in *Rasenna. Storia e civiltà degli Etruschi*, Libri Scheiwiller: Milan, 159–237.

Torelli, M. 1997a: *Il rango, il rito e l'immagine. Alle origini della rappresentazione storica romana*, Electa: Milan.

Torelli, M. 1997b: 'Limina Averni. Realtà e rappresentazione nella pittura tarquiniese arcaica', *Ostraka* 6: 63–86.

Torelli, M. 1999: '*Funera etrusca*: Reality and Representation in Archaic Tarquinian Painting', in Bergmann & Kondoleon (eds), 147–61.

Torelli, M. 2007: 'Linguaggio ellenistico e linguaggio 'nazionale' nella pittura ellenistica etrusca', *Ostraka* 16: 149–70.

Torelli, M. (ed.) 2000: *The Etruscans*, Rizzoli international publications: New York.

Treasures 2004: *Treasures from Tuscany – The Etruscan Legacy* (exhibition at the National Museums of Scotland from 16 July to 31 October 2004), National Museums of Scotland Enterprises Publishing: Edinburgh.

Toynbee, J. M. C. 1971: *Death and Burial in the Roman World*, Thames & Hudson: London.

Vaccaro, V. 2011: 'Caroni e finte porte', in La Torre & Torelli (eds), 349–59.

van der Meer, L. B. 2011: Etrusco Ritu. *Case Studies in Etruscan Ritual Behaviour*, Peeters: Louvain & Walpole, MA.

van Essen, C. C. 1927: *Did Orphic Influence on Etruscan Tomb Paintings exist? Studies in Etruscan Tomb Paintings I*, H. J. Paris: Amsterdam.

van Gennep, A. 1960: *The Rites of Passage*, The University of Chicago Press: Chicago (English translation of French original text, published in 1908).

Ville, G. 1981: *La gladiature en occident des origins à la mort de Domitien* (Bibliothèque de les Écoles françaises de Athène et de Rome 245), École française de Rome: Rome.

Vincenti, V. 2007: 'La Tomba Bruschi di Tarquinia', *Ostraka* 16: 93–103.

von Vacano, O.-W. 1957: *Die Etrusken in der Welt der Antike*, Rowohlt Taschenbuch Verlag GmbH: Hamburg.

Walberg, G. 1986: 'The Tomb of the Baron Reconsidered', *Studi Etruschi* 54: 51–59.

Weber-Lehmann, C. 2004a: 'Die etruskische Grabmalerei: Bilder zwischen Tod und evigem Leben', in Andreae, Hoffmann & Weber-Lehmann (eds), 122–26.

Weber-Lehmann, C. 2004b: 'Tomba delle Pantere', in Andreae, Hoffmann & Weber-Lehmann (eds), 127–28.

Weber-Lehmann, C. 2004c: 'Tomba degli Auguri', in Andreae, Hoffmann & Weber-Lehmann (eds), 129–35.

Weber-Lehmann, C. 2004d: 'Tomba della Caccia e Pesca', in Andreae, Hoffmann & Weber-Lehmann (eds), 136–43.

Weber-Lehmann, C. 2004e: 'Tomba del Letto Funebre', in Andreae, Hoffmann & Weber-Lehmann (eds), 144–49.

Weber-Lehmann, C. 2004f: 'Tomba della Scrofa', in Andreae, Hoffmann & Weber-Lehmann (eds), 150–53.

Weber-Lehmann, C. 2005a: 'Tomba dei Pigmei: *Addenda et corrigenda* II', in Gilotta (ed.), 93–101.

Weber-Lehmann, C. 2005b: 'Überlegungen zum Bildprogram der Tomba François', in Gilotta (ed.), 103–14.

Weber-Lehmann, C. 2012: 'Ritus und Kultus. Taugliche Topoi zur Interpretation der etruskischen Grabmalerei?', in P. Amann (ed.): *Kulte – Riten – religiöse Vorstellungen bei den Etruskern und ihr Verhältnis zu Politik und Gesellschaft* (Akten der 1. Internationalen Tagung der Sektion Wien/Österreich des Istituto Nazionale di Studi Etruschi ed Italici (Wien 4.–6.12. 2008), 273–86.

Weege, F. 1921: *Etruskische Malerei*, Max Niemeyer Verlag: Halle.

Whitehead, J. K. 1996: 'Towards a Definition of Etruscan Humor', *Etruscan Studies. Journal of the Etruscan Foundation* 3: 9–32

Wikan, U. 1990: *Managing Turbulent Hearts: A Balinese Formula for Living*, University of Chicago Press: Chicago.

Wikan, U. 2008: *Om ære* (On Honour), Pax forlag: Oslo.

Woodford, S. & Spier, J. 1992: 'Kerberos', in *LIMC* VI: 25–32, pls 12–16.

"WHETHER BY DECAY OR FIRE CONSUMED …":[1]

Cremation in Hellenistic and Roman Asia Minor

Sven Ahrens

The eastern Mediterranean has been considered, in terms of general studies on cremation, an area where inhumation rites were practiced nearly exclusively since the Hellenistic Period. But was this really the case? This article gives a summary of the evidence for cremation as recorded in the ethnically complex Asia Minor and discusses the reasons for its presence and introduction (or refusal), which can be linked to either religious, political, social, or personal explanations; it will also be assessed if cremation was an indigenous or 'Greek' rite in some parts of the region. The primary evidence, such as architectural tomb features, burial containers and epigraphic evidence are used to reconstruct the chronological development and the geographical spread of this rite in Asia Minor. This allows the delimitation of chronological phases and distribution patterns of the cremation rite from the late 4th century BC to the 3rd century AD. These time limits define the onset and the end of a phase when archaeologically traceable cremation was practised, that is between the Macedonian conquest and the early Late Roman Empire. The chronological survey will also discuss the possible impact of Persian religious beliefs on the rituals practiced under Persian rule.

Keywords: Asia Minor, cremation, funerary architecture and inscriptions, Hellenistic Period, inhumation, Macedonian, ostothecae, Persian, Roman

The opinion that cremation was not a Greek rite in the Roman Empire, and in particular in Asia Minor, can be found in several of the general works on cremation and inhumation (Audin 1960: 526; Morris 1996: 52–53; Nock 1932: 337). This assumption is based

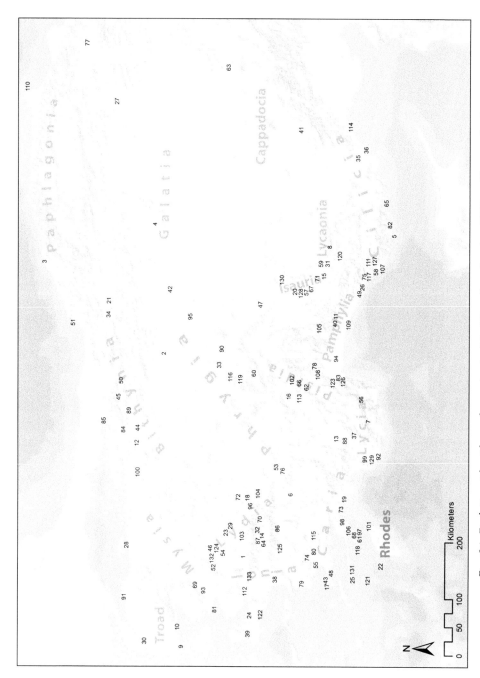

Fig. 6.1. Find sites with evidence of cremation in Asia Minor (map based on ESRI world terrain base)

on comments by ancient writers who referred to cremation as the '*mos romanus*' and to inhumation as '*mos graecus*' (e.g. Morris 1996: 31, 52 after Tacitus, *Annales* 16.6, and Petronius, *Satyricon* 111.2). Superficial surveys of the archaeological record seemed to confirm that assumption, showing overwhelming evidence for inhumation in the area as a whole. However, in a recent article, Marcello Spanu (2000: 174) justifiably draws attention to the fact that cremation was practiced in Asia Minor to an unknown extent. This is of course no surprise for those scholars devoted to the study of cinerary urns or funerary inscriptions, who have been aware of hundreds or rather thousands of finds confirming the practice of cremation in Asia Minor. A closer look at the extensive evidence further confirms that the rites practiced in that area were subject to multiple regional and super-regional changes.

This article gives a summary of the evidence for cremation in order to establish a precise definition of its chronological and geographic distribution in the ethnically complex Asia Minor. Such a framework is necessary to understand possible causes of the significant changes from inhumation to cremation and vice versa. For this purpose a wide range of material has been covered and presented in an appendix with distribution maps. The evidence was gathered from four groups of sources: cremations, inscriptions, receptacles (ostothecae), and architecture. The time limits from the late 4th century BC to the 3rd century AD were chosen because they define the onset and the end of a phase when archaeologically traceable cremation was practiced. The time frame starts two centuries before the inheritance of the Pergamene kingdom by the Romans in 133 BC. This should allow us to clarify if cremation indeed was practiced as an indigenous or 'Greek' rite or just as a consequence of Roman domination.

The study undertaken had to overcome major obstacles: very few published regional studies exist and most of the information had to be gathered from very dispersed sources. Lack of dates and the existence of hundreds of yet unpublished finds make such a study a sketchy and preliminary affair. The survey only included finds with a provenance. Furthermore, as the available dates were in most cases extracted directly from archaeological publications, it is possible that some dating is erroneous. It should also be taken into account that many places may have had a much wider period of cremation, but that the finds or the given dates only allow for a narrow timeframe. However, the large number of sites with cremation evidence (see Fig. 6.1 and Appendix) makes certain patterns clearly visible, regardless of a certain margin of error.

Sources

Cremations
Evidence for cremation, in the form of charred bones and ashes, is scarce in Asia Minor (see table; some data collected by Spanu 2000: 174). This is partially due to the lack of excavations, as well as Medieval and modern destruction of evidence in the necropoleis. Cinerary urns were placed on shelves or benches along the walls in the

numerous chamber-tombs (Schweyer 2002: 40; Söğüt 2001: 252), and hence, in such an exposed position, they were usually removed or destroyed by tomb robbers. The receptacles, often of metal or ceramic, did not have a specific shape or usually differ from utility pottery. Urns with explicit funerary inscriptions, such as those in Sardis are exceptional (Dedeoğlu & Malay 1991: 116–19). Consequently, most simple urns cannot be recognised as cremation containers when taken out of context. Similarly, the larger cinerary chests of stone, ostothecae, could easily be removed and are usually found out of their original context (Rosenbaum et al. 1967: 53).

Six large-scale necropolis excavations and surveys can give an idea of how common cremation was compared to inhumation. In the necropolis of Myrina, 116 graves were excavated dating to the 3rd–1st centuries BC (Pottier 1887: 107). Twelve of the graves contained between one and three cremations (Pottier 1887: 78–100, nos. 39, 51, 69, 93, 95, 98, 101, 105, 108, 110, 113, 114). At least 164 inhumations and 16 cremations, from the second half of the 4th century BC until the Early Imperial Period, were found in the west-gate necropolis of Assos (Freydank 2000: 103). The two datasets from Myrina and Assos indicate that cremation was used in the Hellenistic Period in up to one tenth of the burials at these sites. This relatively similar ratio should, however, not be generalised. At Sagalassos, cremation in urns and cinerary chests was the predominant or even exclusive rite in the Hellenistic Period, and inhumation gained importance in the Imperial Period (Köse 2005: 164–166). A comparable development through time can also be observed in the northeast necropolis of Laodicea, where 32 cremation vessels have been found among 183 graves (Şimşek 2011: 32–37). A rough browsing through the findings of the extensive excavations in the northeast necropolis of Laodicea (Şimşek 2011: 347–805) shows that about 70% of the graves of the mid-2nd to the mid-1st century BC are cremations, while only about 20–25% of the graves of the mid-1st century BC to the mid-1st century AD contained cremations. Later on cremations seemed to have been exceptions and disappear in the course of the 2nd century AD. The ratio of the rites could also vary greatly from location to location as the two sites Gordion and Pessinus can demonstrate. Located at a distance of only 50 km and dating roughly from the Late Hellenistic to the Early Byzantine Period the sites have revealed quite differing ratios. Among several hundred graves found in Gordion only two cremations could be identified (Goldman 2007: 304), while excavations in nearby Pessinus uncovered 60 cremation and 78 inhumation graves (Devrecker et al. 2003: 40).

The finds presented in the maps and appendix show that cremation was practiced throughout the period under consideration and in large parts of western, southern and central Anatolia. The range of rites is as broad as the ethnic composition of Asia Minor. Cremation was carried out inside tombs, in cremation pits or a grave was dug under the pyre (Devrecker et al. 2003: 40–46; Goldman 2007: 304; Pottier 1887: nos 98, 101). Indeed, cremated remains have been found in simple cooking pots (Waelkens 1993: 41), luxurious ceramic (Forbeck 2005: 57, fig. 4) and bronze vessels (Akok 1948:

fig. 10), in rock-cut pits (Çevik 1997; Çevik & Iplikçioğlu 2003; Peschlow 1990: 384, fig. 9–10) or marble ostothecae (Walker 1985: 55–56). Urns could be buried directly in the earth (Verzone 1961–62: 637), in small cists (Newton 1862–63: 338) or placed in tomb monuments (Anderson 2007: 477–78). Cremated bones have also been placed in sarcophagi (Çelgin 1994: 164; İplikçioğlu et al. 1991: 25, no. 11; Nock 1932: 333; Stupperich 1996: 11), though it is impossible to estimate to what extent this was practiced, because of the lack of archaeological evidence. Cremated remains were frequently placed in the same tomb as inhumations and may, if contemporary, provide proof that both rites were practiced within the same family (Kubinska 1999: nos 30–33; Pottier 1887: no. 95; Şimşek 2011, 717–718).

Inscriptions

Inscriptions mentioning ostothecae and kaustrai have been gathered by Kubinska (1999) and the catalogue adds substantially to the evidence. The term ὀστοθήκη (ostotheca) was applied to small receptacles which housed calcified bones and ashes (Korkut 2006: 1). Uncertainties regarding the usage of ostothecae have been present until recently (Cormack 2004: 109, note 522). However, the latest studies leave no doubt about their main function as receptacles for the remains of cremations (Korkut 2006: 77; Kubinska 1999: passim; Köse 2005: 37–38). In some cases, ostothecae could have been used as sarcophagi for children or for secondary burials (Koch 1990: 154; Köse 2005: 38, note 208; see further: Koch 2008). In Side (Inan 1963: 69) and Ephesus (Thomas & Içten 1999: 550; Thomas & Içten 2007: 338, note 27) ostothecae have been found containing non-cremated bones of several individuals, though the interments may also have occurred during a secondary use of the chests (see similar find in Boeotian Akraiphnio: Flämig 2007: 81).

The term καύστρα (kaustra) may have been used for the site of the pyre or the burial place of cremated bones, but in most cases it was probably a synonym for ostotheca (Kubinska 1999: 55). A further term, λάρναξ (larnax), was used for cinerary urns and altars, as well as for sarcophagi or *loculi* (Kubinska 1968: 52–55). Because of its wide applicability this term has not been considered here.

Eight funerary epigrams, dating at least from the 2nd century BC to the 2nd century AD mention cremations directly or indirectly, and provide a few hints on why it was practiced (Merkelbach & Stauber 1998–2004: 03/06/04, 03/07/17, 03/07/19, 05/03/05, 09/05/05, 09/05/12, 14/13/04, 16/52/02). Five of these cremations mentioned were carried out abroad for the purpose of repatriating the ashes. Two of these five inscriptions were found in the coastal city of Erythrae, which leaves little doubt that repatriation of the earthly remains may have been the main reason for the practice of cremation, particularly in places with mobile populations such as harbour towns. Repatriation is attested by further inscriptions, which describe the transfer of bones after the putrefaction of the soft tissue and the subsequent burial in a container (10/02/03, 10/03/02). A certain comfort in burial at home in contrast to the sorrow of being buried in foreign earth is omnipresent in Greek epigrams, and hence explains the importance of such repatriation (see, for example, Merkelbach & Stauber 1998–2004: 02/06/14, 02/13/03, 03/02/66, 06/01/01, 08/01/42, 08/07/07, 08/01/45, 08/02/01, 09/09/16, 10/03/07, 14/16/03, 15/02/11, 16/23/14, 16/52/02).

One inscription mentions that the deceased was burned to death in his house and his ashes were placed in an urn (02/03/01). House fire was a constant threat in the ancient world and such accidental cremations may have subsequently received a burial, which would be impossible to distinguish from planned cremations using archaeological methods. Because of repatriation and accidental cremation, isolated examples in Asia Minor should never be considered as evidence of indigenous cremation rites.

Receptacles (ostothecae)

Ostothecae of circular or rectangular shape have been found at many sites in Asia Minor. Numerous occurrences have not been published, while new specimens appear constantly. The ostothecae used for the present analysis represent only a fraction of what have been uncovered in Turkey.

Although ostothecae are excellent cremation indicators it should be kept in mind that cremations were also buried in other receptacles. The period of use of ostothecae does not necessarily indicate the exact period of cremation at a site. Assos, for example, has a tradition of cremation from the late 4th century BC until the Early Imperial Period, although ostothecae do not appear before the second half of the 2nd century BC (see, for example, Freydank 2000: 93).

The simplest form of ostothecae are rock-cut shafts or pits. In Trebenna, circular rock-cut pits with conical lids (Çevik 1997: 138) have recently been identified as incineration receptacles dating to the 3rd century AD. Similar pits have also been discovered in other necropoleis of Asia Minor, but a funerary function is not always evident (Çokay-Kepçe 2006: 171, note 46; Diler 2002: 64–65;). Rectangular rock-cut chests are known from Elaiussa Sebaste, Korykos, Kanytelleis, Adrasus, and Balboura (Equini Schneider 2003: 270), although they have been interpreted as charnel pits for the nearby tombs rather than as cinerary receptacles. If a quadrangular pit close to a rock-cut sarcophagus in Alinda served a similar purpose or indeed presents a cremation receptacle is not clear (Özkaya & San 2003: 121).

Besides the use of improvised receptacles, such as the reworked stone vessel in Alpu (Atasoy 1974: 258) and occasional terracotta chests (McLean 2002: 195–97), more luxurious stone ostothecae in the form of chests or vases, often with relief decoration, were produced locally in many regions of Asia Minor (Koch 1990: 154–62; 2010: 130–33) and even exported (e.g.: Koch 1990: 158). Production of ostothecae began: in Pisidia and Rhodes during the Early Hellenistic Period; in Lydia and Ionia during the 2nd and 1st centuries BC; in Pamphylia and Cilicia during the Late Hellenistic and Imperial Period. In the 2nd century AD, craftsmen in Bithynia and Isauria/ Lycaonia also developed their own ostotheca types. In the middle of the 2nd century

AD, the market for ostothecae was seemingly so lucrative that the famous producer for luxurious sarcophagi, the quarries of Docimeium in Phrygia exported ostothecae (Koch 1990: 155; Waelkens 1982: 50). While some of the early production areas had a decisive decline in the 1st and 2nd centuries AD, some of the new centres appear to have peaked in production during the 2nd century AD, followed by a decline in the 3rd century AD. There is no evidence for the production of luxurious ostothecae after the 3rd century AD.

Architecture

In Sardis (Greenewalt 1977: 50) and Cnidus (Berns in press; Newton 1862–63: 478), ostothecae were found standing in niches in the walls of tombs. Comparable architectural solutions for the placement of ostothecae can be observed in loculi and chamber tombs on Rhodes, with inhumations and cremations often placed in the same tomb monuments (Fraser 1977: 12, 52–53). These finds open up an interpretation of similar constructions as niches for cremation receptacles. A similar function has been proposed for tombs in Hisarlik (Söğüt 2001: 251), Elaiussa Sebaste (Berns 2003: 109, 186–87, cat. 10A1; Durukan 2005: 110, 114, figs 7, 8; Durukan 2007: 151) and the niches and shelves in tombs or tomb yards at several other places in Cilicia (Alföldi-Rosenbaum 1971: 100, note 53, 169; Korkut 2006: 78; Rosenbaum et al. 1967: 53; Söğüt 2001: 252–53). However, other findings suggest a careful and critical interpretation of such architectonical features is required, because niches may also have served other purposes, such as for the placement of grave goods (Abbasoğlu 2001: 187; Söğüt 2001; 2002).

Columbaria are a distinctly Roman architectural type. The partially rock-cut columbarium G15 in the N4 necropolis of Elaiussa Sebaste (Machatschek 1967: 56, 112–13, pl. 37b) is unique in Cilicia. The walls contain about 60 small niches where cinerary urns were immured with stucco and the large amount of niches indicates that a collegium rather than a family had built and used the tomb. Furthermore, the architecture is so distinct from the tomb architecture of the region, one would suspect that foreigners were responsible for the commission of this building. Columbaria were more common in Caria and along the West coast, such as in Miletus (Forbeck 2005: 58), as well as rock-cut examples from Ephesus (Wood 1877: 122) and Caunus (Diler 2002: 70–71). Rock-cut niches at several sites on the Halicarnassus Peninsula may also have served the same purpose (Diler 2002: 71–72). In Sagalassos, arcosolium tombs from the late 2nd or early 3rd century, hewn into steep cliffs, contained ostothecae partially constructed of slabs (Köse 2005: 146–47). Other forms include two-storied conical monuments in the necropolis of Anemurium, which were too small to house inhumations (Alföldi-Rosenbaum 1971: 94–95, 122). Similarly, a monumental obelisk tomb in Nicaea, according to its inscription, was constructed for a cremation, hence proving that cremations could be placed in any tomb type (*Anthologia Palatina* 15.4–7).

Social status

There is very little evidence for social distinction being attributable to cremation in the Hellenistic Period. Cremation burials in Assos were for the most part very simple, though some were placed in more luxurious cinerary urns (Stupperich 1992: 9–10; Freydank 2000: 92–93). However, cremations in important heroa (Miletus: Schörner 2007: 237–38, no. A 16; Termessos: Pekridou 1986: 67–73) indicate that the rite was also practiced in the highest strata of society.

In Roman Asia Minor, no apparent social pattern explains why cremation was practiced, since the rite occurs in very different social classes (Kubinska 1999: 51–52). In Trebenna, ostothecae were most likely reserved for slaves and poorer members of the family, while the head of the family was buried in a sarcophagus (Çevik & Iplikçioğlu 2003: 151; Kubinska 1999: 46–47, no. 38). In Ephesus and Smyrna, ostothecae were also used in connection with large funerary complexes, though it is not clear if they were reserved for particular groups within a household (Kubinska 1999: nos I 20–21, I 26–27). There is the possibility that cremation could be reserved to particular age-groups as the excavated cremations in Labraunda only comprise of adolescents and adults. However, this phenomenon could also have a taphonomic explanation (Henry & Ingvarsson-Sundström 2011: 194).

Inscriptions connected to ostothecae mention the following professions: A *nomenclator* (*IK* 15,5: no. 1665), a *dispensator* of the emperor, a *vicarius* of a *dispensator*, a scribe, a soldier (*IK* 16: nos 2255A, 2270, 2283, 2319), a *speculator* (*MAMA* 1962: no. 558), a bath attendant (*IK* 22,1: no. 1227), the clerk of a tolling station (*IK* 49,1: no. 102), a possible fishing net mender (Swoboda, Keil & Knoll 1935: 59–60, no. 123), a veteran (*SEG* 55, 2005: no. 1497), a courier, a linen merchant and twice councillors (Kubinska 1999: nos I 1, I 14, I 27, I 44). In the inscriptions of the councillors, however, it is made very clear that the ostothecae were only one element within larger and probably sumptuous funerary complexes. Indeed, cremations ranged from being placed in monumental tombs such as the tumulus in Lerdüge (Akok 1948: 854), to representative ostothecae that could claim a place among the sarcophagi in the necropolis of Perge (Abbasoğlu 2011: 84–85, fig. 1), as well as mass burials of the poor's cremated remains in Ephesus (cfr. Ephesus: Thomas & Içten 2007: 337). Consequently, although cremation was conducted by the different social classes, it seems that burials with only an ostotheca as a monument was practiced in preference by people with modest incomes. Usually the grave goods and the tomb monument gives indications of the economic status of an individual or a family, not the rite (Korkut 2006: 44; Strocka 1978: 885–886). Although cremation was certainly a more expensive solution for the treatment of the body itself compared to inhumation burials (Korkut 2006: 44; for Classical Athens, see De Schutter 1989: 56; Humphreys 1980: 100), the ashes could subsequently be placed in very small containers and graves, or be disposed of otherwise. The purchase of a burial place would in extreme cases be unnecessary and thus cremation could certainly be the best affordable solution for many of the poor.

Chronology

The Classical Period

After the first half of the 5th century BC cremation is difficult to trace in the archaeological record, despite its frequent use in the 7th, and its rare use in the 6th century BC (see Philipp 1981: 153) and it seems that it was rarely practiced or completely abolished. A classical cremation is known from Assos (Stupperich 1996: 11); in Lycia, cremation was possibly practiced until the second half of the 5th century BC (Blakolmer 2005: 4–5; Hülden 2006: 29–30, 212, 284; 2010: 6–7; Marksteiner 1994: 83–84). Although, there is evidence for cremation in Classical Sinope (*IK* 64: no. 74), the preliminary publication of the numerous cremation graves does not give enough chronological data for further analysis (Akurgal & Budde 1956: 4–5, 35). There have been found Classical cremations in the necropolis of Ainos (Başaran et al. 2010: 152 and passim) and two urnae from Nagidos further proof the rare practice of cremation in the early 4th century (Durugönül 2007: 33. 36, no. 14. 412). There is also an abrupt decline or even abolishment of cremation at Rhodian sites during the Late Archaic Period (Gates 1983: 41; Laurenzi 1936: 14), though the rite was still practiced rarely until the 5th century BC (Jacopi 1931: 17). The possibility exists that the decrease in cremation was part of a super-regional development in the Aegean, since there was also a remarkable decline during the 5th century BC in Athens. However, the rite was still frequently practiced in 4th century Athens, particularly at lavish funerals (Houby-Nielsen 1998: 135–36), and remained common in Classical Olynthos (Robinson 1942: 144), necessitating the discussion of another explanation.

Cremation decreased at a time when the Persian conquerors established their rule over Asia Minor and Rhodes. It has even been suggested that Zoroastrianism may have been a decisive factor for this remarkable development, though others have contested whether the Achaemenid Persians were Zoroastrians at all (Jacobs 2001: 87). However, Zoroaster's god, Ahuramazda, played the major role in the official religious system of Darius the Great, and the Persians continued to venerate other gods only as far as they were compatible with Zoroastrian lore (Koch 1977: 174–78). Audin (1960: 525–26) explained the beginning of the use of sarcophagi in Asia Minor with the Zoroastrian purity laws. Furthermore, Kolb and Thomsen (2005: 137) suspected Persian religion as a factor for the increase and final dominance of inhumation in Lycia, particularly because of the otherwise obvious Persian influence on tomb architecture and decoration. The purity laws of the Vendidad strictly forbade the contact of the corpse with fire and water to prevent pollution of the elements (Avesta Vendidad 7.25–27). The interdiction applied to both Zoroastrians and other religions, and the violation of this law, according to the Vendidad, had to be punished with death (Grenet 1984: 32–33). Burial was also considered a serious transgression (Grenet 1984: 33), but obviously this purity law had little impact on the rites practiced in the multiethnic Achaemenid Empire (Basirov 2001: 103–104).

The Lydian-Persian elite developed an eclectic mortuary behaviour that accounts for a polyethnic society anxious to demonstrate a new unifying identity of the elite (Basirov 2001: 101–102; Baughan 2002/2004: 227–28; Cahill 1988: 500–501; Dusinberre 2003: 145–57). Indeed, a strong mutual exchange of architectural and customary features becomes evident in the tomb architecture and decoration of the dynastic elites of Classical Asia Minor (Cahill 1988: 499; Dusinberre 2003: 133–45; Fedak 1990: 29–37; Henry 2009: 142–44, 160–61, 187; Jacobs 1987). Consequently, it seems possible that acceptance of the Persian abhorrence for cremation and the observance of some essential purity laws was necessary for the construction of such a hybrid society and for the success of political and commercial processes between Persians and the local elite. The coast was only temporarily under Persian rule during the Classical Period and many poleis remained allies of Greek powers. However, it seems unlikely that Persian customs and constant contact with neighbours under Persian rule would not have influenced the coastal towns. Similarly, the Persian religion is known to have been studied intensively by the Greeks of the Classical Period and further found its way into Greek philosophical thought (e. g. Kingsley 1995; McEvilley 2002: 172–73; Miller 2011: 63–70). A direct reference to Zoroastrian beliefs in connection with cremation is given by a source ascribed to Xanthus of Lydia, a historian of the 5th century BC. He gives an account of the attempted execution of Croesus on a pyre by the hand of Cyrus. But fearing the darkening sky as a sign, the participants recollected the lore of Zoroaster and abstained from the execution. Xanthus explains further that Zoroaster had interdicted the burning of bodies or any other defiling of the fire (*FrgHG* 90 Nikolaos von Damaskus 68; Boyce 1982: 183). The knowledge of Zoroastrian purity laws distinguishes the text from other versions of this narrative, which do not include any reference to Persian beliefs (Bacchylides, Odes 3.31–62; Herodotus I.87; see: Evans 1978: 34, 39). Unfortunately, the text of Xanthus may have been revised by Nikolaos (Erbse 1992: 23; Parke 1988: 60–61) and thus it cannot be certain if the connection of Zoroaster, cremation and pollution of the fire was Xanthus' own comment on funerary customs and beliefs in Achaemenid Asia Minor or later Hellenistic knowledge. If Nicolaos' reference to Zoroaster belongs to the original source, then it is very likely that the awe for Zoroaster's lore as described reflects an attitude experienced by Xanthus in 5th century BC Lydia. Despite the suggestive arguments discussed, any impact of Zoroastrianism on the cremation rite in Asia Minor must remain hypothetical.

Phase 1: Late 4th–2nd centuries BC (Figs 6.2 & 6.3)

Cremation experienced a revival in several regions along the west coast of Asia Minor and in Pisidia in the late 4th and early 3rd centuries BC. An ostotheca in Bithynia confirms isolated cases of cremation, which in a period of constant war and intensive sea trade could very well originate from repatriated ashes. Cremation continues into the Hellenistic Period in the same areas, but evidence occurs at more sites.

Fig. 6.2. Phase 1. Cremation in the late 4th–early 3rd centuries BC (map based on ESRI world terrain base)

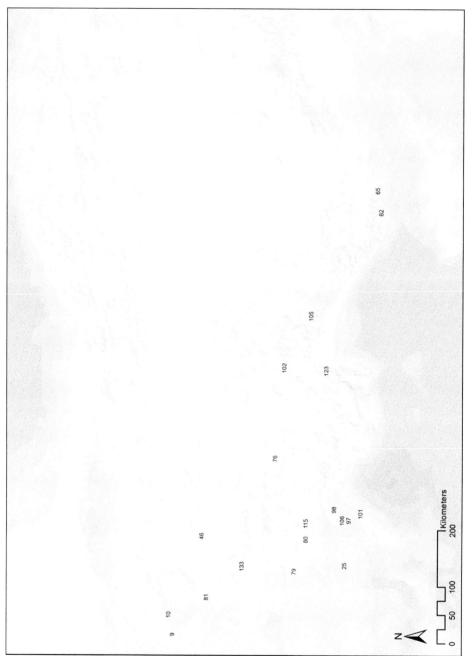

Fig. 6.3. Phase 1. Cremation in the 3rd–2nd centuries BC (map based on ESRI world terrain base)

Two of the earliest cremations, both in Pisidia, are probably linked to the Macedonian incursions of Alexander the Great. The tomb with ostotheca in Termessos is ascribed to Alkestas, a commander in Alexander's army (Çelgin 1994: 158–160; Pekridou 1986: 121–27). Fourteen cinerary urns from a hasty mass burial in Sagalassos might have a connection with the Macedonian campaigns and clearly date to that period (Waelkens et al. 1991: 212; Waelkens 1993: 41). Indeed, it is tempting to link the revival of cremation to the power shift after the defeat of the Persians.

In the course of the Macedonian conquest and the following wars between the Diadochs, soldiers from Macedonia, Greece, and other parts of the Greco-Persian world moved for decades through Asia Minor and would have practiced cremation there, either because it was their indigenous rite or to make the transport of mortal remains possible. The Macedonian cremation rite becomes popular in the royal necropolis of Aigai in the 5th and 4th century BC and is the predominant rite in Hellenistic Macedonia (Barr-Sharrar 2008: 30; Chilidis 2012: 232–33; Kottaridou 1998: 114). Elite funerals were characterised by rich grave goods and spectacular funerary pyres, which may have been inspired by Homeric descriptions of heroic funerals (Barr-Sharrar 2008: 30; Chilidis 2012: 244–49; Kottaridou 1998: 113–16; Musgrave 1990a: 277; 1990b: 321). The impression with which the audience of the Macedonian rite was left may certainly have stimulated emulation. The cultural exchange under the rule of the Macedonians and Diadochs possibly also left its fingerprint on Pisidian funerary art. The Pisidian workshops, which frequently decorated ostothecae with round 'Macedonian' shields, are believed to have drawn their inspiration from Macedonian art (critically discussed in: Köse 2005: 49–54). Such influences have been explained with the presence of Macedonian settlements in Pisidia, particularly in the Sagalassos area (Kosmetatou & Waelkens 1997: 289–90; Kosmetatou 2005: 221; compare Macedonian shields in the Hellenistic Gerdekkaya tomb in Phrygia: Kortanoğlu 2008). However, it is surprising that the power shift and subsequent Diadoch rule should have left such a deep impact on the Pisidians that they adopted the cremation rite as their primary practice for the centuries to come. Only future archaeological finds can evaluate if cremation played a more dominant role in Pisidia in the Classical Period.

Political and commercial contacts and an increased mobility in the Early Hellenistic Period may have facilitated the spread and assimilation of funerary rites along the western and southern coast. Cremation was practiced throughout the Hellenistic Period on Rhodes and the Peraia, the part of Asia Minor ruled by Rhodes, where the earliest ostotheca, belonging to a citizen of Kasara, is dated to the first half of the 3rd century BC. At that time Rhodes had developed into one of the most prosperous harbours for overseas trade through its fruitful commercial ties with Alexandria (Van Dessel & Hauben 1977: 335–37), which may have contributed to the assimilation or spread of rites. Proof for the impact of Alexandria on burial customs in Asia Minor are so-called Hadra hydriai. The typical Alexandrinian rite to place the ashes of Greeks in Hadra hydriai imported from Crete (Breccia 1933: 18–19; Dunand and Lichtenberg 1995:

3223, 3251; Forti 1992; Nock 1932: 327–28; Venit 2002: 11, 12, 24) was adopted on Rhodes during that period (Giannikoure 1996–1997: 256), and is further documented by a cremation in a Hadra hydria from Early Hellenistic Miletus (Forbeck 2005: 57 fig. 4). Hadra hydriai were also used in the Cilician cities Nagidos (Durugönül 2007: 41, no. 32. 412) and Kelenderis (Zoroğlu 2000: 115, 132) probably during the Ptolemaic occupation of the Cilician coast.

The distribution of cremation remained quite stable during the 3rd and the first two thirds of the 2nd centuries BC (Fig. 6.3), with the heartlands in southern Caria, Rhodes and Pisidia. Early ostothecae appear in Lydia already before the organisation of the province Asia in 129 BC. Indeed, the substantial finds along the western coast suggest that cremation may have occurred at even more places, but which lack archaeological finds.

Phase 2: Late 2nd century BC–early Imperial Period *(Fig. 6.4)*

In the late Hellenistic and the Early Imperial Period, the use of ostothecae takes off in Ionia, Lydia, and Pamphylia. The increase in monuments linked to cremation occurs particularly after the establishment of the Roman province Asia, though there is little evidence for long distance distribution. However, in the early 1st century BC, cremation graves also appear in Pessinus as the first site of what later would become the Roman province Galatia.

Phase 3: 1st–3rd centuries AD *(Fig. 6.5)*

There is evidence for cremation in the 1st and 2nd centuries AD in new areas of Asia Minor: Bithynia (2nd century AD; Koch 1990: 155–56; 2010: 131)); Isauria and Lycaonia (probably 2nd –3rd centuries AD; Doğanay 2010: 43–47; Koch 1990: 160–61; 2010: 132), and Galatia/east Phrygia (see Appendix). Cremation continues and spreads within Ionia, to new parts of Caria (Late Hellenistic–2nd century AD: Koch 2010: 131), Lydia, Pamphylia, and Cilicia Trachea (see Appendix). Isolated examples also occur from sites in Paphlagonia, Cilicia, and Cappadocia; in addition a few examples are attested from Lycia, most of them probably from the Imperial Period, though it remains uncertain if cremation had a longer tradition there or began in the Imperial Period. Evidence from Ağva indicates that cremation may have been practiced in the Pisidian-Lycian borderland in the 3rd century BC or earlier (Özoral 1980: 95–96, 98).

In the case of Ephesus, inscriptions have revealed that more than 50% of the ostothecae were used by Roman citizens or freedmen (Thomas & Içten 1999: 550, 552; 2007: 339–342). Some ostothecae even bear bilingual or Latin inscriptions (Thomas & Içten 1999: 552, note 23). It has been suggested that the increase in the use of ostothecae in Ephesus in phase 2 should be seen as the adoption or reflection of Roman funerary practices (Thomas & Içten 2007: 338). Ostothecae in Smyrna (*IK* 23: nos 366, 383, 472) and Laodicea (*IK* 49: nos 102, 117) also support the assumption that burial in ostothecae may have been particularly common among Westerners or 'Romanised' slaves

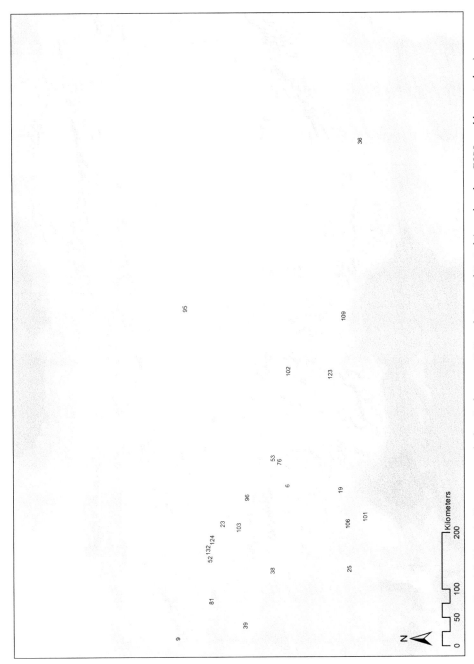

Fig. 6.4. Phase 2. Cremation in the late 2nd century BC–early Imperial Period (map based on ESRI world terrain base)

in administrative positions. The re-introduction of cremation in Early Imperial Miletus (Forbeck 2005: 59) may be a further indicator of Western influence. It is notable that several of the columbaria in Asia Minor were found in Miletus and Ephesus.

At two sites in Greece the practice of cremation can also be seen as a direct result of an acculturation process. At Cenchreai (Rife 2007), the eastern port of Corinth, thirty chamber tombs built in the Early Imperial Period were recorded with niches for both inhumations and cremations. The cremated were upper class Greeks who adopted the rite, probably under Western influence. In Greece, cremation seems to have been common in important centres and colonies during the 1st century AD, with strong links to the West: Corinth, Patras, and Nicopolis (Flämig 2007: 89; Ubelaker & Rife 2007: 40). Cremation was also introduced due to the emulation of Western customs during the reign of Augustus on Samothrace, where it was practiced for only about half a century (Dusenbery 1998: 22–24). Indeed, at both Corinth and Samothrace cremation was not a rite practiced before the 1st century BC.

However, the obvious impact of the Roman presence on cremation and the use of ostothecae is restricted to areas along the west coast of Asia Minor. The few published examples from Isauria/Lycaonia gathered for this article are hardly representative (numerous examples of cinerary containers were not presented on the map or in the Appendix: Bean & Mitford 1970: 98, 100, 106, 108, 110, 119, 136–37, 141, 144, 148; Doğanay 2010: 43, 45, 47), as very few inscriptions mention possible Westerners (Kubinska 1999: I 44; Swoboda, Keil & Knoll 1935: 30, no. 66), and it would seem that the percentage is much lower than in the examples from Ionia. The 251 recently published ostothecae from Pamphylia and Cilicia are rarely inscribed and none bears a Latin name (Korkut 2006: 86–105). The owner of one of the early ostothecae in Sardis, dated from before the organization of the Roman province Asia in 129 BC, bears a Latin name, but he is apparently the son of a Greek (Malay 1994: no. 439). Of 64 inscribed ostothecae with certain provenance from Lydia (Akyürek Şahin & Onur 2008; Dedeoğlu & Malay 1994; Malay 1994; 1999; Malay & Petzl 2005; Malay & Ricl 2006; examples from the Cayster Valley have not been considered here), there is only one example belonging with all probability to a Westerner. It must remain open if the onset of the use of ostothecae could somehow be linked to Roman dominance in Lydia and similarly if the use of ostothecae starts at the same time as the practice of cremation. A late 2nd or 1st century BC family tomb in Sardis, containing nine cremated relatives with Greek names, indicates that cremation was a well-established tradition by that time (Dedeoğlu & Malay 1991; Malay 1994: 440–48).

A direct impact of Roman art on the shape or decoration of incineration receptacles in Asia Minor has certainly occurred. The use of ostothecae in Asia Minor is much older than the quite similar cinerary urns in Rome and both groups follow local traditions (Sinn 1987: 11). However, a new Roman type of ostothecae appears in Early Imperial Sagalassos and demonstrates that Roman funerary art became fashionable and added to the variety of local products (Köse 2002: 120–21; 2005: 164). It has also been argued that the sudden and successful decoration with garlands on the Ephesian ostothecae,

Fig. 6.5. Phase 3. Cremation from the 1st–3rd centuries AD (map based on ESRI world terrain base)

produced since the second half of the 1st century BC, was introduced by Roman citizens living in Ephesus (Cormack 1997: 148; Thomas & Içten 1999: 552–53). Indeed, cinerary urns with garland decoration were mass-produced in Rome from the middle Augustan Period (Sinn 1987: 23, 57). The influential workshops of Ephesus contributed to the spread of garland decoration to other areas (Köse 2005: 82–83). However, the development of garland decoration in Pamphylia is considered independent of Roman decorative systems (cfr. Korkut 2006: 16).

As a conclusion, the decisive impact that Romans, their freedmen and slaves had on the practice of cremation and the decoration of burial containers is only traceable in the coastal towns of Ionia. From here Roman funerary art spread eastwards to, for example, Sagalassos. The use of ostothecae seems to have spread from the west to the east and from the coast inland via Pamphylia to Cilicia and Lycaonia, and from Bithynia to Galatia. The most obvious explanation for the pattern observed in phases 2 and particularly 3 is that the spread is not an indigenous development independent of the new political situation, but an adoption of coastal fashions facilitated by the improved security and economic realities of the Pax Romana and the enormous increase of mobility. Mobility both voluntary and involuntary has contributed significantly to the transfer of ritual practices in the Roman Empire (Chaniotis 2009: 20). The Western influence in Pisdia, where cremation was practiced and ostothecae were produced long before any intense contact with the Roman West, is of course only superficial. However, it should be asked if the regions where the use of ostothecae emerged during the Roman administration had a tradition for cremation earlier or if the rite was adopted? There is of course also the possibility that cremation in some of these regions was an older rite, which was only monumentalised through the use of ostothecae. Nevertheless, it is likely that particular groups of the local populations adopted the cremation rite under the influence of new trends. If these groups were aware of the indirect Western impact on their practices, however, remains uncertain. It was probably often rather an emulation of trends in neighbouring regions that led to the use of ostothecae in connection with cremation. The ostothecae show particular local styles and the inscriptions do not reveal a strong Western presence. Possibly comparable is the diffusion of the Roman rosalia ritual which conquered the provinces East probably spreading from the Balkans (Chaniotis 2009: 21).

The pattern of distribution in Galatia, East Phrygia, and along the Pontic coast does not pose any particular interpretation problems. The only site with extensive evidence, Pessinus, is also the site with the oldest finds. At Pessinus, cremation was already practiced before the annexation of Galatia in 25 BC, with the type of tomb showing some similarities with Celtic rites (Devreker et al. 2003: 343; compare also a cremation tomb with Mid-Latène fibula in Assos, Stupperich 1996: 11). The cremations in Alpu and Gordion date to the 1st century AD, while ostothecae and inscriptions in Ancyra and Synnada provide evidence for cremation at least in the 2nd century AD. All five sites, in addition to one of the main production centres for ostothecae, Docimeium, are situated along one of the major traffic roads, identified by some scholars as the "royal highway" (Levick 1967: 10), or the road leading from Ancyra via Dorylaeum to the Bosporus (Mitchell 1995: 129); the cities Amastris, Heraclea Pontica, and Sinope were important trading ports. Cultural contacts along the roads and the coast, movement of merchants, establishing garrisons, settlement of foreigners during the reconstruction of Pessinus and Ancyra under Augustus (Mitchell 1995: 87) and the foundation of Caesar's colonies in Heraclea Pontica and Sinope (MacMullen 2000: 9), contributed to the distribution pattern observed there. For example, the inscriptions mentioning ostothecae from Ancyra use formulae according to the Bithynian habit (Kubinska 1999: 51), which makes it likely that migrating Bithynians spread their funerary customs to other regions.

Phase 4: 3rd century AD *(Fig. 6.6)*

Evidence for cremation in the 3rd century AD is scarce. However, this is probably much more due to inadequate dating than lack of evidence. Indeed, an increase in the practice of cremation is evident at Trebenna (Çevik & Iplikçioğlu 2003: 151). In Ephesus, Sagalassos and Pamphylia, the production or use of ostothecae and other cinerary receptacles lasts until the middle of the 3rd century AD or even later (Korkut 2006: 83; Köse 2005: 147; Thomas & Içten 1999: 552). Many of the Isaurian/Lycaonian ostothecae most probably date to the 3rd century AD, but lack detailed studies (Koch 2010: 132). In one cemetery in Pessinus, 23 inhumations and 24 cremations were found dating from the 3rd to the late 5th centuries AD (Lambrechts 1969: 127–31). The amount of sites, however, has obviously decreased from the previous period, based on the finds of ostothecae. Indeed, ostothecae production comes to a halt in many areas in the late 2nd century AD. Large production centres such as Docimeium had stopped production already around AD 170 (Koch 1990: 155), probably because of a decrease in demand. There is also the possibility that the market was saturated and that a continuous production was unnecessary due to the reuse of old ostothecae. However, lack of cremation evidence and late 3rd century AD inscriptions add to the impression that this practice was indeed receding in large parts of Asia Minor after the 2nd century AD.

It is tempting to link such a possible decline to the general reduction of cremation in the west of the Empire, where inhumation gained more importance in the course of the 2nd century AD and became the primary rite in the 3rd century AD. The development in the West has been discussed extensively in order to identify the cause(s) for the increase of inhumation and the successful introduction of sarcophagi shortly after AD 100. The latest debate asserts that no particular reason can be identified (Koch & Sichtermann 1982: 27–30; Morris 1996: 31–68; Schrumpf 2006: 70–77) from the written sources. For the time being neither religious nor ideological causes can be directly linked to changes from cremation to inhumation in the Roman Empire before the 4th century AD (Scheid 2007: 19) and vice versa. The assumption is that the shift in Rome was the result of social fashion (Morris 1996: 33; Nock 1932: 357–59; Schrumpf 2006: 76). The change from cremation to inhumation may have had its onset under the Flavian

Fig. 6.6. Phase 4. Cremation in the 3rd century AD (map based on ESRI world terrain base)

emperors, who increasingly recruited senators from inhumating areas of Italy and the Greek East to fill the seats emptied by the civil war (Schrumpf 2006: 75–76). Recently, more archaeological evidence has become available for inhumation in Rome in the 1st century AD to show that the shift in funerary rites in the early 2nd century AD was less abrupt, than previously assumed (Steinby 2003: 28–34; Taglietti 2001: 150).

Personal freedom in the choice of the burial rite is supported by the literary sources. Greek accounts from the 2nd century AD– Athenaeus and Lucian – indicate that the selection could have been entirely personal and sometimes made freely by the relatives (Robinson 1942: 149). For the following short discussion both Latin and Greek sources have to be considered because of the extremely meager literary evidence. This is surprising considering that inhumation replaced cremation almost completely and millions of people changed their funerary habits radically in the course of only 150 years. In the 1870s, thousands of contributions were published for or against cremation during the debate around its introduction in Germany (Thalmann 1978: 9, 13–15). In the Roman Empire, however, there was seemingly no noteworthy debate on this issue. The difference between the two periods may be that European cremationists of the 19th century had to overcome a religious dogma that had determined funerary rites for far over one millennium and thus felt an enormous pressure to defend their cause. Such a religious consensus simply did not exist in the multi-religious Roman Empire, and consequently a discussion was unnecessary.

There was obviously no philosophical objection against any burial rite. Lucretius argues that the treatment of the body after death is of no importance for the dead because death would mean the end of self (*De rerum natura* 3.870–93). Lucin sees the body dissolve into the cycle of nature independently of any funerary treatment (*Pharsalia* 7.27–28). These Epicurean and Stoic notions may not have applied to everybody at that time, but may be representative of a considerable part of Roman society. The Stoic notion is further interpreted by Minucius Felix, a 2nd or 3rd century AD Christian writer (*Octavia* 34.10). He believes that even though the corpse is transformed by whatever funerary rite or treatment after death into whatever element, it will still exist for God, who is the preserver of the elements. Minucius mentions further that the Christians prefer the old tradition of inhumation, additionally hinting at the resurrection of the body at the last judgment (*Octavia* 34.11–12). The characterization of inhumation as a tradition can also be found in the Syriac version of Aristides' *Apology* (14). He praises the Jews for burying their dead because this is agreeable to god and a tradition from their forefathers.

From the other sources we may extract two more arguments against cremation. The first is the pity and respect for the corpse, which is particularly evident in the Early Christian sources (Rebillard 2009: 84–85; Volp 2002: 187–88). Tertullian writes that the body may exercise a reduced activity after death, basing his argument on Democritus' observation of corpses growing hair and nails after death and the possibility of revivication exemplified by Plato's Er (*De Anima* 51.2–4). He adds that many choose not to cremate because of these remains of life in the corpse and/or because of respect for the body that does not deserve such a harsh treatment (see also Turcan 1958: 341). Pity for the body is not a new or even Christian argument; the 1st century AD description of a man who did not cremate his wife because he could not bear the smell and noise of the cremation process already points to such emotions (Statius *Silvae* 5.1.225–28). Everybody who reads the vivid ancient reports on cremations (Noy 2000) will understand that the extreme transformation of the burning body could have been a traumatic experience for the audience and evoked a strong sensation of pity. This may indeed have been a factor for the decision for a "peaceful end" (Bynum 1995: 53; Davies 2011: 50).

According to Philostratus *Vitae Sophistarum*, the Sophist, Apollonius, a contemporary of Septimius Severus, allegedly held the declamation 'Callias tries to dissuade the Athenians from burning the dead' (602). In the passage, Apollonius argues that fire is an ethereal element linked to the divine rather than to the underworld, which would be polluted by the corpse. The Greeks had their own tradition of rituals including purification with fire (Burkert 1970: 3–7), which places Apollonius' argument in an understandable context. However, a Hadrianic funerary inscription from Nicaea contains the contradictory argument that the burning of the corpse by fire was by others considered an act of purification (*Anthologia Palatina* 15.6). Apollonius' notion of the divine character of fire might rather have been inspired by Pythagorean philosophy and it has to be considered whether the argument reflected Apollonius' own belief. According to the meager written sources (Pliny the Elder, *Naturalis Historia* 35.160), inhumation was part of the Pythagorean funerary rite (Kahn 2001: 88, 90). There are further indications that the sect indeed tried to avoid pollution of the fire (Diogenes Laertius, *Lives* 8.17), probably under the influence of Zoroastrian lore (Miller 2011: 65–66). Apollonius might also have drawn his inspiration directly from Persian (Turcan 1958: 337–40) or Hellenistic sources discussing the Persian abhorrence of cremation (Dioscorides, *Anthologia Palatina* 7.162). The fascination of the sophists with Zoroaster is already attested some hundred years earlier in the oration 36 of the Bithynian Dio Chrysostomos. Whatever his sources, Apollonius must have been very clear about the religious connotation of the argument.

This does not necessarily mean that Apollonius was agitating against cremation or that he acted as the follower of a religious sect. The declamation was probably held *ex tempore* and in this case the topic would be proposed by the audience. Indeed, Apollonius possibly had a repertoire of excellent arguments against inhumation if the audience had chosen to hear that instead. Nevertheless, it should be assumed that this argument against cremation was considered a good one at that time and it cannot be excluded that Apollonius even used a popular idea for the persuasiveness of his declamation. It was the profession of the sophistic teachers in their function as speakers and embassies, at the highest level of Roman politics, to persuade the audience of their declamations, both with an elaborate rhetoric style and a powerful argumentation. Apollonios probably held this speech at the Academy in Athens where he held a chair for political oratory.

The declamation was not only heard of by a considerable part of the richest and most influential intellectuals in the Greek world, but the oral and written transmission of such teachings also spread philosophical ideas to all the Greek intellectuals. Thus, it could have influenced the decision for the funerary rite of the listeners and readers.

The examples cited above show that diametric ideas like pity for the deceased or the pollutive nature of the corpse may have been used against cremation. It is clear that there were a variety of personal, religious, and philosophical reasons for the choice of a funerary rite and no consensus that actuated the decrease in cremation. This strongly suggests that the decline was not an isolated ritual change, originating directly from a single or multiple source(s), but only one symptom of a much wider psychological shift.

Cremation offered an abrupt separation from the deceased and an omission of the putrefaction process. Dio Chrysostomos (*Oration* 4.32) mentions as a particular attribute of cremation that it dissolves the corpse completely except for the teeth, a characteristic that Pliny the Elder (*Naturalis Historia* 36.27) had shortly before imputed to sarcophagi from Assos and Lycia. It seems that the radical consumption of the corpse by fire was a desirable effect for those who practiced cremation. Inhumation, however, would extend the period of separation. Hence, even if the corpse was placed in a sealed tomb, a sarcophagus or a grave, the awareness of the presence of the body, which had been seen intact at the funeral, must have made the separation feel less finite. The prolongation of separation gave the possibility of prolonged mourning, particularly when the deceased had been placed in a tomb or sarcophagus. The preference for an extended separation process and the increasing respect for the body, as extracted from the written sources, may be connected to the heightened concern for a lasting monument and epigraphic commemoration in the 2nd century AD.

Analyses of funerary inscriptions have established an unprecedented increase of Latin inscriptions in the 2nd century AD in the Roman Empire, peaking around AD 200 (MacMullen 1982: 241–46; Morris 1996: 167–68). A second analysis of the inscriptions from Lydia, most of them epitaphs, reached a comparable result, but with a peak in the reign of Marcus Aurelius (MacMullen 1986). In Paphlagonia, the chronological distribution is also comparable (French 1991; Højte 2006: tables 1–2, 4). MacMullen (1982: 246) gives the following hypothesis: '... people... counted on their world still continuing in existence for a long time to come, so as to make nearly permanent memorials worthwhile'. Indeed, the extreme increase can only be the result of a heightened desire for a lasting memory.

The enormous increase in sarcophagi in 2nd century AD Asia Minor points in the same direction. Only a few received a lasting or individual monument in early Imperial Asia Minor and most were probably interred in family monuments or in simple graves. The stelae and ostothecae used at that time were too easy to remove, which is shown by the fact that they are rarely found in their original context. In the 2nd and 3rd centuries AD, large parts of the population in certain regions acquired sarcophagi, which by their weight and size alone could guarantee a long lasting memorial. Sarcophagi would have been a considerable expense, but at the same time could serve for multiple interments (for example Asgari & Firatli 1978: 34), while the burial spot would not cost more than a simple shaft grave. Because of the possibility of a lasting memorial and these additional benefits, more people may have been inclined to save money for their own burial during their lifetime or spend large sums on deceased relatives than was the case before the 2nd century AD. This further implies that money was rather spent on the funerary monument, than on a sumptuous funeral including the pyre.

Concluding remarks

Cremation had a renaissance during and subsequent to the Macedonian incursions, after its almost complete abolishment under Persian rule. An impact of Persian religion on the practice of cremation in the 6th and 5th centuries BC is possible but must remain hypothetical. However, the comeback of cremation after the Macedonian conquest in the late 4th century BC certainly reflects the adaption and emulation of foreign customs enabled by new cultural and economic contacts under Macedonian and Ptolemaic rule. The rite spread from regions in western and southern Asia Minor to large parts of western Anatolia during the Hellenistic and Roman Imperial Periods, but regional differences are evident. **Emulation was probably a decisive factor behind the long distance spread of the use of ostothecae in the 1st and 2nd centuries AD. The distribution pattern in Galatia and Paphlagonia makes migration the most plausible factor for the spread of cremation under the Pax Romana.** Even though the distribution patterns and epigraphic evidence for some regions clearly show an increased spread of cremation, the Roman rule appears not to have caused a significant ritual change for the area as a whole. **Cremation was practiced side by side with inhumation and often was a matter of practical considerations, personal preferences (Ubelaker & Rife 2007: 41), traditions or even fashions. Indeed, it is impossible to trace any discrimination of cremation between the late 4th century BC and the 3rd century AD. Hence, it seems that the two rites were not seen as something contrary, but rather as just two options in the multifaceted range of mortuary rites available in Asia Minor.**

The evidence gathered for this summary demonstrates, indeed, that cremation was a 'Greek' rite in Asia Minor or maybe rather an Ionian, Pisidian, Rhodian, Carian rite, and so forth. Cremation was practiced in Pisidia and Rhodes for a period of 500–600 years, and thus longer than for example in Rome. However, on a super-regional level inhumation was much more common than cremation at least in the Imperial Period. An uncritical and unsystematic search in the Packhard Humanities database gives over 800 mentions of the term σορὸς (sarcophagus) in inscriptions from Asia Minor, most of them from the Imperial Period. Additionally, there are hundreds of inscriptions, mentioning other terms for sarcophagi, for example, σωματοθήκη, ἀνγεῖον, πυαλίς, πύελος (collected in Kubinska 1968: 32–57). A comparison with the 60 inscriptions mentioning ὀστοθήκη and καύστρα (Kubinska 1999: passim) makes the overriding dominance of inhumation in the epigraphic record very clear. Such preeminence was already visible in the Hellenistic necropoleis of Assos and Myrina.

Appendix

In the table below are summarised the cremations discussed in the text.

Abbreviations used in the table: Hel= Hellenistic; Imp = Roman Imperial; E = Early; L = Late; 1/2 = first half; 2/2 = second half; 2/4 = second quarter; 1/3 third quarter; Aug = Augustan. The numbers refer to those on the maps in Figs 6.1–6.6. Receptacle always refers to monumental cinerary containers of stone and terracotta. Clearly identifiable urns of metal or ceramics have been grouped with cremations. Docimeium has been inserted in the table as a producer of ostothecae. If cremation was practiced there is not known.

no	site	architecture	receptacle	inscription	cremation	publications	Chronology
1	Akçapinar (Troketta?)		X			Malay & Ricl 2006: 50 no. 3.	Imp
2	Alpu		X		X	Atasoy 1974: 258.	I AD
3	Amastris		X			Koch 1990: 162; Marek 2003: 134 fig. 196.	2/2 II AD
4	Ancyra (and area)		X	X		Kubinska 1999: nos I 11–18, II 2–3.	Imp
5	Anemurium	X				Alföldi-Rosenbaum 1971: 94–95, 100 note 53, 122, 169.	Imp
6	Aphrodisias		X			Işik 2007: 285 pl. 111.1; *MAMA* 1962: no. 558.	L Hel–E Imp
7	Arneai			X		Kubinska 1999: no. I 41.	
8	Aşağieşenler		X			Scarborough 1995: 340–41 fig. 6.	
9	Assos		X		X	Freydank 2000: 92–94, 100; Stupperich 1996: 9–11.	III–II BC; E Imp
10	Atandros				X	Polat 2008: 277 ; Polat 2010 : 110, 114.	III–II BC ; Hel
11	Avasun			X		Kubinska 1999: no. II 5.	
12	Ayaz		X			Ötüken 1996: no. MKP 15 b pl. 44,4–5.	L IV BC
13	Balboura		X			Hallett & Coulton 1993: 66.	
14	Bezdegüme		X			*IK* 17,2: 3702.	I AD
15	Bozkir area				X	McLean 2002: nos 185–190; Scarborough 1995: 342–43 figs 21–22, 24; Swoboda, Keil & Knoll 1935: 56 no. c, 57 no. g, 59 no. 123, 61 no. 127.	Imp; III AD
16	Burdur district				X	Asgari 1983: nos B.366, 133; Horsley 2007: nos 246, 256–7, 278, 287.	I–III AD
17	Burgaz Tepesi	X				Diler 2002: 71–72.	
18	Caberfakili		X			Malay 1999: 160 no. 186.	Imp
19	Caunus	X				Diler 2002: 70–71.	L Hel–Imp
20	Çavus				X	Swoboda, Keil & Knoll 1935: 20 nos a–d., 21 nos 29–30.	Imp
21	Çaygökpinar Köyü		X			Adak et al. 2008: 113–14 no. 50.	Imp
22	Chalke		X			Fraser 1977: 93 note 48	
23	Charakipolis				X	Deodoğlu & Malay 1994: 130–132. nos 1–4.	Augustan

no	site	architecture	receptacle	inscription	cremation	publications	Chronology
24	Clazomenae		X			Malay 1994: 475.	Imp
25	Cnidus	X	X		X	Berns in press; Newton 1862–63: 478; Pastutmaz 2008: 526.	E II–3/4 I BC
26	Coracaesium		X			Asgari 1983: nos B.363, 131.	II AD
27	Çorum			X		Kubinska 1999: no. II 2.	
28	Cyzicus		X			Koch 1990: 158.	
29	Daldis		X			Malay 1994: nos. 465, 467.	Aug–I or II AD
30	Dardanos		X			Duyuran 1960: 11 pl. XIII.	Hel (?)
31	Dereiçi		X			Scarborough 1995: 339 fig. 2.	
32	Devrent		X			IK 17,7, 2: no. 3718.	
33	Docimeium					Koch 1990: 155; 2010: 130; Waelkens 1982: 50.	Ca. AD 140–170
34	Doğanci Köyü/Bolu		X			Adak et al. 2008: 112–13 no. 47.	II AD
35	Efrenk				X	Durukan 2007: 148 figs. 7–8.	Imp?
36	Elaiussa Sebaste	X				Berns 2003: 109, 186–87 no. 10A1; Durukan 2005: 110, 114 figs. 7. 8; Durukan 2007: 151; Machatschek 1967: 56, 112–13 pl. 37b.	L Hel–Imp
37	Eldessos		X			Milner 2004: 72–74 no. 34.	II–III AD
38	Ephesus		X	X	X	Kubinska 1999: nos. I 22–33. 45, II 9–17; Thomas & Içten 1999: 552–53; Walker 1985: 55–56.	1/2 I BC–III AD
39	Erythrae			X		Merkelbach & Stauber 1998–2004: 03/07/17, 03/07/19.	II BC; I AD
40	Etenna?			X		Kubinska 1999: no. II 6.	
41	Faustinopolis			X	X	Kubinska 1999: no. II 4; IK 55, 1: no. 123.	Imp
42	Gordion				X	Goldman 2007: 304.	I AD
43	Gündoğan	X				Diler 2002: 71–72.	
44	Günece Köy			X		SEG 14: no. 770.	Imp
45	Günsalar Köyü		X			Adak & Akyürek Sahin 2005: 165 no. 37.	
46	Gökçeahmet		X			Malay 1994: 478–80.	Hel
47	Hadrianoupolis		X			Merkelbach & Stauber 1998–2004: 16/52/02.	
48	Halicarnassus				X	Newton 1862–63: 338.	
49	Hamaxia		X			Korkut 2006: no. 32.	2/2 II AD
50	Harkköy		X			Adak & Akyürek Sahin 2005: 166 no. 38.	
51	Heraclea Pontica		X			IK 47: no. 16.	Imp
52	Hermokapeleia		X			Petzl & Pleket 1979: 284–85 nos 2–3.	I BC–I AD
53	Hierapolis		X		X	Anderson 2007: 477–78; Okunak 2005: 57; Verzone1961–62: 637. Unpublished ostotheca	L Hel/E Imp; Imp
54	Hieroceasarea		X			Malay & Ricl 2006: 50–51 nos 5–6.	Imp
55	Iasos				X	Levi 1961–62: 567 fig. 100.	Imp
56	Idebessos		X			Kizgut et al. 2009: 156.	
57	Inçesu		X			Swoboda, Keil & Knoll 1935: 30 no. 66.	Imp
58	Iotape		X	X		Bean & Mitford 1965: 30, 32; Rosenbaum et al. 1967: 59.	
59	Isaura Nova			X		Merkelbach & Stauber 1998–2004:	Imp

no	site	architecture	receptacle	inscription	cremation	publications	Chronology
60	Karaadilli		X			İlaslı & Üyümez 2008: 198 fig. 162.	Imp
61	Kasara		X			*IK* 38: no. 58; Bresson 1991: 155 no 163	1/2 III BC
62	Kaynar Kale (Kodrula?)		X			Bean 1960: 48.	
63	Kayseri		X			Koch 1990: 162.	2/2 II AD
64	Kazanli		X			Asgari 1977: 376.	
65	Kelenderis				X	Zoroğlu 2000: 115, 132	Hel
66	Kepez Kalesi		X			Waelkens et al. 1997: 71.	
67	Kesecik		X	X		*SEG* 49: nos 1938–39.	II–III AD
68	Kirbaşi		X			Bresson 1991: nos 89, 99; *IK* 38: no. 231–32.	Hel?
69	Koca Kuru Tepe				X	Yaraş 2004	2/2 I–1/2 II AD
70	Koloe (Kaleköy)		X			Malay & Ricl 2006: 70 no. 43.	Imp
71	Küçük Öz			X		Kubinska 1999: no. I 44.	Imp
72	Kula		X			Asgari 1977: 338 fig 17; Malay 1994: 466.	AD 61/62
73	Küyükkaraagaç		X			Fraser 1977: 94 note 48.	
74	Labraunda				X	Henry & Ingvarsson-Sundström 2011: 189.	Imp
75	Laertes		X			Korkut 2006: 83.	2/2 II AD
76	Laodicea		X		X	*IK* 49: nos 102. 117; *IK* 59: no. 57; Kahil 1969: 207–8 no. 31; Şimşek 2007: 323–325; Şimşek 2011: 15.	II BC–II AD
77	Lerdüge				X	Akok 1948: 854.	I BC–II AD
78	Melli		X			Vandeput & Köse 2001: 141.	
79	Miletus	X			X	Forbeck 2005: 57, 59–60; Schörner 2007: 237–38 no. A 16.	L IV–III BC; II BC?; Imp
80	Mylasa		X	X	X	Akarca 1952; Kızıl 2009: 403–404. nos M32–33 figs. 103, 125; Kubinska 1999: no. I 36.	L IV–III BC; Hel; Imp
81	Myrina				X	Pottier 1887: 73, 78–100 nos 39, 51, 69, 93, 95, 98, 101, 105, 108, 110, 113, 114.	III–I BC
82	Nagidos				X	Durugönül 2007: 41 no. 32, 412.	2/2 III BC
83	Neapolis		X			Özdilek 2008: 239.	
84	Nicaea		X	X		Asgari 1983: nos B.367, 369; Durugönül & Şahin 1993: 57; Koch & Sichtermann 1982: 511; Kubinska 1999: nos I 6, 8; Merkelbach & Stauber 1998–2994: 09/05/12, 09/05/08.	II AD
85	Nicomedia		X	X		Kubinska 1999: nos I 1–5.	Imp
86	Nysa		X			Asgari 1977: 363; Koch & Sichtermann 1982: 527	
87	Ödemiş		X			Malay & Ricl 2006: 74 no. 53.	Imp
88	Oinoanda		X			Milner 2004: 73.	II–III AD
89	Osmaneli		X			Asgari 1983: B.368, 133	II AD
90	Özburun (Polybotos?)		X			Asgari 1983: nos B.360, 130.	I AD
91	Parion				X	Başaran 2009, 393–95; Başaran & Tavukçu 2006: 621–22.	Imp
92	Patara			X	X	Kubinska 1999: no. I 40; Yilmaz 1992: 391 fig. 10.	Hel?

no	site	architecture	receptacle	inscription	cremation	publications	Chronology
94	Perge		X		X	Abbasoğlu 2008: 58–60 ; Abbasoğlu 2009: 4–5. 13; *IK* 61: no. 403; Korkut 2006: nos 167, 175.	Imp
95	Pessinus				X	Devreker 1994: 105–6; Devreker et al. 2003, 40–43; Lambrechts 1969: 127–31.	E I BC–V AD
96	Philadelphia		X			Malay 1994: nos 453–55, 457, 459, 62–463, 471–74; Malay & Petzl 2005: nos 1–7; Akyürek Şahin & Onur 2008: 131–33 nos 3–5.	Hel–Imp
97	Phoinix		X			Bresson 1991: 138 no. 146; *IK* 38: no. 117.	Hel
98	Physkos		X			*IK* 38: no. 518; Bresson 1991: 56 no. 21	Hel
99	Pinara			X		Schweyer 2002: 40.	
100	Prusa ad Olympum		X			*IK* 39, I: nos 126, 169; Koch & Sichtermann 1982: 512–13.	I–II AD
101	Rhodes	X	X			Fraser 12. 52–53.	Hel–III AD
102	Sagalassos	X	X		X	Köse 2005: 146–47, 163; Waelkens et al. 1991: 208–12.	3/4 IV BC–I AD; 2/2 II–III AD
103	Sardis		X		X	Asgari 1977: 337; Asgari 1983 nos. B356.129, B357.130; Dedeoğlu & Malay 1991: 116–119; Gibson 1981: 216; Greenewalt 1977: 50; Koch 1990: 156, 158; Malay 1994: nos 438–52. Malay & Petzl 2005.	Before 129 BC–L II AD
104	Sarigöl		X			Malay 1994: 485.	
105	Selge		X			Fleischer 1978: 43–44.	Hel
106	Selimiye		X			*IK* 38: nos 258, 262; Bresson 1991: 96 no 71.	Hel–L Hel
107	Selinous		X			Korkut 2006: 83.	I–3/4 II AD
108	Sia		X			*IK* 57: no. 147.	Imp?
109	Side		X			*IK* 44: nos 212–15; Korkut 2006: nos 224, 231.	I BC–2/2 III AD
110	Sinope		X			Koch 1990: 161–62.	2/2 II AD
111	Sivasti			X		Kubinska 1999: no. I 43.	
112	Smyrna		X	X		*IK* 23: nos 366, 383, 437, 443, 449, 472, 480, 480, 486; Kubinska 1999: nos I 19–21.	Imp
113	Soğanlı			X		*SEG* 19: no. 799.	
114	Soli-Pompeiopolis				X	Kaya 2006: 41, 43, 54–57, 60.	Imp
115	Stratonicaea		X	X	X	Civelek 2006: 51; *IK* 22,1: nos 1226a, 1227, 1250, 1256; Koch 1990: 158; Kubinska 1999: I 34–35; Söğüt 2010: 198–99.	II BC; Imp
116	Sülün/Afyonkarahisar		X			İlaslı & Üyümez 2008: 198 fig. 161.	Imp
117	Syedra		X			Korkut 1999: 83.	2/4 II–2/4 III AD
118	Syme		X			Fraser 1977; 93 note 48.	
119	Synnada		X			Asgari 1977: B.362, 132.	Mid II AD
120	Taşkent		X			Baldiran 2007: 27–30.	

no	site	architecture	receptacle	inscription	cremation	publications	Chronology
121	Telos		X			Fraser 1977: 93 note 48.	
122	Teos		X			Merkelbach & Stauber 1998–2004: 03/06/04	Imp
123	Termessos		X	X		Çelgin 1994: 169–171; Fleischer 1978: 42; İplikçioğlu 1991: no. 11; Kubinska 1999: nos I 37, II 8; Lanckoronski 1892: 69–70; Pekridou 1986: 67–73; Pietrograhde 1935: 29–30.	319 BC–III AD
124	Thyateira		X			Malay 1994: 461, 468; 1999: 43 no. 28.	L Hel–Imp
125	Tralleis			X	X	Ertuğrul 2005: 29–28; Kubinska 1999: no. II 7; Yener & Özkan 1997: 221 fig. 22.	L IV–E III BC, Imp
126	Trebenna		X	X		Çevik 1997: 138; Çevik & İplikçioğlu 2003; Kubinska 1999: no. I 38.	Imp–III AD
127	Tülü Asar		X			Söğut 2003, 284–85.	Imp?
128	Vasada		X			Laminger-Pascher 1973: 71 no. 21.	
129	Xanthos			X		Kubinska 1999: no I 39.	
130	Yatağan		X			Swoboda, Keil & Knoll 1935: 8.	
131	Yazıköy		X			*IK* 41: no. 519.	
132	Zeytinliova		X			Malay 1994: 456, 484.	Hel–L Hel
133	Nif (Olympos) Dağı*				X	Tulunay 2009: 391	E Hel

Databases

Two internet databases have been used constantly for research on texts and Greek epigraphy:

http: //epigraphy.packhum.org/inscriptions/main
http: //www.perseus.tufts.edu/hopper/collections

Acknowledgements

I want to express my gratitude to Christof Berns, Andrew Goldman, and Patrick Lee Miller for sending me unpublished manuscripts of interest for the arguments presented above.

Note

1   Lucin, *Pharsalia* 7.945–46.

Bibliography

Abbasoğlu, H. 2001: 'The Founding of Perge and its Development', in D. Parrish (ed.): *Urbanism in Western Asia Minor* (Journal of Roman Archaeology, Suppl. 45): 172–88.

Abbasoğlu, H. 2008: 'Perge 2007', *News of Archaeology from Anatolia* 6: 58–62.

Abbasoğlu, H. 2011: 'Perge 2010. Anatolia's Mediterranean Areas', *ANMED (News from Anatolian Mediterranean Areas)* 9: 82–89.

Adak, M. & Akyürekşahin, N. E. 2005: 'Katalog der Inschriften im Museum von Adapazari', *Gephyra* 2: 133–72.

Adak, M. et al. 2008: 'Neue Inschriften im Museum von Bolu (Bythinion/Klaudiopolis)', *Gephyra* 5: 73–120.

Akarca, A. 1952: 'Mylasa'da Hellenistik bir mezar. A Hellenistic Tomb in Mylasa', *Belleten* 16: 367–405.

Akok, M. 1948: 'Samsun ili havza ilçesinin Lerdüge köyünde bulunan tümülüsler', *Belleten* 12: 835–54.

Akurgal, E. & Budde, L. 1956: *Vorläufiger Bericht über die Ausgrabungen in Sinope* (Türk Tarih Kurumu Basımevi 14).

Akyürek Şahin, N. E. & Onur, F. 2008: 'New Funerary Inscriptions from Lydia in the Kütahya Museum', *Gephyra* 5: 125–38.

Alföldi-Rosenbaum, E. 1971: *Anamur nekropolü. The Necropolis of Anemurium*, Türk Tarih Kurumu Basımevi: Ankara.

Anderson, T. 2007: 'Preliminary Osteo-Archaeological Investigation in the North Necropolis', *Hierapolis di Frigia I. Le attività delle campagne di scavo e restauro 2000–2003*, Ege Yayinlari: Istanbul, 473–93.

Asgari, N. 1977: 'Die Halbfabrikate kleinasiatischer Girlandensarkophage und ihre Herkunft', *Archäologischer Anzeiger* 1977: 329–82.

Asgari, N. (ed.) 1983: *The Anatolian Civilisations: Istanbul. May 22–October 30, 1983: 18th European Art Exhibition*, Turkish Ministry of Culture and Tourism: Istanbul.

Asgari, N. & Firatli, N. 1978: 'Die Nekropole von Kalchedon', in M. J. Vermaseren (ed.): *Études préliminaires aux religions orientales dans l'Empire Romain*, E. J. Brill: Leiden, 1–92.

Atasoy, S. 1974: 'The Kocakızlar Tumulus in Eskişehir, Turkey', *American Journal of Archaeology* 78: 255–63.

Audin, A. 1960: 'Inhumation et incineration' *Latomus* 19: 312–22, 518–32.

Bakır, T., Sancisi-Weerdenburg, H., Gürtekin, G., Briant, P. & Henkelman, W. (eds): *Achaemenid Anatolia. Proceedings of the First International Symposium on Anatolia in the Achaemenid Period, Bandırma, 15–18 August 1997*, Nederlands Instituut voor het Nabije Oosten: Leiden.

Baldiran, A. 2007: '2005 yılı Taşkent (Konya) yüzey araştırması', *Araştırma Sonuçları Toplantısı* 25.1: 27–42.

Barr-Sharrar, B. 2008: *The Derveni Krater. Masterpiece of Classical Greek Metalwork* (Ancient Art and Architecture in Context 1), The American School of Classical Studies at Athens: Princeton, N.J.

Basirov, O. 2001: 'Achaemenian Funerary Practices in Western Asia Minor', in Bakır et al. (eds), 101–7.

Başaran, C. et al. 2009: 'Parion 2008 kazıları', *31. Kazı Sonuçları Toplantısı* 1: 393–410.

Başaran, S. et al. 2010: 'Enez (Ainos) 2009 yılı kazı ve onarım-koruma Çalışmaları', *32. Kazı Sonuçları Toplantısı* 4: 145–68.

Başaran, C. & Tavukçu, A. Y. 2006: 'Parion kazısı', *28. Kazı Sonuçlari Toplantisi* 1: 609–28.

Baughan, E. P. 2002/2004: 'Aspects of Empire in Sardis (Review)', *Journal of Field Archaeology* 29: 225–28.

Bean, G. E. 1960: 'Notes and Inscriptions from Pisidia. Part II', *Anatolian Studies* 10: 43–82.

Bean, G. E. & Mitford, T. B. 1965: *Journeys in Rough Cilicia in 1962 and 1963*, H. Böhlau: Vienna.

Bean, G. E. & Mitford, T. B. 1970: *Journeys in Rough Cilicia 1964–1968* (Tituli Asiae Minoris, Suppl. 3), H. Böhlau: Vienna.

Berns, C. 2003: *Untersuchungen zu den Grabbauten der frühen Kaiserzeit in Kleinasien* (Asia Minor Studien 51), R. Habelt: Bonn.

Berns, C. in press: 'Grabbezirke von Knidos. Zwei Standards der Repräsentation in klassischer Zeit', in K. Sporn (ed.): *Griechische Grabbezirke klassischer Zeit – Normen und Regionalismen, Kolloquium Berlin 2009*.

Blakolmer, F. 2005: 'Die Nekropole V von Zemuri-Limyra', in İşkan & Işık (eds), 1–27.

Boyce, M. 1982: *A History of Zoroastrianism II*, E. J. Brill: Leiden & Cologne.

Breccia, E. 1933: *Le musée gréco-romain*, Bergamo.

Bresson, A. 1991: *Recueil des inscriptions de la Pérée Rhodienne*, Les Belles Lettres, 95 Boulevard Raspail: Paris.

Burkert, W. 1970: 'Jason, Hypsipyle, and New Fire at Lemnos: A Study in Myth and Ritual', *The Classical Quarterly n.s.* 20.1: 1–16.

Bynum, C. W. 1995: *The Resurrection of the Body in Western Christianity, 200–1336*, Columbia University Press: New York.

Cahill, N. 1988: 'Taş Kule. A Persian-Period Tomb near Phokaia', *American Journal of Archaeology* 92: 481–501.

Çelgin, A. V. 1994: 'Termessos ve çevresinde nekropol ve epigrafya araştırmaları': 1975–1991, *Anadolu Araştırmaları* 13: 153–77.

Çevik, N. 1997: 'Yuvarlak kaya ostothekleri. Trebenna'da belgelenen yeni bir mezar tipi ve onun ışığında benzeri çukurların yeniden irdelenmesi. Circular Rock-Cut Ostotheques. A New Type of Grave discovered at Trebenna and a Reexamine of Similar Hollows', *Adalya* 2: 127–50.

Çevik, N. & İplikçioğlu, B. 2003: 'Epigraphische Mitteilungen aus Antalya X. Neues zu den Felsostotheken in Trebenna', *Epigraphica Anatolica* 35: 147–56.

Chaniotis, A. 2009: 'Dynamics of Rituals in the Roman Empire', in: O. Hekster, S. Schmidt-Hofner & C. Witschel (eds), *Ritual Dynamics and Religious Change in the Roman Empire*, E. J. Brill: Leiden, 3–29.

Chilidis, K. 2012: *The Construction of Knowledge in Archaeology – the Case of "Philip's Tomb" at Vergina in Northern Greece*, PhD Thesis, University of Oslo.

Civelek, A. 2006: 'Stratonikeia-Akdağ nekropolisi'nden bir mezar', *Anadolu* 20: 47–64.

Çokay-Kepçe, S. 2006: *The Karaçalli-Necropolis near Antalya* (Adalya Supplement Series 4), Suna – İnan Kiraç – Akdeniz Medeniyetleri Araştırma Enstitüsü: Antalya.

Cormack, S. H. 1997: 'Funerary Monuments and Mortuary Practice in Roman Asia Minor', in: S. Alcock (ed.): *The Early Roman Empire in the East*, Oxbow Books: Oxford, 137–56.

Cormack, S. H. 2004: *The Space of Death in Roman Asia Minor* (Wiener Forschungen zur Archäologie 6), Phoibus: Vienna.

Davies, G. 2011: 'Before Sarcophagi', in J. Elsner & J. Huskinson (eds): *Life, Death and Representation*, De Gruyter: Berlin & New York, 21–53.

De Schutter, X. 1989: 'Rituel funéraire et coût des obsèques en Grèce à l'époque classique', *Kernos* 2: 53–66.

Dedeoğlu, H. & Malay, H. 1991: 'Some Inscribed Cinerary Chests and Vases from Sardis', in *Erol Atalay memoria. Arkeooji Dergisi* 1, Ege Üniversitesi Basimevi: Izmir, 113–20.

Dedeoğlu, H. & Malay, H. 1994: 'Kuzey Lydia'da ortaya çıkan geç hellenistik bir mezar', *Arkeoloji Dergisi* 2: 129–35.

Devreker, J. 1994: 'New Excavations at Pessinus', *Forschungen in Galatien* (Asia Minor Studien 12), Dr. Rudolf Habelt: Bonn, 105–30.

Devreker, J. et al. 2003: *Excavations in Pessinus: the so-called Acropolis. From Hellenistic and Roman Cemetery to Byzantine Castle* (Archaeological Reports Ghent University 1), Academia Press: Gent.

Diler, A. 2002: 'The Northern Rock Necropolis of Caunus', *Studien zum antiken Kleinasien 5* (Asia Minor Studien 44), Dr. Rudolf Habelt: Bonn, 63–95.

Doğanay, O. 2010: 'Isauria bölgesi ölü gömme âdetlerine genel bir bakış', *Arkeoloji ve Sanat* 133, 39–57.

Dunand, F. & Lichtenberg, R. 1995: 'Pratiques et croyances funéraires en Egypte romaine', *Aufstieg und Niedergang der römischen Welt*, 2.18.5, Walter de Gruyter & Co.: Berlin & New York, 2801–3730.

Durugönül, S. 2007: *Nagidos, Results of an Excavation in an Ancient City in Rough Cilicia*, (Adalya Supplement 6), Suna–İnan: Antalya.

Durugönül, S. & Şahin, S. 1993: 'Begräbnisstätte einer Familie bei Nikaia', *Epigraphica Anatolica* 21: 55–60.

Durukan, M. 2005: 'Monumental Tomb Forms in the Olba Region, *Anatolian Studies* 55: 107–26.

Durukan, M. 2007: 'Dead Cult in Olba Region in Hellenistic and Roman Periods', *Anatolia Antiqua* 15: 147–64.

Dusenbery, E. B. 1998: *Samothrace. The Nekropoleis*, Princeton University Press: Princeton N. J.

Dusinberre, E. R. M. 2003: *Aspects of Empire in Achaemenid Sardis*, Cambridge University Press: Cambridge.

Duyuran, R. 1960: 'Découverte d'un tumulus près de l'ancienne Dardanos', *Anatolia* 5: 9–12.

Equini Schneider, E. 2003: 'Some Considerations on Elaiussa's North-Eastern Necropolis', *Olba* 7: 263–73.

Erbse, H. 1992: *Studien zum Verständnis Herodots*, Walter de Gruyter & Co.: Berlin.

Ertuğrul, F. 2005: 'Tralleis'de bulunan bir kremasyon kabi', *Arkeoloji ve Sanat* 120: 29–38.

Evans, J. A. S. 1978: 'What Happened to Croesus?', *The Classical Journal* 74: 34–40.

Fedak, J. 1990: *Monumental Tombs of the Hellenistic Age*, University of Toronto Press: Toronto.

Flämig, C. 2007: 'Grabarchitektur der römischen Kaiserzeit in Griechenland', M. Leidorf: Rahden/Westfalen.

Fleischer, R. 1978: 'Eine späthellenistische Ostothek aus Pisidien', in *Classica et provincialia. Festschrift Erna Diez*, Akademische Druck- u. Verlagsanstalt: Graz, 39–50.

Forbeck, E. 2005: 'Die Nekropolen von Milet', in İşkan & Işık (eds), 55–64.

Forti, L. 1992: 'Appunti sulla ceramica di Hadra', *Alessandria e il mondo ellenistico-romano* (reprint), "L'Erma" di Bretschneider: Rome, 222–41.

Fraser, P. M. 1977: *Rhodian Funerary Monuments*, Clarendon Press: Oxford & New York.

French, D. H. 1991: 'Dated Inscriptions at Amasia', *Arkeoloji Dergisi* 1: 65–70.

Freydank, J. 2000: *Die Westtor-Nekropole von Assos in klassischer und hellenistischer Zeit*, Dissertation Universität Mannheim.

FrgHG: K. & T. Müller (eds): *Fragmenta historicorum Graecorum* 1841–1870.

Gates, C. 1983: *From Cremation to Inhumation. Burial Practices at Ialysos and Kameiros During the Mid-Archaic Period, ca. 625–525 B.C.* (Occasional Papers 11), University of California: Los Angeles.

Giannikoure, A. 1996–1997: 'Μελανόγραφες υδρίες Hadra από την ελληνιστική νεκρόπολη της Ρόδου. Συμβολή στη μελέτη της γραπτής ελληνιστικής', *Αρχαιολογικόν Δελτίον* 51,1: 231–256.

Gibson, E. 1981: 'The Rahmi Koç Collection. Inscriptions, 8. A Cinerary Chest from Sardis', *Zeitschrift für Papyrologie und Epigraphik* 42: 215–16.

Goldman, A. L. 2007: 'The Roman-Period Cemeteries at Gordion in Galatia', *Journal of Roman Archaeology* 20: 299–320.

Greenewalt, C. H. 1977: 'The Eighteenth Campaign at Sardis (1975)', *Bulletin of the American Schools of Oriental Research* 228: 47–59.

Grenet F. 1984: *Les pratiques funéraires dans l'Asie centrale sédentaire de la conquête Grecque à l'islamisation*, Centre National de la Recherche Scientifique: Paris.

Hallett, C. H. & Coulton, J. J. 1993: 'The East Tomb and Other Tomb Buildings at Balboura', *Anatolian Studies* 43: 41–68.

Henry, O. 2009: *Tombes de Carie. Architecture funéraire et culture Carienne, VIe –IIe s. av. J.-C.*, Presses Universitaires de Rennes: Rennes.

Henry, O. & Ingvarsson-Sundström, A. (eds), 2011: 'The Story of a Tomb at Labraunda', in L. Karlsson & S. Carlsson (eds), *Labraunda and Karia (Boreas 32)*, Uppsala: Uppsala Universitet, 177–97.

Horsley, G. H. R. 2007: *The Greek and Latin Inscriptions in the Burdur Archaeological Museum*, The British Institute at Ankara: London.

Højte, J. M. 2006: 'From Kingdom to Province: Reshaping Pontos after the Fall of Mithridates VI', in T. Bekker-Nielsen (ed.): *Rome and the Black Sea Region: Domination, Romanization and Resistance* (Black Sea Studies 5), Århus University Press: Århus, 15–30.

Houby-Nielsen, S. 1998: 'Revival of Archaic Funerary Practices in the Hellenistic and Roman Kerameikos', *Proceedings of the Danish Institute at Athens* 2: 127–45.

Hülden, O. 2006: *Gräber und Grabtypen im Bergland von Yavu (Zentrallykien). Studien zur antiken Grabkultur in Lykien*, Dr. Rudolf Habelt: Bonn.

Hülden, O. 2010: *Die Nekropolen von Kyaneai in Zentrallykien*, Dr. Rudolf Habelt: Bonn.

Humhreys, S. C. 1980: 'Family Tombs and Tomb Cult in Ancient Athens', *Journal of Hellenic Studies* 100: 96–126.

İlaslı, A. & Üyümez, M. 2008: *Afyonkarahisar, Museums and Sites*, Metgraf Maatbacılık: Istanbul.

Inan, J. 1963: 'Die Skulpturen', in A. M. Mansel (ed.): *Die Ruinen von Side*, Walter de Gruyter & Co.: Berlin, 63–77.

IK: Inschriften griechischer Städte aus Kleinasien.

İplicioğlu, B. 1991: *Epigraphische Forschungen in Termessos und seinem Territorium* I, Verlag der Österreichischen Akademie der Wissenschaften: Vienna.

Işik, F. 2007: 'Werkstätten der Girlandensarkophage der kleinasiatischen Hauptgruppe', in Koch (ed.), 279–89.

İşkan, H. & Işık, F. (eds) 2005: *Grabtypen und Totenkult im südwestlichen Kleinasien* (Lykia VI), Akdeniz Universitesi: Antalya.

Jacobs, B. 1987: *Griechische und persische Elemente in der Grabkunst Lykiens zur Zeit der Achämenidenherrschaft*, Paul Åström Förlag: Jonsered.

Jacobs, B. 2001: 'Kultbilder und Gottesvorstellungen bei den Persern', in Bakır et al. (eds), 83–90.

Jacopi, G. 1931: 'Scavi nelle necropoli camiresi 1929–1930', *Clara Rhodos* IV, Officine dell'Istituto Italiano d'Arti Grafiche: Bergamo.

Kahil, L. 1969: 'Sculpture', in J. des Gagniers et al. (eds): *Laodicée du Lycos. Le Nymphée*, Presses de L'Université Laval: Quebec, 87–234.

Kahn, C. H. 2001: *Pythagoras and the Pythagoreans. A Brief History*, Hackett Publishing Company: Indianapolis.

Kaya, F. H. 2006: *Soli/Pompeiopolis mezar tipolojisi*, Unpublished MA Thesis, Dokuz Eylül University Izmir.

Kingsley, P. 1995: Meetings with the Magi: Iranian Themes among the Greek, from Xanthus of Lydia to Plato's Academy, *Journal of the Royal Asiatic Society* 5, 173–209.

Kizgut, I. et al. 2009: 'An East Lycian City: Idebessos', *Adalya* 12: 145–72.

Kızıl, A. 2009: '1990–2005 yılları arasında Mylasa'da kurtarma kazıları yapılan mezarlar ve buluntuları üzerinde genel bir değerlendirme', in F. Rumscheid (ed.): *Die Karer und die Anderen. Internationales Kolloquium Berlin 2005*, Dr. Rudolf Habelt: Berlin, 397–461.

Koch, G. 1990: *Sarkophage der römischen Kaiserzeit*, Wissenschaftliche Buchgesellschaft: Darmstadt.

Koch, G. 2008: 'Kinder-Sarkophage der römischen Kaiserzeit in Kleinasien', *Adalya* 11: 165–87.

Koch, G. 2010: 'Sarkophage der römischen Kaiserzeit in der Türkei. Ein Überblick (mit einer Bibliographie)', *Adalya* 13: 111–82.

Koch, G. & Sichtermann, H. 1982: *Römische Sarkophage; mit einem Beitrag von Frederikke Sinn-Henninger* (Handbuch der Archäologie 3), C.H. Beck'sche Verlagsbuchhandlung: Munich.

Koch, G. (ed.) 2007: *Akten des Symposiums der Sarkophag-Corpus 2001*, Verlag Philipp von Zabern: Mainz am Rhein.

Koch, H. 1977: *Die religiösen Verhältnisse der Dareioszeit* (Göttinger Orientforschungen III. Reihe Iranica 4), Otto Harrassowitz: Wiesbaden.

Köse, V. 2002: 'Die Grabdenkmäler von Sagalassos. Kontinuität und Diskontinuität zwischen Hellenismus und früher Kaiserzeit', *Patris und Imperium: kulturelle und politische Identität in den Städten der römischen Provinzen Kleinasiens in der frühen Kaiserzeit; Kolloquium Köln, November 1998*, Peeters: Leuven, Paris & Dudley (MA), 117–33.

Köse, V. 2005: *Nekropolen und Grabdenkmäler von Sagalassos in Pisidien in hellenistischer und römischer Zeit* (Studies in Eastern Mediterranean Archaeology 7), Turnhout: Brepols.

Kolb, F. & Thomsen, A. 2005: 'Gräber und Grabkult auf dem Avşar Tepesi', in İşkan & Işık (eds), 131–50.

Korkut, T. 2006: *Girlanden-Ostotheken aus Kalkstein in Pamphylien und Kilikien. Untersuchungen zu Typologie, Ikonographie und Chronologie* (Sarkophag-Studien 4), Verlag Philipp von Zabern: Mainz am Rhein.

Kortanoğlu, R. E. 2008: 'Phrygia'da Makedonia kalkan bezemeleri ile süslenmişbir kaya mezarı ve mezar sahibinin kökeni üzerine', in İnci Delemen et al. (eds): *Euergetes, Prof. Dr. Haluk Abbasoğlu'na 65. Yaş Armağanı 2*, Zero Prodüksiyon Ltd.: Antalya, 735–45.

Kosmetatou, E. & Waelkens, M. 1997: 'The "Macedonian" Shields of Sagalassos', *Sagalassos* IV, 277–91.

Kosmetatou, E. 2005: 'Macedonians in Pisidia', *Historia* 54: 216–21.

Kottaridou, A. 1998: 'Macedonian Burial Customs and the Funeral of Alexander the Great', in Διεθνές Συνέδριο Ἀλέξανδρος ὁ Μέγας: ἀπὸ τη Μακεδονία στην ᾽οικουμένη. Nomarchiakē Autodioikēsē Ēmathias: Veroia, 113–20.

Kubinska, J. 1968: *Les monuments funéraires dans les inscriptions grecques de l'Asie Mineure*, PWN: Warsaw.

Kubinska, J. 1999: *Ostothèques et kaustrai dans les inscriptions grecques d'Asie Mineure* (Światowit. Supplement series, A. Antiquity 3), Warsaw University: Warsaw.

Lambrechts, P. 1969: 'Les fouilles de Pessinonte. La nécropole' *L'antiquité classique* 38: 121–46.

Laminger-Pascher, G. 1973: 'Kleine Nachträge zu den isaurischen Inschriften II', *Zeitschrift für Papyrologie und Epigraphik* 12: 63–74.

Lanckoronski, K. 1892: *Städte Pamphyliens und Pisidiens 2*, F. Tempski: Prag, Vienna & Leipzig.

Laurenzi, L. 1936: 'Necropoli Ialisie', *Clara Rhodos* VIII, Officine dell'Istituto Italiano d'Arti Grafiche: Bergamo, 7–207.

Levi, D. 1961–62: 'Missioni in Levante. Le due prime campagne di scavo a Iasos', *Annuario della Scuola archeologica di Atene e delle missioni italiane in Oriente* 34–35: 505–71.

Levick, B. 1967: *Roman Colonies in Southern Asia Minor*, Clarendon Press: Oxford.

Machatschek, A. 1967: *Die Nekropolen und Grabmäler im Gebiet von Elaiussa Sebaste und Korykos im Rauhen Kilikien* (Tituli Asiae Minoris, Suppl. 2), H. Böhlau: Vienna.

MacMullen, R. 1982: 'The Epigraphic Habit in the Roman Empire', *The American Journal of Philology* 103.3: 233–46.

MacMullen, R. 1986: 'Frequency of Inscriptions in Roman Lydia', *Zeitschrift für Papyrologie und Epigraphik* 65: 237–38.

MacMullen, R. 2000: *Romanization in the Time of Augustus*, Yale University Press: New Haven & London.

Malay, H. 1994: *Greek and Latin Inscriptions in the Manisa Museum* (Tituli Asiae Minoris, Suppl. 19), Verlag der Österreichischen Akademie der Wissenschaften: Vienna.

Malay, H. 1999: *Researches in Lydia, Mysia and Aiolis* (Tituli Asiae Minoris, Suppl. 23), Verlag der Österreichischen Akademie der Wissenschaften: Vienna.

Malay, H. & Petzl, G. 2005: 'Aschenkisten aus Lydien', *Epigraphica Anatolica* 38: 37–41.

Malay, H. & Ricl, G. 2006: 'Some Funerary Inscriptions from Lydia', *Epigraphica Anatolica* 39: 49–83.

MAMA 1962 = W. M. Calder & J. M. R. Cormack (eds): *Monuments from Lycaonia, the Pisido-Phrygian borderland, Aphrodisias* (Monumenta Asiae Minoris antiqua. Publications of the American Society for Archaeological Research in Asia Minor VIII), The Manchester University Press: Manchester

Marek, C. 2003: *Pontus et Bithynia. Die römischen Provinzen im Norden Kleinasiens*, Verlag Philipp von Zabern: Mainz am Rhein.

Marksteiner, T. 1994: 'Brand- und Körperbestattung; Tumulus und Fassadenkammergräber: Überlegungen zu Veränderungen der Bestattungsbräuche im vorhellenistischen Lykien', *Lykia* 1: 78–88.

McEvilley, T. 2002: *The Shape of Ancient Thought: Comparative Studies in Greek and Indian Philosophies*, Allworth Press: New York.

McLean, B. H. 2002: *Greek and Latin Inscriptions in the Konya Archaeological Museum*, British Institute of Archaeology Ankara: London.

Merkelbach, R. & Stauber, J. (eds) 1998–2004: *Steinepigramme aus dem griechischen Osten I-V*, K.G. Saur Verlag: Munich & Leipzig.

Miller, P. J. 2011: *Becoming God. Pure Reason in Early Greek Philosophy*, Continuum International Publishing Group: London.

Milner, N. P. 2004: 'Ancient Inscriptions and Monuments from the Territory of Oinoanda', *Anatolian Studies* 54: 47–77.

Mitchell, S. 1995: *Anatolia. Land, Men, and Gods in Asia Minor 1. The Celts and the Impact of Roman Rule*, Clarendon Press: Oxford.

Morris, I. 1996: *Death-Ritual and Social Structure in Classical Antiquity*, 2nd edition, Cambridge University Press: Cambridge.

Musgrave, J. 1990a: 'Dust and Damn'd Oblivion: A Study of Cremation in Ancient Greece', *The Annual of the British School at Athens* 85: 271–99.

Musgrave, J. 1990b: 'Cremated Remains from Nea Mihaniona and Derveni', *The Annual of the British School at Athens* 85: 301–25.

Newton, C. T. 1862–63: *A History of Discoveries at Halicarnassus, Cnidus, and Branchidae I–II*, Day & Son: London.

Nock, A. D. 1932: 'Cremation and Burial in the Roman Empire', *The Harvard Theological Review* 25: 321–59.

Noy, D. 2000: 'Half burnt on an Emergency Pyre': Roman Cremations which went Wrong. *Greece & Rome* 47.2: 186–96.

Okunak, M. 2005: *Hierapolis kuzey nekropolü (159D nolu tümülüs) anıt mezar ve buluntuları*, Unpublished MA thesis Pamukkale University, Denizli.

Ötüken, S. Y. 1996: *Forschungen im nordwestlichen Kleinasien: Antike und byzantinische Denkmäler in der Provinz Bursa* (Istanbuler Mitteilungen, Suppl. 41), Wasmuth: Tübingen.

Özdilek, B. 2008: 'Neapolis nekropolleri üzerine bir ön-rapor', in *III.–IV. Ulusal arkeolojik araştirmalar sempozyumu* (Anadolu Suppl. 2), Ankara, 235–52.

Özkaya, V. & San, O. 2003: 'Alinda. An Ancient City with its Remains and Monumental Tombs in Caria', *Revue des Études Anciennes* 108, 1: 103–25.

Özoral, T. 1980: 'Ağva kazısı/Fouilles dans la nécropole d'Ağva', in *Actes du colloque sur la Lycie Antique,* Librairie d'Amérique et d'Orient Adrien Maisonneuve: Paris, 95–100.

Parke H. W. 1988: *Sibyls and Sibylline Prophecy in Classical Antiquity*, Routledge: London.

Pastutmaz, D. 2008: 'Knidos – Das Grab N4 und seine Funde', *Asia Minor Studien 65: Vom Euphrat bis zum Bosporus 2*, Dr. Rudolf Habelt: Bonn, 526–32.

Pekridou, A. 1986: *Das Alketas-Grab in Termessos* (Istanbuler Mitteilungen, Suppl. 32), Wasmuth: Tübingen.

Peschlow, A. 1990: 'Die Nekropole von Herakleia am Latmos', 8. *Araştirma Sonuçlari Toplantısı*, 383–99.

Petzl, G. & Pleket, H. W. 1979: 'Inschriften aus Lydien', *Zeitschrift für Papyrologie und Epigraphik* 34: 281–95.

Philipp, H. 1981: 'Archaische Grabtypen in Ostionien', *Istanbuler Mitteilungen* 31: 149–66.

Pietrograndе A. L. 1935: 'Nuova serie asiatica di urne e di piccoli sarcofagi', *Bullettino della Commissione archeologica comunale di Roma* 6: 17–37.

Pirson, F. et al. 2011: 'Der Tumulus auf dem İlyastepe und die pergamenischen Grabhügel', *Istanbuler Mitteilungen* 61, 117–203.

Polat, G. 2008: 'Antandros nekropolü ölü gömme gelenekleri', in *III.–IV. Ulusal arkeolojik araştirmalar sempozyumu* (Anadolu Suppl. 2), Ankara, 271–80.

Polat, G. et al. 2010: 'Antandros 2009 Yılı Kazıları', 32. *Kazı Sonuçları Toplantısı* 3, 98–121.

Pottier, E. 1887: *La nécropole de Myrina: récherches archéologiques exécutées au nom et aux frais de l'École française d'Athènes*, E. Thorin: Paris.

Rebillard, E. 2009: *The Care of the Dead in Late Antiquity*, Cornell University Press: Ithaca & London.

Rife J. L. 2007: 'Inhumation and Cremation at Early Roman Kenchreai (Corinthia), Greece, in Local and Regional Context', in *Körpergräber des 1.–3. Jahrhunderts in der römischen Welt: internationales Kolloquium Frankfurt am Main, 19.–20.11.2004* (Schriften des Archäologischen Museums Frankfurt 21), Archäologisches Museum: Frankfurt, 99–120.

Robinson, D. M. 1942: *Necrolynthia. A Study in Greek Burial Customs and Anthropology. Excavations at Olynthus XI*, Oxford University Press: London.

Rosenbaum E. et al. 1967: *A Survey of Coastal Cities in Western Cilicia: Preliminary Report; with an Excursus by Roderich Regler* (Türk Tarih Kurumu yayınlarindan; 6. seri, no. 8), Türk Tarih Kurumu Basımevi: Ankara.

Scarborough, Y. E. 1995: '1994 Isaura yüzey araştırması', 13. *Araştırma Sonuçları Toplantısı* 1: 339–56.

Scheid, J. 2007: 'Körperbestattung und Verbrennungssitte aus der Sicht der schriftlichen Quellen', in *Körpergräber des 1.–3. Jahrhunderts in der römischen Welt : internationales Kolloquium Frankfurt am Main, 19.–20.11.2004* (Schriften des Archäologischen Museums Frankfurt 21) Archäologisches Museum: Frankfurt, 19–25.

Schörner, H. 2007: *Sepulturae graecae intra urbem. Untersuchungen zum Phänomen der intraurbanen Bestattungen bei den Griechen* (Boreas Suppl. 9), Bibliopolis: Möhnesee.

Schrumpf, S. 2006: *Bestattung und Bestattungswesen im Römischen Reich*, V&R Unipress: Bonn.

Schweyer, A.-V. 2002: *Les Lyciens et la mort. Une ètude d'histoire sociale* (Varia Anatolica XIV), Institut Français d'Études Anatoliennes d'Istanbul: Paris.

SEG: *Supplementum Epigraphicum Graecum.*

Şimşek, C. 2007: *Laodikeia*, Ege Yayınları: Istanbul.

Şimşek, C. (ed.) 2011: *Laodikeia nekropolü (2004–2010 yılları)*, Ege Yayınları: Istanbul.

Sinn, F. 1987: *Stadtrömische Marmorurnen* (Beiträge zur Erschließung hellenistischer und kaiserzeitlicher Skulptur und Architektur 8), Verlag Philipp von Zabern: Mainz am Rhein.

Söğüt, B. 2001: 'Dağlık Kılıkıa bölgesi mezar nişleri', *Olba* 7: 239–60.

Söğüt, B. 2002: 'Dağlık Kilikia'da Tülü Asar (Lamos?) yüzey araştırması-2002', 21. *Araştırma Sonuçları Toplantısı* 1: 279–90.

Söğüt, B. 2010: 'Stratonikeia 2009 yılı çalışmaları', 32. *Kazı Sonuçları Toplantısı* 4, 194–211.

Spanu, M. 2000: 'Burial in Asia Minor during the Imperial Period with a Particular Reference to Cilicia and Cappadocia', in *Burial, Society and Context in the Roman World*, Oxbow Books: Oxford, 169–77.

Steinby, E. M. 2003: *La necropoli della Via Triumphalis. Il tratto sotto l'Autoparco Vaticano*, Quasar: Rome.

Strocka, V. M. 1978: 'Die frühesten Girlandensarkophage. Zur Kontinuität der Reliefsarkophage in Kleinasien während des Hellenismus und der frühen Kaiserzeit. Studien zur Religion und Kultur Kleinasiens', in *Festschrift für Friedrich Karl Dörner zum 65. Geburtstag am 28. Februar 1976* (Etudes préliminaires aux religions orientales dans l'empire romain 66), E. J. Brill: Leiden, 882–913.

Stupperich, R. 1992: 'Zweiter Vorbericht über die Grabung in der Westtor-Nekropole von Assos im Sommer 1990', in Ü. Sedaroğlu & R. Stupperich (eds): *Ausgrabungen in Assos 1990* (Asia Minor Studien 5), Dr. Rudolf Habelt: Bonn, 1–31.

Stupperich, R. 1996: 'Vierter Vorbericht über die Grabung in der Westtor-Nekropole von Assos im Sommer 1992', in Ü. Sedaroğlu & R. Stupperich (eds): *Ausgrabungen in Assos 1992* (Asia Minor Studien 21), Dr. Rudolf Habelt: Bonn, 1–31.

Swoboda, H., Keil, J. & Knoll, F. 1935: *Denkmäler aus Lykaonien, Pamphylien und Isaurien: Ergebnisse einer im Auftrage der Gesellschaft von Julius Jüthner... durchgefürten Forschungsreise*, R. M. Rohrer: Brünn-Prag.

Taglietti, F. 2001: 'Ancora su incinerazione e inhumazione: la necropoli dell'Isola Sacra', in M. Heinzelmann, J. Ortalli, P. Fasold & M. Witteyer (eds): *Römischer Bestattungsbrauch und Beigabensitten* (Palilia 8), Dr. Ludwig Reichert Verlag: Wiesbaden, 149–58.

Thalmann, R. 1978: *Urne oder Sarg? Auseinander Setzungen um die Einführung der Feuerbestattung im 19. Jahrhundert*, Peter Lang: Bern.

Thomas, C. M. & Içten, C. 1999: 'The Ephesian Ossuaries and Roman Influence on the Production of Burial Containers', in *100 Jahre österreichische Forschungen in Ephesos. Akten des Symposions, Wien 1995*, Verlag der Österreichischen Akademie der Wissenschaften: Vienna, 549–54.

Thomas, C. M. & İçten, C. 2007: 'The Ostothekai and the Rise of Sarcophagus Inhumation', in Koch (ed.), 335–44.

Tulunay, E. T. 2009: 'Nif (Olympos) Dağı araştırma ve kazı projesi: 2008 yılı kazısı', 31. *Kazı Sonuçları Toplantısı* 2: 387–408.

Turcan, R. 1958: 'Origines et sens de l'inhumation à l'époque impériale' *Revue des études anciennes* 60: 323–47.

Ubelaker, D. H. & Rife, J. L. 2007: 'The Practice of Cremation in the Roman-Era Cemetery at Kenchreai, Greece', *Bioarchaeology of the Near East* 1: 35–57.

Van Dessel, P. & Hauben, H. 1977: 'Rhodes, Alexander and the Diadochi from 333/332 to 304 B.C.', *Historia* 26.3: 307–39.

Vandeput, L. & Köse, V. 2001: 'The 1999 Pisidia Survey at Melli', *Anatolian Studies* 51: 133–45.

Verzone, P. 1961–1962: 'Le campagne 1960 e 1961 a Hierapolis di Frigia', *Annuario della Scuola archeologica di Atene e delle missioni italiane in Oriente* 34–35: 633–47.

Venit, M. S. 2002: *Monumental Tombs of Ancient Alexandria: the Theater of the Dead*, Cambridge University Press: Cambridge.

Volp, V. 1012: *Tod und Ritual in den christlichen Gemeinden der Antike*, E. J. Brill: Leiden.

Waelkens, M. 1982: *Dokimeion. Die Werkstatt der repräsentativen kleinasiatischen Sarkophage* (Archäologische Forschungen 11), Gebr. Mann Verlag: Berlin.

Waelkens, M. 1993: 'Sagalassos. History and Archaeology', in M. Waelkens (ed.): *Sagalassos I*, Leuven University Press: Leuven, 37–82.

Waelkens, M. et al. 1991: 'The Excavations at Sagalassos 1990', *Anatolian Studies* 41: 197–213.

Waelkens, M. et al. 1997: 'The 1994 and 1995 Surveys on the Territory of Sagalassos', in M. Waelkens & J. Poblome (eds): *Sagalassos IV*, Leuven University Press: Leuven, 11–102.

Walker, S. 1985: *Memorials to the Roman Dead*, British Museum: London.

Wood, J. T. 1877: *Discoveries at Ephesus including the Site and Remains of the Great Temple of Diana*, James R. Osgood and Company: Boston.

Yaraş, A. 2004: 'Die "Koca Kuru Tepe" Nekropole', *Istanbuler Mitteilungen* 54: 227–42.

Yener, E. & Özkan, M. K. 1997: 'Aydin Merkez alihanoğlu İsmail türbesi yanındaki Roma mezarı kurtarma kazısı 1996', *VIII. Müze Kurtarma Kazıları Semineri*, 219–33.

Yilmaz, H. 1992: 'Patara 1991 – Tepecik nekropolü', *Kazı Sonuçları Toplantısı* 14.2: 389–92.

Zoroğlu, L. 2000: 'Kelenderis nekropolü', *Olba* 3: 115–33.

A 'CIVILISED' DEATH?
The Interpretation of Provincial Roman Grave Good Assemblages

John Pearce

This paper reviews change in funerary rituals in northwest Europe from the 1st century BC to early 3rd century AD. Burial practice in this period is often perceived by scholars as conservative, reflecting greater continuity of indigenous Iron Age tradition than other aspects of life under Roman rule. This paper argues that this characterisation is flawed, since it underestimates change and, more importantly, evaluates burial practice in isolation, making insufficient use of the contextual evidence available to interpret Roman Period mortuary rituals. Taking its cue from the study of prehistoric burials, particular attention is given to the identity for the dead constructed by participants during the funerary ritual from the objects placed with the body or its cremated remains. These recurring symbols embody and evoke an urbane sociability that epitomises 'Roman'-style savoir faire *as much, if not more, than adherence to local tradition.*

Keywords: Belgica, Britain, funerary assemblages, Gallia, mortuary ritual, Roman burial, Roman *savoir-faire*

The interpretation of funerary assemblages from Rome's northwest provinces provides the subject matter for this article. I focus in particular on those assemblages with abundant grave goods, sometimes of prestigious character, which are considered to accompany the burials of the elite dead, urban magistrates and villa-owners. Interpretation of the burial practice of which these are the residue has emphasised their continuity with pre-Roman Iron Age tradition. This 'traditional' character has often been taken to signify that burial customs change less than others after incorporation within the Roman world, or even that they manifest resistance to Rome. This, I will argue, is misleading, since these burials demonstrate continuity only when considered in isolation: reading them against the changed material and social world around them allows a different perspective. In re-reading these assemblages, I hope to draw attention to the richness of evidence for burial rituals from the Roman world for a contextualised study of burial practice, since it scarcely features in the broader literature in the archaeology of death (Parker Pearson 1999). Unlike some other types of data, such as public buildings or villas, limited use of burial evidence has also been made for characterising provincial Roman societies: in the study of Roman Britain, for example burial data have played little role in the 'Romanisation' debate (James & Millett 2001; Millett 1990). This is particularly striking when compared to the importance of funerary archaeology for the study of those periods preceding and succeeding the Roman centuries. I hope therefore to use this case study to follow up Ian Morris' (1992) advocacy of the potential for contextualised reading of burial practice to enhance understanding of provincial societies.

The paper first outlines changing burial rituals in the northwest provinces of the Empire from the Late Iron Age to the 3rd century AD, with a particular focus on characterising the funerary rituals traditionally associated with elites. The characterisation of Roman Period rituals uses examples from southern Britain and eastern Belgium and the Netherlands. The individual assemblages discussed are described and referenced in Tables 7.1 and 7.2. I review previous interpretations and outline an alternative perspective, drawing on recent studies of burial practice beyond the Classical world. Contextual information, especially comparison with other contexts of deposition, allows us to 'calibrate' the burial of the dead as a focus of display and as a medium for negotiating power relations, but also to consider the capacity of the objects placed with the remains of the dead to evoke other areas of social practice. These allusions and connotations can be reconstructed through comparison with non-funerary archaeological and textual sources. While multiple readings were possible, I argue that from the *mise-en-scène* in the grave, in particular the objects placed with the dead, many participants in the burial ritual could construct an identity for the dead as epitomising 'Roman' cultivation and *savoir faire*.

'Princely' burials of the 1st century BC and early 2nd century AD, Britain and northern Gaul

During the Iron Age in northwest Europe burial practice is only intermittently visible to archaeologists. From the late 2nd century BC a mosaic of regional funerary traditions can however be documented, of which the most widespread is the so-called 'North Gallic culture', discontinuously distributed across northern Gaul and southeastern Britain, where it is known as the 'Aylesford-Swarling' tradition. This is a cremation tradition in which burials were accompanied by a range of grave goods, most commonly wheel-turned ceramics and dress accessories (Fitzpatrick 2000; 2007; Roymans 1990). In some areas in the 1st century BC, for example the Aisne and Moselle valleys and Essex/ Herfordshire, burial hierarchies have been identified on the basis of major differences in the number and range of artefacts buried or consumed on the pyre (Haselgrove 1987). The earliest examples of tombs with very substantial burial assemblages (termed 'Welwyn' burials in Britain after a key type-site), are first manifested in the early 1st century BC, for example at Baldock in Hertfordshire (*c*. 100–50 BC) and Clemency in Luxembourg (*c*. 80–60 BC). Examples described in Table 7.1 illustrate their development on either side of the Channel up to the early 1st century AD: despite the absorption of northern Gaul into the Roman Empire several decades before Britain, burial rituals appear to have changed in tandem.

Hearth furniture and vessels for storing, serving and consuming food and drink dominate these assemblages. The former includes cauldrons, suspension chains, and iron firedogs, the latter copper alloy and copper alloy-bound buckets, tankards and drinking horns, as well as ceramics made locally and elsewhere within northwest Europe, especially terra nigra and terra rubra from *c*. 15–10 BC. Mediterranean imports include silver, copper alloy, Arretine and occasionally glass vessels associated with serving and drinking wine. Dressel 1A and later 1B wine amphorae, predominantly from west central Italy, are found in some graves in numbers: later the repertoire is extended by amphorae from southern France and Tarraconensis, the latter containing fish sauce. Animal bones from burials and their environs comprise the principal direct evidence for foodstuffs consumed by the participants and/or burnt on the pyre.

Weapons buried with the dead include panoplies and individual items. Spears and shields (represented by their bosses) are the most common, but rarer items were also deposited, for example visors from parade armour (Feugère 1996). Some burials also contain horse gear and, occasionally, evidence for the deposition of vehicles or their parts. In Britain copper alloy mirrors decorated in La Tène style are sometimes documented in burials in this tradition, primarily, but not exclusively with women (Joy 2010). Other items documented include gaming pieces, laid out on the game board in the 'doctor's' burial at Stanway (Essex), bear claws from cremation of the deceased in a bearskin (for example at Baldock, Clemency, Welwyn Garden City, and Folly Lane), a carved bier from Folly Lane, medical and divining equipment. Excavations of tomb settings shows deposition of grave goods to be part of a longer ritual sequence, which also saw destruction of objects on the pyre and in post-burial ceremonies, sometimes in monumentalised settings. The latter are perhaps most spectacularly attested in the massive ditched enclosures and funerary chambers at Stanway and Folly Lane.

These tombs have been central to writing the social and cultural history of Late Iron Age northwest Europe. Once primarily discussed as indicators of migration, attention shifted during the 1980s to exploring the socio-political dimension of the funerary ceremonies of which these are the residue. In an influential paper Colin Haselgrove argued (1987) that innovation in burial practice in northern Gaul represents a re-alignment of Gallic elite behaviour on Roman models after the Caesarean conquest:

'At burial sites such as Goeblingen-Nospelt the message is re-iterated in everything from large-scale wine consumption to the cremation rite: the power and continued success of the ruling groups was indissolubly linked to the Roman alliance.' (Haselgrove 1987: 116).

John Creighton (2006) has also seen (in the British examples) an emphatic statement of connections to Rome in these funerary ceremonies, arguing that hostages and ambassadors returned to Britain with a new form of political theatre to legitimate their position. Others have argued that the emphasis on Romanisation may be exaggerated or misplaced. Fitzpatrick (2000; 2007) proposes that exotic artefacts and foodstuffs were assimilated within an existing feasting culture in different ways across northwest Europe. Pitts' (2005) recent analysis of pot forms and capacities suggests that beer rather than wine-drinking remained the focus of feasting; only with such evidence can the limited and problematic textual documentation for beer drinking be complemented (Nelson 2005: 38–67). Others argue that the external or exotic connections displayed in these ceremonies are those within north-west Europe, rather than to the Mediterranean (Crummy et al. 2007; Haselgrove 1996: 174–75). It is perhaps not helpful to choose definitively between a Roman and a local aspect, since the reading may well vary according to the context of the participant, with a specifically 'Roman' value to some objects or ceremonies only being available to some. Burial with arms may derive from local martial culture, but take on additional meaning where individuals have served under Roman leaders as clients or in the *auxilia* (Feugère 1996).

Whatever their cultural resonance, the special character of these objects seems indisputable, as does their restricted circulation, since they are rarely found in settlement deposits. Arguably the objects deposited in the grave were both objects of gift exchange in their own right and evoke the other occasions in which these objects were made and exchanged, for example the gift giving, especially the feasting documented in the Classical authors such as Posidonius (Athenaeus, *Deipnosophistae* IV 151–2; Gosden & Garrow 2012: 196–255). Some objects may have served as symbols of office or priestly status, their use requiring restricted knowledge: for example the enigmatic rods associated with the medical equipment and gaming pieces in the 'doctor's' tomb at Stanway are argued to have had a possible role in divination. However, the particular status of the buried individuals, whether that be 'princely' (*Fürstengräber)* or 'noble' (*Adelsgräber*), is less significant than the central place of burial ceremonies in contesting successions (Haselgrove 1987: 117), particularly perhaps where monumentalised burials cluster near central places, as at *Camulodunum*-Colchester. The near contemporary tomb of Caecilia Metella on the Appian Way outside Rome reminds us that the burial of politically insignificant individuals could be exploited to project group ambition (Gerding 2002).

Display in funerary ritual in the 1st–3rd centuries AD, Britain and northern Gaul

As already indicated there is no radical break in funerary traditions in the decades after the Roman conquest on either side of the English Channel. Instead the further development of existing trends can be documented, including a long term increase in the proportion of the dead being afforded an archaeologically visible burial. The reconfiguration of settlement space, especially around towns, further distanced the dead from the living. Lining the roads that radiate from towns, urban cemeteries are regularly attested in chartered towns such as St Albans and Tongres, reflecting the requirements of city foundation charters attested elsewhere in the Empire, for example for Urso, a Caesarian colony in southern Spain (*Lex Ursonensis* 73–74). The same is true of *agglomérations secondaires*, such as Baldock (Hertfordshire) or Wederath (Rheinland-Pfalz) and in farms and villas too the dead were similarly placed on the periphery of settlement space. The relative infrequency of intercutting between graves suggests that many were marked. Perhaps the most obvious funerary innovation is the commissioning of stone monuments bearing inscriptions or carved image to mark a small number of burials. In Britain they are scarce outside garrison communities, even in London and other major towns (Hope 1997), but in eastern Gallia Belgica, especially among the *Treveri* they are as abundant and diverse as those in any provincial setting and the rich sculptural decoration as well as extensive epigraphic habit gives unique insights into provincial culture (Wightman 1985: 164–5; Freigang 1997). Elsewhere barrows, usually in rural settings, are the commonest monument, abundant in southeast England, eastern Belgium and on the Moselle (Wigg 1993).

Rituals too show a substantial degree of continuity. In the early Roman Period (1st and 2nd centuries AD) the dead were usually cremated but non-infant inhumation was also widely practised prior to becoming the norm during the 3rd century AD: its wide distribution makes it difficult to attach specific ethnic explanations to its occurrence (Jones 1987; Faber et al. 2004). The cremation tradition varies: in a minority of burials, for example, the same pit served as pyre and grave – the *bustum* (Struck 1993). The evidence for pyre rituals is limited, though well-studied pyre debris suggests that objects were often destroyed in substantial quantities by burning (see below).

After cremation the remains of the dead were usually collected and buried in a variety of containers, typically a pottery jar. In some cases pyre debris, including charcoal, further cremated bone and artefact fragments was also placed in the burial or buried with the remains of the dead unsorted (*Brandschuttgräber*). A complex typology has evolved to describe the varied modes of incorporating pyre debris in the grave, but its terms are not consistently applied and without full documentation it may not be possible to distinguish between burials, pyre sites, and other deposits of pyre debris or the residue of commemorative ceremonies (Bechert 1980; Scheid ed. 2008; Weekes 2008).

Grave goods were frequently placed with the dead, especially table ceramics (Table 7.2: Figs 7.1–7.4). These have received the majority of scholarly attention, their cataloguing comprising a major component of cemetery publications, and they form the backbone of Roman provincial museum collections. As in the later Iron Age there is considerable regional variability in the quantity and type of grave goods deposited. This variability is only partly understood, the major survey for northern Gaul having been published more than 40 years ago (Van Doorsaeler 1967), whilst two decades have

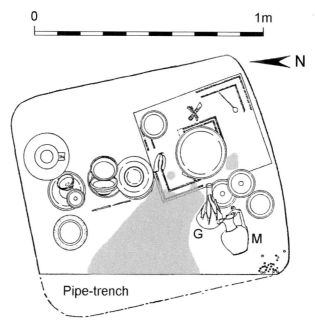

Fig. 7.1. Plan of a Flavian Period cremation burial (2) from Winchester Grange Road. The shaded area indicates the location of the cremated bone (after Biddle 1967, 232, fig. 5; G = glass vessel, M = metal vessel). For assemblage see Table 7.2.

elapsed since Philpott's (1991) synthesis of Romano-British burial. As in the Iron Age, where grave goods are commonly deposited it is possible to identify a hierarchy among burials, at the apex of which a small number of burials with very substantial grave good assemblages. Some of these are associated with monuments, especially barrows (Jones 1987; Struck 2000; Wigg 1993). Evidence for pre-interment rituals reminds us that deposition on the pyre could be an alternative or complementary stage in the deposition or destruction of objects. This aspect of funerary rituals is not yet well understood (see above), but can be illustrated in the range of pyre and feasting deposits from Belgium (Table 7.2, especially Helshoven and Berlingen) and in the remnants of a spectacular barbecue from Biberist-Spitalhof (Solothurn, Switzerland). In this instance a late second century cremation burial contained the burnt remains of at least 333 ceramic vessels, molten glass and metal, and foodstuffs including carbonised lentils, grain, and fruit and at least seven pigs and a cow (Schucany & Delage 2006: 113–30). The instructions to burn hunting equipment and textiles in the extensive will of a second century AD Gallic aristocrat recorded in a Medieval manuscript the so-called 'Testament of the Lingon' indicate that other items were sometimes destroyed on the pyre (Woolf 1998: 167). Burnt fragments of writing equipment in a tomb at Nersingen (Ulm, Bavaria) provide an archaeological illustration of this (Ambs and Faber 1998).

Fig. 7.2. Reconstruction of Winchester Grange Road burial 2, Winchester Museum. The cremated bone was found beside and on the shale tray. Gaming pieces and other small items were placed in the SW corner of the grave (bottom left) (Reproduced with kind permission of Winchester City Council).

These large grave good assemblages will be the focus of the rest of the paper. Their characterisation (Table 7.2) is based on two sample areas, southeast Britain and eastern Belgium and the south Netherlands. In the former area examples are taken from the *civitates* of the Catuvellauni and Belgae, in particular the environs of St Albans/*Verulamium* (Hertfordshire) and Winchester/*Venta Belgarum* (Hampshire). There is a direct continuity here with the (British) Late Iron Age burials discussed above. Philpott's (1991) synthesis of Romano-British burial practice includes extensive discussion from the territory of the Catuvellauni, while Millett (1987) focuses on the Hampshire burial tradition. The sample area in Belgica comprises Belgian and Dutch Limburg and Brabant, especially the central area of the *civitas* of the Tungri bisected by the Cologne-Bavai road. Here the tradition of rich burial rarely pre-dates the later 1st century AD. Some of the most spectacular assemblages cannot be reconstructed in detail because of poor documentation, but their contents are summarised and lavishly illustrated by Mariën (1980: 243–308). Examples listed in Table 7.2 are selected from more recent excavations: results from projects undertaken in the 1970s and 1980s are discussed by Roosens (1976) and van den Hurk (1984), while de Groot (2006) reports a key assemblage excavated in 2003 and notes other recent work. The following discussion draws on these and other examples to characterise the recurring aspects of these grave groups under approximate functional headings (dining, bathing, hunting or ritual). While this is a typical approach to these grave assemblages (Nuber 1972; van den Hurk 1984), it should be noted that the function of specific objects is not securely established in all cases, as Cool's (2006) discussion of Roman dining equipment illustrates. Many objects were also used in multiple settings, for example the jug and pan set at the sacrifice or the meal, cosmetic gear at home or the baths. The relationship between objects, their purpose and their symbolic significance will be evaluated after this description.

In both sample areas the deposition of substantial grave groups continues from the first into the early third centuries AD. In Britain the cremated remains of the dead are more likely to have been deposited in perishable containers, either bags or wooden boxes, of which the fittings sometimes survive, such as caskets with lionhead studs from Essex and Hertfordshire (Philpott 1991: 12–16). Stone or metal cists or glass containers also commonly served as containers for these burials. In Belgica massive stone coffins of a size sufficient to contain an unburnt body are sometimes used for cremation, most famously the Simpelveld sarcophagus with its unique carved interior surface (de Groot 2006: 55, 116).

Ceramics account for the vast majority of grave goods, especially dishes, bowls, and cups for consumption of food and drink, often in terra sigillata. Vessels for food preparation or storage are represented in small numbers and unlike earlier burials amphorae were infrequently deposited, usually in single instances. Examples in Table 7.2 illustrate the frequently consistent ratio between numbers of different vessel forms. A nine or 12 piece 'service' for an individual is sometimes proposed, but numbers of pots vary widely and some dining ware, especially decorated terra sigillata bowls, is absent from burial assemblages (Martin-Kilcher 1976: 84–87). Whether this 'service' represents the equipment of a single or multiple diners also cannot be known: larger numbers of vessels would however have provided for more than a single individual, for example in the pyre debris from Biberist-Spitalhof discussed above.

Glass vessels were more frequently found in these larger assemblages than in other burials, jugs and bottles for storing and serving liquids being the commonest forms (van Lith & Randsborg 1985). Multiple deposits are sometimes of identical types, for example boxed square glass bottles at Helshoven. Later in the 2nd century AD they also comprise 'services' of cups and plates for eating and drinking, as at Esch and Bocholtz (Massart 2001).

Iconographic evidence shows that the paired copper alloy jugs and handled pans found in many of these assemblages were used for hand washing at a meal or sacrifice: some graves substitute glass or ceramic vessels in these forms (Nuber 1972). Other less common metal vessels include double handled jugs, drinking cups, and shallow pans ('bath saucers') as well as strainers. Among other dining items are knives and spoons, the latter in bone, copper alloy, and occasionally silver, as at Cortil-Noirmont and Bocholtz.

Furniture and lighting equipment were also often deposited in these graves. After the early 1st century AD ivory- and bone-inlaid couches, as documented at Folly Lane were rarely used for cremation (Eckardt 1999: 77), but folding seats of the type documented at Bocholtz have been found in other second century tombs in Belgica and Britain (de Groot 2006: 112–13). These are conventionally interpreted as *sellae curules* (portable seats symbolising holding or magistracies or civic honour), or *sellae castrenses* (portable seats indicating military rank), but both have a common origin in a domestic form and it does not seem possible to differentiate between the latter and signifiers of rank (Nuber 1972: 171–72). Tripods from St Albans and Bois-et-Borsu probably supported trays of food (cf. Nuber 1984). Lighting equipment is frequently attested, most commonly ceramic lamps, less often iron or copper alloy lamps or candelabras.

Many items related to the manipulation of physical appearance (cf. Crummy & Eckardt 2008). As well as mirrors, sometimes plain, as at Stansted, less often decorated, as at Simpelveld, the panoply of items for modifying personal appearance include razors, tweezers, nail cleaners, ear scoops, as well as palettes and mortars for grinding cosmetic powders or medicines. Glass unguent bottles containing cosmetics and perfumes (and spatulas for extracting them) regularly occur amongst these assemblages, though they are also to be found in less-well furnished burials. Among the dress-related items copper alloy brooches are found widely among provincial Roman tombs. Precious metal jewellery is rare but documented in a small number of burials, often of juveniles or young adults across the Roman west (Rottloff 1995). Some individuals were dressed or shod in fabrics incorporating gold thread. Both instances are illustrated at Southfleet, Kent, where gold thread survived on leather shoes in a 2nd century cremation burial and a child burial was accompanied by a gold necklace, ring and snake-headed bracelets of 3rd century AD date.

Other artefacts served as equipment for leisure or labour. Bathing gear, primarily strigils and glass or metal oil flasks and perfume bottles, is restricted to these larger

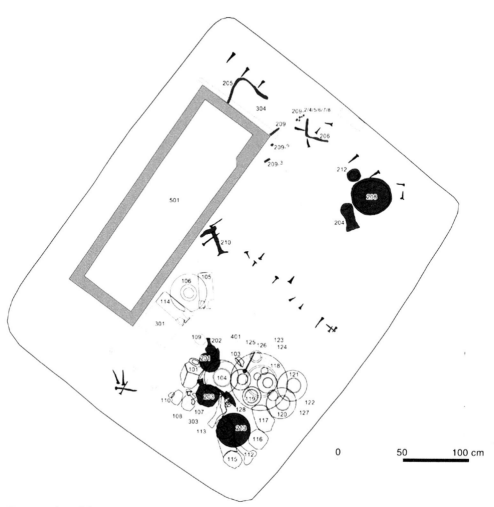

Fig. 7.3. Plan of the grave pit at Bocholtz, Limburg, Netherlands. The cremated bone was placed in the stone chest (501). For assemblage see Table 7.2 (with kind permission of T. de Groot, Rijksdienst voor Archeologie, Cultuurlandschap en Monumenten, Amersfoort).

assemblages. The metal examples are sometimes richly figured: the Bocholtz flask takes the form of a bust of Antinous while the Herstal example bore relief images of lovers and philosophers (Braun 2001). Gaming pieces, usually in glass, but occasionally in other materials, for example amber at Cortil-Noirmont, are recorded in varying numbers and combinations, placed in a bag or scattered across the tomb floor (Schädler 2007: 366). Of writing implements styli are the most commonly attested, sometimes with silver-inlay (Simpelveld). Less common are spatulas and inkwells, while small knives and rulers like those found at Berlingen may also be writing-related (Ambs & Faber

Fig. 7.4. Reconstruction of the grave pit at Bocholtz, Limburg, Netherlands (with kind permission of T. de Groot, Rijksdienst voor Archeologie, Cultuurlandschap en Monumenten, Amersfoort).

1998: 441–44; Bozic & Feugère 2004). After the mid-1st century AD burial of weapons was largely given up in Britain, but spears, axes, and daggers were sometimes deposited in Dutch and Belgian tombs (Nicolay 2007: 199–206). The daggers are sometimes identified as *parazonia*, i.e. parade swords worn by Roman army officers, but they do not correspond well with the limited textual and artistic evidence for these (Devijver & van Wonterghem 1990: 95–96). These arms may have served for hunting or combat. Horse harness and vehicles or their parts are also better documented in Belgica (de Groot 2006: 43, 104). Other tools were very occasionally deposited with the dead, medical instruments being the most widely distributed (Künzl 1982).

The Dutch and Belgian tombs are richer in exceptional items than those from Britain. Instances include the portrait cameo of Augustus deposited in a 2nd century grave from Tienen, knife handles, distaffs and figures in amber, and, exceptionally, a piece of amber carved in the form of a shell with relief decoration showing a Capricorn carrying a vessel between its front paws. A rock crystal lizard and ring were deposited in the same tomb group as the amber shell from Cortil-Noirmont (Mariën 1980). Occasionally inscriptions explicitly indicate that objects have been given as gifts, for example the dedication *Iunoni meae* on the Simpelveld ring, although we do not know if the deceased was the original recipient (Zinn 1997). At Tienen and in other cases objects were sometimes several decades or centuries old when deposited and it seems likely that their 'biographies' may be significant in their selection to accompany the dead (cf. Gosden & Garrow 2012).

No single arrangement of objects within the tomb can be identified and it is often not possible from older excavations to differentiate objects placed in direct association with the grave and those above it (Gaeng & Metzler 2008). At Berlingen grave goods were packed tightly and with little apparent order in a wooden case, but at Bocholtz they were spaced in groups in and around the stone chest containing the cremated bone as well as elsewhere in the timber chamber. Spatial grouping of artefacts sometimes relates to function: at Esch, for example, pairs of jugs and bowls were regularly placed above the timber chests containing the cremated remains, while at Bocholtz washing gear (a metal jug, bowl, and bath flask) was placed in the east corner of the tomb chamber (Figs 7.3–7.4). Yet in the same tomb other washing gear was placed elsewhere in the grave, strigils in its north corner with weapons, and a further jug and pan with glass eating and drinking vessels in the south. Ceramic and glass vessels were stacked, boxed or laid out, sometimes on trays of wood, shale or pewter with animal remains sometimes placed on them, pig being the most common species (Cool 2006: 82–84) (Figs 7.1–7.2). The disposition is suggestive of place settings, but the variability must, for the moment at least, frustrate reconstruction of table layout (*contra* Cool 2006: 193–97) and it is not certain that vessels were in simultaneous use. Disappearance of perishable items, especially food, textiles, or wooden items poses an obstacle, not only to understanding layout but also to whether and how some items were wrapped.

Interpreting the civilised dead

The post-conquest tombs, like burial practice in general, have played a somewhat marginal role in the study of the Roman Period (see above). Individual types of grave goods have often been considered in isolation as a key source of evidence for artefact chronology, typology, and function, since burials often offer the most complete examples. As such, museums often display them in isolation from their funerary context to illustrate Roman lifestyle. Nevertheless burial rituals have attracted some interest as evidence for social and cultural change under the Empire. Robert Philpott's (1991) emphasis on the continuity of Iron Age traditions and beliefs in Roman burial rituals in Britain exemplifies an enduring view of burial practice in the early Roman northwest. Change is primarily conceded in the materials used within the rituals, rather than in the essentials of their performance and their significance: it has been widely proposed that burial practice is not fully 'Romanised' until the spread of inhumation from the late 2nd century AD (van Doorsaeler 1967: 67; Morris 1992: 68; Wightman 1985: 188). Other scholars have given this characterisation greater theoretical weight by connecting it to general models for cultural change, i.e. to the Romanisation debate. Greg Woolf's (1998: 247) proposal for a 'formative' phase in the adoption of Roman culture, primarily by (male) elites engaged in urban public life and manifested in the creation of Roman-style public buildings, leaves other areas, including burials, as cultural 'backwaters'. This position is explicitly articulated by Nicola Terrenato (1998: 24), in whose formulation oppositions of public and private, male and female, and home and tomb differentiate areas at the interface with Roman power and culture from those which are not. In this view change to burial practice comes later and serves to differentiate within provincial society more than to demonstrate cultural community with Roman incomers. Taking up the cudgels of an older argument, Manuela Struck (1995) has argued that the apparent endurance of Iron Age burial practice and the limited adoption of Roman customs may even indicate cultural resistance in Britain and elsewhere.

This emphasis on continuity does not however take sufficiently into consideration significant changes in the form of the ritual itself, for example the disappearance of hearth furniture or amphorae from the funerary repertoire or the reduced frequency of weapon burial. More to the point though, it takes limited account of contextual information to interpret the assemblages, in particular of the rich archaeological and documentary evidence for the circulation of these artefacts and their social contexts. Paradoxically more attention has been given to the very limited evidence for the afterlife beliefs that may be indicated by these rituals (Morris 1992).

Parker-Pearson (1993; 1999) has proposed that through comparison of settlement, votive and funerary contexts it is possible to assess burial as a sphere of display in comparison to other arenas. I noted above that the many objects placed in Late Iron Age tombs derived from socially restricted exchanges, especially gift-giving. The special status of these artefacts and their rarity in other contexts, as well as the creation of monumental complexes in which to perform sometimes protracted burial ceremonies, indicate the central role of burial in the reproduction of social relations, especially amongst competing elites. The significance of burial from the mid-1st to early 3rd century AD is not so clear cut as in the preceding period. With incorporation in the Roman world other contexts have attracted more attention as the media in which elites have competed, especially, from the Augustan Period, urban public buildings, and later, town and rural housing. Within burial assemblages, some of the most numerically significant elements, such as terra sigillata and glass, occur widely on contemporary settlements as well as generally in burial practice. It therefore seems unlikely that these were derived from restricted circuits of exchange, although the frequency of terra sigillata and glass is higher in these graves than in others (van Lith & Randsborg 1985) and as a proportion of an assemblage it is often higher than on settlement sites. Some grave goods may also have been badges of civic or military rank, and thus also restricted in circulation, but these identifications can be challenged (see above). A limited group of objects, for example the Tienen cameo or rock crystal or amber figurines, would have been restricted to a class integrated within circuits of elite gift-giving and able to commission or buy artefacts in materials which counted as luxuries even at an imperial level. Taken together with the monuments with which they are sometimes associated, the assemblages outlined above suggest that burial should not be ignored as an arena for display and the negotiation of status into the mid-Roman Period. In the absence of epigraphic evidence the status of competing groups is not clear. However, inscriptions from other substantial funerary monuments in the Roman northwest commemorating individuals such as veteran *milites*, merchants, or freedmen suggest that they need not have been restricted to civic elites.

To focus on the tomb as a conspicuous removal from circulation of objects or greater or lesser prestige by destruction or deposition does not, however, explain why burial display should take this particular form. It ignores the *mise-en-scène* created by the burial ritual, in which the identity given to the deceased is shaped by the associations prompted among the participants by the combination of symbols placed with the body. In examining British Bronze Age 'Beaker' burials Julian Thomas (1991: 40) argues that the short-lived burial ceremony derived its effect from the presentation of highly stereotyped images of the dead 'in which particular identities for the deceased had to be produced and fixed in the minds of the onlookers'. This 'fixing' was achieved by signifiers whose connotations resonated beyond burial to other contexts, in the case of Beaker burials feasting and warfare. Paul Treherne's (1995: 124) study of prehistoric European male weapon burials develops this perspective further. He proposes that the groomed male corpse, furnished with artefacts related to personal care, such as shears or razors, and weapons responds to the 'Angst' of death by presenting the epitome of heroic male virtue, at the same time reinforcing the status of that virtue. Thus the display of the dead gives access to areas of social reproduction beyond the mortuary sphere. Others have developed a similar argument in relation to early Medieval burials (e.g. Williams 2006: 118–20). That visual symbols were prompts to 'reading' identities for the deceased, is of course also a commonplace in study of Roman commemorative monuments. An understanding of funerary art as *Selbstdarstellung*, a representation of identity through portraiture, other symbols and text, has allowed insights into group ideologies, particularly of non-elites: monuments to traders or craftspeople for example, often of freed status, present legitimate families supported by economic activity whose instruments and processes are also represented and celebrated (Zanker 1975). This paper proposes that the presentation of the dead in the grave can be approached in a similar way.

For prehistoric societies evidence for other contexts against which to assess the reading of burial is often lacking, but the Roman Period burial assemblages can be much more fully contextualised. The overwhelming emphasis of grave assemblages lies on objects related to the consumption of food and drink. The commodities consumed are rarely represented, perhaps as a function of preservation. The disappearance of amphorae suggests that prestige relies less on access to commodities such as wine, which by the later 1st century AD was much more widely available. Instead an increasingly elaborate etiquette of consumption lies behind the proliferation of vessel forms and materials, with many vessels required for one or more courses implying the *savoir-faire* necessary to correct use of these vessels. Depictions of Dionysiac scenes on copper alloy vessels are also appropriate to the symposium setting.

Another area of allusion is the manipulation of physical appearance. Here again the grave goods, in particular the multiplication of gear related to bath house routines, washing before eating or sacrifice, depilating and the application of cosmetics and perfumes embody an increasing complexity in this area. Dress items and jewellery are sporadically attested and it is impossible to know how the dead would have been dressed for cremation or burial. Funerary monuments from Germany and Gallia Belgica suggest the continuity of local dress styles for men and women and these may be more trustworthy than literary commonplaces which suggest the widespread adoption of the toga; even in Rome textual evidence suggests an increasing restriction of the latter to ceremonial occasions from the 1st century AD onwards (Freigang 1997; Stone 1994).

Other activities are evoked which might be grouped under the heading of *otium*, i.e. of relaxation, dignified leisure and sociability. The dining and bathing already discussed can be included under this rubric, as can the gaming represented by the glass gaming pieces. Beyond the ability to write (in Latin) the writing equipment might allude to *paideia*, literary cultivation and participation in epistolary culture (Bowman and Woolf 1996). In contrast to Iron Age tombs, reference to martial achievements symbolised by arms is less frequent in Roman Period graves: when present they may evoke the hunt rather than combat. Seats may mark civic honour or military status, but this can be challenged (see above). As in funerary monuments and grave goods from Gallia Belgica, the generation of wealthy economic power may be symbolized in for example writing equipment, with potential use for accounting and inventorising. In general however funerary assemblages comprise symbols of consumption rather than production of wealth.

The references to dining, grooming of the body and to varied forms of sociability are, at one level, common to funerary culture across much of European prehistory and the early historic period. They are generic signifiers of an elite lifestyle with a substantial leisure component, i.e. of conspicuous consumption demonstrating the ability of a leisured class to devote substantial resources to non-productive activity (Veblen 1902). There is, however, a more culturally specific perspective from which the recurring associations in the grave goods can be read, using evidence from Roman textual sources, which indicate how conduct in public and private settings marks possession of the virtues and cultural expertise necessary to assert membership of a Roman elite (Toner 1995). The *Laus Pisonis*, a short verse panegyric of unknown authorship dated to the 1st century AD for a male member of the Piso family, perhaps Gaius Calpurnius Piso, consul in AD 57, provides an illustration (Wight Duff & Duff 1982). The qualities it praises include not only ancestral glory, participation in public affairs, especially forensic eloquence and *amicitia* to clients, but also accomplishments in the sphere of *otium*, including athleticism in the bath house palaestra, and, in a long excursus, skill in board games, especially games of strategy with 'glass soldiers' (*milites vitrei*; *Laus Pisonis* 193).

Closer to Britain, the historian Tacitus reports changes in elite behaviour among the Britons at the prompting of the governor, his father-in-law, Agricola:

> '… little by little the Britons went astray into alluring vices: to the promenade, the bath, the well-appointed dinner table (*porticus et balnea et conviviorum elegantiam*). The natives gave the name of *humanitas* to this factor of their slavery' (*Agricola* 21.3).

From the Britons' perspective at least, this behaviour is emblematic of *humanitas*, their new lifestyles expressed metaphorically and metonymically by reference to public and domestic spaces and pastimes (the *porticus* may refer to colonnaded urban streets or peristyles within houses). *Humanitas*, often translated as 'civilisation' or 'culture', includes both intellectual cultivation and sophistication in lifestyle, separating Roman from barbarian and elite from non-elite (Woolf 1998: 54–60). *Savoir faire* in public life and in *otium* is emblematic of *humanitas*, even if reworked for ironic effect by Tacitus. The burial assemblages can be read to have the same emblematic character: the recurring symbols in this *mise-en-scène* evoke the same involvement in civic life and sociability, the dead embodying and presenting to the living the qualities that differentiate by class and culture. In analysis of grave assemblages scholars have sometimes tried to differentiate between the property of the deceased and gifts to them by the living (van den Hurk 1984; Roosens 1976). Not only is this impossible to apply in practice, but it also neglects the strong similarities between grave assemblages and relative lack of idiosyncrasy: the recurring symbols associated with the dead evoke and reinforce highly conventionalised qualities. Grave goods of the type discussed have often been seen as evoking domestic space in tombs considered as eternal homes for the deceased (e.g. '*Spiegelbild eines Wohnzimmers*': Roosens 1976: 149). However, if the house is evoked, it is as interface where patronage and friendship were extended in the *salutatio* and dinner party (Wallace-Hadrill 1988). The range of allusions in funerary assemblages is, however, wider than this, to a civic routine that takes in public as well as private space.

Against this 'Roman' reading it may be objected that deposition of grave goods in large quantities is not a Roman custom, although we might note (see above) that the 'Iron Age' tradition had only developed in the last century before conquest by Rome. Certainly the tradition considered here is evolutionary, with a gradual change in grave good assemblages over decades which continued to contain objects evocative of an indigenous milieu, for example the *carnyx* and vehicle fittings of the Folly Lane burial. Its strength was perhaps that it could be read either as traditional or as innovative depending on the perspective of the participant. The same argument has been made to explain the popularity of the barrow/tumulus as funerary monument in the Roman northwest (Wigg 1993). However, to label the burial practice represented by these grave good assemblages as 'non-Roman' is to adopt a metropolitan definition of Roman culture. The rituals I have described from Britain and Belgica are widely practised across central and northern Europe. Similar examples could have been given from other parts of Gaul, Germany and along the Danube, often, like Belgica, without local pre-Roman antecedents: Nuber's (1972: Beilage 1) map of copper alloy jug and pan sets from burials in Roman Europe illustrates the general distribution of such assemblages. Common social practice across the Empire need not only radiate from Rome, but develop within the interaction of provincial elites. But in any case rather than privileging either 'Roman' or 'non-Roman' readings of this burial practice, we might better seek polyvalency in the potential for variant 'Roman' readings. The passage from Tacitus' *Agricola* cited above, as well as other textual sources, remind us of negative constructions which might be put on behaviours symbolised in burial and that excessive indulgence at the *convivium* or bath house might signal physical and moral debilitation rather than cultivation (Toner 1995).

Concluding remarks

This paper has argued for more significant change than previously allowed for in burial practice in Rome's northwest provinces to the early 3rd century AD. The common emphasis on continuity has been argued to be misplaced. Burial traditions evolved during this period rather than changing radically, but the cumulative effect of changes in burial ritual and, more importantly, its context allows a different interpretation to be advanced. The combined resonance of the symbols associated with the dead and of the behaviours and values linked to these is with Roman-style urbanity and cultivation. The association with the dead asserted the status of these behaviours as norms for the living, though the possibility of variant 'readings' has also been noted. It has also been argued that the significance of burial as a sphere of display has been under-estimated, even if this is not as clear-cut as in the Late Iron Age. My approach was influenced by approaches to burial evidence outside the Classical world, but is analogous in some respects to reading Roman funerary art as a representation of identity (*Selbstdarstellung*).

Several important aspects have of course received insufficient attention. I have given little attention to variability within the group of burials discussed and chronological and spatial nuances have been downplayed in order to assess the general interpretative position. The relationship with broader contemporary burial practice, from which these assemblages are not sharply differentiated, also requires further consideration. Key dimensions of social identity have not been considered, especially age and gender. Osteological evidence indicates that that both men and women were buried in the style discussed above but the implications of this, or indeed of gender-related variation in general in Roman burial practice have received limited attention. There is very significant scope to investigate further the selection of objects for burial from the material culture in circulation in this period, not only in terms of form or fabric of ceramics, for example, but also other aspects like colour or iconography and to consider the exchange mechanisms through which these items circulated before their deposition with the dead. My argument has emphasised the generic significance of these objects, but as for Late Iron Age graves, as recently argued by Gosden and Garrow (2012), it is equally likely that the history of individual objects (for example older or inscribed objects) and their previous circulation evoked the specific social relationships that gave meaning to the ceremony. The spatial organisation of cremation graves, has also received little attention compared to later Roman inhumations. Nonetheless I hope this article has shown how the evidence of Roman burial rituals can be further exploited to address developing interests in funerary archaeology, not only because of the richness of the record of the burials themselves, but also because of the extensive evidence for context in which they can be situated.

Acknowledgements

This paper presents aspects of an argument that is more specifically rehearsed, with particular reference to a broader body of data from Britain, in my doctoral thesis (1999), currently in preparation for publication. My supervisor, Martin Millett, and examiners, Colin Haselgrove and Greg Woolf, are thanked for their comments on the argument of the thesis, as are Hella Eckardt and Jake Weekes and the anonymous referees for their observations on draft versions of this paper. Tessa De Groot, Rijksdienst voor Archeologie, Cultuurlandschap en Monumenten, Amersfoort, kindly allowed the use of illustrations from the Bocholtz tomb.

Table 7.1 – Summary of burial assemblages from c. 100 BC–AD 50, Britain and Luxembourg.
(NB Items such as nails which may be part of burial structures are omitted from the descriptions in both tables, as are unidentified fragments. The character of associated non-burial deposits is briefly indicated).

1. *'The Tene' Baldock, Hertfordshire* (Stead & Rigby 1986: 51–61): 100–50 BC.
Context: A burial on SW side of *oppidum*. Burial in a circular pit, some damage prior to excavation. Limited excavations of environs revealed some ritual deposits and a 3rd century AD cremation burial.
Assemblage: A small quantity of cremated human bone and bear phalanges in a copper alloy cauldron and on the floor of the pit. Surviving grave goods include: 2 firedogs, a iron cauldron, a single Dr1A amphora, vertebrae of a pig, 2 decorated copper alloy-bound wooden buckets, 2 bronze bowls.

2. *Clemency, Luxembourg* (Metzler et al. 1991): 80–60 BC.
Context: Robbed wooden burial chamber under barrow within ditched enclosure, with evidence for exposure platform, pyre site, feasting debris and commemorative rituals.
Assemblage: Cremated bone of an adult (40–50) with bear phalanges on base of chamber.
Surviving grave goods: 10+ Dr 1A amphorae, 36 locally made vessels, a small black gloss lamp, a copper alloy dish, remains of 4 pigs and, originally placed above the chamber, part of a chimney from a furnace.

3. *Welwyn Garden City, Hertfordshire* (Stead 1967): 50–25 BC.
Context: Sub-rectangular grave pit discovered through laying a pipe-trench. Limited excavations of environs revealed further contemporary burials.
Assemblage: Cremated bone of adult (?M) with bear phalanges heaped on base of grave. *Grave goods:* 5 Dr 1B amphorae, 36 other vessels including pedestal urns, bowls, beakers, tazze, 2 platters, flagons, 24 gaming pieces, 6 bead and bracelet fragments, a silver cup, copper alloy dish with strainer, nail cleaner,

many copper alloy studs, burnt copper alloy fragments, wooden vessels with copper alloy fittings and wooden objects with iron fittings, iron razor, straw mat.

4. *Tomb B Goeblingen-Nospelt, Luxembourg* (Böhme-Schonberger 1993; Gaeng & Metzler 2008; Metzler 1984): 20–10 BC.

Context: The latest of five richly furnished tombs excavated from a small cemetery of second half of 1st century BC date associated with a pyre site, feasting debris and evidence for commemorative rituals as well as other burials.

Assemblage: Cremated bone on base of tomb. *Grave goods*: 2 decorated copper alloy-bound wooden buckets, 2 copper alloy basins, 2 flagons, handled pan, sieve, sword with decorated sheath and fittings, spur, spearhead, brooch; Gallo-Belgic ceramics: 1 dolium, 13 jars and beakers, 2 bowls, 15 dishes; Imported ceramics: 4 Spanish amphorae, including 1 Haltern 69 for garum, 3 for wine (Pascal 1, Dressel 12), 1 lamp, 1 ACO beaker, 1 dish, 3 flagons.

5. *Stanway, Essex* (Crummy et al. 2007): AD 40–50 'doctor's' burial.

Context: In the NW corner of 0.38 ha ditched enclosure 5, with 'mortuary enclosure', funerary chamber, and four further burials of similar date.

Assemblage: Cremated human bone heaped on wooden gaming board. *Grave goods*: 11 ceramic cups and platters, mostly in terra nigra and terra rubra, flagon, decorated terra sigillata bowl (form 29), copper alloy pan and strainer; gaming board with white and blue glass counters, 8 rods and 8 rings (for divination?), surgical instruments, 2 brooches and jet bead; metal fittings for wooden objects and traces of textiles in corrosion products on metal objects. Fish sauce amphora (Dressel 8) originally placed above wooden board over other grave goods.

6. *St Albans, Folly Lane, Hertfordshire* (Niblett 1999): AD 45–55.

Context: Rectilinear ditched 2 ha enclosure, shaft with wooden chamber at base, pyre site and burial.

Assemblage: Shaft back fill: sherds from 35 broken and scattered vessels, including: 1 flagon, 4 amphorae, 10 platters (5 terra sigillata, 5 Gallo-Belgic), 10 cups (5 terra sigillata, 1 butt beaker, 1 terra nigra cup and 3 imitation Gallo-Belgic imitation vessels), and 10 dishes (5 terra sigillata, 4 imitation Gallo-Belgic and 1 grog-tempered). Burial pit containing a single adult cremation and cremated items. *Grave goods*: burnt fragments of amphorae, imitation terra nigra and imitation Gallo-Belgic wares, fragments from a *carnyx*, a cart or chariot, a bridle bit and a cheek piece, iron chain mail, molten copper alloy, 4 kg of molten silver, fragments from ivory-inlaid furniture, bear claws, animal bones.

Table 7.2. Summary of burial assemblages from c. AD 50 – AD 250, Britain, Belgium, and Holland.

1. *Burial 2, Winchester Grange Road, Hampshire* (Biddle 1967): AD 70–90.

Context: One of two rich tombs excavated *c.* 1.5 km south of *Venta Belgarum*.

Assemblage: Cremated bone heaped on base of grave pit and on tray (immature (?) female (?)). *Grave goods*: flagon, beaker, 13 terra sigillata vessels including a larger form 18R dish, 4 form 18 dishes, 4 larger and 4 smaller form 27 cups (S. Gaul); glass jug, metal jug, shale tray, copper alloy spoon, 2 iron knives, copper alloy pin, copper alloy finger ring, iron finger ring, seal box lid, 2 iron styli, glass gaming pieces, iron tool, bell, 8 melon beads, fossil, pig and bird bones.

2. *'William Old' burial, St Albans, Hertfordshire* (Niblett & Reeves 1990): AD 80–90
Context: Excavation of single burial south of *Verulamium*.
Assemblage: Adult cremation in glass jar. *Grave goods*: 13 terra sigillata vessels including 1 large form 18 dish, 4 form 18 dishes, 4 larger and 4 smaller form 27 cups (southern Gaul); glass flask, copper alloy bowl, 4 ceramic lamps, 2 strigils, folding iron tripod; black and white glass gaming pieces.

3. *Burials 25 and 26, Stansted DCS, Essex* (Havis & Brooks 2004: 216–31): Early–mid-2nd century AD.
Context: Rural cemetery.
Assemblage: 25. Cremation on pewter tray, probably in wooden box. *Grave goods*: carrot amphora, beaker, form 18 and 2 form 42 dishes, four form 35 and 1 form 33 cups (terra sigillata primarily from southern Gaul); 6 glass vessels (pillar moulded bowl, 2 cups, flask, small bottle and large bottle); copper alloy jug and pan, hemispherical bowl, bath saucer, vessel foot and rim; iron lamp, knife; pig.
Assemblage: 26. (incomplete due to damage) Boxed cremation, adult (& juvenile?); *Grave goods*: form 37 decorated bowl, form 18/31 dish, 2 form 35 and one form 27 cups, flagon, beaker, vessel; (terra sigillata from central and southern Gaul); glass bowl and bottle, fragmentary and molten pieces; mirror, hobnailed footwear.

4. *Berlingen, Limburg, Belgium* (Roosens & Lux 1973): AD 70–80.
Context: Wooden box in grave chamber beneath barrow contains burial and grave goods, pyre debris also spread in grave chamber, ritual pits also under barrow.
Assemblage: Cremated bone young man and animal remains in glass jar. *Grave goods*: 7 form 18 dishes, 4 form 27 cups (southern Gaul) and 1 terra sigillata bowl, 2 beakers and 1 jar, 3 flagons, glass oil flask and 3 unguent bottles, 2 glass handled pans, 2 lamps, writing equipment including a stylus and wax spatula, compasses and folding ruler, iron spearhead and axe, shears, bone plaque; animal bones on some vessels.

5. *Helshoven, Limburg, Belgium* (Roosens & Lux 1974): Second quarter of 2nd century AD.
Context: Wooden box in burial pit under barrow contained burial and grave goods, pyre debris on and around the box and in separate pit. A further well-furnished

burial, postholes and cremation area beneath same barrow.

Assemblage: Cremated bone (young woman and burnt animal bone) in glass jar. *Grave goods*: 6 form 27 cups and 6 form 18/31 dishes (central and eastern Gaul), 2 beakers, 2 jars, another vessel, a lid and mortarium, 5 dishes and 1 bowl, 5 flagons, lamp, 2 glass beakers, 5 square glass bottles, metal bath flask, 15 melon beads, 2 strigils, leather shoes, animal bone, worked bone fragments.

6. *Bocholtz, Limburg, Netherlands* (de Groot 2006): Late 2nd/early 3rd century AD.

Context: Square timber-lined pit, with stone capping, probably beneath barrow.

Assemblage: Cremated bone (adult) in large sandstone chest (1.8 m long). *Grave goods* in chest and tomb include at least 28 glass objects, including bottles, dishes, jugs, cups and bowls and an unguent bottle, a copper alloy basin, 3 jugs and a bath flask, a handled pan, iron knife, silver spoon (cochlear), a folding stool, oil lamp on a stand, 2 strigils, iron folding seat, spearhead, axe, horse bit, horse harness, spur, dagger and sheath, copper alloy ink well, wax spatula.

Other tombs and assemblages referred to in text:

Britain

Southfleet, Kent (Davies 2000); Turnershall Farm, Wheathampstead, Hertfordshire (Faulkner 2003, 97–98); Holborough, Kent (Jessup 1954).

Belgium

Clavier-Vervoz, Liège (Massart 2001); Bois-et-Borsu, Liège; Cortil-Noirmont, Walloon Brabant; Herstal, Liège; Tienen-Grimde, Flemish Brabant (Mariën 1980: 245–48).

Netherlands

Esch, north Brabant (van den Hurk 1984); Belfort, Limburg (de Grooth and Mater 1997); Simpelveld, Limburg (Zinn 1997; de Grooth and Mater 1997).

Bibliography

Ambs, R. & Faber, A. 1998: 'Ein Bestattungplatz der provinzialen Oberschicht Raetiens an der Donausüdstraße bei Nersingen-Unterfahlheim', *Bericht der Römisch-Germanischen Kommission* 79: 383–478.

Bechert, T. 1980: 'Zur Terminologie provinzialrömischer Brandgräber', *Archäologisches Korrespondenzblatt* 10: 253–58.

Biddle, M. 1967: 'Two Flavian Burials from Grange Road, Winchester', *Antiquaries Journal* 47: 224–50.

Böhme-Schonberger, A. 1993: 'Die reichen Gräber von Goeblingen-Nospelt als Zeichen der Romanisierung der einheimischen Bevölkerung', in Struck (ed.), 337–44.

Bozic, D. & Feugère, M. 2004: 'Les instruments de l'écriture', *Gallia* 61: 21–41.

Bowman, A. & Woolf, G. 1996. 'Literacy and Power in the Ancient World', in A. Bowman & G. Woolf (eds): *Literacy and Power in the Ancient World*, Cambridge University Press: Cambridge, 1–16.

Braun, C. 2001: *Römische Bronzebalsamarien mit Reliefdekor*, British Archaeological Reports International Series 917: Oxford.

Cool, H. 2006: *Eating and Drinking in Roman Britain*, Cambridge University Press: Cambridge.

Creighton, J. 2006: *Britannia. The Creation of a Roman Province*, Routledge: London.

Crummy, N. & Eckardt, H. & 2008: *Styling the Body in Late Iron Age and Roman Britain – A Contextual Approach to Toilet Instruments*, Instrumentum: Montagnac.

Crummy, P., Benfield, S., Crummy, N., Rigby, V. & Shimmin, D. 2007: *Stanway: An Elite Burial Site at Camulodunum*, Britannia Monograph 24: London.

Davies, M. 2000: 'Death and Social Division at Roman Springhead', *Archaeologia Cantiana* 121: 157–69.

van Doorsaeler, A. 1967: *Les nécropoles d'époque romaine en Gaule Septentrionale*, Dissertationes Archaeologicae Gandenses 10: Bruges.

Devijver, H. & van Wonterghem, F. 1990: 'The Funerary Monuments of Equestrian Officers of the Late Republic and Early Empire in Italy (50 B.C.–100 A.D.), *Ancient Society* 21: 59–98.

Eckardt, H. 1999: 'The Colchester "Child's Grave"', *Britannia* 30: 57–90.

Faber, A., Fasold, P., Struck, M. & Witteyer, M. (eds) 2004: *Körpergräber des 1.–3. Jh. in der römischen Welt*, Archäologisches Museum Frankfurt: Frankfurt am Main.

Faulkner, N. 2003: *Hidden Treasure*, BBC: London.

Feugère, M. 1996: 'Les tombes à armes de l'aristocratie gauloise sous la paix romaine', in M. Reddé (ed.): *L'armée romaine en Gaule*, Errance: Paris, 165–76.

Fitzpatrick, A. 2000: 'Ritual, Sequence and Structure in Late Iron Age Mortuary Practices in North-West Europe', in Pearce et al. (eds), 15–29.

Fitzpatrick, A. 2007: 'The Fire, the Feast, the Funeral: Late Iron Age Burial Rites in Southern England', in V. Kruta & G. Leman-Delerive (eds): *Feux des morts, foyers des vivants. Les rites et symbols du feu dans les tombes de l'Age de Fer et de l'époque romaine*, Revue Du Nord Hors Série. Collection Art et Archéologie 11: Lille, 123–42.

Freigang, Y. 1997: 'Die Grabmäler der gallo-römischen Kultur im Moselland. Studien zur Selbstdarstellung einer Gesellschaft', *Jahrbuch des römisch-germanischen Zentralmuseums Mainz* 44.1: 278–440.

Gaeng, C. & Metzler, J. 2008: 'Observer les abords du sepulture pour comprendre le rituel funéraire', in Scheid (ed.), 161–70.

Gerding, H. 2002: *The Tomb of Caecilia Metella: Tumulus, Tropaeum and Thymele*, PhD Thesis, Lund University.

Gosden, C. & Garrow. D. 2012: *Technologies of Enchantment. Exploring Celtic Art 400 BC to AD 100*, Oxford University Press: Oxford.

De Groot, T. 2006: *Resultaten van de opgraving een Romeins tumulusgraf in Bocholtz (gem. Simpelveld)*, Rapportage Archeologische Monumentenzorg 127: Amersfoort.

De Grooth, M. E. T. & Mater, B. 1997: *Een huis voor altijd*, Bonnefantenmuseum: Maastricht.

Haselgrove, C. 1987: 'Culture Process on the Periphery: Belgic Gaul and Rome during the Late Republic and Early Empire', in M. Rowlands, M. Larsen & K. Kristiansen (eds): *Centre and Periphery in the Ancient World*, Cambridge University Press: Cambridge, 104–24.

Haselgrove, C. 1996: 'Roman Impact on Rural Settlement and Society in Southern Picardy', in

N. Roymans (ed.): *From the Sword to the Plough. Three Studies on the Earliest Romanisation of Northern Gaul*, Amsterdam University: Amsterdam, 127–88.

Havis, R. & Brooks, H. 2004: *Excavations at Stansted Airport, 1986–91. Volume 1: Prehistoric and Romano-British*, East Anglian Archaeology 107: Chelmsford.

Hope, V. 1997: 'Words and Pictures: The Interpretation of Romano-British Tombstones', *Britannia* 28: 245–58.

van den Hurk, L. 1984: 'The Tumuli from the Roman Period of Esch, Province of North Brabant V', *Berichten van de Rijksdienst voor het Oudheidkundig Bodemonderzoek* 34: 9–38.

James, S. & Millett, M. (eds) 2001: *Britons and Romans. Advancing an Archaeological Agenda*, Council for British Archaeology Research Reports 125: York.

Jessup, R. 1954: 'Excavation of a Roman Barrow at Holborough', Snodland, *Archaeologia Cantiana* 68: 1–61.

Jones, R. F. J. 1987: 'Burial Customs of Rome and the Provinces', in J. Wacher (ed.): *The Roman World*, Routledge: London, 812–38.

Joy, J. 2010: *Iron Age Mirrors: A Biographical Approach*, British Archaeological Reports 518: Oxford.

Künzl. E. 1982: 'Medizinische Instrumente aus Sepulkralfunden der römischen Kaiserzeit', *Bonner Jahrbuch* 82: 1–131.

van Lith, S. & Randsborg, K. 1985: 'Roman Glass in the West: A Social Study', *Berichten van de Rijksdienst voor het Oudheidkundig Bodemonderzoek* 35: 413–532.

Mariën, M. 1980: *Empreinte de Rome: Belgica Antiqua*, Fonds Mercator: Antwerp.

Martin-Kilcher, S. 1976: *Das römische Gräberfeld von Courroux im Berner Jura*, Basler Beiträge zur Ür- und Frühgeschichte 2: Derendingen-Solothurn.

Massart, C. 2001: 'Les services de table en verre dans les tumulus gallo-romains de Hesbaye', *Bulletin des Musées Royaux d'Art et d'Histoire (Bruxelles)* 72: 189–211.

Metzler, J. 1984: 'Treverische Reitergräber von Goeblingen-Nospelt', in *Trier. Augustusstadt der Treverer. Stadt und Land in vor- und frührömischer Zeit*, von Zabern: Mainz, 87–99.

Metzler, J., Waringo, R., Bis, R. & Metzler-Zens, N. 1991: *Clemency et les tombes de l'aristocratie en Gaule Belgique*, Dossiers d'Archéologie du Musée National d'Histoire et d'Art 1: Luxembourg.

Millett, M. 1987: 'An Early Roman Burial Tradition in Central Southern England', *Oxford Journal of Archaeology* 6: 63–68.

Millett, M. 1990: *The Romanization of Britain*, Cambridge University Press: Cambridge.

Morris, I. 1992: *Death Ritual and Social Structure in Classical Antiquity*, Cambridge University Press: Cambridge.

Nelson, M. 2005: *The Barbarian's Beverage: A History of Beer in Ancient Europe*, Routledge: London & New York.

Niblett, R. 1999: *The Excavation of a Ceremonial Site at Folly Lane, Verulamium*, Britannia Monograph 14: London.

Niblett, R. & Reeves, P. 1990: 'A Wealthy Roman Cremation from Verulamium', *Antiquaries Journal* 70.2: 441–46.

Nicolay, J. 2007: *Armed Batavians: Use and Significance of Weaponry and Horse Gear from Non-Military Contexts in the Rhine Delta (50 BC–AD 450)*, Amsterdam University Press: Amsterdam.

Nuber, H. 1972: 'Kanne und Griffschale. Ihr Gebrauch im täglichen Leben und die Beigabe in Gräbern der römischen Zeit', *Bericht der Römisch-Germanischen Kommission* 53: 1–232.

Nuber, H. 1984: 'Römische Metallklapptische', *Alba Regia* 21: 53–57.

Parker Pearson, M. 1993: 'The Powerful Dead: Archaeological Relationships between the Living and the Dead', *Cambridge Archaeological Journal* 3.2: 203–29.

Parker Pearson, M. 1999: *The Archaeology of Death and Burial*, Sutton: Stroud.

Pearce, J., Millett, M. & Struck, M. (eds) 2000: *Burial, Society and Context in the Roman World*, Oxbow: Oxford.

Pitts, M. 2005: 'Pots and Pits: Drinking and Deposition in Late Iron Age South-East Britain', *Oxford Journal of Archaeology* 24.2: 143–61.

Philpott, R. 1991: *Burial Practices in Roman Britain. A Survey of Grave Treatment and Furnishing A.D. 43–410*, British Archaeological Reports, British Series 219: Oxford.

Roosens, H. 1976: 'Bestattungsritual und Grabinahlt einiger Tumuli im Limburger Haspengouw', *Helinium* 16: 139–56.

Roosens, H. & Lux, G. 1973: *Grafveld met Gallo-Romeinse Tumulus te Berlingen*, Archaeologia Belgica 147.

Roosens, H. & Lux, G. 1974: *Gallo-Romeinse Tumulus te Helshoven onder Hoepertingen*, Archaeologia Belgica 164.

Rottloff, A. 1995: 'Der Grabfund von der Blauen Klappe in Augsburg. Bemerkungen zu römischen Frauengräbern des 2. und 3. Jahrhunderts n. Chr. mit Goldschmuck', in W. Czysz (ed.): *Provinzialrömische Forschungen: Festschrift für Günther Ulbert zum 65. Geburtstag*, Marie Leidorf: Espelkamp, 371–86.

Roymans, N. 1990: *Tribal Societies in Northern Gaul*, Universiteit van Amsterdam: Amsterdam.

Schädler, U. 2007: 'The Doctor's Game: New Light on the History of Ancient Board Games', in Crummy et al., 359–75.

Scheid, J. (ed.) 2008: *Pour une archéologie du rite. Nouvelles perspectives sur l'archéologie funeraire*, Collection de l'École rrancaise de Rome 407: Rome.

Schucany, C. & Delage, R. 2006: *Die römische Villa von Biberist-Spitalhof/SO*, Greiner: Remshalden.

Stead, I. M. 1967: 'A La Tène III Burial at Welwyn Garden City', *Archaeologia* 101: 1–62.

Stead, I. M. & Rigby, V. 1986: *Baldock: The Excavation of an Iron Age and Romano-British Settlement, 1968–1972*, Britannia Monograph 7: London.

Stone, S. 1994: 'The Toga: From National to Ceremonial Costume', in J. L. Sebesta & L. Bonfante (eds): *The World of Roman Costume*, University of Wisconsin Press: Madison: 13–45.

Struck, M. 1993: '*Busta* in Britannien und ihre Verbindungen zum Kontinent', in Struck (ed.): 81–94.

Struck, M. 1995: 'Integration and Continuity in Funerary Ideology', in J. Metzler Millett, M. N. Roymans & J. Slofstra (eds): *Integration in the Early Roman West. The Role of Culture and Ideology*, Musée National d'Histoire et d'Art: Luxembourg, 139–47.

Struck, M. 2000: 'High Status Burials in Roman Britain (1st–3rd Centuries AD)', in Pearce et al. (eds), 85–96.

Struck, M. (ed.) 1993: *Römerzeitliche Gräber als Quellen zu Religion, Bevölkerungsstruktur und Sozialgeschichte*, Johannes Gutenberg Institut für Vor- und Frühgeschichte: Mainz.

Terrenato, N. 1998: 'The Romanisation of Italy; Global Acculturation or Cultural Bricolage', in C. Forcey (ed.): *Proceedings of the 7th Annual Theoretical Roman Archaeology Conference*, Oxbow: Oxford: 20–27.

Thomas, J. 1991: 'Reading the Body: Beaker Funerary Practice in Britain', in P. Garwood, D. Jennings, R. Skeates & J. Toms (eds): *Sacred and Profane*, Oxford University Committee for Archaeology: Oxford, 33–42.

Toner, J. 1995: *Leisure and Ancient Rome*, Polity Press: Cambridge.

Treherne, P. 1995: 'The Warrior's Beauty: The Masculine Body and Self Identity in Bronze Age Europe', *Journal of European Archaeology* 3.1: 105–44.

Veblen, T. 1902: *The Theory of the Leisure Class: An Economic Study of Institutions*, Macmillan: New York.

Wallace-Hadrill, A. 1988: 'The Social Structure of the Roman House', *Papers of the British School at Rome* 56: 43–97.

Weekes, J. 2008: 'Classification and Analysis of Archaeological Contexts for the Reconstruction of Early Romano-British Cremation Funerals', *Britannia* 39: 145–60.

Wigg, A. 1993: *Grabhügel des 2. und 3. Jahrhunderts n. Chr. an Mittelrhein, Mosel und Saar*, Rheinisches Landesmuseum: Trier.

Wight Duff, J. & Duff, A. (eds) 1982: *Minor Latin Poets: In Two Volumes*, Harvard University Press: Cambridge, MA.

Wightman, E. 1985: *Gallia Belgica*, Batsford: London.

Williams, H. 2006: *Death and Memory in Early Medieval Britain*, Cambridge University Press: Cambridge.

Woolf, G. 1998: *Becoming Roman: The Origins of Provincial Civilization in Gaul*, Cambridge University Press: Cambridge.

Zanker, P. 1975: 'Grabreliefs römischer Freigelassener', *Jahrbuch des deutschen archäologischen Instituts* 90: 267–315.

Zinn, F. 1997: 'Überlegungen zum Sarkophag von Simpelveld', *Oudheidkundige Mededeelingen van het Rijksmuseum van Oudheden te Leiden* 77: 135–58.

8

FRIENDS, FOES AND HYBRIDS
The Transformation of Burial Ritual
in Roman Dalmatia

Marina Prusac

This paper will examine changes in burial ritual from the perspective of the evolving cultural identities which appeared in Illyria/Dalmatia in the early Roman Period. Different cultural identities were expressed through burial customs among Illyrians and Romans respectively in the earliest period of Roman rule, and later mainly through the iconography of grave stelae and sarcophagi. The variation in cultural identities in Illyria, especially in the Imperial Period, probably reflects a similarly rich spectrum of religious beliefs and therefore also different burial rituals. Numerous grave stelae from Dalmatia illustrate the combination of indigenous iconography and Roman epigraphic tradition, which was a hybrid result of the encounters between Illyrian and Roman funerary cultures. Hybrid elements reveal that memories of the indigenous past were transformative and individually manageable cultural values. Over time, however, burial customs changed into a predominantly 'Roman' style, as also seen in other parts of the Roman Empire, but they were not 'standardised'. In the following it is argued that the changes and adjustments in burial rituals that took place during the 'Romanisation' of Dalmatia allowed for new expressions of individual ideas about the afterlife.

Keywords: burial ritual, changes, cultural encounters, Dalmatia, hybrid memories, Illyria.

In the Imperial Period, the cultural identities of Illyria/Dalmatia underwent considerable changes. The various groups adhered to different cults, which are reflected in the heterogeneous funerary material of the province. The variety in the material remains indicate that the burial practices, including the rituals, were of rather local character.

From the last decades of the first century BC and throughout the first decades of the 1st century AD, different cultural identities were expressed in funerary contexts through distinctively different burial customs among Illyrians and Romans. From the 1st century AD onwards cultural identities were expressed mainly through grave stelae, followed by sarcophagi. We cannot discern the full details of the burial rituals themselves, but the evidence does allow us to glean a great deal about the cultural identity of the deceased.

Illyria and Illyricum were the names used for the western Balkans until most of the area was reorganised as the Roman province of Dalmatia in AD 9 (Wilkes 1969: 74–75). The various indigenous groups in Illyria have often been given the generic label 'Illyrians,' but there were several cultural differences between the different tribes. Syntheses of the different burial customs and rituals in the western Balkans and their interrelationship have been rare, apart from brief treatments by John Wilkes (1992: 241–53) and Aleksandar Štipčević (1977: 229–42), and a thoroughly anti-'Romanisation' interpretation by Aleksandar Jovanović (1984). More recently, the results of investigations of changes in local burial customs over an extended time span have become available (e.g. Girardi Jurkić 2002).

'Romanisation' and change of burial practices

The burial evidence indicates that various, heterogeneous local customs were still present in Dalmatia in the Imperial Period (cf. Štipčević 1977: 230). Local, traditional and 'Romanised' rituals were preformed parallel to each other. Although the Roman traits seem to dominate, the archaeological material shows that a full homogenisation was never completed. What appears as 'Romanised' has in many cases elements of a pre-Roman tradition, and the 'standardised' result was a blend of indigenous elements and cultural traits from different parts of the Roman world. This blend of cultural traits is best described through the post-colonial term *hybridity*, which defines cultural elements and traits such as pattern and iconographic renderings which are revealed or 'frozen' in a given moment in the unavoidable, continuous process of change (Bhaba 1994: 2–5). Cultures are never static but in perpetual change, and the term *hybridity* is here used on examples which demonstrate cultural changes in transformation. The hybridities which were expressed in the Illyrian-Roman funerary iconography indicate the presence of 'collective memories' of the Illyrian past blended with Roman traditions. 'Collective memories' are understood as formative elements for group identities, such as the Illyrian tribal identities by the time of the Roman takeover. Maurice Halbwachs (1925) was the first to use the term 'collective memories'. To Halbwachs, 'collective memories' were always social constructs defined by time and space (1992: 38–39). In the last decades, his theory has become much used in studies of places where memories of a certain past are manifested in hybrid forms within a given geographical area (Nora 1984: 1–2 for the introduction of the phrase *lieux de mémoires* or 'spaces of memory'). The use of pre-Roman elements in the cultural practices and iconography of Dalmatia was not necessarily on a conscious level but rather the opposite: 'hybrid memories' are usually understood as expressions of persistent ideas and beliefs which survive the encounter with others. Burial rituals in Early Roman Dalmatia includes several blended cultural traits, which are best explained through the term 'hybrid memories.'

The different indigenous burial customs and rituals, which existed side by side at the beginning of the Roman immigration, and the ways by which they were transformed, provide a complicated blend of local cult- and burial-practices, which are here perceived as carriers of traditions and markers of group identities during a period of political and cultural transformation.

During the Imperial Period, when the burial customs in Dalmatia became more homogenised, with cremation burials marked by inscribed grave stelae dominating completely, each individual had more options for expressing his or her own individual ideas and beliefs. Seen in relation to the post-colonial research (following Said 1978), which is generally considered applicable to studies of 'Romanisation' processes (Cooper & Webster 1996; Huskinson 2000: 1), Ulrich Beck's statement that standardisation is a parallel form to individualisation is central (1986: 210): The rituals and material expressions of the memory of an individual, perceived through his or her grave, correspond to the burial trends introduced by the dominating powers. Concurrently, local features occur in the burials and express a cultural substratum which is not necessarily an expression of resistance, but merely preservation of an older tradition.

Despite the ritual changes, which took place when the Romans imposed their burial customs on the indigenous populations, there seems to have been continuity in some perceptions of death. This continuity informs us about beliefs, which differ from the mainstream ideas of the dominating power. The hybridities in the grave materials in Roman Dalmatia mirror the encounters between the heterogeneous pre-Roman inhabitants and the immigrant groups from various parts of the Empire.

The most thorough changes took place during the encounters between the indigenous populations and Italic and other settlers from the Empire in the 1st century BC and the 1st and 2nd centuries AD. The ritual changes and exchange of ideas which were caused by the negotiations between immigrating soldiers and the 'Romanised' inhabitants, in particular in the 2nd and 3rd centuries AD, were of a more subtle character, but of significance in the negotiation between the different cultural groups and their burial customs and ideas about the afterlife. Interpretations of specific meanings of shape and decoration provide contextualisation (Hodder 2000: 96) and connection between the mortuary rituals and the social organisation (Parker Pearson 2000: 246).

Diversity

From the Bronze Age and until the 3rd century BC, the size and location of the Illyrian tumuli indicated the social status of the buried. The social elite and aristocracy in this period demonstrated their power through the monumentality of their graves (Earl 1987: 279), but the actual relations of power were not always necessarily expressed (Parker

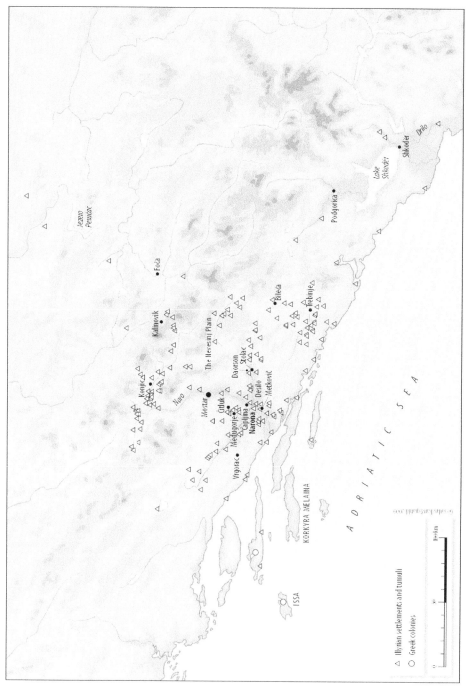

Fig. 8.1. Map with clusters of Illyrian burial mounds in South-Illyria (M. Prusac. Graphics by Gerd Kielland at Geoatlas/Kartõgrafikk, Oslo).

Fig. 8.2. Illyrian tumulus, at Ograđ, Croatia (photo: M. Prusac).

Pearson 2000: 249). Despite the many variations in the burial traditions in Illyria from the Bronze Age to the Late Iron Age and the Roman annexation it is possible to distinguish two main customs: inhumation graves beneath tumuli and cremation burials in rectangular urns (Štipčević 1977: 230).

The Illyrian tumuli are generally located along the main communication arteries and near settlements (Fig. 8.1). A circle of stones outlined the graves. On top, large quantities of stone formed the mound. The mounds contain inhumation graves with the bodies outstretched on their backs or in a crouching position in stone slab coffins. The presence of tumuli with both outstretched bodies and bodies in crouching position indicates that parallel rituals were probably undertaken contemporaneously by groups with different social or cultural identities. The Illyrian graves which contained bodies in crouching position are often marked out by smaller tumuli which contained only one grave, such as, for example, at Baćina and Ograđ, both in Croatia, in the vicinity of the Bosnia-Herzegovian border (Fig. 8.2). The tumuli and Roman grave markers in the Late Hellenistic Neretva Valley, a divided funerary landscape, reflect the clear distinction between the Illyrian and Roman cultural identities despite the proximity of the settlements and their close connections.

Apart from the rare occurrence of 'princely' graves such as the one in Stična, Slovenia, there are little, if any, grave goods present in the Illyrian tumuli to indicate social status or the organisation of the communities, or to distinguish between male and female (Wilkes 1992: 241). The few examples that have produced grave goods were generally large mounds, which probably indicate elite warrior status and perhaps a kind of 'hero' status, although they carry no markers of identity. The few equipped graves often include several secondary burials inserted into the mound in a regular arrangement, probably containing companion warriors.

The grave goods share a number of Iron Age symbols, which traditionally have been interpreted as solar cult signs, such as the spiral, wheel, serpent, birds, and female dancing figures. These symbols remain popular in grave iconography throughout the Roman Period and into the Middle Ages. Vast numbers of massive stone sarcophagi, 'stećci' (alternatively 'stećaci'), with crudely carved iconographic renderings of such symbols, mainly in Herzegovina, suggest a strong continuity of local symbolic language. The encounters with Roman culture influenced the style and design in a way which makes the renderings of such symbols and figures manifestations of cultural hybridities in the material.

Lost rites and the problem of reconstructing them

The Illyrian burial rituals are largely unknown and the available material is too scarce to allow for valid reconstruction, but some general observations can be made on the basis of the archaeological remains and a few examples of grave contexts which provide more information than others.

At Atenica near Čačak in Serbia there is a rare example of a large 'princely' grave, which contained grave goods such as imported Greek pottery and glass beads. A construction that was interpreted as a small shrine was also included in the grave (Štipčević 1977: 231; Wilkes 1992: 105). The purpose of the shrine is unknown, but its presence seems to indicate a more institutionalised burial ritual than most in Illyria, at least among the ruling classes.

The majority of the Illyrian tumuli have yielded very little material except pottery shards, which suggest a ritual breaking of clay vessels on the mound – a practice which is known to have been performed throughout the Prehistoric Period (Marović 1980; Štipčević 1977: 231). It is possible that wine, which gained a foothold among the Illyrians in the Hellenistic Period (Lindhagen 2009), was included in the ritual, and that the fragments of amphorae, which have been found on the surface of the tumuli along the river Neretva, derive from burial rituals (Basler et al. 1988: 298, no. 24.161). In this context, the interesting finds from Desilo (southwestern Bosnia-Herzegovina near the Croatian border, not far from the Roman site Vid/Narona) should be mentioned. In a small lake, vast amounts of amphora fragments and amphora stoppers (*c.* 800) together with animal bones and pottery were found together with the remains of Illyrian boats, everything blackened by fire. It is possible that these finds further testify to the importance of wine drinking in Illyrian ritual.

It has been suggested, based on the frequent occurrence of ornamentation on funerary stone coffins, that the Illyrians performed a ritual dance during the burial ceremony (Štipčević 1977: 230). This is of course difficult to prove, but the continuity in the much-used dance motif in funerary art indicates that traditional dance was maintained in Illyria-Dalmatia during the Roman Period as well. Iconographical renderings such as the Japodian urn from Ribić (Fig 8.3), indicate that in the 5th century BC there was a connection between a ritual dance and the consumption of intoxicating beverages. As Rasmus Brandt demonstrates, the combination of consuming intoxicating beverages and ecstatic ritual dance was common in funerary practices in Etruria (Brandt, this volume). The Etrurians descended from the Villanova culture which we know negotiated culturally with the Illyrians, and among European Iron Age populations in general there was more or less frequent contact and negotiation of cultural practices.

When foes become friends: from diversity to 'standardisation'?

Considering the blend of indigenous groups, the variation in burial customs during the Roman Period is not surprising. Although the practice of tumuli burials continued as late as into the second century in the more distant areas, cremation according to Roman burial tradition became the dominant way of depositing the dead in the 1st century AD (Wilkes 1992: 242–43). The grave stelae became popular in Dalmatia at the same time as the simple, Roman cremation urns began to dominate. However, it should not be excluded that some groups may still have practiced inhumation and marked the graves with stelae. It seems, nevertheless, that the stelae in Dalmatia, as in most parts of the Roman Empire, were erected in connection with cremation burials.

During the 1st century BC, the Greek colonists on the islands off the Illyrian coast still performed their traditional burial rites. The Roman settlers along the coast and in the emerging centres followed the Roman way of burying their dead, which in this period had many features in common with the Greek or Hellenistic grave customs. In the indigenous communities, the combination of indigenous iconography and grave inscription illustrates a hybrid result of the encounters between Illyrian, Greek, and Roman burial cultures (Rendić-Miočević 1967: 139–56). Local customs did not disappear easily and grave urns of the typical 'Japodian' style as well as the 'Liburnian'

Fig. 8.3. Japodian cremation urn (drawing after Wilkes 1992 fig. 1992b).

and south Illyrian grave markers, or *cippi,* continued to be used during the Roman Period; not even the tumuli were completely out of fashion yet (Rendić-Miočević 1961: 144; Sergejevski 1949–1950: 45–93; Rendić-Miočević 1961). The options for burial type were many and there is no clear pattern for how and why a certain choice of burial was made.

Burial practice soon became quite uniform once under the sway of the Roman Empire. The most important variations appear in the iconography of the grave stelae. The iconography reflects rituals and attitudes towards the afterlife and differences within society, social and cultural. In many cases, however, it is difficult to discern the origin of the different practices, as the general image soon contained impulses from many parts of the Roman Empire. In the provinces the interpretation of form and ritual content on the basis of iconography is complicated, as there was a transformation from indigenous practices to the more 'standardised' Roman customs, which in turn caused ritual changes. In addition, large numbers of slaves, soldiers and military veterans immigrated from every corner of the Empire, bringing their own traditions and rituals along.

It is possible to distinguish the more Roman mainstream style and iconography on the stelae of the colonies from the more crude expressions of the local workshops, which traditionally have been referred to as 'provincial' monuments. These stelae are, however, not merely low quality imitations of the 'Stadtrömische' grave stelae, but indications of the beliefs about afterlife in this part of the Roman Empire. They carry symbols which had cultural and religious significance for these areas and its inhabitants. The differing containers and iconographic expressions seem to be reflections of local variations.

From the site of the Roman colony Narona (Vid) near Metković on the Dalmatian coast, simple cremation urns (Figs 8.4a–b), tituli, cippi, and grave stelae with architectonic and military elements are all represented through several examples. Further south along the coast, at the site of Butua (Budva) in Montenegro, cinerary urns with indigenous symbols have been found side by side with the more 'mainstream' Roman cylindrical urns. In the same contexts, there were small conical tombstones interpreted as grave markers (Wilkes 1992: 243; Rendić-Miočević 1966: 151 with attempted reconstruction).

In the 1st and 2nd centuries there was another practice with hut-like, erect cippi with conical roofs, among the Liburnian branch of the Illyrians, situated in the northern part of Illyria (Wilkes 1992: 243; Cambi 2005: 58). The variations in burial practice seem to rely on trends and local tastes rather than being indications of diverging ideas about death and the afterlife or ritual changes. Often it seems that the burials were marked with what was at hand, with a somewhat casual result. This is in itself an interesting observation, as the heterogeneity in the grave markers indicates that the burial rituals were of individual, negotiable and hybrid character during the first centuries of Roman rule in Dalmatia. The general image seems to reflect multiple choices rather than a clear-cut shift in tradition caused by the immigrating groups.

The find contexts of the various cinerary containers (compare Figs 8.4a–b) are located close to slightly earlier indigenous settlements and burial mounds, and it is

Fig. 8.4. Roman cremation urns. Vid, Archaeological Museum (Narona) (photo: M. Prusac).

common to find Roman cemeteries adjacent to Illyrian mounds. This indicates both population continuity and a break with tradition from the beginning of the Imperial Period. The landscape, with a chain of mountains limiting the settlement areas to valleys and plains, caused the Roman immigrants to settle in areas that were already inhabited by indigenous groups. The Roman settlers with time blended with the indigenous populations; intermarriage between Roman soldiers and local women was common from the middle of the 2nd century onwards (Wilkes 1969: 317). By then the distinctions between the tombs of people of indigenous descent and those of immigrant descent had almost disappeared, although cultural differences remained between the iconographic expressions on the grave markers in the urban coastal areas and those in the more remote inland settlements. In these remote areas the frequent use of symbols, which can be traced back to pre-Roman times, suggests that pre-Roman cultural traits survived more exclusively and unblended than along the coast

In the second half of the 2nd century AD, there was a dramatic change in Roman burial customs, from cremation of the dead and the use of cremation urns with grave reliefs to inhumation, often in sarcophagi of stone. This change of tradition happened in Dalmatia, as elsewhere in the Roman Empire (e.g. Cambi 2005: 107–8). Examples from Rome suggest that the changes in the burial practices from cremation to inhumation pertained merely to the form, and not the ritual content, which may partly explain why the production of grave reliefs could continue so freely (Morris 1992: 33). Sarcophagi were expensive, and with some exceptions, the grave reliefs continued to be used as markers on simple inhumation graves until Late Antiquity. In this period, sarcophagi became popular along the coast and in particular at Salona, where a local sarcophagus style emerged, influenced by eastern Greek workshops. The accumulation of simple stone sarcophagi beneath the floors of churches and along the roadside is characteristic of the burial practices of Dalmatia in the Early Christian Period.

There is no doubt that the uniformity and standardisation of both burial customs and rituals increased with the arrival of Christianity from the fourth century onwards. However, within the boundaries of the seemingly homogeneous Christian Roman Empire and one single religion, there also would have been great variation between different social strata and geographical areas.

The ritual significance of funerary art

The grave reliefs remained in use throughout the 2nd and 3rd centuries. In the hinterlands of the larger coastal towns the 'Romanised' motifs flourished in funerary art. In the remote mountain settlements the local iconography dominated and often included pre-Roman deities such as versions of a triad of mother goddesses, or nymphs, and solar and fertility symbols (e.g. Basler 1966: 151). The symbols which appear in the Illyrian-Roman stelae are known from large parts of Iron Age Europe, but they seem to have been more persistent in the interior of Dalmatia, perhaps due to the inaccessible terrain of the mountainous landscape, which isolated the inhabitants from foreign cultural influence. The examples abound. In the funerary reliefs from Zenica and from Opačić near Glamoč, both in Bosnia-Herzegovina, from the 2nd and 3rd centuries AD, there are several examples of non-Roman traits (e.g. Cambi 2005: 39, 202). Swastikas, spirals and wheels are rendered in a crude style. These symbols, which are traditionally interpreted as solar signs, appear most frequently in the Illyrian-Roman funerary art.

In the example from Zenica the swastikas which can be interpreted as solar symbols are rendered in the garment of one of the four depicted, which represent the deceased (Fig. 8.5). This relief is particularly interesting as it has been argued, on the basis of stylistic interpretations, that it may reference pre-Roman woodcarving art (e.g. Abramić 1928: 53; Sergejvski 1943: 163; 1949–1950: 86–87; Rendić-Miočević 1955: 7; Benac & Pašalić 1966: 265; Prusac 2007: 265; in comparison, see Cambi 1968: 133–34).

Such symbols, which can be traced back to pre-Roman times, appear frequently in grave reliefs in Dalmatia during the Roman Period. They are not unique to the Illyrians and many of them had probably already been imported from the Aegean during the Bronze Age (Harding 1976; Štipčević 1977: 186), but the survival of these elements in the Roman Period are interesting because they suggest ritual adaption to new burial forms among groups with local traditions. The pre-Roman symbols in the Romanised grave forms are examples of hybrid memories which indicate that there was a change in form, but a certain continuity in pre-Roman ideas and beliefs.

The votive reliefs of Roman Dalmatia show a similar pattern of hybridisation. Here, the popularity of the cult of the nymphs, a version of the *matronae* (Herz 2003: 144), suggests that the tradition was ancient, already in Roman times (Fig. 8.6). The *translatio romano* of these female deities shows continuity in local beliefs at the same time as they clearly exemplify the adjustment to Rome as the dominating power, and the 'Romanised' versions of nymphs can thus be perceived as examples of hybrid memories.

The arrival of Others: shared symbols – different meanings

New rituals and beliefs in the afterlife came with the arrival of soldiers from the eastern parts of the Empire. The soldiers observed the customs of the host community and reconstructed a required selection of rules for practical conduct (Schutz 1944: 503–7). Migration theories often consider the social consequences of the hybrid customs of the immigrants as a kind of identity creation (Barth 1969). When the newcomers changed their positioning towards the locals, a 'we-relationship' emerged (Naum 2008: 264–67). Within the 'standardised' Roman world, there were great opportunities for 'we-relationships.' This is visible in the funerary iconography, which mirrors conformity to social practices and ritual adjustment together with the wish to be remembered (D'Ambra 1998: 114).

Soldier veterans composed one such group of the population in Dalmatia which to some extent sought to conform to social practices. Grave monuments erected in memory of immigrant soldiers appear in large numbers in Dalmatia from the beginning of the 1st century AD and throughout the 2nd century, particularly at Salona and Narona and at the *castra* of Tilurium and Bigeste (Figs 8.7–8.8). The majority of these reliefs commemorate military veterans from the *Legio VII*. The reliefs are decorated with

Fig. 8.5. Grave stele from Zenica in Bosnia-Herzegovina. Sarajevo, Zemaljski Muzej, courtesy of Adnan Busuladžić.

Fig. 8.6. Cult relief with nymphs from Opačić near Glamoč, in Bosnia-Herzegovina. Sarajevo, Zemaljski Muzej, courtesy of Adnan Busuladžić.

architectural elements carved in a regional style, and their iconographic details and the cultural identity of the commemorated soldiers have received a lot of interest (Sanader 2003; Paškvalin 1985b; Medini 1984; Dodig 1985; Cambi 1993: 154–56; Waelkens 1986: 17; Hoffmann 1905: 54–59; see Cambi 2003: 511 note 5 for several others). The discussion is mainly about the extent to which the reliefs indicate a presence of individuals from the East. Sculpted heads which appear on the gable of the reliefs have been interpreted as representations of the mythological figure Attis, the lover of the mother goddess from the Near East, Cybele. Belief in resurrection was an important feature in the myth of Attis (Vermaseren 1977). The cult of Cybele and Attis thus conveyed the popular message of life after death, which attracted soldiers in particular, who were constantly faced with the danger of losing their lives in battle.

In the beginning the Romans were sceptical about the fertility cult of Cybele and its adherents. The rites of the cult included the castration of priests, which in Roman eyes was an utterly barbaric custom. However, through the large number of eastern soldiers in the Roman army, the cult of Cybele gained importance during the 3rd century AD. It became fused with more traditional Roman mother goddess cults, such as that of Magna Mater.

The cult of Cybele is important here, because it found some of its most loyal worshippers among the members of the *Legio VII*, the veterans of which settled at Bigeste near Narona (Medini 1984: 107–27; Hofmann 1905: 54–59). The identification of Attis in the soldier reliefs of the *Legio VII* is congruent with identifications of the lion heads and lion protomes as symbols used in the cult of Cybele (Paškvalin 1985: 119–23). Some scholars argue, however, that two other figures in these reliefs, previously also interpreted as Attis, are instead Roman barbarian captives from the East, as they are generally represented in couples, and in a state of mourning (Cambi 2003, esp. 520; see also, Cambi 2005: 52–55). It is worth questioning whether the figures had a single meaning, or if they could be perceived in more than one way. To the common Roman soldier they could symbolise captives at the same time as they could be understood as references to the Cybele-Attis cult by its followers. The different interpretations would depend on the cultural references of the beholder and an individual's experiences at the time of encountering 'the Other'.

It has been argued that these funerary reliefs may have been made in one particular workshop, probably at Tilurium, a plausible argument with regard to the style and technique in which they are executed (Cambi 2003: 512; Sanader 2003: 510; Cambi 2005: 55). The view that they are not to be interpreted in relation to the many eastern soldiers in Dalmatia is untenable though, as the presence of soldiers from Asia Minor is well testified here through epigraphic evidence (Alföldy 1965: 136; also, Dodig 2003: 365–66). The argument is equally unfounded that they would not be comparable because the doors of the reliefs differ from those on monuments in Asia Minor. Both style and iconography were transformed when introduced to new areas, in the same way as cultic rituals (cf. Cambi 2003: 511–12). The fact that similar doors, with lion protomes, exist on sarcophagi from the second century AD from Salona proves neither that they represent a local tradition nor an external influence (cf. Cambi 2005: 92 fig. 130). The bronze figurines of Attis from the areas of Humac and Muć, and an altar from Klis which refers to a sanctuary of Cybele, confirm the presence of the cult of Cybele among soldiers here (Vermaseren 1977: 142–43).

Two of the three inscriptions known from these reliefs leave no doubt that the deceased were from the East, clearly expressing that their hometowns were Amblada and Pessinus (Vermaseren 1977: 511 with reference to Hoffmann 1905: 56–57 and

CIL 3.9726 and 9737 for Pessinus and Amblada respectively). A direct influence from Pessinus, the place of origin of the cult of Cybele, may be possible, as it is well known that Syrian soldiers in foreign lands remained loyal to their goddess (Vermaseren 1977: 142; see also Cumont 19). The third inscription indicates that one soldier came from Hispania Tarraconensis (Cambi 2003: 511), but this cannot prove that this kind of grave stelae emerged independently of the eastern soldiers. Rather, it was common for soldiers to practice the cults of the areas where they stayed (Mellor 1992: 390), and this soldier, more precisely of the *Cohors I Bracaraugustorum*, may have adapted to local cult practices. Considering the significance of eastern cults in military communities, there is no reason why a western soldier could not have venerated an eastern god. The connection between the Phrygian figures and the lions in a funerary context can only be an allusion to life after death and to the important message of rebirth transmitted by the Cybele cult. It is difficult not to assume that soldiers from Asia Minor were commonly followers of the Cybele cult, and that an individual from Pessinus, the city of origin of Cybele, must have related to Cybele's lions and Attis as at least one of maybe several interpretations of the stele. After all, ambiguity and polysemy was not new in the Roman world (Elsner 1995: 191), nor was manipulation of iconography to create contrasting or common identities (Berry & Lawrence 1998: 8).

Some groups, which maintained more local traditional cult practices with elements handed down over time in the renderings of pre-Roman symbols, were probably also particularly open to eastern cults brought there by the soldiers, such as that of Cybele and Mithras. Like the cult of Cybele, that of Mithras flourished in the Balkans from the 3rd century AD onwards because of the strong military presence in the area (Mellor 1992: 39; Rendić-Miočević 1982: 121–40).

Hybrid memories and blended burial customs

At the outset, during the 1st century AD, distinctly different burial customs changed into more uniform practices and rituals of a 'Romanised' character. The monumental tumuli which earlier had expressed the status of the deceased were gradually abandoned on behalf of smaller grave markers with iconography. There was a shift in focus from the demonstration of social status and control of the landscape into the demonstration of social position in urban societies. Through the iconography introduced by Greek and Roman culture, the indigenous and 'Romanised' groups could express their ideas in a common iconographic language, often combined with traditional symbols. References to indigenous beliefs and rituals were used side by side with, and often expressed through, a Roman iconographic language.

The iconography reveals some of the ideas and beliefs connected with afterlife, since it often refers to solar and fertility cults, sometimes connected with versions of a mother goddess cult. The indigenous solar and mother goddess cults evidently found new expressions through Greek and Roman art, resulting in hybrid representations. The

Fig. 8.7. Military grave stele, of Quintus Metius. From Salona. Split, Archaeological museum, courtesy of the museum. (Photo: Tonci Šešer).

Fig. 8.8. Military grave stele, of Quintus Metius. From Salona. Split, Archaeological museum. Courtesy of the museum. (Photo: Tonci Šešer).

'Romanised' or 'Roman provincial' grave stelae represent the general 'trend', which was the burial practice of the dominating power; a structuralising and standardising element.

The Roman tradition provided the indigenous groups with multiple possibilities in the choice of ornamentation. The local and individual freedom discernible in funerary art reveals continuity in pre-Roman beliefs. These elements could, however, carry different connotations to different groups. Various ideas could meet in shared symbols. The differences expressed social identities between local groups, whereas shared symbols indicate negotiation and translation. Thus, the hybrid memories, which are represented in the grave material, reveal a combination of ideas which at the outset were contrasting and sometimes conveyed by force of arms, but which gradually, after the Roman annexation, reflected a peaceful exchange of beliefs and negotiation of common features. On a larger scale, the Roman burial customs reflect the central power of Rome in Dalmatia, whereas on a smaller scale local memories continued, and immigrants brought their own variants of the 'Romanised' burial tradition. Dominance, influence and negotiation between different groups about shared interests changed the burial rituals into a more equal form with an unequal content (Parker Pearson 2000: 247).

Conclusions

We know very little in detail of the burial rituals performed in Dalmatia in the Late Illyrian and Roman Periods. The many Illyrian tumuli are relatively mute regarding burial ritual, yet they often tell us more than burials of the Roman Period; very few intact graves are known from the period of cremation graves (mid-1st to mid-2nd century AD), only their grave markers. Even the later inhumation graves tell us little in this regard, since Romans did not express their rituals in their burials to the same extent as the Illyrians. However, important information can nevertheless be gathered from the grave stelae of the Roman Period. In the first stage, the various burial customs clearly express very distinct and different burial rituals among the Illyrian inhabitants on the one hand and the Italic settlers on the other. They coexisted in this first stage of contact, but Illyrian burial customs disappear in the course of the 1st century AD, and more uniform 'Roman' burial customs become ubiquitous. The standardisation of the eclectic Roman world offered opportunities for more individual choices to be made. By the 3rd century AD the funerary iconography had become a suitable point of reference for all, despite the diverse social and cultural groups involved. While it may have appeared uniform at one level, the funerary iconography had multiple meanings and could be read or understood in different ways, thus satisfying the needs of a broad range of peoples.

The inhabitants of the province Dalmatia encompassed a vast spectrum of cultural identities; from the rural inhabitants in the distant hinterland with their still vivid memory of past Illyrian traditions to the immigrant soldiers from different corners of the Empire with their specific religious traditions. The burial custom of the Roman Empire was on the surface uniform everywhere. Naturally, this does not mean that the burial *rituals* were identical everywhere, since its inhabitants had so many different religious and cultural identities. It is safe to presume that religious beliefs differed quite markedly from the 'Roman Illyrian' peasant of the hinterland to the Italic urban magistrate and the Asian or Spanish legionnaire, although all were inhabitants of the province Dalmatia in the Roman Empire and shared similar burial customs. With such different religious and cultural identities it is probable that the rituals carried out in connection with burial were diverse and differed from each other.

Bibliography

Abramić, M. 1928: 'Nekoliko skulptura antiknih božanstva', *Vjesnik za arheologiju i historiju dalmatinsku* 50: 52–61.

Alföldy, G. 1965: *Bevölkerung und Gesellschft der Römischen Provinz Dalmatien*, Akadémiai Kiadó: Budapest.

Barth, F. 1969: *Ethnic Groups and Boundaries. The Social Organization of Cultural Difference*, Universitetsforlaget: Oslo.

Basler, Đ. 1966: 'Arhitetura kasnoantičkog doba u Bosni i Hercegovini, kasnoantički doba', in *Kulturna istorija Bosne i Hercegovine*, Veselin Masleša: Sarajevo.

Basler, Đ., Čović, B. & Miletić, N. (eds) 1988: *Arheološki leksikon Bosne i Hercegovine*, vol. 3, Zemaljskog muzeja Bosne i Hercegovine: Sarajevo.

Beck, U. 1986: *Risikogesellschaft. Der Weg in eine andere Moderne*, Suhrkamp: Frankfurt.

Benac, A. & Pašalić, E. et al. (eds) 1966: *Kulturna istorija Bosne i Hercegovine, Cetinska krajina od prethistorije do dolaska Turaka*, Veselin Masleša: Sarajevo.

Berry, J. & Laurence, R. (eds) 1999: *Cultural Identity in the Roman Empire*, Routledge: London.

Bhabha, H. K. 1994: *The Location of Culture*, reissued edition 2004, Routledge: London.

Cambi, N. 1968: 'Silvan – Atis, primjer kultnog sinkretisma', *Diadora* 4: 131–42.

Cambi, N. 1993: 'Stele iz kasnoantičke grobnice u Dugopolju', *Vjesnik za arheologiju i historiju dalmatinsku* 86: 154–56.

Cambi, N. 2003: 'Attis or someone else on Funerary Monuments from Dalmatia?', in Noelke (ed.), 511–21.

Cambi, N. 2005: *Kiparstvo rimske Dalmacije*, Književni krug: Split.

Cooper, N. J. & Webster, J. (eds) 1996: *Roman Imperialism. Post-Colonial Perspectives*, School of archaeological studies, University of Leicester: Leicester.

Cumont, F. 1906: *Les religions orientales dans le paganisme romain*, E. Leroux: Paris.

D'Ambra, E. 1998: *Art and Identity in the Roman Empire*, Weidenfeld and Nicolson: London.

Dodig, R. 1985: 'De Lubussa disputationes archeologicae et epigraphicae', in Zelenika, A. et al. (eds): *100 godina muzeja na Humcu*, Samuopravna interesna zajednica kulture Općine: Ljubuški, 110–12.

Dodig, R. 2003: 'Spomenik kvinta Valerija iz Hardomija kod Ljubuškoga (Monumentum Quinti Valeri e Hardomilje apud Ljubuški)', *Vjesnik za arheologiju i historiju dalmatinsku* 95: 363–74.

Earl, T. K. 1987: 'Chiefdoms in archaeological and ethnohistorical perspective', *Annual Review of Anthropology* 16: 279–308.

Elsner, J. 1995: *Art and the Roman Viewer*, Cambridge University Press: Cambridge.

Girardi Jurkić, V. 2002: 'Najznačanije nekropole i groblja', *Histria antiqua* 8: 11–36.

Halbwachs, M. 1925: *Les cadres sociaux de la mémoire*, Librairie Félix Alcan: Paris.

Halbwachs, M. 1992: *On Collective Memory*, Chicago University Press (English translation of Halbwachs 1952): Chicago.

Harding, A. F. 1976: 'Illyrians, Italians and Mycenaeans. Trans-Adriatic Contacts during the Late Bronze Age', *Iliria* 4: 157–62.

Herz, P. 2003: 'Matronenkult und kultische Mahlzeiten', in Noelke (ed.), 139–48.

Hodder, I. 2000: 'Symbolism, Meaning and Context', in Thomas (ed.), 86–96.

Hoffmann, J. 1905: *Römische Militärgrabsteine der Donauländer* (Sonderschriften Archäologisches Österreichisches Instituts 5), A. Hölder: Vienna.

Huskinson, J. (ed.) 2000: *Experiencing Rome. Culture, Identity and Power in the Roman Empire*, Routledge: London.

Jovanović, A. 1984: *Rimske nekropole na teritoriji Jugoslavije.* University of Belgrade (Cyrillic script): Belgrade.

Lindhagen, A. 2009: 'The Lamboglia 2 and Dressel 6A Transport Amphorae: A Central Dalmatian Origin?', *Journal of Roman Archaeology* 21: 83–108.

Marović, I. 1980: 'Prahistorijska istrazivanja u okolici Narone (Recherches préhistoriques aux environs de Narona)', in *Dolina rijeke Neretve od prethistorije do ranog srednjeg vijeka (La vallee du fleuve Neretva depuis la prehistoire jusqu'au debut du Moyen age*, Hrvatsko Arheološko Društvo: Split, 45–105.

Medini, J. 1984: 'Spomenici s Atisovim likom na području Sinjske krajine', in Benac & Pašalić et al. (eds), 107–27.

Mellor, R. 1992: 'The Local Character of Roman Imperial Religion', *Athenaeum* 80: 385–400.

Morris, I. 1992: *Death Ritual and Social Structure in Classical Antiquity*, Cambridge University Press: Cambridge.

Naum, M. 2008: *Homelands lost and gained. Slavic Migration and Settlement on Bornholm in the Early Middle Ages* (Lund studies in historical archaeology), PhD diss., Lund University: Lund.

Noelke, P. (ed.) 2003: *Romanisation und Resistenz im Plastik, Architektur und Inschriften der Provinzen des Imperium Romanum. Neue Funde und Forschungen. Akten des VII internationalen Colloquiums über Probleme des Provinzialrömischen Kunstschaffens, Köln 2. bis 6. Mai 2001*, Philipp von Zabern: Mainz.

Nora, P. 1984: *Les lieux de mémoire I: La République XVII–XLII*, Gallimard: Paris.

Parker Pearson, M. 2000: 'Mortuary Practices, Society and Archaeology', in Thomas (ed.), 246–65.

Paškvalin, V. 1985: 'Stele arhitektonske kompozicije na Humcu kod Ljubuškog', in Zelenika A. et. al (eds): *100 godina muzeja na Humcu*, Samuopravna interesna zajednica kulture, Općine: Ljubuški, 119–23.

Prusac, M. 2007: *South of the Naro, North of the Drilo, from the Karst to the Sea. Cultural Identities in South Dalmatia 500 BC–AD 500* (Acta Humaniora 312), PhD diss., University of Oslo: Oslo.

Prusac, M. 2011: 'Hybrid Deities in South Dalmatia', in *Bollettino di archeologia online, Direzione per le antichità. International Congress of Classical Archaeology. Meetings between Cultures in the Ancient Mediterranean* (http: //151.12.58.75/archeologia/bao_document/ articoli/2_PRUSAC.pdf).

Rendić-Miočević, A. 1982: 'Uz dva Silvanova svetišta u okolici Salone (A propos des deux sanctuaries de Silvan dans les environs de Salone)', *Arheološki radovi i rasprave* 8–9: 121–40.

Rendić-Miočević, D. 1955: 'Ilirske prestave Silvana na kultnim slikama s područja Dalmata (Représentations illyriennes de Sylvanus sur les monuments du culte dans le domain Dalmate)', *Glasnik Zemaljskog muzeja u Sarajevu* 10: 5–40.

Rendić-Miočević, D. 1961: 'La tombe illyro-romaine à la lumière des nouvelles fouilles et decouvertes en Yugoslavie', in Susini (ed.), 143–54.

Rendić-Miočević, D. 1967: 'Problemi romanizacije Ilira s osobitim obzirom na kultove i onomastiku', *Centar za balkanološka ispitivanja* 2: 139–56.

Said, E. W. 1978: *Orientalism*, Pantheon: New York.

Sanader, M. 2003: 'Grabsteine der Legio VII aus Tilurium – Versuch einer Typologie', in Noelke (ed.), 501–10.

Schutz, A. 1944: 'The Stranger: An Essay in Social Psychology', *American Journal of Sociology* 49.6: 499–507.

Sergejevski, D. 1949–1950: 'Japodske urne', *Glasnik Zemaljskog muzeja u Sarajevu* 4-5: 45–93.

Štipčević, A. 1977: *The Illyrians. History and Culture*, Noyes Press: Park Ridge (N. J.).

Susini, G. (ed.) 1961: *Atti del settimo Congresso internazionale di archeologia classica*, "L'Erma" di Bretschneider: Rome.

Thomas, J. (ed.) 2000: *Interpretive Archaeology. A Reader*, Leicester University Press: London.

Urso, G. (ed.) 2004: *Dall'Adriatico al Danubio. L'Illirico in età greca e romana. Atti del convegno internazionale, Cividale dei Friuli, 25–27 settembre 2003*, Edizioni ETS: Pisa.

Vermaseren, M. J. 1977: *Cybele and Attis, the Myth and the Cult*, Thames and Hudson: London.

Waelkens, M. 1986: *Die kleinasiatische Türsteine, typologische und epigraphische Untersuchungen der kleinasiatischen Grabreliefs mit Scheintür*, Philipp von Zabern: Mainz.

Wilkes, J. J. 1969: *Dalmatia*, Harvard University Press: Cambridge (MA).

Wilkes, J. J.1992: *The Illyrians*, Blackwell: Oxford.

COMMEMORATING THE DEAD IN NORTH AFRICA
Continuity and Change from the Second to the Fifth Century CE

Eric Rebillard

This paper argues that a major change occurred in the ritual commemoration of the dead in North Africa during the third century when the sacrifice to the dead was abandoned and the banquet became the focus of attention. This hypothesis is based on the delicate conjunction of archaeological and textual data.

Keywords: Banquet, commemoration; Early Christianity, North Africa, sacrifice.

Funerary meals in the Graeco-Roman world seem to be one of those rituals that do not change. Attested abundantly from the 1st century BCE, they are still mentioned by Christian sources in the 5th or 6th century and even beyond. Ramsay MacMullen claimed that 'for hundreds of years, the pagan cult of the dead was a common part of Christianity'.[1] He was walking in the footsteps of Paul-Albert Février, who called the attention of scholars to a variety of evidence that attested the practice of funerary meals by Christians in the 3rd century.[2] After a long period during which any continuity between pagan and Christian practices was denied,[3] it was salutary to emphasise the similarities, and today nobody would argue against such a continuity.[4] However, historians and archaeologists tended to understand these rites in the light of the classical evidence and to conflate written and archaeological evidence of the 1st century with those of later periods.[5] Dealing with the Merovingian Period, Bonnie Effros underlined the danger of such an approach and proposed instead to focus exclusively on the early Medieval Christian communities in Gaul.[6] However, late antique Christian writers did compare the practices of their fellow Christians to what they usually describe as 'pagan' practices. Despite the difficulties involved, it is therefore worth trying to determine if commemorating rites changed between the 2nd century and the 5th. My own choice of North Africa as a test case is dictated by the availability of both written and archaeological evidence.

Dining with the dead in the 1st and 2nd centuries

We need first to outline the rituals as they are known from 1st and 2nd century evidence. The best starting point is the reconstitution recently proposed by John Scheid.[7] Even if our focus is on the commemoration of the dead,[8] we will consider first the funerals to which the commemorative rites are strictly parallel.[9]

On the day of the funerals, the Romans performed the sacrifice of a sow to Ceres next to the tomb.[10] The meat was then shared between the goddess, who received the *exta*, the dead, whose share was burned on the pyre, and the relatives, who ate together the remaining meat next to the tomb. Apuleius (*c.* 125–180), in the *Florida*, shed important light on this ritual when he relates how the famous doctor Asclepiades revived an apparently dead man:

> He immediately shouted out that the man was alive and that they should therefore do away with the torches, that the fire should be scattered far and wide, that the pyre should be demolished, and that they should take the funeral banquet from the tomb back to the table.[11]

The funeral meal thus reverted into an ordinary meal.[12] Apuleius indirectly attests that a table was set up next to the grave and that the living and the dead ate their respective share of the sacrifice.[13] This meal was known as the *silicernium* at the end of the Republic.[14]

Eight days later, on the *novemdialis*, the Romans performed a sacrifice to the Manes at the grave.[15] It was a sacrifice in holocaust in which the offering was completely burned. We also know that a banquet concluded the period of mourning.[16] Its location and even its date seem to have varied according to the importance of the dead and the family,[17] but Petronius in the *Satyricon* attests that it could be celebrated at the grave. A guest of Trimalchio, who arrived late to the dinner, explains where he had spent the first part of his evening:

> Scissa was having a funeral feast on the ninth day for her poor dear slave, whom she set free on his deathbed. [...] anyhow it was a pleasant affair, even if we did have to pour half our drinks over his lamented bones.[18]

John Scheid tentatively suggests that this banquet was associated with a sacrifice to the Lares.[19] What matters most, however, is that the banquet that concludes the funerals serves to separate the dead and the living. The food that the living eat at the banquet is different from the offerings sacrificed in holocaust to the Manes of the dead.[20]

According to John Scheid's reconstitution, the rituals commemorating the dead were parallel to the rituals for funerals. There was an individual commemoration of the dead, the *parentatio*, that took place on the anniversary of the death. The ritual is known through the decrees that describe the funeral honors for the heirs of Augustus, in particular the Pisan decrees for Lucius.[21] It was customary to perform a sacrifice in holocaust to the Manes of the dead at the grave every year, and no banquet followed.

There was also a collective commemoration of the dead, each year in February.[22] It was a period of ten days, starting with the *Parentalia* on February 13, followed by the *Feralia* eight days later on 21 February and completed on the 22nd by the *Caristia*. *Parentalia* and *Feralia* appeared to have been used for each other quite often in our sources, creating some confusion. Our understanding of the *Parentalia* depends on Virgil's description of the commemoration of Anchises' death in *Aeneid* 5.42–105 and Ovid's description of the *Feralia* in *Fasti* 2.533–570. Two elements are clearly attested on the *Feralia*: a sacrifice to the Manes of the dead and a banquet at the grave.[23] The following day, on the *Caristia*, another banquet was celebrated at home.[24] John Scheid tentatively proposes that a sacrifice to the Lares was done before the banquet of the *Feralia*.[25] Thus the parallel with the funerals would be total.

In 1st and 2nd century evidence, two kinds of rites are therefore attested at the grave for the commemoration of the dead: food offerings to the dead that are sacrificed in holocaust and banquets of the living that were probably also included in a sacrificial context.

Dining with the dead from the 3rd to the 5th century

Written evidence on funerary meals after the 2nd century are all Christian, making it difficult to trace any changes without simultaneously considering the impact of Christian practice.

According to Church historians, in the 2nd and 3rd centuries, funerary meals were forbidden to Christians because of their pagan character, but they came to be tolerated with the mass conversions following the conversion of Constantine, until a few clerics put an end to the practice in the second half of the 4th century.[26] The same evidence is always mentioned: Tertullian's affirmation in the *De spectaculis* that Christians do not sacrifice to the gods nor give any food to the dead, and that they do not eat from sacrifice or offerings to the dead;[27] Augustine's letter in which he says that 'when peace came to the Church, a mass of pagans who wished to come to Christianity were held back because their feast days with their idols used to be spent in an abundance of eating and drinking' and that '[his] predecessors thought it was opportune to tolerate these habits temporarily';[28] and finally the story of Augustine's mother, Monica, compelled in Milan to abandon her African custom to bring offerings of pottage, bread, and wine to the tombs of martyrs.[29] I have argued elsewhere against such an account that depends too much on Augustine's own 'piece of clerical euhemerism', as Peter Brown had called it.[30] Christian bishops at the end of the fourth century did not attempt to forbid funerary meals in general. Their reform was limited to martyr tombs and they left out of their sphere of control the private commemorative practices, especially as most of the dead who mattered for the people were not Christian.[31]

Tertullian makes several allusions to the pagan commemorative rites and always exhorts Christians not to perform them.[32] However, we cannot assume that Christians followed his recommendations and more often than not the confidence of his tone betrays the fact that at least some Christians were taking part in these rituals whether in remembrance of their own dead or in remembrance of the dead of their neighbors and friends.[33] The verb *parentare* and the noun *parentatio* are used to describe these rites and few details are given.[34] Tertullian establishes a strong parallel between the sacrifice to the gods and the *parentatio*, or sacrifice to the dead, but he also mentions the banquet. Thus in the *De spectaculis*, he says: 'we pay no sacrifice; we pay no funeral rite. No, and we do not eat of what is offered in sacrificial or funeral rite, because "we cannot eat of the Lord's supper and the supper of the demons"' (1 Cor 10: 21).[35] In the *De testimonio animae*, Tertullian does not mention the sacrifice, but describes a banquet at the grave: 'You call them in repose if you are venturing outside the gate to the tombs with dainty dishes and delicacies to entertain yourself in the name of the dead or if you are returning somewhat inebriated from the tombs. But I am demanding your sober opinion. You refer to them as miserable when you are speaking from your own perspective, when you are at a distance from them. You really cannot find fault with the state of the dead when you are reclining and carousing as if in their actual presence. You have to extol those on whose account you are at the moment living festively.'[36] The polemical intention certainly influences this description, but we can note that not only there is no allusion to a sacrifice, but that the meal is brought from home to the grave.[37] It is only in a figurative way that Tertullian implies that this meal was shared with the dead: what matters is that it takes place near or on the grave.

We should probably not put too much weight on such testimonies, but it is worth noting that in the only text where he is not interested in stressing that the gods are in fact divinised dead (by emphasising that their cult and the cult of the dead are one and the same), Tertullian does not associate the commemoration of the dead with a sacrificial context.

Cyprian may allude to funerary meals in Letter 67 addressed to the Christians of Legio, Asturica and Emerita in Spain. Cyprian accuses the bishop Martialis, in addition to obtaining a certificate of sacrifice, of being 'a habitué of the shameful and obscene banquets of a pagan *collegium*'.[38] As Martialis is also accused of having buried his sons in the funerary monument of the *collegium*, we can assume that some of these banquets were funerary meals, which were very often part of the activities of the *collegia*. Cyprian does not explicitly associate these banquets with idolatry, but denounces their excesses and immorality.[39] We should note, however, that the purpose of the excursus is to show that Martialis was living more like a pagan than like a Christian, up to the point of sacrificing during the persecution.

The testimony of Augustine is less ambiguous: when he mentions funerary meals, he does not associate them with sacrifices. In the *Confessions*, Augustine records that in Milan his mother Monica was stopped by the doorkeeper as she was bringing pottage, bread, and wine to the tombs of the martyrs as she was accustomed to do in Africa. She complied, explains Augustine:

> once she had ascertained, that Ambrose, illustrious preacher and exemplar of piety as he was, had forbidden the celebration of these rites even by those who conducted them with restraint, lest any opportunity might be given to drunkards to indulge in excess, and also because these quasi *parentalia* were so close kin to the superstitious practices of the pagans.[40]

The main concern of Ambrose is very clearly the risk of intemperance as is confirmed by mentions of funerary meals in his own works.[41] The mention that this practice resembles the *parentalia* – but *only* resembles them – could be taken as an indication that the Christian practice differs from the pagan one as no sacrifice was performed, but it might also only be due to Augustine's apologetic concerns about his mother that pervade all this anecdote.[42] It makes it difficult to use this incident as a testimony of actual practices. Augustine's description of what Monica was used to do in Africa is thus all about her temperance and restraint:

> She would bring her basket containing the festive fare which it fell to her to taste first and then distribute; but she would then set out no more than one small cup, mixed to suit her abstemious palate, and from that she would only sip for courtesy's sake. If it happened that there were many tombs of the dead to be honored in this manner she would carry round the same single cup and set it forth in each place. She thus served to her relatives extremely sparing allowances of the wine, which was not only heavily diluted, but by this time no more than lukewarm. What she sought to promote at these gatherings was piety, not intemperance.[43]

Despite this strong bias, a few details can be usefully pointed out. First, there is no reason to assume that in Africa Monica visited only the tombs of martyrs. The presence of some relatives rather suggests that she intended to honor the memory of her family's dead. Second, there is no trace of a sacrifice, or even of offerings brought to the dead. She was sharing with her relatives' food and drink brought from home at the grave of each departed she wanted to honor.

Other texts of Augustine attest similar practices. In a sermon preached in 410–412, he rails against the dying rich who, giving little thought to salvation, rejoice to be surrounded by children and grandchildren, for, according to verse 12 of Psalm 48, 'they will remember his name':

> 'These will invoke their names in their own lands.' What does that mean? They will carry bread and wine to the tombs, and there call upon the names of the dead. Just think how fervently the name of that rich man in the gospel must have been invoked after his death! People would have been getting drunk at his monument, yet not a drop found its way below to his burning tongue. The celebrants are providing a treat for their own bellies, not for the spirits of their ancestors. Nothing reaches the spirits of the dead except what they did for themselves while they were alive; if they did no good in their lifetime, nothing will avail them when they are dead.[44]

The parable of the rich man (Luke 16: 19–31) was mentioned by Augustine earlier in his sermon to emphasise the vanity of funerals and explains the reference to the impossibility of the rich man to quench his thirst. It should probably not be taken as a testimony for the practice of libations to the dead. The bread and the wine were for the living gathered around the grave for the commemoration of their departed parent.

In another sermon preached in the same years, Augustine explicitly mentions the *parentalia*:

> When we're dead, even if our parents, or dear ones, or relatives bring things along to our graves, they will bring them for themselves, the living, not for us, the dead. Scripture too, in fact, has mocked such practices, when it says about people who are insensible to good things that are presented to them, 'As if you were to lay a banquet', it says, "around a dead person' (Sir 30: 18) . . . It's obvious that this doesn't benefit to the dead, and that it's a custom of the pagans, and that it doesn't flow from the channel of justice derived from our fathers the patriarchs; we read about their funerals being celebrated; we don't read of *parentalia* being offered for them.[45]

Augustine underlines that these rites are useless, but does not denounce them as a form of sacrifice. The allusion to the *parentalia* is an attack against those Christians who seek to defend funerary meals by citing the verse from Tobit: 'Break your bread and pour out your wine on the tombs of the just' (Tob. 4: 17). Augustine rejects the literal interpretation and explains, in veiled terms, because not all of his listeners were baptised, that the bread and wine had to be understood allegorically as the Eucharist. If the mention of the *parentalia* in the *Confessions* was ambiguous, in this sermon, it seems to be just a label that the bishop uses to give authority to his claim that Christians reform their habits,[46] and therefore it does not say anything about what non-Christians actually did in their celebration of the *parentalia*.

There is an interesting inscription from Aïn-Kebira, in Mauretania Sitifiensis, dated 299 CE, that says:

> To the memory of Aelia Secundula. We all already have sent a lot of worthy things for the funeral of our mother Secundula and, above the place where she rests, we have decided to put up a stone table, where we will together remember all the things that she did. When the food has been brought and the cups have been filled and the cushions have been laid around, then in order to heal the painful wound, until late in the evening we will discuss gladly and with praises our honorable mother – and the old lady will sleep. Now she who nourished us lies here in eternal sobriety. She lived 72 years. Provincial year 260. Erected by Statulenia Julia.[47]

It is difficult to determine the exact location of the *mensa* in relation to the tomb, but the bringing of food to the tomb, the meal of the living and the evocation of the deceased is a striking parallel to what Augustine describes in his sermons and sometimes calls *parentalia*. The Christian character of the inscription cannot be unambiguously established,[48] and this suggests that the form of ritual for the *parentalia* here described might not be specific to Christians, but one shared with the non-Christians. It puts the emphasis on a meal of the living as an occasion for remembrance of the dead rather than on offerings made to the dead.

If these texts offer a valid testimony, it appears that, by the end of the fourth century at the latest, bishops alluded to the *parentalia* without referring to a sacrifice and that the ritual was now just a meal of the living at the grave.[49] The bishops deem the practice useless, but not contrary to Christianity. It consists of bringing food and drink to the tomb and sharing part of it on the spot with relatives and friends.

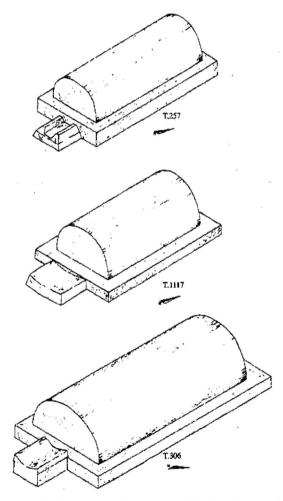

Fig. 9.1. Pupput, Cupula tombs 257, 1117, and 306 (drawings by F. Giomblanco, in Ben Abed & Griesheimer 2004: 319).

Material installations for the cult of the dead in North-African necropoleis from the 2nd to the 5th century

If we now turn to the material installations for the cult of the dead evinced in North-African necropoleis, there is some evidence that between the 2nd and the 5th century material installations for the sacrifice to the dead disappeared, to be replaced by installations for the banquet of the living. Before spelling out the difficulties attached to this conjunction between material and textual evidence, we need to review the archaeological data.[50]

In the necropolis located to the west of the ancient city of Tipasa (Algeria), some areas have been in use continuously from the 2nd to the 5th century and thus provide us with a rare situation in which we can see a change in the material installations for the cult of the dead.[51] This evidence is focused on 'ensemble II' and its 5 enclosures.[52] The earliest enclosure (*area* 2) comprised some 30 cupula tombs of the common North-African type (Fig. 9.1),[53] generally equipped with an offering table and also, in most cases, with a libation conduit. These tombs have been dated to the second and early third century.[54] Unfortunately the area around the tombs and the surface of the *mensae* are not documented in the publication, but we can probably assume that these *mensae* were used to burn offerings to the dead.[55] A masonry base (80 × 80 cm) built between tombs 4 and 5 has been interpreted as an intermediary type between the offering table attached to the tomb and the 4th and 5th century *mensa*-tomb that we will describe next. The table accordingly could have been used for the offerings to the dead, but also for the banquet of the living, the guests being seated on the basis of the cupula tombs that are around it.[56] However, the structure is too badly preserved and too poorly documented for any conclusive interpretation.

In *area* 3 we find both the cupula tombs and the so-called *mensa*-tombs. A very common type of *mensa*-tomb is represented by tomb 2.[57] On top of the tomb itself is built a rectangular masonry base of 3.13 × 2.50 m with a semi-circular depression in the centre of one side. The *mensa*-tomb therefore comprised both the reclining couches and the table itself. This type of installation is well represented in other Tipasa cemeteries.[58] More impressive is the installation associated with tomb 11.[59] The monument occupies some 65 square metres and is constituted of the following elements (Fig. 9.2): a U-shape masonry base of 6.6 × 6 m with a rectangular depression on the east side. The *mensa* is 80 cm high. The depression opens up on a rectangular room (5.5 × 3.4 m); along its northern side, a bench; a well was built on the southern side. Two sarcophagi (12 and 13 on the map) have been placed at some later point in the depression – a basin, to the southeast of the *mensa*, was providing water for cleaning the floor of the room and also through a canalisation for the cleaning of the surface of the *mensa*.

Even if absolute dating is not available, the *mensa*-tombs are clearly more recent than the cupula tombs of the enclosure.[60] There are many more *mensa*-tombs in the necropolis, all dated to the fourth and fifth century.[61] While the *mensae* in *area* 1 of 'ensemble I' are Christian,[62] there is no evidence that the *mensae* in other *areae* are.[63]

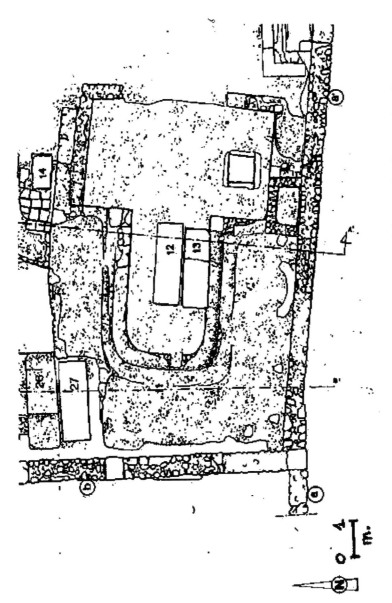

Fig. 9.2. Tipasa-Matarès, Mensa-tomb 11, 'ensemble II, area' (copied from Bouchenaki 1975: fig. 10).

There are *mensae* in other cemeteries at Tipasa, but none has been fully published.[64] They date for the most part to the fourth and fifth centuries and are usually built on top of sarcophagi.[65]

The western necropolis of Caesarea Mauretaniae (Cherchel, Algeria) is not as well documented.[66] In one sector, sector II, cupula tombs with offering tables and *mensae* are found side by side,[67] but only one *mensa* and its associated tomb have been excavated and published according to modern standards.[68] The *mensa* has the shape of a *triclinium* and covers a cremation. The grave-goods place the tomb in the second half of the 2nd century.[69] This *mensa* is thus the oldest one archeologically attested in North Africa. For Leveau, this proves that this type of installation is originally pagan, and not Christian.[70] There is very likely another *mensa* in the same sector, but no data were recoverable about it.[71] In the absence of a systematic excavation of the cemeteries of Caesarea, it is impossible to determine if there was a shift from one type of installation to the other.

The necropolis of Pupput (Hammamet, Tunisia) is not fully excavated yet, but an interim report is dedicated to the tables for food offerings.[72] Out of a total of 1,393 tombs excavated in 2000, 156 offering tables have been discovered (11%). They are mainly associated with cupula housing primary cremations: up to 22% of these tombs are equipped with an offering table. In most cases it is attached to one of the short sides of the tomb and typically where the head of the deceased is placed. These rectangular bases are usually 50–60 by 40 cm. The surface is very often burned and ashes and charcoal have been found in the ground around them, as well as a significant number of broken dishes attesting to the practice of libations. It is worth noting that libation conduits are otherwise rare at Pupput: five for a total of 1,393 tombs. The offering tables, which were quite common in the first half of the 2nd century, disappeared rather quickly at the beginning of the 3rd.[73] As the authors of the report conclude, they were thus associated with a Roman or a recently 'Romanised' population.[74] So far only one semi-circular installation for banqueting has been unearthed in façade of a mausoleum, but it is not yet published.[75]

At Leptiminus (Lamtah, Tunisia), a Roman cemetery was excavated in 1989, 1990 and 1991 on the north side of an aqueduct. Out of a total of 189 recorded burials, 48 have been fully excavated.[76] The cemetery was first laid out in the later second century and was mainly used during the 3rd and early 4th century. It was then buried in rubbish deposits in the later 4th and 5th centuries and has been partially destructed in modern time by the construction of lime kilns. There are also evidence of destruction and/or desecration of the tombs in Late Antiquity. That explains why the living layers were not preserved and that no evidence for commemorative rites could be recovered, except a few offering tables attached to cupula tombs.[77] The surface of the offering tables did not bear any trace of burning, but I am not sure that this is significant. No *mensa*-tomb has been found.

There are thus only a few cemeteries where we can compare installations for the cult of the dead from the 2nd to the 5th century. The change evinced at Tipasa in the western necropolis from offering tables to dinner tables cannot be confirmed directly in any other site. On the other hand no archaeological data invalidates the hypothesis of a more general shift. Moreover, there is some indirect evidence that such a shift took place. First, Lea Stirling has well established that the cupula tomb disappeared after the 3rd century.[78] The cupula tomb flourished during the 2nd and 3rd centuries as its shape was particularly well suited to marking and covering bodies laid out either for cremation *in situ* or for burial. There are some later examples, but they are much rarer. With them also disappeared the attached offering tables. Second, the use of the term *mensa* on epitaphs to designate the tomb itself dates to the end of the 3rd century in Mauretania where Paul-Albert Février was able to study a series of well-dated inscriptions.[79] Finally, there is an undeniable multiplication of *mensae* in later and Christian contexts in Africa and elsewhere in the Mediterranean world. Paul-Albert Février already pointed to this in his report on the cult of the dead at the Christian Archeology Congress of 1975 in Rome.[80]

Concluding remarks

North-African material installations for the cult of the dead show that the banquet becomes the focus of attention during the 3rd century, at the expense of the sacrifice to the dead. At the same time, written evidence abundantly attests that the banquet for the commemoration of the dead is an important act of piety, in a context in which sacrifices are unlikely to be performed. Without more excavations carried out with scientific methods, we do not have enough evidence to draw any definitive conclusions. Analysis of residues on the surfaces of the offering tables and the *mensa*-tombs, for instance, or the recovery of faunal and botanical remains on and around the tombs could bring important information on the rituals of commemoration.[81]

The conjunction of archaeological and textual data, though difficult to elaborate, presents us with convincing enough evidence to formulate the hypothesis that an important change in the ritual commemoration of the dead takes place during the third century. I think it is important to emphasise that this shift does not seem to be the result of a Christianisation of death nor does it seem to emerge from the context of new eschatological or cosmological circumstances. It takes place more or less at the same time as inhumation is replacing cremation as the dominant mode of disposing of the body in North Africa as in the rest of the Roman Empire. This latter change now tends to be explained as a shift in trends. I recently proposed that it should also be related to a new concern for the body.[82] Future explanations will have to take into account both changes and to look at all the other aspects of the relations of the living and the dead.

Notes

1   MacMullen 1997: 111.
2   Février 1978 [1996].
3   For a good example of this attitude, see Leclercq 1907. Some scholars had suggested that

the Christians who were commemorating their dead as the pagans were Donatists: Doignon 1969; Marrou 1949.

4   For a *status quaestionis*, see Jensen 2008.

5   A good example of this tendency is Giuntella, Borghetti & Stiaffini 1985; see a severe review by Duval 1986–1987.

6   Effros 2002: 71.

7   Scheid 2005: 161–209; see Lindsay 1998 for a general overview.

8   It must be emphasised right at the start that it is quite impossible to determine if the material installations were used for the funerals, the commemorative rites or both.

9   Cf. Scheid 1984.

10   Cicero: *Laws* 2.55, 57; Festus, 296–98 Lindsay. See Scheid 2005: 167–74.

11   Apuleius: *Florida* 19. 6: *Confestim exclamauit uiuere hominem: procul igitur faces abigerent, procul ignes amolirentur, rogum demolirentur, cenam feralem a tumulo ad mensam referrent.* English translation by J. Hilton, in Apuleius, *Rhetorical works*, Oxford: Oxford University Press, 2001, 172.

12   Scheid 2005: 169–70; see the commentary in Huninck 2001: 200.

13   Asclepiades died at an advanced age at the end of the 1st century and was active in Rome where the anecdote probably took place (see Huninck 2001: 198). The anecdote is related by Pliny (*Natural History* 26.12–15), but the details on the pyre and the food offerings are from Apuleius (see Harrison 2000: 126). So we can consider it valid testimony for the middle of the 2nd century.

14   Scheid 2005: 170–72.

15   See Porphyrio (3rd c.) on Horace: *Epodes* 17.48 (ed. F. Hauthal, Berlin, 1894, 535): *nam nouemdiale dicitur sacrificium, quod mortuis fit nona die, qua sepulti sunt.* On this sacrifice, Scheid 2005: 175–77; on the period of eight days, see Belayche 1995.

16   Scheid 2005: 175, wrongly indicates that Porphyrio mentions a *cena nouendialis.* The expression is found in Tacitus: *Annals* 6.5.1 on which see Bragantini 1991: 219–21. She contends that *nouendialis* is used as a substantive and that the passage in Tacitus means 'this banquet is like a funerary banquet' and not 'this is a funerary banquet'. On a similar use of *nouendiale* as a substantive, see Petronius: *Satyricon* 65.

17   Scheid 2005: 175.

18   Petronius: *Satyricon* 65: *Scissa lautum nouendiale servo suo misello faciebat, quem mortuum manu miserat. […] tamen suauiter fuit, etiam si coacti sumus dimidias potiones super ossucula eius effundere.* English translation by M. Heseltine & E. H. Warmington, Cambridge 1969 (Loeb Classical Library), 147.

19   Scheid 2005: 176–77, based on Cicero: *Laws* 2.55.

20   Scheid 2005: 182–88.

21   Pisan Decrees: *CIL* XI, 1420–21 (*ILS* 139–140). See Marotta d'Agata 1980 for a commentary and, more generally on this ritual, Scheid 2005: 193–200.

22   I leave aside the *Lemuria*, celebrated in May, as the rituals took place at home, and not at the grave. See Danka 1976 with Scheid 1984: 134–36.

23   Virgil: *Aeneid* 5.75–99: sacrifice of Aeneas to the Manes of Anchises; 100–104: preparations for the banquet of the Trojans.

24   Ovid: *Fasti* 2.571–638.

25   Scheid 2005: 182, based on Virgil: *Aeneid* 5.63–64 where the banquet of the Trojans is

anticipated by Aeneas' gift of bulls to them and his asking them to invite the Penates to their banquet. However, he adds: 'C'est possible, mais on peut tout aussi bien supposer que la famille apportait au cimetière des offrandes végétales. Dans ce cas, les célébrants consacraient des aliments spécifiques aux Mânes de la personne défunte, ou ils lui sacrifiaient une victime; avec d'autres aliments, qui ne faisaient pas partie de l'offrande précédente, et n'avaient donc pas été consacrés aux Mânes, ils préparaient ensuite un repas.'

26   For North Africa, see Quasten 1940; Saxer 1980; Kotila 1992; cf. Jensen 2008.

27   Tertullian: *De spectaculis* 13: see below.

28   Augustine: *Epistula* 29. 9.

29   Augustine, *Confessions* 6.2.2.

30   Brown 1981: 29.

31   Rebillard 2005.

32   Saxer 1980: 47–52 reviews the different texts.

33   In *De idolatria* 16, Tertullian makes the difference between performing pagan rites and attending them because of social or familial obligation and concedes that it is fine just to attend even a sacrifice. This text is quoted by Saxer 1980: 51, but not given the right relevance.

34   See Saxer 1980: 47–50.

35   Tertullian: *De spectaculis* 13: *Non sacrificamus, non parentamus. Sed neque de sacrificio et parentato edimus.* English translation by T. R. Glover, Cambridge 1931: 267 (Loeb Classical Library).

36   Tertullian: *De testimonio animae* 4: *Vocas porro securos, si quando extra portam cum obsoniis et matteis tibi potius parentans ad busta recedis aut a bustis dilutior redis. At ego sobriam tuam sententiam exigo. Misellos uocas mortuos, cum de tuo loqueris, cum ab eis longe es. Nam in conuiuio eorum quasi praesentibus et conrecumbentibus sortem suam exprobrare non possis.*

37   This does not exclude the possibility of a sacrifice to the Lares at home, but shows that the emphasis is on the meal at the grave itself.

38   Cyprian: *Ep.* 67.6.2: *gentilium turpia et lutulenta conuiuia in collegio diu frequentata.* English translation (modified) by G. W. Clarke, *The Letters of Cyprian. 4*, Newman Press: New York 1989 (Ancient Christian writers, 47), 25.

39   The point is made by Saxer 1980: 100–2; see Saxer 1984: 298–300.

40   Augustine: *Confessiones* 6.2.2: *Itaque ubi comperit a praeclaro praedicatore atque antistite pietatis praeceptum esse ista non fieri nec ab eis qui sobrie facerent, ne ulla occasio se ingurgitandi daretur ebriosis, et quia illa quasi parentalia superstitioni gentilium essent simillima, abstinuit se libentissime.* English translation by Maria Boulding: *The Works of Saint Augustine: A Translation for the 21st Century 1*, New City Press: New York 1997. See Courcelles 1968: 87–91.

41   Ambrose: *De Helia et ieiuno* 17.62 and *Expositio euangelii secundum Lucam* 7.43. See Rebillard 2003: 167–68.

42   O'Donnell 2005: 55–56, on Monica's religious practices as a cause of embarrassment for Augustine. O'Donnell suggests that bringing foods to the graves is a practice that Monica kept from the time she was Donatist, but, despite Marrou 1949 there is no evidence that it was more a Donatist practice than a 'Catholic' one.

43   Augustine: *Confessiones* 6.2.2: *illa cum attulisset canistrum cum sollemnibus epulis praegustandis atque largiendis, plus etiam quam unum pocillum pro suo palato satis sobrio temperatum, unde*

dignationem sumeret, non ponebat, et si multae essent quae illo modo uidebantur honorandae memoriae defunctorum, idem ipsum unum, quod ubique poneret, circumferebat, quo iam non solum aquatissimo, sed etiam tepidissimo cum suis praesentibus per sorbitiones exiguas partiretur, quia pietaem ibi quaerebat, non uoluptatem.

44   Augustine: *Enarratio I in Psalmum 48* 15: *Quid? Audi: Inuocabunt nomina eorum in terris ipsorum. Quid est hoc? Tollent panem et merum ad sepulcra, et inuocabunt ibi nomina mortuorum. Putas quantum inuocatum est nomen illius diuitis postea, quando inebriabant se homines in memoria ipsius, nec descendebat una gutta super linguam ipsius ardentem? Ventri suo seruiunt homines, non spiritibus eorum.* Translated by Maria Boulding: *The Works of Saint Augustine: A Translation for the 21st Century 3, no. 16,* New City Press: New York 2000.

45   Augustine: *Sermo 361* 6.6: *cum autem mortui fuerimus, etiamsi parentes nostri, aut cari, aut propinqui afferant ad sepulcra nostra, sibi afferent qui uiuunt, non nobis mortuis. Et haec quidem irrisit etiam scriptura, dicens de quibusdam bona praesentia non sentientibus : Tamquam si epulas, inquit, mortuo circumponas. [...] Et manifestum est hoc ad mortuos non pertinere, et consuetudinem hanc esse paganorum, non uenire de propagine illa et uena iustitiae patrum nostrorum patriarcharum, quibus exsequias celebratas esse legimus, parentatum esse non legimus.* Translated by Edmund Hill: *The Works of Saint Augustine: A Translation for the 21st Century 3,* no. 10, New City Press: New York 1995.

46   On paganisation as an issue of authority, see the comments of Brown 1995: 24.

47   CIL VIII, 20277 = ILCV, 1570. Text revised by Février 1964: 151: *Memoriae Aeliae Secundulae / Funeri multa quid(e)m condigna jam misimus omnes / insuper arequ(e) deposite Secundulae matri(s) / lapideam placuit nobis atponere mensam / in qua magna ejus memorantes plurima facta / dum cibi ponuntur calicesqu(e) et copertae / vulnus ut sanctur nos rod(ens) pectore saevum / libenter fabul(as) dum sera redimus ora / castae matri bonae laudesq(ue) vetula dormit / ipsa o nutrix, jaces, et sobriae semper. V(ixit) a(nnis) lxxv. A(nno) p(rovinciae) cclx. Statulenia Julia fecit.* English translation adapted from F. Van der Meer: *Augustine the Bishop: The Life and Work of a Father of the Church,* translated by B. Battershaw and G. R. Lamb, Sheed & Ward: London 1961: 501.

48   As the inscription was included by E. Diehl in his collection of *Inscriptiones Latinae Christianae veteres,* the Christian character of the inscription has usually not been discussed, but Février 1964: 129 expressed some serious reservations, comforted by his study of all the dated inscriptions from Mauretania.

49   A confirmation that sacrifice was not involved can be found in the *Apostolic Constitutions* (8.44), written in the area of Antioch around 380: priests who are invited to participate to commemorations of the dead are asked to eat and drink with moderation. Of course all sacrifices were officially forbidden by imperial laws since 391, but, as we know, such an interdiction was quite impossible to enforce.

50   I did not include in this review cemeteries excavated in the 19th or early 20th century because of the difficulties that their interpretation presents.

51   See Bouchenaki 1975.

52   The 'ensemble II', as the other ones, has arbitrary limits; the enclosures, or *areae,* are delimited by walls.

53   Cupula tomb have a half-barrel shaped top, placed on a rectangular basis: see Stirling 2007.

54   Bouchenaki 1975: 80–95. The dates are established by the grave-goods.

55   See the case of Pupput, *infra,* where it is archaeologically documented.

56 Bouchenaki 1975: 84, 95. He compares this type of installation to that described by Lancel 1970: 166.
57 Bouchenaki 1975: 105–6.
58 Bouchenaki 1975: 191–92 (n. 511) for a list with bibliography.
59 Bouchenaki 1975: 113–18; at 117 he notes that the presence of a tomb has not been positively established.
60 Bouchenaki 1975: 119; the relative chronology is based on the topography of the enclosure.
61 Bouchenaki 1975: 170–71.
62 Bouchenaki 1975: 16. On the *mensa* with an inscribed mosaic, see also Marrou 1979.
63 The inscription on *mensa*-tomb 8 in the area 3 of 'ensemble II' contains no evidence of Christianity: see Bouchenaki 1975: 110.
64 See *supra* n. 59.
65 See Février 1970: 191–99.
66 On the different funerary areas of Cherchel, see Leveau 1987. The western necropolis is described in Leveau 1971–1974; Leveau; 1975–1976; 1983.
67 Leveau 1983: 119–36.
68 Leveau 1975–1976.
69 Leveau 1975–1976: 129–30.
70 Leveau does not make explicit the criterion he uses for determining the 'religion' of the monument; I assume that it is the fact that it covers a cremation.
71 Leveau 1983: 130.
72 Ben Abed & Griesheimer 2004. For a general presentation, see Ben Abed & Griesheimer 2001.
73 Ben Abed & Griesheimer 2001: 585.
74 The eastern necropolis of Sitifis (Stif, Algeria) offers an interesting parallel to Pupput. Here too tombs housing primary cremations are quite regularly equipped with an offering table (22%), an installation that is rare otherwise in the necropolis. These tombs are dating from the second century and seem to be associated with the arrival of Roman veterans in the new colony; Février & Guéry 1980: 112, 124. The necropolis is published in Guéry 1985.
75 Ben Abed & Griesheimer 2001: 585.
76 See Mattingly, Stirling & Ben Lazreg 1992; Mattingly, Pollard & Ben Lazreg 2001. Another cemetery (site 200) is briefly described (but not published) in Ben Lazreg 2001.
77 Five offering tables were found: Ben Lazreg, Mattingly & Stirling 1992: 315–16.
78 Stirling 2007.
79 Février 1964.
80 Février 1978 [1996]: 222–26; see also Duval 1985: 437–41; 1995: 199–200. Février thought that the same shift happened in Ostia, but we now know that there the two kinds of installations seem to have coexisted and that banqueting couches were not built after the 2nd century; see Bragantini 1990: 70.
81 The difficulty is that sealed contexts allowing such analysis are available only in very few cases. Stirling 2004 considers only remains found in the tomb itself.
82 Rebillard 2003: 101–5.

Bibliography

Belayche, N. 1995: 'La neuvaine funéraire à Rome ou "la mort impossible"', in F. Hinard (ed.): *La mort au quotidien dans le monde romain*, de Boccard: Paris, 155–69.

Ben Abed, A. & Griesheimer, M. 2001: 'Fouilles de la nécropole romaine de Pupput (Tunisie)', *Comptes rendus de l'Académie des Inscriptions et Belles-Lettre*, 553–90.

Ben Abed, A. & Griesheimer, M. 2004: 'Les supports des offrandes funéraires dans la nécropole de Pupput (Hammamet, Tunisie)', in M. Fixot (ed.): *Paul Albert Février de l'Antiquité au Moyen Age: actes du colloque de Fréjus, 7 et 8 avril 2001*, Publications de l'Université de Provence: Aix-en-Provence, 309–24.

Ben Lazreg, N. 2001: 'Un cimetière romain sur Jebel Lahmar (Site 200) près de Dhahret Slama: fouille de sauvetage', in Stirling, Mattingly & Ben Lazreg (eds), 409–11.

Ben Lazreg, N., Mattingly, D. J. & Stirling, L. 1992: 'Summary of Excavations in 1990 and Preliminary Typology of Burials', in Ben Lazreg & Mattingly (eds), 301–33.

Ben Lazreg, N. & Mattingly, D. J. (eds) 1992: *Leptiminus (Lamta): A Roman Port City in Tunisia: Report no. 1* (Journal of Roman Archaeology. Supplementary Series 4), University of Michigan: Ann Arbor, MI.

Bouchenaki, M. 1975: *Fouilles de la nécropole occidentale de Tipasa (Matarès)*, Publications de la Bibliothèque nationale: histoire et civilisation 1: Alger.

Bragantini, I. 1990: in S. Angelucci, I. Baldassarre, I. Bragantini, M. G. Lauro, V. Mannucci, A. Mazzoleni, C. Morselli, F. Taglietti: 'Sepolture e riti nella necropoli di Porto all'Isola Sacra', *Bollettino di Archeologia* 5–6: 49–113.

Bragantini, I. 1991: '*Cena novendialis?*', *Annali dell'Istituto Universitario Orientale di Napoli. Sezione di archeologia e storia antica* 13: 219–21.

Brown, P. 1981: *The Cult of the Saints: Its Rise and Function in Latin Christianity* (The Haskell Lectures on History of Religion. n.s. 2), The University of Chicago Press: Chicago.

Brown, P. 1995: *Authority and the Sacred: Aspects of the Christianization of the Roman World*, Cambridge University Press: Cambridge.

CIL = *Corpus Inscriptionum Latinarum*, de Gruyter: Berlin 1863–.

Courcelles, P. 1968: *Recherches sur les Confessions de saint Augustin*, 2nd ed., de Boccard: Paris.

Danka, I.R. 1976: '*De Feralium et Lemuriorum consimile natura*', *Eos* 64: 257–68.

Doignon, J. 1969: '*Refrigerium* et catéchèse à Vérone au IVe siècle', in J. Bibauw (ed.): *Hommages à Marcel Renard* (Collection Latomus 102.2), Latomus: Bruxelles, 220–39.

Duval, N: 1985: 'Piscinae et mensae funéraires: de Salone à Aquilée', in *Aquileia, la Dalmazia e l'Illirico* (Antichità altoadriatiche, 26), Chiandetti: Udine, 1: 437–62.

Duval, N. 1986–1987: 'Review of Giuntella, Borghetti & Stiaffini', in *Karthago* 21: 163–70.

Duval, N. 1995: 'Les nécropoles chrétiennes d'Afrique du Nord', in P. Trousset (ed.): *L'Afrique du Nord antique et médiévale. Monuments funéraires, institutions autochtones* ([actes du] VIe Colloque international sur l'histoire et l'archéologie de l'Afrique du Nord, Pau, octobre 1993), Éditions du centre des travaux historiques et scientifiques: Paris, 187–205.

Effros, B. 2002: *Creating Community with Food and Drink in Merovingian Gaul*, Palgrave Macmillan: New York.

Février, P.-A. 1964: 'Remarques sur les inscriptions funéraires datées de Maurétanie césarienne orientale (IIe-Ve siècle)', *Mélanges d'Archéologie et d'Histoire de l'École française*, 76.1: 105–72.

Février, P.-A. 1970: 'Le culte des martyrs en Afrique et ses plus anciens monuments', in *Corso di cultura sull'arte ravennate e bizantina* 17: 191–215.

Février, P.-A. 1978 [1996]: 'Le culte des morts dans les communautés chrétiennes durant le

IIIe siècle', in *Atti del IX Congresso Internazionale di archeologia cristiana, Roma, 21–27 settembre 1975*. Vol. 1, *I monumenti cristiani precostantiniani* (Studi di antichità cristiana 32.1), Pontificio Istituto di archeologia cristiana: Città del Vaticano, 211–74 [= P.-A. Février: *La Méditerranée de Paul-Albert Février*, Rome: École française de Rome: Rome & Université de Provence: Aix-en-Provence 1996 (Collection de l'École française de Rome 225), vol. 1: 39–129].

Février, P.-A. & Guéry, R. 1980: 'Les rites funéraire de la nécropole orientale de Sétif', *Antiquités africaines* 15: 91–124.

Giuntella, A. M., Borghetti, G. & Stiaffini, D. 1985: *Mensae e riti funerari in Sardegna: la testimonianza di Cornus* (Mediterraneo tardoantico e medievale. Scavi e ricerche 1), Scorpione: Taranto.

Guéry, R. 1985: *La nécropole orientale de Sitifis (Sétif, Algérie): fouilles de 1966–1967*, Éditions du Centre national de la recherche scientifique (Études d'antiquités africaines): Paris.

Harrison, S. J. 2000: *Apuleius a Latin sophist*, Oxford University Press: Oxford.

Huninck, V. 2001: *Apuleius of Madauros, Florida*, ed. with a comment by Vincent Jan Christian Hunink, Gieben: Amsterdam 2001.

ILCV = *Inscriptiones Latinae Christianae veteres* (ed. E. Diehl), Weidmann: Berlin 1925–31.

ILS = *Inscriptiones Latinae Selectae* (ed. H. Dessau), Weidmann: Berlin 1892–1916.

Jensen, R.M. 2008: 'Dining with the Dead: From the *mensa* to the Altar in Christian Late Antiquity', in L. Brink & D. Green (eds): *Commemorating the Dead: Texts and Artifacts in Context*, de Gruyter: Berlin, 107–43.

Kotila, H. 1992: Memoria mortuorum*: Commemoration of the Departed in Augustine* (Studia Ephemeridis Augustinianum, 38), Institutum Patristicum Augustinianum: Rome.

Lancel, S. 1970: 'Tipasitana IV: la nécropole romaine occidentale de la porte de Césarée, rapport préliminaire', *Bulletin d'archéologie algérienne* 4: 149–266.

Leclercq, H. 1907: 'Agape', in *Dictionnaire d'archéologie chrétienne et de liturgie*, vol. 1.1: Paris, cols. 775–848.

Leveau, P. 1971–1974 : 'Une area funéraire de la nécropole occidentale de Cherchel', *Antiquités Africaines* 5: 73–152.

Leveau, P. 1975–1976: 'Une mensa de la nécropole occidentale de Cherchel', *Karthago*: 127–31.

Leveau, P. 1983: 'Recherches sur les nécropoles occidentales de Cherchel (Caesarea Mauretaniae), 1880–1961', *Antiquités Africaines* 19: 85–173.

Leveau, P. 1987: 'Nécropoles et monuments funéraires à Caesarea de Maurétanie', in H. von Hesberg & P. Zanker (eds): *Römische Gräberstrassen: Selbstdarstellung – Status – Standart (Kolloquium in München vom 28. bis 30. Oktober 1985)*, Verlag der Bayerischen Akademie der Wissenschaften (Abhandlungen/Bayerische Akademie der Wissenschaften, Philosophisch-Historische Klasse. n.F. 96): Munich, 281–90.

Lindsay, H. 1998: 'Eating with the Dead: The Roman Funerary Banquet', in I. Nielsen & H. S. Nielsen (eds): *Meals in a Social Context: Aspects of the Communal Meal in the Hellenistic and Roman World* (Aarhus Studies in Mediterranean Antiquity 1), Aarhus University Press: Aarhus, 67–80.

MacMullen, R. 1997: *Christianity and Paganism in the Fourth to Eighth Centuries*, Yale University Press: New Haven.

Marotta d'Agata, A. R. 1980: *Decreta Pisana (CIL, XI, 1420–21)*, edizione critica, traduzione e commento a cura di Alida Rosina Marotta D'Agata, Marlin: Pisa.

Marrou, H.-I. 1949: 'Survivances païennes dans les rites funéraires des donatistes', in *Hommages à J. Bidez et F. Cumont* (Collection Latomus 2.2), Latomus: Bruxelles, 193–203.

Marrou, H.-I. 1979: 'Une inscription chrétienne de Tipasa et le *refrigerium*', in *Antiquités africaines* 14: 261–69.

Mattingly, D. J., Stirling L. M. & Ben Lazreg, N. 1992: 'Excavation at Site 10: a Roman Cemetery on the Southeast Edge of Leptiminus', in Ben Lazreg & Mattingly (eds), 177–252.

Mattingly, D. J., Pollard, N. & Ben Lazreg, N. 2001: 'Stratigraphic Report, Site 10, 1991', in Stirling, Mattingly & Ben Lazreg (eds), 107–68.

O'Donnell, J. J. 2005: *Augustine: A New Biography*, Harper Collins: New York.

Quasten, J. 1940: '*Vetus superstitio et nova religio*: The Problem of *refrigerium* in the Ancient Church of North Africa', *Harvard Theological Review* 33: 253–66.

Rebillard, E. 2003: *Religion et sepulture: l'église, les vivants et morts dans l'antiquité tardive*, École des hautes études en sciences sociales: Paris.

Rebillard, E. 2005: '*Nec deserere memorias suorum*: Augustine and the Family-Based Commemoration of the Dead', *Augustinian Studies* 36.1: 99–111.

Saxer, V. 1980: *Morts, martyrs, reliques en Afrique chrétienne aux premiers siècles: les témoignages de Tertullien, Cyprien et Augustin à la lumière de l'archéologie africaine* (Théologie historique 55), Beauchesne: Paris.

Saxer, V. 1984: *Vie liturgique et quotidienne à Carthage vers le milieu du IIIe siècle: le témoignage de saint Cyprien et de ses contemporains d'Afrique*, 2nd ed. (Studi di antichità cristiana, 29), Pontificio Istituto di archeologia cristiana: Vatican City.

Scheid, J. 1984: '*Contraria facere*: renversements et déplacements dans les rites funéraires', *Annali dell'Istituto Universitario Orientale di Napoli. Sezione di archeologia e storia antica* 6: 117–39.

Scheid, J. 2005: *Quand faire, c'est croire: les rites sacrificiels des Romains* (Collection historique), Aubier: Paris.

Stirling, L. M. 2004: 'Archaeological Evidence for Food Offerings in the Graves of Roman North Africa', in R. B. Egan & M. A. Joyal (eds): *Daimonopylai: Essays in Classics and the Classical Tradition presented to Edmund G. Berry*, University of Manitoba Centre for Hellenic Civilization: Winnipeg, 427–51.

Stirling, L. M. 2007: 'The Koine of the Cupula Roman North Africa and the Transition from Cremation to Inhumation', in D. L. Stone & L. M. Sterling (eds): *Mortuary Landscapes of North Africa* (Phoenix. Supplementary volume, 43), University of Toronto Press: Toronto, 110–37.

Stirling, L. M., Mattingly, D. J. & Ben Lazreg, N. 2001: *Leptiminus (Lamta): A Roman Port City in Tunisia: Report no. 2* (Journal of Roman Archaeology. Supplementary Series 41), University of Michigan: Ann Arbor, MI.

CHURCHES AND GRAVES OF THE EARLY BYZANTINE PERIOD IN *SCYTHIA MINOR* AND *MOESIA SECUNDA**
The Development of a Christian Topography at the Periphery of the Roman Empire

Irina Achim

During the Proto-Byzantine Period (4th–6th centuries AD), the Roman provinces on the Lower Danube – such as Scythia Minor *and* Moesia Secunda, *nowadays located in the territory of Dobroudja (southeastern Romania and northeastern Bulgaria) – underwent profound political, administrative, cultural and social transformations. These changes coincided with the significant growth of Christianity in this geographical space. Recent research on Paleochristian basilicas and associated necropoleis and graves in* Scythia Minor *and* Moesia Secunda *has reopened the discussions on the processes behind the creation of a Christian topography in relation to Greek-Roman towns in this peripheral area of the old Empire. Since the relationship between churches and graves is important for understanding early Christian re-use of urban space, the archaeological funerary material has been organised into two major groups: graves found* intra ecclesiam *versus* extra ecclesiam. *By considering the development of a Christian landscape and the related social Christian topography, the analysis demonstrates the existence of two rather centripetal processes. Firstly, cemeterial churches appear to have been established exclusively outside the city walls in connection with or without existing necropoleis, before the graves move inside the walls in association with new or already established churches. Secondly, burials start outside the church walls and move progressively inside and towards the sanctuary of the church. A peculiar category, geographically limited to* Scythia Minor, *comprises the graves of martyrs. This study indicates a gradual development of a specific Christian space, followed by the crystallisation of a local tradition of relic worship.*

Keywords: Centripetal processes, *extra ecclesiam* graves, *intra ecclesiam* graves, martyr graves, *Moesia Secunda*, Paleochristian churches, re-use of urban space, *Scythia Minor*.

Burials, all inhumations, inside and in proximity to Paleochristian churches, represent an interesting manifestation of the spiritual life of Christian communities in Late Antiquity. By studying this phenomenon, one can obtain precious information concerning the topography of funerary areas in the 4th–6th centuries AD, the funerary practices, as well as the successive changes in the perception of the ecclesiastic architectural context that included burial sites, whether isolated or organised into cemeteries. An analysis of graves and churches in relation to each other will further the understanding of the processes operating behind the transformation of the ancient *polis/urbs* into a Christian city (Dagron 1977: especially pp. 11–19; Dagron 1991; Ivison 1996; Bonnet & Privati 2000; Karagiorgou 2001: especially pp. 194–96, concerning the burial sites of Thebes; Rebillard 2003; Snively 2006).

We shall focus on a limited number of Christian monuments and their related graves, nowadays located in Dobrudja (southeastern Romania and northeastern Bulgaria, which covers an area bordered by the Black Sea to the east, the Balkan Mountains to the south, and the Danube River to the north, respectively. This area corresponds to the territory, once comprising the provinces of *Scythia* (so-called *Minor*) and *Moesia Secunda*, which were part of the diocese *Thracia* and the Prefecture of the Orient (Fig. 10.1). The comparative study of graves and related Paleochristian churches, in a pre-defined provincial area, allows us to recreate the use of funerary customs or practices in a wider geographical area by placing into a similar perspective the finds from neighbouring regions, especially Eastern Illyricum (Snively 1984; Sodini & Kolokotsas 1984: 211–41, for a theoretical approach concerning inhumations in or around Christian basilicas; Văleva 1989; Aleksova 1997: *passim*; Snively 1998; Marki 2002).

Archaeological research has in the course of the 20th century managed to draw a quite precise image of the process behind the merging of burials with ecclesiastic contexts during the Early Byzantine Period in different regions of the Late Empire. Thus, the fusion of graves with churches or the development of necropoleis in their vicinity can be followed in: *pars Occidentis* (Reekmans 1968; Cortesi 1982; Duval 1988: 100–6; Mérel-Brandenburg 1995; Solier 1995; Picard 1998: 197–254; Guyon 2000: especially pp. 392–94, n. 13; Meneghini & Santangeli Valenzani 1994); Greece (Laskaris1991); North Africa (Christern 1976: 81–85, 271–73, fig. 38, pls 1, 5a, c; Février 1987: 919–23; Bonacasa Carra 1989: especially pp. 1921–22, figs 9–12; Duval 1982: *passim*; Stevens 1993: 55; Ennabli 1997: 7–11, fig. 3; Leone 2002; Stevens, Kalinowski, van der Leest et al. 2005: 557–77, figs 12.1, 12.3), and the Christian East (Macridy 1912: 37, fig. 5; Lassus 1938; Donceel-Voûte 1988: 21–23, 78, 80, 138, 298, figs 4, 46, 107, 280; Falla Castelfranchi 1989; Goldfus 1997: *passim*; Piccirillo & Alliata 1998: 413–24; Ribak 2007: 41–43, appendix 2, 107–14; Grossmann 2002: 127–36).

However, the research on the appearance and spread of burials in an ecclesiastic context in the 4th–6th centuries AD describes a phenomenon in obvious opposition to

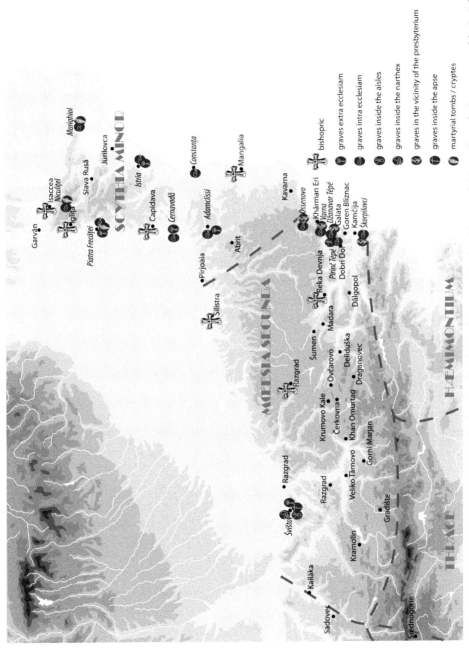

Fig. 10.1 The map of the geographic distribution of Paleochristian churches with graves in Scythia Minor and Moesia Secunda (map prepared by I. Achim and D. Iacovache 2009).

the reality drawn by written sources. As G. Dagron (1977: 11–19) stressed over three decades ago, the Roman juridical tradition and practice, codified in the middle of the 5th century BC by the *Lex Duodecim Tabularum*, forbade the dead – considered to be impure – the right of *intra urbem* burial and reserved for them extra urban locations, at least until the end of antiquity or to the reign of Theodosius the Great and beyond (Picard 1988: 1–8; 1998: especially pp. 312–16; Saradi 2006: 432–39). From then on, we witness a change from the established tradition to a new reality: the slow and sporadic accession of burials into the city (Cantino Wataghin 1999; Costambeys 2002; Capponi & Ghilardi 2002; di Gennaro & Griesbach 2003; Nieddu 2003). This change of mentality is confirmed by the position of the legislators, as visible in the *Codex Iustinianus* 1.2.2 from the 6th century AD, which formally forbade any burial in *apostolorum vel martyrium sedem* (see *Corpus iuris civilis* ed. Krueger 1959: 12), though did not clearly ban burials inside towns. To the strong opposition adopted by the laic authorities against *intra muros* inhumations, we must add the catechistic and homiletic literature, which emphasises that only a pure soul can find its rest inside a church (see the discourse of St Gregory the Great: *Dialogues* 4.52.2, 176–77:[1]

> [...] *quos grauia peccata non deprimunt, hoc prodest mortuis si in ecclesiis sepeliantur, quod eorum proximi, quotiens ad eadem sacra loca conueniunt, suorum, quorum sepulcra aspiciunt, recordantur et pro eis Domino preces fundunt. Nam quos peccata grauia deprimunt, non ad absolutionem potius quam ad maiorem damnationis cumulus eorum corpora in ecclesiis ponuntur* [...]).

In the geographical area of the Danubian provinces in the diocese of *Thracia*, namely *Scythia* so-called *Minor* and *Moesia Secunda*, the problem of burials in an ecclesiastic context has never been the subject of either a detailed or a synthetic study. This lacuna is explained partly by the state of the archaeological research, and partly by insufficient or incomplete field excavations of Christian monuments. We owe to J.-P. Sodini (1986), the first attempt to classify the 'privileged graves' in the Christian East, as well as a detailed discussion on burials associated with churches, which he presented in his publication of the results of excavations at Aliki (Sodini & Kolokotsas 1984: 219–38). The archaeological information available has since been augmented both with examples which were not discussed by Sodini, as well as by more recent archaeological discoveries. Such new findings in Romania and Bulgaria (namely in the ancient provinces of *Scythia* and *Moesia Secunda*) have led to the identification and field exploration of a series of Christian monuments with graves in their vicinity or even inside the churches.

We are therefore in a better position to investigate the complex process of Christianisation of the ancient cities in *Scythia* and *Moesia Secunda*. In spite of its incomplete character, archaeological information available on the history and evolution of urban structures in the Danubian sector of the diocese *Thracia* allows us to follow the slow crystallisation of a Christian landscape, specific to this peripheral area of the Roman world. We witness the progressive insertion of Christian churches into urbanism, as well as the symbolic redefining of cult building as an architectural context into which relics or martyrial graves started to be associated. Indeed, such a process followed patterns/traditions visible in other parts of the Empire. At the same time, the constant concern for defining the sacred space was doubled by the invention of a new type of Christian sensibility that permitted the admission, even if only in certain cases, of the dead *intra urbem*. This relatively sporadic phenomenon in the Lower Danube area during the 4th–6th centuries AD indicates the gradual change of the city's image (by desacralising the urban space) and the development of a new social Christian topography (by creating a hierarchy of the dead in terms of the burial place reserved for them). For the discussions which follow, two major categories of burials can be clearly recognised and examined: *extra ecclesiam* and *intra ecclesiam* graves. The division may seem arbitrary with some scholars, but it is used with purpose in order to arrange the available data in some clearly distinguishable categories which may also be useful for distinguishing possible topographical developments.

Extra ecclesiam graves

When considering *extra ecclesiam* graves in connection with churches, two main sub-groups can be defined: the first sub-group contains churches which 'attracted' contemporary necropoleis around them; the second sub-group is made up of isolated graves or small groups of burials in the proximity of churches or their annexes.

The first sub-group: Basilicas around which necropoleis were formed

To this sub-group belong three churches surrounded by contemporary necropoleis (Table 10.1): the cemeterial church on the northeastern hill at Adamclisi (ancient *Tropaeum Traiani*, Constanța County, Romania); the extra-mural basilica at Istria (ancient *Histria*, Constanța County, Romania), and; the extra mural church at Švištov (ancient *Novae*, Bulgaria). The presence of graves near these three churches automatically classified them as cemeterial basilicas.

At Adamclisi, the so-called *basilica coemeterialis* was built several hundred meters north of the city, on the highest point of a hill, where a significant number of graves (dating from the Early Roman Period up to the 6th century AD) were identified (Table 10.1, No. 1). A series of Roman and Roman-Byzantine graves were also noted on the hills northeast and east of the defensive wall of the ancient city. It is remarkable that, from a topographical point of view, in the entire area north and east of the ancient city of *Tropaeum Traiani*, necropoleis seem to have developed in the same defined areas during both the Roman and Roman-Byzantine Periods; on the hill north of the city, Roman-Byzantine burials appear to be directly connected to the Christian basilica.

The graves were dug on terraces in order to use the hilly scenery efficiently, occurring with no obvious structural pattern, north, south and west of the basilica, which contains as yet an unexcavated crypt for relics. Only a series of monumental Roman graves with cradle vaults were identified (west and south of the basilica), one

Table 10.1. Extra ecclesiam graves. Subgroup 1: Basilicas around which necropoleis were formed.

Cat. no.	Site (current name, followed by ancient name)	Monument	Context of discovery	The necropolis associated with the basilica	Graves with a special location within the necropolis or in connection with the church	Bibliography
1	Adamclisi / *Tropaeum Traiani*, Constanţa County, Romania; *Scythia Minor*	Cemeterial church on the north-eastern hill	Basilica discovered and partially investigated in 1896 by architects H. Jacobi (from Cologne) and J. Fakler (from Bucharest) at the initiative of the National Museum of Antiquities (Bucharest); – the church was discovered several hundred meters N of the city; – 1908: small test excavations near the basilica; – after 1992 research was resumed by the Universities of Bucharest and Iaşi in order to clarify the plan of the church and the situation of the necropolis.	Two successive funerary levels: graves that predate the basilica (Roman period); graves contemporary with the basilica (Late Roman period); – 25–30 graves identified at the end of the 19th c; – other Roman and Late Roman graves were discovered in the last decades of the 20th c.; – funerary rite: inhumation (Late Roman graves); – dual funerary rite (inhumation/cremation) for the Roman graves; – the graves are grouped around the basilica.	– no such grave was discovered	Barnea (coord.) 1979: 19; Papuc & Custurea 1989: 296; Zugravu & Barnea 1993: 397; Zugravu & Barnea 1994: 377; Zugravu & Barnea 1995: 281; Zugravu & Barnea 1996: 421; Zugravu & Barnea 1997: 373; Zugravu & Barnea 1998: 291–92; Netzhammer 2005: 165–66.

| 2 | Istria/ *Histria*, Constanța County, Romania; *Scythia Minor* | Extra mural basilica | Basilica discovered in 1914–1915 by Vasile Parvan, 200 meters away from the post-Gothic defense wall;
– necropolis identified and researched by E. Popescu between 1955 and 1956 and by N. Hampartumian between 1961 and 1964; other graves were identified between 2001 and 2010 (N and S of the basilica). | Two successive funerary levels: one that predates the basilica (flat cemetery, dated to the 4th–5th c. (necropolis I; *sub divo* necropolis, contemporary to the basilica necropolis II);
– 13 graves discovered between 1954 and 1955;
– 74 graves discovered between 1961 and 1964;
– over 10 graves discovered between 2001 and 2010;
– funerary rite: inhumation;
– grave orientation: variable (necropolis I); relatively stereotypical (necropolis I); (W–E for necropolis II);
– inhumated population: mostly adults, only a small number of children;
– relatively limited use of coffins (indicated by the presence of nails and wood remains);
– the graves are grouped around the basilica, to its N, E and S sides;
– M58 has a special location, E of the apse, in its axis (priviledged grave?) | *Grave 58*: found in a precinct (courtyard?) located E of the basilica, which also contained graves belonging to both necropoleis;
– placed 1.2 m E of the apse, in its axis;
– rite: inhumation;
– type of grave: individual;
– shape of the grave: rectangular;
– grave's architecture: stone cist bound with mortar and brick floor; dimensions: 2 × 0.80 m;
– the deceased was laid in a dorsal position, probably in a wooden coffin (wood fragments found inside the grave), head to the W, legs parallel, hands on the pelvis;
– funerary inventories: gold clothes accessories laid in a non-functional position (buckles, a tongue belt, adornments/footwear appliques, all concentrated at the feet) and remains of golden threads (probably from the costume's embroidery);
– according to Hampartumian, the anthropological analysis confirmed that the bones found in the grave belonged to a female, probably of a Gothic–Alanic origin;
– datation: second quarter of the 6th c. AD;
– grave partially superposed by another (M59). | Popescu 1957: 16–24, pl. IV;
Popescu 1959: 291–96, fig. 4;
Nubar 1971a: 199–215;
Nubar 1971b: 335–47;
Fiedler 1992: 59–60, fig. 6;
Rusu-Bolindeț & Bădescu 2003–2005: 104–12, figs 1–4 (with previous bibliography);
Rusu Bolindeț et al. 2009: 128;
Rusu Bolindeț et al. 2010: 88–89. |

| 3 | Švištov/ *Novae*, the site at Stăklan, Švištov District, Veliko Tărnovo County, Bulgaria; *Moesia Secunda* | Extra mural basilica | Basilica discovered and researched in the 1990's, 100 m W of the city's defence wall and its western gate | *Sub divo* necropolis (approx. 100 inhumation graves), located exclusively N of the basilica; the graves superpose and affect the remains of the classical Roman building with peristyle; – funerary rite: inhumation; – graves' orientation: E–W; – manner of depositing the deceased: stereotype, in a dorsal position, arms along the body or on the pelvis; – the deceased are rarely accompanied by jewellery, clothes' accessories or other funerary ware. | 4 graves were identified inside the basilica: one in the narthex, one in each aisle and one in the centre of the apse (see description in *Table 3*) | Fiedler 1992: 66–67, notes 162–67; Dimitrov 1995: 703, pl. 89 c–e; Čičikova 1997: 57–69, figs III/1–3. |

of which was partially destroyed by the construction of the basilica's atrium. Salvage excavations during the last three decades of the 20th century showed the bi-ritual character of the necropoleis at Adamclisi, between the 2nd and the middle of the 3rd centuries AD, when both inhumation and cremation rites were practiced (Panaitescu 1976; Constantin et al. 2007: 265, n. 60).

The partial and unsystematic archaeological research conducted in the area of the *basilica coemeterialis* at Adamclisi does not provide any further clues concerning the necropolis that developed around the church. Even so, the presence of a crypt for relics in the sanctuary of the basilica could indicate an *ad sanctos* burial. Future archaeological excavations will not be able to dissociate research on the *basilica coemeterialis* and the burials in its proximity, from the funerary discoveries on the plateau in front of the city's western gate, where a second *extra muros* Christian basilica was identified during the last decades of the 20th century.

The *extra muros* basilica at Istria presents an even more complex archaeological situation (Table 10.1, No. 2). The drastic reduction of the urban area from the Early Roman to the Roman-Byzantine Period made it possible to build this Christian monument in a suburban area, only 200 m west of the post-Gothic defence wall, a structure dated to the second half of the 3rd century AD (Suceveanu 2007: 88–90, pls 54–55). As in the case at Adamclisi, the *extra muros* basilica at

Istria was built on ground previously used, during the 4th century and first decades of the 5th century AD, for a necropolis (which for convenience here shall be referred to as necropolis I). The funerary function of this Christian monument is uncertain for its first two phases (according to Rusu-Bolindeț & Bădescu 2003–2005: 111–12, the first phase is dated to the end of the 5th century AD and beginning of the 6th century AD, and the second phase being dated to the middle/second half of the 6th century AD), but during its third phase (dated to the last decades of the 6th century AD and the beginning of the 7th century AD) the basilica 'attracted' in its immediate proximity a necropolis whose period of function lasted up to the beginning of the 7th century AD (which also for convenience here shall be referred to as necropolis II).

After the post-Gothic defence wall was built, thus reducing the size of the Roman town, the area between the latter and the Early Roman defence wall was covered by extra-mural dwellings that gradually changed this area's former monumental character. In addition, archaeological research conducted up to the present indicates that, as early as the last quarter of the 4th century AD, burials started to fill this area between the two defence walls, expanding east towards the new defence wall and the ditches in front of it (Ștefan 1976: 45, 48, 50–51, nn. 48–51, 70, fig. 2); Suceveanu 2007: 97, n. 54, pl. 56). This process marked a breach from the urban topography at Istria during the Classical Roman Period. During the 1st–3rd centuries AD, the area covered by necropoleis – barrow and flat (inhumation) cemeteries – was limited to the plateau west of the 2nd century AD defence wall, thus strictly following the polis/necropolis delimitation (Ștefan 1975: 54–55, n. 40, fig. 3). Both cremation and inhumation rites were used, but inhumation was already preferred by the 1st–2nd centuries AD (Oța & Domăneanțu 2010: 393–400, especially p. 394). Primary and secondary barrow burials gradually stopped and, towards the end of the 3rd century AD, the necropolis became entirely a flat cemetery (Ștefan 1975: 54).

The 4th–5th centuries AD necropolis which preceded the foundation of the *extra muros* basilica was a flat cemetery. The present archaeological investigations conclude that no graves belonging to the necropolis II, contemporary with the basilica, were ever placed inside it (Fig. 10.2). The few graves identified by E. Popescu (1994: 312), during excavations in the 1950s inside the basilica, belong to necropolis I and lie beneath its pavement. The largest proportion of the graves in the two necropoleis were concentrated at the sides of the basilica, especially north and east of the apse (Nubar 1971a: 199–215, fig. 1). The courtyard that extends eastwards from the apse contained graves belonging to both necropoleis (see above) and included the apsed annex in the church's northeastern corner. This eastern courtyard has no direct parallels in religious architecture in *Scythia* or in a larger regional context. A similar funerary precinct was uncovered at Knossos (Crete), where the 5th century AD cemetery church, discovered near the University of Medicine, was surrounded by a *peribolos*, defined as *campo santo* (Megaw 1984: 321–29, figs 1–5, especially fig. 5; Varalis 1999: 197–99, fig. 1). This elaborate structure also contained twenty ossuaries and a large Roman funerary monument. In Rome, the cemeterial basilica of Saints Marcellinus and Peter has an

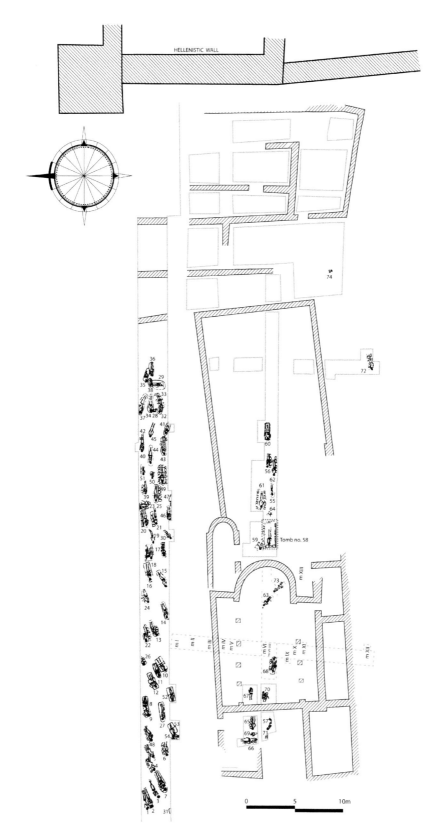

HELLENISTIC WALL

Tomb no. 58

0   5   10m

Fig. 10.2. Istria. The extra muros basilica and the surrounding necropolises (after Nubar 1971b: 335–47, fig. 2).

enclosure (precinct) to the north, containing a number of mausoleums, as well as a courtyard with a portico to the south (Guyon, Strueber & Manacorda 1981; Guyon 2002: 1157–73, figs 6–7).

Even if no *intra ecclesiam* burial was documented, a special emplacement can be seen in Grave 58 (which belongs to necropolis II), and is located immediately east of the apse of the basilica. Its particular position in the topography of necropolis II and the golden clothes' accessories discovered in the grave (Fig. 10.3) suggest that the deceased was a person of a high social status in the local community. The inventory of Grave 58 belongs to a group of similar discoveries in the Lower Danube region and *Thracia*, namely a territory occupied by Goth federates from the second half of the 5th century to the first half of the 7th century AD (Kazanski 1991: 137/plate). The animal style decoration of the belts discovered in the grave has caused major debate in terms of whether to connect it to a Late Roman influence or an Early Avar innovation specific to the Empire's periphery (Kidd & Pekarskaya 1995).

Grave 58 has a direct parallel with the episcopal basilica at Istria, the only difference being that in this latter case the graves are isolated and attracted towards an *intra muros* basilica (see Table 10.2, No. 2). In this context, should also be considered: a double burial – found east of the apse – of the Stamata/Amygdaleza Basilica, in Attica (Greece)

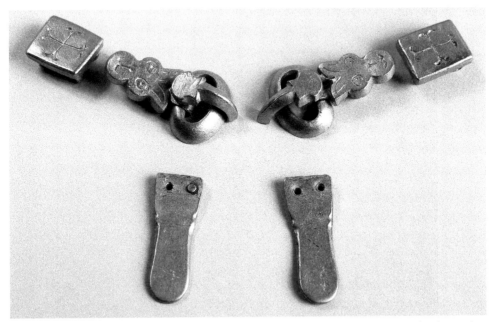

Fig. 10.3. Istria. The extra muros basilica, gold objects from the inventory of grave 58 (from the photo archive of the National History Museum of Romania, Bucharest, inventory nos.: 9527–9528/buckles; 9531-9532/ appliqué; 9529-9530/belt ends).

(Gkine-Tsophopoulou 1995); two graves identified in the Povlja Basilica in Dalmazia (Ostojić 1963: 144–45, fig. 1; Chevalier 1996, 1: 296 and 2: pl. xlviii/2), and; the collective cist grave (ossuary) discovered at Vaste nel Salento Basilica in Italy, datable to the second half of the 6th century AD (see D'Andria, Mastronuzzi & Melissano 2006: 271–72, figs 22, 27).

In spite of the scarce archaeological information from the two necropoleis, identified near the *extra muros* basilica at Istria, several remarks can be made: the orientation of the graves is variable, with only a minority (i.e. graves in stone/brick cists or with stone walls) being oriented more notably W–E or SW–NE; in graves with a W–E orientation the corpse was laid in a dorsal position, with the legs parallel to each other and the hands placed on the pelvis; graves containing pottery, coins, and clothes' accessories are relatively rare; food offerings are rather frequent in graves of necropolis I. Three double burials were also identified (M18, M23 and M73), as well as several cases where graves of necropolis II, contemporary with the basilica, superposed graves from necropolis I. Adults seem to have represented the majority of the graves, though child burials in limited numbers have been recorded in both necropoleis. Children were buried either in amphorae (necropolis I, M68: Nubar 1971a: 203), or in stone cists (necropolis II, M38: Nubar 1971a: 203, 209). The practice of inhumating infants in amphorae is attested at a provincial scale during the 4th–5th centuries AD in the necropoleis at Slava Rusă, Tulcea County, and Mangalia, Constanța County (see Soficaru 2007: 304, nn. 89–90). At Istria, as yet child graves appear not to have had a preferential location; on the contrary, they seem to have been integrated in a arbitrary way in a funerary space reserved for adults. In a single, recently documented case, (M14/09 located south of the basilica: Rusu Bolindeț et al. 2010: 88–89), a frontoparietal skull deformation was recorded, a practice specific to Germanic or other barbarian populations (Buora 2010: 190).

The third example in this sub-group is the extra mural basilica at Švištov (Table 10.1, No. 3). In this particular case, the necropolis, grouped exclusively on its northern side, was occupied by an important building with peristyle up to the middle of the 3rd century AD (Fig. 10.4), and identified as the residence of the *legatus legionis I Italicae* (see Ivanov 1997: 569, nn. 382–84, fig. 32a). There is no sign that the area of the *extra muros* basilica at Švištov had previously been used for funerary purposes. Unlike the *extra muros* basilicas at Adamclisi and Istria, the *extra muros* church at Švištov combines the use of *extra ecclesiam* and *intra ecclesiam* graves. The co-existence of the two categories of graves indicates an incontestable bipolarity of the cult complex and an obvious tendency to redefine the Christian funerary space in the 5th–6th centuries AD at Švištov. The presence of a smaller number of graves inside this *extra muros* basilica confers to the monument a symbolic ambivalence: a cult building and a place of burial for a (privileged?) minority at the same time. In the absence of any epigraphic information, the architectural characteristics of the *intra ecclesiam* graves – in brick cists – seem to at least indicate a different social status of the deceased when compared to that of the people buried in the necropolis near the basilica. Moreover, the different topographic situation of the *intra ecclesiam* burials indicates a certain concern for the hierarchy of graves in the building's internal space: a sacred topography, in which it seems impossible to contest that the grave located in the apse had the largest symbolic value.

The basilica was built sometime during the first half of the 5th century AD, as determined using coins discovered from the reigns of the Emperors Arcadius, Honorius and Theodosius II. During its second phase – also dated by coins, from the end of the 5th to the second half of the 6th centuries AD – the church's narthex was enlarged and divided into three compartments, each corresponding to the nave and aisles (Ivanov 1997: 574, n. 394, fig. 32b). Based on the available archaeological documentation, we agree with M. Čičikova's theory (1997: 61) that the necropolis significantly developed in the second half of the 5th century AD, but for now we cannot establish if the necropolis appeared during the initially phase of the basilica. Nevertheless, the necropolis lying north of the basilica is attributed to a Germanic population (Dimitrov 1995: 703,

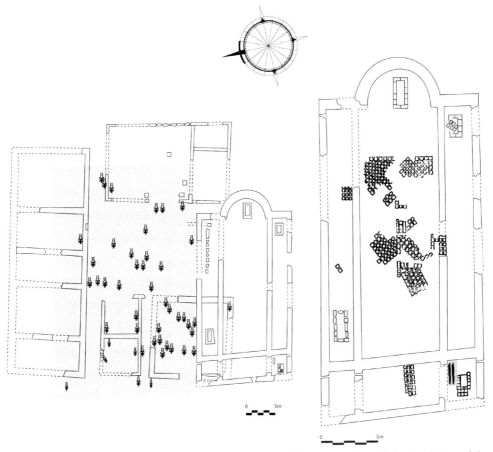

Fig. 10.4. Švištov. The extra muros basilica, plans of the church, the necropolis and the distribution of the intra ecclesiam graves (after Čičikova 1997: 64, figs. III/2–3).

pls 89c–e), as revealed by a limited number of gold jewels and clothes' accessories discovered in some of the graves: a bracelet with thick ends (a comparable object of silver is recorded at Ficarolo, in Italy, see Bierbrauer 1994: 46–47, fig. 5/1), a bee-type *fibula* (see the similar fibula from Domagnano, San Marino, Giunta 1984: 53–96, fig. 16), and an eagle shaped *fibula*. This last type of *fibula* is an object characteristic of a certain Ostrogothic female costume, popular in Italy and in the provinces of Illyricum at the end of the 5th century and the first half of the 6th century AD (Kazanski 1991: 136/plate; also see Bierbrauer 1984: 449–50, figs 379–80/*fibulae* from the hoard of Domagnano, San Marino). Nevertheless, the *fibula* discovered at Švištov is typologically similar to other pieces found in the area of the San Valentino basilica on via Flaminia, in Rome (Salvetti 1994: 523–32; Nieddu 2003: 580–81, n. 118, fig. 19).

The second sub-group: Isolated graves or small groups of graves near churches

A second sub-group of *extra ecclesiam* graves contains examples of churches that 'attracted' in their immediate vicinity isolated or small groups of graves, which could exceptionally be sheltered by an annex of the cult building (Table 10.2). This is the case of the basilica C at Adamclisi, the cathedral at Istria (both of them in Constanța County, Romania), and the main church of the cathedral complex at Švištov. The extra mural church at Cernavodă (ancient *Axiopolis*, also in Constanța County, Romania) can be added as a fourth example. Three of the four churches that attracted isolated graves in their proximity are *intra muros* monuments (Basilica C at Adamclisi, the cathedral at Istria, and the main church of the Episcopal complex at Švištov), and two of these were identified as cathedrals of the city. From a topographical point of view, the graves identified there seem to spread in a random manner around the churches, both east of the apse, as well as along their northern and southern flanks. Thus, at Istria, three graves east of the apse and a fourth to its north can be associated with the Episcopal basilica (Table 10.2, No. 2; Fig. 10.5). Similarly at Miletus, several burials were found east of the apse of the great basilica (see Müller-Wiener 2005: 366–71, fig. 2). At the Great Basilica in the Episcopal complex at Švištov, an isolated grave and an independent chapel identified with a *martyrium* were discovered along its southern flank (Fig. 10.6).

If at Istria the graves are rather modest (simple-pit graves, with bones *in situ*), at Švištov, the tomb placed in the external southwestern corner of the southern aisle is an elaborate masonry structure that rigorously respects the orientation of the basilica and is perfectly aligned to its southern peripheral wall (Table 10.2, No. 3). At Louloudies, in Greece, a double monumental tomb is located in a similar topographical position, near the southwestern corner of the basilica's narthex. As at Švištov, the tomb is built in masonry and covered by a cradle vault (Marki 1997a: 19–24, figs 1–10). A second grave at Švištov was placed in an independent space, namely an apsed chapel built east of the southern aisle. A. Biernacki (2005: 58–59, figs 5C–D) has tentatively identified the chapel as a *martyrium*, but firm evidence is lacking. The chapel communicates directly with the southern aisle and also with the outside, but no burial has been found on site. A similar chapel was built in Church A II 1, a cemeterial church, in *Anemurium* (Cilicia)

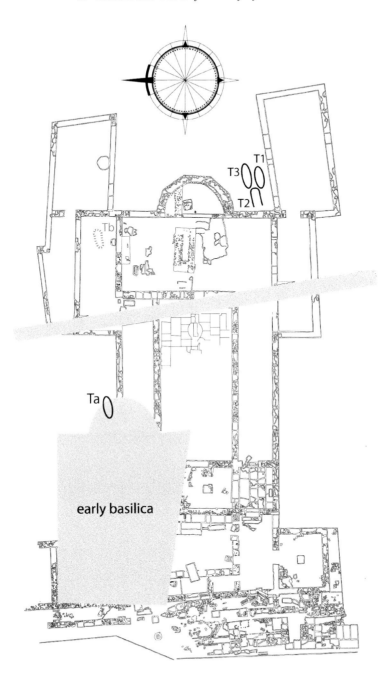

T1, T2, T3, Ta: 6th century graves
Tb: 7th century grave

Fig. 10.5. Istria. The episcopal basilica, plan of the church and distribution of graves around the monument. (Courtesy of Al. Suceveanu).

Table 10.2. Extra ecclesiam graves. Subgroup 2: Isolated graves or small groups of graves near churches.

Crt. no.	Site (current name followed by the ancient name)	Monument	No. of graves	The topography of the graves	Description of the graves	Dating of the graves	Bibliography
1	Adamclisi/ *Tropaeum Traiani* Constanța County, Romania, *Scythia Minor.*	The Cistern Basilica (Basilica C)	– 3? graves discovered in 1908 by German architect H. Brötz; – other inhumation graves (unspecified number) signaled by I. Barnea in 1976	Graves located east of the E side and on the S side of the basilica, inside a masonry precinct (peribolos) surrounding the basilica.	– Tomb E of the E side of the basilica, 'behind the altar' – (multiple burial?); – grave E of the basilica, on its axis, inside the precinct (single burial, traces of the coffin); – on the S side of the church: simple pit containing bones composed without an anatomical connection and four human skulls, along with a ceramic pot that contained coins and jewellery? – inhumation graves on the S side of the basilica (no description); – other inhumation graves identified on the S side of the basilica.	– Graves on the S side of the basilica: 6th c. AD?; – pit with bones on the S side of the church: *terminus post quem* provided by coins from Justin II and Sophia (565–578), Tiberius Constantine (574–582).	Barnea 1977a: 225, 233, figs 4–5; Barnea (coord.) 1979: 21–22, figs 2–3;
2	Istria/ *Histria* Constanța County, Romania, *Scythia Minor*	Basilica with transept / cathedral	4 graves contemporary with the basilica and one dated after the latter's abandonment	– 3 graves grouped E of the apse, between the latter and the annex in the basilica's SE corner; – 1 grave to the N, in the area near the apse of the basilica, a burial pre-dating the cathedral	– Burials E of the apse: simple pit inhumation graves, with the deceased laid in a dorsal position, head to the W, arms along the body; no funerary inventory, except for T2, which was disturbed in Antiquity and contained a piece from a buckle; – grave on the N side of the basilica: the pit was made of bricks set on their side; inhumation, with the deceased laid in a dorsal position, with no funerary inventory or clothes' accessories; – grave dug near the N transept after the basilica was abandoned: inhumation in stone cist, with the body laid in a dorsal position, head to the W, no funerary inventory or clothes' accessories.	– The graves E of the apse and N of the basilica are contemporary with the monument's second phase (second half of the 6th c. AD); – grave in the N transept: 7th c. AD.	Suceveanu 2007: 37–38, 43, pls IV, VI.

	Location	Church	No.	Graves (summary)	Description	Chronology	Bibliography
3	Svištov /*Novae*, (site at Stăklan, near Svištov, Svištov District, Veliko Tărnovo County, Bulgaria); *Moesia Secunda*.	Main church of the cathedral complex	2 graves	– Grave in a lower room of the independent chapel in the SE corner of the basilica; – grave located in the external SW corner of the S aisle	– Martyrium in an apsed chapel E of the S aisle, in the SE corner of the basilica; grave dug in this chapel's lower room (chapel's internal dimensions: 5.47 × 3.38 m; dimensions of its lower room: 1.35 × 0.90 m); – grave located in the external SW corner of the S aisle; dimensions: 2.48–2.50 m × 1.17–1.27 m; typology: stone masonry grave, with a brick vault; entrance on the E side; vault completely destroyed in time; no signs of a burial inside the grave	– Grave in the lower room of the chapel (martyrium?) located in the SE corner of the church: phase III of the cathedral (5th–6th c. AD); – grave in the external SW corner of the S aisle: phases I–II of the cathedral (5th c. AD)	Parnicki-Pudelko 1980 (1982): 120–21, figs 7–12; Parnicki-Pudelko 1983: 266–67, figs 24–25; Biernacki 2005: 58–59, figs 5A–D.
4	Cernavodă/ *Axiopolis*, Constanţa County, Romania, *Scythia Minor*.	Extra mural church	2? or more	– Grave in the annex located on the S side of the church; – other inhumation graves were signalled by P. Polonic around the church between 1899 and 1901	– Grave of Anthousa, daughter of Gibastes: marble inscription discovered in the apsed annex on the S side of the church; – Greek inscription, discovered in the debris of the nave, mentioning a certain Euphrasius, whose (soul and body) were entrusted to the martyrs Cyril, Kindeus, and Tasius	– Anthousa's epitaph: 5th–6th c. AD; – Euphrasius' inscription: 3rd–4th c. AD; – unclear chronology for the graves around the church	Romanian Academy Library, Manuscripts Section, Personal archive P. Polonic, I Mss. 8 (*Săpăturile cetăţilor romane*), Notebook 11, 12–23; Barnea 1977b: 158–60, fig. 53/5, with previous bibliography; Popescu 1976: 206–8, no. 195; Barnea 1977b: 104–5, no. 72, fig. 31; Popescu 1976: 205–6, no. 194; Barnea 1977b: 101–4, no. 71, fig. 31; Handley 2010: 130, 139.

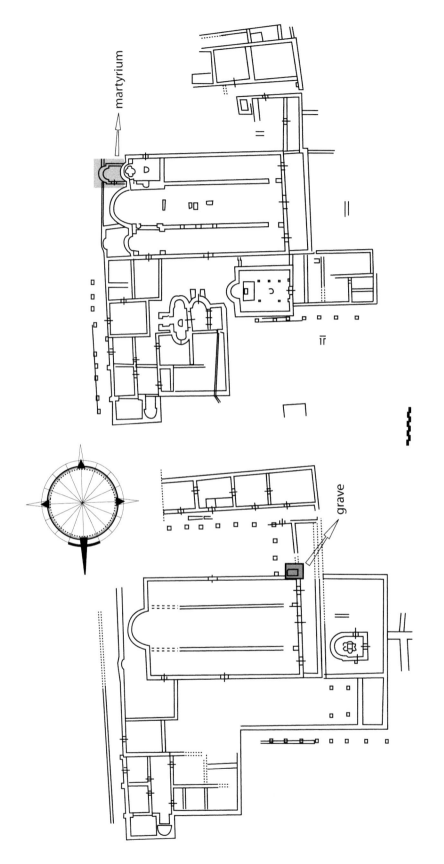

martyrium

grave

Fig. 10.6. Švištov. The cathedral, plan of the complex on various progressive phases of evolution (after Biernacki 2005: 57, figs 3A–B).

around 400 AD (Russell 1979: 184–45; Hellenkemper 1990: cols 270–273, fig. 36 a–e). Besides the initial grave in the southeastern chapel, a series of other graves were placed there after the church had been abandoned at the end of the 7th century AD.

The situation of basilica C at Adamclisi is singular (Table 10.2, No. 1; Fig. 10.7). It is the only known case in the area under scrutiny in which an *intra muros* basilica is protected by a peribolos with graves inside; the graves were grouped on the southern side and only sporadically on the eastern side of the basilica. New archaeological excavations are needed in order to find out more about the characteristics and the exact chronology of the necropolis developing outside the basilica. In the absence of conclusive data, we can only suppose that the graves were attracted to the basilica by the crypt for relics which was identified in the nave.

From a chronological point of view, at Švištov, the graves associated with the Great Basilica in the cathedral complex are dated to the basilica's first three phases, which correspond to the 5th and the beginning of the 6th centuries AD. After this period and during the building's later phases, the *martyrium* chapel, east of the southern aisle, stopped functioning and the eastern side of the basilica was profoundly modified by the addition of the lateral apses that flank the main apse (first half of the 6th century AD). At Istria, however, the graves were dated on stratigraphical observations to the second half of the 6th century AD, a chronology that corresponds to the second phase of the basilica. The only grave dated to the first half of the 7th century AD discovered there suggests a sporadic funerary use of the site in the period after the basilica had been abandoned.

Another special situation is that of the extra mural church at Cernavodă (Table 10.2, No. 4). In this case, a grave belonging to a member of the provincial aristocracy – Anthousa, daughter of *comes* Gibastes, as written on an epitaph discovered there – was installed in a chapel added to the southern face of the church (Fig. 10.8). The placement of this funerary chapel finds a direct parallel in the southern church at Hemmaberg (Glaser 1991: 56–58, n. 86, figs 2, 7).

A second inscription discovered in the ruins of the nave reveals the name of a Christian, Euphrasius, and could constitute in *Scythia* a rare example of an *ad sanctos* burial documented epigraphically (Fig. 10.9). The text mentions that Euphrasius was entrusted to the martyrs Cyril, Kindeus, and Tasius. The last person's name is most probably a corrupted form of Dasius, a martyr who died for the Christian faith at *Durostorum* (Pillinger 1988: 39–40, 49–50, n. 71, 130–39, fig. 3). Apart from the graves of Anthousa and Euphrasius, other burials are mentioned in the same area by the topographer P. Polonic (see the reference indicated in Table 10.2, No. 4) at the beginning of 20th century. Due to incomplete archaeological investigations, we can only presume that the graves identified near this small church at Cernavodă were all *ad sanctos* burials, placed under the protection of the martyrs mentioned by the inscription of Euphrasius, and probably patrons of the church.

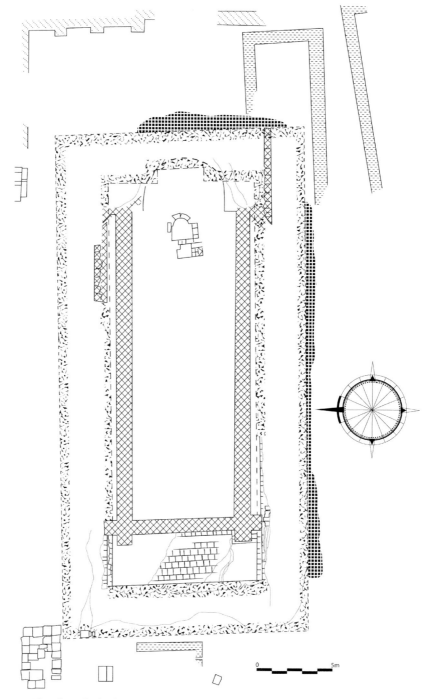

Fig. 10.7. Adamclisi. The basilica C, plan of the church and its courtyard (after M. Mărgineanu-Cârstoiu 1977, 236, fig. 1).

Table 10.3. Intra ecclesiam *graves.*

Crt. no.	Site (current name followed by the ancient name)	Monument	The location of the grave inside the church	Identity of the deceased	Description of the graves	Dating of the graves	Bibliography
1	Švištov/*Novae*, (site at Stăklan, Švištov District, Veliko Tărnovo County, Bulgaria); *Moesia Secunda*	The extra mural basilica	In the S section of the narthex	Unknown	Single inhumation grave under the brick pavement of the narthex; pit coated with *tegulae* set vertically; orientation: E–W	Second phase of the church: 6th c. AD?	Čičikova 1997: 60, fig. III/3, III/10.
2	Pirinč Tepe/ Varna County, Bulgaria; *Moesia Secunda*	Basilica	NW corner of the N aisle	Unknown	Inhumation grave; typology: stone cist; dimensions: 1.7 × 1.32 m.	Uncertain date; according to Škorpil's brothers, the basilica had two phases, the first in the 4th c., the second in the second half of the 5th c.	Škorpil 1910: 15–21, especially p. 16, with a plate on the volume's front page and not part of the article's text. On the plate the grave is marked by the letter R
3	Švištov/*Novae*, (site at Stăklan, Švištov District, Veliko Tărnovo County, Bulgaria); *Moesia Secunda*	The extra mural basilica	W extremity of the N aisle	Unknown	Inhumation grave; no other archaeological information available.	5th–6th c. AD	Čičikova 1997: 59, fig. III/3.

No.	Site	Church	Location	Patron	Description	Dating	Reference
4	Švištov/*Novae*, (site at Stăklan, Švištov District, Veliko Tărnovo County, Bulgaria); *Moesia Secunda*	The extra mural basilica	E extremity of the S aisle	Unknown	Inhumation grave under the pavement of the S aisle; single burial?; cist with walls made of 7 courses of bricks; orientation: E–W; ext. dimensions: 1.78 × 1.08 m; int. dimensions: 1.22 × 0.54 × 0.62 m; – no traces of human remains inside the grave; – metallic parts of a coffin or a wooden box were identified in the fill of the grave.	5th–6th c. AD	Čičikova 1997: 57–69, fig. III/3.
5	Švištov/*Novae*, (site at Stăklan, Švištov District, Veliko Tărnovo County, Bulgaria); *Moesia Secunda*	Basilica no. 1, located in sector 12, near the Eastern Gate	The SE area of the nave of the church	Unknown	Grave dug between the opening of the apse and the first pillar of the S colonnade; there are no archaeological arguments to explain its relation to the area of the sanctuary.	Uncertain dating	Biernacki 2005: 54, fig. 2A.
6	Švištov/*Novae*, (site at Stăklan, Švištov District, Veliko Tărnovo County, Bulgaria); *Moesia Secunda*	The extra mural basilica	E, in the centre of the apse	Saint Louppos? (according to Čičikova)	Grave in the axis of the apse; single burial?; cist with walls made of 8 courses of bricks, covered with two stone slabs; ext. dimensions: 2.70 × 1.35 m; int. dimensions: 2.20 × 0.95 × 0.58 m; orientation: E–W; – architecture of the grave: the cist walls were covered in plaster and the floor was paved with bricks; – inside the grave: highly decomposed human remains, mixed with black soil.	5th–6th c. AD	Čičikova 1997: 59, fig. III/3.
7	Džanavar Tepe?/ Varna County, Bulgaria; *Moesia Secunda*	Church with a single nave	E, near the sanctuary	Unknown	The grave located in the axis of the nave, between the W limit of the sanctuary and the pulpit; double burial; – typology: vaulted brick structure; – the grave is connected with the *enkainion* in the apse by a corridor or *dromos* located on its E side; – two different-size coffins, one containing the remains of an adult and the other bones wrapped in a golden embroidery.	Uncertain dating; the church: first half of 6th c. AD	Bojadjiev 1995: 70–71, figs 2, 4–5; Pillinger, Popova & Zimmermann (eds.) 1999: 18, pl. 2, fig. 15/3; pl. 3, fig. 17.

No.	Site	Building	Location in church		Description	Dating	References
8	Škorpilovci/ Varna County, Bulgaria; *Moesia Secunda*	Basilica	E extremity of the nave, near the sanctuary	Unknown	Grave in the axis of the nave, W of the limit of the sanctuary; – typology: vaulted tomb with access stairs to the W, a niche to the E (tomb defined as a crypt); – decoration: painted crosses and stucco cornices at the base of the vault.	4th–5th c. AD	Văleva 1979–1980: 119–20, 123, fig. 16; Pillinger, Popova & Zimmermann (eds.) 1999: 18–19, pl. 3/fig. 18; Minčev 1996–1997: 132–33, fig. 2; Văleva 2001: 171, fig. 7.
9	Varna/*Odessos* Varna County, Bulgaria; *Moesia Secunda*	Basilica near the junction of A. Gačev st., Tsar Simeon st. and Kozloduj st.	E extremity of the nave?	Unknown	Vaulted brick tomb, with access stairs blocked by a sculpted marble block with Latin inscription.	Uncertain dating	Beševliev 1975: 149–50, pl. I/4.
10	Piatra Frecăței/*Beroe* Tulcea County, Romania; *Scythia Minor*	Basilica *extra muros*	Partially in the apse, partially in the nave	Unknown	Grave in the axis of the church, partially under the floor level of the apse, partially in the nave; – typology: grave with brick vault and stone walls, entrance through a W dromos; – multiple inhumation?	4th c. AD?	Baumann 2006: 826–27, pl. 20, fig. 1; pl. 21, figs 2–4.
11	Constanța/*Tomis*, Constanța County, Romania; *Scythia Minor*	Large basilica	Partially in the apse, partially in the nave	Unknown	Large cross-shaped crypt (50 m2) with 7 interconnected chambers and a W dromos, covered by a brick vault; no traces of human remains inside the crypt.	5th–6th c. AD.	Rădulescu 1966: 32–45, figs 11–14, 20–26; Barnea 1981, 492–95, figs 5–6; Sodini 1981: 445, fig. 5.
12	Constanța/*Tomis*, Constanța County, Romania; *Scythia Minor*	Small basilica	Partially in the apse, partially in the nave.	Unknown	Rectangular brick crypt with entrance to the W and no traces of human remains inside the crypt.	6th c. AD.	Rădulescu 1966: 24–25, fig. 9; Barnea 1981: 497, fig. 9.

	Location	Basilica	Position	Martyrs	Description	Date	References
13	Constanța/ *Tomis*, Constanța County, Romania; *Scythia Minor*	Basilica in the courtyard of the M. Eminescu High School	Under the floor level of the sanctuary	Unknown	Large crypt under the floor level of the sanctuary of the basilica; – dimensions: 6.15 × 3.75 m; orientation: E–W; – brick vaulted structure with a W dromos and three, approx. equally-sized loculi to the E; decoration al fresco imitating *opus sectile*	4th–5th c. AD.	Barnea 1981: 491–92, figs. 3–4; Sodini 1981: 445; Barbet & Monier 2001: 221–28.
14	Murighiol/ *Halmyris*, Tulcea County, Romania; *Scythia Minor*	Basilica *intra muros*	Partially in the apse, partially in the nave	Martyrs Epictet and Astion	Grave in the axis of the church, partially under the floor level of the apse, partially in the nave; – typology: brick vault and stone walls, W dromos; counters on both sides of the funerary room; decoration al fresco imitating *opus sectile*; – double inhumation, remains belonging to two males identified *in situ*, skeletons with perimortem traces of violence; – burial in the dromos after the abandonment of the basilica	4th–6th c. AD	Zahariade & Phelps 2002: 241–45, figs 15–17, 19; Miriţoiu & Soficaru 2001–2003 (2007); Miriţoiu & Soficaru 2003; Zahariade 2009: 141–50, figs 13–21; Miriţoiu & Soficaru 2009: 151–81.
15	Niculiţel/ *territorium* of ancient *Noviodunum*, Tulcea County, Romania; *Scythia Minor*	Basilica	Partially in the apse, partially in the nave	Martyrs Zotikos, Attalos, Kamasis, and Philippos	Martyrium located partially under the floor level of the apse, partially under that of the nave; square structure of mixed masonry (brick and stone), covered by a hemispherical cupola; entrance to the W, blocked by a limestone slab; – 2 chambers: multiple burial in a collective coffin (upper room) – 4 adult males; – double burial in the lower room; bones with distinct traces of burning; 2 ceramic pots; – inscription mentioning the names of the 4 martyrs laid in the *martyrium*'s upper room.	End of the 4th c. AD?	Barnea 1981: 489–91, figs 1–2; Sodini 1981: 445–46; Baumann 2004: 90–128, 153–74, pls. 1–9; Baumann 2006: 827–30, pl. 22, figs. 5–7; pl. 23, figs 8–9.

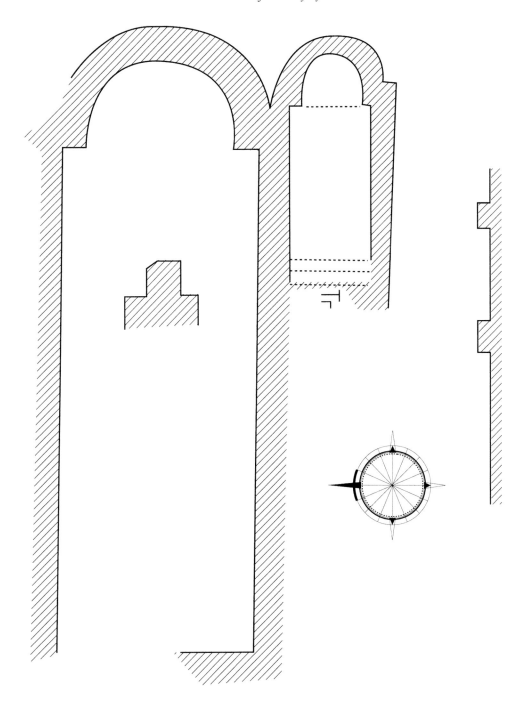

Fig. 10.8. Cernavodă. The extra mural church, plan (courtesy of the Library of the Romanian Academy, Manuscripts Section, personal archive of P. Polonic, I varia I: 22 pachete cu planuri și desene arheologice, envelope 3, pl. I varia 78).

Fig. 10.9. Cernavodă. The extra mural church, the inscription of Euphrasius (from the photo archive of the National History Museum of Romania, Bucharest, inventory no. 18 881).

Intra ecclesiam graves

The second major category of graves to be discussed here are the *intra ecclesiam* ones (Table 10.3). Archaeological excavations have identified only a relatively small number of such burials in *Scythia* and *Moesia Secunda*. There may be more reasons for this, as probably confirmed by field research on Christian monuments north of the Balkans. One fact is certain: both civilian and ecclesiastic authorities controlled the placement of the burials inside the city and inside the churches. A significant testimony of this is offered by an African funerary inscription: Rogata, mother of the deacon Tiberinus, was buried in the centre of the northern aisle of Alexander's Church in Tipasa *ex permissu/ Alexandri/ episcopi* (Leschi 1957: 373), a monument dated to the late 5th/6th centuries AD.

The archaeological reports on the *intra ecclesiam* graves seem to imply that the graves were placed inside the church without any certain rules. In both provinces, the Christian epigraphy is rather poor and offers just a few clues on the identity of the individuals granted permission to be buried inside the churches.

Moving from west to east inside the architectural space of the churches, the narthex seems to be the area least used for funerary purposes. At present, there are practically no graves placed in the narthex in *Scythia*. In *Moesia Secunda*, on the other hand, there is one well-documented case, namely the extra mural basilica in Švištov, where a grave was placed in the southern chamber of the narthex (Table 10.3, No. 1; Fig. 10.4). The positioning of a grave with a modest architecture in the entrance area of the basilica should most likely be dated after the primitive narthex had been replaced by a three-chambered narthex, an architectural modification that – according to M. Čičikova (1997: 61–62, fig. III/3) – took place during the first half of the 6th century AD.

The apparent lack of burials inside the narthex in *Scythia* and *Moesia Secunda* stands in contrast to the situation documented in the neighbouring regions of Eastern Illyricum (Nikolajević 1980: 366–67; on the subject of 'common martyrium' see also Donceel-Voûte 1998: 122–24, fig. 15/3), and *Thracia*, where burials were more frequently located in the western area of the church, therefore also in the narthex. For the 5th–6th centuries AD, graves inside the narthex have been documented, for example in: Serbia, at Caričin Grad, Church B (Guyon & Cardi 1984: 40–44, figs 38–43, pl. iii), at Jelica, Churches A (Milinković 2001: 111–13, figs 30, 32) and B (Milinković 2001: 114–17, figs 33–34), and in the cemetery church in Niš (Milošević 2006: 173–86, especially pp. 179–82, figs 2, 11); the little church in Ljutibrod, Bulgaria (Djingov & Mašov 1985: 41–43, fig. 3), and; *Thracia*, at Kran (Tabakova-Čanova & Ovčarov 1975: 46, fig. 6).

If the funerary use of the narthex proved sporadic in *Scythia* and *Moesia Secunda*, burials in the space of the *quadratum populi* were more frequent. This category of burials is also defined by the absence of rules regarding their position. Even so, the disproportion between the number of graves located in the aisles (less numerous) and those in the nave is striking.

As in the case of the narthex, the aisles seem to have had a reduced funerary role, limited to only three examples in the area of our two provinces. Concomitantly, we notice a certain polarisation of the position of graves inside the aisles, namely at their extremities. Thus, one grave was placed at the western end of the northern aisle at Pirinč Tepe, near Varna (Table 10.3, No. 2; Fig. 10.10) and at Švištov, in the extra mural basilica (Table 10.3, No. 3; Fig. 10.4). The simultaneous use of both aisles is exceptional, as the only such case is that of the basilica *extra muros* at Švištov. Here, apart from the grave in the northern aisle, a second was dug near the sanctuary area, at the eastern end of the southern aisle (Table 10.3, No. 4; Fig. 10.4). Its architecture is similar to that used for the grave located in the apse of the church. The deceased, whose remains disappeared at an unknown date, was most probably laid in a coffin made of perishable material, of which only the metal parts were preserved.

During the 5th–6th centuries AD, in the Aegean and Balkan regions, the aisles played a more important funerary role than in *Scythia* and *Moesia Secunda* and seem to have been more frequently used as burial places reserved for the clergy, even if not as a rule. At Stobi, in Macedonia, inside the Episcopal Church, the only grave found until now is

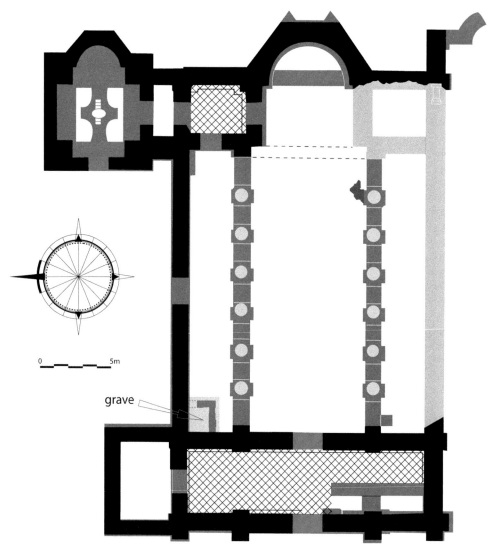

grave

Fig. 10.10. Pirinč Tepe. The basilica, plan (after Škorpil & Škorpil 1910: 15–21).

located at the eastern end of the southern aisle. The grave at Stobi, contemporary with the second phase of the monument, built at the beginning of the 6th century AD by Bishop Philip, contained the remains of one individual, dressed in a rich costume and wearing leather sandals (Aleksova 1986: 19–20; Sodini 1986: 233–34). The eastern ends of the aisles in the extra mural basilica in Philippi (Macedonia) were reserved for the clergy: Paul, priest and also doctor, was buried inside grave A, located in the northern aisle of the church (Pelekanides 1977: 369–70, 379–80, fig. 9, pls 28, 37); two priests, *Faustinus* and *Donatus*, were buried in the southern aisle, inside grave B (Pelekanides

1977: 370–72, fig. 9, pls 29, 38). In Hissar (ancient *Diocletianopolis*, in *Thracia*) in the Basilica 3 – dedicated to Saint Stephanus – a certain *Theodoros* was buried in the eastern end of the northern aisle as the identity of the grave's occupant was revealed by the text of his Greek epitaph (Ivanova 1937: 217, 223–24, 226–29, figs 198, 206). A 6th century AD double tomb with vault, erected in masonry, was inserted in the centre of the southern nave of the basilica of Arethousa, near Thessaloniki (Adam-Velene 1995: 354–55, figs 2–4, pl. 1), while at Eressos (in Lesbos) a grave occupies the eastern extremity of the southern nave (Orlandos 1929: 31, fig. 30). As in the case of the *extra muros* basilica in Švištov, the Episcopal complex at Louloudies – near Pydna, in Greece – sheltered, during its second phase (dated to the second half of the 6th century AD) a grave at the western extremity of the northern aisle and two others at the eastern extremity of the southern aisle, while other burials were concentrated around the monument (Marki 1997b: 293–94, fig. 1; 2001: 19–25, 82, figs 2, 8–9). The Basilica D from Byllis (Albania) housed – in the centre of the northern aisle – a cradle vaulted tomb (Chevalier et al. 2003: 161, figs 3, 6).

If graves inside the narthex and the aisles are rare, the presence of graves in the nave is, on the other hand, much better documented in the geographical area under scrutiny. Intriguingly, no graves were located at the entrance of the nave. One also notices an increased tendency to place the graves in the eastern end of the nave, exceptionally inside the apse and much more frequently in the vicinity of the sanctuary. When graves are discovered near the sanctuary we notice that they are constantly placed in line with the axis of the church. Even so, the grave discovered in the eastern extremity of the nave of basilica no. 1, located in sector 12, near the Eastern Gate at Švištov (Table 10.3, No. 5; Fig. 10.11) seems to elude the usual pattern followed by churches in *Scythia* and *Moesia Secunda*. In this particular case, the grave was placed south of the axis, towards the southern colonnade of the nave and seeming to ignore any concern for an axial location. The monument's poor state of conservation and insufficient archaeological documentation do not allow us to determine the exact position of the grave in relation to the enclosure of the sanctuary, whose western extension and limits are not known. A grave in a similar position was discovered in the Eressos basilica at Lesbos (Orlandos 1929: 31, fig. 30).

The presence of graves in the apse is exceptional. In the entire area considered only one example was discovered in the extra mural basilica at Švištov (Table 10.3, No. 6; Fig. 10.4). The grave, well built as a brick cist, is probably among the most elaborate in the entire necropolis that developed around the basilica. The disappearance of any trace of pavement inside the apse makes it impossible to comment on the grave-Eucharistic altar relationship. The axial position, precisely in the centre of the apse, seems to underline the particular concern that the person in charge of the burial had to make it well visible. Unlike the grave in the southern aisle of the same church, the burial in the apse does not preserve any indication of the use of a coffin. No artefact was discovered inside the grave and in the absence of any other evidence, be it archaeological or epigraphic, the identity of its occupant could not be determined. M. Čičikova (1997: 59) suggests

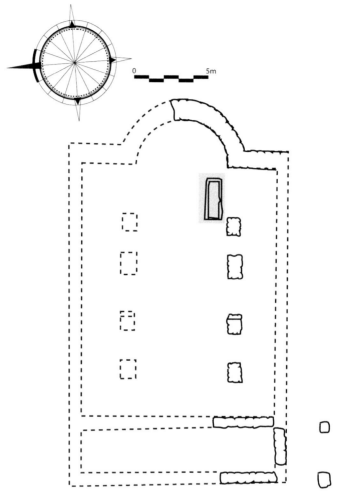

Fig. 10.11. Švištov. The basilica no 1, located in sector 12, near the Eastern Gate, plan (after Biernacki 2005: 55, fig. 2A).

that the grave could have been destined for a local martyr, perhaps to Saint Louppos, mentioned by Theophylact Simocatta, *Hist.* 7.2.17, 249. In neighbouring Serbia, in Ulpiana, Kosovo, a similar position can be noted for a grave that comprised a lead sarcophagus (Nikolajević 1978: 688–89, 693, figs 12–13). According to Nikolajević, the grave housed the bones of two local martyrs, *Florus* and *Laurus*, later venerated in Constantinopolis. Another similar example is recorded in the S Basilica at Sidi Jdidi, Tunis (Ben-Abed-Ben Khader et al. 2004: 87–108, especially pp. 87–95, figs 47–48, 50–51). The grave was placed in the centre of the apse, at a moment subsequent to the first phase of the mosaic pavement covering this space. The mosaic epitaph, which covers the grave, indicates that its occupant was a certain *Cyprianus, presbyter.* Other examples of graves in the apse are found in the area of the Diaporit basilica, in Butrint, Albania (Bowden, Hodges, Lako et al. 2002: 216, figs 12, 17–18).

In and around Varna (ancient *Odessos,* Bulgaria) a group of three graves was discovered, placed in an axial position at the western limit of the sanctuary enclosure (Table 10.3). It is regrettable that these discoveries, made several decades ago, have not yet been published in detail. Moreover, their archaeological publication does not clearly indicate them as privileged graves, crypts, or martyrial graves. Two of these graves were identified in churches in the territory of the bishopric of *Odessos* (a single nave church in Džanavar Tepe and a basilica in Škorpilovci), while the third was discovered in an *intra muros* building (a basilica in Varna, near the crossing of the streets A. Gačev, Tsar Simeon, and Kozloduj).

At Džanavar Tepe, the tomb, located at the western limit of the sanctuary enclosure, was partially superposed by the latter and at the same time by the pulpit (Table 10.3, No. 7; Fig. 10.12). The burial has a direct connection to the *loculus* where relics were preserved inside the sanctuary. In the well-built tomb the remains of two individuals were laid in separate coffins. As far as the funerary rite is concerned, S. Bojadjiev (1995: 70–71, figs 2, 4–5) – one of the scholars who analysed the monument – indicated that the bones in the smaller coffin were wrapped in a golden embroidery. This practice is actually attested at Džanavar Tepe, where, in the *loculus* located in the apse, a group of three reliquaries set one inside the other was discovered: a marble reliquary contained a second of silver which housed a third reliquary made of gold. The latter was wrapped in a yellow silk cloth (Minčev 2003: 15–18, especially p. 17).

Should we admit that this tomb's occupant was given special permission to be buried near the relics preserved in the sanctuary? New interpretations of the funerary use of the ecclesiastic context at Džanavar Tepe seem to be suggested by the discovery of four inhumation graves immediately east of the the church's eastern façade (Minčev & Tenekedjiev 2010: 277–79, fig. 1). Until their exact chronology is established we can only stress, along with the other investigators involved, that the pits are oriented approximately E–W and that their walls were built using Roman bricks. No further graves were recorded inside this church. The basilica of Siagu, in Tunisia, illustrates this association of a grave with a deposit of relics, both incorporated in the area of the sanctuary. However, at Siagu the grave is located behind the *loculus* for relics, on the axis of the apse (see Duval 1984–1985: 173–74, figs 2–3). The basilica on the September 3rd Street in Thessaloniki (Marki 2006: 97–98, fig. 35) provides the nearest analogy for this singular *intra ecclesiam* tomb, as it has the same position in the church vis-à-vis the western limit of the sanctuary enclosure.

Unlike the grave at Džanavar Tepe, the one at Škorpilovci is remarkable through its distinctive elements (Table 10.3, No. 8; Fig. 10.13): *al fresco* decoration; accessibility by a western staircase that probably opened into the nave; the eastern niche could have served for rituals associated with the tomb (worship?). According to A. Minčev (2003:

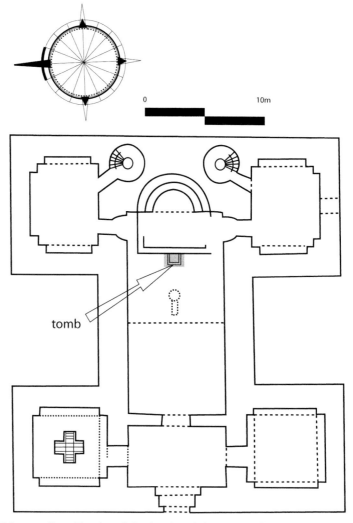

Fig. 10.12. Džanavar Tepe. The plan of the church and the grave in the vicinity of the presbyterium (after Bojadjiev 1995, fig. 2).

24–25, cat. no. 10 a–d, figs 10 a–d), the marble reliquary with a lid provided with an orifice (used for taking out contact relics), discovered by chance at the mouth of River Škorpilovska, could be a part of the grave's inventory. The association of relics with a simple grave, in theory inaccessible after burial, is attested in neighbouring regions by the discovery of a silver reliquary in grave no. 3 of the Saint Sophia Basilica in Sofia (see Filow 1913: 70–72, figs 57–59, pl. 8/1–4; Duval 1988: 126–29). As far as the chronology of the basilica is concerned, Minčev proposed the end of the 5th and beginning of the 6th centuries AD, based on architectural characteristics and the style of the pavimental

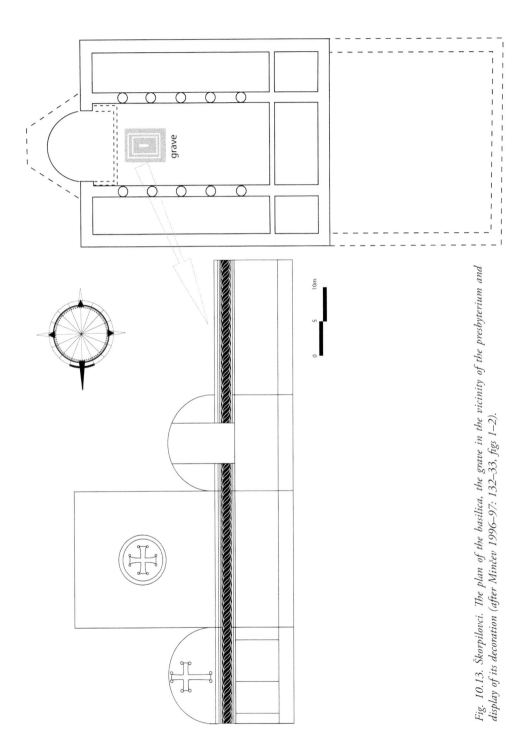

Fig. 10.13. Škorpilovci. The plan of the basilica, the grave in the vicinity of the presbyterium and display of its decoration (after Minčev 1996–97: 132–33, figs 1–2).

Fig. 10.14. Varna. The basilica located on the crossroad A. Gačev, Tsar Simeon, and Kozloduj streets, the inscription which blocked the entrance of the grave located in the vicinity of the sanctuary (Varna Regional History Museum, inventory no.: II 5018; photo I. Achim 2008).

mosaics. The dating of the grave is a more delicate problem; J. Văleva (2001: 171, fig. 7) has proposed a time span ranging between the 4th and the 5th centuries AD. The dates put forward by the two scholars could hypothetically constitute an argument in favour of the hypothesis that the grave in the nave preceded the basilica, which was later built precisely above to shelter this primitive funerary structure.

The basilica discovered near the crossing of the streets A. Gačev, Tsar Simeon, and Kozloduj in Varna – in the southwestern part of the late antique city – constitutes the third example of graves from this series (Table 10.3, No. 9; Fig. 10.14). The grave is inaccessible, its entrance blocked by a marble slab with a metrical Latin inscription. The text has eight lines and its connection with a grave is testified twice by the use of the terms *tumulus* and *sepulchrum*, terms not unusual in a late antique context. The term *tumulus* appears, for example, in the text of a 6th century AD Christian inscription from *Tomis* (Popescu 1976: 65–66, no. 30, 1 = Barnea 1977b: 56, no. 23, fig. 11). Under the form *tumolo* this word is also mentioned in the epitaph of *Dessideratus* discovered at Kobern-Gondorf, Germany, now in the Rheinisches Landesmuseum, Bonn (Schmitz 2004: 57, fig. 4), and on the gravestone inscription of Leo, in the cemetery of St

Gereon in Cologne (Schmitz 2004: 55, fig. 3). The term *sepulchrum* is mentioned – in a corrupted form – by two late antique inscriptions in Bulgaria (Beševliev 1964: 32, no. 47.3, fig. 45/Ratiaria, *sepulhro*; and on pp. 177–78, no. 246.1–2, fig. 264/unknown place of discovery, *sepulhcrus*). In Romania, the Christian epigraphy provides an example of the use of this term in the text of a Latin inscription from Rasova (Popescu 1976: 201–3, no. 191.4). In North Africa, at Cherchel, a dedicatory inscription in verses was also noted from a cemetery, where the term is used in plural form (*sepulchra*) (Duval 1982: 1, 380–83, no. 179, fig. 248).

Finally, the last category to be discussed here is that of funerary or martyrial structures located in the eastern extremity of the churches (Table 10.3, Nos 10–15). This series of monumental structures or *hypogea*, located invariably under the pavement of the apse and sanctuary, forms a homogenous group of six examples found exclusively in the territory of *Scythia*. All examples included in this series have constantly been presented in the archaeological literature as martyrial crypts which, due to their considerable dimensions, could contain entire bodies of one or several venerated persons (martyrs and saints) (Barnea 1981: 489–97, figs 1–8). At a provincial scale, the starting point of this kind of *hypogea* integrated in the sanctuary seems to be the ecclesiastic metropolis *Tomis* (at present the city of Constanța, Romania), from where it was exported to other centres in the province. Four of the six churches that make up this group are *intra muros* buildings; the other two are outside and at a considerable distance from the urban centre.

The basilica at Piatra Frecăței (ancient *Beroe*, Tulcea County, Romania), which is unfortunately insufficiently excavated, is an *extra muros* structure built in the area of a previous Roman necropolis (Petre 1987, 104–6; Baumann 2000, 247–48, pl. 2; 2006, 826–27, pls 21.2–4) (Table 10.3, No. 10). The tomb, mentioned as a crypt by the author of the discovery, was initially located probably inside a commemorative architectural context (an apsed, single-naved hall dated to the 4th–5th centuries AD). During the 6th century AD, this primitive building, which focused on the burial structure, was extended and transformed into a three-aisled church surrounded by a cemetery. Thus, the pre-existing grave was included in the apse and nave of the basilica (Fig. 10.15). The tomb has the appearance of a room with a cradle vault, accessible (as in the case of the monuments in the Varna region) through a west-facing staircase which opened into the nave and contained multiple inhumations at the time of discovery.

Other examples in this series are recorded at Constanța (ancient *Tomis*, Romania), the administrative and religious capital of *Scythia*. Six *intra muros* churches mark the Christian topography of the Proto-Byzantine city, but no Christian cult building was identified outside the urban centre. Three of the six churches known at present in Constanța have *hypogea* integrated in the sanctuary: the large (Fig. 10.16) and the small basilicas in the city's western district (Table 10.3, Nos 11–12) and the basilica discovered in the courtyard of the M. Eminescu High School (Table 10.3, No. 13; Fig. 10.17). If we consider the topographical position inside the church, we can say that all these *hypogea* occupied the area covering the apse and part of the nave in front of it.

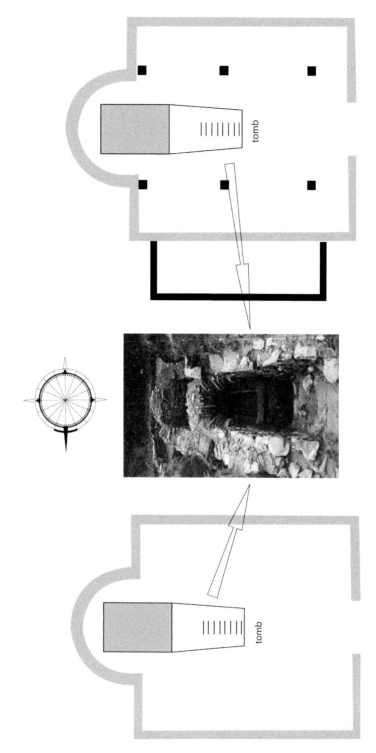

Fig. 10.15. Piatra Frecăței. The basilica, plan and view over the crypt (plan after Baumann 2000: 253, pl. II; photography representing a view over the crypt. Courtesy of Gh. Mănucu-Adameșteanu).

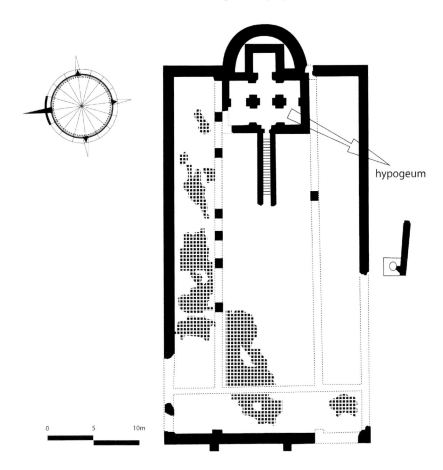

hypogeum

0   5   10m

Fig. 10.16. Constanța. The great basilica, plan and view over the crypt (plan of the church after Barnea 1981: 494, fig. 5. From the National History and Archaeology Museum, Constanța, inventory no. 2246b).

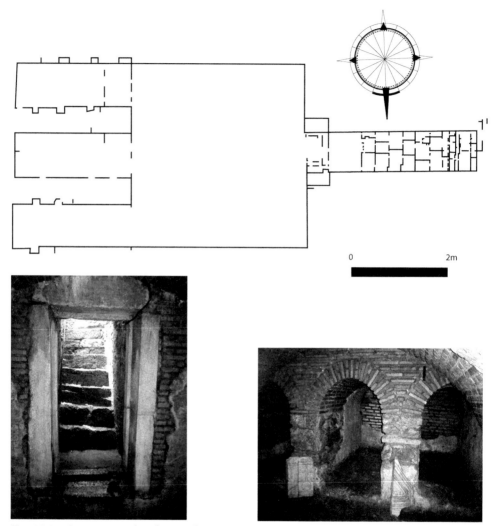

Fig. 10.17. Constanţa. Basilica discovered in the courtyard of M. Eminescu Highschool, plan and view over the crypt (from the National History and Archaeology Museum, Constanţa).

However, their architecture and decoration vary according to the taste and resources of the persons who ordered their construction, as well as to specific cult necessities. A certain monumental tendency can be noticed in the *hypogea* integrated in sanctuaries in Constanţa. The large dimensions and sometimes excessive internal division of all these subterranean constructions support the supposition that all were used for multiple-inhumations. The occupants might have been local martyrs, as widely attested by hagiographic sources at *Tomis*, whose remains could have been moved into the city. We can therefore witness a symbolic fusion of the relics with the church and, at the same time, a significant development of the cult of martyrs in the area of the provincial capital. In this context, the access to the above-mentioned structures (which all have access staircases) could indicate the establishment of regional pilgrimage itineraries.

This typical tradition of the province of *Scythia* has recently been confirmed by the Episcopal Basilica discovered in Murighiol (ancient *Halmyris*, Tulcea County, Romania) (Table 10.3, No. 14; Fig. 10.18). Here, a martyrs' grave, according to M. Zahariade (2009: 141–50, figs 13–21), was associated with the *intra muros* basilica as early as its first phase, dated to the first half of the 4th century AD. The martyrs' grave has the appearance of a room with a cradle vault, which finds a direct provincial analogy at Piatra Frecăței, with the only difference being that at Murighiol two masonry benches were built, on which the bodies were laid. This funerary structure (crypt) is accessible through a *dromos* on the western side and was decorated *al fresco*. A Greek inscription surrounded by eight concentric circles was written in black paint on the eastern wall of the funerary chamber. The text mentions twice the word *martys*. Inside the *hypogeum* were recorded several ceramic artifacts and a lamp hook. A Romanian laboratory (Mirițoiu & Soficaru 2003: 531–80; 2001–2003 (2007): 169–90), undertook the anthropological examination of the two skeletons discovered both disarticulated in the

Fig. 10.18. Murighiol. The episcopal basilica, view over the eastern side of the nave and crypt (courtesy of M. Zahariade 2002).

main chamber, which indicates a double, probably secondary burial (two male adults, one in his sixties and the other 30–40 years old). For both individuals, the skulls were missing, the younger one showing signs of having been beheaded; in addition, both individuals revealed evidence of perimortem violence. All this, corroborated with the hagiographic sources, has lead to the identification of the two individuals buried in the basilica at Murighiol as the local martyrs *Epictet* and *Astion*, executed at *Halmyris* on July 8th AD 290. Along with the remains of the two martyrs were identified a series of disparate bones belonging to both adults and infants, as well as animals. The *hypogeum* was also used for funerary purposes after the abandonment of the cult monument, as shown by an inhumation in the *dromos* (an adult female in a crouched position, with two lamps set near the body – Zahariade 2009: 141, fig. 13).

The last example of martyrs' graves, being probably one of the most interesting of the category discussed here, is the *martyrium* in Niculiţel, in the *territorium* of ancient *Noviodunum* (nowadays Isaccea, Tulcea County) (Table 10.3, No. 15; Fig. 10.19). In this particular case, the person who paid for the monument used a different architectural scenario from that of the other *hypogea* known in *Scythia*: the *martyrium*, placed in the basement of the sanctuary, was associated with a rural basilica, built above and at the same time with a monumental grave. The monumental tomb contained the remains of six individuals (two of them unknown and buried in the lower chamber). This unusual situation could be the result of the basilica being probably built on the site of a pre-existing martyrs' grave, which did not attract other *ad sanctos* burials in its vicinity. V. H. Baumann (2004: 90–128, 153–74, pls 1–9) supposed that, when the church was erected, the two unknown martyrs' remains were placed in a commemorative architectural structure whose traces were conserved west of the *martyrium* included in the sanctuary. These two martyrs were moved from this original burial site into the lower chamber of the *martyrium*; the primitive martyrial grave was later included into the basilica's sanctuary, near its western end. When the church was built, the partially burned remains of the two martyrs (45–55 year old adult males) were laid into the monumental tomb with a cupola, together with four other martyrs: Zotikos, Attalos, Kamasis, and Philippos. These four *martyres Christou* were placed in dorsal *decubitus*, in a collective coffin, into the upper chamber of the *martyrium*. The state of preservation of their skeletons, discovered in anatomical position, suggests that the four were buried at the same moment, which excludes a supposed relocation – inside the church – of the bodies from another pre-existing grave. Two of the skeletons bear traces of *perimortem* violence (Charlier 2009: 83, 86, fig. 21). An interesting detail is that the entrance into the *martyrium* was blocked with a reused limestone slab on which the Greek letter 'Chi' was incised (Popescu 1976: 276–78, no. 267). This detail indicates that the martyrs' grave was isolated and sealed under the floor level of the sanctuary, and remained inaccessible.

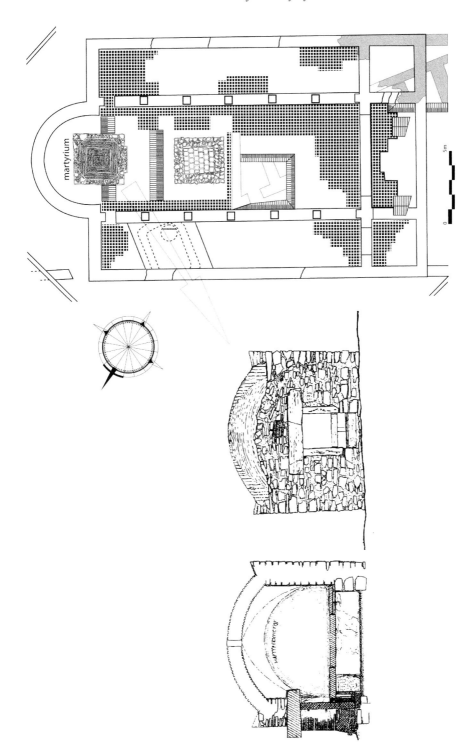

Fig. 10.19. Niculițel. Plan of the basilica and the martyrium under the level of the sanctuary (after Baumann 2004, pls. 4–5).

Concluding observations

The data presented in this contribution is based on a collection of information gathered through publications and excavation reports covering many decades. The disparity of information presented, mainly due to the authors' various methodological approaches and aims, makes it often difficult to get sets of comparable data to be used in a coherent analysis. The purpose of this article has been to collect the data available in order to prepare a better foundation for further studies. In fact, much more detailed studies are necessary in order to reconsider this archaeological evidence and its significance in understanding burial customs in the new Christian cities. Despite this unsatisfactory situation a certain image, even if partial, can be sketched with precaution.

In *Scythia* and *Moesia Secunda* – as for the rest of the Empire – the 5th century AD seems to be the crucial period when the first burials started to move from the outside into the area of the city, even if during the Proto-Byzantine Period funerary areas were still located beyond the city ramparts. The penetration of graves inside the walls was a relatively isolated phenomenon, specific for highly urbanised centres. If we consider the case of Istria, where the urban topography is well-studied, archaeological research has already shown that the suburban space between the new post-Gothic defence wall (dated around the middle of the 3rd century AD) and the classical Roman defence wall further west constantly reinvented itself throughout the 4th–6th centuries AD. On one hand, we witness the extension of the necropoleis eastwards, towards the post-Gothic defence wall, but without having a definitive funerary use for this space. On the other hand, the land around the post-Gothic defence wall was also used for dwellings, and graves were dug as early as the 4th century AD in and around the already ruined (Suceveanu 1982: 36–39, 86–92) Thermae 2 complex (located west of the *extra muros* basilica).

However, parallel with this situation, an increasing association can be noted between burials and churches, be they Eucharistic or cemeterial ones. The archaeological contribution is crucial, yet it alone cannot provide the answers to all the problems raised by the Christian topography (Périn 1987: 9–17; Fiocchi Nicolai 2002: 159–60, n. 6; 2003), whether by the location and inner organisation of cemeteries, or by the association between a church and isolated graves. As C. Snively (2003: 61) noticed, the deliberate and symbolic fusion between burial and church is affiliated to a series of Christian monuments of exceptional theological and architectural value: St Peter's Church in Rome (Deichmann 1982; Krautheimer 1980: 26–28, 86; de Blaauw 1994: 2, 451–55, 470–79, 493–503; Brandt 2001: 110–11; Brandenburg 2005: 91–102, pl. xi); St Paul's Church in Rome (Brandenburg 2005–2006; Filippi 2005–2006); the Church of the Holy Sepulcher in Jerusalem (Krautheimer 1967; 1993: 512–19; Corbo 1982: 39–117, pl. 3; David 2000), and; the *Apostoleion* in Constantinople (Krautheimer 1964; Dagron 1974: 405; Mango 1990). In the area of *Scythia* and *Moesia Secunda*, the process of moving martyrial relics inside the city seems to have already started during the 4th century AD, probably under the influence of models from the Holy Land, Constantinople or Rome.

In some cases, however, the presence of isolated burials does not seem to be connected to the cemeterial use or funerary function of the church. As a general rule, the churches in *Scythia* and *Moesia Secunda* did not play the role of proper cemeteries, unlike the North African ones (Février 1965: 38–39, 55, 145–52, figs 5, 22; Duval 1971–1973, II: 331–38; Yasin 2002: 96–120), the Hispanic ones (Ulbert 1978: 20–44, fig. 11: the basilica of Casa Herrera, Mérida; pp. 86–87, figs 32, 35: the basilica of San Pedro de Alcántara, Córdoba; p. 91, fig. 38: the basilica of El Germo, Córdoba), and the '*a deambulatorio*' basilicas in Rome (Krautheimer 1960; La Rocca 2002). However, if cemeterial churches are not considered, during the 5th and 6th centuries AD, the presence of graves inside or around ecclesiastical monuments continued to represent a rare, special situation in *Scythia* and *Moesia Secunda*. This reality, barely visible and difficult to decipher, suggests a powerful distinction among the dead, based on a Christian sociology that developed slowly. From this point of view, the location of the graves became an important criterion in order to classify and differentiate the deceased (Delahaye 1998: especially pp. 716–17). The diversity of grave forms – from simple graves to more elaborate ones (namely tile graves, burials in stone cists or elaborate constructions involving masonry) – corresponds to a multitude of possible locations.

According to the presently available archaeological data there appears to have been no intermediary stage between the burial of the dead outside the city walls and those buried inside, in association with the churches. The cemeterial basilicas are a minority and seem to appear exceptional in areas of previous necropoleis. The adjacent necropolis grows mainly outside the cult monuments, especially on their flanks. At Švištov, where the necropolis around the *extra muros* basilica seems to have developed at the same time with the neighbouring ecclesiastic context, we can suppose the cemetery was mostly Christian. This may be supported by the dominant E–W orientation of the graves and the considerable decrease, even if not complete disappearance, of the funerary inventory. In this case the church contained graves only occasionally. This controlled and selective process illustrates best the particular status of the graves located in eminent positions very close to or inside the cemeterial churches. Once more, this particular feature is outlined by the direct and indissoluble relation between the cult place and the burial place. When the burial was a martyrial grave, it became subordinated to the cult monument (Pani Ermini 1989: 837–67).

From the outer to the inner space of the basilica, the graves were distributed without a certain topographical pattern in relation to the ecclesiastic monument; however, the 'topographical' repartition of the graves inside or around the church demonstrates a permanent centripetal tendency. Thus, from outside to the inside, the graves converged more and more towards the basilica's sanctuary, and in this process became more and more elaborate as they approached the central ritual area of the church. Relics are not considered in this context, as they seem to be exceptions having penetrated earlier inside the urban area, as witnessed by the case at Murighiol (ancient *Halmyris*).

An attempt to classify such graves in or around the churches on social criteria appears more delicate. Christian funerary inscriptions from our two regions are few in number and limited in content, making it difficult to reveal if the privileged position of the burial is based on 'holiness' criteria or just on the deceased's position as a layman. At Istria, the inventory of the grave located east of the apse of the *extra muros* basilica seems to indicate the high social rank of the deceased, possibly an influential member of the local community. Even in the absence of any epigraphic indication, the presumed external *martyrium* of the cathedral in Švištov might be interpreted as a privileged burial (tomb), maybe of the founding bishop (see the specific elements for the identification of a martyrial chapel proposed by Donceel-Voûte 1995).

In *Scythia*, a number of large underground structures shelter the remains of certain martyrs, whose bodies were moved from their original graves. The presence of martyrial installations, which in this particular geographical area seem to be invariably located *intra ecclesiam*, in the eastern part of the church, within the sanctuary (Brandenburg 1995), indicates in fact the crystallisation of a local martyrial relics worship tradition and, at the same time, a change in the function of the building, admirably theoreticised by C. Sotinel (2005: 411–34). The association of relics with the ecclesiastic context adds to the Eucharistic dimension of the church a commemorative function that supposes the celebration of the martyr's commemorative mass on his *dies natalis* and the pilgrimage at a regional scale. This phenomenon of liturgical fragmentation has been well studied at the Roman Christian basilicas (Bauer 1999: 385–93, 399–401; Emerick 2005: 50–55, figs 6–9), and it is illustrated by many cemetery churches in Rome, among them San Lorenzo fuori le mura (Geertman 1995; 2002).

Finally, we have already seen that, in the Danubian provinces of the Eastern Empire, the creation of a Christian topography and urbanism seems to have been rather a linear process, with extra mural churches first occupying Roman necropoleis, followed by the churches quickly attracting new burials when moving inside the city walls. The traditional Roman city became a city of Christians, even if it remained profoundly attached to the traditional Roman civil values. This is clearly indicated by the large amount of (ordinary) interments in the cemeteries outside the ramparts and only a minority of singular tombs absorbed during the 4th–6th centuries AD into the city and associated with Christian monuments. Such observations lead to a closing question: could the church-grave dichotomy discussed here have been considered a testimony of these urban communities' attachment to the monumental heritage and the material image of their cities, which they wanted to remain unaltered, or was this reality caused by a conservative opposition to the Christian faith in this peripheral region of the troubled Empire?

Acknowledgements

The author is very grateful to Adela Bâltâc, Corina Borş, Dana Iacovache (National History Museum of Romania, Bucharest), Valentin Bottez (University of Bucharest), Costin Băjenaru (National History and Archaeology Museum, Constanţa) for their invaluable help and support. I would also like to thank the anonymous peer-reviewer and the editors of this volume for their helpful advice, suggestions and criticism.

Note

1   Translation: […]For the dead that are not burdened by the heavy sins, it is of use if they are buried inside churches, as those very close to them that come together to the same holy places remember their dead, whose graves they behold and say prayers for them to the Lord. As for those that are burdened by heavy sins, not for forgiveness, but for a hardening of punishment are their bodies laid in churches […].

Sources

Corpus iuris civilis, 2, P. Krueger (ed.), Berlin: Weidmannsche Verlagsbuchhandlung 1959.

Gregory the Great (= Grégoire le Grand): *Dialogues* 4, texte critique et notes A. de Vogüé, traduction P. Antin (Sources Chrétiennes 265), Paris: Les Éditions du Cerf 1980.

Theophilactus Simocattes: *Historiae*, C. de Boor and P. Wirth (eds) (Bibliotheca scriptorum Graecorum et Romanorum Teubneriana), reprinted in Stuttgart: Teubner 1972.

Bibliography

ACIAC 11 = *Actes du XIe Congrès international d'archéologie chrétienne, Lyon, Vienne, Grenoble, Genève et Aoste (21–28 septembre 1986)* (Studi di antichità cristiana 41.1–3/Collection de l'École française de Rome 123.1–3), Vatican City & Rome 1989.

ACIAC 12 = *Akten des XII. Internationalen Kongresses für christliche archäologie, Bonn 22.–28. September 1991* (Studi di antichità cristiana 52.1–2/Jahrbuch für Antike und Christentum suppl. 20.1–2), Vatican City & Münster 1995.

ACIAC 13 = *Acta XIII Congressus internationalis archaeologiae christianae, Split-Poreč, 25.9.– 1.10.1994* (Studi di antichità cristiana 54.1–3/Vjesnik za arheologiju i historiju dalmaninsku, suppl. 87–89), Vatican City & Split 1998.

ACIAC 14 = *Akten des XIV Internationalen Kongresses für christliche archäologie, Wien 19.–26. 9. 1999* (Studi di antichità cristiana 62.1–2/Österreichische Akademie der Wissenschaften. Philosophisch-Historisch Klasse. Archäologische Forschungen 14), Vatican City & Vienna 2006.

Adam-Velene, P. 1995: 'Anaskaphe palaiochristianikes basilikes se these ellenistikon-palaiochristianikon chronon sten Arethousa n. Thessalonikes', *To Archaiologiko ergo ste Makedonia kai Thrake* 9: 351–65.

Aleksova, B. 1986: 'The Early Christian Basilicas at Stobi', *Corsi di cultura sull'arte ravennate e bizantina* 33: 13–81.

Aleksova, B. 1997: *Loca sanctorum Macedoniae. The Cult of Martyrs in Macedonia from the 4th to the 9th Centuries*, Macedonian Civilization-Scopje-Prilep, Institute for Old Slav Culture: Skopje.

Barbet, A. & Monier, F. 2001: 'La crypte funéraire de la basilique sous le lycée M. Eminescu à Constantza (Roumanie)', in *La peinture funéraire antique IVe siècle av. J.-C.-IVe siècle ap. J.-C.* (Actes du VIIe Colloque de l'Association Internationale pour la peinture murale antique (AIPMA), 6–10 octobre 1998, Saint-Romain-en-Gal-Vienne), Éditions Errance: Paris, 221–28.

Barnea, I. 1977a: 'La basilique citerne de Tropaeum Traiani à la lumière des dernières fouilles archéologiques', *Dacia* N.S. 21: 221–33.

Barnea, I. 1977b: *Monuments paléochrétiens de Roumanie* (Sussidi allo studio delle antichità cristiane pubblicati per cura del Pontificio Istituto di archeologia cristiana 6), Pontificio Istituto di archeologia cristiana: Vatican City.

Barnea I. (coord.) 1979: *Tropaeum Traiani I. Cetatea*, Editura Academiei Republicii Socialiste România: Bucharest.

Barnea, I. 1981: 'Le cripte delle basiliche paleocristiane della Scizia Minore', *Revue des Études sud-est européennes* 19.3: 489–505.

Bauer, F. A. 1999: 'La frammentazione liturgica nella chiesa romana del primo medioevo', *Rivista di Archeologia Cristiana* 75: 385–446.

Baumann, V. H. 2000: 'À propos des premières basiliques chrétiennes découvertes aux embouchures du Danube', in M. Iacob, E. Oberländer-Târnoveanu, Fl. Topoleanu (eds): *Istro-Pontica. Muzeul tulcean la a 50 a aniversare 1950–2000. Omagiu lui Gavrilă Simion la 45 de ani de activitate 1955–2000*, Institutul de Cercetări Eco-Muzeale: Tulcea, 247–56.

Baumann, V. H. 2004: *Sângele martirilor* (Izvoarele creştinismului românesc), Editura Arhiepiscopiei Tomisului: Constanţa.

Baumann, V. H. 2006: 'À propos des premières basiliques paléo-chrétiennes découvertes à l'embouchure du Danube', in *ACIAC* 14.1: 825–31.

Ben-Abed-Ben Khader, A. et al. 2004: *Sidi Jdidi I. La basilique sud* (Collection de l'École française de Rome 339), Rome.

Beševliev, V. 1964: *Spätgriechische und spätlateinische Inschriften aus Bulgarien* (Deutsche Akademie der Wissenschaften zu Berlin, Institut für Griechisch-Römische Altertumskunde. Berliner byzantinische Arbeiten 30), Akademie Verlag GmbH: Berlin.

Beševliev, V. 1975: 'Novi starochristijanski nadpisi ot Varna', *Izvestija na narodnija Muzej Varna* 11 (26): 148–150.

Bierbrauer, V. 1984: 'Aspetti archeologici di Goti, Alamanni e Longobardi', in *Magistra barbaritas*, 445–508.

Bierbrauer, V. 1994: 'Germanen des 5. und 6. Jahrhunderts in Italien', in R. Francovich & G. Noyé (eds): *La Storia dell'alto medioevo italiano (VI–X secolo) alla luce dell'archeologia. Convegno internazionale (Siena, 2–6 dicembre 1992)* (Biblioteca di archeologia medievale 11), All'Insegna del Giglio: Florence, 33–56.

Biernacki, A. B. 2005: 'A City of Christians: Novae in the 5th and 6th c. A.D.', *Archaeologia Bulgarica* 9.1: 53–74.

de Blaauw, S. 1994: *Cultus et decor. Liturgia e architettura nella Roma tardoantica e medievale Basilica Salvatoris, Sanctae Mariae, Sancti Petri* (Studi e testi 356–357), Biblioteca apostolica vaticana: Vatican City.

Bojadjiev, S. 1995: 'L'église de Djanavar Tépé près de Varna', in B. Borkopp, B. Schellewald & L. Theis (eds): *Studien zur byzantinischen Kunstgeschichte. Festschrift für Horst Hallensleben zum 65. Geburtstag*, A. M. Hakkert: Amsterdam, 65–71.

Bonacasa Carra, R. M. 1989: 'Il complesso paleocristiano a nord del teatro di Sabratha: una revisione critica', in *ACIAC* 11.3: 1909–26.

Bonnet, C. & Privati, B. 2000: 'De la ville antique à la ville chrétienne. Les chantiers archéologiques de Genève', in *Romanité*, 381–90.

Bowden, W., Hodges R., Lako, K. et al. 2002: 'Roman and Late-Antique Butrint: Excavations and Survey 2000–2001', *Journal of Roman Archaeology* 15: 199–229.

Brandenburg, H. 1995: 'Altar und Grab. Zu einem Problem des Märtyrerkultes im 4. und 5. Jh.', in M. Lamberigts & P. van Deun (eds): *Martyrium in Multidisciplinary Perspective. Memorial Louis Reekmans* (Bibliotheca ephemeridum theologicarum lovaniensium 117), Peeters: Leuven, 71–98.

Brandenburg, H. 2005: *Ancient Churches of Rome. From the Fourth to the Seventh Century. The Dawn of Christian Architecture in the West* (Bibliothèque de l'antiquité tardive 8), Brepols: Turnhout.

Brandenburg, H. 2005–2006: 'Die Architektur der Basilika San Paolo fuori le mura. Das Apostolgrab als Zentrum der Liturgie und des Märtyrerkultes', *Römische Mitteilungen* 112: 237–75.

Brandt, O. 2001: 'Constantine, the Lateran, and Early Church Building Policy', in J. R. Brandt & O. Steen (eds): *Imperial Art as Christian Art – Christian Art as Imperial Art. Expression and Meaning in Art and Architecture from Constantine to Justinian* (Acta ad archaeologiam et artium historiam pertinentia 15 (N.S. 1), 109–14.

Buora, M. 2010: 'La ricerca sui goti nell'Italia nordorientale e nelle regioni contermini', *Peuce* S.N. 8: 185–202.

Cantino Wataghin, G. 1999: 'The Ideology of Urban Burials', in G. P. Brogiolo & B. Ward-Perkins (eds): *The Idea and Ideal of the Town Between Late Antiquity and the Early Middle Ages* (The Transformation of the Roman World 4), E. J. Brill: Leiden, Boston & Cologne, 147–63.

Capponi, M. & Ghilardi, M. 2002: 'Scoperta, nel *Templum Pacis*, di un area sepolcrale probabilmente contemporanea alla fondazione dei SS. Cosma e Damiano', in Guidobaldi & Guiglia Guidobaldi I: 733–56.

CCA = *Cronica cercetărilor arheologice din România* [*Chronicle of Archaeological Researches in Romania*], Bucharest, followed by the year of publication of the field research results (available on http: //www.cimec.ro).

Charlier, P. 2009: *Male mort. Morts violentes dans l'Antiquité*, Fayard: Paris.

Chevalier, P. 1996: Ecclesiae Dalmatiae. *L'architecture paléochrétienne de la province de Dalmatie (IVe–VIIe s.)* [*en dehors de la capitale, Salone*]. Tome 1: *Catalogue*. Tome 2: *Illustrations et conclusions*, in *Salone II. Recherches archéologiques franco-croates dirigées par N. Duval et E. Marin* (Collection de l'École française de Rome 194.2), De Boccard & «L'Erma» di Bretschneider: Paris & Rome.

Chevalier, P., Raynaud, M.-P., Vanderheyde, C., Wurch-Koželj, M., Beaudry, N., Muçaj, S. & Sodini, J.-P. 2003: 'Trois basiliques et un groupe épiscopal des Ve–VIe siècles réétudiés à Byllis (Albanie)', *Hortus Artium Medievalium. Journal of the International Research Center for Late Antiquity and Middle Ages* 9: 155–66.

Christern, J. 1976: *Das frühchristliche Pilgerheiligtum von Tebessa. Architektur und Ornamentik einer spätantiken Bauhütte in Nordafrika*, Franz Steiner: Wiesbaden.

Čičikova, M. 1997: 'La basilique et la nécropole paléochrétiennes *extra muros* de Novae (Mésie Inférieure)', in A. B. Biernacki & P. Pawlak (eds): *Late Roman and Early Byzantine Cities on the Lower Danube from the 4th to the 6th Century A.D., International Conference. Poznań, Poland 15–17 November 1995. Studies and Materials*, Instytut Historii Uniwersytetu im. Adama Mickiewicza w Poznaniu: Poznań, 57–69.

Constantin, R., Radu, L., Ionescu, M. & Alexandru, N. 2007: 'Mangalia. Cercetări arheologice de salvare', *Peuce* S.N. 5: 241–96.

Corbo, V. 1982: *Il Santo Sepolcro di Gerusaleme. Aspetti archeologici dalle origini al periodo crociato* (Studium Biblicum Franciscanum. Collectio maior 29), 3 vols. (I. *Testo*, Jerusalem

1982; II. *Tavole con annotazioni in italiano e in inglese*, Jerusalem 1981; III. *Documentazione fotografica con annotazioni in italiano e in inglese*, Jerusalem 1981), Franciscan Printing Press: Jerusalem.

Cortesi, G. 1982: 'I principali edifici sacri ravennati in funzione sepolcrale nei secc. V et VI', *Corsi di cultura sull'arte ravennate e bizantina* 29: 63–107.

Costambeys, M. 2002: 'The Culture and Practice of Burial in and around Rome in the Sixth Century', in Guidobaldi & Guiglia Guidobaldi I: 721–31.

Dagron, G. 1974: *Naissance d'une capitale: Constantinople et ses institutions de 330 à 451*, Presses universitaires de France: Paris.

Dagron, G. 1977: 'Le christianisme dans la ville byzantine', *Dumbarton Oaks Papers* 31: 1–25.

Dagron, G. 1991: '"Ainsi rien n'échappera à la réglementation." États, Église, corporations, confréries: à propos des inhumations à Constantinople (IVe–Xe siècle)', in V. Kravari, J. Lefort & C. Morrisson (eds): *Homme et richesses dans l'Empire byzantin*, 2. *VIIIe–XVe siècle* (Réalités byzantines 3), Éditions P. Lethielleux: Paris, 155–82.

D'Andria, F., Mastronuzzi, G. & Melissano, V. 2006: 'La chiesa e la necropoli paleocristiana di Vaste nel Salento', *Rivista di Archeologia Cristiana* 82: 231–322.

David, M. 2000: 'Le Saint-Sépulcre de Jérusalem: genèse et métamorphose d'un modèle', in R. Cassanelli (ed.): *La Méditerranée des Croisades*: Milan, 85–95.

Deichmann, F. W. 1982: 'Märtyrerbasilika, Martyrion, Memoria und Altargrab', in *Rom, Ravenna, Konstantinopel, Naher Osten: Gesammelte Studien zur spätantiken Architektur, Kunst und Geschichte*, Franz Steiner: Wiesbaden, 375–400.

Delahaye, G.-R. 1998: 'Organisation d'un cimetière du VIIe siècle autour d'une église: le cas de Villemomble (France)', in *ACIAC* 13.2: 711–22.

Dimitrov, K. 1995: 'Novae on the Lower Danube as an Early Christian Centre (5th–6th Century AD)', in *ACIAC* 12.2: 700–4.

Djingov, G. & Mašov, S. 1985: 'Arheologičeski proučvanija kraj Ljutibrod, Vračanski okrăg', *Izvestija na muzeite ot Severozapadna Bălgarija* 10: 39–70.

Donceel-Voûte, P. 1988: *Les pavements des églises byzantines de Syrie et du Liban. Décor, archéologie et liturgie* (Publications d'histoire de l'art et d'archéologie de l'Université catholique de Louvain 69), Institut supérieur d'archéologie et d'histoire de l'art: Louvain-la-neuve.

Donceel-Voûte, P. 1995: 'L'inévitable chapelle des martyrs: identification', in M. Lamberigts & P. van Deun (eds): *Martyrium in Multidisciplinary Perspective. Memorial Louis Reekmans* (Bibliotheca ephemeridum theologicarum lovaniensium 117), Peeters: Leuven, 179–96.

Donceel-Voûte, P. 1998: 'Le fonctionnement des lieux de culte aux VIe–VIIe siècles: monuments, textes et images', in *ACIAC* 13.2: 97–156.

Duval, N. 1971–1973: *Les églises africaines à deux absides. Recherches archéologiques sur la liturgie chrétienne en Afrique du Nord*. Tome I: *Recherches archéologiques à Sbeitla. Les basiliques de Sbeitla à deux sanctuaires opposés (Basiliques I, II et IV)*. Tome II: *Inventaire des monuments – interprétation* (Bibliothèque des Ècoles françaises d'Athénes et de Rome 218 e 218 bis), Paris.

Duval, N. 1984–1985: 'Le chœur de l'église de Siagu (Tunisie). Études d'archéologie chrétienne nord-africaine: XII', *Felix Ravenna* quarta serie, 127–130.1–2: 159–99.

Duval, N. 1995 (coord.): *Les premiers monuments chrétiens de la France. 1. Sud-Est et Corse*, Ministère de la Culture – Picard : Paris.

Duval, Y. 1982: *Loca sanctorum Africae. Le culte des martyrs en Afrique du IVe au VIIe siècle* (Collection de l'École française de Rome 58.1–2), De Boccard & «L'Erma» di Bretschneider : Paris & Rome.

Duval, Y. 1988: *Auprès des saints, corps et âme. L'inhumation «ad sanctos» dans la chrétienté d'Orient et d'Occident du IIIe au VIIe siècle* (Collection des Études Augustiniennes: Antiquité 121), Études Augustiniennes: Paris.

Emerick, J. J. 2005: 'Altars Personified: The Cult of the Saints and the Chapel System in Pope Paschal I's S. Prassede (817–818)', in J. J. Emerick & D. M. Deliyannis (eds): *Archaeology in Architecture: Studies in Honor of Cecil L. Striker*, Philipp von Zabern: Mainz am Rhein, 43–63.

Ennabli, L. 1997: *Carthage une métropole chrétienne du IVe à la fin du VIIe siècle* (Études d'antiquités africaines), CNRS Éditions: Paris.

Falla Castelfranchi, M. 1989: 'Le sepolture di vescovi e monaci in Mesopotamia (IV–VIII secolo)', in *ACIAC* 11.2: 1267–79.

Février, P.-A. 1965: *Fouilles de Sétif. Les basiliques chrétiennes du quartier nord-ouest*, Éditions du Centre National de la Recherche Scientifique: Paris.

Février, P.-A. 1987: 'La mort chrétienne', in *Segni e riti nella chiesa altomedievale occidentale* (Settimane di studio del Centro italiano sull'Alto medioevo 33.2), Presso la sede del Centro: Spoleto, 881–942.

Fiedler, U. 1992: *Studien zu Gräberfeldern des 6. bis 9. Jahhunderts an der unteren Donau* (Universitätsforschungen zur prähistorischen Archäologie 11), Dr. Rudolf Habelt GmbH: Bonn.

Filippi, G. 2005–2006: 'Die Ergebnisse der neuen Ausgrabungen am Grab des Apostels Paulus. Reliquienkult und Eucharistie im Presbyterium der Paulusbasilika', *Römische Mitteilungen* 112: 277–92.

Filow, B. 1913: *Sofiiskata cărkva Sv. Sofija* (Materiali za istorijata na Sofija 4), Sofija: Carska Pridvorna Pečatnica.

Fiocchi Nicolai, V. 2002: 'Santuario martiriale e territorio nella diocese di "Nomentum": l'esempio di S. Alessandro', *Rivista di Archeologia Cristiana* 78: 157–89.

Fiocchi Nicolai, V. 2003: 'Elementi di trasformazione dello spazio funerario tra tarda antichità ed altomedioevo', in *Uomo e spazio nell'Alto Medioevo* (Settimane di studio del Centro italiano sull'Alto Medioevo 50.2), Presso la sede del Centro: Spoleto, 921–69.

Geertman, H. 1995: 'Cripta anulare "ante litteram". Forma, contesto e significato del monumento sepolcrale di San Lorenzo a Roma', in *Martyrium in Multidisciplinary Perspective. Memorial Louis Reekmans* (Bibliotheca ephemeridum theologicarum lovaniensium 117), Peeters: Leuven, 125–55.

Geertman, H. 2002: 'La basilica maior di San Lorenzo f.l.m.', in Guidobaldi & Guiglia Guidobaldi II: 1225–47.

di Gennaro, F. & Griesbach, J. 2003: 'Le sepolture all'interno delle ville con particolare riferimento al territorio di Roma', in Pergola, Santangeli Valenzani & Volpe (eds), 123–66.

Giunta, F. 1984: 'Gli ostrogoti in Italia', in *Magistra barbaritas*, 53–96.

Gkine-Tsophopoulou, E. 1995: 'Stamata. Palaiochristianike basilike', *Archaiologikon Deltion* 50, B1, Chron., 71–73.

Glaser, F. 1991: *Das frühchristliche Pilgerheiligtum auf dem Hemmaberg* (Aus Forschung und Kunst 26), Verlag des Geschichtsvereins für Kärnten: Klagenfurt.

Goldfus, H. 1997: *Tombs and Burials in Churches and Monasteries of Byzantine Palestine (324–628 A.D.)*, Ph. D. Thesis, Princeton University, Princeton (N. J.), Microform available from University Microfilms International, Ann Arbor, Michigan.

Grossmann, P. 2002: *Christliche Architektur in Ägypten* (Handbook of Oriental Studies. The Near and Middle East 62), E. J. Brill: Leiden, Boston & Cologne.

Guidobaldi, F. & Guiglia Guidobaldi, A. (eds) 2002: Ecclesiae Urbis, *Atti del congresso internazionale di studi sulle chiese di Roma (IV–X secolo), Roma, 4–10 settembre 2000*, I–III (Studi di antichità cristiana pubblicati a cura del Pontificio Istituto di archeologia cristiana 59), Vatican City.

Guyon, J. 2000: 'La topographie chrétienne de Marseille pendant l'Antiquité tardive et le Haut Moyen âge. Retour sur un dossier toujours ouvert', in *Romanité*, 391–407.

Guyon, J. 2002: 'À l'origine de la redécouverte et de l'interprétation du monument de la via Labicana: l'iconographie de la basilique cémétériale des Saints Marcellin-et-Pierre', in Guidobaldi & Guiglia Guidobaldi II: 1157–73.

Guyon, J. & Cardi G. 1984: 'L'église B, dite "basilique cruciforme"', in N. Duval & V. Popović (eds): *Caričin Grad I* (Collection de l'École française de Rome 75), Belgrade & Rome, 1–90.

Guyon, J., Strueber, L. & Manacorda, D. 1981: 'Recherches autour de la basilique constantinienne des saints Pierre-et-Marcellin sur la via Labicana à Rome: le mausolée et l'enclos au nord de la basilique', *Mélanges de l'École française de Rome. Antiquité* 93: 999–1061.

Handley, M. A. 2010: 'Two Hundred and Seventy-Four Addenda and Corrigenda to the *Prosopography of the Later Roman Empire* from the Latin-Speaking Balkans', *Journal of Late Antiquity* 3.1: 113–57.

Hellenkemper, H. 1990: s.v. Kommagene–Kilikien–Isaurien, *Reallexikon zur Byzantinische Kunst* 4, Anton Hiersemann: Stuttgart, cols 182–355.

Ivanov, R. 1997: 'Das römische Verteidigunssystem an der unteren Donau zwischen *Dorticum* und *Durostorum* (Bulgarien) von Augustus bis Maurikios', *Bericht der Römisch-Germanischen Kommission* 78: 467–640.

Ivanova, V. 1937: 'Tri novorazkopani baziliki vă Hissarija', *Izvestija na bălgarskija arheologičeski institut. Bulletin de l'Institut archéologique bulgare* 11: 214–42.

Ivison, E. A. 1996: 'Burial and Urbanism at Late Antique and Early Byzantine Corinth (c. AD 400–700)', in N. Christie & S. T. Loseby (eds): *Towns in Transition. Urban Evolution in Late Antiquity and the Early Middle Ages*, Scolar Press: Aldershot Hants, 99–125.

Karagiorgou, O. 2001: 'Demetrias and Thebes: The Fortunes and Misfortunes of Two Thessalian Port Cities in Late Antiquity', in L. Lavan (ed.): *Recent Research in Late-Antique Urbanism* (Journal of Roman Archaeology, Suppl. Ser. 42), Portsmouth, Rhode Island, 183–215.

Kazanski, M. 1991: *Les Goths (Ier–VIIe après J.-C.)* (Collection des Hespérides), Éditions Errance: Paris.

Kidd, D. & Pekarskaya, L. 1995: 'New Insight into the Hoard of 6th–7th Century Silver from Martynovka (Ukraine)', in F. Vallet & M. Kazanski (eds): *La noblesse romaine et les chefs barbares du IIIe au VIIe siècle* (Mémoires. Association française d'archéologie mérovingienne 9), Association française d'archéologie mérovingienne, Musée des antiquités nationales: Saint-Germain-en-Laye, 351–60.

Krautheimer, R. 1960: 'Mensa–Coemeterium–Martyrium', *Cahiers archéologiques* 11: 15–40.

Krautheimer, R. 1964: 'Zu Konstantins Apostelkirche in Konstantinopel', in A. Stuiber & A. Hermann (eds): *Mullus. Festschrift Theodor Klauser* (Jahrbuch für Antike und Christentum, Ergänzungsband 1), Aschendorff: Münster Westfalen, 224–29.

Krautheimer, R. 1967: 'The Constantinian Basilica', *Dumbarton Oaks Papers* 21: 117–40.

Krautheimer, R. 1980: *Rome, Profile of a City, 312–1308*, Princeton University Press: Princeton, New Jersey.

Krautheimer, R. 1993: 'The Ecclesiastical Building Policy of Constantine', in G. Bonamente & F. Fusco (eds): *Costantino il Grande. Dall'antichità all'umanesimo. Colloquio sul cristianesimo nel mondo antico. Macerata 18–20 Dicembre 1990*, vol. 2, Università degli Studi di Macerata: Macerata, 509–52.

La Rocca, E. 2002: 'Le basiliche cristiane "a deambulatorio" e la sopravvivenza del culto eroica', in Guidobaldi & Guiglia Guidobaldi II: 1109–40.

Laskaris, N. 1991: *Monuments funéraires paléochrétiens (et byzantins) de la Grèce*, Athènes: Paris.

Lassus, J. 1938: 'L'église cruciforme Antioche–Kaoussié', in *Antioch-on-the-Orontes, 2. The Excavations of 1933–1936*, Department of Art and Archaeology of Princeton University: Princeton, 5–44.

Leone, A. 2002: 'L'inumazione in "spazio urbano" a Cartagine tra V e VII secolo d.C.', *Antiquité tardive. Revue internationale d'histoire et d'archéologie* 10: 233–48.

Leschi, L. 1957: 'Fouilles à Tipasa dans l'église d'Alexandre', in *Études d'épigraphie, d'archéologie et d'histoire africaines*, Arts et métiers: Paris, 371–76.

Macridy, T. 1912: 'Antiquités de Notion. II', *Jahreshefte des Österreichischen Archäologischen Institutes in Wien* 15: 36–67.

Magistra barbaritas = *Magistra barbaritas. I barbari in Italia*, Libri Scheiwiller: Milan 1984.

Mango, C. 1990: 'Constantine's Mausoleum and the Translation of Relics', *Byzantinische Zeitschrift* 83.1: 51–61, and 'Constantine's Mausoleum: Addendum', *Byzantinische Zeitschrift* 83.2: 434.

Marki, E. 1997a: 'Deux tombeaux monumentaux protobyzantins récemment découverts en Grèce du Nord', *Cahiers archéologiques* 45: 19–24.

Marki, E. 1997b: 'Louloudies 1997', *To Archaiologiko ergo ste Makedonia kai Thrake* 11: 289–96.

Marki, E. 2001: *Kitros mia pole kastro tes byzantines periphereias. Archaiologike kai istorike prosegnise*, Thessaloniki: Tramakia.

Marki, E. 2002: 'Ta christianika koimeteria sten Hellada. Organosi, typologia, taphiki zographiki, martyria, koimeteriakes basilikes', *Deltion tes christianikes archaiologikes hetaireias* 23: 163–75.

Marki, E. 2006: *He nekropole tes Thessalonikes stous hysteroromaikous kai palaiochristianikous chronous (meta tou 3ou eos meta tou 8ou ai. m.Ch.)* (Demosieumata tou 'Archaiologikon Deltion' 95), Hypourgeio Politismou: Athens.

Mărgineanu-Cârstoiu, M. 1977: 'Problèmes d'architecture concernant la citerne romaine et la basilique chrétienne de Tropaeum Traiani', *Dacia* N.S. 21: 235–50.

Megaw, A. H. S. 1984: 'A Cemetery Church with Trefoil Sanctuary in Crete', in *ACIAC* 10, 2, 321–29.

Meneghini, R. & Santangeli Valenzani, R. 1994: 'Corredi funerari, produzioni e paessagio sociale a Roma tra VI e VII secolo', *Rivista di Archeologia Cristiana* 70: 321–37.

Mérel-Brandenburg, A.-B. 1995: 'Montferand. Église cimétériale', in Duval (coord.), 26–31.

Milinković, M. 2001: 'Die Byzantinische Höhenanlage auf der Jelica in Serbien – ein Beispiel aus dem nördlichen Illyricum des 6. Jh.', *Starinar* 51: 71–130.

Milošević, G. 2006: 'Late Roman Martyrium and Basilica at the Necropolis in Niš (Naissus)', in *Early Christian Martyrs and Relics and their Veneration in East and West, International Conference, Varna, November 20th–23rd 2003* (Acta Musei Varnaensis 4), Reghionalen istoričeski muzej: Varna, 173–86.

Minčev, A. 1996–97: 'Novi danni za rannochristijanskata bazilika s mozaiki s. Škorpilovci, Varnensko', *Izvestija na Narodnija Muzej Varna. Bulletin du Musée National de Varna* 32–33 (47–48), 130–50.

Minchev, A. 2003: *Early Christian Reliquaries from Bulgaria (4th–6th Century AD)*, Varna Regional Museum of History/Stalker: Varna.

Minčev, A. & Tenekedjiev, V. 2010: 'Razkopki na rannohristiianska cărkva v M. Djanavara krai Varna', *Arheologičeski otkritiia i razkopki prez 2009 g.*, Bălgarska Akademija na Naukite/ Nacionalen Istoričeski Institut i Muzej: Sofia, 277–79.

Mirițoiu, N. & Soficaru, A. D. 2001–03 (2007): 'Osteobiographical Study of the Human Remains Discovered in the Crypt of Murighiol (antique Halmyris) Basilica', *Il Mar Nero. Annali di archeologia e storia* 5: 169–90.

Mirițoiu, N. & Soficaru, A. 2003: 'Studiu antropologic al osemintelor descoperite in cripta basilicii de la Murighiol (anticul Halmyris)', *Peuce* S.N. 1 (14) 531–80.

Müller-Wiener, W. 2005: s.v. Milet, *Reallexikon zur Byzantinische Kunst* 6, Anton Hiersemann: Stuttgart, cols 362–77.

Netzhammer, R. 2005: *Antichitățile creștine din Dobrogea²*, Editura Academiei Române: Bucharest.

Nieddu, A. M. 2003: 'L'utilizzazione funeraria del suburbio nei secoli V e VI', in Pergola, Santangeli Valenzani & Volpe (eds), 545–606.

Nikolajević, I. 1978: 'Sahrahjivanje u ranohrišćanskim crkvama na područiju Srbije', *Arheološki vestnik* (Ljubljana) 29: 678–93.

Nikolajević, I. 1980: 'Nécropoles et tombes chrétiennes en Illyricum oriental', in *Rapports présentés au Xe Congrès international d'archéologie chrétienne (Thessalonique, 28 septembre – 4 octobre 1980)*, Société d'études macédoniennes (= Ellinika. Revue de la Société d'études macédoniennes. Supplement 26): Thessalonique, 349–67.

Nubar, H. 1971a: 'Contribuții la topografia cetății Histria în epoca romano-bizantină. Considerații generale asupra necropolei din sectorul bazilicii "extra muros"', *Studii și cercetări de istorie veche* 22.2: 199–215.

Nubar, H. 1971b: 'Ein gotisch-alanisches Grab in Histria', *Dacia* N.S. 15: 335–47.

Orlandos, A. 1929: 'Hai palaiochristianikai bazilikai tes Lesbou', *Archaiologikon Deltion* 12: 1–72.

Ostojić, I. 1963: 'Basilica paleocristiana con battistero a Povlja (Dalmazia)', *Rivista di Archeologia Cristiana* 39.1–2: 139–49.

Oța, L. & Domăneanțu, C. 2010: 'Remarques sur les tombes du Haut-Empire d'Histria', in M. V. Angelescu, I. Achim, A. Bâltâc, V. Rusu-Bolindeț & V. Bottez (eds): *Antiquitas istro-pontica. Mélanges d'archéologie et d'histoire ancienne offerts à Alexandru Suceveanu*, Editura Mega: Cluj-Napoca, 393–400.

Panaitescu, A. 1976: 'Morminte din necropolele cetății Tropaeum Traiani', *Pontica* 9: 207–11.

Pani Ermini, L. 1989: 'Santuario e città fra tarda antichità e altomedioevo', in *Santi e demoni nell'Alto Medioevo (secoli V–XI)* (Settimane di studio del Centro italiano sull'Alto medioevo 36, 2), Presso la sede del Centro: Spoleto, 837–77.

Papuc, G. & Custurea, G. 1989: 'Adamclisi. Necropolă', in A. Barnea: *Cronica cercetărilor arheologice efectuate în anii 1981–1988 de Institutul de Arheologie din București* (Studii și cercetări de istorie veche și arheologie 40.3): 295–313.

Parnicki-Pudełko, St. 1980 (1982): 'Novae – Sektor zachodni, 1978. Sprawozdanie tymczasowe z wykopalisk ekspedycji archeologicznej Universytetu im. Adama Mickiewicza w Poznaniu', *Archeologia* (Warszawa) 31: 113–66.

Parnicki-Pudełko, S. 1983: 'The Early Christian Episcopal Basilica in Novae, *Archaeologia Polona* 21–22: 241–270.

Pelekanides, S. 1977: 'He exo ton teichon palaiochristianike basilike ton Philippon', in *Meletes palaiochristianikes kai byzantines archaiologias* (Idruma Meletôn Hersonêsou tou Aimou 174), Idruma Meletôn Hersonêsou tou Aimou: Thessaloniki, 333–94.

Pergola, P., Santangeli Valenzani, R. & Volpe, R. (eds) 2003: Suburbium. *Il suburbio di Roma dalla crisi del sistema delle ville a Gregorio Magno* (Collection de l'École française de Rome 311), Rome.

Périn, P. 1987: 'Des nécropoles romaines tardives aux nécropoles du Haut-Moyen Âge. Remarques sur la topographie funéraire en gaule mérovingienne et à sa périphérie', *Cahiers archéologiques* 35: 9–30.

Petre, A. 1987: *La romanité en Scythie Mineure (IIe–VIIe siècles de notre ère). Recherches archéologiques*, AIESEE: Bucharest.

Picard, J.-C. 1988: *Le souvenir des évêques. Sépultures, listes épiscopales et culte des évêques en Italie du Nord des origines au Xe siècle* (Bibliothèque des Écoles françaises d'Athénes et de Rome 268), Rome.

Picard, J.-C. 1998: *Évêques, saints et cités en Italie et en Gaule. Études d'archéologie et d'histoire* (Collection de l'École française de Rome 242), Rome.

Piccirillo, M. & Alliata, E. 1998: *Mount Nebo. New Archaeological Excavations 1967–1997* (Studium biblicum franciscanum. Collectio maior 27), Franciscan Printing Press: Jerusalem.

Pillinger, R. 1988: *Das martyrium des Heiligen Dasius (Text, Übersetzung und Kommentar)* (Österreichische Akademie der Wissenschaften. Philosophisch-historische Klasse Sitzungsberichte 517. Band), Verlag der Österreichischen Akademie der Wissenschaften: Vienna.

Pillinger, R., Popova, V. & Zimmermann, B. (eds) 1999: *Corpus der spätantiken und frühchristlichen Wandmalereien Bulgariens* (Schriften der Balkankommission/ Österreichische Akademie der Wissenschaften. Antiquarische Abteilung 21), Verlag der Österreichischen Akademie der Wissenschaften: Vienna.

Popescu, E. 1957: 'Sectorul de la vest de zidul de incintă din valul al III-lea', in E. Condurachi et al.: 'Şantierul arheologic Histria', *Materiale şi cercetări arheologice* 4: 16–24.

Popescu, E. 1959: 'Sectorul de la V de zidul de incintă din valul III', in D. M. Pippidi et al.: 'Raport asupra activităţii şantierului Histria în campania 1956', *Materiale şi cercetări arheologice* 5: 291–96.

Popescu, E. 1976: *Inscripţiile greceşti şi latine din secolele IV–XIII descoperite în România*, Editura Academiei Republicii Socialiste România: Bucharest.

Popescu, E. 1994: 'Les antiquités paléochrétiennes d'Histria', in *Christianitas daco-romana. Florilegium studiorum*, Editura Academiei Române: Bucharest, 306–96.

Rădulescu, A. 1966: *Monumente romano-bizantine din sectorul de vest al cetăţii Tomis*, Muzeul Regional de Arheologie Dobrogea: Constanţa.

Rebillard, É. 2003: *Religion et sépulture: L'Église, les vivants et les morts dans l'Antiquité tardive* (Civilisations et société 115), Éditions de l'École des Hautes Études en Sciences Sociales: Paris.

Reekmans, L. 1968: 'L'implantation monumentale chrétienne dans la zone suburbaine de Rome du IVe au IXe siècle', in *Miscellanea in onore di Enrico Josi 3–4 = Rivista di Archeologia Cristiana* 44.1–4: 173–207.

Ribak, E. 2007: *Religious Communities in Byzantine Palestina. The Relationship between Judaism, Christianity and Islam, AD 400–700*, British Archaeological Reports, International Series 1646, Archaeopress: Oxford.

Romanité = Romanité et cité chrétienne. Permanences et mutations, intégration et exclusion du Ier au VIe siècle. Mélanges en l'honneur d'Yvette Duval (De l'archéologie à l'histoire), De Boccard: Paris 2000.

Russell, J. 1979: 'Recent Archaeological Research in Turkey. Anemurium, 1978', *Anatolian Studies. Journal of the British Institute of Archaeology at Ankara* 29: 182–86.

Rusu-Bolindeț, V. & Bădescu, A. 2003–2005: 'Histria. Sectorul Basilica extra muros', *Studii și cercetări de istorie veche și arheologie* 54–56: 103–30.

Rusu Bolindeț et al. 2009: 'Istria. Sectorul Basilica extra muros', *CCA* 2009 = *Valachica* 21–22: 127–29.

Rusu Bolindeț et al. 2010: 'Istria. Sectorul Basilica extra muros', *CCA* 2010: 87–90.

Salvetti, C. 1994: 'Qualche considerazione sulle tombe gote della via Flaminia', in *Historiam pictura refert. Miscellanea in onore di padre A. Recio Veganzones O.F.M.*, Pontificio Istituto di Archeologia Cristiana: Vatican City, 523–32.

Saradi, H. G. 2006: *The Byzantine City in the Sixth Century: Literary Images and Historical Reality*, Society of Messenian Archaeological Studies: Athens.

Schmitz, W. 2004: 'Der neidische Tod und die Hoffnung auf das Paradies. Die frühchristlichen Inschriften als Zeugnisse der Christianisierung des Rhein-Mosel-Raums', in S. Ristow (ed.): *Neue Forschungen zu den Anfängen des Christentums im Rheinland* (Jahrbuch für Antike und Christentum. Ergänzungsband Kleine Reihe 2), Aschendorff: Münster Westfalen, 51–70.

Škorpil, C. & Škorpil, K. 1910: 'Odesus i Varna', *Izvestija na Varnenskoto Arheologičesko Družestvo* 3: 3–23.

Snively, C. S. 1984: 'Cemetery Churches of the Early Byzantine Period in Eastern Illyricum: Location and Martyrs', *The Greek Orthodox Theological Review* 29.2: 117–24.

Snively, C.S. 1998: 'Intramural Burial in the Cities of the Late Antique Diocese of Macedonia', in *ACIAC* 13.2: 491–98.

Snively, C. S. 2003: 'Churches and Cemeteries: Religion and Death in Early Byzantine Macedonia', in *Starohristijanskata arheologija vo Makedonija. Prilozi od naučen Sobir*, Makedonska Akademija na Naukite i umetnostite: Skopje, 59–74.

Snively, C. S. 2006: 'Old Rome and New Constantinople. The Development of Late Antique Cemeteries', in *ACIAC* 14: 711–16.

Sodini, J.-P. 1981: 'Les cryptes d'autel paléochrétiennes: essai de classification', *Travaux et mémoires* 8 = *Hommage à P. Lemerle* (Centre de recherche d'histoire et civilisation de Byzance), De Boccard: Paris, 437–58.

Sodini, J.-P. 1986: 'Les tombes privilégiées dans l'Orient chrétien (à l'exception du diocèse d'Egypte)', in Y. Duval & J.-C. Picard (eds): *L'inhumation privilégiée du IVe au VIIIe siècle en Occident. Actes du colloque tenu à Créteil les 16–18 mars 1984*, De Boccard: Paris, 233–43.

Sodini, J.-P. & Kolokotsas, K. 1984: *Aliki II: la basilique double* (École française d'Athènes. Études thasiennes 10), De Boccard: Paris.

Soficaru, A. D. 2007: 'Propunere pentru o tipologie uniformă a mormintelor romano-bizantine din Dobrogea', *Peuce* S.N. 5: 297–312.

Soler, E. 2006: *Le sacré et le salut à Antioche au IVe siècle apr. J.-C. Pratiques festives et comportements religieux dans le processus de christianisation de la cité* (Institut français du Proche-Orient. Bibliothèque archéologique et historique 176), Beyrouth.

Solier, Y. 1995: 'Narbonne. La basilique funéraire du Clos-de-la-Lombarde', in Duval (coord.), 32–38.

Sotinel, C. 2005: 'Les lieux de culte chrétiens et le sacré dans l'Antiquité tardive', *Revue de l'histoire des religions*, 222.4: 411–34.

Stevens, S. T. 1993: *Bir el Knissia at Carthage: A Rediscovered Cemetery Church. Report no. 1* (Journal of Roman Archaeology, Suppl. Ser. 7), Ann Arbor.

Stevens, S. T., Kalinowski, A. V., van der Leest, H. et al. 2005: *Bir Ftouha: A Pilgrimage Church Complex at Carthage* (Journal of Roman Archaeology, Suppl. Ser. 59), Portsmouth, Rhode Island.

Suceveanu, Al. 1982: *Histria VI. Les thermes romains*, Éditions de l'Académie Roumaine & De Boccard: Bucharest & Paris.

Suceveanu, Al. 2007: *Histria XIII. La basilique épiscopale, Les résultats des fouilles*, Éditions de l'Académie Roumaine: Bucarest.

Ştefan, A. S. 1975: 'Cercetări aerofotografice privind topografia urbană a Histriei: II. Epoca romană târzie (sec. III–IV e.n.)', *Revista muzeelor şi monumentelor. Monumente istorice şi de artă* 44.2: 51–62.

Ştefan, A. S. 1976: 'Cercetări aerofotografice privind topografia urbană a Histriei: III. Epoca romană târzie (sec. IV–VII e.n.)', *Revista muzeelor şi monumentelor. Monumente istorice şi de artă* 45.1: 43–51.

Tabakova-Čanova, G. & Ovčarov, D. 1975: 'Rannovizantijska bazilika pri s. Kran, Starozagorski okrăg', *Arheologija. Organ na arheologiceskija Institut i Muzei pri bălgarskata Akademija na naukite. Sofia* 17.3: 43–51.

Ulbert, T. 1978: *Frühchristliche Basiliken mit Doppelapsiden auf der Iberischen Halbinsel. Studien zur Architektur- und Liturgiegeschichte* (Deutsches Archäologisches Institut, Archäologische Forschungen 5), Gebr. Mann: Berlin.

Varalis, Y. D. 1999: 'Deux églises à chœur triconque de l'Illyricum oriental. Observations sur leur type architectural', *Bulletin de correspondance hellénique* 123: 195–225.

Văleva, J. 1979–1980: 'Sur certaines particularités des hypogées paléochrétiens des terres thraces et leurs analogies en Asie Mineure', *Anatolica* 7: 117–50.

Văleva, J. 1989: 'Les nécropoles paléochrétiennes de Bulgarie et les tombes peintes', in *ACIAC* 11.2: 1243–58.

Văleva, J. 2001: 'La peinture funéraire dans les provinces orientales de l'Empire romain dans l'Antiquité tardive', *Hortus Artium Medievalium. Journal of the International Research Center for Late Antiquity and Middle Ages* 7: 167–208.

Yasin, A. M. 2002: *Commemorating the Dead – Constructing the Community: the Church Space, Funerary Monuments and Saints' Cults in Late Antiquity*, Ph. D. Thesis – The University of Chicago, Chicago (Ill.), Microform available from University Microfilms International, Ann Arbor, Michigan.

Zahariade, M. 2009: 'The Episcopal Basilica from Halmyris and the Crypt of Epictetus and Astion', *Thraco–Dacica* S.N. 1 (24).1–2: 131–50.

Zahariade, M. & Phelps, M. K. 2002: 'Halmyris, a Settlement and Fort near the Mouth of the Danube', *Journal of Roman Archaeology* 15: 230–45.

Zugravu, N. & Barnea, A. 1993: 'Adamclisi. Basilica coemeterialis', in A. Barnea: *Cronica cercetărilor arheologice efectuate în 1992 de Institutul de Arheologie din Bucureşti* (Studii şi cercetări de istorie veche şi arheologie 44.4): 397.

Zugravu, N. & Barnea, A. 1994: 'Adamclisi. Basilica coemeterialis', in A. Barnea: *Cronica cercetărilor arheologice efectuate în 1993 de Institutul de Arheologie din Bucureşti* (Studii şi cercetări de istorie veche şi arheologie 45.4): 377.

Zugravu, N. & Barnea, A. 1995: 'Adamclisi. Basilica coemeterialis', in A. Barnea: *Cronica cercetărilor arheologice efectuate în 1994 de Institutul de Arheologie din Bucureşti* (Studii şi cercetări de istorie veche şi arheologie 46.3–4): 281.

Zugravu, N. & Barnea, A. 1996: 'Adamclisi. Basilica coemeterialis', in A. Barnea: *Cronica cercetărilor arheologice efectuate în 1995 de Institutul de Arheologie din Bucureşti* (Studii şi cercetări de istorie veche şi arheologie 47.4): 421.

Zugravu, N. & Barnea, A. 1997: 'Adamclisi. Basilica coemeterialis', in A. Barnea: *Cronica cercetărilor arheologice efectuate în 1996 de Institutul de Arheologie din București* (Studii și cercetări de istorie veche și arheologie 48.4): 373.

Zugravu, N. & Barnea, A. 1998: 'Adamclisi. Basilica coemeterialis', in A. Barnea: *Cronica cercetărilor arheologice efectuate în 1997 de Institutul de Arheologie din București* (Studii și cercetări de istorie veche și arheologie 49.3–4): 291–92.

11

SOCIAL ANXIETY AND THE RE-EMERGENCE OF FURNISHED BURIAL IN POST ROMAN ALBANIA

William Bowden

This paper examines the so-called Komani cemeteries in present-day central and northern Albania, which represent the re-emergence of the practice of furnished burial in this region around the 7th century AD. These cemeteries have previously been studied within the confines of a nationalist culture-historic archaeological tradition that stresses their relationship with pre-Roman Illyrian burial practice, rather than seeing them as part of a wider phenomenon of Early Medieval furnished burial. This paper focuses in particular on the diversity of burial practice that can be observed in the Komani cemeteries and argues that this diversity reflects the uncertainties and anxieties that accompanied the adoption of new practices in a rapidly changing world. It is further argued that, while we can never fully understand the multiplicity of meanings attached to burials from archaeological evidence alone, the complex multiple meanings attached to the commemoration of death in contemporary and historic contexts compel us to be aware of the complex social nuances that surround the burial ritual.

Keywords: Albania, anxiety, grave goods, Komani cemeteries, status, transformation.

The commemoration of death is an area of extraordinary complexity. Funerary rituals and memorials to the dead send out a multiplicity of messages. The way that these messages are received and indeed what messages are received varies according to the recipient and the circumstances in which they are encountering the funeral or memorial.

The memorials to Dodi al Fayed and Diana, Princess of Wales, in Harrods department store in London are an interesting example of this, inspiring reverence, sadness, pity or derision depending on the point of view of the onlooker. For Mohammed al Fayed, who erected them, they are a representation of grief at the loss of his son, but at the same time they embody his attempt to create a permanent link with the British establishment, which has denied him citizenship and, according to him at least, murdered the subjects of the memorial. The now unbreakable link with Diana has thus been used by al Fayed as part of his perpetual campaign for greater legitimacy within the UK. For others, however, they are extraordinary pieces of kitsch, emphasising al Fayed's ultimate failure to understand the cultural values of the British social elite that he aspires to join.

Our ability to read this multiplicity of meanings from the Harrods memorials depends on the fact that we can contextualise them – we know the historical circumstances in which they were created and the personalities involved. However, in prehistoric contexts or in circumstances in which historic data is limited or altogether absent, how can we glean these multiple meanings from the archaeological data? Is it legitimate to even try?

When dealing with funerary remains, we have certain advantages. We can usually assume that, when death occurred in circumstances where burial or disposal of the remains could take place according to customary practice, the actions that took place in relation to the corpse would be deliberate actions. These actions were intended to explicitly or implicitly convey certain messages about the dead person, their relationship to those who were burying them, and the way in which the deceased and those who were carrying out the funerary rite viewed their position in relation to other members of society.

The extent to which we can decode these explicit and implicit messages from the archaeological evidence alone is inevitably limited. This paper discusses some elements of one particular group of cemeteries in relation to these possibilities. These cemeteries, situated in present-day central and northern Albania, date to between the 6th and 9th centuries AD and represent the apparently rapid re-emergence of a burial rite involving grave goods in an area where this practice had previously been abandoned. The largest of these cemeteries were at Koman and Kruja and as such they are often referred to by Yugoslavian archaeologists as representing the Komani-Kruja culture, although Albanian archaeologists generally refer to them in terms of the Arbër or proto-Albanian culture. For ease of reference, I use the term 'Komani cemeteries' when talking about these sites although that should not be taken to imply adherence to any of the nationalist archaeological theories that have been applied to this material.

The Komani cemeteries

The Komani cemeteries were first noted in the 19th century by the French consul, M. Degard, and aroused considerable interest as to their date and origin (Popović 1984: 214; Bowden 2003a; 2003b: 203–11 with references to earlier literature). The first to be discovered were those at Koman (Spahiu 1971; 1979–1980) and Kruja (Anamali & Spahiu 1979–1980), and further cemeteries were subsequently discovered at Lezhë (Prendi 1979–1980), Shurdhah (Komata 1979–1980), Bukël (Anamali 1971), and

Fig. 11.1. Map of Albania (drawing by W. Bowden).

Prosek (Doda 1989), together with a series of smaller cemeteries and isolated finds spread across the remote mountainous areas of central and northern Albania. Similar cemeteries are also known from Mijele in present-day Montenegro and Radoliste and St. Erasme in Macedonia, while a related cemetery was also excavated in the 1930s at Aphiona on the island of Corfu (Bulle 1934). In southern Albania and northwest Greece, burials which shared some of the characteristics of the Komani cemeteries were found as secondary insertions in Bronze Age tumuli at Piskova, Cepuni, Merope and Kato Pedina (Bodinaku 1983; Andreou 1980; 1983; 1986; 1987) (Fig. 11.1). Most of the cemeteries were poorly excavated, with relatively little detail being recorded of individual graves.

The most striking characteristic of the cemeteries was the range of objects that accompanied some of the burials (although by no means all of them). Jewellery and dress fittings appeared in many of the graves, occasionally including gilded disc brooches and crescent shaped gold earrings, which were probably imported from Byzantine Sicily. There were also local variants of the same types of items (Anamali 1993). Buckles were also common, of a type widely known in the southern Balkans as well as in Italy, Hungary, Crimea, and Constantinople, together with large rectangular-backed bronze fibulae of a type found in the Danubian provinces, Dalmatia, Thessalonica, and northern Italy (Popovič 1984: 217–18).

Other metal finds included frequent examples of bronze and iron pendants (Prendi 1979–1980: pl. xxii, which recall similar objects known from Avar cemeteries, bronze rings, many of which were decorated with Christian cryptograms (Spahiu 1971: pl. v), and the radiate headed brooches (Anamali & Spahiu 1979–1980: pl. vii; Prendi 1979–1980: pl. xx), characteristic of the period and widely found in Frankish, Lombard, Slav, and Avar contexts. Glass necklaces (sometimes including *millefiori* beads) are also common (Anamali & Spahiu 1979–1980: 75), again of a type widely paralleled in Migration Period contexts elsewhere.

The graves also contain pottery in a hard fired buff fabric and painted with wide red stripes similar to examples found in southern Italian cemeteries. These are usually in the form of two-handled flasks and trilobal jugs, and were found for example at Kruja (Anamali & Spahiu 1979–1980: pls v–vi), Lezhë (Prendi 1979–1980: graves 3, 8, 11, 12, 20, 31, 35). With the exception of examples from the Aphiona cemetery on Corfu (Bulle 1934), finds of glass vessels are very rare.

Some of the burials contain weapons, including axes, as well as arrowheads and short daggers. The axes can be of a lightweight, broad bladed form suitable for combat (for example those from Koman illustrated by Spahiu 1979–1980: pl. iii.1–3), or alternatively of a more narrow bladed, wedge-shaped form suitable for use as a splitting axe (e.g. the example from grave 7 at Lezhë, illustrated by Prendi 1979–1980: pl. iii). In general, axes are more common at Koman than at the other cemeteries, as are spear heads and swords. Swords are rare even at Koman, where they were found in a form that Popović suggests is paralleled in Merovingian and Lombard contexts (1984: 221–22).

The burials were usually placed in tombs constructed of slabs of limestone although occasionally a tent-like roof was adopted reminiscent of Roman 'cappuccina' burials. This style of tomb construction including the use of limestone slabs and pitched covers is very similar to that which can be seen in Late Roman contexts in Albania, although in most cases the dating of unfurnished burials of this type is far from certain and could often date from any time between the 5th century and the Late Medieval Period. The apparent continuity of this type of cyst burial is often cited in support of the claims of cultural continuity discussed below (Prendi 1979–1980: 143).

In terms of their location, the Komani cemeteries showed a marked break with the past, in that they were not associated with the population centres of the Roman Period. The latter were predominantly concentrated on the coastal plain or along the principal north–south routes which ran along the river valleys of Albania. The Komani cemeteries, by contrast, were in mountainous and isolated locations, sometimes close to the fortified hill-top sites that were occupied in both the prehistoric and post-Roman periods (a fact that was made much of by communist period archaeologists keen to forge links between Early Medieval Albania and the pre-Roman Period). There is also a concentration of surviving Latin toponyms in the vicinity of the main cemetery group, accompanied by a marked absence of the Slavic names that frequently occur elsewhere in Albania (Popović 1984: 211–13) Although no contemporary settlements have been conclusively identified, the cemeteries suggest that new population foci developed in the changed political and social circumstances of the post-Roman Period.

Status representation in the Komani cemeteries

When I first approached the question of the Komani cemeteries (Bowden 2003a; 2003b), I devoted some attention to demonstrating that the Albanian communist period interpretation of these cemeteries as representing a proto-Albanian ethnic identity was a construct rooted in a nationalistic culture-historic archaeological tradition. Most of the cemetery excavations were carried out during the 1960s, '70s, and '80s as part of an explicit agenda on the part of the ruling communist party of Enver Hoxha to provide archaeological evidence for the modern Albanian population's direct descent from the ancient Illyrians, the group of tribes who inhabited the western Balkans in the pre-Roman Period. As with most attempts to establish links with an ancient population, the principal intention was to reinforce the territorial primacy of the Albanian people, particular against the Greeks to the south and east, who continue to argue that much of southern Albania is in fact Greek.

In the Albanian interpretation (summarised for example by Anamali 1979–1980; 1982) the Illyrians had been subjugated by the Romans, but had never been fully assimilated into the Roman world. They had consequently remained ethnically independent while under the Roman political control. When the Roman 'occupation' ended, the Illyrians had reasserted their independence, reoccupying the sites of their earlier settlements and reviving pre-Roman forms of material culture and burial. The period from the 6th–11th century (the date when there is the first textual reference to the Albanians in the *Alexiad* of Anna Comnena) was of crucial importance to this thesis. The settlement sites of the Early Medieval Period in particular have proved extraordinarily difficult to find, and so the Komani cemeteries were fundamental to this reconstruction of Albanian history with considerable resources put into their investigation. The interpretation of the grave goods and the skeletal remains was driven by the need to support this narrative. External parallels for the objects and the presence of possible Slavic items were played down in favour of often questionable parallels with objects from Illyrian tumulus burials.

The problem of the relatively limited distribution of these cemeteries, which unsurprisingly bore little resemblance to the area claimed by modern Albania, was solved by the identification of the so-called southern Arbër culture. This was the name given to burials containing similar items to the Komani burials, that were found inserted into Bronze Age tumuli in the south of Albania. These included a series of tumuli excavated at Piskova in the upper reaches of the Aoos river valley. Similar Late-Antique or post-Roman burials have been found within prehistoric tumuli on the Greek side of the border for example at Merope and Kato Pedina, which contained materials described by the excavators as 'Slavic' (evidence summarised in Bowden 2003b, 211). This adoption of tumulus burial in the post-Roman Period was also used to bolster the case for Illyrian-Albanian continuity.

All the arguments rested on the assumption inherent in culture-historic archaeology, that material culture is a manifestation of the activities of a particular ethnic group. Indeed, given the apparently rapid appearance of objects and burial practices, a classic culture historic explanation of the Komani cemeteries would favour the sudden appearance of a migrant population. This idea of incomers was untenable within the model favoured by Albanian archaeologists, which saw the cemeteries as representing the survival of a pre-Roman Illyrian population. The result was an awkward nationalist construct which sat uncomfortably within the culture-historic explanatory framework in which most of Albania's archaeologists had been trained. Interestingly, although in the immediate post-communist period some Albanian archaeologists consciously distanced themselves from the extremes of the nationalist model (e.g. Miraj & Zeqo 1993), the basic reconstruction of Albanian history in this period remains largely unchanged (repeated for example in Korkuti 2003).

In attempting to move beyond this culture-historic construct, I argued that the Komani-Kruja graves were part of a wide sphere of burial practice that related to individual rather than to group identity, in which hierarchies were expressed through the interment of high-status objects (Bowden 2003a). Migrant groups including the Avars, Slavs, and Lombards, who were probably the closest geographically to Epirus Nova, buried their dead with jewellery, weapons, and other goods. The Komani-Kruja material indeed conforms to patterns of status-related burial elsewhere, for example in Avar contexts, in which great emphasis was placed on the presence of imported objects. The Albanian graves contain a wide variety of imported materials, most notably the gold earrings, which probably originated in Byzantine Sicily. Also of note in this context are the glass vessels which are unique to the Aphiona cemetery on Corfu.

In my explanation, therefore, material culture was not used as a medium through which ethnic difference was conveyed, but rather as a means through which the Komani-Kruja populations participated in a set of social relations.

I also argued that a primary function of these 'means of representation' was of engendering stability within a fragmented society. The post-Roman world was one of uncertainty and high mobility, in terms of location of settlement or residence and in terms of identity and status. The speed of change within 7th-century Epirus was rapid. Historical sources suggest that in the late 6th and 7th centuries, groups of Avars and Slavs reportedly overran, among other areas, the provinces of Epirus Nova and Epirus Vetus, forcing much of the existing population to migrate elsewhere. Although the scale and timing of these events are contested, there can be little doubt that during the late 6th and 7th centuries far reaching changes occurred within the provinces.

In the space of perhaps two generations, an urbanised or semi-urbanised society with recognisable affinities with the Roman past was transformed into one that was essentially rural, the leadership structures of which had also dramatically altered (Bowden 2003b). Power became individualised in Late Antique Epirus, a situation that may have its origins in the patronage systems of the Late Empire and which was exacerbated by the ascendance of powerful churchmen in the late 5th and 6th centuries. Epirus also became increasingly peripheral in relation to the administrative structures of the Empire. This perhaps created a situation in which power coalesced around individuals rather than being focussed on town or state. The result was a far more fluid and localised network of relationships based around fluctuating allegiances and competition. In terms of social and political cohesion these localised networks may not have been dissimilar to those of incoming migrant groups, whose arrival doubtless exacerbated the process.

This explanation sees the rapid re-emergence of a furnished burial rite as a response to an entirely new and continually changing set of social relations. The representation of individual identity and status in relation to peer groups proved more compelling than previous strictures of the Christian church regarding furnished burial. If the occupants of the Komani-Kruja graves were Christian, their religion was not an aspect of their identity that was expressed within the burial ritual (and perhaps not within other areas of social relations). Although Christian items were placed within the graves, as with the presence of Christian objects within the context of pagan graves elsewhere in Europe, their symbolic value lay in their status as objects rather than as a means of religious representation.

Ultimately, however, an interpretation that sees the transition to furnished burial as related to individual status remains unsatisfactory as an explanatory framework for the nature of the grave assemblages themselves. How did the grave assemblages work? What messages were they supposed to be communicating? And what about the graves that didn't have any grave goods at all? What messages were they communicating?

The idea that grave goods demonstrate social status has some validity in the very broadest sense. It would be hard to argue, that the Sutton Hoo ship burial, or the Oslo Viking ship burials belong to individuals who were of little account in their respective communities. It gets more difficult at apparently lower levels of the social order if one attempts to ascribe status value to individual items. Indeed, in this sense the 'wealth scoring' pioneered in a number of cemetery studies (Parker Pearson 1999: 78–82) seems very difficult to apply in any but the most general sense. For example in Esmeralda Agolli's (2006) table of graves with arrowheads from Lezhë, it is extremely hard to rank these graves in terms of the social status of the occupants. Grave 7 clearly has more material than the others, although grave 8 is also an individual of some account by this reckoning. The remainder of the furnished graves, however, have little to separate them in terms of the quality of their contents. Equally when there is little or no chronological differentiation between the graves themselves, even if one suggests that a given object was perceived as having a greater status than another, one cannot assume that these relative values remained constant, particularly in the case of objects which are often utilitarian (Parker Pearson 1999: 85; Bradley 1990).

The attachment of values to different objects is in fact inherently dangerous, even in the case of objects which have a clear intrinsic worth such as gold or silver. The social value of such objects can only be understood in their social context, particularly in circumstances where rigid and complex social codes exist. These codes can mean that different values are attached by different sections of society to the same body of material. While Renfrew, in his study of Chalcolithic burials at Varna on the Black Sea, suggested that gold had a 'prime value' (Renfrew 1986; Parker Pearson 1999: 79), this value must be understood as being subject to a range of social imperatives to which we are not party. Who was entitled to wield the gold-embellished symbols of power such as the maces and spears of the Varna burials and how was that status ascribed? Was that status earned or inherited and was it part of the deceased's identity in life as well as death? Perhaps most importantly, was that status acknowledged by all members of the community?

We are particularly well-informed about these socially ascribed values for the Roman Period, where it is quite clear that the most ostentatious funerary monuments were often those of freedmen and women. It is also clear that these tombs were built within the context of a strict social code in which purchasing power was not necessarily commensurate with status. This is apparent from Petronius's 'Dinner with Trimalchio' in which the eponymous wealthy freedman hosts a dinner of colossal extravagance, which culminates in a reading of his will and his instructions to his architect as to the nature of his tomb (*Satyricon* 10.71). Through this caricature Petronius mocks Trimalchio's pretensions and lack of taste in a way that reminds us that in the Roman world, wealth was not a mark of status in its own right, but had to be accommodated within a wider set of social values involving one's background and one's role in public life.

Nowhere was this more so than funerary monuments. These were aspirational, serving to demonstrate the status that the deceased and the builder of the monument had reached, and their place within the hierarchy of Roman society. Death was used to commemorate connections with class, wealth and power, as freedmen and women erected monuments to their patrons who had often freed them in their wills. The socially mobile were particularly anxious to have their achievements recorded and it is for this reason that freedmen and women are more heavily represented in the epigraphic record and funerary record than any other social group. However, the process was clearly a social minefield, in which individuals had to tread a fine line between display and humility, ostentation and awareness of one's place in the social hierarchy. Although Trimalchio is a caricature, Petronius's lampooning of him would have only worked for his audience if they were implicitly aware of the social transgressions that Trimalchio was committing.

Is it possible to detect these types of anxieties or other related concerns within the Early Medieval cemeteries in Albania? To my mind it is not an unreasonable proposition. As noted above, during the later 6th and 7th centuries the provinces of Epirus and

Prevalitaine had undergone an extraordinary degree of social upheaval, at the end of which their inhabitants were to all intents and purposes outside the Roman Empire, the political system that they had been a part of for some 6–700 years. Small wonder that this upheaval coincided with changes in funerary practice.

Perhaps the most striking aspect of the Albanian cemeteries is the sheer level of variation present within the burial practices represented. This variation can be seen on two distinct levels. First there is variation in burial practice within individual cemeteries and second there is significant variation between cemeteries in different locations. This level of variation suggests that 'normative behaviour' was ill defined and probably very localised, and is therefore likely to have been the cause of social (and perhaps spiritual) anxiety. One would be hard pushed to identify cultural norms within the cemeteries and indeed the communist period archaeologists of Albania only managed to create a coherent 'culture' by ignoring or downplaying significant areas of the evidence. The 'southern Arber' culture, with its reuse of tumuli has relatively little in common with the main Komani graves, apart from the presence of certain types of material. Unfortunately the level of recording of most of the excavations is not sufficient for a reliable analysis of the cemeteries, but a few points can be highlighted regarding the wide variation in burial practice.

Variable factors within the Komani cemeteries

There is variation present in almost all aspects of the burial ritual within the Komani cemeteries, ranging from the orientation of the graves, to the presence or absence of grave goods, or even the presence or absence of a body. These variations are not, however, consistently present within cemeteries in different areas, to the extent that one or more of the cemeteries often display marked characteristics that are wholly absent from the others. Given that it is very unlikely that any of the cemeteries have been excavated in their entirety it is possible that these variations simply reflect the selection of excavated graves, although this seems improbable.

One of the most marked variations concerns the presence or absence of grave goods. While the Albanian scholars were particularly concerned with the objects found within the tombs, it should be remembered that a significant proportion of the graves had no grave goods at all. In understanding the graves, these unfurnished burials are clearly as important as those that include quantities of objects. In a situation where half the burials are furnished and half are not, it is likely that a lack of grave goods was intended to convey as important and explicit a message as those that were buried with a large number of items.

The ratio of unfurnished to furnished burials varies from cemetery to cemetery (Table 11.1), ranging from approximately equal proportions of each at Aphiona, Koman, and Shurdhah, to the situation at Lezhë, Kruja, Bukël, and Prosek where the furnished graves vastly outnumber the unfurnished ones. It is unclear as to whether there is a chronological aspect to this differentiation. Some cemeteries almost certainly stayed in

Table 11.1. Ratios of furnished and unfurnished burials (where known) (data from Agolli 2006 with additions).

Site	Furnished	Unfurnished
Aphiona	9	10
Lezhë	33	4
Koman (Dalmace)	22	18
Kruja	26	2
Shurdhah	9	12
Bukël	53	4
Prosek	36	7

use into the 2nd millennium AD, and it may be that the unfurnished tombs relate to this later period. Certainly it seems unlikely that the deceased and their relatives were too impoverished to furnish a burial with the most utilitarian of objects if they so desired. Consequently we should look for other explanations as to why some sections of some communities were simply not participating in the rite of furnished burial.

It is possible that the deceased and their relatives had different religious beliefs than those with furnished burials (e.g. they were Christian or belonged to a sub-group of a wider Christian community who rejected the use of grave goods). This is certainly possible, and may have a chronological element also. Christianity was firmly established in the region by the late 4th century (Bowden 2003b: 108–10), and unless one considers that the existing population was wiped out or left the area entirely (neither of which is impossible) it is likely that a section of the population remained Christian into the Early Middle Ages. The cemeteries also have associated churches in some cases or at least buildings that are interpreted as such, as for example at Shurdah and Aphiona, although the relationships between these buildings and the graves are inconclusive. Indeed the nearest burials to the churches are in fact furnished. There is no indication as to whether the cemeteries and the churches were in use contemporaneously and these buildings may reflect a later recognition of the significance of the location rather than a direct association. This is particularly likely in the case of Shurdah (Komata 1979–1980), where the remains of the settlement may well date to the Late Medieval Period.

Although it has often been suggested that the occupants of the graves are Christian, there is little in the orientation of the graves to suggest this (although in many late antique Christian contexts orientation is also apparently of little account). Although considerable effort seems to have been made at Aphiona, to maintain an E–W orientation (and there is some evidence for E–W orientation at Shurdah) elsewhere orientation seems to have been of little consideration (see Table 11.2). At most other cemeteries, the E–W orientated graves appear to be in the minority and there seems to be little obvious adherence to any other orientation.

We should also consider the possibility that the occupants of the unfurnished burials and their relatives belonged to a social group defined by factors other than religion for which grave goods were also inappropriate. This group may have been defined by class, gender, ethnic origin, or other factors. It is of course possible that we are looking at groups of newcomers or at least communities that were partly made up of newcomers. The wide variations in practice that can be identified in a relatively small area of Albania

Table 11.2. Orientation of graves at Komani cemeteries (where known).

Site	E-W	N-S	NW-SE	NE-SW	Unknown
Kruja		14	8		6
Lezhë	10		24		
Koman	11	8	7	11	
Aphiona	50+				
Shurdah	11		7	1	4

may reflect the arrival of immigrants from a variety of locations who all brought their own localised variation of burial traditions with them.

At Aphiona, Koman, and Shurdah the approximately equal ratio of unfurnished and furnished burials could be suggested to reflect the gender of the occupants. This of course makes the considerable assumptions that a cross section of an entire community is represented within the cemeteries and that both male and female infants were equally encouraged to survive. It also assumes that cultural differences between different groups of people in a relatively small area were sufficiently pronounced to allow fundamental differences in the treatment of male and female bodies.

The assignation of gender to the Komani graves is generally very problematic. In the Albanian archaeologists' interpretation dress items and jewellery are associated with female graves while weapons are associated with male graves. The fibulae are suggested to be common to both sexes. None of these attributions, however, are based on osteology, but rely rather on the excavators' perceptions of gender roles, with which the drawbacks are self-evident. Indeed, close examination of the assemblages suggests that many items (including possibly arrowheads) were present in graves of both sexes and that this association between objects and gender is unreliable. This can be seen for example at Bukël, in a table from Esmeralda Agolli's recent work (2006), where the single burials clearly contain both weapons (i.e. arrowheads) and dress items. At Prosek, which is the only cemetery where analysis of the skeletal remains has been carried out, it was impossible to associate grave goods with individual bodies, because of their occurrence in multiple burials (Doda 1989). Only at Aphiona are the items that occurred with the burials all those that the Albanian archaeologists have associated with female burials.

The picture of associations between grave goods is confused by the very high incidence of multiple burials at certain sites, although there is also considerable variation in this aspect. At Lezhë, Prendi (1979–1980: 144) suggested that most were 'family' tombs, containing 2–5 skeletons. At Kruja, however, 22 of the 28 graves contained single inhumations, while two graves contained two skeletons, two contained three skeletons, and a single example contained four bodies. The remaining grave is not mentioned in this context (Anamali & Spahiu 1979–1980: 81). The multiple burials suggest that the graves may have been used over more than one generation, although there is no evidence that all the bodies were not inserted contemporaneously or had been transferred from elsewhere. It has not been established whether the occupants of the graves have familial

Table 11.3. Graves containing arrowheads (after Agolli 2006).

Site	Total graves	Total graves with arrowheads
Lezhë	37	7
Koman (Dalmace)	40	6
Kruja	28	2
Shurdhah	21	1
Bukël	57	5
Prosek	43	9

relationships although with the continued improvement in extraction of mitochondrial DNA this is clearly both possible and desirable (see Bejko, Fenton & Foran 2006 on DNA work in Albania).

At the opposite end of the scale both Bukël and Prosek also include a number of apparent cenotaphs, where deposits had been buried in circumstances where a body was not available for interment, but where the relatives clearly considered it important to conduct a funerary rite, either for social or religious reasons or both (Agolli 2006: 293). Interestingly at Koman, a number of graves (2, 13, 23, 28, 32, 37) were excavated which lacked both grave goods and skeletal remains (Spahiu 1979–1980: 29–31), although the apparently poor preservation of the skeletal remains from Koman means that we should be wary of drawing too many conclusions from this. It is not impossible, however, that the occupants of these cenotaph graves were removed some time after burial to be added to one of the multiple graves. The practice of constructing cenotaphs is seemingly restricted to these sites, with no recorded examples at Lezhë, Shurdah or Kruja.

There is also considerable divergence between the cemeteries in terms of the types of objects present. The idea of a homogeneous 'Komani culture' was attractive to the excavators, and the assemblages do share the defining characteristic of their existence in a milieu where furnished burial had previously fallen from favour. Nonetheless, there is considerable diversity between the cemeteries in terms of the types of material present, which may in part be explained by the fact that different groups of people in different locations would not all have had access to the same range of objects. Of note in this context are the glass vessels from Aphiona, the presence of which may suggest that Aphiona, by dint of its location, may have remained in contact with Mediterranean trading routes from which the central Albanian cemeteries had been cut off.

Weapons were present in some, but by no means all of the cemeteries and the types varied widely. Swords and spears are exceptional, the latter appearing most at Koman, although single swords are known from Kruja and Koman (Anamali & Spahiu 1979–1980: 56–57), and the most common weapons are axes, daggers, and arrowheads. It should be noted that all the latter items also have functions off the battlefield and may have been included in this context.

The arrowheads, on which Agolli (2006) focuses (Table 11.3), are particularly interesting. Their inclusion must be as a symbolic token – a single arrow is of limited practical use as a weapon in the afterlife and an act of conspicuous consumption – demonstrating status by the disposal of goods – would surely require multiple arrowheads. What could these signify? Agolli does not go beyond stating that they were an important part of the male burial rite. However, the numbers suggest that not all males were buried with arrowheads, while the single and cenotaph arrowhead graves at Bukël contain items that could also be associated with female burials. Did arrowheads imply a particular social status or a symbolic allegiance or claim to membership of a particular social group, in the same way that weapon burials may have worked in Anglo Saxon England to demonstrate Germanic descent as Heinrich Härke (1992) demonstrated?

One final point that is worthy of comment is the relatively small size of the cemeteries of which the largest with consistent records only contains 57 burials. While it is likely that few, if any, of the cemeteries have been investigated in their entirety, the picture that emerges suggests that the cemeteries, if in use for any length of time, were serving very small communities, perhaps comprising a mere handful of families. There is also nothing to say that the cemeteries were consistently in use, or whether they were used seasonally or periodically. Given that Albanian archaeologists have postulated that these cemeteries belong to a period that lasts through the 7th and 8th centuries and sometimes into the 9th century, this is a question that needs to be seriously addressed.

Conclusion: interpreting burials in a period of transition

The Komani-Kruja burials represent the re-emergence of furnished burials in a period of profound transition, in which Roman society effectively fragmented into a semi-tribal system based around fluid and localised loyalties and allegiances. It would be stretching credulity to claim that these changes in burial practice were not somehow connected with the fundamental changes that were occurring within society. Nonetheless with new social mores came additional anxieties as people struggled to accommodate and adapt to new practices within their own lifestyles. The significant levels of variation between cemeteries suggest that this fragmentation of society is reflected in burial practice, with different groups adapting burial practices that were specific to that location. The adoption of furnished burial must have been a process that was fraught with social danger, seemingly indicated by the fact that not all members of the community adopted it.

In conclusion, however, although the possibilities for decoding explicit and implicit messages from the burial evidence alone are limited by comparison with what can be achieved in historic periods, I am optimistic that possibilities exist for significant advances in our understanding of the Komani graves and other grave groups from non-historic contexts. The possibilities of extracting ever greater levels of information from the skeletal remains themselves in terms of diet and health (and hence wealth and social status) and genetic background are increasing exponentially, and it is now possible to ask and answer questions that were impossible to consider even 20 years ago. Equally the application of basic excavation techniques and clear publication would also aid our understanding of these cemeteries very considerably.

Finally, we must continually seek to nuance the questions that we ask of funerary assemblages. We must attempt to chart the social boundaries that are implicit in these assemblages, and be alive to the possibilities that these boundaries were continually being pushed and transgressed. Death is a moment when the social aspirations of the living come to the fore. The fluid social structures of the post-Roman world provided ample opportunity for social mobility. However, the graves of Roman freedmen and women remind us that social mobility is articulated through a complex vocabulary in which meanings are both implicit and explicit. Who knows what social censure may have befallen the man who included an arrow in his wife's grave, when her life and social background did not merit such an object in the eyes of his neighbours?

Bibliography

Agolli, E. 2006: 'The Distribution of Arrowheads in Koman Culture Burials (6th–8th Centuries A.D.)', in L. Bejko & R. Hodges (eds): *New Directions in Albanian Archaeology*, International Centre for Albanian Archaeology: Tirana, 287–93.

Anamali, S. 1971: 'Një varrezë e mesjetës së hershme në Bukël të Mirditës', *Iliria* 1: 209–26.

Anamali, S. 1979–1980: 'Antikiteti i vonë dhe mesjeta e hershme në kërkimet shqiptare', *Iliria* 9–10: 5–21.

Anamali, S. 1982: 'Le probleme de la formation du peuple Albanais a la lumiere des donées archeologiques', *Studia Albanica* 19.2: 53–73.

Anamali, S. 1993: 'Oreficerie, gioelli bizantini in Albania: Komani', *XL Corso di cultura sull'arte Ravennate e bizantina. Seminario Internazionale su: 'L'Albania dal Tardoantico al Medioevo, aspetti e problemi di Archeologia e Storia dell'Arte', Ravenna, 29 aprile – 5 maggio 1993*, Edizioni del Girasole: Ravenna, 435–46.

Anamali, S. & Spahiu, H. 1979–1980: 'Varreza arbërore e Krujës', *Iliria* 9–10: 47–104.

Andreou, E. 1980: Μερόπη και Παληόπυργος Πωγωνίου, *Archaiologikon Deltion* 35: 303–7.

Andreou, E. 1983: Μερόπη, *Archaiologikon Deltion* 38: 229–30.

Andreou, E. 1986: Κάτω Πεδινά Ζαγορίου, *Archaiologikon Deltion* 41: 113.

Andreou, E. 1987: Παληόπυργος Πωγωνίου, *Archaiologikon Deltion* 42: 7–8.

Bejko, L., Fenton, T. & Foran, D. 2006: 'Recent Advances in Albanian Mortuary Archaeology, Human Osteology and Ancient DNA', in L. Bejko & R. Hodges (eds): *New Directions in Albanian Archaeology*, International Centre for Albanian Archaeology: Tirana, 309–22.

Bodinaku, N. 1983: 'Kultura e varrezës së hershme mesjetare Shqiptare në lunginën e sipërme të Vjosës të rrethit të Përmetit', *Iliria* 13.1: 241–50.

Bowden, W. 2003a: 'The Construction of Identities in Post-Roman Albania', in L. Lavan & W. Bowden (eds): *Theory and Practice in Late Antique Archaeology*, E. J. Brill: Leiden, 57–78.

Bowden, W. 2003b: *Epirus Vetus: The Archaeology of a Late Antique Province*, Duckworth: London.

Bradley, R. 1990: *The Passage of Arms*, Cambridge University Press: Cambridge.

Bulle, H. 1934: 'Ausgrabungen bei Aphiona auf Korfu', *Athenische Mitteilungen* 59: 147–240.

Doda, N. 1989: 'Varreza arbërore e Prosekut (rrethi i Mirditës)', *Iliria* 19.1: 137–77.

Härke, H. 1992: 'Changing Symbols in a Changing Society: The Anglo-Saxon Weapon Burial Rite in the Seventh Century', in M. O. H. Carver (ed.): *The Age of Sutton Hoo*, Boydell and Brewer: Woodbridge, 149–65.

Komata, D. 1979–1980: 'Varreza arbërore e Shurdahut', *Iliria* 9–10: 105–22.

Korkuti, M. 2003: *Parailirët, Ilirët, Arbërit,. Histori e Shkurtër*, Toena: Tirana.

Miraj, L. & Zeqo, M. 1993: 'Conceptual Changes in Albanian Archaeology', *Antiquity* 67 (254): 123–25.

Parker Pearson, M. 1999: *The Archaeology of Death and Burial*, Sutton: Stroud.

Popovič, V. 1984: 'Byzantines, Slaves et autochthones dans les provinces de Prévalitaine et Nouvelle Épire', in V. Popovič (ed.): *Villes et peuplement dans l'Illyricum Protobyzantin. Actes du colloque organisé par l'École Française de Rome. Rome, 12–14 mai 1982,* Collection de l'École française de Rome 77: 181–243.

Prendi, F. 1979–1980: 'Një varrezë e kultorës arbërore në Lezhë', *Iliria* 9–10: 123–70.

Renfrew, A. C. 1986: 'Varna and the Emergence of Wealth in Prehistoric Europe', in A. Appadurai (ed.): *The Social Life of Things: Commodities in Cultural Perspective*, Cambridge University Press: Cambridge, 141–68.

Spahiu, H. 1971: 'Gjetje të vjetra nga varreza mesjetare e kalasë së Dalmaces', *Iliria* 1: 227–62.

Spahiu, H. 1979–1980: 'Varreza arbërore e Kalasë së Dalmaces, *Iliria* 9–10: 23–46.

12

CHANGING RITUALS
AND REINVENTING TRADITION:
The burnt Viking Ship at Myklebostad, Western Norway

Terje Oestigaard

At Myklebostad in Eid in Nordfjord, western Norway, five large grave mounds were discovered. In 1874, a large Viking ship was excavated in grave mound no. 1. However, contrary to the Oseberg and Gokstad Viking ships, the ship at Myklebostad was burnt. Only half of the mound was excavated, but the ship may have been the size of Gokstad or perhaps even larger. The most spectacular find was the urn in which the cremated bones of a 30–35 year old man were found. In mound no. 2 there were six burials dating from the 8th to the 10th century AD, including both inhumations, cremations and two smaller boats – one burnt and one unburnt. Mounds nos 3 and 5 were not excavated, but in mound no. 4 cremated remains from a woman in a small boat were found. The most striking feature at this cemetery regarding rituals is that all of these funerals were conducted in a different manner, even those within mound no. 2. Nevertheless, the deceased belonged to the same cultural and religious sphere, and may have been one family or at least part of the same community. Thus, the different practices must have been used deliberately and this cemetery enables therefore a discussion of why the rituals vary, the relationship between cremation and inhumation, the invention and reinvention of tradition, and the ritual transformation of the society in the development of the Norwegian kingdom.

Keywords: Cremation, inhumation, Norwegian kingdom, ritual mobilisation, tradition, Viking ship

Fig. 12.1. Map of Myklebostad in Eid in Nordfjord, Norway (courtesy of Ragnar Børsheim and Arkikon).

The most famous Viking ship in the world is most likely the Oseberg ship. In Norway, ever since the first Viking ship was excavated at Borre in Vestfold in 1852, Snorre's sagas (he himself being an Icelandic poet, historian and politician, 1179?–1241) have been used to interpret which chieftains and kings were given ship burials, thus linking the Viking ships to the Ynglingatal, the Ynglinga Saga, and the foundation of the Norwegian kingdom. According to history, King Harald Hårfagre (Fairhair) started the conquest of Norway, which ended with the formation of the Norwegian kingdom, hence unifying the previous former petty kingdoms or chiefdoms. Traditionally, Harald Hårfagre and the development of the Norwegian kingdom have been located to Vestfold in eastern Norway (Andersen 1977). However, although the final battle in Hafrsfjord where Hårfagre unified Norway has traditionally been set at AD 872, it is now believed that Harald Hårfagre started his conquest from his strongholds in southwestern Norway and that the unification took place somewhat later (Krag 1995: 86, Opedal 1998; 2005; Myhre & Gansum 2003).

Next to Oseberg's fame is the Gokstad Viking ship. These, together with the lesser known Borre ship, are all buried in Vestfold, while the Tune ship was buried across Oslofjord in Østfold. The Oseberg burial took place in AD 834, while those at Gokstad, Borre and Tune occurred around AD 900. In addition, in southwestern Norway, two ship burials have been found at Avaldsnes: Storhaug dating to *c.* AD 690–750 and Grønhaug to *c.* AD 930, respectively. It is commonly agreed that those who were given these extraordinary burials were part of the elites, political centres, processes and even the conquests that led in one way or another to the unification of Norway as a kingdom. It is, however, highly problematic to link these graves to historical figures or persons described in the sagas. Noteworthy, all these ship burials were unburnt and the deceased inhumated, but perhaps the largest of all Viking ships found in Norway and the least discussed, the Myklebostad ship in Eid in Nordfjord, western Norway, was burnt and the deceased cremated.

Thus, I will present and discuss the Myklebostad ship burial in the context of the unification of the kingdom of Norway (Fig. 12.1). Although it is possible that this funeral represents something ritually and cosmologically unique with regards to the circumstances of the deceased's death necessitating such a massive cremation, in a political context (which will be discussed) one may assume that the deceased was a local

Gravene paa Myklebostad, efter skisse af EILERT MEHL.

Fig. 12.2. The Myklebostad cemetery (after Shetelig 1905: 6, fig. 1).

Fig. 12.3. Mound no. 1, Rundehogjen, at Myklebostad (courtesy of Ragnar Børsheim).

king or chieftain. Why was *this* ship burnt? Why only was this local king or chieftain cremated when the common practice for royal burials was inhumation? How can this ritual practice be contextualised in relation to the local traditions at Myklebostad, the foundation of the Norwegian kingdom, and the religious beliefs in the Viking Age?

The Myklebostad ship burial

Originally, there were five large grave mounds at Myklebostad (Fig. 12.2). In grave mound no. 1. (Fig. 12.3), a large Viking ship was excavated in 1874 by Anders Lorange (Lorange 1875). The mound measured 31 m in diameter with a height of 4 m. Around the mound there was a ditch measuring 4 m in width and 1 m in depth. As indicated, contrary to the Oseberg and Gokstad burials, the Viking ship at Myklebostad was burnt. Only half of the mound was excavated and 44 shield bosses were found (Shetelig 1912: 201), which indicates the large size of the ship, and the fact that more shields may still be *in situ*. The Gokstad ship may have had 64 shields, but only 32 were found (Nicolaysen 1882: 62). Thus, the Myklebostad ship may have been the size of Gokstad, which was 24 m long, or perhaps even longer. However, since this ship was burnt and excavated as early as 1874, the documentation is rather poor according to today's standards. There are no drawings or maps of the site from the excavation; indeed, the original documentation is also lost (Magnus 1967: 60). In fact, the only information about the excavation is a nine page published report describing the context (Lorange 1875: 153–61). Thus, in the absence of excavating the remaining mound, our interpretations are restricted to the 1875 publication, which nevertheless reveals information about the stratigraphy, the cremation, and the successive rituals.

Before the mound was built, a layer of charcoal and burnt soil was deposited on the field. The layer had the same diameter as the mound itself, around 30 m, and was a bit thicker at the centre than at the edges. Above this layer, fine sand was deposited covering most of the charcoal beneath, but leaving the outer edges bare. Subsequently, another layer of charcoal was deposited with the same diameter as the one beneath, thus connecting the two charcoal layers at the edge of the mound, but separated by about 20 cm of sand at the centre. In both the charcoal layers, scattered ship nails, spikes, cremated remains, shield bosses and intentionally destroyed weapons were found (Lorange 1875: 154–55). Based on the description of the context, it is for the time being impossible to decide whether the ship was burnt on the spot where the mound was raised or if the material for the charcoal layers was transported to the site and thereafter scattered. It is possible to argue for both alternatives.

The most remarkable find is nevertheless the urn, which was deposited in a pit in the gravel beneath the lower charcoal layer (Fig. 12.4). Twelve shield bosses covered the urn which was filled 2/3 with a mixture of burnt bones, ashes, and charcoal. In between the cremated bones there were found pieces of burnt iron tools and smelted bronze, together with an arrowhead, three bone dices and six counters (Lorange 1875:

Fig. 12.4. The urn with shield bosses from grave mound no. 1, Myklebostad (courtesy of Bergen Museum, Bergen).

155). All the cremated bones in the urn belonged to a 30–35 year old man, but he might have been younger. The total weight of the bones was 1712 g. In the shoulder there was an indication of a cut, which may stem from a battle or *post mortem* treatment (Holck 1983).

The urn itself is one of the most spectacular finds in Norwegian archaeology. The three figures (Fig. 12.5) and the decoration at the bottom of the urn (Fig. 12.6), in particular, show unique craftsmanship, with the figures bearing a resemblance to the 'Buddha-bucket' in the Oseberg burial. It is uncertain what kind of cauldron this urn originally was. Paralleling hanging bowls in Anglo-Saxon graves, it is most likely Irish, though whether it was made in Ireland or in Irish monasteries in England is not known. Indeed, its original function may have been as a liturgical bowl for washing during Mass in early Christian communities (Liestøl 1953) or as a baptismal font. The bowl is dated to the middle or the end of the 8th century AD (Henry 1936; 1965: 93; Magnus 1967: 111), and some time have elapsed before being used as an urn and deposited in the grave.

Although there are no radiocarbon dates or exact typological dates for the ship burial, it has generally been considered to date from the end of the 9th century AD or the first

Fig. 12.5. The urn of grave mound no. 1: 'The Myklebostad Man' on the urn (courtesy of Bergen Museum, Bergen).

half of the 10th century AD (Shetelig 1906; Magnus 1967; 1978; 1992). This chronology would place the funeral within a similar timeframe as the formation of the Norwegian state and King Harald Hårfagre's conquest of the petty kingdoms along the west coast. According to Snorre Sturlasson (1993), there was a political centre in Nordfjord resisting King Harald Hårfagre's unification, and both the local kings, Audbjørn and Vemund, were killed by Harald Hårfagre's men. However, it is difficult to relate Snorre's sagas to historical events. Even if there were two local kings named Audbjørn and Vemund in Nordfjord at this time, it is not obvious that one of them was buried with the burnt ship in the Myklebostad grave. Thus, in order to contextualise this unique ship one has to look closer at the local ritual and religious practices, which took place at this farmstead, and how they deviate from other funerary practices at the same time.

The Myklebostad grave field

The political centre in Nordfjordeid from AD 600 to 1000 was situated at Myklebostad, where five large grave mounds were constructed, including the one with the burnt Viking ship (Table 12.1). In grave mound no. 2, there were six burials (Fig. 12.7) dating from the 8th to the 10th century AD, which were excavated by Håkon Shetelig in 1902–3. The first and second graves were the eldest of these (Grave II), which was a double burial of a man and a woman – both inhumated. The third was a cremation burial of a man (Grave III), consisting of a cremation patch measuring 1.60 × 1 m scattered with human bones, but the grave also contained a concentration of cleaned bones together with intentionally destroyed weapons (Shetelig 1905: 24–32). The fourth grave was a ship burial. Throughout large parts of the mound ship nails were scattered, and by their size it must have been a ship of considerable proportions. It is possible that later graves disturbed this burial of an unburnt ship (Grave V), as the distribution of nails and pieces of wood seemed unstructured (Shetelig 1905: 38, 51). The fifth grave was a cremation burial where a smaller boat was burnt (Grave I), which left an imprint of its size, measuring 7 m in length. In the charcoal layer there were

Table 12.1. Relative and absolute dating of the grave-mounds (from Shetelig 1905).

Graves		Sex	Date	Contents
Mound no. 1	R727	Man	End of 9th century?	Burnt ship
Mound no. 2	Grave II	Man	8th century, may be older	Inhumation
	Grave II	Woman	8th century, may be older	Inhumation
	Grave III	Man	8th century	Cremation
	Grave V	Man?	?	Unburnt boat
	Grave I	Man	End of 9th century, may be younger	Burnt boat
	Grave IV	Woman	End of 9th century, may be younger	Cremation, boat?
Mound no. 3				Unburnt boat/ship
Mound no. 4		Woman	10th century	Burnt boat
		Man	10th century	Inhumation
Mound no. 5				Two graves?

Fig. 12.6. The urn of grave mound no. 1: The décor at the bottom of the urn (after Shetelig 1905, folio at the end).

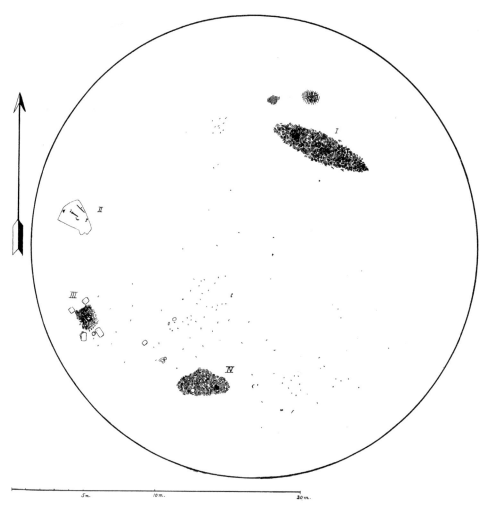

Fig. 12.7. Grave mound no. 2 with the six graves (after Shetelig 1905, folio at the end).

numerous nails, a sword and eight shield bosses. The cremated bones were collected and cleaned, and piled together under a cauldron. Finally, there was a cremation of a woman (Grave IV) consisting of two cauldrons: one of iron and one of bronze, stemming from the British Islands. Most of the cremated bones together with the grave gifts, such as two bronze fibulae, were scattered in the charcoal layer of 2 × 3 m in extension. The cremation had not taken place on the spot; furthermore ten unburnt boat nails were also found in the layer, indicating that parts of a boat were involved in the funerary procedures, although one would not label this as a boat grave (Shetelig 1905: 32–37).

Grave mound no. 4 was severely damaged and in 1847 large parts were removed as part of a road construction. Nevertheless, it seems that there were at least two burials in this mound. In one part, a sword, a spear and a cauldron were found, indicating that it was a male burial. In another part, Shetelig found a layer of charcoal of 1.80 × 1.30 m in extension, with a maximum thickness of six cm, containing about 350 boat nails, of which the majority measured between 2.5 cm and 3.5 cm in length. The deceased was a woman who had been cremated in a boat, but not where the mound was made because the charcoal layer, in which the bones were scattered, was too small for such a cremation. Grave mounds nos 3 and 5 were not excavated by archaeologists, though numerous boat nails in mound no. 3 were found earlier during construction work, but no other finds (Shetelig 1905: 40–41). Grave mound no. 5 was removed around 1875, from which two swords, two axes and a spear had been recovered and taken care of, indicating at least two male funerals in the mound (Magnus 1967: 60). Thus, there may have been other graves apart from the ones described.

Changing rituals and 'death myths'

The term 'religion' is contested in Iron Age studies. On the one hand, it is commonly acknowledged that there was no pre-Christian religion as such. On the other hand, depending upon definitions, one may also say that religion focuses on answering three main questions: 1) What becomes of us after death?, 2) How should we lead a moral life?, and 3) How and why were the universe, life, and human beings created? (Davies 1999). This relates to ritual practices and why certain rituals are performed and conducted the way they are. In this sense, death is the door to religion.

The grave mounds in this cemetery date from the 8th century AD, perhaps even earlier, to the end of the 10th century AD, thus giving a ritual continuity covering the Merovingian and the Viking Periods (*c.* AD 550–1000). The most striking feature with regards to rituals is that all of these funerals were conducted differently. Although there were some inhumations, the majority of men and women were cremated. The burnt Viking ship is an anomaly as a funeral practice, but also two smaller boats were burnt. There are also indications of one unburnt Viking ship of considerable size, as well as nails from two other unburnt ships or boats. To add to the variation, men and women were cremated or inhumed with burnt and unburnt ships or boats. Nevertheless, the deceased belonged to the same cultural and religious sphere, possibly originating from one family or at least the same community.

Death is contra-social and the funerary rites may meet the threat that death makes to the social system (Goody 1962: 26). Before addressing the question of inventing and reinventing tradition and why cremation is the dominant funeral practice in this region as opposed to inhumation which the elite practiced in other parts, it is necessary to put emphasis on the observed variation in the mortuary rituals: why are there differences in funeral practices when the descendants are assumed to share the same cosmological ideas and worldviews? The differences cannot be explained by different religions or ethnicities. Gender or social identities may have influenced the wealth of grave gifts, but prescribing cremation or not to both men and women cannot explain the variation within the respective rituals.

An approach that may explain part of the variation is through an analytical perspective, which we have called 'death myths' (Kristoffersen & Oestigaard 2006; 2008). If one assumes that the variation in rituals conducted by the descendants was intentional, then the differences are meaningful in themselves. Each funeral was carried out individually according to an overall cosmological or mythological scheme, which one may label a 'death myth'. In death there are a set of ritual possibilities, whereby the descendants can compose and conduct the funeral in accordance to: specific causes of death; the ancestors; the spiritual world, or; using the deceased as a medium for social outcomes in the reconstruction of society. Hence, a funeral is not a fixed set of ritual sequences, but an open field of mediations and interactions between the descendants and the divinities. Consequently, the participants may compose and perform particular rites to obtain a special desired result. Despite the differences in funeral practices, a large degree of homogeneity existed in burial customs. There are variations on a theme and a religious code must have defined and prescribed what was allowed: this is what a 'death myth' is. It is a collective conception of how, why, and who can perform death rituals at a given time. Variation in funeral customs can thus be seen as an expression where different rituals have been performed according to certain objectives based on a given repertoire of ritual possibilities. By seeing a ritual as a practice in social and religious life, it opens up a sphere of negotiations, manipulations and constructions of political and cosmological orders (Kristoffersen & Oestigaard 2006; 2008).

In pre-modern societies, tradition is intimately connected to truth. Based on analogies, one may also assume that this is true for the Viking Age. The access to truth or the possibility and capacity to make true statements about certain domains of reality are restricted to only some actors (Boyer 1990: 94). This is not limited to statements, but includes ritual participation and performance, particularly in funerals of the elite in a society. Not everybody can perform the most important and auspicious parts of the rituals, and hence, there will be a hierarchy among the descendants and ritual participants in a funeral (Oestigaard & Goldhahn 2006). In the words of Geertz (1980: 120), 'A royal cremation was not an echo of a politics taking place somewhere else. It was an intensification of a politics taking place everywhere else'. Political rituals and the state cult were not a cult of the state, but a repeated argument in the vocabulary of rituals that worldly status had a cosmic origin and that hierarchy was the governing principle of the universe (Geertz 1980: 102). Political rituals construct power and they are elaborate and efficacious arguments about power and how it is made. Indeed, the political order was often perceived as coming from divine sources (Bell 1997: 129).

Traditions may be created in two ways: new inventions acquiring legitimacy from tradition by being seen as a *direct continuity*, or; through being explicitly perceived as a *re-creation of a lost tradition*. Hence, an invented tradition may not bear any direct or visible relationship to the past, although believers may perceive it differently. Consequently, the re-creation or the presence of an authentic past in the present is often seen as an invention of tradition (Gombrich & Obeyesekere 1988: 241).

All social and ritual practices change through time, and the belief in tradition as a timeless continuity without change is a construction. Indeed, continuity is more remarkable than change. Roy Rappaport (2001: 6–7) has emphasised that 'structural transformations in some subsystems [have] made it possible to maintain more basic aspects of the system unchanged', and he stresses that the crucial question to ask is '*What does this change maintain unchanged?*' Changes in parts of the subsystems may preserve the continuity of the system as a whole living entity (Rappaport 2001: 7), in this case the religious and political institutions, and thus it is necessary to invent traditions and change rituals in order to preserve the existing ideologies and hierarchies of power in a time of transition.

The variation in funeral practices at Myklebostad indicates that death was an active medium by which the descendants or the elite probably reconstructed the deceased and their relationship to the ancestors, society and cosmos. Moreover, if one looks at the Myklebostad grave field with a particular emphasis on the burnt Viking ship, there are several factors suggesting that the funerals were mass mobilisations recreating or reinventing a former tradition with its roots in the Migration Period (*c.* AD 400–550), or in other words, re-creating a lost tradition.

Reinventing tradition

The political and religious context in which the Myklebostad complex appears is characterised by two overall processes: the formation of the Norwegian kingdom and the process of Christianisation. In the context of these processes one may interpret the ritual scenario which unfolded at Myklebostad. Harald Hårfagre unified Norway and conquered his enemies by force. Harald's eldest son, Eirik Bloodaxe, married Gunnhild, the daughter of the Danish King, Gorm the Old, thus unifying the two dynasties. However, his youngest son, who later became King Håkon the Good, was raised as a Christian by King Athelstan of England. Thus, on the one hand, religion or Christianity seems to have been a political and strategic tool, but on the other hand, religion can often be the key building block of identity (Insoll 2004a) and 'conceived as the superstructure into which all other aspects of life can be placed' (Insoll 2004b: 12), structuring all aspects of a given material culture and practices (Insoll 2004b: 13). It is in this light, funerals played a particularly important role.

With Christianity cremation was forbidden, but one cannot interpret inhumations in the Viking Period as influenced by Christianity; this practice started among the elite in the Late Roman Period, with for instance 'Flagghaugen', which is the richest grave in Norway from that period. However, cremation is undoubtedly a heathen practice, and coincidentally one of the closest parallels to the Myklebostad ship burial is found in France. In Île de Groix, Morbihan in Bretagne, a Viking ship was burnt in a Viking context for the 930s or '40s. The ship nails together with cremated bones, burnt soil, sand, and clay were deposited in a layer measuring 5.4 m in diameter with a thickness of 10–12 cm, but this size is only partial since half of the grave had eroded over a cliff when it was excavated. There were at least 20 shield bosses together with weapons and other artefacts collected in an iron cauldron (Shetelig 1945, Price 1989). This funeral in a Viking colony may hint that the Myklebostad practice may be more common than usually thought (see Price 2010; 2013). Still, with regards to Myklebostad in the particular cultural-religious Norwegian context, one may suggest that the funeral reinforced and reinvented earlier practices on a massive scale:

1. *Cremation.* Even though this was a common funeral practice in the Viking Period, its dominant position during the Migration Period was gradually replaced by inhumation which culminated with Christianity. The burnt Myklebostad ship is unique in the Norwegian context although it is described in written sources such as Ibn Fadlan (2005) and Saxo Grammaticus [1975]. Smaller boats have been burnt in Norway, but the cremation of a large Viking ship especially must have been a demonstration of power and wealth. This ritual manifested a particular religious belief and political ideology, since the other Viking ships such as Oseberg, Gokstad, Borre and Tune were unburnt.

2. *Urn.* During the Roman Iron Age and the Migration Period (until *c.* 550 AD) the use of urns in cremations was the ordinary practice, but with the transition to the Late Iron Age (from *c.* 550 AD) this practice disappears with some few exceptions in Norway (although quite common in for instance Sweden). In Norway, the production of pottery ends abruptly with the transition to the Merovingian Period (*c.* AD 550) and consequently no ceramic urns are made locally. In the Late Iron Age, the common practice was that the bones were scattered in the cremation patch, and using urns may relate to former traditions and practices from the Early Iron Age (Oestigaard 1999; 2000).

3. *Celtic cauldrons.* If one assumes that those living at Myklebostad knew the original meaning of this cauldron, the use of an alleged Christian liturgical cauldron as an urn would then be a deliberate manifestation and replacement of a religious idea with another, which desecrated Christianity, particularly since it was used as an urn. Utilising a liturgical bowl (Henry 1936; 1965; Liestøl 1953) in such a way may also relate to, and have a symbolic parallel to, older Celtic practices, such as employing skulls for ritual purposes. Early baptismal fonts have been interpreted as a continuity of the pagan skull cult and use (Bord & Bord 1985: 8–9; Green 1998), and the cauldron in the Myklebostad grave may relate to Irish heathendom. The double symbolism of cauldrons and skulls may reflect pagan beliefs, and hence the iconic motifs of the three figures on the urn may point backwards to the heathen past rather than towards the process of Christianisation.

4. *Intentional destruction of weapons.* This is a practice only found in cremations and it is a direct continuity of rituals from the Early Iron Age, which may relate to ancestral worship and cult. In the process of smelting and making swords, charcoal derived from the bones of animals and humans was used to transform

iron into steel. Thus, smelting brought life and identities into the objects, and this process may have been considered reversed in the ritual destruction of the weapons during the cremation ritual (Gansum 2004a; 2004b; 2004c; Goldhahn & Oestigaard 2007; Oestigaard 2007).

All together, it seems that the cremation and the burning of the Viking ship at Myklebostad reinvented former cremation practices, which had their roots in the Migration Period. Although former traditions were reinvented, there also appears to be a bricolage of syncretistic practices probably influenced by inhumation and beliefs of the body as a unity. Per Holck (1987: 55–56) analysed the cremated remains from eastern Norway: Of 1,082 samples, 919 were from the Early Iron Age and 147 from the Late Iron Age, with a further 16 from the Bronze Age. Based on measurements from the Asker Crematorium outside Oslo, the average weight of cremated bones from modern individuals is 3,075 grams (3375 g for men, 2,625 g for women), whereas other analyses of cremated modern individuals indicate that the average weight is 2,700 g for men and 1,840 g for women (Holck 1987: 71–73, 121). In contrast, the average weight of the cremated bones found in the archaeological record in general in eastern Norway is 269.7 g for single deposits. In many of these contexts it was impossible to determine the sex because too few fragments were available, but where possible the average weight was 637.9 g for men (with a range of 10–3,175 g) and 455.6 g for women (with a range of 30–1,950 g) (Holck 1987: 119). Since the majority of these cremations were conducted in the Early Iron Age, the traditional practice was that only 10–20% of the deceased's bones were placed in the urn and the rest were used for other purposes (Goldhahn & Oestigaard 2007; 2008). In the urn at Myklebostad, there were 1,712 g of bones, and although not a complete skeleton, it seems that the descendants aimed to collect all or most of the cremated bones. This observation appears to indicate a belief that it was necessary to preserve the complete body – a belief which is more in accordance with inhumation and contradicting the Early Iron Age cremation practices.

The massive scale and dimensions of this funeral bears testimony to a ritual mobilisation at a time of transition when the Norwegian kingdom was being established, and concomitant with the Christianisation process taking place (e.g. Gansum & Oestigaard 1999; 2004). The numerous shields deposited may indicate that the deceased king's men paid homage and tribute to their dead leader, who may have been killed in battle as indicated by the cut on his shoulder. If this was the case, one may relate this event to the unification of the kingdom and local chieftains or kings fighting against this process, as they stood to lose part or all of their own political power and sovereignty. This interpretation is, of course, based on a number of assumptions. Nevertheless, given the scale of the cremation in the time era when it took place, it could be of interest to pursue such a line of reasoning and propose some additional interpretations.

Importantly, if the deceased was killed in battle, the successor, who most likely was responsible for conducting the funeral, could have used this ritual as a means for mobilising forces in the ongoing struggle. The massive dimensions of the cremation, including the burning of the ship, is a strong manifestation of the pagan religion and its practices with continuity from earlier traditions and beliefs. Thus, older beliefs and power structures were emphasised as elite funerals linked the future with the past, which gave the present a divine legitimacy. This deeply rooted heathen tradition is also evident in the other grave mounds at Myklebostad, which seem to indicate a similar ritual and political manifestation, although not on the same scale.

However, if the local king at Myklebostad lost the war, another scenario is also possible. If the grave dates to the first half of the 10th century AD, it is one of the last funerals to have been conducted at Myklebostad, perhaps with a few minor burials later. Nevertheless, such a grandiose funeral can be seen as the final manifestation of a religious tradition. The tradition died with the king. In written sources there are references to the practice and ideal that when the king was killed, the battle was over. In Saxo Grammaticus, a battle is referred to where the Danish King Harald Hildetann went with his fleet to Kalmar in Sweden and attacked King Ring and his men. However, Ring's warriors killed Harald Hildetann, and when Ring became aware of his death, he ended the battle and ordered his men to search for the king's corpse. They searched among the corpses for half a day before they found the king's body. King Ring then prepared a funeral pyre and let the Danes put the deceased king's ship on the pyre before it was lit. When the cremation was completed, the bones of the king were collected in an urn and transported back to Leire in Denmark (Saxo Grammaticus [1975]: 312–16). Thus, the Myklebostad King may have lost the battle, and it was the victorious king's duty to prepare and conduct an honourable funeral for the deceased leader. If this was the case and his death was part of the unification of Norway, the political and ideological resistance against this process from this region would have been crushed. However, the massive dimensions of the funeral at Myklebostad as a continuity of existing tradition may suggest that the funeral was used as a unifying mobilisation within the community.

The Myklebostad king may even have been killed somewhere else and been cremated where he died, whereupon his men collected the bones, ashes and charcoal from the pyre and brought it back home. The uppermost of the two charcoal layers in the mound may provide hints supporting this hypothesis. Since the cremated material was placed upon a layer of sand, this would indicate that the remains from the pyre were collected at a certain stage during the funeral and deposited afterwards. As mentioned, however, the evidence at present is too vague to confirm whether the ship was burnt at the place where the mound was constructed or if the funeral took place somewhere else. In the latter scenario, the possibility exists that the king lost the battle elsewhere or even overseas, and this event may not relate to the unification of Norway, since the urn stems from the British Islands.

If a person died abroad or far from home, the urn may have been procured from that region and transported back. Hence, the origin of the urn may give indications of where the deceased died unless urns were procured prior to death (Oestigaard

1999). The parallel find of a burnt Viking ship in France suggests that the funeral was arranged where the battle was lost and that the ship was burnt *in situ* upon which the mound was built.

Changes in rituals, traditions and ritual variation

Making theoretical elaborations about social processes on a micro-level based on changes in material culture are always a challenge. Complex rituals such as those at Myklebostad can be solely local developments not relating to grander narratives of renegotiating traditions. If, however, they are, it can be of interest to relate the Myklebostad complex to theories of tradition and social change through time.

The past is always a created ideology with a purpose designed to control individuals or to motivate societies and inspire classes (Plumb 1969: 17). The past can be seen as an elaborate house of cards, which the present has been constantly upsetting and using for political purposes. Power needs legitimacy and legitimacy needs justification. Legitimacy can be justified in three ways: from religion, from philosophy, and from the past. More often than not, legitimacy is an amalgam of the three, which is evident at Myklebostad where the past and religion (or possible philosophy) were two sides of the same coin used in the formation of society. The past has constantly been involved in the present, and everything from the past including monuments and funerals were securing the authority (Plumb 1969: 36–38). Hence, tradition is an ideological interpretation and uses the past in the present for the future.

Tradition constitutes a broadly significant phenomenon. A major characteristic of tradition is that the temporal distance separating us from the past or the living from the dead, is not value-free or objective. The time and relation between the past and the present is a transmission which generates and gives legitimacy to meaning, which then gives legitimacy to social control and institutions. Tradition is the outcome of the exchange between an interpreted past and an interpreted present. Within a tradition nobody is an absolute inventor, but rather the contrary, the past is a source for constructing the future, which creates a situation where everybody is an heir of the past. Tradition enables us therefore to understand what has been said and done when this knowledge is transmitted historically through chains of interpretations and reinterpretation, which create some structural properties of societies (Ricoeur 1990: 221, 227):

1. Traditions create an interconnectedness which assures the continuity of understanding the past. Thus, the past becomes a source for making history and the future, whereby the actors are affected by the past.
2. Traditions are bearers of meaning, and it is through tradition that received heritage is given symbolic and moral value. In this sense traditions are not only bearers of meaning, but also proposals and creators of meaning.

3.   Traditions are justifying legitimacy, and claims for truths can be found in tradition, particularly when argumentation is offered within the public space of discussion or performed in rituals.

The last point directs the attention from the dead to the living and emphasises that death is a matter of transactions and re-negotiations. From a societal perspective, death is often more important for the living than for the dead (Oestigaard & Goldhahn 2006). It is in this light important to distinguish between changes in tradition, rituals and ritual variation. As I have suggested, it seems that there is an intentional reinvention of tradition at Myklebostad, which had an explicit, political, ideological, and religious reason and pre-conceived outcome. In the conquest of Norway, which ended with the formation of a unified kingdom, the past was a source giving religious and political legitimacy to opposition and resistance, and the evidence for this can be traced in the actual funerals. However, there is a lot of contemporary, ritual variation, and an archaeological challenge remains how to distinguish between synchronic variation and diachronic change. The Myklebostad complex is, nevertheless, such an empirical case study, which enables one to analyse and propose suggestions with regard to why ritual change took place.

Concluding remarks

The burnt Viking ship at Myklebostad in western Norway is a unique example of a funeral which breaks both with tradition, and at the same time reinvents tradition. The death of high-profile individuals provides a political and religious platform, which was arguably more important for the living than the dead. Funerals were events where the descendants could legitimise future hierarchies by transforming the deceased's social and ritual status and power to themselves (Oestigaard & Goldhahn 2006). Funeral rituals were a part of political strategies interwoven and legitimised by religion giving the successors divine power and authenticity. The dead were a means and used as mediums for other social and religious purposes, thus combining social strategies, political ambitions, and religious beliefs. In this process rituals were composed, changed, and reinvented creating the preferred and ideological platform necessary for social change and re-establishing hierarchies. This change was within an overall religious framework, which one may call a 'death myth' prescribing and legitimising what was allowed to be done. Within this ritual sphere it seems that almost every kind of new invention was possible, so long as it was conducted by the right person and rooted in a real or imagined tradition. In particular, such a situation as the unification of Norway and the concomitant Christianisation would have necessitated the ritual mobilisation that occurred.

Acknowledgements

I would like to thank Ragnar Børsheim for discussions of the Myklebostad complex and for giving me permission to use his illustrations. My thanks also go to Joakim Goldhahn, who has contributed with many ideas regarding the Myklebostad grave, and finally, I would like to thank Neil Price for constructive suggestions as a reviewer.

Bibliography

Andersen, S. P. 1977: *Samlingen av Norge og kristningen av landet 800–1130*, Universitetsforlaget: Oslo.

Bell, C. 1997: *Ritual. Perspectives and Dimensions*, Oxford University Press: Oxford.

Bord, C. & Bord, J. 1985: *Sacred Waters. Holy Wells and Water Lore in Britain and Ireland*, Granada: London.

Boyer, P. 1990: *Tradition as Truth and Communication. A Cognitive Description of Traditional Discourse*, Cambridge University Press: Cambridge.

Davies, C. 1999: 'The Fragmentation of the Religious Tradition of the Creation, After-life and Morality: Modernity not Post-Modernity'. *Journal of Contemporary Religion* 17.3: 339–60.

Gansum, T. 2004a: *Hauger som konstruksjoner – arkeologiske forventninger gjennom 200 år* (Gotarc Series B. Gothenburg Archaeological Thesis No. 33), Gothenburg University: Gothenburg.

Gansum, T. 2004b: 'Role the Bones – from Iron to Steel', *Norwegian Archaeological Review* 37.1: 41–57.

Gansum, T. 2004c: 'Jernets fødsel og dødens stål. Rituell bruk av bein', in Å. Berggren, S. Arvidsson & A.M. Hållans (eds): *Minne och myt. Konsten att skapa det förflutna*, Nordic Academic Press: Lund, 121–55.

Gansum, T. & Oestigaard, T. 1999: 'En haug med ritualer – Haugar og rikssamlingen', *Vestfoldminne* 1998/1999: 74–99.

Gansum, T. & Oestigaard, T. 2004: 'The Ritual Stratigraphy of Monuments that Matter', *European Journal of Archaeology* 7.1: 61–79.

Geertz, C. 1980: *Negara. The Theatre State in Nineteenth-Century Bali*, Princeton University Press: New Jersey.

Goldhahn, J. & Østigård, T. 2007: *Rituelle spesialister i bronse- og jernalderen*, vols. 1–2 (Gotarc Series C, No. 65), Gothenburg University: Gothenburg.

Goldhan, J. & Oestigaard, T. 2008: 'Smith and Death. Cremations in Furnaces in Bronze and Iron Age Scandinavia', in K. Chilidis, J. Lund & C. Prescott (eds): *Facets of Archaeology. Essays in Honour of Lotte Hedeager on her 60th Birthday*, Unipub Forlag: Oslo, 215-41.

Goody, J. 1962: *Death, Property and the Ancestors*, Stanford University Press: California.

Gombrich, R. & Obeyesekere, G. 1988: *Buddhism transformed. Religious Change in Sri Lanka*, Princeton University Press: Princeton, New Jersey.

Green, M. J. 1998: 'Vessels of Death: Sacred Cauldrons in Archaeology and Myth', *The Antiquaries Journal* 78: 63–84.

Henry, F. 1936: 'Hanging Bowls', *Journal of the Royal Society of Antiquarians of Ireland* 66: 209–46.

Henry, F. 1965: *Irish Art during the Early Christian Period to AD 800*, Methuen: London.

Holck, P. 1983: 'Analyse av B2978. Innberetning', Topografisk arkiv, Bergen Museum: Bergen.

Holck, P. 1987: *Cremated Bones. A Medical-Anthropological Study of Archaeological Material on cremated Burials* (Antropologiske skrifter nr. 1, Anatomisk Institutt), University of Oslo: Oslo.

Ibn Fadlan, A. 2005: *Ibn Fadlan's Journey to Russia: A Tenth-Century Traveller from Baghdad to the Volga River*, translated with commentary by Richard N. Frye, Markus Wiener Publishers: Princeton.

Insoll, T. 2004a: 'Are Archaeologists afraid of Gods? Some Thoughts on Archaeology and Religion', in T. Insoll (ed.): *Belief in the Past. The Proceedings of the Manchester Conference on Archaeology and Religion* (British Archaeological Reports, International Series 1212), Archaeopress: Oxford, 1–6.

Insoll, T. 2004b: *Archaeology, Ritual, Religion*, Routledge: London.

Krag , C. 1995: *Vikingtid og rikssamling 800–1130* (Norges Historie bind 2), Aschehoug: Oslo.

Kristoffersen, S. & Oestigaard, T. 2006: '"Dødsmyter" – regissering av ritualer og variasjon i likbehandling i folkevandringstid', in Oestigaard (ed.), 113–32.

Kristoffersen, S. & Oestigaard, T. 2008: '"Death Myths": Performing of Rituals and Variation in Corpse Treatment during the Migration Period in Norway', in F. Fahlander & T. Oestigaard (eds): *The Materiality of Death. Bodies, Burials, Beliefs* (British Archaeological Reports, International Series 1768), Archaeopress: Oxford, 127–39.

Liestøl, A. 1953: 'The Hanging Bowl: A Liturgical and Domestic Vessel', *Acta archaeologica* 24: 163–70.

Lorange, A. 1875: *Samlingen af norske oldsager i Bergens museum* (J.D. Beyers Bogtrykkeri), Bergen Museum: Bergen.

Magnus, B. 1967: *Studier i Nordfjords yngre jernalder* (Magistergrad thesis, Arkeologisk Institutt), University of Bergen: Bergen.

Magnus, B. 1978: 'De eldste tider i Gloppen og Breim', in *Soga om Gloppen og Breim. Band 1. Frå dei eldste tider til om lag år 1800*, Gloppens Sparebank: Sandane, 103–227.

Magnus, B. 1992: 'Småkonger og politiske sentra i Fjordane i tidlig vikingtid', *Nytt fra utgravningskontoret i Bergen* 1992.3: 71–82.

Myhre, B. & Gansum, T. 2003: *Skipshaugen 900 e. Kr. Borrefunnet 1852–2002*, Midgard Forlag: Borre.

Nicolaysen, N. 1882. *Langskibet fra Gokstad ved Sandefjord*, Alb. Cammermeyer: Kristiania.

Oestigaard, T. 1999: 'Cremations as Transformations: When the Dual Cultural Hypothesis was cremated and carried away in Urns', *European Journal of Archaeology* 2.3: 345–64.

Oestigaard, T. 2000: 'Sacrifices of Raw, Cooked and Burnt Humans,' *Norwegian Archaeological Review* 33.1: 41–58.

Oestigaard, T. 2006: 'Lik og ulik – introduksjon til variasjon i gravskikk', in Oestigaard (ed.), 9–44.

Oestigaard, T. 2007: *Transformatøren – Ildens mester i jernalderen. Vol. 2* (Gotarc Series C, No. 65), Gothenburg University: Gothenburg.

Oestigaard, T. 2006 (ed.): *Lik og ulik: Tilnærminger til variasjon i gravskikk* (Universitetet i Bergens Arkeologiske Skrifter 2), University of Bergen: Bergen.

Oestigaard, T. & Goldhahn, J. 2006: 'From the Dead to the Living. Death as Transactions and Re-negotiations', *Norwegian Archaeological Review* 39.1: 27–48.

Opedal, A. 1998: *De glemte skipsgravene* (AmS-Småtrykk 47), Arkeologisk museum i Stavanger: Stavanger.

Opedal, A. 2005: *Kongens død i et førstatlig rike: skipsgravritualer i Avaldsnes-området og aspekter ved konstituering av kongemakt og kongerike 700–950 e. Kr.* (Acta Humaniora 228), D. Phil. Thesis, University of Oslo: Oslo.

Plumb, J. H. 1969: *The Death of the Past*, Macmillan: London.

Price, N. 1989: *The Vikings in Brittany*, Viking Society for Northern Research: London.

Price, N. 2010: 'Passing into Poetry: Viking-Age Mortuary Drama and the Origins of Norse Mythology'. *Medieval Archaeology* 54: 123–56.

Price, N. 2013: *Viking Brittany: Revisiting the Colony that failed*. Festschrift. In press.

Rappaport, R. A. 2001: *Ritual and Religion in the Making of Humanity*, Cambridge University Press: Cambridge.

Ricoeur, P. 1990: *Time and Narrative. Vol. 3*, The University of Chicago Press: Chicago.

Saxo Grammaticus [1975]: *Danmarks Krønike*, translated by Dr. Fr. Winkel Horn, A. Christiansens Forlag: Copenhagen.

Shetelig, H. 1905: *Gravene ved Myklebostad paa Nordfjordeid* (Bergen Museums Aarbog 1905 No. 7), Bergen Museum: Bergen.

Shetelig, H. 1906: *Ship Burials*, reprinted from the Saga Book of the Viking Club.

Shetelig, H. 1912: *Vestlandske graver fra jernalderen* (Bergens Museums skrifter. Ny række. Bd. II. No. I), A/S John Griegs Boktrykkeri: Bergen.

Shetelig, H. 1945: 'The Viking Graves in Great Britain and Ireland', *Acta Archaeologica* 16: 1–56.

Snorre Sturlasson [1993]: *Snorres kongesoger*, Det Norske Samlaget: Oslo.

13

TRANSFORMING MEDIEVAL BELIEFS
The Significance of Bodily Resurrection
to Medieval Burial Rituals

Roberta Gilchrist

The most significant changes in Medieval burial practices developed in response to the conversion to Christianity. This paper focuses on the transitional period of the 9th to the 11th centuries in England, when distinctively Christian burial rites emerged that placed a new emphasis on the treatment of the corpse and the structure of the grave. Recent interpretations have emphasised economic and political factors in prompting the demise of the furnished inhumation rite. In contrast, it is argued here that Christian eschatology played a central role in shifting emphasis to maintaining the material continuity of the body, to allow its literal resurrection at Judgement Day. Christian burial rites of this period exhibit three broad tendencies: the marking of graves with distinct materials, the containment of the body, and the dressing of religious corpses. It is proposed that these traits relate to Christian beliefs about the bodily resurrection, the embodied experience of the afterlife, and the perceived reality of corporeal transformation in death. Investigation of funerary rites at the junctures of the boundaries between Early and later Medieval Periods also reveals long-term continuities and the reworking of older traditions, such as the placement of amulets with the dead.

Keywords: amulets, body, Christian eschatology, conversion, England, resurrection, transformation.

Introduction: material continuity and the Medieval body

The Medieval Period witnessed stark changes in death rituals: the practice of cremation ceased and the rite of furnished inhumation declined dramatically. However, comprehensive evaluation of this major transition has been lacking, perhaps prevented by the rigid periodisation of the discipline of Medieval archaeology into early and later phases. The resulting tendency is for later Medieval archaeologists to chronicle subtle variations in established modes of Christian burial (11th–15th centuries CE), while their Early Medieval colleagues explore more diverse pagan funerary customs as expressions of social identities in life (5th–8th centuries CE). The most significant watersheds occur at the junctures and limits of these period boundaries, when distinctively Christian burial rites developed from the 8th–11th centuries, and much later, when Medieval Catholic rites were reinterpreted by the Protestant Reformation in the 16th century (Gilchrist 2003).

Traditionally, Early Medieval burials were studied in terms of race and religion, with patterns in grave goods used as indices of migration and conversion. Over the past three decades, in contrast, Early Medieval archaeologists have emphasised more symbolic and ideological elements in mortuary ritual (Williams 2005: 195). In particular, they have interpreted the demise of the furnished burial rite as being linked to economic and political factors, rather than stemming from any intrinsic connection to Christian belief (Hadley 2001: 92–93). To the contrary, I will argue that Christian eschatology played a central role in redefining the meaning of the grave and the treatment of the corpse. Of primary importance was the Christian premise of the material continuity of the body for its resurrection at Judgement Day.

I will focus particularly on the transitional period of the 9th to the 11th centuries in England, when distinctively Christian burial rites emerged that placed a new emphasis on the corpse and the structure of the grave. These innovations continued to be used in later Medieval churchyards and monastic cemeteries from the 11th century up to at least *c.* 1300. Many of these rites were prevalent across western and northern Europe, with the precise chronology and diversity of practice varying in each locality according to the dates of Christianisation. My interpretative approach uses mortuary evidence to explore changing beliefs about the body in life and death, drawing on the premise that burials actively represent social theories of the body (after Joyce 1998; Lacquer 1990). My reassertion of the centrality of religious belief to the meaning of Medieval graves is consistent with a wider movement in interpretative archaeology that calls for the reintegration of ritual with other aspects of social life (Brück 1999; Insoll 2004; Bradley 2005).

To many today, the belief in bodily resurrection seems entirely implausible. Did Medieval people truly accept that at the end of time God would reassemble their fragmented remains, granting eternal life to these reanimated bones? The historian Caroline Bynum has traced the doctrine of bodily resurrection from its development between the 2nd and the 5th centuries up to its formalisation in the later Middle Ages.

Theological treatises leave little doubt that Medieval belief was deeply material (Bynum 1991; 1995). Theologians debated the smallest details of the embodied afterlife: What age and sex would the resurrected be? Would they wear clothes? Would they smell, eat or taste? These concerns are expressed, for example, by the 10th-century English homilist Ælfric of Eynsham (*c.* 955–1010): 'Each person yet shall have his own height in the size that he was before as a person, or that he should have had, had he become fully-grown, those that departed in childhood or adolescence' (quoted in Thompson 2002: 237). In 1215, the doctrine was confirmed by the 4th Lateran Council: 'all rise again with their own individual bodies, that is, the bodies which they now wear' (Bynum 1991: 240).

The doctrine of purgatory was also formalised by the 4th Lateran Council in 1215, with the Medieval concept evolving from much earlier roots. The central tenet of purification in the afterlife is based in Judaism, while the idea that sins should be expurgated by trial emerged as early as the 3rd or 4th century. The Medieval construction of purgatory also drew upon classical traditions of the otherworld and European folkloric associations of fire with rejuvenation and rebirth (Le Goff 1984: 1–14). Purgatory was not conceived as a distinct physical space until the 12th century, but the premise was long established of a preliminary stage of the afterlife in which sins were cleansed. Did Medieval people perceive a material connection between the corpse in the grave and the soul that was physically purged in the afterlife? In his classic study of Medieval purgatory, Jacques Le Goff dismisses this question as unproblematic: 'Once separated from the body, the soul was endowed with a materiality *sui generis*, and punishment could then be inflicted upon it in Purgatory as though it were corporeal' (Le Goff 1984: 6). In contrast, Bynum identifies the question of *bodily continuity* as a persistent challenge for Medieval theologians, who pondered how personal identity could endure the ravages of death and decay and the miraculous resurrection of the body (Bynum 1991: 254). But to what extent did these theological tenets permeate popular practice? Archaeological evidence for Medieval funerary rites provides additional insight to social theories of the body, and in particular, to changing concerns over the *integrity* of the Christian body in death.

Anglo-Saxon burial rites in transition

Recent interpretations of the richly furnished Anglo-Saxon burials of the 5th to 7th centuries have assessed them as 'theatrical tableaux'. The setting of the corpse was staged as a funerary performance for the living to express their social memory of the dead. Spectacular burials such as Sutton Hoo (Suffolk) or Prittlewell (Essex) have been compared by Martin Carver to 'a theatre, in which each burial is a composition, offering, with greater or lesser authority, a metaphor for its age' (Carver 1998: 139). It is commonly argued that lesser burials in Anglo-Saxon cemeteries were also laid out with the emphasis on the *viewing* of the tableau, with weapons, jewellery, and other grave furnishings selected and arranged to display the identity of the deceased during life (Geake 2003: 260; Devlin 2007: 33). There was broad consistency within the Germanic burial tradition that was shared by the Franks, Burgundians, Alamans, Bavarians, Saxons and Anglo-Saxons: jewellery, amulets, and chatelaines accompanied female burials; and weapons, tools, and horse-equipment were provided for men; both sexes were associated with knives, buckles, coins, and food vessels and offerings (Marzinzik 2000: 149).

From the 8th century onwards, only the most modest artefacts were deposited in graves, items such as beads, rings, coins, small knives, and dress fasteners, perhaps reflecting the continued practice of clothed burial (Hadley 2001: 96). As grave furnishings declined in importance, greater significance was placed on the location of the interment. Seventh and 8th century rites included burial in barrows and on the boundaries of ancestral territories. Radiocarbon dating has confirmed that some 8th century cemeteries remained independent of churches and maintained the traditional use of grave goods to at least some degree. There was a gradual shift toward row-cemeteries on sites that were either associated with churches or pre-dated their development on the same site, such as Barrow-upon-Humber (Lincolnshire) (Hadley 2002: 221); churchyard burial seems to have been the usual practice by the 10th century (Hadley & Buckberry 2005: 125–26).

The impact of the Christian conversion is usually assessed with reference to the disappearance of grave goods, but there is no evidence that the early church was either prescriptive or consistent in its views on burial practice. Numerous early churchyards have yielded graves containing single artefacts such as coins, combs, bracelets, and knives (Morris 1983: 50, 60–61). While most categories of grave good declined in variety and occurrence, one type actually increased during this transitional period. The range and frequency of amulets expanded to include fossils, the teeth of wild animals (such as boar and beaver), antique Roman coins, and waist bags, which may have held herbal charms or even Christian relics (Geake 1997; Meaney 1981). These amulets were almost exclusive to the graves of women and perhaps reflect the role of women as religious or funerary specialists (Geake 2003). Throughout Early Medieval Europe, the association is repeated of amulets with the graves of women and children. Their frequency increases during the conversion period in respective regions, for example in the later 10th century in Denmark (Zeiten 1997: 45). John Blair has proposed that this use of amulets may have been consistent with Christian practice and integral to the mortuary display of religious affiliation by newly converted women (Blair 2005: 174). Others have argued precisely the opposite: that the increased use of amulets indicates resistance to Christianity, even that the distinctive change in amulet use may represent the development of paganism as a more cohesive and political theology (Zeiten 1997: 49; Geake 1997: 98). The relationship between Christianity and amulets may be clarified with reference to both earlier and later practice, and I will return to discuss the meaning of their occurrence in later Medieval graves.

Christian burial rites: marking, containing and dressing the body

A range of Christian mortuary practices had emerged by the 9th century that focused more closely on the corpse and its framing within the grave. Some of these were variations on the furnished burial rite, but greater emphasis was now placed on the cadaver itself. Three themes can be identified among the diverse range of rites that are evidenced in urban, rural and ecclesiastical sites of the period.

1. The marking of graves with distinct materials

Grave constructions were used to distinguish the corpse from the surrounding soil, making it both visually and physically discrete (Thompson 2002: 231). These included grave linings of stone and tile, the framing of the head and body with stones, and the addition of distinctive materials to the grave. The practice of elaborating the grave with stones is well illustrated by excavations at the 9th to 12th century church of Raunds (Northamptonshire). Stones were represented in approximately half of the excavated graves: they occurred singly or in clusters, lining the entire grave or placed more strategically, under the head or either side of it, along the body, or at the feet (Boddington 1996: 38–42). A similar pattern is repeated at Worcester Cathedral (Worcestershire), where a late Saxon cemetery sealed by the Norman chapter house contained 180 interments of men, women and children (Fig. 13.1). Stones were used to mark approximately 30% of burials, associated particularly with the head: as 'ear-muffs' to support the head on either side, or as 'pillow stones' placed beneath the head (Guy 2010). In the Worcester cemetery, stones were sometimes used in conjunction with coffins. Stone and tile grave linings continued into the later Middle Ages, but the use of 'ear-muff' stones became less common after the 11th century (Gilchrist and Sloane 2005: 138).

The addition of charcoal to graves is well attested and linked especially with religious settlements of the 9th–12th centuries, where it is often interpreted as a penitential rite (Thompson 2004: 118–22). But foreign substances such as clay, chalk and lime were also used to line graves, mixed with grave soils or used to pack coffins. For example, at the parish church of Barton-on-Humber (Lincolnshire), two distinct groups of 37 burials (dated *c.* 950–1150) had liquid mud poured into the coffins (Rodwell 2007: 26). The use of visually distinctive base linings continued into the later Middle Ages, with chalk, mortar, and plaster commonly used to create plain white floors for graves, and more localised traditions of using crushed or chipped stone, sand and gravel (Gilchrist & Sloane 2005: 142–44)

Victoria Thompson (2002: 240) has argued that this range of mortuary innovations aimed to provide a 'clean burial', both spiritually and materially, to display humility and to protect the body from decay. The concept of the cemetery as sacred space was fully developed by the 10th century (Gittos 2002), resulting in significant pressure to reuse burial space within consecrated churchyards. Demarcation of the grave may also have protected it from disturbance by subsequent grave-digging. At the 10th century

WORCESTER CATHEDRAL

CHAPTER HOUSE

☐ STONES

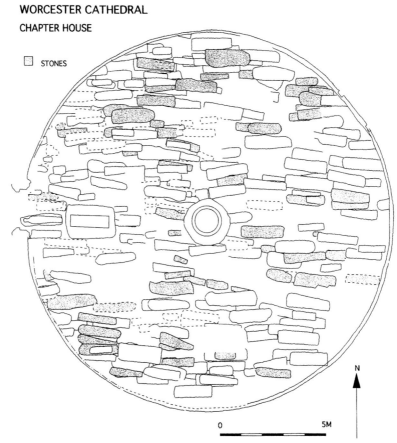

0   5M

N

*Fig. 13.1. Plan of late Saxon burials excavated within the chapter house at Worcester Cathedral; stones were used in c. 30% of graves (shown shaded) (**plan by Christopher Guy, Worcester Cathedral Archaeologist; reproduced with the kind permission of the Dean and Chapter of Worcester Cathedral**).*

church of St Mark's, Lincoln, attempts to minimise disturbance involved the use of flat and upright grave markers, stone slabs, and wooden markers held in post-holes, all used alongside timber coffins and stone cists (Gilmour & Stocker 1986). At Barton-on-Humber there is clear evidence that efforts were made to carefully remove and translate burials when the church was rebuilt. A group of 29 early burials at Barton were meticulously exhumed and removed before the erection of the late Saxon church (Rodwell 2007: 30). At Addingham (West Yorkshire), which fell out of use by the 11th or 12th century, bodies were deliberately exhumed from the western part of the cemetery for re-interment within new graves in the eastern cemetery: the disinterred remains were placed neatly in a pile at one end of the new grave (Adams 1996: 186).

Occasionally, we recover discrete, secondary inhumations of translated remains. 'Translated' burials are the disarticulated bones of a single individual that have been repackaged for reburial. Translated remains at Raunds were inhumed in sacks or pits (Boddington 1996: 28–29), while later Medieval practice favoured the use of chests or caskets (Gilchrist & Sloane 2005: 116–17). For example, a small wooden casket excavated from St Oswald's, Gloucester, contained the neatly packed bones of an adult male, including the tiny bones of the hands and feet (Heighway & Bryant 1999: 205–6).

2. Containment of the body

Within the grave, the corpse was enveloped by a winding sheet or enclosed within a coffin. The white linen shroud indicated that the Christian body had been shriven, denoting a 'good death' that followed the deathbed rites of confession, communion and the sacrament of extreme unction (Woolgar 2006: 50). The white shroud was symbolic of spiritual purity: St Cuthbert of Lindisfarne (d. 687) ordered that he should be buried only in a precious white cloth (although his monastic community actually buried him in rich vestments and with grave goods of a golden pectoral cross, a gold chalice, an ivory comb, scissors and a book of Gospels (Bonner et al. 1989). White shrouds may have been in regular use by the 11th century, as suggested by the depiction of the funeral of Edward the Confessor on the Bayeux Tapestry (Hadley & Buckberry 2005: 123). The late Saxon cemetery at Worcester Cathedral produced nine fragments of woolen textile that may be remnants of shrouds; however, these examples derive from coffined burials and could alternatively represent clothing (Guy 2010).

The common use of coffins can be demonstrated at sites where water-logged conditions have facilitated their survival. At Barton-on-Humber, radiocarbon and dendrochronology dates have confirmed that use of timber coffins was the norm by the 10th century. These were oak coffins, lightly-constructed with few nails or metal components, and occasionally incorporating bases woven from wattles (Rodwell 2007: 29, 22). At Worcester Cathedral, late Saxon timber coffins survived due to the very dry conditions beneath the chapter house: 106 coffins were identified in association with 180 burials (Guy 2010). The difficulties in detecting coffins archaeologically may have led to under-estimates of their use, particularly if wooden dowels rather than iron nails were typically used for fastening. The incidence of coffin use at later Medieval monastic cemeteries has been estimated to range from between 4% and 34% (Gilchrist & Sloane 2005). However, the 60% rate of coffin use at late Saxon Worcester Cathedral may call this estimate into question.

Other receptacles were sometimes employed to contain the corpse for burial. Occasionally domestic chests were used, complete with locks and hinges, a practice known in Scandinavia in the 10th century, and occurring in England from the 8th up to the 12th century (Fig. 13.2). Four chest-burials from York Minster were dated to the 9th or 10th centuries, so close together that they were intercutting: they contained one elderly male, a middle-aged female, a young adult male, and an adolescent of unknown sex (Kjølbye-Biddle 1995: 517). The close proximity of the chests suggests that these individuals may have formed a distinctive social group in life. Other chest-burials are known principally from the north of England, including Repton (Derbyshire), Ripon

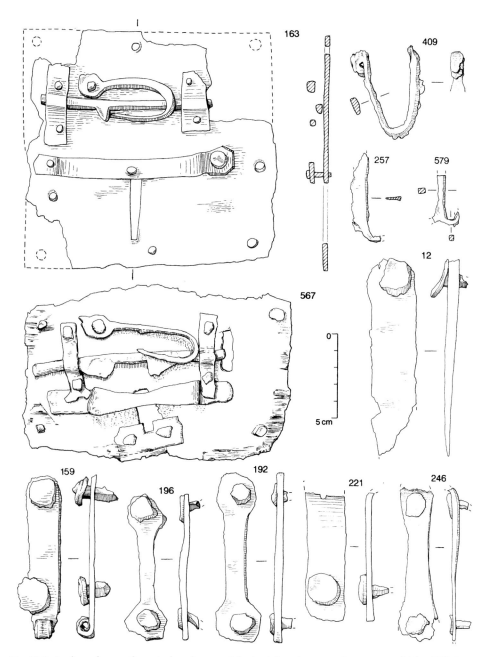

Fig. 13.2. Locks and straps from timber chests used for burial at the monastic cemetery of Ailcy Hill, Ripon, North Yorkshire, c. 7th–10th century (reproduced with the kind permission of York Archaeological Trust from Hall & Whyman 1996, 107: fig. 25).

Fig. 13.3. A barrel padlock and key were placed between the knees of a young adult female buried in a coffin at Worcester Cathedral (photograph by Christopher Guy, Worcester Cathedral Archaeologist; reproduced with kind permission of the Dean and Chapter of Worcester Cathedral).

(Yorkshire), Flixborough (Lincolnshire), Partney (Lincolnshire) and Fishergate (York), but isolated examples have also been recorded from Winchester and Hereford (Kjølbye-Biddle 1995: 517; Hall & Whyman 1996: 113). This practice appears to have been reserved for burials occurring within a discrete area of a monastic or cathedral cemetery, and the rite perhaps denoted a particular religious status. The latest dated example is the burial of a 'possible' male in a locked chest or coffin at the hospital of Partney (Lincolnshire), radiocarbon dated AD 1080–1160 (Atkins & Shepherd Popescu 2010).

The chest-burials seem to convey a deliberate symbolism of locks and containment. The locking metaphor may also be pertinent to barrel padlocks, which were occasionally deposited deliberately with Medieval burials. They were first used as grave goods during the conversion period: of six known examples dating from the late 7th to 8th centuries, five occurred with women (Geake 1997: 82). A young adult female from the late Saxon cemetery at Worcester Cathedral was interred in a coffin with a barrel padlock placed between her knees (Fig. 13.3). Analysis of the padlock showed that it was locked and intact, with the key in place; remains of pupa cases were incorporated in the corrosion crust of the lock, confirming that the object was in contact with the corpse during decomposition (Guy 2010). In later Medieval contexts, padlocks were also associated principally with women. Two 11th century padlocks from graves in

Hereford retained textile impressions, confirming that they were contained within the shroud: the padlocks were placed on the respective pelvic areas of an adolescent and an adult female. Two later Medieval examples from the Cistercian monastery of St Mary Graces in London (1350–1538) were also associated with women, one adjacent to the pelvic area (Gilchrist & Sloane 2005: 178). The gender correlation is uncertain in some cases: a barrel padlock recovered from the chapter house of Benedictine Sandwell Priory (Staffordshire; dated 1250–1450) was deposited with an adult of unknown sex (Hodder 1991: 91).

The social context of the chest and padlock burials suggests that this particular treatment may represent some distinct religious status, rather than a general effort to contain and protect the body, or even to imprison the 'dangerous' dead. The position of the padlocks in association with the pelvic region may indicate the signaling of chastity, the sexual purity of the body. Virginal bodies were believed to remain incorrupt in death, as indicated by contemporary hagiography (Thompson 2002: 235–36). The symbolism of chests and locks may have been used to represent the integrity of the virginal body, while barrel padlocks seem to have been reserved especially for deposition with the female corpse. Incorruptibility of the body after burial was regarded as the definitive miracle for proving sanctity, particularly in the case of female saints (Bynum 1991: 266).

3. Dressing religious corpses

Christian burials show an increased emphasis on the marking and containment of the body, and small numbers of associated artefacts imply that the practice of clothed burial continued to some extent. But the use of grave goods and funerary costume was deliberately enhanced for one category of the Christian dead: religious personnel were given special treatment to denote the consecrated status of their bodies. Bishops, abbots, and priests were accompanied by religious grave goods that signaled their ranking in the ecclesiastical hierarchy: mortuary crosses and plaques, crosiers, and the chalice and paten that were symbolic of the office of the priest (Gilchrist & Sloane 2005). Perhaps most significantly, religious corpses were fully dressed in their monastic habits or consecration robes. This clothing did not merely represent the identity or status of the deceased, it was perceived to *protect* the physical body of the corpse in purgatory.

This belief is vividly expressed in the story of a lay-brother of the Cistercian monastery of Stratford Langthorne (Essex), recounted in Peter of Cornwall's *Liber revelationum* of 1200–6 (Holdsworth 1962: 196–97; Woolgar 2006: 180). This particular lay-brother had demonstrated some uncertainty in his vocation: on one occasion he fled the abbey to resume his secular life as a shepherd, only to return subsequently to his calling. He was allowed re-entry to the abbey, but as punishment the lay-brother was permitted to wear only the black tunic that represented his position, and not the customary black hood. When the lay-brother eventually died he was buried in his tunic, but without the hood. Both the abbot and the prior of Stratford Langthorne reported oneiric visions of the dead lay-brother, who told them that he needed his full habit in order for his soul to be saved. The apparition was singed and scarred because he had lacked the protection of the lay-brothers' hood during the purgation of his sins. His hair, head and shoulders had been burnt by drips of burning pitch, sulphur and lead from a cauldron that the lay-brother had passed under during his judgement. The impact of the vision was immediate: the next day the monks exhumed the lay-brother's body and redressed it in the full habit. The symbolism of the lay-brother's hood is consistent with the metaphoric use of clothing in oneiric literature. In his study of Medieval ghost stories, Jean-Claude Schmitt emphasises the dual role of clothing to represent the identity of the deceased and to convey the fate of their soul in the afterlife; clothing also provides a concrete medium through which exchanges are made between the worlds of the Medieval living and the dead (Schmitt 1998: 201–5). The significance of the cape or hood is a recurring theme particularly of monastic apparitions and ghost stories. Schmitt connects this motif with folkloric attributions of the hood providing supernatural protection in the afterlife; in common with traditional grave goods, the monastic hood was perceived to hold amuletic properties.

The monastic cemetery of Stratford Langthorne has been partially excavated, providing an opportunity to examine the actual burial practices among the community associated with the lay-brother of the vision recounted by Peter of Cornwall. The cemetery to the northeast of the church was excavated by Museum of London Archaeology and 651 burials were recovered (Barber et al. 2004) (Fig. 13.4). These were predominantly male and are likely to represent the graves of the monastic community: only eleven burials were associated with dress accessories, and two corpses were interred with medical poultice discs that were used to promote healing of leg injuries (Fig. 13.5). The absence of preserved textiles at the site prevents full understanding of burial rites that may have involved monastic dress. However, the poultice discs are indicative of a broader practice of inhuming Medieval corpses with therapeutic devices such as metal plates and supports, crutches, and even hernia trusses (Gilchrist & Sloane 2005: 103–5).

The lay-brother's tale underlines the emphatic materiality of Medieval beliefs surrounding the dead: the condition of the corpse in the grave was consonant with that of the soul in purgatory (Bynum 1995: 206). Through preparation and dressing of the dead body for the grave, the living were empowered to assist the progress of the soul through purgatory.

Transforming the body in death

Victoria Thompson (2002: 232) has interpreted these new modes of burial as increasingly elaborate means of controlling and confining the Christian body. But what prompted these innovations in funerary rites? The belief in bodily resurrection must have heightened anxieties surrounding the decay and fragmentation of the corpse. Efforts to mark, contain and protect the cadaver in the grave may be interpreted as strategies to preserve continuity of the body for its resurrection. Further efforts were sometimes made to transform the body, as if to heal or enhance its physical form in anticipation of it rising again.

Fig. 13.4. Typical earthen graves from the north-east cemetery at the Cistercian abbey of St Mary Stratford Langthorne, Essex (reproduced with kind permission of Museum of London Archaeology).

Fig. 13.5. Copper alloy plate (medical poultice disc) from the burial of a man at the Cistercian abbey of St Mary Stratford Langthorne, Essex (diam. 58 mm) (reproduced with kind permission of Museum of London Archaeology).

In addition to the medical items that were left adhering to corpses, a considerable number of amulets were placed with the Medieval dead (Gilchrist 2008). The ancient practice of placing apotropaic objects in graves reached a peak during the conversion period, and continued right up to the 15th century. Many of the same artefact types and natural materials were selected for deposition with conversion period and later Medieval corpses: fossils, animal teeth, white stones, antique coins, rings and bracelets, and single beads. For example, boar tusks were included in adult graves at the monastic sites of Wearmouth (county Durham) and St Oswald's, Gloucester (Cramp 2005: 80). The example at St Oswald's dates to the 11th century: the tusk was placed near the right shoulder of a female who was buried in a charred coffin (Heighway & Bryant 1999: 202, 214) (Fig. 13.6). At Barton-on-Humber, the coffined burial of a 3-year old child contained an amulet fashioned from a worn pig canine; the date bracket of the grave spanned the 10th–13th centuries (Waldron 2007: 158). Boar tusks were used as amulets in Early Medieval graves (Meaney 1981: 131) and are also well known from prehistoric burial contexts. Tusks may have been retained initially as hunting trophies, but some appear to have been handed down as heirlooms: for example, a radiocarbon-dated tusk from the Bronze Age barrow at Irthlingborough (Cambridgeshire) was hundreds of years old when it was deposited (Woodward et al. 2005: 45). We may postulate a common tradition of 'curating' selected objects such as boar tusks for amuletic use, a practice that was familiar to many prehistoric and historic communities across Europe. The deposition of ancient, fragmented and worn items in graves suggests that the resulting heirlooms were occasionally placed with the dead for apotropaic motives (Woodward 2002).

While Early Medieval amulet use was almost exclusively associated with female graves, amulets in later Medieval burials were also linked with those of infants and

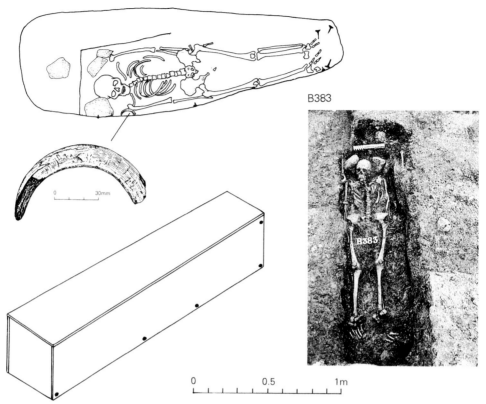

*Fig. 13.6. Burial 383 from St Oswald, Gloucester, displays many of the late Saxon mortuary rites discussed in the text. This 11th century burial of a woman was placed in a nailed timber coffin on a thick layer of oak charcoal. Two stones were placed within the coffin to support the head, and to the right of the shoulder was placed a very large, left canine tusk of wild boar (*Sus scrofa*) (Heighway & Bryant 1999: 202, 214) (drawing by Wayne Loughlin, reproduced with the kind permission of Carolyn Heighway).*

children. Some limited correlation can also be demonstrated for the placement of amulets with inhumations of physically disabled individuals, particularly those with impaired mobility (Gilchrist 2008). Perhaps amulets were intended to transform the immature or disabled body: was special assistance given to those deemed too young or impaired to rise at Doomsday? If this interpretation seems far-fetched, we should return to the contemporary commentary offered by Ælfric of Eynsham: 'Nor shall the holy ones who are to enter heaven have any blemish or ill-health, or be one-eyed, although he was lame in his life, but his limbs shall be all sound to him, in shining brightness, and tangible in his spiritual body' (quoted in Thompson 2002: 237).

The increased use of amulets during the conversion period has been interpreted previously as evidence of deliberate pagan resistance to Christianity (Geake 1997: 98; Zeiten 1997: 49). To the contrary, I would argue that the tradition of amulet use was adopted and developed as a Christian strategy to transform the body in readiness for the resurrection. The general concept of corporeal transformation is entirely consistent with Christian rites: during the mass, the consecrated materials of the wafer and wine were believed to transform miraculously into the body and blood of Christ. These same apotropaic materials accompanied the burials of priests, contained in the chalice and paten that were placed with the priest's corpse, to protect his soul on its journey through purgatory.

Concluding remarks: the materiality of the Christian afterlife

For the past three decades, the study of Early Medieval burial practice has been dominated by questions of social identity: how furnished burials were constructed to convey aspects of an individual's identity during life. With noteworthy exceptions (Marzinzik 2000; Effros 2002; Thompson 2002, 2004; Crawford 2004; Blair 2005; Hadley 2009), even burials of the transitional and Early Christian Periods have been discussed in terms of lifetime identity, neglecting the potential impact of Christian eschatology on burial rites. The emerging funerary practices of the 9th–11th centuries reveal the fundamental significance and shared comprehension of three Christian beliefs about the afterlife: bodily resurrection, continuity of embodied experience, and the reality of corporeal transformation in death. But alongside these new tenets, some long-held traditions persisted. Investigation of funerary rites at the junctures between the Early and later Medieval Period boundaries reveals the extent of this syncretism. Consideration of longer-term trends also promotes the recognition of important continuities and the reworking of older traditions, such as the placement of amulets with the dead.

Widespread acceptance of the belief in the resurrection seems to have prompted efforts to preserve the *integrity* of the body in the grave. This was expressed by marking of the grave through the use of linings, stones, and visually distinctive materials, that both created a symbolic boundary for the burial and helped to protect it from subsequent disturbance in consecrated cemeteries that were subject to regular reuse. Some human remains were 'curated' by the Christian community, including the careful exhumation of graves that were to be disturbed by new buildings, and the translation of disinterred bones for reburial. The corpse was contained in a shroud or coffin as a practical intervention to impede decay, while serving simultaneously as an act of ritual enclosure or containment of the cadaver. More unusual rites seem to have represented the symbolic integrity of the body, with the use of locking chests and barrel padlocks for some members of religious communities, perhaps to convey the incorruptibility of the chaste Christian body (and particularly that of the pious female cadaver). This example emphasises that the meaning of Christian grave goods can be highly nuanced, with ordinary domestic chests and padlocks holding the potential to convey aspects of gendered embodiment in specific contexts.

From the 11th and 12th centuries, the developing concept of purgatory heightened anxiety surrounding the continuity of the body: the progress of the soul in judgement was directly affected by the condition of the corpse in the grave (Bynum 1995). The tale of the lay-brother of Stratford Langthorne confirms the popular perception that items of dress could provide amuletic protection on the soul's journey, while the distinctive garb of religious personnel could hasten their salvation. The experience of the dead in purgatory was embodied and sensory, and the living could alleviate their suffering by undertaking the appropriate preparations of the corpse and the grave.

Finally, the Christian belief in corporeal transformation impacted on burial rites. The transformation and resurrection of Christ's body represented the salvation of humanity, through its transubstantiation during the sacrament of the mass, and through its resurrection at the Sepulchre. The transformative materials of the mass were deposited in priests' burials, with the sacrificial wine held in the chalice and the Eucharistic wafer placed on the paten; these were symbolic of the priest's office and offered powerful protection on the journey through purgatory (Gilchrist 2009). Amulets and medical devices were sometimes placed with the most vulnerable of the dead: those perceived to require special assistance in achieving the transformation from withered bones to 'shining brightness', to rise from their graves whole.

Current scholarship characterises Medieval Christian funerary practices in sharp opposition to those of the preceding Anglo-Saxons. 'Theatrical tableaux' of pagan corpses were replaced by Christian rites that emphasised the integrity and continuity of the physical body. Motives of display, and celebration of the individual in life, were transplanted by themes of transformation for benefit in the afterlife. But perhaps some continuities can be discerned, some elements of pagan belief that were selected and developed for incorporation into Christian funerary practice? Many of the objects deposited in Anglo-Saxon furnished burials were used in the protection or modification of the body, including weapons, grooming implements and amulets (Devlin 2007: 33). Howard Williams (2006) has argued that the lavishly staged funerary tableaux represent the *transformation* of the Anglo-Saxon dead, emphasising the emotive force of grief, rather than the static display of their identity in life.

The theme of corporeal transformation was further elaborated by the processes of syncretism that connected Medieval pagan and Christian funerary rites. The materiality of death was developed in relation to the emerging tenets of purgatory and the bodily resurrection: judgement and the afterlife were imagined as fully embodied, introducing an imperative to protect the integrity of the dead body. The perceived continuity between the corpse in the grave and the soul in the afterlife sustained the centrality of the mortuary sphere to social life. Christian burial rites continued to channel the emotive force of grief, in an epoch when humble shrouds and modest coffins were the most efficacious gifts from the living to the dead.[1]

Note

1   The manuscript for this article was submitted in July 2008. Since the timing of writing, Dawn Hadley has published an article addressing the possible amuletic qualities of objects deposited in Anglo-Saxon burials dating from the 7th–11th centuries (Hadley 2009).

Bibliography

Adams, M. 1996: 'Excavation of a Pre-Conquest Cemetery at Addingham, West Yorkshire', *Medieval Archaeology* 40: 151–91.

Atkins, R. & Shepherd Popescu, E. 2010: 'Excavations at the Hospital of St Mary Magdalen, Partney, Lincolnshire, 2003', *Medieval Archaeology* 54: 204–70.

Barber, B., Chew, S. & White, W. 2004: *The Cistercian Abbey of St Mary Stratford Langthorne, Essex: Archaeological Excavations for the London Underground Limited Jubilee Line Extension Project*, Museum of London Archaeology Service Monograph 18: London.

Blair, J. 2005: *The Church in Anglo-Saxon Society*, Oxford University Press: Oxford.

Boddington, A. 1996: *Raunds Furnells: The Anglo-Saxon Church and Churchyard*, English Heritage Archaeology, Report 7: London.

Bonner, G., Rollason, D. W. & Stancliffe, E. (eds) 1989: *St Cuthbert, his Cult and his Community to AD 1200*, Boydell: Woodbridge.

Bradley, J. 2005: *Ritual and Domestic Life in Prehistoric Europe*, Routledge: London.

Brück, J. 1999: 'Ritual and Rationality: Some Problems of Interpretation in European Archaeology', *European Journal of Archaeology* 2.3: 313–44.

Bynum C. W. 1991: 'Material Continuity, Personal Survival and the Resurrection of the Body: A Scholastic Discussion in its Medieval and Modern Contexts', in C. W. Bynum (ed.): *Fragmentation and Redemption. Essays on Gender and the Human Body in Medieval Religion*, Zone Books: New York, 239–97.

Bynum, C. W. 1995: *The Resurrection of the Body in Western Christianity, 200–1336*, Columbia University Press: New York.

Carver, M. 1998: *Sutton Hoo: Burial Ground of Kings?*, University of Pennsylvania Press: London.

Cramp, R. 2005: *Wearmouth and Jarrow Monastic Sites. Volume 1*, English Heritage: London.

Crawford, S. 2004: 'Votive Deposition: Religion and the Anglo-Saxon Furnished Burial', *World Archaeology* 36.1: 87–102.

Devlin, Z. 2007: *Remembering the Dead in Anglo-Saxon England. Memory Theory in Archaeology and History*, British Archaeological Reports, British Series 446: Oxford.

Effros, B. 2002: *Caring for Body and Soul. Burial and the Afterlife in the Merovingian World*, Pennsylvania State University Press: Pennsylvania.

Geake, H. 1997: *The Use of Grave-Goods in Conversion-Period England, c. 600–850*, British Archaeological Reports, British Series 261: Oxford.

Geake, H. 2003: 'The Control of Burial Practice in Anglo-Saxon England', in M. Carver (ed.): *The Cross goes North: Processes of Conversion in Northern Europe*, Boydell: Woodbridge, 259–69.

Gilchrist, R. 2003: '"Dust to Dust". Revealing the Reformation Dead', in D. Gaimster & R. Gilchrist (eds): *The Archaeology of Reformation*, The Society for Post-Medieval Archaeology Monograph 1: Leeds, 399–414.

Gilchrist, R. 2008: 'Magic for the Dead? The Archaeology of Magic in Later Medieval Burials', *Medieval Archaeology* 52: 119–59.

Gilchrist, R. 2009: 'Rethinking Later Medieval Masculinity: The Male Body in Death', in D. Sayer & H. Williams (eds): *Mortuary Practices and Social Identities in the Middle Ages: Essays in Honour of Heinrich Härke*, Exeter University Press: Exeter, 236–52.

Gilchrist, R. & Sloane, B. 2005: *Requiem: The Medieval Monastic Cemetery in Britain*, Museum of London Archaeology Service: London.

Gilmour, B. J. J. & Stocker, D. A. 1986: *St Mark's Church and Cemetery*, The Archaeology of Lincoln, Volume 13–1: Lincoln.

Gittos, H. 2002: 'Creating the Sacred: Anglo-Saxon Rites for Consecrating Cemeteries', in Lucy & Reynolds (eds): 195–208.

Guy, C. 2010: 'An Anglo-Saxon Cemetery at Worcester Cathedral', in J. Buckberry & A. Cherryson (eds): *Later Anglo-Saxon Cemeteries, c. 650–1100 AD*, Oxbow: Oxford, 73–82.

Hadley, D. M. 2001: *Death in Medieval England*, Tempus: Stroud.

Hadley, D. M. 2002: 'Burial Practices in Northern England in the Later Anglo-Saxon Period', in Lucy & Reynolds (eds): *Burial in Early Medieval England and Wales*, Society for Medieval Archaeology Monograph 17: Leeds, 209–28.

Hadley, D. M. 2009: 'Burial, Belief and Identity in Later Anglo-Saxon England', in R. Gilchrist & A. Reynolds (eds): *50 Years of Medieval Archaeology*, Society for Medieval Archaeology Monograph 30: Leeds, 465–88.

Hadley, D. M. & Buckberry, J. 2005: 'Caring for the Dead in Late Anglo-Saxon England', in F. Tinti (ed.): *Pastoral Care in Late Anglo-Saxon England*: Boydell: Woodbridge, 121–47.

Hall, R. A. & Whyman, M. 1996: 'Settlement and Monasticism at Ripon, North Yorkshire, from the 7th to 11th Centuries AD', *Medieval Archaeology* 40: 62–150.

Heighway, C. & Bryant R. 1999: *The Golden Minster: The Anglo-Saxon Minster and Later Medieval Priory of St Oswald at Gloucester*, Council for British Archaeology Research Report 117: London.

Hodder, M. 1991: *Excavations at Sandwell Priory and Hall*, South Staffordshire Archaeology and History Society Transactions 31: Stafford.

Holdsworth, C. J. 1962: 'Eleven Visions connected with the Cistercian Monastery of Stratford Langthorne', *Cîteaux* 13: 185–204.

Insoll, T. 2004: *Archaeology, Religion, Ritual*, Routledge: London.

Joyce, R. 1998: 'Performing the Body in Prehispanic Central America', *Res: Anthropology and Aesthetics* 33: 147–65.

Kjølbye-Biddle, M. 1995: 'Iron-bound Coffins and Coffin-fittings from the pre-Norman Cemetery', in D. Phillips & B. Heywood (eds): *Excavations at York Minster Volume 1. From Roman Fortress to Norman Cathedral. Part 2 The Finds*, HMSO: London, 489–521.

Lacquer, T. 1990: *Making Sex: Body and Gender from the Greeks to Freud*, Harvard University Press: Cambridge MA.

Le Goff, J. 1984: *The Birth of Purgatory* (trans. A. Goldhammer), Scolar Press: London.

Lucy, S. & Reynolds, A. (eds): *Burial in Early Medieval England and Wales,* Society for Medieval Archaeology Monograph 17: Leeds.

Marzinzik, S. 2000: 'Grave-goods in "Conversion Period" and Later Burials – a Case of Early Medieval Religious Double Standards?', in K. Pollmann (ed.): *Double Standards in the Ancient and Medieval World*, Göttinger Forum für Altertumswissenschaft: Göttingen, 149–66.

Meaney, A. L. 1981: *Anglo-Saxon Amulets and Curing Stones*, British Archaeological Reports 96: Oxford.

Morris, R. 1983: *The Church in British Archaeology*, Council for British Archaeology Research Report 47: London.

Rodwell, W. 2007: 'Burial Archaeology', in T. Waldron (ed.): *St Peter's Barton-upon-Humber, Lincolnshire. A Parish Church and its Community. Volume 2. The Human Remains*, Oxbow: Oxford, 15–32.

Schmitt, J-C. 1998: *Ghosts in the Middle Ages: The Living and the Dead in Medieval Society*, University of Chicago Press: Chicago.

Thompson, V. 2002: 'Constructing Salvation: A Homiletic and Penitential Context for Late Anglo-Saxon Burial Practice', in Lucy & Reynolds (eds): *Burial in Early Medieval England and Wales*, Society for Medieval Archaeology Monograph 17: Leeds, 229–40.

Thompson, V. 2004: *Dying and Death in Later Anglo-Saxon England*, Boydell: Woodbridge.

Waldron, T. 2007: *St Peter's Barton-upon-Humber, Lincolnshire. A Parish Church and its Community. Volume 2. The Human Remains*, Oxbow: Oxford.

Williams, H. 2005: 'Rethinking Early Medieval Mortuary Archaeology', *Early Medieval Europe* 13.2: 195–217.

Williams, H. 2006: *Death and Memory in Early Medieval Britain*, Cambridge University Press: Cambridge.

Woodward, A. 2002: 'Beads and Beakers: Heirlooms and Relics in the British Early Bronze Age', *Antiquity* 76: 1040–47.

Woodward, A., Hunter, J., Ixer, R., Maltby, M., Potts, P. J., Webb, P. C., Watson, J. S. & Jones, M. C. 2005: 'Ritual in some Early Bronze Age Gravegoods', *Archaeological Journal* 162: 31–64.

Woolgar, C. 2006: *The Senses in Late Medieval England*, Yale University Press: New Haven.

Zeiten, M. Koktvedgaard 1997: 'Amulets and Amulet Use in Viking Age Denmark', *Acta Archaeologica* 68: 1–74.

14

CHANGING BELIEFS ABOUT THE DEAD BODY IN POST-MEDIEVAL BRITAIN AND IRELAND

Sarah Tarlow

The historian, archaeologist, or classicist looking at the past does not have direct access to 'belief', but instead has evidence of ritual practices. In historical periods, we have written discourse, too. Belief discourses and ritual practices surrounding the dead human body in the period from the Reformation to the 19th century related to each other in particularly complex ways. Theologically, Protestant eschatology suggests that place and manner of burial do not matter, but in practice it did. This is most evident in attitudes to deviants – criminals and suicides, where irregular burial and interventions in the body were used as social and legal sanction. Scientific humanism also developed an empirical and medicalised discourse of the body over this period. The incompatibility between a theology which stressed the meaninglessness of the dead body, and a legal system which specified treatments of the dead body (such as dissection, or gibbeting) as part of criminal punishment is to some extent clarified by attention to another belief discourse: folk practice. I will consider two examples of folk practices which were widespread in Early Modern Europe: 'bier-right' (Bahr-Recht) and the curative power of the 'dead hand'. These rituals suggest a belief that power remains in the newly dead body. This unwritten, unspoken belief, asserted neither in theological doctrine nor scientific humanism, also seems to inform legal and social norms and may continue to do so to the present day.

Keywords: Belief, body, Britain, death, folk practice, Ireland, legal system, scientific humanism, theology.

My concern in this article is with the relationship between ritual and belief: that is, how beliefs and what I have chosen to call here 'belief discourses' affect people's ritual practices. As archaeologists, and in common with other scholars of the human past, we often seek explanation for change in ritual practices in the beliefs that inform them. As beliefs change, it may be expected, so too will the ritualised actions which produce and reproduce them in society. This chapter unpacks that proposition through the consideration of one example which suggests that, contrary to expectations, ritual action might have been more stable than belief, and that 'belief' is a contradictory, multiple and complex thing.

The particular ritual practices I am concerned with are those surrounding the dead body in the 16th, 17th, and 18th centuries AD in Britain and Ireland. This was an eventful period in terms of beliefs about the dead. The Protestant Reformation of the mid-16th century should best be understood as a process rather than an event. Part of the process involved the transformation of relationships between the living and the dead. The replacement of Catholicism with Protestant orthodoxy meant that the dead individual no longer went to Purgatory, from whence the prayers and masses of the living could bring about his or her early release. Instead the dead person went directly to Judgement, and nothing that the living did could make any difference to the fate of a dead person's soul.

Theological beliefs, however, are not the only kind of beliefs to affect ritual practices. Social beliefs, scientific beliefs and folk beliefs, among others, all affect the kinds of ritual that surround the dead body. The remainder of this paper considers the operation of some of those kinds of belief.

The work discussed in this paper is part of a project funded by the Leverhulme Trust called 'Changing Beliefs about the Human Body'. When I began the research I was thinking that the critical term in that title was 'body': now, I think that the most interesting and problematic idea is actually 'belief'.

Addressing problems of the relationship between belief and ritual practice in the past is problematic for a number of reasons. In particular there are two problems involved with dealing with interior experience: first, people do not always say or do what they really think; and second (even more seriously) we cannot suppose that belief, even inside the head of a single person, is clear and coherent. Rather than belief, in the sense of interior conviction, therefore, this paper considers 'belief discourse': the way people 'talk', through their words and deeds, about their beliefs.

In this paper I will discuss four kinds of belief discourse in relation to the dead body:

1. Theological belief
2. Social belief
3. Scientific belief
4. Folk belief/practice

I will briefly summarise the main developments in each tradition of discourse.

Theological belief

The Protestant theology which dominated Britain from the mid-16th century onwards was profoundly different to Late Medieval Catholicism in many ways. The treatment of the dead was most affected by the disappearance of Purgatory. But in other ways, ideas about the significance of the dead body were similar to Catholic discussions about the body and the soul. Religious texts of the period do not pay much attention to the dead body, but when they do, it is nearly always to contrast the repugnant body with the divine and eternal soul. The body is thus characterised as only a temporary container for the soul, and its fleshliness is emphasised.

'Is it not your greatest desire to flitte from this bodie which is but a Booth, a shoppe, or Tabernacle of clay? Is not your Soule wearie to sojourne into such a reekie Lodge?' asks Zacharie Boyd (1629: 84).

> Is not this Body wherein now I dwell,
> Nought But my Vassall, Casket, House or Shell?
> Compact of dust and Ashes, things most base

concludes the Soul in William Prynne's poem *The Soule's Complaint against the Body* published in 1641. Scores of similar examples could easily be piled up. Given a dualistic understanding of human nature where the principal distinction is between body and soul, the one being temporary and worldly, the other divine, it makes sense to value the soul more highly, and to value the body principally because it is the container for the soul, a 'temple' is among the more positive metaphors regularly used. But when the soul leaves the body, it is no longer a temple but a 'jakes' [toilet] (Prynne 1641), or even just a 'dead Carkase' (Sherlock 1690). The dualistic opposition between body and soul was a core belief of both Catholics and Protestants, but where the dead body was a focus of prayer for Catholics, Protestant theology downgraded religious funerary ritual to a very brief service, and promoted largely secular commemoration. The corpse itself had minimal importance to the formal and religious part of commemorative ritual but, as we shall see, it continued or even grew in significance in secular mortuary rites.

The treatment of the body at death matters not at all to the future fate of the soul, say Early Modern Protestant theologians, in a rare example of consensus. They do not agree about exactly what our resurrected bodies will be like, but they all concede that God will be able to reconstitute the bodies of the righteous for resurrection, no matter what kind of funerary rites they have received. 'Vile, or no exequies at all hinder nothing the sepulture of the poore saints' wrote Thomas Becon in 1568. Even if evil people, said Oxford preacher Thomas Beconsall (1697: 23):

> tear Infants from the Womb, to sacrifice to Wolves and Tygers; yet after Wit and Malice, and Cruelty have spent themselves, there will still be Materials enough for Omnipotence to perfect his own Designs, in a glorious and triumphant Resurrection.

Social belief

All the dismissive metaphors used to describe the body by Early Modern Protestant theologians might lead one to predict a decrease in the amount of care and attention given to the preparation of the dead body and its disposal. It would also be consistent to expect the abandonment of the crowded churchyard and the hard-to-access underfloor space within the church itself, since the belief that any part of the ground was more holy than any other, or that burial close to saints or churches would in any way enhance your prospects of redemption were seen after the Reformation as Popery of the worst kind.

However, the archaeological evidence of Protestant burial in the 16th and 17th centuries tells a very different story. The amount of care and money spent on the preparation and disposable of the average dead body if anything increased after the Reformation. The use of coffins, which was becoming more common even before the Reformation (Gilchrist & Sloane 2005), became very widespread in this period, even for the burial of people who had died in epidemics, as seems to have been the case at one 17th century cemetery in Abingdon, Oxfordshire, and in what appear to be plague burials in London (Norton et al. 2005; Harding 1993).

The ongoing social significance of the dead body is perhaps most evident, however, at the top and at the bottom of the social scale: at the upper end, the dead body as a material object was at the centre of rites that reinforced relationships and position in society. The decay of the body was denied through embalming, the use of lead coffins (Goodall 1970: 155; Fig. 14.1) and wax-impregnated 'cerecloths' which delayed or prevented decay by creating an anaerobic wrapper for the body.

At Hemingford Grey, in Cambridgeshire, a late 17th century dissenter cemetery eschewed the conventions of west–east burial – still an almost universal custom in Anglican graveyards, but still treated the bodies of the dead with care, dressing them specially for the grave in tailored, lace-up shrouds of the nightdress variety, attested by the presence of copper alloy aglets and numerous shroud pins in the mostly coffined burials (McNichol et al. 2007).

The dead body could also be indexical of the person for the representation of social status. At the bottom of the social scale were criminals and suicides, where irregular burial and interventions in the body were used as social and legal sanction. In the century and a half following the Reformation, suicides were treated with particular intolerance in Britain. Among other sanctions, they were denied Christian burial. Instead they were by custom, and by law, buried in the road – often at a crossroads, with a stake through their body. From the later 17th century, the social treatment of suicides softened, and their bodies were increasingly permitted church burial, as local authorities often decided

Fig. 14.1. Lead coffin of John Belaysus from a vault at Blandford, Dorset (photograph by Reverend Canon Goodall).

Fig. 14.2. The body of John Williams being taken for staked burial at Cannon Street crossroads, London, in 1811. Williams was a convicted murderer who killed himself rather than face judicial execution (The Newgate Calendar, http: //www.exclassics.com/newgate/ngbibl.htm).

that their suicide was driven by mental imbalance and that they could not therefore be held responsible (MacDonald & Murphy 1990). However, folkloric accounts of staked burial in the road exist as late as the early twentieth century in some parts of England, and the criminal who committed suicide as a way of evading execution was still subject to considerable social opprobrium (Fig. 14.2).

An other area where attitudes to the body different to those promulgated by church leaders is very evident is the treatment of the dead criminal body. Up until the mid-19th century the post-mortem fate of the criminal body was often part of their judicial punishment. Moreover, these bodily punishments often specified ways in which the dead body should be treated. Primarily, the corpses of criminals could be stigmatised by the division or segmentation of the body, by its anatomisation, and by special treatment in the place and/ or manner of burial. The broken bodies dumped in the ditch around Oxford castle (Fig. 14.3) are the remains of criminal bodies that had been subjected to anatomical dissection (Norton 2006).

The presentation of a number of criminal corpses to the anatomists of the Colleges, Guilds and Schools was customary in most European countries throughout the Early Modern Period. In Britain and Ireland, the practice was given additional force in 1751 with the passage of the *Act for Better Preventing the Horrid Crime of Murder*. This stipulated that after execution the bodies of murderers should not be given a normal Christian burial, but either given to anatomists or 'hung in chains', a practice also known as gibbeting. Gibbeting involved leaving the body hanging in a cage from a tall edifice, tree or a specially-constructed gibbet, until it fell to pieces and was devoured by animals and the natural processes of decay. Archaeological evidence of a

Fig. 14.3. Remains of an anatomised body buried in the ditch at Oxford Castle (reproduced with the kind permission of Oxford Archaeology).

former gibbet comes from Dunball Island in the mouth of the Avon, where numerous pieces of disarticulated bone were found when the pilings for the Royal Edward Docks were being sunk (Brett 1996). Eyre Square in Galway City also produced disarticulated human bone thought to be gibbeting deposits, as well as a number of crania from just below the city walls, which are likely to be the remains of heads exhibited on the walls (Lofqvist 2004). All this suggests that people cared sufficiently about their bodies for the threat of violation of the body after death to work as a deterrent.

Scientific belief

Scientific humanism also developed an empirical and medicalised discourse of the body over this period. Although the metaphors that came eventually to dominate scientific and medical discourses of the body were those of bodies as machines, the dominant metaphors in the 16th and 17th centuries were geographical – the body was a country or a world to be explored (Sawday 1995). Geographical metaphors also enabled scientific discourses of the body to conform, at last superficially, to another strand of theological discussion about the human body – the idea of the microcosm.

The Early Modern body was not the collection of biological facts that it would become in later centuries. It was an allegory of God, the universe and the world. In 1615 Helkiah Crooke published his *Microcosmographia*, a highly detailed and illustrated anatomy of the human body (Fig. 14.4). The eponymous microcosm is the human body itself, frequently used in literary and philosophical texts of the period as a conceit for the whole universe.

A study of the introductory chapters and dedicatory epistles of anatomy textbooks in the 17th century shows that the ultimate purpose of studying anatomy as advanced by most of the famous anatomists, was a greater knowledge of God. At the start of the 17th century, Anthony Nixon's anatomy text, called *The Dignitie of Man, both in the perfections of his soule and bodie* (1612) describes the practice of anatomy as a meditation upon the divine. The book itself takes the form of a catechistic set of questions and answers. In answer to the question: 'What commoditie commeth by *Anatomy of the body?*' Nixon answers:

> It puts us in minde of our mortality, and teacheth us that if the providence of God bee so wonderful in the composition of the vilest and the earthly partes, It must needes follow that it is farre more great, and admirable in the creation of the Noble parts, especially of the Soule.

Thus, to know the human body was also to know God. Anatomy could, in this way, be justified as a devotional practice.

Anatomical dissection was used punitively, as we have seen, but the majority of subjects of post-mortem investigation were not criminals. Post-mortem autopsy was often carried out on the bodies of the well-to-do to establish cause of death, essentially as an extension of their medical treatment, or as part of the embalming process.

When anatomy was not punitive, efforts were made to repair the body and to present it in an appropriate form for burial. One individual, for example, buried

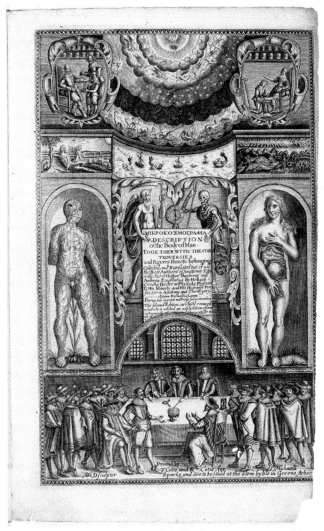

Fig. 14.4. Frontispiece of Helkiah Crooke's Microcosmographia.

at Barton-upon-Humber in England in about 1800, had been subject to extensive post-mortem investigation (Rodwell & Rodwell 1982). The top of his skull had been removed (craniotomy), and all his abdominal and thoracic organs, and his spine were removed. But before burial his body had been restored to an appearance of normality by inserting a length of charred wood to stiffen his back, in place of a spine, and stuffing the body cavity with straw or moss. The skull had been glued together and the join concealed by hair.

Later, the 'unclaimed' bodies of those who died in institutions were also often taken as subjects for anatomists, as were, notoriously, the stolen bodies sold by 'resurrection men' – grave robbers. Grave robbing was the focus of great cultural anxiety, particularly in the 18th and 19th century when demand for dissectable cadavers was at its height (Richardson 1988).

The point to make here is to re-iterate that whatever the general wisdom might have been when discussing the relative properties of the body and the soul, and the theologically coherent teaching on the vanity of caring for the body, and the particular insignificance of the dead body – as a body without a soul, people cared very deeply about what happened to the dead body.

There seems to be an incompatibility between theological beliefs about the dead body which stress its insignificance, scientific beliefs according to which the dead body was valued chiefly for the insights it could provide to the functioning of the living one, an interpretation sometimes glossed in devotional terms, and the social beliefs which subjected the dead body to considerable ritual care, and which continued to use place and manner of burial as a way of constructing and signalling social position.

Folk belief

The incompatibility between a theology, which stressed the meaninglessness of the dead body, and a legal system, which specified treatments of the dead body (such as dissection, or gibbeting) as part of criminal punishment, is to some extent clarified by attention to another belief discourse: folk practice. I will consider two kinds of folk practice, which were both widespread in Early Modern Europe: the curative power of the 'dead hand' and the judicial power of the murdered body, called in German *Bahr-Recht* (the 'Law of the Bier': the English word 'cruentation' is not widely used). Finally I will consider briefly the significance of the dead saintly body among Catholics in the wake of the Reformation.

The 'dead hand'

There is considerable evidence that people sought out the touch of the dead for medicinal reasons. Most widespread was the belief that the touch of a recently hanged man's hand would cure various medical conditions. Peacock's (1896) survey of the significance of executed criminals in folk medicine records the practice throughout France, Switzerland, Denmark, Sweden, Germany, and parts of Italy, particularly Sicily. Balkutė records the

Lithuanian folkloric belief that the hand of a corpse (but not necessarily a hanged one) will cure moles, warts, and similar skin conditions. Similar traditions in the regions of Britain are legion. Wollaston Groome (1895) records the Suffolk belief that the hand of a dead man, passed 3 times over the affected part, will cure wens or 'fleshy excrescences'. The *Stamford Mercury* of March 26th 1830 records that two women, one bringing a child, attended the execution of three men at Lincoln in order to rub the dead men's hands over themselves in order to cure diseased parts of their bodies. A correspondent of the journal *Notes and Queries* (ii: 36) said in 1850 that execution days in Northampton drew crowds of the afflicted hoping to receive the 'death stroke', and an Oxfordshire woman in 1852 was keen to try the cure for her goitre, because it had apparently worked for her father (*Notes and Queries* first series vi: 145). In the late 18th century, John Brand (1777: 97) noted a widespread willingness to subject 'any maculated part to the Touch of the Dead'. Even in the early twentieth century the touch of a dead man's hand was believed effective for curing cancer in Cambridgeshire (Porter 1969: 75), and in the Cambridgeshire fens it was believed that, if woman was able to hold the hand of a dead man for two minutes, she would not conceive for two years, a most desirable reward for the mothers of large, poor Fenland families in an age of rudimentary family planning. In North Yorkshire too unspecified diseases could be cured by the touch of a dead hand (Blakeborough 1898: 201) and in Sussex and Northamptonshire a hanged man's hand would cure a wen or goitre (Sternberg 1851: 116). In County Durham, the hand of a dead child or a suicide would cure a goitre, and Brockie (1974 [1886]: 221) cites the case of a coal miner's wife in that county in about 1853 who, on the advice of a wise woman, spent the night in an outhouse where a suicide had been laid out, with the hand of the corpse against her neck to cure a wen there.

Often the bodies of those who had died a violent death were particularly potent, especially executed criminals. In Thomas Hardy's short story *The Withered Arm* (published in 1888 but set in the 1820s) a desperate young woman seeks out the body of a victim of hanging in the hope that the touch of the young man's still warm neck will cure her own deformity. Even medical men apparently made use of the power of the corpse on occasion. According to Napier (1976 [1879]: 92–3), William Harvey, the 17th century physician who first described the circulation of the blood, successfully removed 'tumours and excrescences' by the application of the hand of one who had recently died of a lingering disease. The curative power of the hanged body, particularly the hand of an executed criminal, is well-attested through much of Europe, and known from Early Modern times. In 1584 Reginald Scot (1964 [1584]: 210) knew of a belief that the touch of a dead hand would cure cysts, wens, goitres, ulcers and the 'King's (or Queen's) evil' (scrofula), and John Aubrey in 1686 knew of a man whose wen had been cured that way, as well as a child who had been cured of a hunchback (1881 [1686]: 198). In Somerset, said Aubrey (1696: 97), it was believed that a man's wen could be cured by the touch of a dead woman's hand, and a woman should use the hand of a dead man. He emphatically affirms the 'Wonderful Effects' proceeding from the touch of a dead hand (1696: 97).

In Denmark, Germany and Switzerland the blood of decapitated criminals was taken as medicine, even in the nineteenth century (Peacock 1896: 270–1) and Christian IV of Denmark is alleged to have taken the powdered skulls of criminals as a cure for his epilepsy (1896: 270).

'Bahr Recht'

The Medieval belief that the body of a murder victim would bleed, if brought into the presence of its murderer, was recognised into the 17th and even the 18th century. Keith Thomas discusses two cases in 1613 and 1636, in Somerset and Lancashire respectively, where a person suspected of murder refused to come into the presence of the corpse for fear, it was alleged, that the corpse would incriminate them in this way (1971: 261). The Somerset man in fact confessed to murder ten years later, having been pursued by the ghost of his victim (Thomas 1971: 714). Holt (1992: 74–76) describes the case of another Somerset man, Robert Sutton, who was murdered around 1729 or 1730. His body was laid out in the church porch and the local clergy and magistrates stood beside it as all the men in the neighbourhood filed past and each in turn laid a hand upon the corpse. When a certain Jack White came past he refused to touch the corpse and was subsequently tried and convicted of Sutton's murder for which he was hanged, although how dependent his conviction was on the mute testimony of the corpse is not clear from Holt's account. A similar story is recorded for Manningford Abbas in Wiltshire (although the source is unreliable): in 1798 Taylor Dyke was robbed and murdered near the Phoenix Inn. The following Sunday the local rector made everyone file out of the church past the body of Dyke and each member of the congregation in turn had to lay a hand on the body and swear their innocence of his murder. A man called Amor refused to swear and was subsequently charged and hanged (Wiltshire 1975: 138). The belief in the power of the corpse to accuse its murderer was also known in Scotland. Napier (1976 [1879]: 85) claims to have heard 'many instances adduced to prove the truth of bleeding taking place on the introduction of the murderer' and asserts that an eleventh-century ballad (which he does not name) alludes to the practice, as does another Medieval ballad called Young Huntin, which must be Child's (1860) ballad 68, versions B, C and J. Napier prefers to explain this phenomenon, in which he clearly believes personally, in terms of Christian belief, acknowledging the Rev. Mr Wodrow's statement that such a marvel could be ascribed to 'the wonderful Providence of God', so that murderers might be found out and His command that 'thou shalt not suffer a murderer to live' be obeyed. The custom was evidently also known in Wales. In the late 19th century, according to Jones (1979 [1930]: 34), O. M. Edwards recorded a story in his journal *Cymru* about a teamsman, who was working away from home, when he heard of the death of the young woman he had been courting. He returned home and encountered the ghost of the young woman who told him that she had been seduced and strangled by the man for whom she had been keeping house. She asked him to have her grave and her coffin opened and to bring the guilty man into her presence. Then, claimed the ghost, her blood would 'leap to his face'. The young man, however, did not do as she had asked and died himself soon afterwards (*Cymru* 4: 43). Also from

Wales comes the belief that the body could announce its innocence from the grave. A Montgomeryshire man executed for murder proclaimed that his innocence would be proven by the fact that no grass would grow on his grave (Jones 1979 [1930]: 217).

Belief in the judicial reliability of corpses was not confined to poorly educated provincial types either. Highly educated and rational men like Francis Bacon and Reginald Scot refer to it, even as they rejected much other folk belief as superstition (although Bacon (apophthegm 144) does refer to the belief as a 'common tradition' and his own position is not clear). Thomas argues that the acceptance of this folk belief was possible because the Neo-Platonic conception of the universe 'pulsating with many undiscovered occult influences' (1971: 691) accommodated numerous relationships of influence and attraction. Even if they were not (yet) properly understood, those laws would eventually provide a scientific explanation of phenomena which were believed to exist. It is interesting that where the phenomenon of the bleeding corpse was accepted as true by the learned middle and upper classes, attempts were made to explain through the belief discourses of either religion (Napier's Rev. Wodrow) or science (Scot).

Perhaps because executed criminals were often healthy and fit young men, their powerful bodies seemed to contain more life than the sick, emaciated and old bodies of those who died natural deaths. This would also explain why the bodies of victims of drowning were sometimes attributed with similar powers to those of executed criminals. Hallam and Hockey's useful distinction between vegetables and vampires is significant here (Hallam & Hockey 2001). Hallam and Hockey use those terms to distinguish categories of person whose social death does not coincide with their biological death. Vegetables are those people whose lengthy declines meant that much of their death processes had happened before they ceased breathing (removal from normal social life into an institution, gradual separation from the people and roles with which they had been familiar in life); vampires those who, cut off in the midst of life, extended their active and social powers further beyond the point of 'natural' death. Murder victims, executed criminals and drowned men were all 'vampires' by this reckoning.

Martyrs and miracles

Peacock's preferred explanation for the widespread folk belief in the power of the criminal corpse, reflecting the vogue for historically deep derivations of folkloric belief in the 19th century, is that the judicially slain take the place of the pre-Christian sacrifice. Modern folklorists are less willing to accept very deep time lines, but the 19th-century beliefs logged by Peacock (1896) and her contemporaries were probably nevertheless descended from the theologically-sanctioned beliefs and practices of Catholic antecedents. The curative and apotropaic power of the body parts of exceptional individuals – and it is worth noting that saints had often met with violent and sudden death while in good health – was controlled by the Church who held the relics. Sufferers would sometimes make long pilgrimages to visit the relics of an appropriate saint.

St Margaret Clitheroe, martyred in 1586 for refusing to plead against the accusation of harbouring a priest, was canonised only in the 20th century, but before that had

had her hand preserved and venerated in the Convent of the Blessed Virgin at York, where it was believed to be effective against throat ailments (presumably because of her own silence). Similarly the hand of St Edmund Arrowsmith, a Jesuit martyred in 1628 is still kept at St Oswald's Church, Ashton in Makerfield. In their collection of Lancashire folklore, Harland and Wilkinson (1882: 158–60) include Arrowsmith's hand as an example of superstitious folk-belief rather than of Catholic orthodoxy. They supply the detail that the hand was kept in a chapel at Bryn Hall, which had been demolished by 1882 and the hand removed to Ashton in a silk bag which was brought out to work cures. Both St Margaret Clitheroe and St Edmund Arrowsmith were among the 'English martyrs', who died during or in the aftermath of the Reformation, and were among the 40 beatified martyrs who were canonised in 1970. In Catholic Ireland the powerful relic was often a body part (but not always: objects associated with the life or, particularly, the death of the saint also frequently have miraculous powers). While some of these belong to ancient saints, corporeal relics of more recent saints are also widespread. The head of St Oliver Plunkett, another of the recently canonised martyrs, was snatched from the flames of the pyre in which he was martyred and taken first to Lambspring in Germany and then to Rome. In the early 18th century it was moved to a new convent in Drogheda, smuggled into Ireland, according to legend, in the top of a grandfather clock (Kilfeather 2002: 232). It is now in St Peter's church Drogheda, near Dublin. There would seem to be some inconsistency between saints' relics where their efficacy is related to the particular blessedness of an individual of extreme virtue, and the powerful body parts of the executed criminal, where the individual certainly was not a person of great virtue or the recipient of divine favour. The particular curative power of a saint often related to the part of the saint's body that was most closely involved with their martyrdom. Thus St Bartholemew (who was flayed) was especially good for skin diseases; St Erasmus (disembowelled) for digestive problems and so on. The notable association between hanged men and conditions of the neck and throat probably related to this tradition.

The rituals of the dead hand and of *bahr-recht* suggest a belief that power remains in the newly dead body. This unwritten, unspoken belief, not asserted in either theological doctrine or scientific humanism, also seems to inform legal and social norms and may continue to do so to the present day, as is evident in the legal protection accorded to bodies and body parts.

Concluding remarks

The dead body was at the centre of a number of ritual practices. These included the burial and commemoration of a social being, as well as a divine soul. The dead body itself, as a material object and an assemblage of substances, was also used in folkloric ritual, for medicinal and divination purposes. All these ritual practices were discussed in terms of belief: not only religious orthodoxy, but also social and scientific beliefs. However, most of the practices discussed here were known from the Medieval Period. The Early

Modern period in Britain witnessed a number of attempts to draw together the beliefs of reformed religion, modern science and new, sophisticated beliefs about social and political organisation, with these older, folk practices. Attempts to incorporate the belief in *Bahr-Recht* into formal judicial process were one example of this; another might be the explanation of the appearance of ghosts by appealing to the hierarchy of Heaven (Kirk 1976 [1690/1]), or the new science of 'palingenesie' (Hibbert 1825), the theory that all living things hold the 'ghost' of all their future generations inside themselves and that this ghost can be released through, for example, the application of heat.

We might tentatively conclude from the evidence of mortuary practices in Early Modern Britain and Ireland that ritual practice appears to be more stable than the beliefs that 'explain' it. 'Belief', by contrast turns out to be complex, contradictory and slippery. Rather that providing a foundation for ritual practice, many belief discourses are drawn upon contextually to provide *post hoc* legitimation for ritual practices whose worth or efficacy is recognised prior to the deployment of the new theology, science or philosophy. Rituals, then, seem less mutable than the beliefs that surround them.

Acknowledgements

Many thanks to the Leverhulme Trust for funding the research on which this paper is based and to Annia Cherryson for reading a draft version. I would also like to thank the editors for their patient copy-editing and an anonymous reviewer for some very thoughtful reflections and suggestions.

Bibliography

Aubrey, J. 1696: *Miscellanies*, Edward Castle: London.
Aubrey, J 1881 [1686]: *Remaines of Gentilisme and Judaisme*, ed. J. Britten, Folklore Society: London.
Balkutė, Rita n.d.: 'Lithuanian Folk Medicine', in *Anthology of Lithuanian Ethnoculture* (http://ausis.gf.vu.lt/eka/EWG/default.htm, accessed 20/8/07).
Beaconsall, T. 1697: *The Doctrine of a General Resurrection: Wherein the Identity of the Rising Body is asserted against the Socinians and Scepticks. A Sermon preached on Easter Monday 1697*, George West: Oxford.
Becon, T. 1568: *The Sicke Man's Salve*, Company of the Stationers: London.
Blakeborough, R. 1898: *Wit, Character, Folklore and Customs of the North Riding of Yorkshire*, Henry Frowde: London.
Boyd, Z. 1629: *The Last Battell of the Soule in Death*, Heires of Andro Hart: Edinburgh.
Brand, J. 1777: *Observations on Popular Antiquities*, J. Johson: Newcastle upon Tyne.
Brett, J. 1996: 'Archaeology and the Construction of the Royal Edward Dock, Avonmouth, 1902–8', *Archaeology of the Severn Estuary* 7: 115–20.
Brockie, W. 1974 [1886]: *Legends and Superstitions of the County of Durham*, E. P. Publishing: Wakefield.
Crooke, H. 1631: *Microcosmographia: A Description of the Body of Man* (2nd edn), Thomas and Richard Cotes: London.

Gilchrist, R. & Sloane, B. 2005: *Requiem: The Medieval Monastic Cemetery in Britain*, Museum of London Archaeology Service: London.

Goodall, H. G. 1970: 'A 17th Century Vault in Blandford Parish', *Proceedings of the Dorset Natural History and Archaeology Society* 92: 153–55.

Groome, W. 1895: 'Suffolk Leechcraft', *Folk-Lore* 6: 117–27.

Hallam, E. & Hockey, J. 2001: *Death, Memory and Material Culture*, Berg: Oxford.

Harding, V. 1993: 'Burial of the Plague Dead in Early Modern London', in J. A. I. Champion (ed.): *Epidemic Disease in London* (Centre for Metropolitan History Working Papers, 1), Institute of Historical Research: London, 53–64.

Harland, J. & Wilkinson, T. 1882: *Lancashire Folk-Lore*, John Heywood: Manchester.

Hibbert, S. 1825: *Sketches of the Philosophy of Apparitions*, Oliver and Boyd: Edinburgh.

Holt, A. 1992: *Folklore of Somerset*, Alan Sutton: Stroud.

Jones, T. G. 1979 [1930]: *Welsh Folklore and Folk Custom*, reissued with and introduction by A. ap Gwynn, D. S. Brewer: Cambridge.

Kilfeather, S. 2002: 'Oliver Plunkett's Head', *Textual Practice* 16.2: 229–48.

Kirk, R. 1976 [1690/1]: *The Secret Common-Wealth and a Short Treatise of Charms and Spells*, edited and with a commentary by Stewart Sanderson, The Folklore Society: London.

Lofqvist, C. 2004: *Osteological Report on Human Skeletal Remains from Eyre Square, Galway City*, unpublished Moore Archaeological and Environmental Services Ltd Report.

MacDonald, M. & Murphy, T. 1990: *Sleepless Souls: Suicide in Early Modern England*, Clarendon Press: Oxford.

McNichol, D., Clough, S. & Loe, L. 2007: *Hemingford Flood Alleviation Scheme, St. Ives, Cambridgeshire. Watching Brief and Excavation Report*, unpublished Oxford Archaeology report.

Napier, J. 1976 [1879]: *Folk Lore: Or Superstitious Beliefs in the West of Scotland within this Century*, Alexander Gardner: Paisley.

Nixon, A. 1612: *The Dignitie of Man, Both in the Perfections of his Soule and Bodie*, Edward Allde: London.

Norton, A. 2006: *Oxford Castle. Post-Excavation Analysis and Research Design*, unpublished Oxford Archaeology Report.

Norton, A., Laws, G. & Smith, A. 2005: *Abingdon West Central Redevelopment Area, Oxfordshire. Post-Excavation Assessment and updated Project Design*, unpublished Oxford Archaeology Report.

Peacock, M. 1896: 'Executed Criminals and Folk-Medicine', *Folk-Lore* 7.3: 268–83.

Porter, E. 1969: *Cambridgeshire Customs and Folklore*, Routledge and Kegan Paul: London.

Prynne, W. 1641: *Mount-Orgueil. A Poem of the Soule's Complaint against the Body hereto annexed*, Michael Sparke Senior: London.

Richardson, R. 1988: *Death, Dissection and the Destitute*, Penguin: London.

Rodwell, W. & Rodwell, K. 1982: 'St Peter's Church, Barton-upon-Humber: Excavation and Structural Study 1978–81', *Antiquaries Journal* 62: 283–315.

Sawday, J. 1995: *The Body Emblazoned*, Routledge: London.

Scot, R. 1964 [1584]: *The Discoverie of Witchcraft*, with an introduction by H. R. Williamson, Centaur Press: Arundel.

Sherlock, W. 1690: *A Practical Discourse concerning Death* (2nd edn), W. Rogers: London.

Sternberg, T. 1851: *The Dialect and Folk-Lore of Northamptonshire*, John Russell: London.

Thomas, K. 1971: *Religion and the Decline of Magic*, Penguin: London.

Wiltshire, K. 1975: *Wiltshire Folklore*, Compton Russell: Salisbury.

INDEX

Please, note the following:

1.   Chapter 3: On p. 49, the caption of Fig. 3.1 gives a list of 127 numbered topographical locations. In the present index only locations mentioned in the running text are entered.
2.   Chapter 5: Appendix A on pp. 154–57 gives a list of names of 156 Etruscan tombs. In the present index only those tombs mentioned in the running text are entered with the exclusion of those in nn. 191–233 on pp. 171–74.
3.   Chapter 6: Appendix, pp. 209–13 gives a list of 133 numbered topographical locations. In the present index only locations mentioned in the running text are entered.

Concepts and names appearing in the illustrations and tables (including their respective captions) are marked in *italics*, while if they appear in an endnote they are marked n. after the page.